Advanced Placement ECONOMICS

Teacher Resource Manual

3rd edition

John S. Morton

Rae Jean B. Goodman

This publication was made possible through funding by

The Goldman Sachs Foundation

NCEE

National Council on Economic Education

Authors

Authors

John S. Morton is Vice President for Program Development at the National Council on Economic Education. Previously, he was a high school economics teacher, director of the Governors State University Center for Economic Education and president of the Arizona Council on Economic Education.

Rae Jean B. Goodman, Director of Teaching and Learning and Professor of Economics, has had more than 30 years of teaching and administrative experience at the U.S. Naval Academy. She served as a table leader and the Chief Faculty Consultant for the Advanced Placement Economics Examinations from 1989 until 1997.

Editor

Melinda Patterson Grenier was a reporter, deputy bureau chief and bureau chief at the print and online Wall Street Journal. A former teacher, she was also the founding editor and publisher of The Wall Street Journal Classroom Edition, an award-winning educational program for high school economics teachers and students.

Artist

Susan A. Mills received her bachelor of fine arts degree in art from the University of Connecticut. She is employed as a Test Publishing Coordinator at Educational Testing Service in Princeton, N.J.

Project Director

Claire Melican is Vice President for Program Administration at the National Council on Economic Education. In addition to teaching economics at the college level, Claire has worked at the Educational Testing Service where she was instrumental in the development and implementation of the Advanced Placement Examinations in Economics until 2000.

Production

Book design and composition by World Composition Services, Inc., Sterling, Virginia.
Printed by PMR Printing, Inc., Sterling, Virginia.

ISBN: 1-56183-566-8

MICROECONOMICS Teacher Resource Manual

MACROECONOMICS Teacher Resource Manual

MACROECONOMICS
Unit 1 Basic Economic Concepts

MACROECONOMICS
Unit 2 Measuring Economic Performance

Advanced Placement Economics: Teacher Resource Manual © National Council on Economic Education, New York, N.Y.

Foreword

The National Council on Economic Education is gratified to publish the third edition of *Advanced Placement Economics*, which is specifically designed to assist high school teachers in teaching the college-level principles of economics courses to their students as part of the Advanced Placement Program™ of the College Board.

NCEE has worked diligently since the mid-1980s to make economics an Advanced Placement subject and to increase student participation in the program. NCEE's involvement has been critical to the success of the AP Economics Program. NCEE worked with representatives of the Committee on Economic Education of the American Economic Association to recommend and support economics becoming an AP subject. NCEE and members of its affiliated state Councils on Economic Education and university-based Centers for Economic Education then worked with the College Board to bring this recommendation to reality. NCEE, through its unique network of affiliated Councils and Centers, has conducted countless workshops and college courses for AP Economics teachers. Economists who are members of the NCEE network have served on the Test Development Committee and as AP readers every year since economics became an AP subject in 1989.

NCEE is proud that the number of students taking the AP Economics Exams increased from about 5,000 in 1989 to more than 60,000 in 2003. AP Economics provides a rigorous standard for high school economics courses. Because AP teachers must be better trained and must teach other economics courses, the entire curriculum benefits.

The third edition of *Advanced Placement Economics* continues NCEE's commitment to AP Economics. We are grateful to the Goldman Sachs Foundation for making this publication possible. I would also like to thank Phillip Saunders who contributed many outstanding activities from his microeconomics and macroeconomics workbooks. I also appreciate Greg Mankiw's leadership of the Blue-Ribbon Committee, which assured that *Advanced Placement Economics* met high standards for economic content and pedagogy. Finally, Rae Jean Goodman, Melinda Patterson Grenier, Claire Melican and John Morton spent more time on this publication than they could have possibly expected to commit, and all of us who are concerned with excellence in economic education are the beneficiaries of this valuable time. I believe the results of all these efforts take *Advanced Placement Economics* to a new level.

Robert F. Duvall, Ph.D.
President and Chief Executive Officer
National Council on Economic Education

Acknowledgments

Acknowledgments

Blue-Ribbon Committee

N. Gregory Mankiw, Harvard University, Cambridge, Mass., Chair
Cecilia Conrad, Pomona College, Claremont, Calif.
David Hakes, University of Northern Iowa, Cedar Falls, Iowa
Mike Johanik, The College Board
Mary Kohelis, Brooke High School, Wellsburg, W. Va.
Richard MacDonald, St. Cloud State University, St. Cloud, Minn.
Claire Melican, National Council on Economic Education, New York, N.Y.
John Morton, National Council on Economic Education, New York, N.Y.
Clark Ross, Davidson College, Davidson, N.C.
Robert Wedge, Massachusetts Council on Economic Education, Waltham, Mass.

Design Committee

Rae Jean B. Goodman, U.S. Naval Academy, Annapolis, Md., Chair
James Chasey, Homewood-Flossmoor High School, Flossmoor, Ill.
Kelly A. Chaston, Davidson College, Davidson, N.C.
Robert Graboyes, University of Richmond, Richmond, Va.
W.C. Kerby, California State University, Sacramento, Calif.
Mary Kohelis, Brooke High School, Wellsburg, W. Va.
Francis McMann, George Washington High School, Cedar Rapids, Iowa
Claire Melican, National Council on Economic Education, New York, N.Y.
John Morton, National Council on Economic Education, New York, N.Y.
James Spellicy, Lowell High School, San Francisco, Calif.

Microeconomics Contributors

Clare E. Adkin, Jr., Cary Academy, Cary, N.C.
Joe Baker, Southern Utah University, Cedar City, Utah
Joanne Beaver, Cumberland Valley High School, Mechanicsburg, Pa.
Ike Brannon, Joint Economic Committee, U.S. Senate, Washington, D.C.
Gregory Breuner, Lakeridge High School, Lake Oswego, Ore.
Kelly A. Chaston, Davidson College, Davidson, N.C.
Jim Clark, Wichita State University, Wichita, Kan.
Janice H. Dukes, Opelika High School, Opelika, Ala.
Rae Jean B. Goodman, U.S. Naval Academy, Annapolis, Md.
Robert Graham, Hanover College, Hanover, Ind.
Margaret Hamilton, Canton Country Day School, Canton, Ohio
Robert J. Heffern, Maryvale High School, Cheektowaga, N.Y.
W.C. Kerby, California State University, Sacramento, Calif.

Mary Kohelis, Brooke High School, Wellsburg, W. Va.

Jimmy D. Lee, Highland Park High School, Dallas, Texas

C. Lee McCarty, Solon High School, Solon, Ohio

Francis McMann, Washington High School, Cedar Rapids, Iowa

John Morton, National Council on Economic Education, New York, N.Y.

Margaret Ray, Mary Washington College, Fredericksburg, Va.

Phillip Saunders, Indiana University, Bloomington, Ind.

Pamela Schmitt, U.S. Naval Academy, Annapolis, Md.

David Stark, Brainerd High School, Brainerd, Minn.

Mary Jo Thomas, South Eugene High School, Eugene, Ore.

Francis Vottero, Shamokin Area High School, Shamokin, Pa.

Gloria Washington, Dillard High School, Ft. Lauderdale, Fla.

Macroeconomics Contributors

Joanne Benjamin, Los Gatos High School, Los Gatos, Calif.

Charles A. Bennett, Gannon University, Erie, Pa.

Ike Brannon, Joint Economic Committee, U.S. Senate, Washington, D.C.

Jim Charkins, California State University, San Bernardino, Calif.

James Chasey, Homewood-Flossmoor High School, Flossmoor, Ill.

Kelly A. Chaston, Davidson College, Davidson, N.C.

Jerry De Young, Riverbank High School, Riverbank, Calif.

Sarah Franklin, Plano Senior High School, Plano, Texas

Rae Jean B. Goodman, U.S. Naval Academy, Annapolis, Md.

Robert Graboyes, University of Richmond, Richmond, Va.

Nancy Griffin, Plano East Senior High School, Plano, Texas

Lisa C. Herman-Ellison, Kokomo High School – South Campus, Kokomo, Ind.

Ruth Kramp, Plano East Senior High School, Plano, Texas

Elaine McBeth, College of William and Mary, Williamsburg, Va.

John Morton, National Council on Economic Education, New York, N.Y.

David Nelson, Western Washington University, Bellingham, Wash.

Robert Nuxoll, Oceanside High School, Oceanside, N.Y.

Karl Ochi, George Washington High School, San Francisco, Calif.

Charles Orvis, Rhodes College, Memphis, Tenn.

Peggy Pride, Saint Louis University High School, St. Louis, Mo.

Helen Roberts, University of Illinois, Chicago, Ill.

Phillip Saunders, Indiana University, Bloomington, Ind.

Betty Shakelford, Maconaquah High School, Bunker Hill, Ind.

James Spellicy, Lowell High School, San Francisco, Calif.

James Stanley, Choate Rosemary Hall, Wallingford, Conn.

Robert Wedge, Massachusetts Council on Economic Education, Waltham, Mass.

Kathleen Whitsett, Princeton High School, Cincinnati, Ohio

Pam Winders, Highland School of Technology, Gastonia, N.C.

Acknowledgments

Reviewers

Curt Anderson, University of Minnesota-Duluth, Duluth, Minn.

Robin Bartlett, Denison University, Granville, Ohio

Morgan Bridge, Mesa State College, Grand Junction, Colo.

Cecilia Conrad, Pomona College, Claremont, Calif.

David Findlay, Colby College, Waterville, Maine

Robert Graham, Hanover College, Hanover, Ind.

David Hakes, University of Northern Iowa, Cedar Falls, Iowa

Margaret Hamilton, Canton Country Day School, Canton, Ohio

Joy Joyce, Willowbrook High School, Villa Park, Ill.

John Karikari, U.S. Government Accounting Office, Washington, D.C.

Andrew Kohen, James Madison University, Harrisonburg, Va.

Richard MacDonald, St. Cloud State University, St. Cloud, Minn.

Karl Ochi, George Washington High School, San Francisco, Calif.

Charles Orvis, Rhodes College, Memphis, Tenn.

Dennis Placone, Clemson University, Clemson, S.C.

Richard K. Rankin, Iolani School, Honolulu, Hawaii

Kathy Ratté, Foundation for Teaching Economics, Littleton, Colo.

Margaret Ray, Mary Washington College, Fredericksburg, Va.

Arthur Raymond, Muhlenberg College, Allentown, Pa.

Elaine Schwartz, Kent Place School, Summit, N.J.

Leah Tesney, Virginia Council on Economic Education, Richmond, Va.

Susan Woodward, Unionville High School, Kennett Square, Pa.

Marty Yopp, University of Idaho, Moscow, Idaho

Introduction

Advanced Placement Economics is designed to help you teach Advanced Placement Economics courses and prepare your students for the AP Economics Examinations.

The AP Program offers two separate examinations in economics: one in microeconomics and one in macroeconomics. Each AP Examination is intended for qualified students who wish to complete studies in a secondary school that are equivalent to a one-semester college introductory course.

The AP Examination in Microeconomics and the AP Examination in Macroeconomics are each a little more than two hours long. Each examination consists of a 70-minute multiple-choice section and a 60-minute free-response section. The free-response section begins with a mandatory 10-minute reading period. Some questions in the free-response section require graphical analysis. In each examination, the multiple-choice section accounts for two-thirds of the student's examination grade and the free-response section for the remaining one-third.

Using *Advanced Placement Economics*

Advanced Placement Economics consists of the microeconomics and macroeconomics Student Activities Books and the Teacher Resource Manual. Each unit in the Student Activities Books begins with a "Key Ideas" section, which provides structure. The Student Activities teach basic economic principles and allow the students to apply economic concepts to a variety of situations. Each unit ends with sample multiple-choice and free-response questions, which are written in the same format as the questions on the AP Examinations. You could use these as a test, but it is better to use them for review. We recommend buying one Student Activities Book for each student.

The Teacher Resource Manual provides form and structure to your course. In addition to microeconomics and macroeconomics course outlines, it contains unit and lesson overviews, unit and daily lesson plans, planning suggestions, lesson objectives, Visuals and answers to the Student Activities. The procedures in the lessons sometimes include instructional activities that are not in the Student Activities Books. The Teacher Resource Manual is not designed as a cookbook. Teachers of an AP Program should design their own curriculum; *Advanced Placement Economics* will make this process easier.

Advanced Placement Economics is designed to be used with a college principles of economics textbook. The textbook provides the basic content, and the activities in *Advanced Placement Economics* provide both drill and practice with the content and the application of this content to a wide variety of situations. Because different textbooks provide different topic sequences, you may have to use the activities in a different order than they appear in the *Advanced Placement Economics* books.

The New and Improved *Advanced Placement Economics*

The new state-of-the-art *Advanced Placement Economics* has been revised, updated and polished. We modestly believe that it is now the best supplementary package published for use for any Advanced Placement subject.

The content and instructional activities of *Advanced Placement Economics* were designed by two committees. A blue-ribbon committee chaired by Dr. N. Gregory Mankiw established the goals of the revision and developed criteria to assure that the components of the new publication would consist of sound economics and innovative pedagogy. A design committee chaired by Dr. Rae Jean B. Goodman then laid out the lessons and instructional activities.

Authors were hired to revise existing activities and write new activities. The instructional activities address the latest content changes in the AP Course Description. The committee members, authors and reviewers include high school AP Economics teachers, college professors of economics, members of the AP Economics Test Development Committee and AP Economics readers. The activities reflect the essence of the content of the Advanced Placement Economics Examinations and a sound understanding of the struggles students have had with this content over the years.

While all of the content changes in this edition are too numerous to list here, the following is a representative sample.

Changes in Microeconomics Lessons

- Extending the discussion of supply and demand to include consumer and producer surplus
- Expanded activities on derivation of the demand curve and price and income elasticities of demand
- Activities on allocative and productive efficiency
- New activities on game theory, price discrimination, the Coase Theorem, information costs and income distribution

Changes in Macroeconomics Lessons

- Reorganization of the aggregate demand and aggregate supply unit
- Differentiation of short-run aggregate supply from long-run aggregate supply
- More emphasis on economic growth
- Realistic and expanded coverage of Federal Reserve mechanics and monetary policy
- New activities on aggregate demand and aggregate supply, the equation of exchange, the money market, monetary policy, and real and nominal interest rates

Top 10 Keys to Teaching an Effective AP Economics Course

You have been assigned to teach an AP Economics course, and it is a daunting task. You are being asked to teach at a higher level than before, and the school administration will see the scores of your students. In fact, everyone may see them. Here are a few tips from veteran teachers that will help you be successful.

1. Order AP Publications from the College Board

You will need four publications from the College Board. Go to the College Board's online store at http://apcentral.collegeboard.com for information on prices and ordering.

- The AP Economics Course Description (Acorn Book) provides a detailed outline of content areas for the AP Microeconomics and AP Macroeconomics Examinations. The percentage goals for the multiple-choice questions are very important. For example, if 8 percent to 12 percent of the Microeconomics Test is on basic economics questions and the exam has 60 questions, expect five to seven questions on this topic. The Acorn Book also has sample multiple-choice and free-response questions.

- The latest released exam has that exam's multiple-choice questions and answer key as well as the free-response questions with scoring guidelines, sample student responses and scoring commentary. There is also statistical information about student performance. The sample exams are excellent practice for the real exams.

- The Microeconomics and Macroeconomics Teacher's Guides have information on starting an AP Economics course, techniques and strategies for teaching the course, sample outlines for high school and college courses, and a bibliography of textbooks and other resources.

- Each year the free-response questions, the scoring rubrics and sample answers are available through the College Board's regional offices or on the College Board Web site, http://apcentral.collegeboard.com.

2. Get Teacher Training

The College Board offers several one-day workshops that will provide you with background for AP Economics courses. These workshops focus on the content covered and an analysis of past multiple-choice and free-response questions. The workshop leader, who may be an AP reader, will provide valuable information to improve student performance. It also helps to attend longer summer workshops that focus on the subject matter of AP Economics in more detail. These workshops cover the content more comprehensively and demonstrate individual activities that teach this content. State Councils on Economic Education and university Centers for Economic Education offer courses and workshops for AP Economics teachers. Some of these affiliates of the National Council on Economic Education can also provide advice to individual teachers. To locate the Council or Center nearest you, log on to the NCEE Web site at http://www.ncee.net.

3. Buy a Textbook You Can Live With

Most textbooks for the college principles of economics course are similar. Choose a textbook that is compatible with your teaching style. Be sure to tell the publisher that you are teaching AP Economics so that the publisher will send you a sample copy. Whichever textbook you choose, be sure to ask about ancillary materials including the student activities book, transparencies, teacher's manual and test bank. Many test banks are on CDs to make the construction of your tests easier. For a review of textbooks and other instructional materials, go to the College Board Web site at http://apcentral.collegeboard.com.

4. Organize the Course in Advance

The sample course outlines, sample unit plans and lesson plans in this book are based on 75 class periods each semester. Each class period is 45 minutes long. Although most semesters have more periods, disruptions reduce the real seat time. Extra days can be used for quizzes, review and additional instruction in areas in which your students are weak. The time is given in minutes for each unit and lesson so you can plan block periods.

You probably do not want to follow these unit and lesson plans in a lock-step fashion, but you must be careful to allocate your time efficiently and stick to your schedule. If you drift and don't finish the last unit, your students will be at a serious disadvantage when they take the test.

5. Quiz and Test Often

The students need frequent assessments. We recommend a brief multiple-choice quiz on every textbook chapter. Unit tests should have both multiple-choice and free-response questions. When possible, include past AP questions, and grade the questions according to the rubrics constructed by the AP readers. Economics builds one concept on top of another. If the students do not understand the earlier concepts, they will be lost as the course progresses. Therefore, the more feedback you can provide, the better off your students will be.

It is essential for you to use writing assignments or quick in-class exercises so your students will gain experience in answering free-response questions. Answering free-response questions in economics is very different from answering free-response questions in other social sciences. The required answers are very succinct.

6. Teach an Economic Way of Thinking

Content is very important in AP Economics, but a quality course goes beyond teaching a bundle of concepts. Economics is a unique way of thinking that offers insights into the seemingly chaotic confusion of human behavior in a world of different values, resources and cultures.

If your students think in an economic way, they will understand each concept better and, more importantly, understand how each concept relates to the others. Even if the students haven't studied a concept covered on the exam, they will be able to use techniques of thinking to draw the correct conclusion. Help your students to see the forest and not just the trees. Constantly focus on the big picture. A good resource of ready-to-use lessons that reinforce the economic way of thinking is *Capstone: Exemplary Lessons for High School Economics* (New York: National Council on Economic Education, 2003).

7. Use Active Learning

In an AP class it is easy to fall into the trap of having the students memorize definitions, information and rules. The lecture-discussion method seems ideal for a course that has so much information. Efficiently presenting information is important, but economics can be more relevant and stimulating if the students are actively involved in the lessons. Involve the students in different types of simulations, group decision making, problem solving, role-playing and group presentations. The students should be doing — not just hearing and seeing.

For active-learning activities that can help your students understand concepts critical to their performing well on the AP Economics Exams, we recommend *Economics in Action: 14 Greatest Hits for High School Economics* (New York: National Council on Economic Education, 2003). For example, "A Market in Wheat" illustrates the behavior behind supply, demand and equilibrium. This publication has activities that illustrate negative and positive externalities, marginal analysis, labor productivity, inflation and the effects of fiscal policy. After the students complete these activities, the concepts and graphs will make a lot more sense to them. Begin by illustrating the behavior and then analyze it.

8. Practice Makes Perfect

Many of the activities in the *Advanced Placement Economics* Student Activities Books focus on drill and practice. The students are given multiple scenarios on supply, demand, perfect competition, monopoly, aggregate demand and supply, monetary policy and fiscal policy. The goal is not to cover every possible situation but to develop economic reasoning from constant practice. Practice is essential and is another form of active learning.

9. Graph Early and Often

The students must be able to perform graphical analysis to do well on the AP Economics Examinations. Important graphs in Microeconomics include production possibilities, supply and demand, perfect competition, monopoly and factor markets. Graphs in Macroeconomics include production possibilities, aggregate demand and aggregate supply, investment demand, the money market and exchange rates.

It is essential for the students to understand that they are graphing behavior. If they try to memorize the graphs, they will have trouble. Emphasize multiple shifts that cannot be memorized. Tell stories about changes in supply and demand, changes in aggregate supply and demand, or changes in a firm's revenues and costs. Then have the students graph the changes.

Finally, graphs must be clearly labeled. If the axes and lines are not labeled, the students will not receive credit for their graphs on the AP Exams. When you correct your students' graphs, always point out labeling omissions.

10. Emphasize Historically Weak Areas

Each year the AP Economics Chief Faculty Consultant identifies areas in which students have done poorly. Because these areas will be covered again in future tests, it pays to get this letter from the College Board. Here are some past student shortcomings that have been identified by Chief Faculty Consultants.

- The students must be able to do multiple time-period analysis. For example, in perfect competition, analyze the perfectly competitive firm's short-run and long-run equilibrium. In Macroeconomics, explain the short-run and long-run effects of a change in fiscal or monetary policy.

- Integrate international economics into the analysis of monetary and fiscal policies. For example, how does an easy money policy affect interest rates, the international value of the dollar and the balance of trade? How does it affect economic growth and the price level?

- Explain the process of policy interpretation. If a student says a tax cut will increase real GDP and the price level, he or she may receive a point on a free-response question. To do well, the students must explain how a tax cut affects aggregate demand and why. Then they must explain how aggregate demand affects the price level and real GDP and why. "Why" and "how" are important questions to ask your students.

And Now It's Time to Get Your Act Together and Take Your Show on the Road

Once you have the right tools and the right training, your students should be able to do well on the AP Economics Exams. More importantly, you will be giving them a new lens through which to view the world. They will learn a systematic and disciplined way of thinking that will serve them well throughout their lives. This is the real contribution of a well-taught AP Economics course.

Advanced Placement ECONOMICS

Microeconomics
Teacher Resource Manual

Outline for an Advanced Placement Microeconomics Course

75 class periods of 45 minutes each

Unit 1 Basic Economic Concepts
(10 class periods or 450 minutes)
A. The Economic Way of Thinking
B. Scarcity: The Nature of Economic Systems
  1. Opportunity costs
  2. Trade-offs
  3. Production possibilities curves
  4. Explicit costs and implicit costs
  5. Interdependence and the circular flow of income
  6. The functions of any economic system (what, how and for whom to produce)
C. Specialization, Trade and Comparative Advantage
D. Applying Basic Economic Concepts

Unit 2 The Nature and Functions of Product Markets
(17 class periods or 765 minutes)
A. Demand
  1. Relationship between price and quantity demanded
  2. Consumer choice behind the demand curve
  3. Income and substitution effects
  4. Law of diminishing marginal utility
  5. Introduction to elasticity of demand
  6. Consumer surplus
  7. Determinants of demand
  8. Changes in quantity demanded vs. changes in demand
B. Supply
  1. Relationship between supply and quantity supplied
  2. Introduction to elasticity of supply
  3. Producer surplus
  4. Determinants of supply
  5. Changes in quantity supplied vs. changes in supply
C. Equilibrium Price, Equilibrium Quantity and Interrelationship of Markets
  1. Why and how price and quantity move toward equilibrium
  2. Effects of shifts in supply and demand on equilibrium price and quantity
  3. Markets as providers of information, creators of incentives and allocators of resources
  4. Basic manipulation of the supply and demand model

D. Elasticity of Demand and Supply
   1. Price elasticity of demand
      a. Total revenue method of calculation
      b. Arc method of calculation
      c. Calculation along demand curve of constant slope
      d. Determinants of price elasticity of demand
      e. Tax incidence and price elasticity of demand
   2. Income and Cross Elasticity of Demand
   3. Elasticity of Supply
      a. Time periods
      b. Applications
E. Price Ceilings and Floors
   1. Effects in terms of surpluses and shortages
   2. Analysis of why shortages and surpluses are created
F. Analysis of Market Behavior Using Supply and Demand

Unit 3 The Theory of the Firm
(25 class periods or 1,125 minutes)

A. Introduction to Market Structure
B. The Costs of Production
   1. Fixed cost and average fixed cost
   2. Variable cost and average variable cost
   3. Total cost and average total cost
   4. Marginal cost
   5. Marginal product and diminishing marginal cost
   6. Relationships among costs
   7. Short-run and long-run cost curves
   8. Economies and diseconomies of scale
C. Perfect Competition
   1. Nature of demand curve or marginal revenue curve
   2. Profit-maximizing assumption
   3. Short-run equilibrium
   4. Long-run equilibrium
   5. Normal and economic profit
   6. Long-run adjustment of firm and industry to short-run economic profits and losses
   7. Effect of perfect competition on allocative efficiency
D. Monopoly
   1. Nature and relationship of demand curve to marginal revenue curve
   2. Monopoly firm profit-maximizing equilibrium
   3. Effects of monopoly behavior on consumer and producer surplus
   4. Comparison of the monopolist's profit-maximizing price, output and price with those of a perfect competitor
   5. Efficiency and government policy toward regulating monopoly

E. Monopolistic Competition and Oligopoly
- 1. Monopolistic competition
  - a. Short-run and long-run equilibrium
  - b. Comparison with perfect competition, monopoly and oligopoly
- 2. Oligopoly
  - a. Nature of oligopoly
  - b. Types of nonprice and price competition
  - c. Game theory
  - d. Comparison with perfect competition, monopoly and monopolistic competition

    F. Application of Market Structure to Conventional and Unconventional Situations

Unit 4 Factor Markets
(12 class periods or 540 minutes)

    A. Differentiation of Factor Markets and Product Markets

    B. Marginal Productivity and Factor Demand
- 1. Resource demand as derived demand
- 2. Marginal physical product, marginal revenue product and marginal resource cost
- 3. Rule for employing resources (MRP = MRC)
- 4. Changes in resource demand and effects on factor prices

    C. The Effects of Resource Market Structure on Wages and Employment
- 1. Competitive labor markets
- 2. Monopsonistic labor markets
- 3. Effects of minimum-wage laws on competitive and monopsonistic labor markets
- 4. Effects of labor unions on competitive and monopsonistic labor markets

    D. Determination of Economic Rent and Interest

Unit 5 The Role of Government
(11 class periods or 495 minutes)

    A. Government and Allocation of Resources
- 1. Economic functions of government
- 2. Nature of public goods

    B. Government and Market Failures
- 1. Positive externalities
- 2. Negative externalities
- 3. Coase Theorem
- 4. Information costs

    C. Government Failures and Public-Choice Theory

    D. Efficiency, Equity and the Effects of Government Policies
- 1. Benefits-received theory of taxation
- 2. Ability-to-pay theory of taxation
  - a. Progressive tax
  - b. Proportional tax
  - c. Regressive tax
- 3. Taxation, government spending and the distribution of income

Microeconomics | Unit 1

Basic Economic Concepts

10 class periods or 450 minutes
(13 percent of course time)

Unit Overview

Unit 1 focuses on basic economic concepts. These concepts account for 8 to 12 percent of the Advanced Placement Microeconomics Examination. More importantly, if the students do not understand these concepts, they will have a difficult time throughout the course.

The most important introductory concept is scarcity. In any economy, scarce resources and unlimited wants result in the need to make choices. The students must understand scarcity, opportunity cost and trade-offs. They should be able to illustrate these concepts on a production possibilities curve.

Because of scarcity, every economic system must determine which goods to produce, how to produce them and for whom to produce them.

Much of a microeconomics course will focus on how specialization and exchange increase the total output of goods and services. The students must be able to differentiate between absolute advantage and comparative advantage. Comparative advantage is the key to specialization and trade. Do not neglect this concept.

Finally, Unit 1 emphasizes an economic way of thinking that is key to ideas that come up over and over again in the course. The students should not memorize the concepts; instead, they should use the concepts as a framework for organizing the course.

The Lesson Planner

Lesson 1 emphasizes the economic way of thinking. It uses **Activity 1** and **Visual 1.1**.

Lesson 2 emphasizes scarcity, opportunity cost and production possibilities curves. It also applies these concepts to organizing an economy. It uses **Activities 2, 3, 4** and **5** and **Visuals 1.2** and **1.3**.

Lesson 3 focuses on comparative advantage and uses **Activity 6** and **Visuals 1.4** and **1.5**.

Lesson 4 reinforces the activities from the previous lessons by applying them to a variety of conventional and unconventional situations. This lesson uses **Activities 7** and **8**.

Week 1

■ Day 1

Give lecture on economic way of thinking, using Visual 1.1.

■ Day 2

Reinforce economic way of thinking, using Activity 1.

■ Day 3

(A) Give lecture on scarcity.

(B) Use Visual 1.2 to illustrate PPC.

(C) Have the students begin Activity 2 and complete as homework.

■ Day 4

(A) Go over Activity 2.

(B) Discuss the differences between explicit and implicit costs.

(C) Have the students complete Activity 3 and discuss answers.

■ Day 5

(A) Give lecture on how economies deal with scarcity.

(B) Have the students complete Activity 4 and discuss answers.

Week 2

■ Day 6

(A) Give lecture on circular flow of resources, using Visual 1.3.

(B) Have the students complete Activity 5 and go over answers.

■ Day 7

(A) Give lecture on comparative advantage, using Visuals 1.4 and 1.5.

(B) Have the students complete Activity 6 during class or as homework.

■ Day 8

(A) Go over Activity 6.

(B) Discuss marginal benefits and costs.

(C) Have the students complete Activity 7 and discuss answers.

(D) Assign Activity 8 as homework.

■ Day 9

(A) Go over answers to Activity 8.

(B) Review for unit test.

■ Day 10

Give unit test.

The Economic Way of Thinking

Introduction and Description

Advanced Placement Economics has thousands of details that can confuse students. The students need a framework to organize these details. This lesson acquaints the students with basic economic concepts and methodology. It begins with some key economic ideas, which represent a new set of lenses through which the students may view the world. The lesson ends with a test of economic myths that should get the students' attention. This exercise also gives the teacher a way of reinforcing the economic concepts taught at the beginning of the lesson.

Objectives

1. Define *opportunity cost.*
2. Define the *economic way of thinking.*
3. Apply *scarcity* concepts to a variety of economic and noneconomic situations.

Time Required

Two class periods or 90 minutes

Materials

1. Activity 1
2. Visual 1.1

Procedure

1. Project Visual 1.1 and discuss the economic way of thinking. Here are some discussion ideas for each point on the transparency.

   ▓ **Everything has a cost.**
   This is the basic idea that "there is no such thing as a free lunch," meaning that every action costs someone time, effort or lost opportunities to do something else. Introduce the term *opportunity cost* here. Stress the concept that people incur costs when making decisions, even when people appear to pay nothing.

▓ **People choose for good reasons.**
People always face choices, and they should choose the alternative that gives them the most advantageous combination of costs and benefits. You might stress here that if people have different values, they may make different choices. This might be a good place to discuss *normative* versus *positive economics.* Economists tend to be a tolerant lot because they realize people choose for good reasons. Also stress that *people* choose. Much of the AP Economics course concerns business and government decision making. But business and government decisions are made by people.

▓ **Incentives matter.**
This course is really about incentives. It has been said that economics is about incentives and everything else is commentary. *Supply and demand analysis* is about incentives. The *theory of the firm* and *factor markets* are about incentives. Government decision making is about incentives. When incentives change, people's behavior changes in predictable ways.

▓ **People create economic systems to influence choices and incentives.**
Cooperation among people is governed by written and unwritten rules that are the core of an economic system. As rules change, incentives and behavior change. The success of market systems and the failure of communism are rooted in incentives.

▓ **People gain from voluntary trade.**
People trade when they believe the trade makes them better off. If they expect no benefits, they don't trade. Part of the AP Economics course focuses on international trade. However, once again it is people, not countries, that trade. A market system is about trade. Economics is about trade.

■ **Economic thinking is marginal thinking.**
Marginal choices involve the effects of additions and subtractions from current conditions. Much of this course is about marginal costs and benefits. Marginal thinking will be stressed in Units 3 and 4, where the theory of the firm and factor markets are discussed. Nevertheless, marginal decision making should be discussed in every unit.

■ **The value of a good or service is affected by people's choices.**
Goods and services do not have intrinsic value; their value is determined by the preferences of buyers and sellers. Because of this, trading moves goods and services to higher-valued uses. This is why trading is so important. The price of a good or service is set by supply and demand.

■ **Economic actions create secondary effects.**
Good economics involves analyzing secondary effects. For example, rent controls make apartments more affordable to some consumers. Controls also make it less profitable to build and maintain apartments. The secondary effect is a shortage of apartments and houses for rent.

■ **The test of a theory is its ability to predict correctly.**
Students will discuss dozens of theories in an AP Economics course. All these theories have simplifying assumptions. However, the proof of the pudding is in the eating. If the theory correctly predicts the consequences of actions, it is a good theory. Nothing is "good in theory but bad in practice."

2. Tell the students that they are going to take a brief quiz. Have the students turn to Activity 1 in the student workbook. Give them a few minutes to answer the questions.

3. When everyone is finished, either poll the students on their answers, or simply announce that all the answers are false. Students will think this is a cheap trick.

4. Discuss the answers, and as you do, explain some of the basic laws of economics. Economics is the study of human behavior, and principles have been developed to explain this behavior.

Do You Think Like an Economist?

All the answers are false.

Questions 1 through 4 concern scarcity. Goods are scarce because we have limited resources and unlimited wants. Therefore, one can't have everything one wants. Whenever people make a choice, they sacrifice something else. The "something else" we sacrifice is called the *opportunity cost*. To be scarce, something must be limited and desirable. Scarce goods have prices.

Question 1. Sunshine isn't scarce because it isn't limited; it is a free good.

Question 2. Polio isn't scarce because it isn't desirable.

Question 3. Scarcity is a relative, not an absolute, concept. Because resources are scarce and wants are unlimited, almost everything is scarce. If you pay an opportunity cost to use a good or service, it is scarce. If you pay a positive price for a good or service, it is scarce. Water may cover three-fourths of the earth, but we pay an opportunity cost and a positive price for clean water everywhere. Of course, water may be scarcer in the desert than in the wetlands. Only a government can actually make water cheaper in a desert.

Question 4. An important opportunity cost of going to college is lost earnings. If you could earn $20,000 a year by working, you will sacrifice $80,000 during four years of college.

Questions 5 and 6 concern the laws of supply and demand. People tend to buy more of something when the price is lower and less when the price is higher. This price includes money as well as such things as time, aggravation, inconvenience and moral guilt. Sellers will try to sell more of something if the price is higher and less of it if the price is lower. This conflict is resolved through the market.

Question 5. Question 5 is false because, if all other things are equal, less mass transportation will be purchased if the price is higher. The price could be increased in terms of dollars, inconvenient schedules, crime and filthy cars. The demand curve for transportation would have to be perfectly inelastic, or vertical, for the answer to this question to be True.

Question 6. The price of something depends on supply and demand, not on usefulness or on some criterion of quality. Water is more useful than diamonds, but it has a lower price. What you pay for a good or service depends on the market price determined by supply and demand.

Questions 7 and 8 concern gains from trade. When people trade voluntarily, both parties expect to gain, or they wouldn't trade. One reason for this gain is the law of *comparative advantage*. If one person does legal work better than another and if a second person word-processes documents better than the first, they would gain by trade. But would a lawyer who is the fastest word processor in town hire a secretary? Yes, because of comparative advantage: Each person would specialize in what he or she does comparatively better. An hour spent word processing is an hour not spent in legal work, and the opportunity cost for the lawyer would be very high. The lawyer will specialize in legal work and the secretary in word processing. The total output of goods and services will increase. This concept can also be applied to countries.

Questions 9 and 10 concern businesses and the role of profits.

Question 9. A monopoly charges a higher price than a competitive market price, but the monopolist cannot repeal the law of demand. If the price is too high, the monopolist might sell nothing. A monopolist will try to establish a price at a point that will make the greatest profit. This price is higher than a competitive price and will result in less production.

Question 10. *Profits* are an incentive for business to succeed. A business that doesn't care about its customers will not make high profits. As Adam Smith (1723-1790) said, "It is not from the benevolence of the butcher, the brewer or the baker that we expect our dinner, but from their regard for their own interest. We address ourselves not to their humanity but to their self-love, and never talk to them of our own necessities but of their advantages."

Scarcity, Opportunity Cost and Production Possibilities Curves

Introduction and Description

This lesson deals with *opportunity cost*, one of the most important concepts in economics. Start with a lecture on scarcity and *production possibilities curves*. Then reinforce the lecture by using Activity 2, which develops the central economic problem of scarcity.

Opportunity costs include not only out-of-pocket expenses (*explicit costs*) but also the value of resources that could be used elsewhere (*implicit costs*). Understanding explicit and implicit costs will be essential as the students analyze product markets. Explicit and implicit costs are the focus of Activity 3.

In all societies, people must organize to deal with the basic problems raised by scarcity and opportunity cost. A society must decide which goods and services to produce, how to produce them and how to distribute them. Societies use three systems — tradition, command or market — to solve the basic problems. This is the focus of Activity 4. It is easier to analyze campus parking than a complex economic system.

Finally, the United States has a mixed market system. The circular flow diagram (Activity 5) describes in a nontechnical way the major flows of goods, services, resources and money in a market economy.

Objectives

1. Define *scarcity*, *opportunity cost* and *trade-offs*.
2. Identify the conditions that give rise to the economic problem of scarcity.
3. Identify the opportunity costs of various courses of action involving a hypothetical problem.
4. Construct production possibilities curves from sets of hypothetical data.
5. Apply the concept of opportunity cost to a production possibilities curve.

6. Analyze the significance of different locations on, above and below a production possibilities curve.
7. Identify the three questions every economic system must answer.
8. Analyze the advantages and disadvantages of each of the three economic systems (market, command and tradition).
9. Describe and analyze the different economic goals of different economies.
10. Determine the mix of tradition, command and market in different economies.
11. Analyze a market economy using the circular flow of income.

Time Required

Four class periods or 180 minutes

Materials

1. Activities 2, 3, 4 and 5
2. Visuals 1.2 and 1.3

Procedure

1. Give a lecture on scarcity.

   (A) Wants are unlimited.

   (B) Resources are limited and fall into four categories: land, labor, capital and entrepreneurship.

   (C) There is a need to make decisions. The cost of choosing one good is giving up another. This is called opportunity cost.

2. Use Visual 1.2 of a production possibilities curve (PPC) and make points such as these:

   (A) What trade-offs are involved?

   (B) Why is the PPC concave, or bowed out, from the origin?

   (C) What does a point inside the PPC illustrate?

(D) What is an historical example of a point inside the PPC? *The Great Depression of the 1930s*

(E) What is the significance of a point outside the PPC? *It is a point that cannot be achieved with current resources and technology.*

(F) Under what conditions can a point outside the PPC be reached? *With more resources and improved technology*

3. Have the students complete Activity 2 as homework.

4. Go over Activity 2. When discussing the answers, consider these points:

(A) The law of increasing opportunity cost is hard for students to grasp. If opportunity cost is constant or increasing for one of the goods, it is constant or increasing respectively for both goods.

(B) The free-good case is an exercise in graphic interpretation, which can be used to emphasize that there are very few free goods in the world. A free good has zero opportunity cost.

5. Discuss with the students the difference between explicit costs and implicit costs. Give some examples of each.

6. Have the students complete Activity 3 and go over the answers.

7. Give a lecture on scarcity as the fundamental economic problem and explain how a combination of tradition, command and market solutions is used to deal with this problem. Every economic system uses some combination of tradition, command and market to answer the questions of what to produce, how to produce and for whom to produce.

8. Have the students read Activity 4, "Campus Parking." This case study helps the students apply tradition, command and market systems to an issue that is concrete to them. Students should answer the questions at the end of the case study.

9. Discuss the case study. In the discussion, you may want to bring up how parking spaces are distributed at your high school. As in all case studies, encourage the students to differ. Some questions have specific answers, while others have no "right" answer.

10. Use Visual 1.3 to introduce the circular flow diagram. To make the diagram more concrete, trace a single product through the circular flow.

11. Reinforce the circular flow diagram by having the students complete Activity 5.

12. Go over the answers to Activity 5.

Scarcity, Opportunity Cost and Production Possibilities Curves

Scarcity necessitates choice. Consuming or producing more of one thing means consuming or producing less of something else. The opportunity cost of using scarce resources for one thing instead of something else is often represented in graphical form as a *production possibilities curve*.

Part A

Use Figures 2.1 and 2.2 to answer these questions. Write the correct answer on the answer blanks, or underline the correct answer in parentheses.

Figure 2.1
Production Possibilities Curve 1

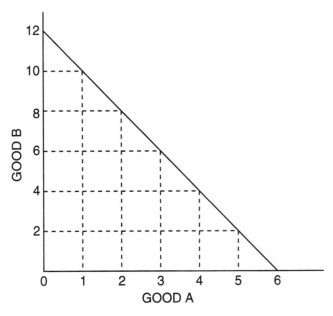

1. If the economy represented by Figure 2.1 is presently producing 12 units of Good B and zero units of Good A:

   (A) The opportunity cost of increasing production of Good A from zero units to one unit is the loss of ___*two*___ unit(s) of Good B.

   (B) The opportunity cost of increasing production of Good A from one unit to two units is the loss of ___*two*___ unit(s) of Good B.

   (C) The opportunity cost of increasing production of Good A from two units to three units is the loss of ___*two*___ unit(s) of Good B.

   (D) This is an example of (***constant*** / increasing / decreasing / zero) opportunity cost per unit for Good A.

✳ Figure 2.2

Production Possibilities Curve 2

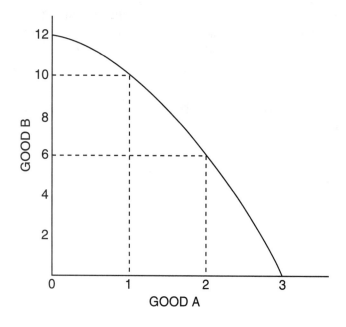

2. If the economy represented in Figure 2.2 is presently producing 12 units of Good B and zero units of Good A:

(A) The opportunity cost of increasing production of Good A from zero units to one unit is the loss of ___*two*___ unit(s) of Good B.

(B) The opportunity cost of increasing production of Good A from one unit to two units is the loss of ___*four*___ unit(s) of Good B.

(C) The opportunity cost of increasing production of Good A from two units to three units is the loss of ___*six*___ unit(s) of Good B.

(D) This is an example of (constant / ***increasing*** / decreasing / zero) opportunity cost per unit for Good A.

Part B

Use the axes in Figures 2.3, 2.4 and 2.5 to draw the type of curve that illustrates the label above each axis.

 Figure 2.3

Production Possibilities Curve 3
Increasing opportunity cost per unit of Good B

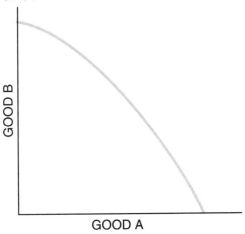

 Figure 2.4

Production Possibilities Curve 4
Zero opportunity cost per unit of Good B

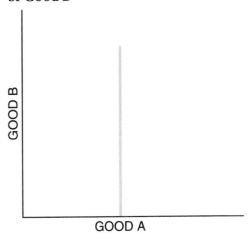

 Figure 2.5

Production Possibilities Curve 5

Constant opportunity cost per unit of Good B

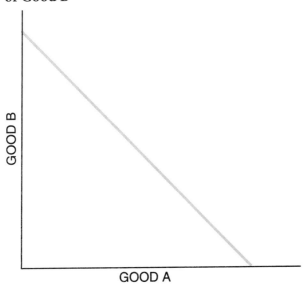

Part C

Use Figure 2.6 to answer the next five questions. Each question starts with Curve BB' as a country's production possibilities curve.

✳ Figure 2.6

Production Possibilities Curve: Capital Goods and Consumer Goods

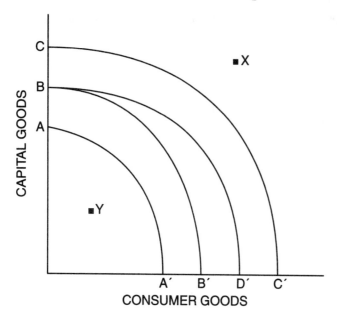

3. Suppose there is a major technological breakthrough in the consumer-goods industry, and the new technology is widely adopted. Which curve in the diagram would represent the new production possibilities curve? (Indicate the curve you choose with two letters.) ___*BD'*___

4. Suppose a new government comes into power and forbids the use of automated machinery and modern production techniques in all industries. Which curve in the diagram would represent the new production possibilities curve? (Indicate the curve you choose with two letters.) ___*AA'*___

5. Suppose massive new sources of oil and coal are found within the economy, and there are major technological innovations in both industries. Which curve in the diagram would represent the new production possibilities curve? (Indicate the curve you choose with two letters.) ___*CC'*___

6. If BB' represents a country's current production possibilities curve, what can you say about a point like X? (Write a brief statement.) *It is impossible for a country by itself to attain with existing resources and technology.*

7. If BB' represents a country's current production possibilities curve, what can you say about a point like Y? (Write a brief statement.) *The economy is not fully using existing resources and technology. An example of Point Y is the Great Depression of the 1930s.*

Part D

Use Figure 2.7 to answer the next three questions.

✳ Figure 2.7

Production Possibilities Curve: Capital Goods and Consumer Goods

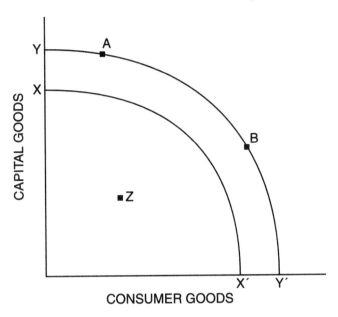

8. What change could cause the production possibilities curve to shift from the original curve (XX')
   to the new curve (YY')? *New resources are discovered. New technologies are developed.*

9. Under what conditions might an economy be operating at Point Z?
   Resources are not being fully employed.

10. Why might a government implement policy to move the economy from Point B to Point A?
    *The government might want to emphasize the production of capital goods so the economy would
    grow more in the future. This would shift the PPC outward in the future.*

You Don't Have to Spend a Buck to Have a Cost

1. For each of the following situations, list at least two explicit costs and two implicit costs. Place them in the correct column.

	Explicit	Implicit
(A) You decide to go to college.	*Tuition, books, travel*	*Income not earned, less job experience*
(B) You take a job after school.	*Work clothes, meals, transportation*	*Less study and social time*
(C) You study for and take an AP Economics Examination.	*Cost of AP Economics books, cost of AP Economics Exam*	*Money earned from part-time job, less social time, less study time for other courses*
(D) A stay-at-home dad returns to work.	*Work clothes, taxes, child-care expenses*	*Less time with family, less time for recreation*
(E) Family members work in their parents' restaurant.		
Child's (employee) viewpoint	*Taxes, work clothes*	*Lower pay than elsewhere, less time for study, less time for recreation*
Parents' (employer) viewpoint	*Payroll taxes, wages for child*	*Less flexibility in hiring and firing, more complex relationship with child*

2. Pick one of the situations in Question 1, and explain why the decision maker must have decided that the benefits he or she received exceeded, equaled or fell short of the opportunity costs to engage in the activity.

(A) You decide to go to college: Consider the benefits of a college education to be your expected extra future income, growth in knowledge and social development. A decision to attend college occurs when the expected explicit and implicit costs are less than expected benefits. If income were the only criterion, individuals who drop out of college to become star professional athletes may have concluded that the costs of missing a professional sports career exceeded the anticipated future income from becoming a better educated, but nonstarring, individual in a career outside of sports.

(B) *You take a job after school:* Working after school may supplement family income, but it normally increases the disposable income of the high school student. More disposable income benefits the income earner. Choice of hours, however, can make the benefits exceed the costs. Total benefits may exceed total costs, even when the cost of an additional hour of work per week exceeds the benefit of the additional hour of work. But the economic way of thinking causes the person to adjust work so the extra benefit from the extra hour just matches the extra cost. If this extra hour of work causes the worker to earn a lower grade in a class, total benefits of work may exceed total costs of work; but the marginal costs of that extra hour of work greatly exceed the marginal benefits of the extra income.

(C) *You study for and take an AP Economics Examination:* While the benefits of studying for an AP Economics Examination are self-evident, there are costs that most students can list in a minute. AP Economics students may take other AP tests, so the management of study time becomes a crucial factor in mastery of all the tests. Marginal decisions determine time allocation among the subject areas: When an extra hour spent on economics adds more expected score points than an hour spent on chemistry, the student spends the hour studying economics.

(D) *A stay-at-home dad returns to work:* Stay-at-home parents sacrifice money income. This stay-at-home dad concluded that the benefits of working for a living exceeded the lost benefits of staying at home. Lost benefits could be explicit in the form of lower or no public-assistance payments. Implicit lost benefits involve control over use of time, ability to bond with and teach children, and the ability to have household chores done without paying someone else. Explicit new costs will include payroll taxes, possibly income taxes, commuting costs, child-care expenses and the costs of work clothes.

(E) *Family members work in their parents' restaurant:* This is the toughest scenario of all. Family decision making frequently follows tradition rather than market criteria. A student may work in a family business that is not the best fit for either the family or the student "just because" other generations worked there. At the other extreme, knowing the business and feeling a sense of ownership in it may bring out the finest service possible from a young worker. Either scenario carries costs and benefits. A student's voluntary work for a family business may generate few perceived benefits. The student works to earn family approval, and this approval is worth more than the perceived costs. Adult members of the family business may want their high school children to sharpen their work ethic. The business may absolutely need the family members to assist as part of family tradition or because a family member has higher productivity than a stranger. Some family restaurants hold secret recipes that are not entrusted to anyone beyond the family. Both parties — the employee and employer — must conclude that the benefits of working exceed the costs, or family labor services will not be purchased.

Campus Parking Activity

1. What central problem does Stanford face in parking spaces? *Because the supply of parking spaces is limited, the scarce good must be allocated among people who want parking spaces.*

2. What are the three ways societies deal with scarcity? *Tradition, command and the market*

3. Categorize the five methods Stanford could use to allocate parking spaces. Which use tradition? Command? The market?

   Leave things as they have been: tradition

   First-come, first-served: tradition and command

   Markets and a price system: the market

   Democracy: a political solution, which is command

   Random choice: command with some market because of reselling

4. For each proposed method, explain what behaviors are encouraged or discouraged by different groups.

   Leave things as they have been: Faculty are rewarded; student parking is discouraged.

   First-come, first-served: People with low opportunity costs for time are rewarded; those who have high opportunity costs for time and many productive activities are penalized. For example, a professor might spend time for research on hunting for a parking space.

   Markets and a price system: People with higher incomes and more important time alternatives are rewarded; those with low opportunity costs for time or with lower incomes are penalized.

   Democracy: People with political clout are rewarded.

   Random choice: People with luck, regardless of cost, are rewarded; the unlucky are penalized.

5. If the goal is equity, which system would you adopt and why? *It is impossible to say because equality or fairness depends on each individual's perspective. Many students will choose first-come, first-served or random choice because everyone has an "equal chance." This could lead to a discussion about what is fair.*

6. If the goal is efficiency, which system would you adopt and why? *The market system leads to the greatest efficiency because every choice has an opportunity cost. There is an incentive to make choices that minimize opportunity cost. Each person makes choices based on his or her costs and benefits.*

7. Which system of allocating parking spaces do you recommend? Why? *Answers will vary. However, students should use equity or efficiency as the basis for their answers.*

Circular Flow Activity

1. Give three examples of resource owners. *Answers will vary because resource owners are anyone who has land, labor, capital or entrepreneurship to sell in the factor market.*

2. Define a business firm. *A business firm buys resources and, in turn, sells goods and services to resource owners.*

3. What is the product market? *A market where finished goods and services are bought and sold*

4. Give three examples of transactions you made this week in the product market. *Answers will vary. Any purchase of a good or service will do.*

5. What is a factor market? *A market where the factors of production (land, labor, capital, entrepreneurship) are bought and sold*

6. Give an example of a transaction you or your family made this month in a factor market. *It probably would be wages for labor, although many other transactions are possible.*

7. How are businesses connected to factor and product markets? *They buy in the factor markets and sell in the product markets.*

8. What determines the prices of land, labor, capital and entrepreneurship in a factor market? *Supply and demand*

9. Where do resource owners get the money to buy goods and services in the product market? *From selling their resources in the factor markets*

10. Where do business firms get the money to pay resource owners for their land, labor, capital and entrepreneurship in factor markets? *From selling the goods and services they produce with the factors of production*

11. Why is it important to know that a market economy is characterized by interdependence? *Interdependence is important because people specialize and trade their production in markets for other products they need. The circular flow of income shows the interdependence of the economy.*

Absolute Advantage and Comparative Advantage, Specialization and Trade

Introduction and Description

Activity 6 introduces *absolute advantage* and *comparative advantage*. Although these concepts are covered in more detail in the international-trade unit in Macroeconomics, they explain economic activities intranationally as well. Students who take the AP Microeconomics Exam will be tested on them.

People trade because both parties stand to benefit when they engage in voluntary exchanges. Comparative advantage is a powerful concept that helps explain how mutual benefits can occur from exchange. A nation and an individual have a comparative advantage when they can make one or more products at a lower opportunity cost than another nation or individual. When producers specialize in the lower-cost product, they can make additional goods, which they can trade to other producers for goods that would have been more costly to make. To determine a comparative advantage, costs must be measured in terms of what other products must be forgone to make a particular product. This relative measure is a subtle, difficult and very important idea for students to understand. A nation's or an individual's comparative advantage will change as the opportunity costs of products made available by different trading partners change.

Objectives

1. Define *comparative advantage* and *absolute advantage*.
2. Describe and give examples of the law of comparative advantage.
3. Explain how both parties in a trade gain from voluntary exchange.
4. Define *specialization* and *exchange*.
5. Use data to determine absolute and comparative advantage.

Time Required

One class period or 45 minutes

Materials

1. Activity 6
2. Visuals 1.4 and 1.5

Procedure

1. Begin with a discussion about the benefits of trade. Ask the students what life would be like if every person had to be totally self-sufficient and could not specialize and trade. Emphasize the point that individuals, not nations, trade. However, specialization and trade can be accomplished both domestically and internationally. The more we trade, the better off we all are.

2. Use Visual 1.4 to distinguish between absolute advantage and comparative advantage. Provide examples of absolute and comparative advantage. Discuss the two examples on Visual 1.4.

    (A) What if a lawyer can do word processing faster than any secretary she can hire? The lawyer has an absolute advantage in the practice of law and in word processing. Should she hire the secretary? *Yes, because the opportunity cost of the lawyer's time spent as a secretary is very high, perhaps $100 an hour or more. She could hire more than one secretary for this amount and still come out ahead.*

    (B) The doctor/nurse situation is the same as the lawyer/secretary situation.

3. Use Visual 1.5 to illustrate absolute and comparative advantage using outputs. You might calculate the opportunity cost of a CD and of a pound of beef for the students; this is similar to what is done in Activity 6. Show that the comparative advantage for each product

depends on which country produces the product at the lower opportunity cost. The example assumes Canada and Japan have the same resources, since the table contains output. Canada has an absolute and comparative advantage in beef. Neither has an absolute advantage in CDs, but Japan has a comparative advantage.

4. Tell the students that they are now going to do an activity that illustrates the same concept of comparative advantage using inputs (minutes or hours to produce a good) and outputs (number of goods produced per hour or per minute). In either case, the key is that if one party trades the good for which it has the lower opportunity cost for the good for which the other party has the lower opportunity cost, both parties gain.

5. Have the students read Activity 6 through Part A. Then carefully review the examples until they get the math right.

6. Now ask questions such as these to make sure the students understand the concept of comparative advantage:

(A) How do you determine who has a comparative advantage in producing a good or service? *The person who can produce the good at the lower opportunity cost has the comparative advantage.*

(B) Why is comparative advantage important? *If people trade on the basis of comparative advantage, they will gain by having more goods at the same cost or the same goods at a lower cost.*

(C) Why does it matter if Ty and Jessica save 35 minutes by specializing in what they do comparatively better? *They can cut and trim more lawns in a week and therefore earn more income, or they can use the 35 minutes to do something else. They are better off.*

(D) Why should Mark and Doreen specialize in what they have a comparative advantage in? *Their output of installations of radios and speakers increases. They earn more income, and consumers obtain more service.*

7. Have the students answer the questions in Part B.

8. Go over the answers to the questions.

Opportunity Cost and Comparative Advantage

Part B: Questions

1. What is the difference between comparative advantage and absolute advantage? *Absolute advantage states that a particular individual or country can produce more of a specific commodity than another individual or country using the same amount of resources. Comparative advantage states that a particular country or individual can produce a specific commodity at a lower opportunity cost (in terms of forgone production in an alternative commodity) than another country or individual.*

2. You're given the following information about a newlywed couple and the time it takes each of them to do two different chores: vacuuming a room or washing a load of dishes.

	Mike	Debbie
Vacuum a room	60 minutes	45 minutes
Wash a load of dishes	30 minutes	45 minutes

(A) What is Mike's opportunity cost of vacuuming in terms of washing dishes? *Washing two loads of dishes*

(B) What is Mike's opportunity cost of washing dishes in terms of vacuuming? *Vacuuming 1/2 of a room*

(C) What is Debbie's opportunity cost of vacuuming in terms of washing dishes? *Washing one load of dishes*

(D) What is Debbie's opportunity cost of washing dishes in terms of vacuuming? *Vacuuming one room*

(E) Who has the *absolute* advantage in vacuuming? _____*Debbie*_____

(F) Who has the *absolute* advantage in washing dishes? _____*Mike*_____

(G) Who has the *comparative* advantage in vacuuming? _____*Debbie*_____

(H) Who has the *comparative* advantage in washing dishes? _____*Mike*_____

(I) Who should do which chore and why? Base your answer only on the information above and on comparative-advantage considerations. *Mike should wash dishes and Debbie should vacuum. They will finish their chores sooner by specializing according to their comparative advantage. The person with the lower opportunity cost should perform the chore.*

3. Now, you're given the following information about Andy and Hannah and the time it takes each of them to clean an office and clean a jail cell:

	Andy	Hannah
Cleaning offices	60 minutes	20 minutes
Cleaning jail cells	30 minutes	15 minutes

(A) What is Andy's opportunity cost of cleaning offices in terms of cleaning jail cells?
Cleaning two jail cells

(B) What is Hannah's opportunity cost of cleaning offices in terms of cleaning jail cells?
Cleaning 4/3 of a jail cell

(C) What is Andy's opportunity cost of cleaning jail cells in terms of cleaning offices?
Cleaning 1/2 of an office

(D) What is Hannah's opportunity cost of cleaning jail cells in terms of cleaning offices?
Cleaning 3/4 of an office

(E) Who has the *absolute* advantage in cleaning offices?_____*Hannah*_____

(F) Who has the *absolute* advantage in cleaning jail cells?_____*Hannah*_____

(G) Who has the *comparative* advantage in cleaning offices?_____*Hannah*_____

(H) Who has the *comparative* advantage in cleaning jail cells?_____*Andy*_____

(I) Who should do which chore and why? Base your answer only on the information above and on comparative-advantage considerations. *Hannah should clean offices and Andy should clean jail cells, and they will finish sooner. The person with the lower opportunity cost should perform the chore.*

4. Consider the following two countries. Assume they produce only these two goods. *Note that productivity is now measured in how many goods can be produced per hour*, the opposite of how we measured it in Questions 2 and 3.

	United States	Japan
Cars	12	10
Computers	4	6

(A) What is the United States' opportunity cost of making cars?
For every car, it must give up 1/3 of a computer.

(B) What is Japan's opportunity cost of making cars?
For every car, it must give up 3/5 of a computer.

(C) What is the United States' opportunity cost of making computers?
For every computer, it must give up three cars.

(D) What is Japan's opportunity cost of making computers?
For every computer, it must give up 5/3 of a car.

(E) Which country has the *absolute* advantage in cars? _____*United States*_____

(F) Which country has the *absolute* advantage in computers? _____*Japan*_____

(G) Which country has the *comparative* advantage in cars? _____*United States*_____

(H) Which country has the *comparative* advantage in computers? _____*Japan*_____

(I) Which country should produce which good and why? Base your answer only on the information above and on comparative-advantage considerations. *The United States should produce cars, and Japan should produce computers because cars and computers would then be produced by the lower-cost country. The total output of cars and computers will be higher.*

5. Use the law of comparative advantage to explain why self-sufficiency leads to a lower standard of living. *If people and nations do not trade on the basis of comparative advantage, there will be fewer goods and services for people to enjoy. People will be poorer. Less trade or self-sufficiency means a lower standard of living.*

Practice in Applying Economic Reasoning

Introduction and Description

This lesson reinforces some of the economic-reasoning ideas that were introduced in Lesson 1. It provides practice in applying economic reasoning to a wide variety of conventional and unconventional situations. Activity 7 emphasizes *marginalism*, a concept used throughout the course. In this case, marginal or additional benefits are compared with marginal or additional costs. Activity 8 is a problem set that illustrates the idea that economic principles affect all kinds of behavior, not just financial, business or consumer behavior.

Objectives

1. Describe and give examples of the law of comparative advantage.
2. Explain how both parties in a trade gain from voluntary exchange.
3. Describe and analyze the *economic way of thinking*.
4. Identify the opportunity costs of various courses of action involving a hypothetical problem.
5. Apply scarcity concepts to a variety of economic and noneconomic situations.

Time Required

Two class periods or 90 minutes

Materials

Activities 7 and 8

Procedure

1. Initiate a discussion on the concept of *marginalism*. In economics, decisions should always be made at the margin. The marginal benefits and marginal costs associated with a choice will determine the effects and wisdom of our decisions. Tell the students they will return to marginal analysis throughout the course.

2. Have the students complete Activity 7, "Is the Benefit of Doing Anything Worth the Cost of Doing It Well?"

3. Go over the answers to Activity 7 with the students.

4. Assign Activity 8 as homework. Tell the students to write out the answers. You could collect this as homework or have the students discuss the answers in small groups.

5. Have a general class discussion on the problems.

Is the Benefit of Doing Anything Worth the Cost of Doing It Well?

1. After reading in *Bartlett's Familiar Quotations* that "knowledge is power," a student decides to be as knowledgeable as possible by devoting the next 20 years, without interruption, to college. From the data below, how would you advise this person to reconsider a career as a professional student? (Write the correct answer in the space, or underline the correct word in parentheses.)

 Figure 7.1
Degree Earned and Expected Lifetime Earnings

Degree Earned	Expected Lifetime Earnings by Degree	Expected Lifetime Costs by Degree
High School	$ 800,000	$ 0
Associate	1,200,000	25,000
Bachelor's	2,000,000	100,000
Master's	2,100,000	200,000
Doctorate	2,500,000	2,500,000

(A) Would a master's degree and a doctorate degree be likely to build the human capital of the student? (*Yes* / No)

In the process of building knowledge, would the doctorate degree be the best example of doing a job well? (*Yes* / No)

(B) Assuming that inflation and interest rates are considered in these data, what is the optimal degree for this person to earn at the university? *Master's degree*

(C) Which criterion did you use to determine the optimal degree this person should obtain? (*Total* / *__Marginal__*) benefits = (total / *__marginal__*) costs   *MB = $100,000   MC = $100,000*

(D) Since inflation is already factored into the data, what is the most likely reason that the costs of a doctorate degree rose to such a high level? *The person's earning power is greater as he or she gets older. The higher degree also increases earning power. Going to school longer means these potential earnings are sacrificed, which increases the opportunity cost.*

2. Wrapping garbage neatly before taking it to the trash can, raking leaves on a windy day, hand-drying dishes after they have been run through a dishwasher's dry cycle and similar tasks seem to push the credibility of any value in doing a job well.

(A) Give examples of job requests you have heard that illustrate severely declining marginal benefits. *Answers will vary. Ironing blue jeans and cleaning up every speck of dust are examples.*

(B) Give estimates of the opportunity cost of accomplishing these tasks. *The opportunity cost depends on the example.*

3. Consider a group of small or large electronic items that you have thought about buying. Do you always choose the highest-priced goods? Explain your answer. *People frequently don't purchase the highest-priced goods because the marginal benefit of the highest quality is not worth the additional cost.*

4. If you wanted to eliminate "senioritis," how would you change the college-acceptance process and/or the incentives offered by high school instructors? *You could make college acceptance conditional on work during the entire senior year. This would raise the cost of senioritis and provide an incentive for seniors to study harder.*

Thinking in an Economic Way

Economics is a way of thinking that views people as rational decision makers who seek to maximize their own welfare within their personal interests and values. Even though people have different values, we all want to maximize benefits and minimize costs. Some people want fast cars and yachts; some want big houses and a good life for their families and others value education. Because of costs, people cannot get everything they want.

As you answer these problems, you must be sure to evaluate costs and benefits. And never forget the concept of scarcity.

1. True, false or uncertain, and explain why? "The best things in life are free." *False. The best things in life are not free. Students may assert that the best things in life are love and friendship, and these are not economic goods. But love and friendship have opportunity costs.*

2. Is life priceless? Give at least four examples to support your opinion. Use the concept of opportunity cost in your answer. *No. This question is controversial. Nevertheless, if life were priceless, we would not use life as an opportunity cost for any other benefit. Yet we fight wars. On a less dramatic level, the "benefits" of smoking, drinking, hang gliding, using illegal drugs, driving without a seat belt and driving at excessive speeds confront people with the risk of an increased probability of death, yet people engage in these activities. If life were priceless, we would use whatever resources were necessary to cure cancer, heart disease and other terminal illnesses.*

3. Teachers are usually displeased when students cheat on tests. Which of these methods intended to stop cheating would be most effective? Why?

   (A) Teachers should say nothing and trust the students to be fair. If people are treated responsibly, they will act responsibly.

   (B) Teachers should give lectures on morality and explain to the students how their actions are not only dishonest but may hurt their classmates.

   (C) Teachers should walk around the room when giving tests, give the students alternate tests and make sure the students understand they will fail if they are caught cheating.

   Only (C) involves opportunity costs for the student who is cheating. For some people, the opportunity cost of cheating is their conscience. Students compare benefits and costs when contemplating cheating. For those with weak consciences, other costs must be substituted to discourage them. If the costs of cheating are greater than the benefits, cheating will not occur.

4. True, false or uncertain, and explain why? "The economic concept of scarcity is not relevant to a modern economy such as the United States. Americans are surrounded by vast quantities of unused goods. For example, food fills the supermarkets, and every car dealer has many cars in the showroom and lot. Americans are surrounded by plenty, not scarcity." *False. Scarcity is a relative concept, not an absolute one. Resources are scarce compared with wants. Unsold stocks of goods do not prove that scarcity does not exist because these goods still have a price. If there were no scarcity, we could produce everything we wanted at a price of zero.*

5. True, false or uncertain, and explain why? "Money is one of America's most important economic resources." *False. Money is not a resource. If the government prints more money, it does not affect the number of goods and services used to satisfy our wants.*

6. An economics professor got a new job in a new town. When she arrived in the new town, she wanted to rent an apartment. She pulled into the first gas station she saw, filled up her tank and drove around inspecting apartments. She rented the tenth apartment she inspected. Does her behavior make sense economically, or did she fail to practice what she preaches? Use marginal benefit and marginal cost analysis in your answer. *Her behavior does make sense economically. The benefits of finding a cheaper gas station were not as high as the opportunity cost. It was not until the tenth apartment that the additional benefits and additional opportunity costs of searching for apartments were equal. This makes sense. After all, a good place to live at a reasonable cost is more important than saving a few cents on a gallon of gas.*

7. Tina is an outstanding lawyer. She also word processes faster than anyone else in her town. Tom word processes at half the speed of Tina. Tom is not a lawyer. Should Tina hire Tom? Why or why not? Use the concepts of absolute and comparative advantage in your answer. *Tina should hire Tom. The key is the law of comparative advantage. Tina sacrifices an hour of legal fees if she does her own word processing. She can probably pay several Toms to word process for less than she can earn in an hour as a lawyer. Therefore, she specializes in law, and Tom specializes in word processing.*

Sample Multiple-Choice Questions

1. *D*	7. *E*	13. *C*	19. *D*	25. *C*
2. *B*	8. *B*	14. *C*	20. *E*	26. *B*
3. *E*	9. *B*	15. *D*	21. *C*	27. *B*
4. *B*	10. *B*	16. *C*	22. *C*	28. *C*
5. *D*	11. *A*	17. *B*	23. *A*	29. *C*
6. *C*	12. *C*	18. *C*	24. *C*	30. *E*

Advanced Placement Economics Teacher Resource Manual © National Council on Economic Education, New York, N.Y.

Sample Short Free-Response Questions

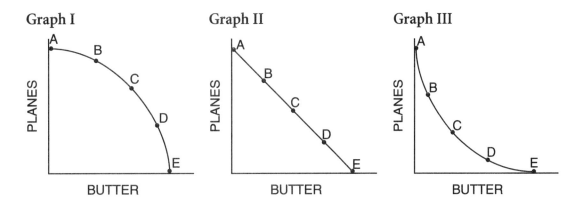

Graph I   Graph II   Graph III

PLANES — BUTTER

1. Explain what would have to be true in each case for the production possibilities curves to be shaped as they are in Graphs I, II and III.

    Graph I assumes increasing opportunity cost. The shape of the curve is concave to the origin or bowed out. If you move from Point A to Point E, you must give up increasing amounts of planes to get more butter. This is what a production possibilities curve should look like.

    Graph II assumes constant opportunity cost. As you go from Point A to Point E, the trade-offs do not change.

    Graph III, a curve convex to the origin, assumes decreasing opportunity cost.

    Economic theory supports Graph I as a graph that correctly represents the law of increasing cost.

2. True, false or uncertain, and explain why? "If you won $1 million in the lottery, you wouldn't have the economic problem of scarcity." *False. People with $1 million cannot spend more than $1 million. Even if people had all the money they could use, time to use it would be scarce.*

Sample Long Free-Response Questions

1. Every society has the fundamental problem of scarcity.

    (A) What is scarcity? *Scarcity exists because there are limited resources to fulfill unlimited wants.*

    (B) What three questions must every society answer because of scarcity? *What to produce and how much of each good or service to produce, how to produce, and for whom to produce*

    (C) What are the three ways societies have dealt with the scarcity problem? *Tradition, command and market*

    (D) Give one example of how each way is used in the United States. *Answers will vary.*

2. Hightechland produces two commodities: movies and computers. Hightechland's resources include workers, factories, electricity and so on. The following schedule indicates some of the points on Hightechland's production possibilities curve.

Commodity	A	B	C	D	E
Movies	100	75	50	25	0
Computers	0	30	55	70	80

    (A) Does movie production exhibit increasing, decreasing or constant per-unit opportunity costs? *Movie production indicates increasing per-unit opportunity costs. As more movies are produced, increasingly more computers must be sacrificed.*

    (B) Graph Hightechland's production possibilities curve, and label it AA.

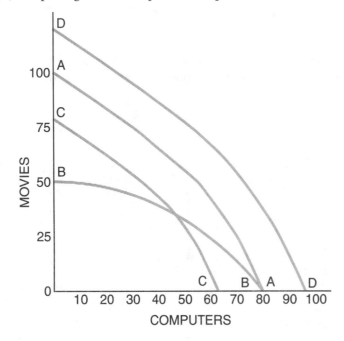

Advanced Placement Economics Teacher Resource Manual © National Council on Economic Education, New York, N.Y.

(C) Suppose Hightechland is operating at Point C but would like to alter production to Point D. What would be the per-unit opportunity cost of producing more computers? *With a move from Point C to Point D, the per-unit opportunity cost of producing one additional computer is 1 ²/₃ movies.*

(D) Suppose Hightechland is operating at Point C but would like to alter production to Point B. What would be the per-unit opportunity cost of producing more movies? *The per-unit opportunity cost of producing one more movie as we alter the production from Point C to Point B is one computer.*

(E) What will happen to Hightechland's production possibilities curve if many of its movie sets are destroyed by fire? (Assume that the sets are not used in the production of computers.) Using the same graph you drew for Question 2(B), draw Hightechland's new production possibilities curve and label it BB. *The point on the axis will shift inward for the movie production, but the point on the axis corresponding to computer production will not change.*

(F) What will happen to Hightechland's production possibilities curve if all the country's resources are reduced (perhaps by natural disaster or war)? Using the same graph as in Question 2(B), draw Hightechland's new production possibilities curve and label it CC. *Shift the production possibilities curve to the left or inward.*

(G) What will happen to Hightechland's production possibilities curve if technology improves both the production of movies and the production of computers? Using the same graph as in Question 2(B), draw Hightechland's new production possibilities curve and label it DD. *Shift the production possibilities curve to the right or outward.*

3. Explain how each of the following may affect the production possibilities curve of the United States or the point at which the economy is operating. Draw a production possibilities curve; put "Capital Goods" on the vertical axis and "Consumer Goods" on the horizontal axis. Now, add a PPC curve or point to the graph to illustrate the scenario.

(A) The Congress and the president decide to provide more funding for higher education with more students attending college and graduating. *More education increases human capital, a resource, and moves the curve outward.*

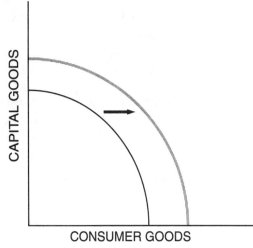

(B) New advances in medicine allow for a healthier lifestyle. *Better medicine improves human capital, a resource, and moves the curve outward.*

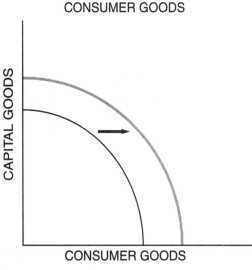

(C) The United States agrees to be a part of a world-trade agreement that will foster international trade. *International trade increases output because of the law of comparative advantage and moves the curve outward.*

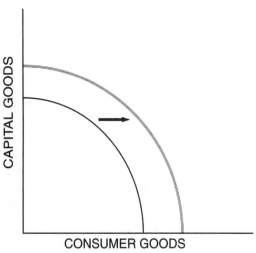

(D) The unemployment rate increases in the economy from 4.2 percent to 5.1 percent of the labor force. *The increase in the unemployment rate results in underemployed resources, which is illustrated by a point inside the curve. The resources (workers) are still available but are not being employed.*

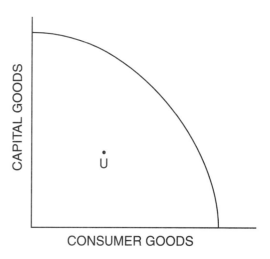

(E) Computer viruses are out of control, and efficiency and output in the economy fall. *The computer viruses take computers out of commission, which shifts the curve inward.*

The Economic Way of Thinking

- Everything has a cost.

- People choose for good reasons.

- Incentives matter.

- People create economic systems to influence choices and incentives.

- People gain from voluntary trade.

- Economic thinking is marginal thinking.

- The value of a good or service is affected by people's choices.

- Economic actions create secondary effects.

- The test of a theory is its ability to predict correctly.

Production Possibilities Curve

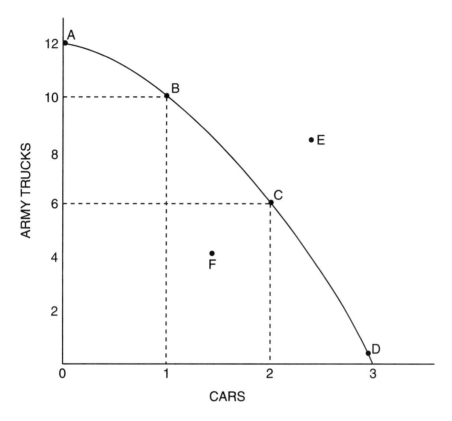

(A) What trade-offs are involved?

(B) Why is the PPC concave, or bowed out, from the origin?

(C) What does a point inside the PPC illustrate?

(D) What is an historical example of a point inside the PPC?

(E) What is the significance of a point outside the PPC?

(F) Under what conditions can a point outside the PPC be reached?

Transparency developed by Faye Ison, Horace Mann High School, Gary, Ind., and Diana Spinnati, Mansfield City Schools, Mansfield, Ohio.

The Circular Flow of Resources, Goods, Services and Money Payments

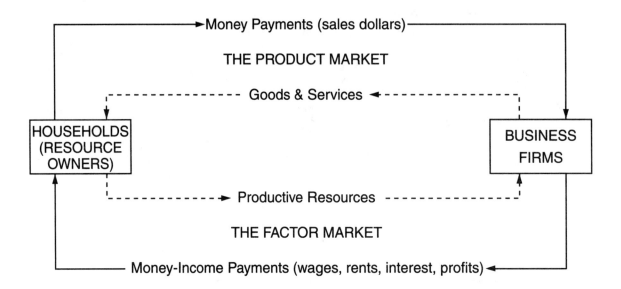

Absolute Advantage and Comparative Advantage

ABSOLUTE ADVANTAGE
- One nation can produce more output with the same resources as the other.

COMPARATIVE ADVANTAGE
- One nation can produce a good at a lower opportunity cost than the other.

EXAMPLES OF COMPARATIVE ADVANTAGE
- Lawyer and secretary
- Doctor and nurse

Determining Comparative Advantage (Output Method)

	CDs	Pounds of Beef
Japan	4	2
Canada	4	6

1. Which nation has an absolute advantage in producing CDs?

2. Which nation has an absolute advantage in producing beef?

3. Which nation has a comparative advantage in producing CDs?

4. Which nation has a comparative advantage in producing beef?

5. Should Japan specialize in CDs or beef?

6. Should Canada specialize in CDs or beef?

Advanced Placement Economics Teacher Resource Manual © National Council on Economic Education, New York, N.Y.

Microeconomics | Unit 2

The Nature and Functions
of Product Markets

17 class periods or 765 minutes
(23 percent of course time)

Unit Overview

Unit 2 focuses on the laws of supply and demand and their effects on the allocation of resources. These concepts account for 20 percent to 30 percent of the Advanced Placement Microeconomics Examination.

The laws of supply and demand are always associated with economics. "Teach a parrot to say demand and supply, and you have an economist," according to some wags.

Supply and demand are tools for understanding a wide variety of specific issues, as well as the operation of the entire economic system. Students need a firm grasp of the laws of supply and demand to understand issues that will be discussed in subsequent units.

In this unit, the students should learn that supply and demand curves are models for understanding human behavior. If the students try merely to memorize the relationships on the graphs, they will not be able to apply supply and demand analysis to a wide variety of issues. Simple memorization will make it difficult to answer the complex application questions on the AP Exam.

This unit contains worksheets on changes in demand, supply, and equilibrium price and quantity. It also covers elasticity of demand and supply, as well as the effects of price ceilings and floors, income effects, substitution effects and diminishing marginal utility. The unit concludes with a series of essays about applying price theory to both conventional and unconventional situations.

Before you begin this unit, it would be a good idea to conduct a supply and demand simulation. By simulating market behavior, the students better understand the behavior behind the curves. There are many simulations available. A good one is "A Classroom Market for Crude Oil" in *Focus: High School Economics*, 2nd ed. (New York: National Council on Economic Education, 2001).

The Lesson Planner

Lesson 1 emphasizes the law of demand and determinants of demand. It uses **Activities 9, 10** and **11** and **Visuals 2.1** and **2.2**.

Lesson 2 emphasizes the law of supply and the determinants of supply. It uses **Activities 12** and **13** and **Visuals 2.3** and **2.4**.

Lesson 3 emphasizes how markets reach equilibrium and the effects of shifts in supply and demand on equilibrium price and quantity. It uses **Activities 14, 15** and **16** and **Visuals 2.5** and **2.6**.

Lesson 4 covers everything anyone ever wanted to know about price and income elasticity of demand. It uses **Activities 17, 18, 19, 20** and **21** and **Visuals 2.7, 2.8, 2.9** and **2.10**.

Lesson 5 emphasizes the effects of price ceilings and price floors. It uses **Activity 22** and **Visuals 2.11** and **2.12**.

Lesson 6 requires the students to apply supply and demand analysis to a variety of conventional and unconventional situations. It uses **Activity 23**.

Week 1

Day 1

(A) Sell an "A."

(B) Use Visual 2.1 to illustrate the difference between a change in demand and a change in quantity demanded.

(C) Discuss determinants of demand using Visual 2.2.

(D) Assign Activity 9 as homework.

Day 2

(A) Go over Activity 9.

(B) Have the students complete Activity 10 and discuss it.

(C) Give a lecture on diminishing marginal utility and illustrate it with a simulation.

(D) Assign Activity 11 as homework.

Day 3

(A) Go over Activity 11.

(B) Illustrate the law of supply using push-up simulation.

(C) Use Visual 2.3 to illustrate the difference between a change in supply and a change in quantity supplied.

(D) Use Visual 2.4 to discuss determinants of supply.

(E) Assign Activity 12 as homework.

Day 4

(A) Go over Activity 12.

(B) Have the students complete Activity 13 and discuss the answers.

Week 1 (continued)

Day 5

(A) Conduct a demonstration of equilibrium.

(B) Use Visual 2.5 to show how markets reach equilibrium.

(C) Assign Activity 14 as homework.

Week 2

Day 6

(A) Discuss answers to Activity 14.

(B) Use Visual 2.6 to illustrate shifts in supply and demand.

(C) Have the students complete Activity 15 and discuss it.

(D) Assign Activity 16 as homework.

Day 7

(A) Go over Activity 16.

(B) Use Visual 2.7 to give a lecture on elasticity of demand.

(C) Use Visual 2.8 to illustrate how to calculate the elasticity coefficient.

(D) Assign Activity 17 as homework.

Day 8

(A) Go over Activity 17.

(B) Have the students complete Activity 18 and discuss it.

Week 2 (continued)

Day 9

(A) Give a lecture on the total revenue test for price elasticity of demand, using Visual 2.9.

(B) Have the students complete Activity 19 and discuss it.

(C) Have the students complete Activity 20 and discuss it.

Day 10

(A) Use Visual 2.10 to discuss tax incidence.

(B) Have the students complete Activity 21, which covers shifts and elasticity of supply and demand applied to an economic-policy question.

(C) Go over Activity 21.

Week 3

Day 11

Conduct a supply and demand simulation such as "A Market in Wheat," "A Classroom Market for Crude Oil" or "A Silver Market." These simulations are in other NCEE publications.

Day 12

(A) Use Visual 2.11 to illustrate a price ceiling.

(B) Use Visual 2.12 to illustrate a price floor.

(C) Have the students complete Activity 22 and discuss the answers.

Day 13

Assign Activity 23. Have the students work on the activity in class.

Week 3 (continued)

Day 14

Go over Activity 23.

Day 15

Review and catch up.

Week 4

Day 16

Give free-response test.

Day 17

Give multiple-choice test.

The Law of Demand

Introduction and Description

In this lesson, the students learn about the law of demand. They first learn that a demand curve is downward sloping and then analyze why it is downward sloping. Finally, they find out which factors other than the price of a product can shift the demand curve for that product. Diagrams are essential for analyzing changes in demand and changes in quantity demanded, but manipulating diagrams is not enough. The students must understand the actual behavior that is illustrated by a demand curve.

Objectives

1. Describe and analyze what demand is and why consumers buy more of a good or service when the price is lower.
2. Differentiate between a *change in demand* and a *change in quantity demanded*.
3. List and explain the *determinants of demand*.
4. Under specific conditions, determine in which direction a demand curve should shift.
5. Define and distinguish between the *income* and *substitution effects*.
6. Define *consumer surplus*, and analyze why markets maximize consumer surplus.
7. Define *diminishing marginal utility*, and explain how the law of diminishing marginal utility affects the behavior of consumers in a market economy.

Time Required

Two and one-half class periods or 113 minutes

Materials

1. Activities 9, 10 and 11
2. Visuals 2.1 and 2.2

Procedure

1. Tell the students that the law of demand describes the behavior of consumers. To illus-

trate this law, you are going to sell an "A" on the next test. Each student will submit a sealed bid. After you receive the bids, develop a demand curve with them. Arrange the bids from the highest to the lowest. In developing the demand curve, point out that the bids are cumulative. That is, a person willing to pay $50 is also willing to pay $25. Develop the demand curve on the chalkboard, and ask the students to describe the behavior of consumers in relation to price and quantity demanded.

2. Use Visual 2.1 to illustrate the difference between a change in demand and a change in quantity demanded. A movement from A to B is a change in quantity demanded. This movement along the curve is caused by a change in the price of the product. Only a change in the price of Greebes will cause a change in the quantity of Greebes demanded. A shift in the curve is caused by factors other than the price of Greebes.

3. Still using Visual 2.1, explain the reason a demand curve shifts. An increase in demand means people are willing and able to buy more at each price. A decrease in demand means people are willing and able to buy less at each price. A movement from D to D_1 is an increase in demand. A movement from D to D_2 is a decrease in demand.

4. Now use Visual 2.2 to discuss the determinants of demand. Give examples in each category.
   - Change in consumer tastes
   - Change in the number of buyers
   - Change in consumer incomes
   - Change in the prices of complementary and substitute goods
   - Change in consumer expectations

5. Have the students complete Activity 9, which presents two equivalent ways of expressing

demand and distinguishes between changes in
the demand curve and movements along the
curve. Be sure to point out that the demand
price is the maximum price consumers would
be willing to pay. Of course, consumers would
be willing to pay a lower price than this maximum price. Activity 9 also covers the concept
of consumer surplus, which is the value
received from the purchase of a good in excess
of the price paid for it. Because there is consumer surplus in a market economy, consumers
are better off. Students have frequently missed
questions on this concept on past AP tests.

6. Reinforce the determinants of demand and
shifts in demand by having the students complete Activity 10 and discuss it.

7. Give a lecture on the substitution and income
effects, which explain why a demand curve is
downward sloping.

8. Give a brief lecture on *diminishing marginal
utility*. Also emphasize *consumer surplus,* which
is the difference between what the good or
service is worth to the consumer and how
much the consumer had to pay for the good or
service in the market. Consumer surplus benefits consumers; this is a major reason that markets benefit consumers.

9. Now illustrate diminishing marginal utility
with a simulation such as the following. You
can use any food in such a simulation.

   (A) Select one student volunteer. Place a dozen
   doughnuts (or other food items) in front of
   the student. Tell the student that you will
   ask him or her to evaluate the utility gained
   from his or her first doughnut. (You might
   want to start with a scale from 0 to 100,
   where 100 is the highest satisfaction.)

   (B) Have the student eat the first doughnut and
   rate the utility gained from that doughnut.
   Keep track of his or her consumption on

the chalkboard with a table that has two
columns: one labeled "Quantity of Doughnuts" and the other labeled "Total Utility."

(C) Now have the student eat a second doughnut. Add the utility gained from this
doughnut to the utility from the first and
place the total in the "Total Utility" column.
Continue until the student refuses to eat
another doughnut; this will be the point at
which negative marginal utility sets in.

(D) Review the "Total Utility" column. At first,
both total and marginal utility may rise;
then total utility may rise, but marginal
utility may fall. Note the increasing total,
but at a decreasing rate. Draw this curve
on the board.

(E) Add a third column to the table, and label
it "Marginal Utility." Review marginal utility. Calculate marginal utility for the second doughnut, then the third. What happens? Emphasize the finding that with one
more unit, the marginal utility decreases.

(F) Continue to calculate until you reach the
point at which the student refused to eat
one more. Ask the student if it would be
fair to say that if he or she were forced to
eat another doughnut, the utility "gained"
might be negative. Add a negative number
to "Total Utility," and then compute the
marginal utility for that last forced doughnut.

(G) With the table still on the board, repeat:
"As more is consumed, the marginal utility
is smaller." Ask how this student could
increase his or her marginal utility of
doughnuts. *Eat fewer: Show the marginal
utility of four doughnuts compared with the
marginal utility of three.*

10. Now have the students complete Activity 11
and discuss it.

Demand Curves, Movements Along Demand Curves and Shifts in Demand Curves

Part A

Figure 9.1 shows the market demand for a hypothetical product: Greebes. Study the data, and plot the demand for Greebes on the axes in Figure 9.2. Label the demand curve D, and answer the questions that follow. Write the correct answer in the answer blanks, or underline the correct words in parentheses.

 Figure 9.1
Demand for Greebes

Price ($ per Greebe)	Quantity Demanded (millions of Greebes)
$.10	350
.15	300
.20	250
.25	200
.30	150
.35	100
.40	50

 Figure 9.2
Demand for Greebes

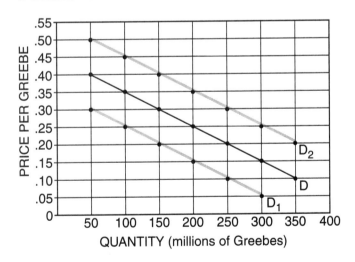

The data for demand curve D indicate that at a price of $0.30 per Greebe, buyers would be willing to buy ___*150*___ million Greebes. Other things constant, if the price of Greebes increased to $0.40 per Greebe, buyers would be willing to buy ___*50*___ million Greebes. Such a change would be a decrease in (demand / **_quantity demanded_**). Other things constant, if the price of Greebes decreased to $0.20, buyers would be willing to buy___*250*___ million Greebes. Such a change would be called an increase in (demand / **_quantity demanded_**).

Now, let's suppose there is a dramatic change in federal income-tax rates that affects the disposable income of Greebe buyers. This change in the *ceteris paribus* (all else being equal) conditions underlying the original demand for Greebes will result in a new set of data, shown in Figure 9.3. Study these new data, and add the new demand curve for Greebes to the axes in Figure 9.2. Label the new demand curve D_1 and answer the questions that follow.

 Figure 9.3
New Demand for Greebes

Price ($ per Greebe)	Quantity Demanded (millions of Greebes)
$.05	300
.10	250
.15	200
.20	150
.25	100
.30	50

Comparing the new demand curve (D_1) with the original demand curve (D), we can say that the change in the demand for Greebes results in a shift of the demand curve to the *(**left** / right)*.

Such a shift indicates that at each of the possible prices shown, buyers are now willing to buy a *(**smaller** / larger)* quantity; and at each of the possible quantities shown, buyers are willing to offer a *(higher / **lower**)* maximum price. The cause of this demand curve shift was a(n) *(**increase** / decrease)* in tax rates that *(increased / **decreased**)* the disposable income of Greebe buyers.

Now, let's suppose that there is a dramatic change in people's tastes and preferences for Greebes. This change in the *ceteris paribus* conditions underlying the original demand for Greebes will result in a new set of data, shown in Figure 9.4. Study these new data, and add the new demand curve for Greebes to the axes in Figure 9.2. Label the new demand curve D_2 and answer the questions that follow.

 Figure 9.4
New Demand for Greebes

Price ($ per Greebe)	Quantity Demanded (millions of Greebes)
$.20	350
.25	300
.30	250
.35	200
.40	150
.45	100
.50	50

Comparing the new demand curve (D2) with the original demand curve (D), we can say that the change in the demand for Greebes results in a shift of the demand curve to the *(left / **right**)*.

Advanced Placement Economics Teacher Resource Manual © National Council on Economic Education, New York, N.Y.

Such a shift indicates that at each of the possible prices shown, buyers are now willing to buy a *(smaller / larger)* quantity; and at each of the possible quantities shown, buyers are willing to offer a *(lower / higher)* maximum price. The cause of this shift in the demand curve was a(n) *(increase / decrease)* in people's tastes and preferences for Greebes.

Part B

Now, to test your understanding, underline the answer you think is the one best alternative in each of the following multiple-choice questions.

1. Other things constant, which of the following would *not* cause a change in the demand (shift in the demand curve) for mopeds?

    (A) A decrease in consumer incomes

    (B) A decrease in the price of mopeds

    (C) An increase in the price of bicycles

    (D) An increase in people's tastes and preferences for mopeds

2. "Rising oil prices have caused a sharp decrease in the demand for oil." Speaking precisely, and using terms as they are defined by economists, choose the statement that best describes this quotation.

    (A) The quotation is correct: An increase in price always causes a decrease in *demand*.

    (B) The quotation is incorrect: An increase in price always causes an increase in *demand*, not a decrease in *demand*.

    (C) The quotation is incorrect: An increase in price causes a decrease in the quantity demanded, not a decrease in demand.

    (D) The quotation is incorrect: An increase in price causes an increase in the *quantity demanded*, not a decrease in *demand*.

3. "As the price of domestic automobiles has inched upward, customers have found foreign autos to be a better bargain. Consequently, domestic auto sales have been decreasing, and foreign auto sales have been increasing." Using only the information in this quotation and assuming everything else constant, which of the following best describes this statement?

    (A) A shift in the demand curves for both domestic and foreign automobiles

    (B) A movement along the demand curves for both foreign and domestic automobiles

    (C) A movement along the demand curve for domestic autos, and a shift in the demand curve for foreign autos

    (D) A shift in the demand curve for domestic autos, and a movement along the demand curve for foreign autos

4. You hear a fellow student say: "Economic markets are like a perpetual see-saw. If demand rises, the price rises; if price rises, then demand will fall. If demand falls, price will fall; if price falls, demand will rise and so on forever." Dispel your friend's obvious confusion in no more than one short paragraph below.

The student is confusing a change in "demand" (shift in the curve) with a change in "quantity demanded" (a movement along the curve). Part of the second sentence, — "if price rises, then demand will fall" — is wrong: The quantity demanded will fall; and since this is not a change in demand, the rest of the statement does not follow.

Part C

Once we have the demand curve, we can define the concept of *consumer surplus*. Consumer surplus is the value received from the purchase of a good in excess of the price paid for it, or stated differently, the difference between the amount a person is willing and able to pay and the actual price paid for each unit.

An approximation of consumer surplus can be shown graphically as the area below the demand curve above the price paid. Redraw the first demand curve (D) from Figure 9.2 on Figure 9.5.

If the price for all the quantities sold is established at $0.30, shade the area above $0.30 up to the demand curve. This is the area of consumer surplus.

Continue to use the demand curve from Figure 9.2, and assume that the price is established at $0.30. There are buyers who will benefit because they are willing and able to pay higher prices than the established price ($0.30). For example, 50 million Greebes are demanded at $0.40, but since the market price is $0.30, there is a gain to the buyers represented by this 50 million. The gain is a total of $5 million ($0.10 x 50 million = $5 million). The buyers of the next 50 million Greebes (always consider the extra or marginal buyers since the buyers at the higher prices will also be willing to buy at the lower price) are willing to pay $0.35, providing a gain of $0.05 of the consumer surplus, for a total of $2.5 million.

Figure 9.5
Consumer Surplus

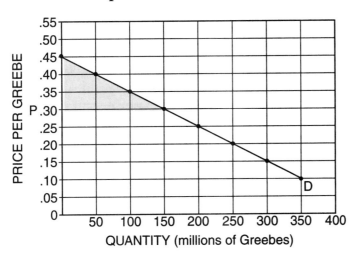

QUANTITY (millions of Greebes)

5. Approximately what will be the total consumer surplus for the buyers of the 150 million Greebes at a price of $0.30? ___ *$7.5 million (50 x $0.10 + 50 x $0.05)* ___

6. If the price consumers pay increases, the shaded area (*increases* / **decreases**). If the price consumers pay decreases, the shaded area (**increases** / *decreases*).

7. If the equilibrium price drops to $0.20, what will happen to consumer surplus? (**Increase** / *Decrease*)

8. At $0.20, calculate the consumer surplus for buyers willing to pay

   (A) $0.40   ___ *$10 million* ___

   (B) $0.35   ___ *$7.5 million* ___

   (C) $0.30   ___ *$5 million* ___

   (D) $0.25   ___ *$2.5 million* ___

   (E) What is the total surplus? ___ *$25 million* ___

9. Will there be any consumer surplus at a price of $0.20 for the buyers willing and able to spend $0.20, $0.15 or $0.10? Why or why not? *No. They are willing to pay equal to or less than the market price.*

Reasons for Changes in Demand

Part A

Read the eight newspaper headlines in Figure 10.2, and use the table to record the impact, if any, of each event on the demand for beef. Use the first column to the right of the headline to show whether the event causes a change in demand. Use the next column to record whether the change is an increase or a decrease in demand. In the third column, decide whether the demand curve shifts left or right. Finally, write the letter for the new demand curve. Use Figure 10.1 to help you. **Always start at curve B**, and move only one curve at a time. One headline implies that the demand for beef does not change.

 Figure 10.1
Beef Consumption in May

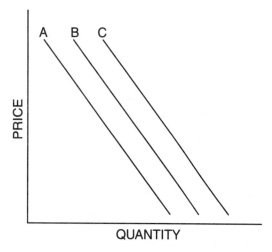

 Figure 10.2

Headline	Demand Shift? (Y/N)	If Demand Shifts, Inc/Dec?	Curve Shifts Left/Right?	New Curve
1. Price of Beef to Rise in June	Y	Inc.	R	C
2. Millions of Immigrants Swell U.S. Population	Y	Inc.	R	C
3. Pork Prices Drop	Y	Dec.	L	A
4. Surgeon General Warns That Eating Beef Is Hazardous to Health	Y	Dec.	L	A
5. Beef Prices Fall; Consumers Buy More	N	—	—	—
6. Real Income for U.S. Drops for Third Month	Y	Dec.	L	A
7. Charcoal Shortage Threatens Memorial Day Cookouts	Y	Dec.	L	A
8. Nationwide Fad: The Disco-Burger	Y	Inc.	R	C

Part B

Categorize each change in demand in Part A according to the reason why demand changed. A given demand curve assumes that consumer expectations, consumer tastes, the number of consumers in the market, the income of consumers, and the prices of substitutes and complements are unchanged. In the table below, place an X next to the reason that the event described in the headline caused a change in demand. One headline will have no answer because it is a change in quantity demanded.

 Figure 10.3

↓ Reason Headline Number →	1	2	3	4	5	6	7	8
A change in consumer expectations	x							
A change in consumer tastes				x				x
A change in the number of consumers in the market		x						
A change in income						x		
A change in the price of a substitute good			x					
A change in the price of a complementary good							x	

Why Is a Demand Curve Downward Sloping?

Part A

Figure 11.1 presents data on Dolores' evaluation of different quantities of polo shirts and different quantities of steak.

1. Use the data to compute the marginal utility of each polo shirt and each steak. The numbers in the figure represent the amount of dollars Dolores is willing to pay for the polo shirts and steaks.

 Figure 11.1

Marginal Utility of Polo Shirts and Steaks

Number of Polo Shirts	Total Utility	Marginal Utility	Number of Steaks	Total Utility	Marginal Utility
0	0		0	0	
1	60	60	1	20	20
2	100	40	2	36	16
3	130	30	3	51	15
4	150	20	4	65	14
5	165	15	5	78	13
6	175	10	6	90	12

2. Using Figure 11.2 (on the next page), plot Dolores' total utility and marginal utility for polo shirts and steaks. Each graph has two points to get you started.

s Unit2Microeconomics
LESSON 1 ■ ACTIVITY 11 Answer Key

* Figure 11.2
Total and Marginal Utility of Polo Shirts and Steaks

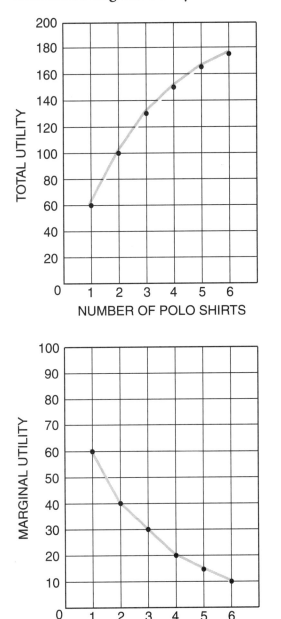

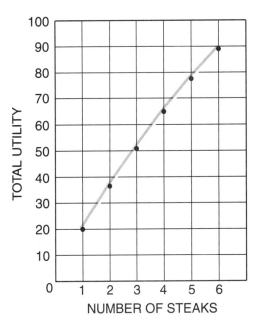

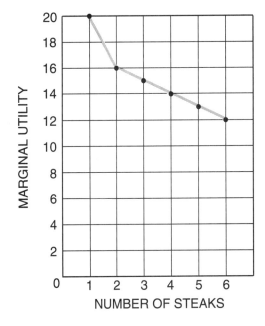

3. Looking at the chart and graphs, you can conclude:

    (A) Total utility is always (***increasing*** / decreasing).

    (B) Marginal utility initially (***increases*** / decreases) and eventually (increases / ***decreases***).

You have demonstrated the law of *diminishing marginal utility*.

Part B

If Dolores has a given budget and must choose between polo shirts and steaks, she will make her choice so that the marginal utility per dollar spent of each good is the same. Using the data in Figure 11.1 and assuming that the price of both goods is $30, let's see what happens if Dolores spends her entire budget of $150 dollars and buys five polo shirts and no steaks. Her marginal utility from the last polo shirt is 15 and from the first steak is 20. So if she buys only four polo shirts and one steak, she loses a utility of 15 on the polo shirt but gains utility of 20 on the steak. Dolores is better off.

Suppose Dolores spends her $150 and buys four polo shirts and one steak. Her marginal utility on the last polo shirt is 20 and on the steak is also 20. She will not want to switch. To buy the next steak gives her an increase in utility of 16, but she would have to give up a polo shirt, which would reduce her utility by 20. Conversely, to buy an additional polo shirt would increase her utility by 15, but she would lose 20 from giving up the steak. Dolores should not change her purchases.

If the prices of the two goods differ, then Dolores will adjust her consumption until the marginal utilities of the two goods, *per dollar spent*, are equal. Or, stated in another way,

$$\frac{MU_x}{P_x} = \frac{MU_y}{P_y}$$

4. Use the information in Figure 11.3 to analyze Frank's choice between gasoline and food. Frank has an income of $130, the price of gasoline is $10 per gallon and the price of food is $20. Complete the table.

Figure 11.3

Gasoline	MU_g	MU_g / P_g	Food	MU_f	MU_f / P_f
1	60	6.0	1	115	5.75
2	55	5.5	2	105	5.25
3	51	5.1	3	98	4.90
4	48	4.8	4	94	4.70
5	47	4.7	5	92	4.60
6	46	4.6	6	90	4.50

(A) Does the combination G = 1 and F = 6 satisfy the income constraint? ___Yes___
Can Frank purchase this combination of goods with his income? ___Yes___

(B) Is this the utility maximizing combination of goods? ___No___

(C) In which direction would Frank like to reallocate his purchases?
Buy less food and more gas

(D) What is Frank's utility maximizing combination of goods, subject to the income constraint of $130? *4 food and 5 gasoline*

Part C

Assume you go into a store to buy a bottle of water. The bottle of water costs you $1. You would have been willing to pay $2. The difference between what you paid and what you would have been willing to pay is *consumer surplus*.

We can calculate Dolores' consumer surplus from buying steak by looking at her demand curve. Look at her marginal utility curve for steak: At three steaks, Dolores is willing to pay $15 for one more; at four steaks, she is willing to pay $14. Dolores will buy steak until the point where the price is equal to the marginal utility of the last steak. Dolores will pay the same price for each of the steaks she buys. Thus if the price of steak is $14, she will buy four steaks; the marginal utility of the fourth steak is $14. Dolores would have been willing to pay more for the earlier steaks. She has gotten a bargain buying four steaks at $14 apiece for a total of $56. She would have been willing to pay $20 for the first, $16 for the second, $15 for the third and $14 for the fourth, for a total of $65. The consumer surplus is the difference between what she was willing to pay ($65) and what she paid ($56). Her consumer surplus is $9.

Consider the following information on Joel's total utility for CD purchases, and then underline the correct answer for each question that follows.

 Figure 11.4
Total Utility of CDs

Number of CDs	Total Utility
1	$ 25
2	$ 45
3	$ 63
4	$ 78
5	$ 90
6	$100
7	$106
8	$110

5. What marginal utility is associated with the purchase of the third CD?

　(A) $18　　　(B) $21　　　(C) $45　　　(D) $63

6. What is Joel's consumer surplus if he purchases three CDs at $11 apiece?

　(A) $30　　　(B) $33　　　(C) $63　　　(D) $96

7. What would happen to Joel's consumer surplus if he purchased an additional CD at $11?

　(A) Consumer surplus declines by $11.

　(B) Consumer surplus increases by $11.

　(C) Consumer surplus increases by $15.

　(D) Consumer surplus increases by $4.

8. How many CDs should Joel buy when they cost $11 apiece?

　(A) 0　　　(B) 3　　　*(C) 5*　　　(D) 7

9. What is Joel's consumer surplus at the optimal number of CD purchases?

   (A) $35   (B) $55   (C) $79   (D) $100

10. If CDs go on sale and their price drops to $8, how many CDs do you expect Joel to buy?

    (A) 5   *(B) 6*   (C) 7   (D) 8

11. Why is consumer surplus important? *Because markets create consumer surplus, many consumers buy the good for less than they would be willing to pay. Consumers like this, but businesses would like to price the goods to collect the consumer surplus.*

Part D
Income and Substitution Effects

Another way of explaining the downward sloping demand curve is through the *income* and *substitution effects.*

Income effect: When the price of a good falls, consumers experience an increase in purchasing power. When the price of a good increases, consumers experience a decrease in purchasing power.

Substitution effect: When the price of a good changes, consumers will substitute toward the now relatively less-expensive good.

You go to your favorite burger place. The price of a burger has increased, but the price of the chicken sandwich stays the same. Over the course of a week, you generally buy both burgers and chicken sandwiches.

12. How will the increase in the price of a burger affect the purchase of burgers? Explain. *You will buy fewer burgers because they are relatively more expensive than chicken sandwiches.*

13. Describe how the substitution effect changes your purchases. *Because the price of burgers increased, chicken is relatively less expensive. Therefore, you substitute chicken for burgers and buy more chicken and fewer burgers.*

14. Describe how the income effect changes your purchases. *The increase in the price of burgers is the same as if you had a decrease in real income or purchasing power. Therefore, you would buy fewer burgers.*

Understanding Supply

Introduction and Description

Prices are determined by demand and supply. This lesson examines the factors that affect supply; these factors are called the *determinants of supply*. The students should also understand the difference between changes in supply and changes in quantity supplied. Students may have more trouble understanding supply than demand. Supply describes the behavior of producers, and the students have had little experience as producers. Of course, they have a lot of experience as consumers.

Objectives

1. Describe the behavior of sellers in a competitive market.
2. Differentiate between a *change in supply* and a *change in quantity supplied.*
3. List and explain the determinants of supply.
4. Under specific conditions, determine in which direction a supply curve should shift.

Time Required

One and one-half class periods or 68 minutes

Materials

1. Activities 12 and 13
2. Visuals 2.3 and 2.4

Procedure

1. Tell the students that supply describes the behavior of sellers. To illustrate this, you are willing to buy push-ups from the students. (WARNING: This activity may not work in some AP classes if all the students will do push-ups for one extra-credit point.)

(A) Tell the students you will give them one extra credit point for 20 push-ups. Ask how many will take your offer. Then make them do the push-ups. If a student says that he or she is injured, tell the student "tough" or

"too bad." You pay for performance. This is how markets work.

(B) Repeat the procedure for two extra-credit points. The students who did push-ups for one point will want to do push-ups for two. Let them. This will show them more clearly that a supply curve is cumulative. Businesses that will sell a product for $1 will also sell it for $2. In any market, some producers have producer surplus.

(C) Repeat the procedure for three extra-credit points.

(D) Construct a supply curve with push-ups (quantity) on the horizontal axis and points (price) on the vertical axis.

(E) Now ask the students why they would sell more push-ups at a higher price. Point out that price is an incentive to producers to produce what consumers want to buy.

2. Use Visual 2.3 to illustrate the difference between a change in supply and a change in quantity supplied. A movement from A to B illustrates a change in quantity supplied. This movement along the curve is caused by a change in the price of a good or service. In other words, only an increase in price can change the quantity of Greebes supplied.

3. Now illustrate a shift in supply. A shift from S to S_2 is a decrease in supply. Less is supplied at each price. A shift from S to S_1 is an increase in supply. More is supplied at each price.

4. Now use Visual 2.4 to discuss the determinants of supply. Give examples of each determinant. Point out that most determinants of supply relate to costs. Any factor that increases costs decreases supply. Any factor that decreases costs increases supply. The determinants of supply are:

- Change in resource prices or input prices
- Change in technology
- Change in taxes and subsidies
- Change in the prices of other goods
- Change in producer expectations
- Change in the number of suppliers

5. Explain the concept of producer surplus to the students. Producer surplus is the amount a seller is paid minus the seller's cost. It is the area below the equilibrium price and above the supply curve. The reason that perfectly competitive markets are so good is that both consumer surplus (studied in Activity 11) and producer surplus are at a maximum. Things just don't get any better than this. Any interference with the equilibrium price under perfectly competitive markets will reduce total consumer and producer surplus. This will be the case with price floors and ceilings, which the students will study later.

6. Have the students complete Activity 12 and go over the answers.

7. Have the students complete Activity 13 and go over the answers.

Supply Curves, Movements Along Supply Curves and Shifts in Supply Curves

In this activity and those that follow, we will assume that the long-run supply curve of Greebes is typically upward sloping.

Part A

Study the data in Figure 12.1 and plot the supply of Greebes on the axes in Figure 12.2. Label the supply curve S and answer the questions that follow. Write the correct answer on the answer blank, or underline the correct answer in parentheses.

 Figure 12.1
Supply of Greebes

Price ($ per Greebe)	Quantity Supplied (millions of Greebes)
$.15	100
.20	150
.25	200
.30	250
.35	300

 Figure 12.2
Supply of Greebes

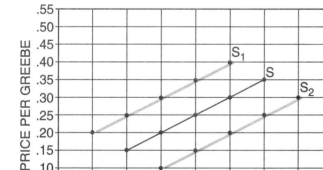

The data for supply curve S indicate that at a price of $0.25 per Greebe, suppliers would be willing to offer ___*200*___ million Greebes. Other things constant, if the price of Greebes increased to $0.30 per Greebe, suppliers would be willing to offer ___*250*___ million Greebes. Such a change would be an increase in (supply / ***quantity supplied***).

Other things constant, if the price of Greebes decreased to $0.20 per Greebe, suppliers would be willing to offer _____*150*_____ million Greebes. Such a change would be called a decrease in *(supply / **quantity supplied**)*.

Now, let's suppose that there is a dramatic change in the price of several of the raw materials used in making Greebes. This change in the *ceteris paribus* conditions underlying the original supply of Greebes will result in a new set of data, such as that shown in Figure 12.3. Study the data, and plot this supply of Greebes on the axes in Figure 12.2. Label the new supply curve S_1 and answer the questions that follow.

 Figure 12.3
New Supply of Greebes

Price ($ per Greebe)	Quantity Supplied (millions of Greebes)
$.20	50
.25	100
.30	150
.35	200
.40	250

Comparing the new supply curve (S_1) with the original supply curve (S), we can say that a change in the supply of Greebes results in a shift of the supply curve to the *(**left** / right)*. Such a shift indicates that at each of the possible prices shown, suppliers are now willing to offer a *(**smaller** / larger)* quantity; and at each of the possible quantities shown, suppliers are willing to accept a *(**higher** / lower)* minimum price. The cause of this supply curve shift was a(n) *(**increase** / decrease)* in prices of several of the raw materials used in making Greebes.

Now, let's suppose that there is a dramatic change in the price of Silopanna, a resource used in the production of Greebes. This change in the *ceteris paribus* conditions underlying the original supply of Greebes will result in a new set of data shown in in Figure 12.4. Study the data, and plot this supply of Greebes on the axes in Figure 12.2. Label the new supply curve S_2 and answer the questions that follow.

 Figure 12.4
New Supply of Greebes

Price ($ per Greebe)	Quantity Supplied (millions of Greebes)
$.10	150
.15	200
.20	250
.25	300
.30	350

Comparing the new supply curve (S_2) with the original supply curve (S), we can say that the change in the supply of Greebes results in a shift of the supply curve to the *(left / **right**)*. Such a shift indicates that at each of the possible prices shown, suppliers are now willing to offer a *(smaller / **larger**)* quantity;

and at each of the possible quantities shown, suppliers are willing to accept a (*lower* / *higher*) minimum price. The cause of this supply curve shift is a(n) (*increase* / *decrease*) in the price of Silopanna,
a resource used in the production of Greebes.

Part B

Now, to check your understanding, underline the answer you think is the one best alternative in each
of the following multiple-choice questions.

1. Other things constant, which of the following would *not* cause a change in the long-run supply of
   beef?
   (A) A decrease in the price of beef
   (B) A decrease in the price of cattle feed
   (C) An increase in the price of cattle feed
   (D) An increase in the cost of transporting cattle to market

2. "Falling oil prices have caused a sharp decrease in the supply of oil." Speaking precisely, and using
   terms as they are defined by economists, choose the statement that best describes this quotation.
   (A) The quotation is correct: A decrease in price always causes a decrease in *supply*.
   (B) The quotation is incorrect: A decrease in price always causes an increase in *supply*, not a
       decrease in *supply*.
   (C) The quotation is incorrect: A decrease in price causes an increase in the *quantity supplied*,
       not a decrease in *supply*.
   (D) The quotation is incorrect: A decrease in price causes a decrease in the quantity supplied,
       not a decrease in supply.

3. You overhear a fellow student say: "Economic markets are like a slide: If supply increases, the price
   increases; if the price increases, then supply will fall. If supply falls, the price will rise; if the price
   increases, supply will increase and so on forever." Dispel your friend's obvious confusion (in no
   more than one short paragraph) below. *The student is confusing a change in quantity supplied*
   with a change in supply. The student also has things backwards: If supply increases, price decreases,
   and that is the end of it, all things equal.

Part C

Once we have the supply curve, we can define the concept of *producer surplus*. Producer surplus is the
amount a seller is paid minus the seller's cost. An approximation of producer surplus can be shown
graphically as the area below the equilibrium price and above the supply curve.

4. Redraw the first supply curve (S) from Figure 12.2 on Figure 12.5. If the price for all the quantities
   sold is established at $0.30, shade the area below $0.30 down to the supply curve. This is the area
   of producer surplus.

✳ Figure 12.5
Producer Surplus

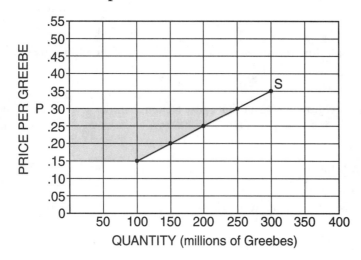

5. Underline the correct answer in parentheses for these questions and for similar questions below.
   (A) If the equilibrium price increases, the shaded area (*increases* / decreases).
   (B) If the equilibrium price decreases, the shaded area (*increases* / *decreases*).

6. Continue to use the supply curve from Figure 12.2 and assume that the selling price is established at $0.25. There are producers who will benefit because some are willing to offer Greebes for a price lower than the established price ($0.25). For example, 100 million Greebes are supplied at $0.15, but since the market price is $0.25, producer surplus for the first 100 million will be $10 million: ($0.25 − $0.15) x 100. Sellers of the next 50 million Greebes (always consider the extra or marginal sellers since the sellers at the lower prices will also be willing to sell at the higher price) are willing to sell Greebes for $0.20, providing a gain of $0.05 for each, resulting in a producer surplus of $2.5 million.

   (A) Approximately what will be the total producer surplus for the sellers if the price is $0.25?
   $12.5 million

   (B) If a seller's price were to increase to $0.30, what will happen to producer surplus?
   (*Increase* / Decrease)

   (C) Calculate the producer surplus for sellers willing to offer
   $0.15   *$15 million (.15 x 100 = 15)*
   $0.20   *$5 million (.10 x 50 = 5)*
   $0.25   *$2.5 million (.05 x 5 = 2.5)*
   $0.30   *$0 million (0 x 50 = 0)*
   What is the total surplus? *$22.5 million*

Reasons for Changes in Supply

Part A

Read the eight newspaper headlines in Figure 13.2, and record the impact, if any, of each event on the supply of cars. Use the first column to the right of the headline to show whether the event will cause a change in supply. Use the next column to record whether the change is an increase or a decrease in supply. In the third column, decide whether the supply curve shifts left or right. Finally, write the letter for the new supply curve. Use Figure 13.1 to help you. **Always start at curve B**, and move only one curve at a time. Two headlines imply that the supply of cars does not change.

 Figure 13.1

Supply of Foreign and Domestic Cars

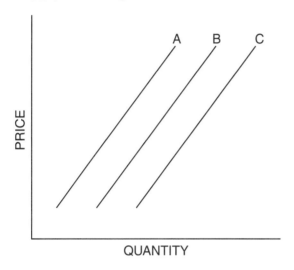

 Figure 13.2

Headline	Supply Shift? (Y/N)	If Supply Shifts, Inc/Dec?	Curve Shifts Left/Right?	New Curve
1. Auto Workers' Union Agrees to Wage Cuts	Y	Inc.	R	C
2. New Robot Technology Increases Efficiency	Y	Inc.	R	C
3. Nationwide Auto Strike Began at Midnight	Y	Dec.	L	A
4. New Import Quotas Reduce Foreign Car Imports	Y	Dec.	L	A
5. Cost of Steel Rises	Y	Dec.	L	A
6. Auto Producer Goes Bankrupt; Closes Operation	Y	Dec.	L	A
7. Buyers Reject New Models	N	—	—	—
8. National Income Rises 2%	N	—	—	—

Part B

Categorize each change in supply in Part A according to the reason why supply changed. In Figure 13.3, place an X next to the reason that the headline indicated a change in supply. In some cases, more than one headline could be matched to a reason. Two headlines do not indicate a shift in supply.

Figure 13.3

↓ Reason Headline Number →	1	2	3	4	5	6	7	8
A change in costs of inputs to production process	x	x			x			
A change in technology		x						
A change in the number of producers in the market			x	x		x		
Government policies				x				

Equilibrium Price, Equilibrium Quantity and the Interrelation of Markets

Introduction and Description

The forces of supply and demand work to establish a price at which the quantity of goods and services people will buy is equal to the quantity suppliers will provide. Activity 14 illustrates this point. If supply or demand changes, equilibrium price and quantity change. Activity 15 drives this point home. Finally, the equilibrium price and quantity of a good or service established by supply and demand affect the equilibrium price and quantity in other markets. Market prices determine what to produce, how to produce and for whom to produce. This is an important point, which is illustrated by Activities 15 and 16.

Objectives

1. Define *equilibrium price* and *equilibrium quantity*.
2. Determine the equilibrium price and quantity when given the demand for and supply of a good or service.
3. Explain why the price of a good or service and the amount bought and sold in a competitive market will be the equilibrium price and quantity.
4. Predict the effects of changes in supply and demand on equilibrium price and quantity and on the price of substitute and complementary goods.
5. Given changes in supply and demand, explain which curve has shifted and why.
6. Analyze how buyers and sellers respond to incentives provided by changing market conditions.
7. Explain how markets provide information that enables consumers and producers to allocate resources more efficiently.
8. Analyze how markets act as rationing devices and how markets allocate resources.

Time Required

Two and one-half class periods or 113 minutes

Materials

1. Activities 14, 15 and 16
2. Visuals 2.5 and 2.6

Procedure

1. Before getting to the graphs, it is helpful to try to define *equilibrium*. Equilibrium is a state of balance between opposing forces. It occurs because everywhere else there is a state of imbalance or *disequilibrium*. In markets, equilibrium is usually a temporary condition. You might illustrate this by putting a ball in a bowl. It will come to rest. Then hit the bowl, and the ball will move and come to rest again. Hitting the bowl is like a shift in demand or supply. However, the difference is that equilibrium occurs at different levels in supply and demand analysis. Each resting place is a different setting, depending on market conditions.

2. Use Visual 2.5 to show how markets reach equilibrium.

   (A) What if the market price were $4? *There would be a surplus of 800 Greebes.* How would sellers get rid of the surplus? *They would lower the price until all the Greebes for sale were sold. The lower price is an incentive that brings more buyers into the market. All the Greebes would be sold at $3, the equilibrium price.*

   (B) What if the market price were $2? *Buyers would demand 800 more Greebes than sellers are willing to sell.* Which buyers will get the Greebes? *The ones who will pay more. The higher price is an incentive that brings more sellers into the market.* Once again, at $3 the number of Greebes offered for sale in a time period is equal to the number of Greebes consumers are willing and able to buy.

   (C) Only at a price of $3 is the number of Greebes sellers are willing and able to sell equal to the number of Greebes consumers are willing and able to buy. This is why the equilibrium price of Greebes is $3 and the equilibrium quantity of Greebes is 1,000.

3. Have the students complete Activity 14 and discuss the answers.

4. Now use Visual 2.6 to illustrate shifts in demand and supply. Each shift changes both the equilibrium price and quantity.

   (A) Graph A shows an increase in demand, causing an increase in price, which causes an increase in quantity supplied.

   (B) Graph B shows a decrease in demand, causing a decrease in price, which causes a decrease in quantity supplied.

   (C) Graph C shows an increase in supply, causing a decrease in price, which causes an increase in quantity demanded.

   (D) Graph D shows a decrease in supply, causing an increase in price, which causes a decrease in quantity demanded.

   (E) In each case, the students should distinguish the difference between a shift and a price effect (in other words, change in quantity demanded or quantity supplied).

5. Have the students complete Activity 15 and discuss the answers.

6. Now it's time for Activity 16, which the students will find difficult. However, the activity shows how markets allocate resources. The activity illustrates how the apparently chaotic billions of individual choices that are made in a market result in an orderly allocation of scarce resources. In this activity, the students should ignore "feedback" effects, which means they should *shift only one curve in each market*. Long-run supply curves are shown so the supply curve shifts only if there are changes in underlying conditions. A change in the equilibrium price and quantity in one market may shift demand or supply in another market. The changes in the other markets are assumed

not to feed back on Market 1 in this time period. Emphasis should be placed on changes in equilibrium quantity as well as changes in equilibrium price. Quantity changes will differ depending on what caused the price change, and quantity changes affect the demand for substitute and complementary goods. Here is the logic that underlies each case:

Question 1. The increased productivity in potatoes results in an increase in supply. Potatoes and bread are substitutes for the consumer (both are starches), so the lower equilibrium price and larger equilibrium quantity of potatoes decrease the demand for bread. With less bread being sold, bakers require less wheat; and with less wheat being sold, farmers require less harvesting machinery, reducing these derived demands.

Question 2. An increased demand for briefcases would result in a higher price and larger quantity of briefcases. This would increase the demand for leather and lead to an increase in its equilibrium price and quantity. The higher price of leather will increase resource costs and decrease the supply of another final product: shoes. Decreased production of shoes results in decreased derived demand for shoelaces and for shoelace-packaging machinery.

Question 3. The destruction of the coffee crop is a reduction in supply. Tea and coffee are probably substitutes for many consumers, so the higher equilibrium price and smaller equilibrium quantity of coffee will increase the demand for tea. Assuming that more cream is used in coffee than in tea, this will reduce the demand for cream and automatic coffee makers, as well as their price and quantity.

Question 4. The change in tastes toward sports shirts will result in an increase in demand for sports shirts. This same change of taste will result in a decrease in the demand for dress shirts. The decline in the equilibrium quantity of dress shirts will result in a decrease in demand for both neckties and tie clips.

Equilibrium Price and Equilibrium Quantity

Figure 14.1 below shows the demand for Greebes and the supply of Greebes. Plot these data on the axes in Figure 14.2. Label the demand curve D and label the supply curve S. Then answer the questions that follow. Fill in the answer blanks, or underline the correct answer in parentheses.

 Figure 14.1

Demand for and Supply of Greebes

Price ($ per Greebe)	Quantity Demanded (millions of Greebes)	Quantity Supplied (millions of Greebes)
$.15	300	100
.20	250	150
.25	200	200
.30	150	250
.35	100	300

 Figure 14.2

Demand for and Supply of Greebes

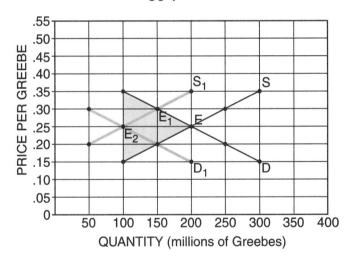

1. Under these conditions, competitive market forces would tend to establish an equilibrium price of _**$0.25**_ per Greebe and an equilibrium quantity of __**200**__ million Greebes.

2. If the price currently prevailing in the market is $0.30 per Greebe, buyers would want to buy __**150**__ million Greebes and sellers would want to sell __**250**__ million Greebes. Under these conditions, there would be a (*shortage* / *__surplus__*) of __**100**__ million Greebes. Competitive market forces would tend to cause the price to (*increase* / *__decrease__*) to a price of __**$0.25**__ per Greebe.

   At this new price, buyers would now want to buy __**200**__ million Greebes, and sellers now want to sell __**200**__ million Greebes. Because of this change in (*__price__* / *underlying conditions*), the

(*demand* / *__quantity demanded__*) changed by ___50___ million Greebes, and the
(*supply* / *__quantity supplied__*) changed by ___50___ million Greebes.

3. If the price currently prevailing in the market is $0.20 per Greebe, buyers would want to buy
___250___ million Greebes, and sellers would want to sell ___150___ million Greebes. Under these
conditions, there would be a (*__shortage__* / surplus) of ___100___ million Greebes. Competitive market
forces would tend to cause the price to (*__increase__* / decrease) to a price of __$0.25__ per Greebe.
At this new price, buyers would now want to buy ___200___million Greebes, and sellers now
want to sell ___200___ million Greebes. Because of this change in (*__price__* / underlying conditions),
the (*demand* / *__quantity demanded__*) changed by 50 million Greebes, and the
(*supply* / *__quantity supplied__*) changed by ___50___ million Greebes.

4. Lightly shade the area of consumer surplus and producer surplus.

   (A) If the government sets the price at $0.35 and the quantity exchanged is 100 million Greebes,
   what will happen to the size of the combined total of consumer and producer surplus?
   It will decrease.

   (B) What does this say about the market system? *The market system results in the maximum
   consumer and producer surplus.*

5. Now, suppose a mysterious blight causes the supply schedule for Greebes to change to the
   following:

Figure 14.3
New Supply of Greebes

Price (\$ per Greebe)	Quantity Supplied (millions of Greebes)
$.20	50
.25	100
.30	150
.35	200

   Plot the new supply schedule on the axes in Figure 14.2 and label it S_1. Label the new equilibrium
   E_1. Under these conditions, competitive market forces would tend to establish an equilibrium price of
   __$0.30__ per Greebe and an equilibrium quantity of ___150___ million Greebes.

   Compared with the equilibrium price in Question 1, we say that because of this change in
   (*price* / *__underlying conditions__*), the (*__supply__* / quantity supplied) changed; and both the equilibrium
   price and the equilibrium quantity changed. The equilibrium price (*__increased__* / decreased), and the
   equilibrium quantity (increased / *__decreased__*).

   Compared with the consumer and producer surpluses in Question 4, consumer surplus has
   (increased / *__decreased__*), and producer surplus has (increased / *__decreased__*).

6. Now, with the supply schedule at S_1, suppose further that a sharp drop in people's incomes as the result of a prolonged recession causes the demand schedule to change to the following:

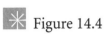 Figure 14.4

New Demand for Greebes

Price ($ per Greebe)	Quantity Demanded (millions of Greebes)
$.15	200
.20	150
.25	100
.30	50

Plot the new demand schedule on the axes in Figure 14.2 and label it D_1. Label the new equilibrium E_2. Under these conditions, with the supply schedule at S_1, competitive market forces would tend to establish an equilibrium price of ___**$0.25**___ per Greebe and an equilibrium quantity of ___**100**___ million Greebes. Compared with the equilibrium price in Question 5, because of this change in (*price* / _**underlying conditions**_), the (_**demand**_ / *quantity demanded*) changed. The equilibrium price (*increased* / _**decreased**_), and the equilibrium quantity (*increased* / _**decreased**_).

Shifts in Supply and Demand

Part A

Fill in the blanks with the letter of the graph that illustrates each situation. You may use a graph more than once.

✳ Figure 15.1
Jelly Beans Supply and Demand

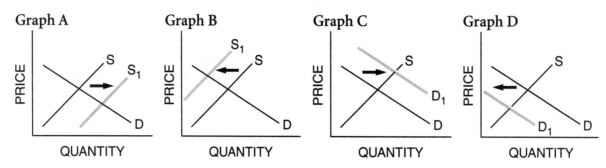

Graph A   Graph B   Graph C   Graph D

1. The price of sugar increases. _____*B*_____

2. The price of bubble gum, a close substitute for jelly beans, increases. _____*C*_____

3. A machine is invented that makes jelly beans at a lower cost. _____*A*_____

4. The government places a tax on foreign jelly beans, which have a considerable share of the market.
_____*B*_____

5. The price of soda, a complementary good for jelly beans, increases. _____*D*_____

6. Widespread prosperity allows people to buy more jelly beans. _____*C*_____

Part B

Connecticut ships large amounts of apples to all parts of the United States by rail. Circle the words that show the effects on price and quantity for each situation, and complete the graphs below, showing how a hurricane that destroys apples before they are picked in Connecticut might affect the price and quantity of each commodity. Then provide your reasoning.

7. **Apples in Boston**

    Price: *Rises*   Unchanged   Falls

    Quantity: Rises   Unchanged   *Falls*

    Reason: *A hurricane destroyed apples.*

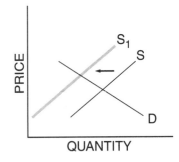

8. **Land devoted to apple orchards in the state of Washington**

    Price: *Rises*   Unchanged   Falls

    Quantity: *Rises*   Unchanged   Falls

    Reason: *Washington farmers grow more apples because the price is higher. To do this, they must buy more land.*

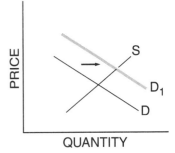

9. **Apples grown in the state of Washington**

    Price: *Rises*   Unchanged   Falls

    Quantity: *Rises*   Unchanged   Falls

    Reason: *Consumers substitute Washington apples for Connecticut apples.*

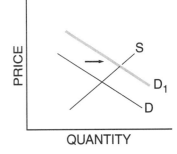

10. **Pears**

Price:	*Rises*	Unchanged	Falls
Quantity:	*Rises*	Unchanged	Falls

Reason: *Consumers substitute pears for apples.*

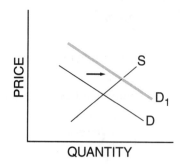

11. **Apple pies**

Price:	*Rises*	Unchanged	Falls
Quantity:	Rises	Unchanged	*Falls*

Reason: *Apples are used to bake pies. Higher priced apples increase the cost of producing pies.*

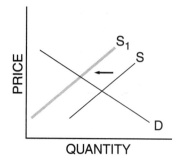

How Markets Allocate Resources

The following questions refer to a group of related markets in the United States during a long period of time. Assume that the markets are perfectly competitive and that the supply and demand model is completely applicable. The figures show the supply and demand in each market *before* the assumed change occurs. Trace through the effects of the assumed change, *other things constant.* Work your way from left to right. Shift only one curve in each market. For each market, draw whatever new supply or demand curves are needed, labeling each new curve S_1 or D_1. Then circle the correct symbol under each diagram (↑ for increase, — for unchanged, and ↓ for decrease). Remember to shift only one curve in each market.

1. Assume that a new fertilizer dramatically increases the number of potatoes that can be harvested with no additional labor or machinery. Also assume that this fertilizer does not affect wheat farming and that people are satisfied to eat either potatoes or bread made from wheat flour.

Figure 16.1
Effects of a New Fertilizer

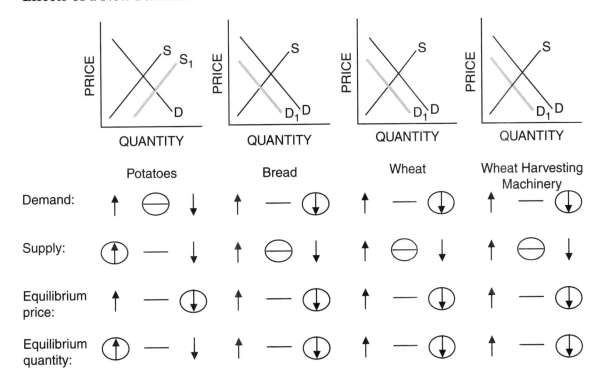

2. Assume people's tastes change and there is an increase in the demand for briefcases and luggage made of leather. How would this affect the leather market and related markets? Draw the new curves and circle the appropriate symbols in all four markets.

Figure 16.2

Effects of Increased Demand for Briefcases and Luggage

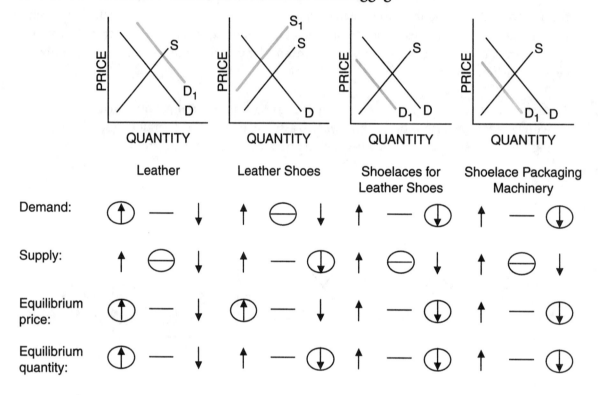

3. Assume that a heavy frost destroys half the world's coffee crop and that people use more cream in coffee than they do in tea.

 Figure 16.3

Effects of a Loss of Coffee Crop

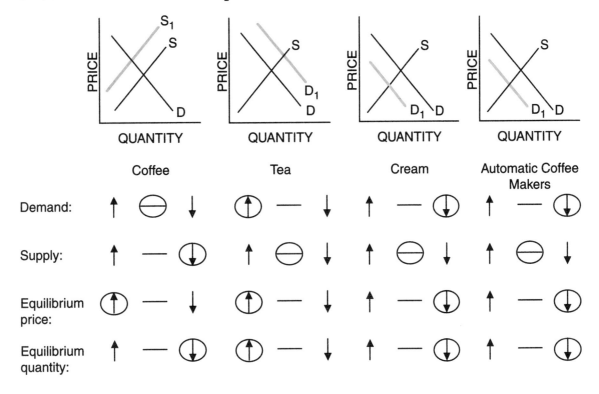

4. Assume people's tastes change in favor of colored sports shirts, which are worn without neckties, and against white dress shirts, which are worn with neckties and tie clasps.

✳ Figure 16.4
Effects of a Shift to Sports Shirts

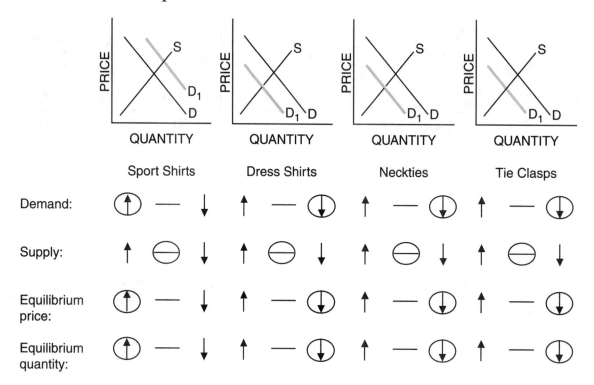

	Sport Shirts			Dress Shirts			Neckties			Tie Clasps		
Demand:	⊕	—	↓	↑	—	⊖	↑	—	⊖	↑	—	⊕
Supply:	↑	⊖	↓	↑	⊖	↓	↑	⊖	↓	↑	⊖	↓
Equilibrium price:	⊕	—	↓	↑	—	⊕	↑	—	⊕	↑	—	⊕
Equilibrium quantity:	⊕	—	↓	↑	—	⊕	↑	—	⊕	↑	—	⊕

Elasticity of Demand and Supply

Introduction and Description

Knowledge of price elasticity of demand and supply helps the students understand how businesses make pricing decisions and how governments make decisions on taxation. These exercises on elasticity become increasingly complex. To answer the elasticity questions on the AP Exam, the students should know the qualities that determine price elasticity of demand and supply, how the total revenue method can be used to determine price elasticity of demand and how to calculate elasticity coefficients. Elasticity lends itself to complex application questions. Knowledge of the factors that determine elasticity may be more important than memorizing formulas. The students should also have some knowledge of other elasticities including income elasticity of demand, cross elasticity of demand and elasticity of supply.

Objectives

1. Define *price elasticity of demand*.
2. Define *price elasticity of supply*.
3. Define and distinguish among *elastic, inelastic* and *unit elastic demand*.
4. Explain the characteristics that tend to make demand more elastic or more inelastic.
5. Determine the prices at which a product has elastic or inelastic demand by observing how total revenue changes in response to changes in price.
6. Apply price elasticity of demand to economic problems.
7. Define and distinguish between a *normal good* and an *inferior good* using income elasticity of demand.
8. Calculate price elasticities of demand using the arc method.
9. Calculate varying price elasticities of demand along a demand curve of constant shape.

Time Required

Three and one-half class periods or 158 minutes

Materials

1. Activities 17, 18, 19, 20 and 21
2. Visuals 2.7, 2.8, 2.9 and 2.10
3. Tennis ball and baseball
4. Paper clip
5. Rubber band

Procedure

1. Remind the students that as price decreases, quantity demanded increases. But does it increase a little or a lot? If it increases a lot, we call it *elastic*. If it increases a little, it is *inelastic*. Later we will define "a lot" and "a little."

2. Illustrate this visually by dropping a tennis ball and a baseball. Elasticity is a measure of responsiveness to any stimulus. Dropping the ball is a stimulus just like a price change is a stimulus. A tennis ball bounces a lot. It is elastic. The baseball doesn't bounce much. It is inelastic. Price elasticity of demand is the response of quantity demanded to a change in price.

3. Using Visual 2.7, give a lecture on the qualities that make demand elastic or inelastic.

   (A) *Substitutability.* The more substitutes there are for the good, the greater the price elasticity of demand.

   (B) *Proportion of income spent on product.* Low-priced goods, which require only a small portion of one's income, tend to be more inelastic than high-priced goods, which require a large portion of one's income.

   (C) *Luxury or necessity.* Luxuries tend to be elastic while necessities tend to be inelastic.

   (D) *Is it habit-forming?* Habit-forming goods

such as cigarettes, alcohol and drugs have more inelastic demand curves.

(E) *Time.* Consumers can respond to a price change more easily if they have more time. The greater the period of time, the greater the price elasticity of demand.

4. Now it is time to put some numbers on "a lot" and "a little." Use Visual 2.8 to explain how to calculate an elasticity coefficient. Make sure the students understand what the coefficients mean.

5. Have the students complete Activity 17 and discuss it. They may need help as they plow through the formulas. You might go over the first two problems before they finish the rest of the activity.

6. Have the students complete Activity 18, which expands upon Visual 2.7. You should also reinforce the concept of income elasticity of demand before the students begin the problem sheet. Income elasticity of demand is the ratio of the percentage change in quantity demanded of a good to the percentage change in income. It measures the responsiveness of consumer expenditures to changes in income. This is important to understand the concept of normal, luxury and inferior goods.

7. Discuss Activity 18.

8. Give a lecture on the total revenue test for price elasticity of demand. Because the relationship between price and quantity demanded is inverse, a total revenue test can be used to determine the price elasticity of demand:

Price x quantity = total revenue

(A) If total revenue moves in the same direction as price, demand is price inelastic.

(B) If total revenue moves in the same direction as quantity or inversely to price, demand is price elastic.

(C) If total revenue remains the same as price increases, the demand is unit elastic.

This is a shortcut way to determine price elasticity of demand and for the students to check if their calculations of price elasticity of demand are at least in the right ballpark.

9. The total revenue test itself is not a very intuitive concept, and the students sometimes have difficulty remembering it. Try this demonstration to explain the concept: Holding a rubber band vertically, consider its top to be price and the bottom total revenue. Note that as you stretch the rubber band, price goes up while total revenue goes down. As you let go, price comes back down and total revenue goes up. They move in opposite directions (inversely), and a rubber band is *elastic.* Now hold a paper clip vertically and label the top price and the bottom total revenue. Note that as the top (price) goes up, so does the bottom (total revenue) of the paper clip. As the top goes down, so does the bottom. They move in the same direction (directly), and a paper clip is *inelastic.* Once the students have the big point about elasticity, it is important that they do not get the impression that the entire market curve for most products can be labeled elastic or inelastic. For most demand curves, elasticity varies at different points on the curve: more elastic at high prices and low quantities and more inelastic at low prices and high quantities. Visual 2.9 summarizes the relationship between elasticity and total revenue.

10. Have the students complete Activity 19 and discuss it.

11. Now it is time to apply elasticity to real-world examples. Have the students complete Activity 20 and discuss it.

12. Use Activity 21 to show how price elasticity of demand can be used to examine an economic policy question: Who really pays a tax? This activity also combines shifts and elasticity in supply and demand. Before beginning the activity, use Visual 2.10 to discuss tax incidence. Cover these points:

(A) Often the person who actually pays the government does not bear the burden of the tax. The person who bears the burden of the tax is said to bear the *incidence* of the tax.

(B) Taxpayers will shift the incidence of a tax whenever possible.

(C) The incidence of a tax can be shifted only when the taxpayer can get a higher price for something he or she sells or a lower price for something he or she buys.

(D) If the taxpayer is able to raise the price of something he or she sells, the tax is shifted forward. If the taxpayer is able to lower the price of something he or she buys, the tax is shifted backward.

(E) How much of the incidence of a tax can be shifted depends on the elasticity of the supply and demand curves. The incidence is heaviest on the most inelastic curve.

13. Now have the students review Activity 21. This problem is an application of the supply and demand model. Actual numbers are supplied so that the students can get practice in interpreting diagrams for quantity and revenue implications as well as for equilibrium prices. Excise taxes can be analyzed by shifting either the supply or demand curve (but only one) by the amount of the tax.

14. Have the students do page 1 of Activity 21 to make sure they know how to analyze data.

15. Go over page 1 of Activity 21.

16. Have the students complete the problem.

17. Discuss the answers. You can make transparencies of the graphs in the answers and illustrate the three cases by coloring in different rectangles as the answers are developed.

Elasticity: An Introduction

Part A
Extra-Credit Problems

1. Now, suppose that your economics teacher currently allows you to earn extra credit by submitting answers to the end-of-the-chapter questions in your textbook. The number of questions you're willing to submit depends on the amount of extra credit for each question. How responsive you are to a change in the extra-credit points the teacher gives can be represented as an *elasticity*. Write the formula for the elasticity of extra-credit problems submitted:

$$\varepsilon_{ps} = \frac{\textit{percentage change in number of questions}}{\textit{percentage change in extra-credit points}}$$

2. Now, consider that your teacher's goal is to get you to submit twice as many questions: a 100-percent increase. Underline the correct answer in parentheses.

   (A) If the number of chapter-end questions you submit *is* very responsive to a change in extra-credit points, then a given increase in extra credit elicits a large increase in questions submitted. In this case, your teacher will need to increase the extra-credit points by (*more than* / ***less than*** / *exactly*) 100 percent.

   (B) If the number of chapter-end questions you submit *is not* very responsive to a change in extra-credit points, then a given increase in extra credit elicits a small increase in questions submitted. In this case, your teacher will need to increase the extra-credit points by (***more than*** / *less than* / *exactly*) 100 percent.

    Advanced Placement Economics Teacher Resource Manual © National Council on Economic Education, New York, N.Y.

Part D
Coffee Problems

Suppose Moonbucks, a national coffee-house franchise, finally moves into the little town of Middle-ofnowhere. Moonbucks is the only supplier of coffee in town and faces the following demand schedule each week. Write the correct answer on the answer blanks, or underline the correct answer in parentheses.

Figure 17.3

Cups of Coffee Demanded per Week

Price (per cup)	Quantity Demanded
$6	80
5	100
4	120
3	140
2	160
1	180
0	200

3. What is the arc price elasticity of demand when the price changes from $1 to $2? ____.18____

$$\varepsilon_d = \frac{\dfrac{\Delta Q}{(Q + Q_1)/2}}{\dfrac{\Delta P}{(P + P_1)/2}} = \frac{\dfrac{20}{170}}{\dfrac{1}{1.5}} = \frac{.12}{.67}$$

So, over this range of prices, demand is (*elastic* / *unit elastic* / *__inelastic__*).

4. What is the arc price elasticity of demand when the price changes from $5 to $6? ____*1.22*____

$$\varepsilon_d = \frac{\dfrac{\Delta Q}{(Q + Q_1)/2}}{\dfrac{\Delta P}{(P + P_1)/2}} = \frac{\dfrac{20}{90}}{\dfrac{1}{5.5}} = \frac{.22}{.18}$$

So, over this range of prices, demand is (*__elastic__* / *unit elastic* / *inelastic*).

Note: Because the relationship between quantity demanded and price is inverse, price elasticity of demand would always be negative. Economists believe using negative numbers is confusing when referring to "large" or "small" elasticities of demand. Therefore, they use absolute or positive numbers, changing the sign on the negative numbers.

Part E

Now, consider Figure 17.4, which graphs the demand schedule given in Figure 17.3.
Recall the slope of a line is measured by the rise over the run: slope = rise / run = ΔP / ΔQ.

Figure 17.4
Elasticity of Demand for Coffee

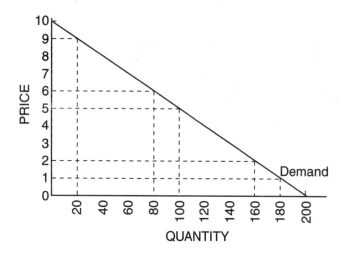

5. Using your calculations of ΔP and ΔQ from Question 3, calculate the slope of the demand curve.
    1/20 or .05

6. Using your calculations of ΔP and ΔQ from Question 4, calculate the slope of the demand curve.
    1/20 or .05 *This is the same slope as for Question 5. These calculations help the students to understand in Question 7 that a demand curve of constant slope has several varying elasticities.*

7. The law of demand tells us that an increase in price results in a decrease in the quantity demanded. Questions 5 and 6 remind us that the slope of a straight line is *constant everywhere along the line.* Along this demand curve, a change in price of $1 generates a change in quantity demanded of 20 cups of coffee a week.

    You've now shown mathematically that while the slope of the demand curve is related to elasticity, the two concepts are not the same thing. Briefly discuss the relationship between where you are along the demand curve and the elasticity of demand. How does this tie into the notion of *responsiveness? At a higher price, you are in the price elastic portion of the demand curve. As you move to a lower price along a demand curve, the demand curve becomes more price inelastic. Thus, at a high price, a small percentage change in price leads to a large percentage change in quantity. As the price decreases, the same percentage change in price generates a smaller percentage change in quantity, so the elasticity of demand decreases.*

The Determinants of Elasticity of Demand

Suppose we don't know the precise demand schedule for electricity and there is a 20 percent increase in the price of a kilowatt hour of electricity. We know that quantity demanded will decrease, but will it be by less than 20 percent (inelastic demand), exactly 20 percent (unit elastic) or more than 20 percent (elastic demand)? What factors influence the price elasticity of demand? (Remember, *ceteris paribus*!)

Part A

Consider the following representative households in our market for electricity:

Household A: Uses electricity for lighting, appliances and heating.

Household B: Uses electricity for lighting, appliances and heating. Has a heating system that can, with one day's labor, be switched to burn natural gas.

1. Household ___B___ will have the more elastic demand because of the presence of a ___substitute___ good.

2. Because Household A has no available substitutes, should we assume that the quantity demanded of electricity will remain unchanged given the increase in price? ___No___

    Do you think Household A's response will be elastic or inelastic? ___Inelastic___

3. Illustrate the same concept identified above by placing a 1, 2 or 3 by each item below, denoting the least price elastic to the most price elastic. Explain your reasoning.

    ___1___ Demand for insulin
    ___3___ Demand for Granny Smith apples
    ___2___ Demand for running shoes

    Rationale: *The smaller the number of substitute goods, the less elastic is the demand for that good. Insulin has no substitutes. There are more substitutes for Granny Smith apples than for running shoes because Granny Smith is a particular type of apple, and running shoes include all running shoes. This is why the demand for Granny Smith apples is most elastic.*

4. To summarize: Demand is (*more* / less) elastic for goods with many available substitutes.

Part B

Consider the following representative households in the electricity market:

Household A: Currently spends $300 a month on electricity.
The household income is $1,200 per month.

Household B: Currently spends $300 a month on electricity.
The household income is $3,600 a month.

5. Household ___*A*___ will have the more-elastic demand, as the expenditures on this good account for a (*smaller* / *__larger__*) proportion of its income.

6. Illustrate the same concept identified above by placing a 1, 2 or 3 by each item below, denoting the least elastic to the most elastic. Explain your reasoning.

___*1*___ Demand for chewing gum

___*3*___ Demand for automobiles

___*2*___ Demand for clothing

Rationale: *Autos take the largest proportion of income, then clothing, then chewing gum.*

7. To summarize: Goods that command a (*small* / *__large__*) proportion of a consumer's income tend to be more price elastic.

Part C

We expect that the price elasticity of demand will also vary with the nature of the good being considered. Is it a necessity? A durable good? Are we considering the short run or the long run? Consider the following alternatives, and underline the option that correctly completes each statement.

8. The price elasticity of demand for cigarettes: A product that is considered to be a necessity will have a relatively price (*elastic* / *__inelastic__*) demand.

9. The price elasticity of demand for automobiles: In the short run, consumers can postpone the purchase of durable goods, and so such goods will have a relatively price (*__elastic__* / *inelastic*) demand.

10. Briefly summarize how the nature of the good — necessity, durable good or luxury good — and the time frame affect the price elasticity of demand for electricity.
Goods that are necessary are less elastic than goods with many substitutes or that are luxuries. The longer the time frame, the more elastic is the demand for electricity.

Part D

Now, suppose that prices in the market for electricity remain constant, but consumers' income increases by 30 percent. Again, we may not know the precise demand schedule but may still be able to use notions of elasticity to speculate about what will happen to demand.

Recall the income elasticity of demand, ε_d:

$$\varepsilon_d = \frac{\textit{percentage change in quantity demanded}}{\textit{percentage change in income}}$$

Note in this case, income and quantity demanded are the relevant variables. All other variables, including the price of electricity, are held constant.

11. In measurements of elasticity, if income and quantity demanded move in the opposite direction — that is, if one increases while the other decreases — then the elasticity coefficient will be (positive / **_negative_**).

12. Remember that if income increases, the demand for a normal good increases and demand for an inferior good decreases. If the good is a normal good, income elasticity will be (negative / **_positive_**). If it is an inferior good, income elasticity will be (**_negative_** / positive).

Note: The formula in almost all principles of economics texts uses "quantity demanded" for income elasticity of demand. However, in the case of income elasticity of demand, the demand curve actually shifts. This can be confusing to the students because we make a big deal out of differentiating a change in quantity demanded from a change in demand. Make sure the students understand that the relationship is between a change of income and the amount of a good or service that buyers are willing to buy.

Elasticity and Total Revenue

Consider the following: total revenue (TR) = price (P) x quantity demanded (Q_d).

The responsiveness of quantity demanded to changes in price will determine whether a price increase leads to an increase or decrease in the total revenue generated.

The law of demand tells us that a price increase (decrease) will result in a decrease (increase) in quantity demanded: They move in opposite directions. What happens to TR when price changes is determined by the dominant effect, either the price effect or the quantity effect. In this case, knowing the price elasticity of demand solves the problem.

Consider that

$\varepsilon_d < 1 \Rightarrow$ $\%\Delta$ in $Q_d < \%\ \Delta$ in price $\Rightarrow$ The *price effect* dominates.
If price is increasing ($Q_d \downarrow$ by less), TR will increase.
If price is decreasing ($Q_d \uparrow$ by less), TR will decrease.

$\varepsilon_d = 1 \Rightarrow$ $\%\Delta$ in $Q_d = \%\ \Delta$ in price $\Rightarrow$ Neither effect dominates. TR remains unchanged.

$\varepsilon_d > 1 \Rightarrow$ $\%\Delta$ in $Q_d > \%\ \Delta$ in price $\Rightarrow$ The *quantity effect* dominates.
If price is increasing ($Q_d \downarrow$ by more), TR will decrease.
If price is decreasing ($Q_d \uparrow$ by more), TR will increase.

Use this information to do the problems below. Fill in the blank or underline the correct answer.

1. Price rises from P = $5 to P_1 = $6, and quantity demanded decreases from Q = 15 to Q_1 = 10.

   (A) The coefficient of elasticity equals ___2.2___.

   (B) P   x   Q   =   TR
       _5_   x   _15_   =   _75_

   (C) P_1 x Q_1 = TR_1
       _6_   x   _10_   =   _60_

   (D) P ($\downarrow$ / $\updownarrow$);   TR($\underline{\downarrow}$ / $\uparrow$)   Demand is (***elastic*** / *unit elastic* / *inelastic*).

2. Price decreases from P = $10 to P_1 = $9, and quantity demanded increases from Q = 100 to Q_1 = 110.

   (A) The coefficient of elasticity equals ___.91___.

   (B) P   x   Q   =   TR
       _10_   x   _100_ =   _1,000_

   (C) P_1 x Q_1 = TR_1
       _9_   x   _110_   =   _990_

   (D) P ($\underline{\downarrow}$ / $\uparrow$);   (TR $\underline{\downarrow}$ / $\uparrow$)   Demand is (*elastic* / *unit elastic* / ***inelastic***).

Advanced Placement Economics Teacher Resource Manual © National Council on Economic Education, New York, N.Y.

Applying Elasticity to the Real World

Each of the following stories contains an assumption about elasticity of demand. In (A) for each story, decide whether the person's conclusion is right or wrong. In (B) explain your reasoning.

1. I.M. Politico, a candidate for the state legislature, is proposing a large increase in the tax on cigarettes and liquor. He says, "I'm not proposing these taxes to raise revenue but to discourage reckless drinking and the filthy smoking habit. If the prices of cigarettes and liquor go up, most people will quit using them. After all, no one needs to drink or smoke."

    (A) *I.M. is wrong.*

    (B) *He assumes that demand for these products is elastic, but it is not. He therefore falsely concludes that a tax increase on cigarettes and liquor will curb their consumption a great deal. In fact, taxes on these commodities will curb their consumption very little.*

2. U.R. Kool, a candidate for Congress, proposes freezing the price of gasoline. "There is no substitute for gasoline," he says. "People have to get from one place to another. Economists who say higher prices will discourage people from buying as much gas as before don't live in the real world."

    (A) *U.R. is wrong.*

    (B) *There are many methods of saving gasoline, including driving cars with smaller engines, car pooling and using public transportation. In fact, following the huge increases in the price of gasoline after 1973, people conserved on the use of gas, and sales were lower than they would have been if prices had not risen.*

3. Councilman Vic Acqua opposed a price increase for water during a recent drought. He claimed that there is no substitute for water. He believes an increase in the price of water (water taxes) will result in the same quantity of water used as before the price went up.

    (A) *Vic is wrong.*

    (B) *Demand for water is inelastic, but raising its price will curb consumption somewhat.*

4. Sky King, world traveler, says if the airlines want to increase total revenue, they should lower fares for business travelers as well as for vacationers. Both groups should respond equally to a price decrease.

    (A) *Sky is wrong.*

    (B) *He assumes that both business travelers and vacationers have an elastic demand for air travel. Business travelers' demand for air travel is inelastic because they cannot as easily postpone or give up their air travel. Vacationers can postpone their air travel, use other means of transportation or change their destination so as not to require air travel or to require less of it.*

Excise Taxes

Suppose Figures 21.1 and 21.2 show the current supply of Greebes.

 Figure 21.1
Table of Current Supply Schedule of Greebes

Quantity (millions)	Supply Price Before Tax ($ per Greebe)	Supply Price After Tax ($ per Greebe)
50	$.10	.25
100	.15	.30
150	.20	.35
200	.25	.40
250	.30	.45
300	.35	.50

 Figure 21.2
Current Supply Schedule of Greebes

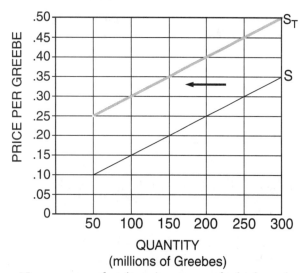

QUANTITY
(millions of Greebes)

Now, suppose that (to raise revenue for higher education) the government enacts an excise (sales) tax of $0.15 per Greebe. *This tax will result in a new supply curve for Greebes.* To determine where this new supply curve lies, reason as follows: If before the tax, firms were willing to supply 50 million Greebes at a price of $0.10, they would now be willing to supply 50 million Greebes only if the price were $0.25. (Remember: $0.15 of the price of each Greebe sold is now going to go to the government. So, if the price is $0.25 and the government is getting $0.15 of this price, then the seller is receiving the remaining $0.10.)

Fill in the blank spaces in the table, and draw in the new supply curve that results from the tax. Label the new supply curve S$_T$.

What will be the result of this excise (sales) tax on the equilibrium quantity of Greebes? The equilibrium price paid by buyers (P_B)? The equilibrium price received by sellers (P_S)? The revenue received by the government? The income, or revenue, received by sellers after the tax?

The answers to these important questions will depend on the nature of the demand for Greebes. The next section of this activity will help you determine the effects of a $0.15 excise tax on Greebes under four different demand conditions.

Part A

Figure 21.3

Relatively Inelastic Demand for Greebes as Compared with D_1 on Figure 21.4

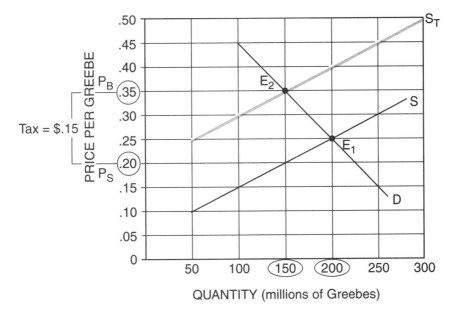

1. On Figure 21.3 above, the equilibrium quantity of Greebes is ___**200**___ million Greebes. Q_{E1}

2. On Figure 21.3, the equilibrium price of Greebes is ___**$0.25**___ per Greebe. P_{E1}

3. Buyers are spending a total of ___**$50**___ million on Greebes. *(.25 x 200 = $50)*

4. Sellers are receiving a total of ___**$50**___ million from selling Greebes. *(.25 x 200 = $50)*

5. If an excise tax of $0.15 for each Greebe sold is levied on the sellers of Greebes, the equilibrium price paid by buyers (P_B) will differ from the equilibrium price received by sellers (P_S) by the amount of the tax. Add the new supply curve incorporating the tax to the graph and indicate P_B and P_S. This $0.15 goes to the government. Under these circumstances:

    (A) The new equilibrium quantity of Greebes would be ___**150**___ million. Q_{E2}

    (B) The new equilibrium price paid by buyers would be ___**$0.35**___ per Greebe. *($P_B = P_{E2}$)*

(C) The new equilibrium price received by sellers (after tax) would be ___*$0.20*___ per Greebe.
   ($P_S = P_B - TAX$ or $\$0.35 - \$0.15 = \$0.20$)

(D) Buyers would spend a total of ___*$52.5*___ million on Greebes.
   ($P_B \times 150 = \$0.35 \times 150$)

(E) Sellers would receive a total of ___*$30*___ million (after tax) from selling Greebes.
   ($P_S \times 150 = \$0.20 \times 150$)

(F) The government revenue from this tax would be ___*$22.5*___ million.
   ($TAX \times 150 = \$0.15 \times 150$)

(G) ___*$15*___ million of this revenue would be paid by buyers in the form of higher prices.
   This is calculated by the equilibrium quantity times the difference in ($P_B - E_1$).
   ($P_B - P_{E1}) \times 150 = (\$0.35 - \$0.25) \times 150 = \$0.10 \times 150$

(H) ___*$7.5*___ million of this revenue would be paid by sellers in the form of reduced income.
   ($P_{E1} - P_S) \times 150 = (\$0.25 - \$0.20) \times 150 = \$0.05 \times 150$

(I) As a result of the tax, buyers will buy a smaller quantity than before the tax. If so, the sellers
   would also have a loss of revenue that is not collected by the government. In this case, the
   uncollected revenue loss would be equal to ___*$12.5*___ million.

$$(200 - 150) \times \$0.25 = 50 \times \$0.25 = \$12.5 \ or \ \$50 \ \ (4)$$
$$\underline{-30} \ \ (5E)$$
$$20$$
$$\underline{-7.5} \ (5H)$$
$$\$12.5$$

Part B

Figure 21.4
Relatively Elastic Demand for Greebes as Compared with D in Figure 21.3

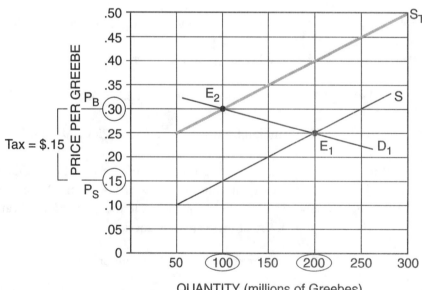

6. On Figure 21.4, the equilibrium quantity of Greebes is ___*200*___ million. Q_{E1}

7. On Figure 21.4, the equilibrium price of Greebes is ___*$0.25*___ per Greebe. P_{E1}

8. Buyers are spending a total of ___*$50*___ million on Greebes. *($0.25 x 200 = $50)*

9. Sellers are receiving a total of ___*$50*___ million from selling Greebes. *($0.25 x 200 = $50)*

10. If an excise tax of $0.15 for each Greebe sold is levied on the sellers of Greebes, the equilibrium price paid by buyers (P_B) will differ from the equilibrium price received by sellers (P_S) by the amount of the tax. This $0.15 goes to the government. Add the new supply curve incorporating the tax to the graph, and indicate P_B and P_S. Under these circumstances:

    (A) The new equilibrium quantity of Greebes would be ___*100*___ million. Q_{E2}

    (B) The new equilibrium price paid by buyers would be ___*$0.30*___ per Greebe. *($P_B = P_{E2}$)*

    (C) The new equilibrium price received by sellers (after tax) would be ___*$0.15*___ per Greebe. *($P_S = P_B – TAX$ or $0.30 – $0.15 = $0.15)*

    (D) Buyers would spend a total of ___*$30*___ million on Greebes. *(P_B x 100 = $0.30 x 100 = $30)*

    (E) Sellers would receive a total of ___*$15*___ million (after tax) from selling Greebes. *(P_S x 100 = $0.15 x 100 = $15)*

    (F) The government revenue from this tax would be ___*$15*___ million. *(TAX x 100 = $0.15 x 100)*

    (G) ___*$5*___ million of this revenue would be paid by buyers in the form of higher prices. *($P_B – P_{E1}$) x 100 = ($0.30 – $0.25) x 100 = $0.05 x 100 = $5*

    (H) ___*$10*___ million of this revenue would be paid by sellers in the form of reduced income. *($P_{E1} – P_S$) x 100 = ($0.25 – $0.15) x 100 = $0.10 x 100 = $10*

    (I) As a result of the tax, buyers will buy a smaller quantity than before the tax. If so, the sellers would also have a loss of revenue that is not collected by the government. In this case, the *uncollected revenue loss* would be equal to ___*$25*___ million.
    (200 – 100) x $0.25 = 100 x $0.25 = $25 or $50 (4)
    $$\begin{aligned} &\underline{-15}\,(5E) \\ &35 \\ &\underline{-10}\,(5H) \\ &\$25 \end{aligned}$$

Part C

Figure 21.5
Perfectly Inelastic Demand for Greebes

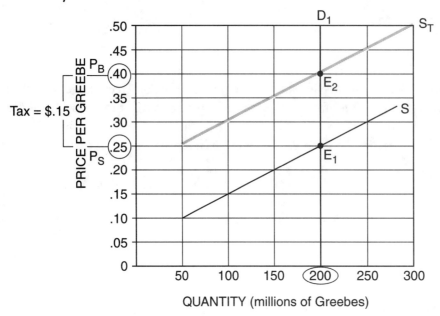

11. On Figure 21.5, the equilibrium quantity of Greebes is ____*200*____ million. Q_{E1}

12. On Figure 21.5, the equilibrium price of Greebes is ____*$0.25*____ per Greebe. P_{E1}

13. Buyers are spending a total of ____*$50*____ million on Greebes. *($0.25 x 200 = $50)*

14. Sellers are receiving a total of ____*$50*____ million from selling Greebes. *($0.25 x 200 = $50)*

15. If an excise tax of $0.15 for each Greebe sold is levied on the sellers of Greebes, the equilibrium price paid by buyers (P_B) will differ from the equilibrium price received by sellers (P_S) by the amount of the tax. This $0.15 goes to the government. Add the new supply curve incorporating the tax to the graph, and indicate P_B and P_S. Under these circumstances:

    (A) The new equilibrium quantity of Greebes would be ____*200*____ million. Q_{E2}

    (B) The new equilibrium price paid by buyers would be ____*$0.40*____ per Greebe. *($P_B = P_{E2}$)*

    (C) The new equilibrium price received by sellers (after tax) would be ____*$0.25*____ per Greebe.
    ($P_S = P_B - TAX = $0.40 - $0.15 = 0.25)

    (D) Buyers would spend a total of ____*$80*____ million on Greebes.
    (P_B x 200 = $0.40 x 200 = $80)

    (E) Sellers would receive a total of ____*$50*____ million (after tax) from selling Greebes.
    (P_S x 200 = $0.25 x 200 = $50)

(F) The government revenue from this tax would be _____$30_____ million.
($TAX \times 200 = \$0.15 \times 200$)

(G) _____$30_____ million of this revenue would be paid by buyers in the form of higher prices.
($(\$0.40 - \$0.25) \times 200 = \$0.15 \times 200 = \$30$)

(H) _____$0_____ million of this revenue would be paid by sellers in the form of reduced income.
($Q_{E1} = Q_{E2}$)

(I) As a result of the tax, buyers will buy a smaller quantity than before the tax. If so, the sellers would also have a loss of revenue that is not collected by the government. In this case, the *uncollected revenue loss* would be equal to _____$0_____ million. *There is no uncollected revenue loss.*

Part D

Figure 21.6
Perfectly Elastic Demand for Greebes

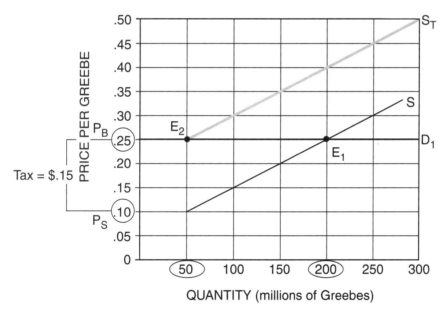

16. On Figure 21.6, the equilibrium quantity of Greebes is _____200_____ million. Q_{E1}

17. On Figure 21.6, the equilibrium price of Greebes is _____$0.25_____ per Greebe. P_{E1}

18. Buyers are spending a total of _____$50_____ million on Greebes. ($\$0.25 \times 200 = \$50$)

19. Sellers are receiving a total of _____$50_____ million from selling Greebes. ($\$0.25 \times 200 = \$50$)

20. If an excise tax of $0.15 for each Greebe sold is levied on the sellers of Greebes, the equilibrium price paid by buyers (P_B) will differ from the equilibrium price received by sellers (P_S) by the amount of the tax. This $0.15 goes to the government. Add the new supply curve incorporating the tax to the graph and indicate P_B and P_S. Under these circumstances:

(A) The new equilibrium quantity of Greebes would be _____50_____ million. Q_{E2}

(B) The new equilibrium price paid by buyers would be _____$0.25_____ per Greebe. ($P_B = P_{E2}$)

(C) The new equilibrium price received by sellers (after tax) would be_____$0.10_____ per Greebe.
($P_S = P_B - TAX = \$0.25 - \$0.15 = \$0.10$)

(D) Buyers would spend a total of _____$12.5_____ million on Greebes.
($P_B \times 50 = \$0.25 \times 50$)

(E) Sellers would receive a total of _____$5_____ million (after tax) from selling Greebes.
($P_S \times 50 = \$0.10 \times 50 = \$5$)

(F) The government revenue from this tax would be _____$7.5_____ million.
($\$0.15 \times 50 = \$7.5$)

(G) _____$0_____ million of this revenue would be paid by buyers in the form of higher prices.
($P_B = P_{E1}$ or $P_B - P_{E1} = 0$)

(H) _____$7.5_____ million of this revenue would be paid by sellers in the form of reduced income.
($P_{E1} - P_S) \times 50 = (\$0.25 - \$0.10) \times 50 = \$0.15 \times 50 = \$7.5$

(I) As a result of the tax, buyers will buy a smaller quantity than before the tax. If so, the sellers would also have a loss of revenue that is not collected by the government. In this case, the *uncollected revenue loss* would be equal to _____$37.5_____ million.
$(200 - 50) \times \$0.25 = 150 \times \$0.25 = \$37.5$ or $\$50$ (4)
                                                        $\underline{-5}$ (5E)
                                                        45
                                                        $\underline{-7.5}$ (5H)
                                                        37.5

Part E

21. A famous Supreme Court justice once said, "The power to tax is the power to destroy" sellers. This is more likely to be true the more the demand for the product taxed is relatively (*elastic* / inelastic). *See Part D.*

22. If you were a government revenue agent interested in getting the most tax revenue possible, you would suggest putting excise taxes on goods whose demand is (*elastic* / *unit elastic* / *inelastic*). *See Part C.*

23. Think of some real-world goods on which excise taxes are placed: liquor, cigarettes, gasoline. Do you think that the demand for these goods is relatively elastic or relatively inelastic? Why? *Relatively inelastic. No good substitutes for the addicted. Also considerable revenue is collected from these taxes.*

Part F

Consider this newspaper quotation and answer the questions that follow: "The city is planning to place a 10 percent tax on auto parking. The tax would fall on every motorist who uses a space in either the garages and the lots operated by the Public Parking Authority or in privately operated lots and garages."

24. Draw the demand curve and the long-run supply curve for parking lots. Explain why each has the shape you show; in other words, why each is relatively elastic or inelastic.
    The long-run supply curve would not be perfectly inelastic. Additional parking places could be added as prices increased. Existing facilities now used for other things could be converted to park-ing garages, and additional stories could be added to existing garages if the price increased enough. The elasticity of the total demand curve is the result of the relative elasticity of demand for different groups of downtown parkers and the strength of the substitution effect and the income effect for these groups. Downtown shoppers have more substitutes (for example, suburban shopping malls with free parking) than do downtown office workers, but even office workers could form car pools and / or use public transportation if the price of parking increased sufficiently. The income effect would be larger for office workers who come every day than for occasional shoppers.

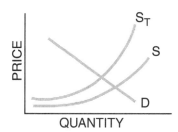

25. Given the curves you have drawn in Question 24, show the effect of introducing a 10 percent tax: How does the equilibrium position after imposition of the tax compare with the initial equilibri-um position? *Price would be higher. Number of spaces used would be smaller. See Part C, except a percentage tax would result in S_T getting progressively farther from S compared with Part C, where a tax was a fixed cents-per-unit amount rather than a percentage.*

26. The newspaper quotation implies that the "burden" of the tax will fall entirely upon the driver. Is this true for the case you have developed in Questions 24 and 25 above? Under what circumstances would this be true? *No, there would most likely be some "sharing" of the burden, since neither supply nor demand is perfectly inelastic. The burden would fall entirely upon the driver if demand were perfectly inelastic. See Part A.*

Price Ceilings and Floors

Introduction and Description

Legislators often have been dissatisfied with the outcomes of free markets. The invisible hand is not good enough for them, so they mandate prices that are lower or higher than the equilibrium price. A *price ceiling* is a legal maximum price that may be charged for a good or service. If a price ceiling is below the equilibrium price, it will cause shortages and illegal, or underground, markets to develop. A *price floor* is a legal minimum price that may be charged for a good or service. If a price floor is above the equilibrium price, it will cause surpluses.

In your presentation of price ceilings and floors, discuss how changing prices are incentives that determine what to produce, how to produce and for whom to produce. Sometimes the students are mechanistic and merely identify shortages and surpluses on a graph. They should instead understand why price ceilings cause shortages and price floors cause surpluses. People react to incentives in predictable ways.

Objectives

1. Define and describe *price ceilings* and *price floors.*
2. Illustrate price ceilings and floors on graphs.
3. Analyze the effects of price ceilings and floors in terms of surpluses and shortages.
4. Analyze how prices act as incentives that influence human behavior.

Time Required

One class period or 45 minutes

Materials

1. Activity 22
2. Visuals 2.11 and 2.12

Procedure

1. Use Visual 2.11 to illustrate a price ceiling. Ask questions such as the following:

   (A) What is the quantity demanded and supplied of Greebes at the equilibrium price? Why?

   (B) What is the quantity demanded if the government mandates a $2 price ceiling? Why? *Emphasize that the lower price is an incentive for buyers to buy more Greebes.*

   (C) What is the quantity supplied at a price ceiling of $2? Why? *Emphasize that a lower price is an incentive for producers to produce fewer Greebes and use their resources to produce something else.*

   (D) With the price ceiling, what is the shortage of Greebes? *800*

   (E) If people want to buy more Greebes, who will get the Greebes? *Market can't determine answer.*

   (F) Why do we call a price that is lower than equilibrium a *price ceiling*? *This confuses the students. Point out that the price cannot go higher than the price ceiling. If they could jump ten feet, the ceiling would keep them from going higher.*

   (G) What would happen if all goods and services were free? Who would produce the goods and services? What would happen to inventories? What would be the long-run effects of such a policy? *Students sometimes have problems conceptualizing the idea that price ceilings can have harmful effects. After all, aren't lower prices a good thing for consumers? Students fail to see the effects of lower prices on producers. The discussion of these questions will help the students visualize these effects.*

2. Use Visual 2.12 to illustrate price floors. Ask questions such as these:

   (A) What is the quantity demanded and quantity supplied at the equilibrium price? Why?

   (B) What is the quantity demanded if there is a price floor of $5? Why? *Emphasize the concept that a higher price makes the opportunity cost of buying a Greebe higher.*

   (C) What is the quantity supplied at a price floor of $5? Why? *Emphasize that a higher price is an incentive to producers to supply more Greebes.*

   (D) At a price floor of $5, what is the surplus of Greebes? *1,600*

   (E) If people want to sell more Greebes than consumers want to buy, who will get the surplus? *The government will probably buy them, or the price floor will not be effective.*

   (F) Why is this called a *price floor*? In economics, why is a price floor above a price ceiling? *The floor keeps the price from going lower, just like the floor in the classroom keeps the students from going lower.*

3. Have the students complete Activity 22 and discuss the answers.

Maximum and Minimum Price Controls

✳ Figure 22.1
Price Floors and Ceilings

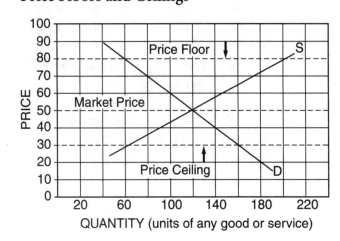

Price floors and ceilings can be plotted with supply and demand curves. Use Figure 22.1 to answer the questions. Fill in the answer blanks or underline the correct words in parentheses.

1. What is the market price? _____ **$50** _____

2. What quantity is demanded and what quantity is supplied at the market price?
   (A) Quantity demanded _____ **120** _____
   (B) Quantity supplied _____ **120** _____

3. What quantity is demanded and what quantity is supplied if the government passes a law requiring the price to be no higher than $30? This is called a *price ceiling*.
   (A) Quantity demanded _____ **160** _____
   (B) Quantity supplied _____ **60** _____
   (C) There is a (**_shortage_** / surplus) of _____ **100** _____ .

4. What quantity is demanded and what quantity is supplied if the government passes a law requiring the price to be no lower than $80? This is called a *price floor*.
   (A) Quantity demanded _____ **60** _____
   (B) Quantity supplied _____ **200** _____
   (C) There is a (shortage / **_surplus_**) of _____ **140** _____ .
   (D) What happens to total consumer or producer surplus? _____ **_It decreased._** _____
   (E) Is society better or worse off after the price floor is imposed? _____ **_Worse off_** _____
   (F) Who gains from the price floor? _____ **_Producers, especially high-cost producers_** _____

Complex Application *Questions in Supply and Demand*

Introduction and Description

This lesson requires the students to apply price theory to a variety of situations. Learning the laws of economics is not enough. Problem solving concentrates the mind and forces the students to really understand an economic concept. Because many AP test questions will be complex application questions, these problems are good practice for the AP test.

Objectives

1. Apply price-theory concepts to analyze market behavior.
2. Analyze how prices act as rationing devices, allocate resources and determine income distribution.

Time Required

Two class periods or 90 minutes

Materials

Activity 23

Procedure

1. You may assign Activity 23 as homework a few days before it is due. An alternative is to have the students work on the problems in groups.

2. Discuss the answers.

Pricing Problems

Write answers to the following questions. Be sure to support your answers with sound economic reasoning and draw graphs where appropriate to illustrate your answers.

1. "Gold is valuable because so many people hunt for it." True, false or uncertain, and why?
   False. Gold is valuable because of supply and demand. People search for gold because it is valuable. There is a fairly small quantity supplied and a high quantity demanded for gold. The price of something does not depend solely on the cost of production.

2. A consumer group believes the prices of necessities such as food, housing, energy and medical care should be controlled by the government. "People can afford higher prices for luxuries," they reason, "but all of us, and especially the poor, suffer when the prices of necessities rise." Evaluate the effects of this plan. *This is a price ceiling and will probably cause a shortage of necessities. This, of course, will happen only if the administered controlled price is lower than the equilibrium price. This administered price will provide incentives for consumers to buy more necessities (an increase in quantity demanded) and incentives for producers to produce less (a decrease in quantity supplied).*

3. State Representative Smith feels that New York can raise revenue 500 percent by increasing license-plate and registration fees by 500 percent. Will the government increase its revenue by 500 percent? Why or why not?
   Representative Smith is wrong. The demand for license plates is inelastic but not perfectly inelastic. Therefore, a 500 percent rise in price would not yield 500 percent more revenue. There are substitutes for cars, such as car pooling and use of mass transit.

4. Make the assumption that one day you will be a college graduate. Would you support a law to raise the legal minimum wage of college graduates to $50,000?
   This is a price floor and would probably increase unemployment among college graduates if the controlled price is above the equilibrium price. There would be incentives for college graduates to work and incentives for employers to hire noncollege graduates at lower wages. This would cause a surplus of workers or higher unemployment.

Advanced Placement Economics Teacher Resource Manual © National Council on Economic Education, New York, N.Y.

5. Recently the price of beef rose. Use graphs to show that the increase in price could be consistent with the following. (Be sure to draw a graph and provide a brief explanation for each situation.)

(A) The quantity of beef consumed falls.

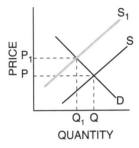

A decrease in supply

(B) The quantity of beef consumed rises.

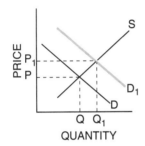

An increase in demand

(C) The quantity of beef consumed stays the same.

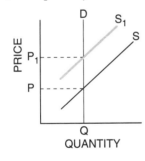 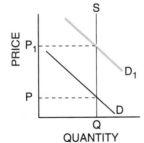 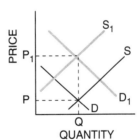

A perfectly inelastic demand curve, a perfectly inelastic supply curve or a simultaneous increase in demand and decrease in supply. Students have the most trouble with this concept. This question also illustrates that the reason for a price change is more complicated than many armchair economists think.

6. You stumble across a heated debate in the cafeteria. It seems that a bunch of friends just bought concert tickets from Ticketmeister, a ticket-handling agency, and paid a $4.00 surcharge for each ticket. "It's outrageous! It's not like they actually do anything worth $4.00," complains a friend. Comment on her complaint. *Ticketmeister brought buyers and sellers together. If Ticketmeister didn't provide a service, people wouldn't pay the $4.00 fee. Evidently, both the concert promoter and the consumer are willing to pay for the service of bringing buyers and sellers together.*

7. You learn that a prominent economist is going to give a lecture, and you rush to get tickets. The economist says, "We economists don't know much, but we know how to create shortages and surpluses."

(A) How can government create a shortage in a competitive market? Illustrate this with a graph. Can you provide examples of this? *Have an administered maximum price below market equilibrium. The students should explain how and why this shortage comes about. Rent controls and price freezes are examples. Use a typical price-ceiling graph such as Visual 2.11 to show this.*

(B) How can government produce a surplus in a competitive market? Illustrate this with a graph. Can you provide examples of this? *Have an administered minimum price above market equilibrium. The students should explain how and why this surplus should occur. Examples are minimum-wage laws and farm-price supports. Use a typical price-floor graph such as Visual 2.12 to show this.*

Sample Multiple-Choice Questions

1. *E*	10. *B*	19. *E*
2. *C*	11. *C*	20. *C*
3. *B*	12. *C*	21. *A*
4. *D*	13. *C*	22. *E*
5. *B*	14. *D*	23. *B*
6. *A*	15. *E*	24. *E*
7. *D*	16. *D*	25. *B*
8. *D*	17. *A*	26. *A*
9. *E*	18. *A*	27. *A*

Sample Short Free-Response Questions

1. Evaluate this statement: "An increase in demand increases price. The higher price increases supply. The higher supply decreases price, and price settles down to the original level."
   The statement is a mixture of accurate economics resulting in nonsense. The first sentence refers to an increase in demand or to a shift in the demand curve to the right. The second sentence says that the higher price will increase the quantity supplied (a movement along the supply curve). The third sentence refers to an increase in supply or a rightward shift in the supply curve.

2. If foreigners demand more American wheat, what will happen to the price and quantity supplied in the momentary situation? In the short run? In the long run? Why?
   In the momentary situation, price would rise and quantity supplied would not change. In the short run, more wheat would come out of storage, and price would fall below momentary equilibrium but above the original equilibrium. In the long run, farmers would plant more wheat, and price would fall more. In a constant-cost industry, price would return to its original level but quantity would increase. In an increasing-cost industry, price would not return to its original level but be higher.

3. I sit in the back row of the barbers' union where they are discussing a proposal to raise the price of haircuts from $18 to $20. The argument gets nowhere, and someone suggests asking me, as an economist, whether it is a good idea or not. I reply, "Many studies have shown that the demand for haircuts is elastic." What are they to make of this? Why? Be as brief as possible in making the major point that the barbers ought to see in this situation.
   If the demand for haircuts is elastic, total revenue would fall if the price were raised.

Advanced Placement Economics Teacher Resource Manual © National Council on Economic Education, New York, N.Y.

4. True, false or uncertain, and explain why? "Other things being the same, the surplus of workers associated with a price floor will be greater the greater the elasticity of both supply and demand." Discuss this statement. Use graphs to illustrate your explanation.

The more elastic the supply and demand curves, the greater the surplus.

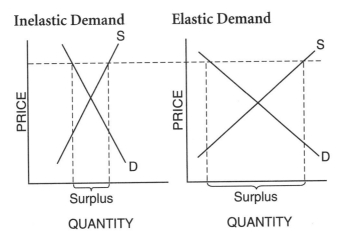

Inelastic Demand **Elastic Demand**

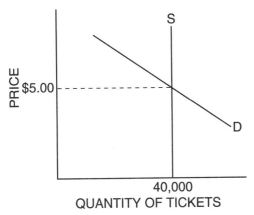

*5. An arena holds a maximum of 40,000 people, as indicated in the graph above. Each year the circus holds eight performances, all of which are sold out.

(A) Analyze the effect on each of the following of the addition of a fantastic new death-defying trapeze act that increases the demand for tickets.

(i) The price of tickets

(ii) The quantity of tickets sold

The trapeze act will cause an increase in demand (shift right in the demand curve) increasing the price, but the quantity will remain the same because the quantity is fixed at 40,000 seats.

Grading Rubric: Part (A) = 2 points
Price increases as a result of the demand increases (1 point)
Quantity remains the same (1 point)

---

* Actual free-response question from a past AP test. Reprinted by permission of the College Entrance Examination Board, the copyright owner. For limited use by NCEE.

UNIT
2 Microeconomics
SHORT FREE-RESPONSE
SAMPLE QUESTIONS
Answer
Key

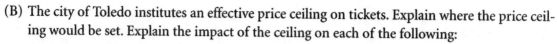

(B) The city of Toledo institutes an effective price ceiling on tickets. Explain where the price ceiling would be set. Explain the impact of the ceiling on each of the following:

(i) The quantity of tickets demanded

(ii) The quantity of tickets supplied

The price ceiling must be set below the equilibrium price with the new trapeze act (1 point). The quantity demanded will increase (1/2 point), however the quantity supplied will remain the same (fixed at 40,000) (1/2 point).

Grading Rubric: Part (B) = 2 points
Setting the price ceiling below the equilibrium price (1 point)
Quantity demand increases (1/2 point)
Quantity supplied unchanged (1/2 point)

(C) Will everyone who attends the circus pay the ceiling price set by the city of Toledo? Why or why not?

No, a secondary market or reselling of tickets or scalping of tickets will have some circus goers paying more than the ceiling price (1 point).

Grading Rubric: Part (C) = 1 point (some version of the above)
(Note: Radio give-aways, coupons and employees do not change with the existence of a price ceiling; therefore that type of answer is incorrect.)

6. A newspaper headline says, "The Coldest Winter in 20 Years Brings Record Prices for Heating Oil."

(A) Using a graph of home heating oil, show and explain how price changed.
The record cold increases the demand for heating oil to run heaters, so the demand increases, raising the price and quantity sold.

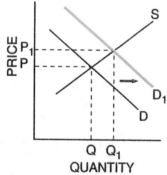

(B) What other factors could cause the price of heating oil to increase?
Any factor that increased demand could increase price and quantity.
Any factor that decreased supply could increase price and decrease quantity.

7. In a recent year, the price of wheat fell. For each of the following, draw a supply and demand graph showing a decrease in prices with the stated impact on quantity.

(A) The quantity of wheat decreasing

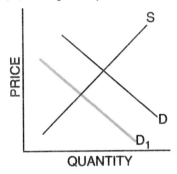

(B) The quantity of wheat increasing

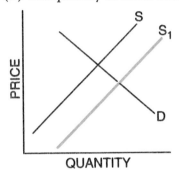

(C) The quantity of wheat staying the same

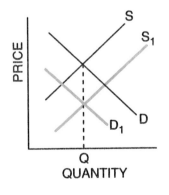 OR 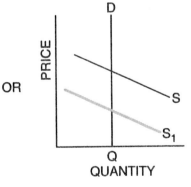 OR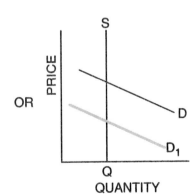

8. The market for many commodities is seasonal in nature. Their sales (equilibrium quantity) increase dramatically during certain times of the year. Christmas cards and fresh strawberries, at least in the North, are two examples. Christmas-card sales increase during the last three months of the year, and the sales of fresh strawberries in the North increase during the summer months. But the (equilibrium) price movement of these two commodities is quite different during their peak sales season: Christmas cards increase in price during the last three months of the year, whereas strawberries decrease in price during the summer.

(A) Show on the graph below how there can be an increase in the equilibrium quantity and an increase in the equilibrium price of Christmas cards during the last three months of the year, and briefly explain what has happened.

Christmas Card Market

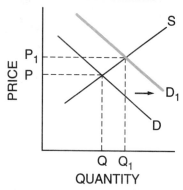

With other things constant, there is an increase in the demand for Christmas cards in the last three months of the year. This causes a rightward shift of demand and causes the price and quantity sold to increase.

(B) Change the graph for fresh strawberries in the North to show how there can be an increase in the equilibrium quantity and a decrease in the equilibrium price of strawberries in the summer, and briefly explain what has happened.

Strawberry Market in the North

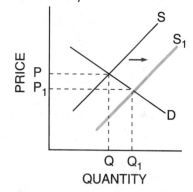

Other things constant, there is an increase in the supply of fresh strawberries in the northern areas of the United States in the warmer months when the berries are harvested in the northern areas. This causes a rightward shift in the supply curve and causes the price to fall and the quantity sold to increase.

UNIT
2 Microeconomics
LONG FREE-RESPONSE
SAMPLE QUESTIONS
Answer
Key

Sample Long Free-Response Questions

1. You are a member of the city council and are considering a law to control rents below the free-market rent. Answer the following questions, and use a graph in your explanation.

    (A) What would be the effect of this rent-control law in the short run? Why?

    (B) What would be the effect of this rent-control law in the long run? Why?

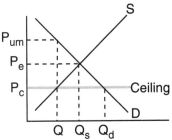

Note: In the figure, P_{um} stands for "Price – underground market."

   (A) *In the short run, this would cause a shortage. There is no time to sell or convert apartments. Quantity supplied (Q_s) stays the same, but quantity demanded increases to Q_d. A shortage from Q_s to Q_d exists.*

   (B) *In the long run, the shortage would be more acute because there would be fewer incentives to build more apartments. Apartments would be converted to condominiums or sold for other businesses. Quantity supplied would move to Q. Also, underground markets could develop, and creative apartment owners could actually charge a price of P_{um}.*

*2. In a perfectly competitive market in long-run equilibrium, what would be the immediate results of imposing and enforcing a price ceiling below the equilibrium price of the product? What would be the long-run effect of continuing to enforce the ceiling price, assuming underground markets don't develop? Be sure to explain why the predicted effects will occur.
   A price ceiling would cause a shortage. Quantity demanded would increase and quantity supplied would decrease. The shortage would be greater in the long run. This is because supply and demand are both more elastic in the long run. This could also be shown by shifting the supply curve leftward in the long run.

---

* Actual free-response question from a past AP test. Reprinted by permission of the College Entrance Examination Board, the copyright owner. For limited use by NCEE.

UNIT
2 Microeconomics
LONG FREE-RESPONSE
SAMPLE QUESTIONS
Answer
Key

*3. Assume the market for unskilled workers is perfectly competitive and in equilibrium. Then a minimum wage is imposed, which increases the wage rate of unskilled workers.

(A) Use supply and demand analysis to explain how this increase in the wage rate will affect each of the following:

(i) The number of workers employed in the market

(ii) The number of unskilled workers seeking employment in the market

(B) Assume that the fast-food industry is perfectly competitive and employs only one factor of production: unskilled workers. Use supply and demand analysis to explain how the increase in the wage rate resulting from the imposition of the minimum wage will affect each of the following in the fast-food industry in the short run.

(i) Price of fast food

(ii) Quantity of fast food produced

(A) *This is a price floor.*

(i) *The minimum wage would decrease the number of workers employed in the industry (quantity of workers demanded).*

(ii) *It would also increase the number of workers seeking employment (quantity of workers supplied).*

(B) *Higher wages increase the costs of production, so supply would decrease, or shift to the left. This would cause the price of fast food to increase and the quantity of fast food produced to decrease.*

---

* Actual free-response question from a past AP test. Reprinted by permission of the College Entrance Examination Board, the copyright owner. For limited use by NCEE.

Advanced Placement Economics Teacher Resource Manual © National Council on Economic Education, New York, N.Y.

Changes in Demand and Quantity Demanded

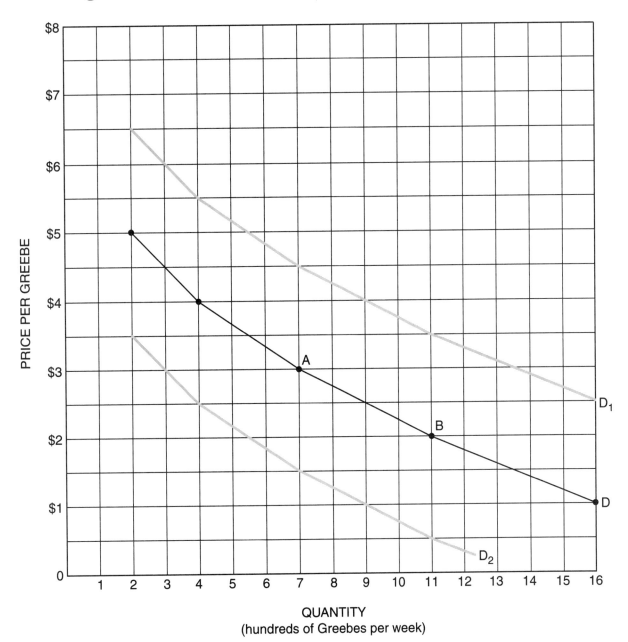

QUANTITY
(hundreds of Greebes per week)

Determinants of Demand

FACTORS THAT SHIFT
THE DEMAND CURVE

- Change in consumer tastes

- Change in the number of buyers

- Change in consumer incomes

- Change in the prices of complementary
  and substitute goods

- Change in consumer expectations

Changes in Supply and Quantity Supplied

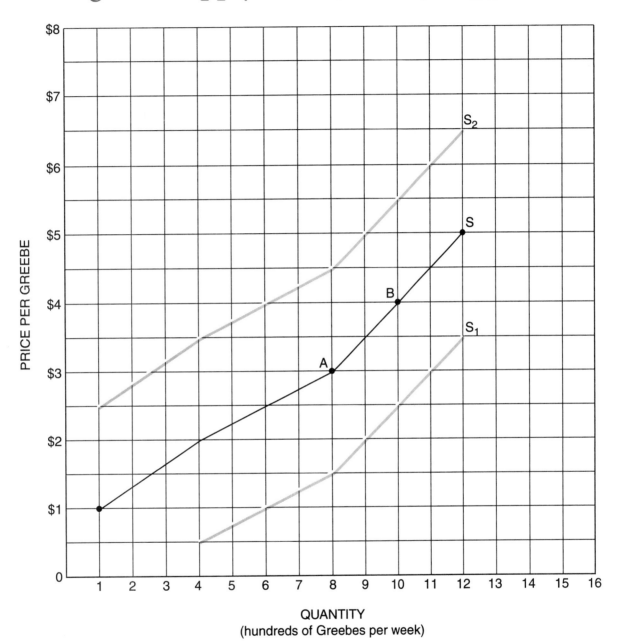

Determinants of Supply

FACTORS THAT SHIFT THE SUPPLY CURVE

- Change in resource prices or input prices

- Change in technology

- Change in taxes and subsidies

- Change in the prices of other goods

- Change in producer expectations

- Change in the number of suppliers

Any factor that *increases* the cost of production *decreases* supply.

Any factor that *decreases* the cost of production *increases* supply.

Equilibrium

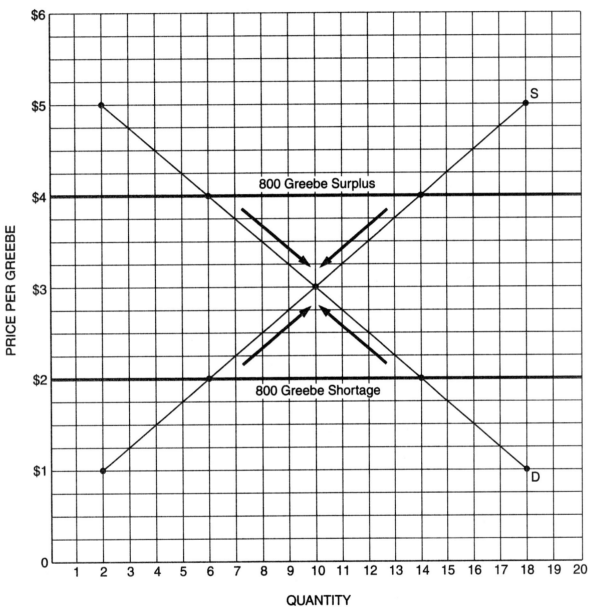

Shifts in Demand and Supply

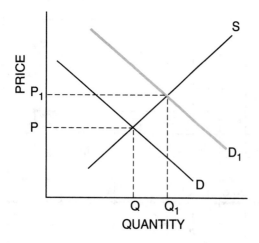

A. INCREASE IN DEMAND

D ↑

P ↑

Q ↑

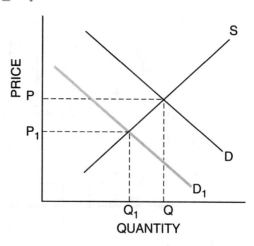

B. DECREASE IN DEMAND

D ↓

P ↓

Q ↓

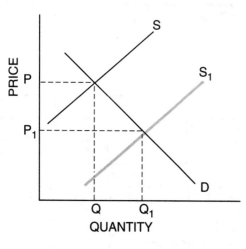

C. INCREASE IN SUPPLY

S ↑

P ↓

Q ↑

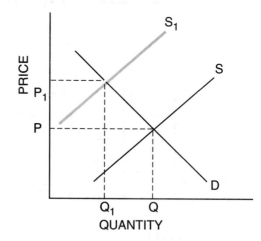

D. DECREASE IN SUPPLY

S ↓

P ↑

Q ↓

Qualities That Affect Elasticity of Demand

(A) Substitutability

(B) Proportion of income spent on product

(C) Luxury or necessity

(D) Is it habit-forming?

(E) Time

Elasticity Coefficients

1. $\varepsilon_d = \dfrac{\text{percentage change in quantity demanded}}{\text{percentage change in price}}$

2. Midpoint or Arc Method

$$\varepsilon_d = \dfrac{\dfrac{\Delta Q}{(Q + Q_1)/2}}{\dfrac{\Delta P}{(P + P_1)/2}}$$

Example: price x quantity = total revenue

$10 x 10 = $100
$ 9 x 12 = $108

$$\varepsilon_d = \dfrac{\dfrac{2}{(10+12)/2} = \dfrac{2}{11} = .18}{\dfrac{1}{(10+9)/2} = \dfrac{1}{9.5} = .10} = 1.8 \text{ elastic}$$

3. What the coefficients mean:

$\varepsilon_d > 1$ Elastic
$\varepsilon_d < 1$ Inelastic
$\varepsilon_d = 1$ Unit elastic

Advanced Placement Economics Teacher Resource Manual © National Council on Economic Education, New York, N.Y.

Summarizing Price Elasticity of Demand

Elasticity Coefficient	Term	Description	Impact on Total Revenue of	
			Price Increase	Price Decrease
Greater than 1 $\varepsilon_d > 1$	Elastic	Quantity demanded changes by a larger percentage than does price	Total revenue decreases	Total revenue increases
Equal to 1 $\varepsilon_d = 1$	Unit elastic	Quantity demanded changes by the same percentage as does price	Total revenue is unchanged	Total revenue is unchanged
Less than 1 $\varepsilon_d < 1$	Inelastic	Quantity demanded changes by a smaller percentage than does price	Total revenue increases	Total revenue decreases

Tax Incidence and Elasticity of Demand

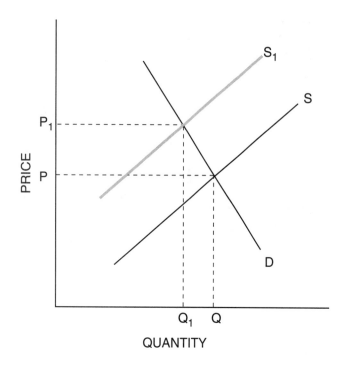

The more inelastic the demand for a good, the more the incidence of an excise tax can be shifted to the consumer.

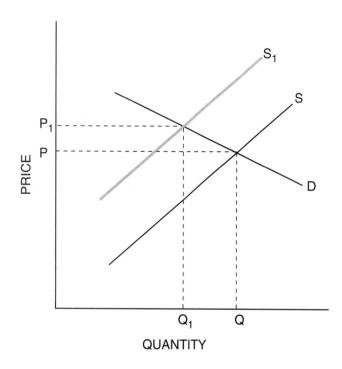

A Price Ceiling

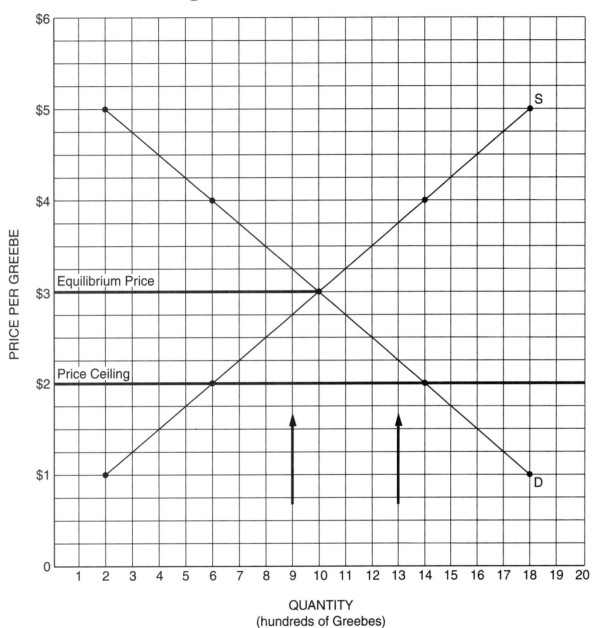

A Price Floor

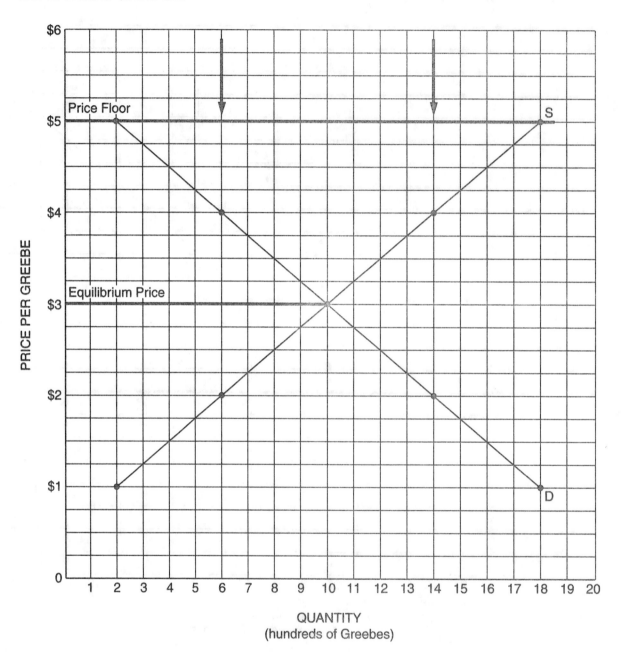

Microeconomics | Unit 3

The Theory of the Firm

25 class periods or 1,125 minutes
(33 percent of course time)

Unit Overview

The theory of the firm is the heart of an AP Microeconomics course. The materials in this unit will account for 40 percent to 50 percent of the AP Microeconomics Exam.

This material is difficult because it is abstract. This is why we have included exercises requiring the students to plot costs and revenue curves before they interpret them. The risk in this approach is that the students may get bogged down in details and miss the major theoretical conclusions. After completing this unit, the students should be able to differentiate between short-run and long-run equilibria for both a profit-maximizing individual firm and for an industry. The students must understand the relationships among price, marginal revenue, average revenue, marginal cost, average cost and profit. They also must be able to compare a monopolist's price, level of output and profits with the price, level of output and profits of a perfect competitor. The students must know why monopoly is bad and competition is good. This unit will help them evaluate government regulation of monopoly. The students must understand the kinds of market structures that range between monopoly and perfect competition, specifically oligopoly and monopolistic competition. On the AP Exam the students will not plot graphs from data; they will have to draw graphs freehand and explain them.

Although the unit plan shows 25 days, this unit may take longer. First, it is wise to start with an overview of business, which is not covered in these activities. In addition to examining the behavior and role of business in a capitalist economy, spend some time on income statements and balance sheets, stocks, bonds and other financial instruments. This will make the cost and revenue curves in this unit more concrete. Most principles of economics books cover this material. Second, try to bring in current controversies regarding the regulation of business. We have not included information about these topics because they rapidly become dated. Nevertheless, teaching the students to evaluate controversial issues is a prime goal of an economics course.

There are several themes to keep in mind while the students plow through this abstract material.

1. Firms should ignore sunk costs when making decisions. Why are marginal costs their primary consideration?

2. This material is based on the assumption that the objective of all firms is to maximize profits. Is this assumption valid?

3. Firms maximize profits where marginal revenue equals marginal cost. Why is this so?

4. When perfectly competitive firms maximize profits, the general good is served. Why? What are the implications of this?

5. When monopolies attempt to maximize profits, the general good is not served. Why? What are the implications of this?

6. Most U.S. markets can be classified as monopolistic competition or oligopoly. Why do we spend so much time on perfect competition and monopoly — forms of market structure that are rare?

7. What type of antitrust policy should government pursue? Why?

It pays to give frequent quizzes in this unit. If the students do not understand costs, they will not be able to understand profit maximization. If they don't understand perfect competition, they will not understand monopoly. If this material is lost on the students, they will have difficulty passing the AP Exam.

The Lesson Planner

Lesson 1 provides an introduction to the market structures of perfect competition, monopoly, monopolistic competition and oligopoly. This lesson uses **Activity 24** and **Visual 3.1**.

Lesson 2 covers the costs of production. This is critical because the relationships among costs hold for all types of firms. This lesson uses **Activities 25** and **26** and **Visuals 3.2, 3.3** and **3.4**.

Lesson 3 covers the short- and long-run equilibria of a perfect competitor for both the firm and the industry. This lesson uses **Activities 27, 28, 29, 30** and **31** and **Visuals 3.5, 3.6, 3.7, 3.8** and **3.9**.

Lesson 4 covers the basics of the monopoly firm. It compares the results achieved by a profit-maximizing monopolist with the results achieved by a profit-maximizing perfect competitor. This lesson uses **Activities 32, 33** and **34** and **Visuals 3.10** and **3.11**.

Lesson 5 examines why monopolies are bad and reviews regulatory policies toward them. This lesson also reinforces monopoly pricing and comparing price and output of a monopolist with price and output of a perfect competitor. Lesson 5 uses **Activities 35, 36, 37, 38** and **39**.

Lesson 6 examines the "in between" market structures of monopolistic competition and oligopoly. Game theory is used to understand how oligopolistic decisions are made. This lesson uses **Activities 40** and **41** and **Visual 3.12**.

Lesson 7 provides practice in solving problems involving market structure and business decision making. It uses **Activity 42**.

Week 1

Day 1

(A) Give lecture on characteristics of perfect competition, monopolistic competition, oligopoly and monopoly.

(B) Have students form groups to complete Activity 24.

(C) Use Visual 3.1 to go over Activity 24.

Day 2

(A) Provide overview of revenue, fixed costs, variable costs and profits.

(B) Use Visual 3.2 to show relationship of marginal product to marginal cost and average product to average variable cost.

(C) Have the students begin Activity 25 and finish it as homework.

Day 3

(A) Discuss answers to Activity 25.

(B) Discuss implicit and explicit costs.

(C) Use Visual 3.3 to show relationships among FC, VC and TC.

(D) Use Visual 3.4 to show relationships among AFC, AVC, ATC and MC.

(E) Use Visual 3.4 to explain why MC crosses ATC at the minimum point. This is always true.

(F) Assign Activity 26 as homework.

Day 4

Discuss the answers to Activity 26.

Day 5

(A) Review costs.

(B) Use Visual 3.5 to show the perfectly competitive firm and industry in short-run equilibrium.

(C) Have the students complete Parts A and B of Activity 27 and discuss answers.

(D) Assign the rest of Activity 27 as homework.

Week 2

Day 6

(A) Go over the rest of Activity 27. You may want to make visuals of the graphs.

(B) Use Visual 3.5 again to summarize what the students have learned.

Day 7

(A) Use Visual 3.6 to illustrate profit, loss and shut-down for a perfectly competitive firm.

(B) Use Visual 3.7 to illustrate a firm in long-run equilibrium.

(C) Have the students complete Part A of Activity 28 and discuss the answers.

Day 8

Have the students complete Part B of Activity 28 and discuss the answers.

Day 9

(A) Use Visuals 3.8 and 3.9 to illustrate how the firm and industry reach long-run equilibrium. This process is critical for a good score on the AP Exam.

(B) Have the students complete Activity 29 and discuss it.

Day 10

(A) Explain the differences between long-run and short-run average cost curves.

(B) Have the students complete Activity 30 and discuss it.

Week 3

Day 11

(A) Review perfect competition.

(B) Have the students complete Activity 31.

(C) Have the students draw the graphs in Activity 31 on the board. Drawing graphs for the firm and industry is a critical skill in AP Economics.

Day 12

Give a test on perfect competition.

Day 13

(A) Use Visual 3.10 to explain why a monopolist is a price seeker and why MR < P.

(B) Have the students complete Activity 32 and discuss it.

Day 14

(A) Use Visual 3.11 to explain the monopolist's profit-maximizing price and to compare the output of a monopolist with that of a perfect competitor.

(B) Have the students complete Activity 33.

Day 15

(A) Discuss the answers to Activity 33.

(B) Illustrate consumer surplus for a monopolist and for a perfect competitor.

(C) Have the students complete Activity 34 and discuss the answers.

Week 4

Day 16

(A) Have the students read Activity 35 and answer the questions.

(B) Discuss the answers to Activity 35.

(C) Give lecture on price discrimination.

(D) Assign Activity 36 as homework.

Day 17

(A) Go over answers to Activity 36.

(B) Give a lecture on regulating monopolies.

(C) Assign Activity 37 and discuss the answers.

Day 18

(A) Have the students complete Activity 38 in small groups.

(B) Discuss the answers to Activity 38.

(C) Have the students do Activity 39 as a quick review of monopoly and perfect competition.

Day 19

(A) Give a test on monopoly.

(B) Assign Activity 42 as homework for Day 22.

Day 20

(A) Use Visual 3.12 to describe the characteristics of monopolistic competition.

(B) Have the students complete Activity 40 and discuss the answers.

Week 5

▓ Day 21

(A) Give lecture on game theory.

(B) Have the students complete Activity 41 and discuss the answers.

(C) Relate game theory to oligopolistic behavior.

▓ Day 22

Go over the answers to Activity 42.

▓ Day 23

Review unit using sample multiple-choice and free-response questions.

▓ Day 24

Give multiple-choice test.

▓ Day 25

Give free-response test.

Note: Tests are not included in the individual lessons but are included in sample lesson plans. This unit has four test days:

   (1) Perfect competition test

   (2) Monopoly test

   (3) Multiple-choice unit test

   (4) Free-response unit test

An Introduction to Market Structure

Introduction and Description

This lesson introduces the students to the kinds of market structures they will be studying during the next several weeks. Because most actual markets do not fit the assumptions of the perfectly competitive market model, it is necessary to examine what happens when these assumptions — such as perfect information and an industry consisting of many small firms — are violated. Economists have developed classifications and market models to explain how other market structures — such as those characterized by monopoly, oligopoly and monopolistic competition — can produce results that differ from those expected under purely competitive conditions.

In this lesson, it is a good idea to point out that throughout the unit we will assume that firms want to maximize their profits. However, depending on the market structure of the industry, such behavior has greatly different effects on society and the economy. Stress that in this unit the students will use models and analytical skills to examine the behavior and effects of firms operating under different types of market structure. As social scientists, the students must support their conclusions.

Objective

Describe the major characteristics of *perfect competition, monopolistic competition, oligopoly* and *monopoly.*

Time Required

One class period or 45 minutes

Materials

1. Activity 24
2. Visual 3.1

Procedure

1. Give a lecture on the characteristics of *perfect competition, monopolistic competition, oligopoly* and *monopoly.*

2. Have the students form groups to complete Activity 24. Allow them to use their textbooks.

3. Use Visual 3.1 as the answer key to discuss the answers to Activity 24. Students may disagree on whether certain examples belong in one category or market structure or another. This may depend on how broadly they define the industry. For example, "canned food" might be monopolistic competition while "canned corn" might be oligopolistic. They may also bring up examples not on Visual 3.1. Stress that it is difficult to determine exactly the market structure in some industries. The real world is messy.

4. Ask questions such as the following to reinforce the students' understanding of the types of market structures:

   (A) What is the difference between homogeneous and differentiated products? *Homogeneous products are identical; differentiated products differ in quality and type. Raw cane sugar is homogeneous; candy bars are differentiated.*

   (B) What is the difference between perfect competition and monopolistic competition? *Under monopolistic competition, products are differentiated, and competition takes place in terms of both price and quality. In perfect competition, products are identical, and market forces set the price.*

   (C) Is monopolistic competition close to monopoly? *No, it is closer to perfect competition because it has many firms and relatively easy entry.*

(D) What are the main characteristics of oligopoly? *Few firms, the ability to influence price, barriers to entry*

(E) What are some examples of barriers to entry? *There are large advertising costs, patents, licenses, large capital investment.*

(F) What is the distinguishing characteristic of monopoly? *Only one supplier in an industry, a particular geographic area or a particular market in which other suppliers are unable to compete*

Different Types of Market Structures

After you have learned about the four types of market structures, complete Figure 24.1.

 Figure 24.1
Market Structures

Characteristics

Market Structure	Number of Firms	Differentiated or Homogeneous Product		Ease of Entry
Perfect Competition	*Very many*	*H*		*Very easy*
Monopolistic Competition	*Many*	*D*		*Relatively easy*
Oligopoly	*Few*	*H/D*		*Not easy*
Monopoly	*One*	*Only product of its kind (no close substitute)*		*Impossible*

Results

Market Structure	Price-Setting Power	Nonprice Competition	Allocative and Productive Efficiency	Long-Run Profits	Examples
Perfect Competition	*Nil (price taker)*	*None*	*Highly efficient*	*0*	*Doesn't exist; agriculture close*
Monopolistic Competition	*Somewhat*	*Considerable*	*Less efficient than PC*	*0*	*Fast food, retail stores, cosmetics*
Oligopoly	*Limited*	*Considerable for a differentiated oligopoly*	*Less efficient than PC*	*Positive*	*Cars, steel, soft drinks, cereals, computers*
Monopoly	*Absolute (price maker)*	*Somewhat*	*Inefficient*	*High*	*Small-town newspaper, rural gas station*

The Costs of Production

Introduction and Description

This lesson helps the students understand the relationship between output and input and ultimately to understand several cost concepts. This lesson is critical if the students are to grasp what follows.

Although there are four types of market structure, the costs of the firm remain conceptually the same for each. Unless the students understand these cost concepts, they will be confused during the entire unit. For this reason, these concepts are repeated as part of Lesson 2. First, this lesson includes the application of opportunity costs (including implicit costs) to determine economic profit. Second, the students learn the interrelationships among these costs. Third, they learn how to graph cost curves in order to see more clearly how the costs are related to each other.

Objectives

1. Define the relationship between inputs and outputs or product and cost.
2. Explain the relationships among marginal product, total product and average product.
3. Explain the relationships among marginal cost, total variable cost and average variable cost.
4. Use explicit and implicit costs to determine economic profit and loss.
5. Distinguish economic profit from normal profit.
6. Define and graph *total fixed cost* (FC), *total variable cost* (VC) and *total cost* (TC).
7. Define and graph *average fixed cost* (AFC), *average variable cost* (AVC), *average total cost* (ATC) and *marginal cost* (MC).
8. Calculate AFC, AVC, ATC and MC given a schedule of the quantity of output and fixed and variable costs at each output level.
9. Explain why MC = ATC at the minimum ATC level.

10. Explain why fixed cost is unrelated to marginal cost.
11. Explain how decreasing marginal product is related to increasing marginal costs.
12. Explain how the law of diminishing marginal returns affects costs.

Time Required

Three class periods or 135 minutes

Materials

1. Activities 25 and 26
2. Visuals 3.2, 3.3 and 3.4

Procedure

1. Start out with a simple discussion of revenue, cost and profit. You might put up a simple income statement like this:

Revenue	$100
Fixed costs	$ 20
Variable costs	$ 70
Profit	$ 10

   You can then define fixed and variable costs, as well as the fact that revenue minus cost equals profit. You can even add normal (or accounting) profit as an implicit cost to determine the difference between economic profit and normal profit.

2. If you have time, you may want to conduct a productivity simulation to show how productivity and diminishing marginal returns affect output and costs. For example, "Getting More or Using Less" is one such activity. It is from NCEE's publication *Focus: High School Economics*, 2nd ed., page 87. There are many other simulations of this type. A simulation probably will add two days to this unit but may make the abstract figures more concrete.

3. Use Visual 3.2 to show the relationship of marginal product to marginal cost and average

product to average variable cost. Discuss how the law of diminishing marginal returns affects costs and the significance of this effect.

4. Have the students complete Activity 25, and discuss the answers. Keep stressing the relationships among total, marginal and average costs. Be sure to close the deal by showing how the law of diminishing marginal returns affects output and, correspondingly, cost. This is critical to each student's future success in this unit.

5. Define and discuss *implicit costs* and *explicit costs*. Relate these to normal profit (sometimes called accounting profit) and economic profit.

6. Use Visual 3.3 to define and show the relationships among FC, VC and TC.

7. Use Visual 3.4 to define and show the relationships among AFC, AVC, ATC and MC.

8. Also use Visual 3.4 to explain why MC crosses ATC at its minimum point.

9. Assign Activity 26 as homework. Here are some things that the students should look out for:

(A) In Part A, the return on investment is a loss when opportunity cost is included. This gives a negative rate of return if "psychic income" from being in business for yourself is ignored.

(B) In Part B, marginal cost is plotted at the midpoints of the quantity intervals, and the quantity intervals are 100 units, not one unit. We will plot marginal cost and marginal revenue at the midpoints. Some textbooks do not do so. Therefore, don't let the students get hung up on this. First the students must calculate marginal cost from the chart. Marginal cost is $\Delta TC / \Delta Q$ or $\Delta TC / 100$. To find MC as output increases from 500 units to 600 units, find the change in total cost over this interval: $4,320 - $3,600 = $720. Divide by the change in quantity (100), and MC = $7.20

at an output of 550 units. The complete steps for all intervals are:

(i) Begin with the schedule of total cost at each output level.

(ii) Calculate the change in total cost, ΔTC, over the output interval.

(iii) Calculate the change in the number of units of output over the output interval, ΔQ.

(iv) Divide ΔTC by ΔQ: $MC = \dfrac{\Delta TC}{\Delta Q}$

(v) Plot at the midpoint of the output interval.

10. Go over Activity 26. Here are some points to consider as you go over the answers.

(A) The accountant's concept of "profit" differs from the economist's because the economist's concept includes implicit opportunity costs. When M.I. Fortunate goes into business for herself, she incurs two implicit opportunity costs:

(i) Her former salary of $50,000

(ii) The 8 percent return on $100,000, which is $8,000

The second is incurred because the $100,000 must be used to invest in the new business. While it earns some return, it does not earn the previous $8,000 realized when it was invested in securities. The "net income" of $55,000 is gross return net of explicit cost only, and it gives an accounting profit only. To find economic profit, the opportunity cost of $58,000 must also be subtracted.

The possibility of "psychic income" from being in business for herself is not considered in establishing her total income of $55,000 after all expenses. If "psychic income" is considered, she may not lose $3,000.

(B) Part B. Students must use these formulas:

Total Cost = Fixed Cost + Variable Cost

$$\text{Average Fixed Cost (AFC)} = \frac{\text{Fixed Cost}}{\text{Quantity}} = \frac{FC}{Q}$$

$$AVC = \frac{VC}{Q}$$

$$ATC = \frac{TC}{Q}$$

$$MC = \frac{\text{Change in Total Cost}}{\text{Change in Quantity}} = \frac{\Delta TC}{\Delta Q}$$

(C) Plot marginal cost at the midpoints.

(D) Question 6 answer: *If marginal cost is below average cost, average cost is falling because the marginal, or additional, cost is pulling AC down. If marginal cost is above average cost, average cost is rising because the marginal, or additional, cost is pulling AC up. Because AC declines and then rises, MC crosses AC at the lowest point on the average cost curve.*

Mirror Images: Marginal Product and Marginal Cost

Part A
The Law of Diminishing Marginal Returns

 Figure 25.2
The Law of Diminishing Marginal Returns

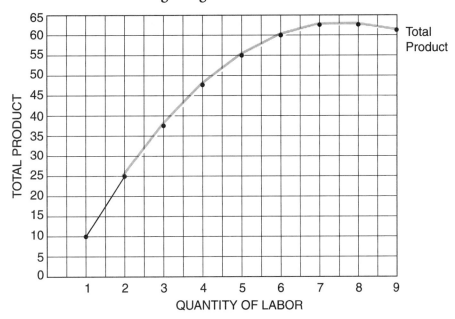

 Figure 25.3
Marginal and Average Product

1. What happens to the total product curve as output (production) increases? *It rises at an increasing rate, continues to rise but at a decreasing rate, levels off and then falls.*

2. What happens to the marginal product curve as output increases? *It rises and then falls.*

3. What happens to the average product curve as output increases? *It rises, levels off and then falls.*

4. Where does the marginal product curve cross the average product curve? *At the highest point on the average product curve*

5. Why do these curves look the way they do? *Because of the law of diminishing marginal returns*

6. What is the law of diminishing marginal returns? *As successive amounts of a variable resource such as labor are added to a fixed resource such as capital or land, at some point the marginal product will decline.*

7. Why is this concept important? *It is important because in the production process, marginal cost and eventually average cost will rise. If marginal cost continued to decline, we could feed the world from a flower pot.*

8. What is the relationship between marginal product and total product? *Marginal product is the slope of the total product curve. When total product is increasing at an increasing rate, marginal product is rising. When total product is increasing at a decreasing rate, marginal product is positive but falling. When total product is at its maximum, marginal product is zero. When total product declines, marginal product is negative.*

9. What is the relationship between marginal product and average product? *When marginal product exceeds average product, average product will rise. When marginal product is less than average product, average product will fall. Therefore, marginal product intersects average product where average product is at its maximum.*

Part B

Products and Costs: A Mirror View

Now look at Figure 25.4, which relates marginal and average product to marginal and average variable costs. Then answer the questions that follow the graph. (*Variable costs* are costs that change with the level of output. *Average variable costs* are total variable costs divided by output.)

Figure 25.4

Marginal Product and Marginal Cost

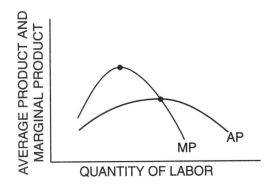 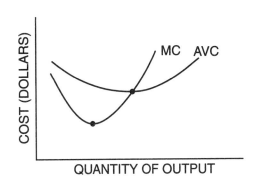

10. Where does marginal product cross average product? *At the AP's maximum*

11. Where does marginal cost cross average variable cost? *At the lowest point on the average variable cost curve*

12. Will this always be true? Why or why not? *Yes. Anything else is mathematically impossible.*

13. How does the law of diminishing marginal returns affect output (product) and costs? *The law of diminishing marginal returns says that the increase to total product (marginal product) will decrease and the total cost curve will increase at an increasing rate (marginal costs will increase).*

Costs of the Individual Firm

Part A
Fill in the blanks and answer the questions.

1. M.I. Fortunate was employed as plant manager for a corporation at a salary of $50,000 a year, and she had savings of $100,000 invested in securities that yielded an 8 percent annual income. She went into business for herself, investing all her savings in the enterprise. At the end of the first year, her accounts showed a net income of $55,000 after all expenses of operation. One accountant said this accounting profit represented a 55 percent return on her $100,000 investment. Another accountant, who had taken introductory microeconomics, said, "No, you should pay yourself the $50,000 salary you would have earned anyway, and your accounting profit of $5,000 represents a return of 5 percent on your investment of $100,000." A serious student of introductory microeconomics, however, should say, "No, your true economic profit from going into business for yourself is __$ –3,000__, and this is a return of __–3__ percent." Was M.I. Fortunate fortunate? Why or why not? *No. The forgone salary of $50,000 and the forgone interest income of $8,000 are opportunity costs, so going into business on her own costs her $3,000. But she might not view this as a loss if she gets "psychic income" from self-employment.*

2. Figure 26.1 (on the next page) shows a comprehensive set of cost data for a firm with a given plant at various levels of output. Study this table to understand how it is set up.

   Marginal cost is the *additional* cost of producing an *additional* unit of output ($\Delta TC / \Delta Q$). If producing an additional 100 units of output adds $700 to total cost, the marginal cost per unit is $700 / 100 = $7.00, etc. Note that in the table, the "marginal" changes are located between ouput levels.

   After you have filled in the blanks in Figure 26.1, finish plotting the aggregate cost data for fixed cost, variable cost and total cost (*not* change in total cost) on Figure 26.2. Also, finish plotting the unit cost data for FC / Q, VC / Q, TC / Q and $\Delta TC / \Delta Q$ on Figure 26.3. Note that marginal cost ($\Delta TC / \Delta Q$) is plotted at the midpoint (between output levels).

3. After you have finished plotting, answer the eight questions in Part B.

✳ Figure 26.1

Aggregate and Unit Cost Structure

	Aggregate Cost Data				Unit Cost Data		
Output	Total Fixed Cost	Total Variable Cost	Total Cost	Marginal Cost ($\Delta TC / \Delta Q$)	Average Fixed Cost	Average Variable Cost	Average Total Cost
0	$500	$0	$500				
100	500	700	1,200	$7.00	$5.00	$7.00	$12.00
200	500	1,300	1,800	6.00	2.50	6.50	9.00
300	500	1,800	2,300	5.00	1.67	6.00	7.67
400	500	2,400	2,900	6.00	1.25	6.00	7.25
500	500	3,100	3,600	7.00	1.00	6.20	7.20
600	500	3,820	4,320	7.20	0.83	6.37	7.20
700	500	4,700	5,200	8.80	0.71	6.71	7.42

✳ Figure 26.2

Graph of Aggregate Cost Data

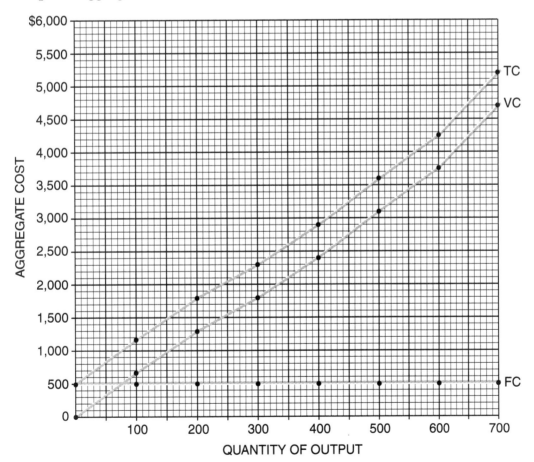

Figure 26.3

Graph of Unit Cost Data

Note: Marginal cost (ΔTC / ΔQ) is plotted between the output levels shown in Figure 26.1.

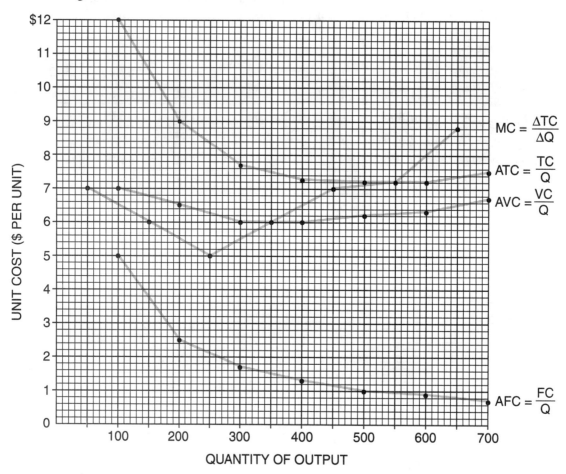

Part B

4. How is marginal cost (ΔTC / ΔQ) represented in Figure 26.2? *It is the slope of the TC curve.*

5. On Figure 26.3, total cost per unit (TC / Q or average total cost) is at a minimum at an output level of __*between 500 and 600*__ units.

6. On Figure 26.3, variable cost per unit (VC / Q or average variable cost) is at a minimum at an output level of __*between 300 and 400*__ units.

7. On Figure 26.3, what is the relation between marginal cost (ΔTC / ΔQ) and average total cost (TC / Q) when average total cost is at its minimum? *They are equal.*

8. On Figure 26.3, what is the relation between marginal cost (ΔTC / ΔQ) and average variable cost (VC / Q) when average variable cost is at its minimum? *They are equal.*

9. Explain why marginal cost on a unit-cost graph always intersects average total cost and average variable cost at their minimum points. *A minimum is the lowest point.*

   If ATC $\left(\frac{TC}{Q}\right)$ and AVC $\left(\frac{VC}{Q}\right)$ fall when MC $\left(\frac{\Delta TC}{\Delta Q}\right)$ is below them (as they must since the cost of one additional unit is less than the average, it pulls average cost down), and if ATC and AVC increase when MC is above them (as they must since the cost of one additional unit is more than the average, it pulls average cost up), and if MC is rising, ATC and AVC must be at a minimum when they are equal to MC since you have to pass through a minimum when you stop falling and start rising. Let's say that a basketball player is averaging 10 points a game. In the next game, she scores eight points. Because the marginal (additional) points are less than her average, her average must fall. On the other hand, what if she scored 12 points? Then her average would rise because the marginal points would be greater than her average.

10. On Figure 26.3, what does the vertical distance between the TC / Q curve and VC / Q curve represent?
    $\frac{FC}{Q}$ *or average fixed cost*

11. Explain why fixed cost has no influence on marginal cost. *Fixed cost, by definition, does not change as output changes. Marginal cost, by definition, is the change in total cost as output changes. Therefore, fixed cost, which does not change, can have no influence on the changes in cost measured by marginal cost.*

Perfect Competition in the Short Run and the Long Run

Introduction and Description

This lesson is designed to help the students understand the profit-maximizing output of the perfectly competitive firm. Any firm maximizes profits by producing at the quantity where marginal revenue equals marginal cost. For a perfectly competitive firm, marginal revenue is equal to the price it receives for selling its product. This is because there are so many firms producing a homogeneous product that no one firm can influence the price. Therefore, a perfectly competitive firm maximizes profits by producing at the quantity where price equals marginal cost.

In the short run, a firm has fixed costs. The firm maximizes profits by producing at the quantity where price equals marginal cost. In the short run, the perfectly competitive firm may make a profit, have a loss or break even. Activity 27 illustrates this point.

The long-run situation is much more complicated, and the students must add an industry graph to the firm graph. Students confuse the firm and the industry. One way to explain this is to say there are many firms in an industry. Another is to tell the students that if they see marginal cost and price curves, they have a firm graph. If they see supply and demand curves, they have an industry graph.

Activities 28 and 29 compare short-run equilibrium with long-run equilibrium and analyze why long-run equilibrium occurs where P = MC = ATC. In the long run, a perfectly competitive firm will earn a normal profit, or break even. The perfectly competitive firm will produce at the quantity where price equals marginal cost equals average total cost; this is also the point where the firm is producing at its minimum average total cost. In long-run equilibrium, a perfectly competitive firm is allocatively and productively efficient. This is terrific for the economy and explains why competitive markets work to the consumer's advantage. Activity

29 emphasizes why a perfectly competitive firm in long-run equilibrium produces at the quantity where P = MC = ATC. If a firm makes an economic profit in the short run, more firms enter the industry and the price decreases. If a firm has short-run economic losses, it will exit the industry, and the price increases. This process has been covered in the AP free-response questions several times, each time with a different twist.

Activity 30 differentiates a long-run cost curve from a short-run cost curve. It is important for the students to understand the difference and to grasp the concepts of economies and diseconomies of scale.

Finally, Activity 31 summarizes both short-run and long-run equilibria. Students can never have enough practice with these graphs.

Objectives

1. List the conditions that must be fulfilled if an industry is to be perfectly competitive.
2. Explain why for a perfectly competitive firm, price, marginal revenue and demand are equal.
3. Compute and graph price, average revenue and marginal revenue when given the demand schedule faced by a perfectly competitive firm.
4. Explain the profit-maximizing rule for a perfect competitor and state the reason the rule works.
5. Given data, determine the price and output of a perfectly competitive firm in the short run.
6. Given data, determine the break-even and shutdown points for a perfect competitor.
7. Given data, determine the price and the output of the individual firm and of the industry in the short run and in the long run.
8. Describe how the entry and exit of firms bring about long-run equilibrium.
9. Evaluate the implications of long-run equilibrium where P = MC = ATC.
10. Derive the firm's short-run supply schedule from cost schedules.

11. Differentiate a long-run average cost curve from a short-run average cost curve.

12. Calculate the firm's economic profit at a given price.

13. Describe the long-run adjustment of the firm and the industry to short-run economic profits and losses.

14. Describe the long-run supply schedules for constant-cost, increasing-cost and decreasing-cost industries.

15. Evaluate the advantages and shortcomings of a perfectly competitive market.

Time Required

Seven class periods or 315 minutes

Materials

1. Activities 27, 28, 29, 30 and 31
2. Visuals 3.5, 3.6, 3.7, 3.8 and 3.9

Procedure

1. Begin with a quick review of costs and basic concepts. Have the students define and explain the following:

   (A) Average fixed cost (AFC): *Fixed cost / output*

   (B) Average total cost (ATC): *Total cost / output*

   (C) Average variable cost (AVC):
   Variable cost / output

   (D) Economic cost: *Any cost that must be incurred to obtain and use a resource*

   (E) Economic profit: *The amount of a firm's total revenue that exceeds all its economic costs including both explicit and implicit costs*

   (F) Explicit cost: *The money payment a firm must make to an outsider to obtain and use a resource*

   (G) Fixed cost (FC): *A cost that does not change with output*

   (H) Implicit cost: *The money income a firm sacrifices when it employs a resource it owns rather than selling it to someone else*

   (I) Law of diminishing marginal returns: *As equal amounts of variable resources are added to a fixed resource, eventually the marginal product (extra output) will decline.*

   (J) Long run: *A period of time long enough to change all inputs. All inputs are variable in the long run.*

   (K) Marginal cost (MC): *The extra cost of producing one more unit of output,* $\dfrac{\Delta TC}{\Delta Q}$

   (L) Normal profit: *A measure of the opportunity cost of capital; a profit that is equal to a firm's implicit costs; the minimum profit needed to stay open in the long run*

   (M) Short run: *A period of time when at least one input is fixed, when existing firms can increase the quantity of their output with their existing plants*

   (N) Total cost (TC): *All of the costs of the firm- both fixed and variable costs*

   (O) Variable cost (VC): *The cost of variable resources (resources that change with output)*

2. Use Visual 3.5 to show the perfectly competitive firm and industry in short-run equilibrium. Ask questions such as these:

   (A) How is the price established at which the firm sells? *By the intersection of the industry supply and demand curves*

   (B) How much control does the firm have over this price? *None*

   (C) Why do we say a perfect competitor is a *price taker? Because the firm has no control over the price and has to "take" the price established in the industry*

   (D) Why does a perfect competitor maximize profits where Price = MC? *All firms maximize profit by producing at the quantity where MR = MC, and for a perfectly competitive firm P = MR since a firm can sell all it wants at the price determined by the industry.*

(E) Is this perfect competitor making a profit? Why or why not? *Yes. P > ATC and TR > TC.*

3. Have the students do Parts A and B of Activity 27, and discuss the answers. These sections of Activity 27 are a review of costs.

4. Have the students complete the rest of Activity 27, and discuss it. This section adds price and revenue to costs.

5. Now, use Visual 3.6 to illustrate profit, loss and shutdown for a perfectly competitive firm.

   (A) At what output will the firm operate at price P_4? Q_4. Will it make a profit? *Yes*

   (B) At price P_3, will the firm make a profit, break even or have an economic loss? *Break even.* What does it mean to *break even*? *TR just covers TC.*

   (C) At P_2, will the firm make a profit, break even or have an economic loss? *Economic loss.* Will it continue to produce? *It will continue to produce.* Why or why not? *Price is greater than AVC or TR > TVC.*

   (D) At P_1, will the firm make a profit, break even or have an economic loss? *Economic loss.* Will it continue to produce? *Indifferent.* Why or why not? *If firm produces, revenue covers variable costs, but firm must pay fixed costs out-of-pocket. Price = AVC or TR = TVC*

6. Use Visual 3.7 to illustrate long-run equilibrium for a perfect competitor. Emphasize these points:

   (A) The market price is determined by supply and demand in the industry.

   (B) Once the price is established, every firm must sell at that price or not sell at all. There is no reason for a firm to lower its price since it can already sell as much as it wants.

   (C) If firms are making economic profits, more firms will enter the industry-an event that reduces price and makes profits disappear.

(D) If firms have economic losses, firms will exit the market-an event that will cause the price to rise.

(E) A perfectly competitive firm in long-run equilibrium is good for society because there is productive and allocative efficiency when the firm is at the lowest point on its average total cost curve.

7. Assign Activity 28. There is a lot of material in this activity, and you may want to assign it in two parts.

   (A) In Part A, marginal cost is plotted at the midpoint of the output interval, and it is assumed the firm can produce any fraction of a unit of output. The profit-maximizing output at a price of $11 is seven units. ATC at seven units equals $7. This yields a short-run profit of $4 per unit and a total profit of $28 ($4 x 7).

   (B) In Question 2, the students may have difficulty connecting market information (such as the equilibrium price of $8) with the firm or difficulty connecting changes in the firm's behavior with the market. Here it may be helpful for the students to draw graphs of the market supply and demand curves and the firm's demand and cost curves. Answers in Question 2(D) depend on whether the student correctly found a positive economic profit in Question 2(C). Some of the answers in Question 2(D) may appear paradoxical since industry output increases while each firm's output decreases.

   (C) The short-run market-supply curve is arrived at by adding the representative firms' short-run supply curves. The long-run supply curve is not derived in the same way and is not so simple. It depends on the firm's cost curves, the existence of economic profit or loss in the short run, and the response of resource prices to changes in the number of firms (or resource demand).

8. Now use Visuals 3.8 and 3.9 to explain how the firm and industry reach long-run equilibrium.

   (A) Visual 3.8 shows what occurs if there is an increase in the demand for Greebes or any other good.

   (B) Visual 3.9 shows what occurs if there is a decrease in the demand for Greebes or any other good.

9. Now have the students complete Activity 29. This activity uses the concept of a competitive firm's marginal cost curve (above minimum AVC) as its short-run supply curve, which was developed in Activity 28. It also uses the concepts of short-run economic profits and short-run economic losses to illustrate the adjustment to long-run equilibrium where each firm is in equilibrium with zero economic profit. The case in which short-run economic profits attract additional firms was illustrated in the last part of Activity 28.

   (A) This problem uses a different set of numerical data to illustrate the effect of short-run economic losses as well as short-run economic profits, and it is much more explicit in setting out the step-by-step calculations used in arriving at total economic profit.

   (B) Students can get too involved in the details of an activity like this and miss the big points. For example, ATC, which is needed to calculate profit, must be read from a graph whose scale is somewhat rough. "About $0.80" and "about $1.05" are good

enough. This is better than trying to fool around with "uneven" numbers such as $0.03, $0.79, $0.81, $1.04, etc.

   (C) In obtaining the answers for questions dealing with the long-run equilibrium price, you may have to explain the steps in the chain of reasoning that lead to the correct answers.

   (D) It is also very important to emphasize that there are completely different cost and demand situations in Parts A and B of the activity. The different conditions lead to different answers, but the adjustment process is the same.

10. Discuss the answers to Activity 29.

11. Explain the differences between long-run and short-run average cost curves. Use the graph in Activity 30 to do this.

12. Have the students complete Activity 30, and discuss the answers.

13. Now if the students are not completely exhausted, assign Activity 31 to see if they have grasped the main points of Lesson 3. They should complete the graphs.

14. Discuss the answers. For each graph, have the students give the reasons why they drew it as they did. You might have the students draw the graphs on the board and then have a different student agree or disagree with the graphs as drawn and give the reasons. The "whys" are the important part of this exercise, and they are provided on the answer key.

An Introduction to Perfect Competition

This activity explains how businesses operate and how their operation affects society. To accomplish this explanation, it is necessary to look at business costs and revenue. This analysis is based on the assumption that the goal of any business is to maximize profits.

Part A

Fill in the blanks in Figure 27.1. Graph the marginal cost data from Figure 27.1 on Figure 27.2 and then answer the questions. MC is on the vertical axis, and output of yo-yos is on the horizontal axis. Plot MC on the midpoint.

 Figure 27.1
Output, Total Cost and Marginal Cost

Output	Total Cost (TC)	Marginal Cost (MC)
0	$55	
1	85	$30
2	110	25
3	130	20
4	160	30
5	210	50

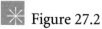 Figure 27.2
Plotting Marginal Cost of Yo-Yos

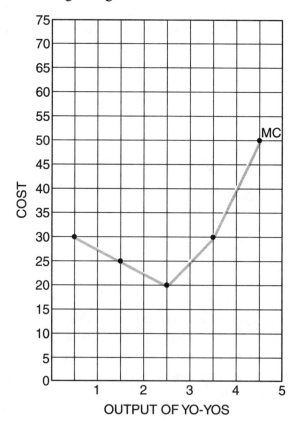

1. What is the relationship between MC and output as shown on your graph?
   As output increases, marginal cost decreases, reaches a minimum and then increases.

2. Explain why MC falls and then rises as output increases. *According to the law of diminishing marginal returns, as variable inputs are added to fixed inputs, output increases at a fast rate (marginal product increases), so the marginal costs of that output decrease. But when MP falls, the marginal cost of producing that output will increase.*

Part B

Complete Figure 27.3. Assume that the firm has a total fixed cost (FC) of $100 and total variable costs (VC) as shown below. Part of the table has been completed for you.

 Figure 27.3

Fixed and Variable Costs of Yo-Yos

Total Product	Fixed Cost	Variable Cost	Total Cost	Marginal Cost	Average Fixed Cost	Average Variable Cost	Average Total Cost
0	$100.00	$0	$100.00				
1	100.00	10.00	110.00	$10.00	$100.00	$10.00	$110.00
2	100.00	16.00	116.00	6.00	50.00	8.00	58.00
3	100.00	21.00	121.00	5.00	33.33	7.00	40.33
4	100.00	26.00	126.00	5.00	25.00	6.50	31.50
5	100.00	30.00	130.00	4.00	20.00	6.00	26.00
6	100.00	36.00	136.00	6.00	16.67	6.00	22.67
7	100.00	45.50	145.50	9.50	14.29	6.50	20.79
8	100.00	56.00	156.00	10.50	12.50	7.00	19.50
9	100.00	72.00	172.00	16.00	11.11	8.00	19.11
10	100.00	90.00	190.00	18.00	10.00	9.00	19.00
11	100.00	109.00	209.00	19.00	9.09	9.90	19.00
12	100.00	130.00	230.00	21.00	8.33	10.83	19.16
13	100.00	160.00	260.00	30.00	7.69	12.31	20.00

3. Graph FC, VC and TC on Figure 27.4. Label each curve. Then answer the questions.

(A) What is the difference between fixed and total costs? *Variable cost*

(B) Why does VC rise as output increases? *In order to increase output, the firm must hire more variable inputs (labor). So the cost of this input (variable cost) must increase.*

(C) Why is FC a horizontal line? *Because fixed costs are constant, regardless of the level of output*

(D) Why does the TC curve have the same slope as the VC curve? *The difference between the TC curve and the VC curve is FC, which is constant.*

✳ Figure 27.4
Total Fixed Costs, Total Variable Costs and Total Costs

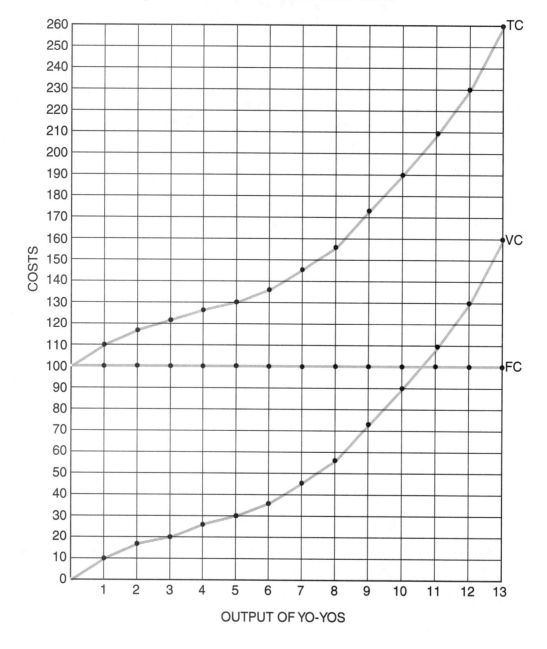

✳ Figure 27.5
Average Variable, Average Fixed, Average Total and Marginal Costs

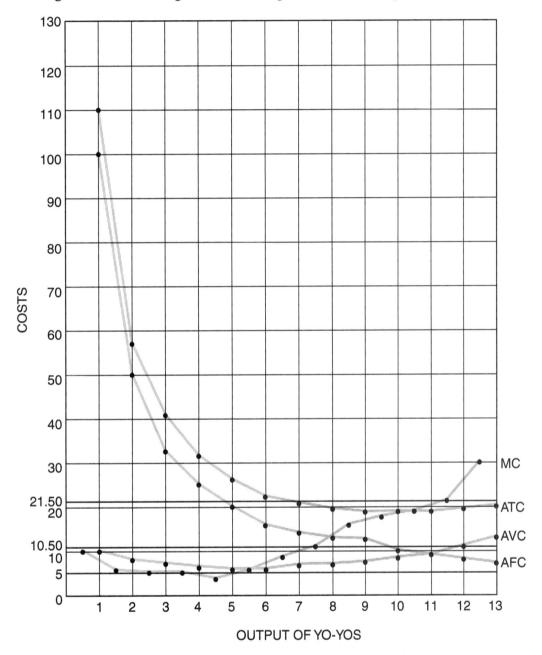

OUTPUT OF YO-YOS

4. Graph AFC, AVC, ATC and MC on Figure 27.5 (be sure to plot MC on the midpoints of output). Label each cost curve. Then answer the questions.

(A) What happens to AFC as output rises? Why? *AFC decreases because total fixed cost is constant. To get AFC, one divides FC by Q, so AFC must decrease.*

(B) What happens to AVC as output rises? Why? *AVC decreases and then increases. When MC is less than AVC, AVC decreases. When MC is greater than AVC, AVC increases.*

(C) What happens to ATC as output rises? Why? *ATC decreases and then increases. When MC is less than AVC, ATC decreases. When MC is greater than ATC, ATC increases.*

(D) What happens to MC as output rises? Why? *MC decreases and then increases. This is because of increasing returns and then diminishing returns.*

(E) At what unique point does marginal cost cross AVC and ATC? Why? *At the minimum of AVC and ATC. If marginal cost is less than average cost, average cost falls. If marginal cost is greater than average cost, average cost will rise, so they are equal when average cost is at its minimum.*

(F) Why is MC the same whether computed from TC or VC? *Fixed costs don't change, and marginal cost is the change in costs divided by the change in output. Change in variable cost always equals the change in total cost.*

Part C
For firms operating under perfect competition define the following terms.

5. Total revenue (TR) $TR = P \times Q$. *The total amount of money brought in from the sale of a good or service*

6. Marginal revenue (MR) $MR = \dfrac{\Delta TR}{\Delta Q}$. *The additional revenue brought in by the sale of one more unit of output*

7. Average revenue (AR) $\dfrac{TR}{Q}$

Part D

Figure 27.6 is a revenue schedule for a perfectly competitive firm. Fill in the blanks.

 Figure 27.6

Revenue Schedule for a Perfectly Competitive Firm

Price	Quantity	TR	MR
$10	1	$10	
10	2	20	10
10	3	30	*10*
10	4	*40*	*10*

8. What generalization can you make about price and marginal revenue under perfect competition? *They are the same.*

9. Why doesn't the perfect competitor lower the price to sell more? *Because the firm can sell all it wants at the equilibrium price. It can't sell more by lowering its price; only its profits would decline because its revenue fell but costs remained the same.*

10. What determines the price at which the perfect competitor sells the product? *P = MR. Firm produces where MR = MC or P = MC.*

Part E

11. Graph prices of $5.00, $10.50 and $21.50 on Figure 27.5. (Hint: Each price is a horizontal line.)

12. At a price of $21.50:

    (A) How many yo-yos will the firm produce in the short run? Why? (Note: Assume you can produce part of a yo-yo.) *Slightly less than 12, because it is at this point where MR = MC*

    (B) Will the firm earn an economic profit or have an economic loss? *Economic profit*

    (C) How much will the approximate profit or loss be per unit? *Profit of about $2.42*

    (D) How much will the approximate total profit or loss be? *Profit of approximately $28 ($2.42 x 11.51 = $27.83)*

13. At a price of $10.50:

    (A) How many yo-yos will the firm produce in the short run? Why? *About 7.5 because P = MC or MR = MC at this output*

    (B) Will the firm earn an economic profit or have an economic loss? *Economic loss*

    (C) How much will the approximate profit or loss be per unit? *Loss of $9.50 ($20 − $10.50 = $9.50)*

    (D) How much will the approximate total profit or loss be? *Loss of $71.25 ($9.50 x 7.5 = $71.25)*

    (E) Will this yo-yo firm stay open or shut down in the short run? Why? *Stay open. P > AVC or TR > TVC. Firm can operate and cover all its variable costs and some fixed costs. If it shuts down, it will have to pay all fixed costs out-of-pocket, so it minimizes losses by producing.*

14. At a price of $5.00:

    (A) How many yo-yos will this firm produce in the short run? Why? *Zero because P = MR below AVC. The firm's revenue is not covering its variable costs, so the firm will shut down.*

    (B) Will this firm stay open or shut down in the short run? Why? *Shut down. It cannot cover its variable costs, so it will lose less money by shutting down than by staying open.*

15. Why will a firm maximize its profits or minimize its losses at the output where MR (price) equals MC? *If output is such that MR < MC, if a firm increases output, then MR will be greater than MC and TR will increase more than TC so profits will increase. If MC > MR, if a firm decreases production, then total cost will decrease more than total revenue decreases, so profits will increase. Therefore, profits are maximized where MR = MC at an output level.*

16. Why are price and MR the same for a perfect competitor? *Price is constant. MR is $\Delta TR / \Delta Q$, but if P is constant, then ΔTR will always be constant and equal to price.*

17. Why is a perfect competitor called a *price taker*? *Because the firm cannot control the price at which it sells the product but takes the price as given by the industry and determines how much output to produce.*

Costs and Competitive Market Supply (Perfect Competition)

Part A

1. The Fiasco Company is a perfectly competitive firm whose daily costs of production (including a "normal" rate of profit) in the short run are as follows:

Figure 28.1

The Fiasco Company's Cost Table

Output (per day)	Total Variable Cost	Total Cost	Marginal Cost	Average Total Cost	Average Variable Cost
0	$0	$12.00			
1	4.00	16.00	$4.00	$16.00	$4.00
2	7.00	19.00	3.00	9.50	3.50
3	9.00	21.00	2.00	7.00	3.00
4	12.00	24.00	3.00	6.00	3.00
5	18.00	30.00	6.00	6.00	3.60
6	27.00	39.00	9.00	6.50	4.50
7	37.00	49.00	10.00	7.00	5.29
8	49.00	61.00	12.00	7.63	6.13
9	63.00	75.00	14.00	8.33	7.00
10	79.00	91.00	16.00	9.10	7.90

(A) Fill in the blanks in Figure 28.1.

(B) On Figure 28.2, plot and label the average variable cost (AVC), average total cost (ATC) and marginal cost (MC) curves. Plot marginal cost at the midpoint. Assume this firm can produce any fraction of output per day so that you connect the points to form continuous curves.

✳ Figure 28.2
The Fiasco Company's Cost Curves

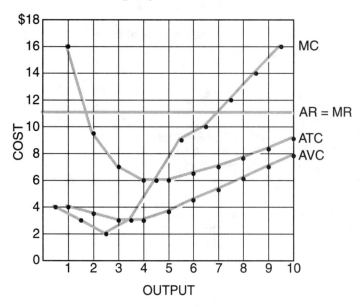

(C) How would you interpret the vertical distance between the average total cost and average variable cost curves? *It is average fixed cost (AFC). As AFC decreases continuously, the ATC and the AVC curves get closer together.*

(D) Why does average total cost decline at first, then start rising as output is increased?
When MC < ATC, ATC declines. When MC > ATC, ATC rises. Why does MC rise? Diminishing MPP

(E) The marginal cost curve intersects both average cost curves (ATC and AVC) at their minimum points. Why? *If the marginal is below the average, the average is decreasing. If the marginal is above the average, the average is increasing. Therefore, the average crosses the marginal at the average's lowest point.*

(F) If fixed costs were $20 instead of $12, how would the change affect average variable costs and marginal costs? *They would not change. (But ATC would increase.) Fixed cost, by definition, does not change when output changes. Therefore, fixed cost has no influence on variable cost or marginal cost.*

2. Given the cost curves for Fiasco Company on Figure 28.2 and the fact that the competitive market price at which the company must sell its output is $11 a unit, fill in the blanks below and add to your graph in Figure 28.2. (Remember, fractions of units are allowed.)

(A) Draw and label the average and marginal revenue curves on your graph.
A horizontal line at $11.00

(B) In order to maximize profits, Fiasco would sell __7__ units, at a price of __$11.00__ . Its average total cost would be__$7.00__ . Its average revenue would be __$11.00__ . It would earn a per-unit profit of __$4.00__ and total profit of __$28.00 ($4 x 7)__ per day.

(C) If the firm produced instead at the quantity that minimized its average total cost, it could sell __4.5__ units, at a price of __$11.00__ . Its average total cost would be _$6.00 (or less than $6.00, say, $5.50)_. If the market price were $11, its average revenue would be __$11.00__ . It would earn a per-unit profit of __$5.50__ and total profit of _$24.75 ($5.50 x 4.5)_ per day.

(D) If the competitive market price fell to $5 a unit, Fiasco would sell __4__ units. Average total cost would be __$6.00__ . It would earn a per-unit (*profit* / *loss*) of __$1.00__ and a total (*profit* / *loss*) of _$4.00 ($1.00 x 4)_ per day.

Part B

3. The long-run cost conditions, including a "normal" rate of profit, for a perfectly competitive firm are as follows:

 Figure 28.3
A Perfectly Competitive Firm Earning a "Normal" Rate of Profit

Output	Total Cost	Marginal Cost	Average Total Cost
1	$9.00		$9.00
2	13.00	$4.00	6.50
3	18.00	5.00	6.00
4	24.00	6.00	6.00
5	31.00	7.00	6.20
6	39.00	8.00	6.50
7	48.00	9.00	6.86
8	58.00	10.00	7.25
9	69.00	11.00	7.67
10	81.00	12.00	8.10

(A) Fill in the blanks in the average total cost and marginal cost columns.

(B) The level of output at which average total cost is at a minimum is _between 3 and 4_ units. At this output, average total cost is __$6.00__ .

(C) What quantities would the firm be willing to supply at each of the following prices for its product?

Figure 28.4
Price and Quantity Supplied

Price	Quantity Supplied
$6	4
7	5
8	6
9	7
10	8
11	9
12	10

(D) In general, the supply schedule (curve) of a perfectly competitive firm coincides with its ___MC___ schedule (curve) in the range where ___MC___ is greater than ___AVC___ .

4. Suppose the perfectly competitive firm in Question 3 is one of 1,000 identical firms currently operating in a competitive industry, all of which have identical cost functions. The market demand for this industry is given in Figure 28.5.

Figure 28.5
Market Demand for an Industry

Price	Quantity Demanded	Quantity Supplied
$12	2,000	10,000
11	3,000	9,000
10	4,000	8,000
9	5,000	7,000
8	6,000	6,000
7	7,000	5,000
6	8,000	4,000

(A) Fill in the industry supply schedule in Figure 28.5. Then answer the following questions by filling in the answer blanks, underlining the correct words in parentheses or writing a sentence.

(B) Explain briefly how the short-run supply schedule (curve) of a competitive industry is derived. *The horizontal sum at each price of all firms' supply curves = MC above minimum AVC.*

(C) Given the present 1,000 firms in the industry, the present market price is ___*$8.00*___; the present equilibrium quantity is ___*6,000*___ units. At this price, each firm will be making (***positive economic profit*** / *zero economic profit* / *negative economic profit* / *economic losses*).

(D) Given the equilibrium above, and assuming that other firms can enter the industry with the same cost as the present firms, the number of firms in the industry in the long run will tend to (***increase*** / *decrease/ remain constant*) and the price will tend to (*increase* / ***decrease*** / *remain constant*). The output of the industry will tend to (***increase*** / *decrease* / *remain constant*), while output per firm will (*increase* / ***decrease*** / *remain constant*).

(E) If this is a constant-cost industry (i.e., costs per unit of output are constant as the industry expands), the long-run equilibrium price for the industry will be ___*$6.00*___; output per firm will be ___*4*___ units. There will be ___*2,000*___ firms in the industry, each earning ___*0*___ economic profits; industry output will be ___*8,000*___ units. The equilibrium price coincides with the ___*minimum*___ per-unit cost of production. *Emphasize minimum ATC*

(F) Can you see why, under the conditions described above, that the long-run market-supply curve for this industry would appear as a horizontal line on a graph? Explain. *Other firms can enter and eliminate any economic profit that appears. Thus, in the long run, all firms will be at minimum ATC.*

(G) Using the cost curves in Figure 28.2, at what price would this long-run horizontal line be plotted? ___*$6.00*___ Explain why it would be at this price. *This is the quantity where MC equals ATC at the minimum level of ATC. The perfectly competitive firm breaks even in the long run at minimum ATC: its most technically efficient point.*

Short-Run and Long-Run Competitive Equilibrium

Part A

Figure 29.1
Competitive Firm and Industry

Diagram A: Cost Situation
for each Greebe Producer

Diagram B: Market Supply
and Demand for Greebes

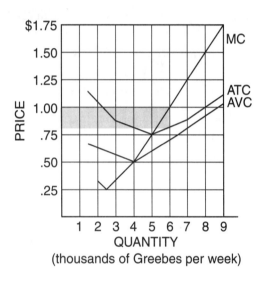 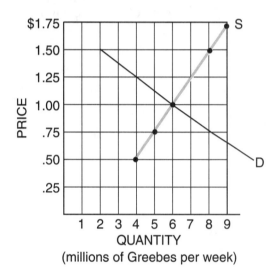

There are currently 1,000 producers of Greebes, each with economic costs like those shown in Diagram A of Figure 29.1. (You should know how to label each of the cost curves.) The market demand for Greebes is shown in Diagram B of Figure 29.1. Assume that the minimum of the short-run average total cost curve occurs at the same output as the minimum of the long-run average total cost curve.

1. Plot on Diagram B the current market supply curve for Greebes and label this curve S. (Ask how much each producer will supply at various prices, and figure how much the total supply *from all 1,000 producers together* will be at those prices. NOTE: One million is a thousand thousand: 1,000,000.)

2. Shade in the appropriate profit (or loss) rectangle in Diagram A, and calculate the total amount of economic profit or loss each typical Greebe producer will make under these conditions. Fill in the blanks below to aid you in your calculations.

(A) Price (P) received by each Greebe producer:____*$1.00*____per Greebe

(B) Quantity (Q) produced by each Greebe producer: __6__ thousand Greebes per week

(C) Average total cost (ATC) for this quantity (approximate): __$0.80__ per Greebe

(D) Economic profit (loss) for each unit produced (P-ATC): __$0.20__ per Greebe

(E) Total economic profit (loss) for each Greebe producer: Profit (loss) per unit x quantity produced = __$1,200__ per week *($0.20 x 6,000 = $1,200)*

3. Is the Greebe market in long-run equilibrium? Why or why not? *No. Short-run economic profits will attract additional firms. This will shift the market supply curve to the right, thus lowering the price.*

4. What is the long-run equilibrium price in this market? __$0.75__ per Greebe

(A) How many Greebes will each firm produce at this price? __5__ thousand Greebes per week

(B) What will be the total market quantity of Greebes produced at this price?
__8__ million Greebes per week

(C) How many firms will be in the market at this price? __1,600__ *(8,000,000 ÷ 5,000 = 1,600)*

Part B

Figure 29.2
Competitive Firm and Industry

Diagram C: New Cost Situation
for each Greebe Producer

Diagram D: New Market Supply
and Demand for Greebes

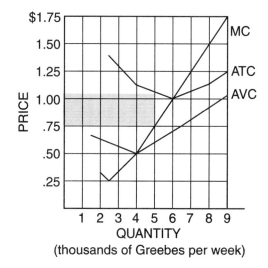

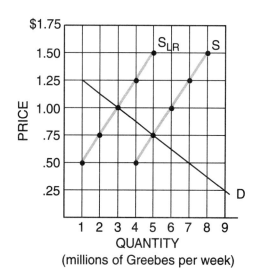

Now, let's start all over again with a new set of cost and demand conditions in the Greebe market. There are again currently 1,000 producers of Greebes, each with economic costs like those shown in Diagram C of Figure 29.2. The market demand for Greebes is shown in Diagram D.

5. Plot on Diagram D the current market supply curve for Greebes and label this curve S.

6. Shade in the appropriate profit (or loss) rectangle in Diagram C, and calculate the total amount of economic profit or loss that each typical Greebe producer will make under these conditions. Fill in the blanks below to aid you in your calculations.

   (A) Price (P) received by each Greebe producer: ___*$0.75*___ per Greebe

   (B) Quantity (Q) produced by each Greebe producer: ___*5*___ thousand Greebes per week

   (C) Average total cost (ATC) for this quantity (approximate): ___*$1.05*___ per Greebe

   (D) Economic profit (loss) for each unit produced (P – ATC): ___*–$0.30*___ per Greebe

   (E) Total economic profit (loss) for each Greebe producer: Profit (loss) per unit x quantity produced = ___*–$1,500*___ per week (*–$0.30 x 5,000 = –$1,500*)

7. Is the Greebe market in long-run equilibrium? Why or why not? *No. Short-run economic losses will cause some firms to leave the market. This will shift the supply curve to the left, thus raising the price.*

8. What is the long-run equilibrium price in this market? ___*$1.00*___ per Greebe

   (A) How many Greebes will each firm produce at this price? ___*6*___ thousand Greebes per week

   (B) What will be the total market quantities of Greebes produced at this price? ___*3*___ million Greebes per week

   (C) How many firms will be in the market at this price? ___*500*___

Long-Run Average Cost Curves

The cost curves that we used in previous activities are short-run cost curves. In the short run, firms can vary output but not plant capacity. Here, we turn to the long run, defined as a time period in which the firm can vary its plant capacity and its output. In the short run, the shapes of the average and marginal cost curves result from diminishing marginal productivity of the resources. In the long run, the shape of the average cost curve results from economies and diseconomies of scale. Sources of economies of scale are specialization of resources, more efficient uses of equipment, a reduction in per-unit costs of factor inputs, an effective use of production by-products and an increase in shared facilities. Sources of diseconomies of scale are limitations on management decision making and competition for factor inputs.

Part A

Use Figure 30.1 to answer the following questions.

 Figure 30.1

Long-Run Average Total Cost Curves

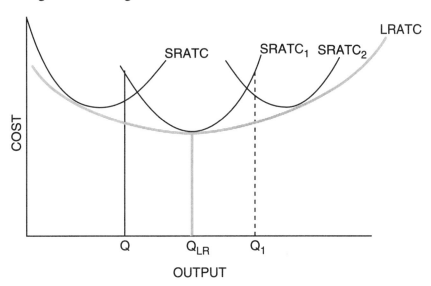

1. What does each of the short-run ATC curves represent? *A different-size plant*

2. The firm can minimize costs by producing output level Q using firm size ___*SRATC*___. This means that it would be *(underutilizing / **overutilizing**)* plant size (***SRATC*** / $SRATC_1$).

3. Label the optimal output level in the diagram as Q_{LR}.

4. To produce output level Q_1, the firm should use plant size **SRATC₂**. This means that it would be (**underutilizing** / overutilizing) plant size (SRATC₁ / **SRATC₂**).

5. Draw in the long-run average total cost curve and indicate its tangency points with each short-run ATC curve. Label the curve LRATC.

6. The firm experiences (**economies** / diseconomies) of scale up to output level **Q_{LR}** and (economies / **diseconomies**) of scale beyond output level **Q_{LR}**.

Part B

7. In the space below, draw the long-run average total cost curve for a firm experiencing constant returns to scale. Explain your diagram. Give an example of a type of firm that experiences constant returns to scale.

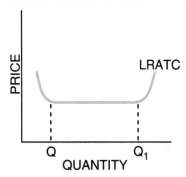

Between Q and Q₁, there are constant costs for all the firm sizes, as shown by a flat LRATC. Examples: furniture industry, household-appliance industry

8. In the space below, draw the long-run average total cost curve for a firm experiencing decreasing returns to scale. Explain your diagram. Give an example of a type of firm that experiences decreasing returns to scale.

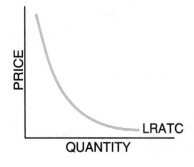

LRATC decreases over the entire relevant levels of output. Example: utilities

9. In the space below, draw the long-run average total cost curve for a firm experiencing increasing returns to scale. Explain your diagram. Give an example of a type of firm that experiences increasing returns to scale.

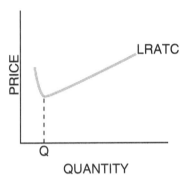

For all levels of output greater than Q, the costs are increasing for all plant sizes. Example: retail trades

Part C

Indicate whether you think the following statements are true, false or uncertain. Explain why.

10. In the long run, a cost-minimizing firm will overutilize its plant when it produces at an output level greater than the optimal level. *True. At output levels > optimum, the points on LRATC are on the upward sloping part of SRATC → overutilizing a plant size.*

11. The short-run average total cost curve declines and then increases as a factor input increases because of economies and diseconomies of scale. *False. SRATC is U-shaped because of diminishing returns. As additional units of variable inputs are added to the fixed plant size, the additional output gets smaller.*

Graphing Perfect Competition

The following firms or industries are all operating in a perfectly competitive market.

(A) Illustrate each situation on the graph provided.

(B) Label all curves in your answers.

(C) Explain the reasoning for your graphs in each situation.

1. A firm experiencing economic profit in the short run.

 Figure 31.1
Short-Run Economic Profit

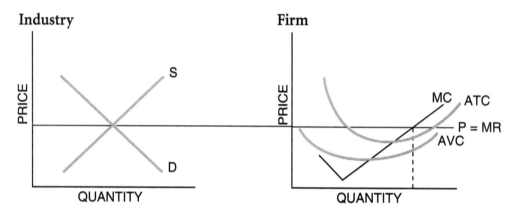

Explanation: *The firm will maximize profits where MR = MC and will enjoy profits because price is above its ATC curve.*

2. A firm operating with an economic loss in the short run.

✳ **Figure 31.2**
Short-Run Economic Loss

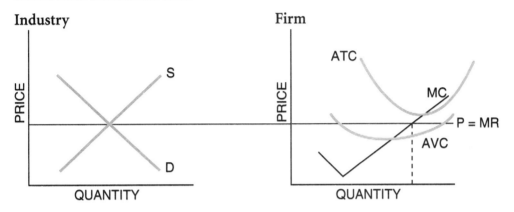

Explanation: *The firm will minimize losses where MR = MC. At this level of output, the firm is covering all of its variable costs and a portion of its fixed costs. In this example, the firm will minimize its losses in the short run by continuing to produce because price is above its AVC curve.*

3. A firm in a classic shut-down position in the short run.

 Figure 31.3
Classic Shutdown Position

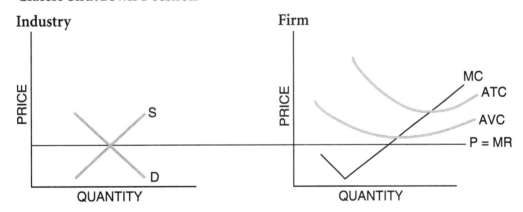

Explanation: *Price is below the AVC curve, and the firm will minimize its losses by closing down. However, it will still experience fixed costs.*

4. Long-run equilibrium for a firm and industry

 Figure 31.4
Long-Run Equilibrium

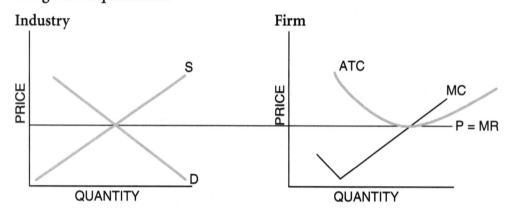

Explanation: *The firm will be in long-run equilibrium where MC = minimum ATC = MR. The firm is breaking even; there is no incentive for other firms to enter the market.*

5. Illustrate how economic profits will disappear in the long run.

 Figure 31.5
From Short-Run Profit to Long-Run Equilbrium

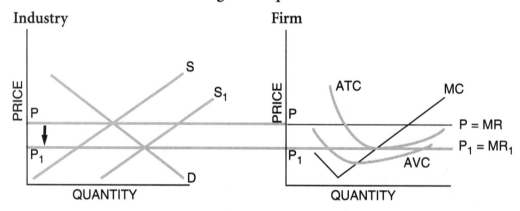

Explanation: *Reports of firms making an economic profit will cause other firms to enter the market. This will shift the supply curve to the right, causing prices to drop and eliminating profits. The firm will then be in long-run equilibrium at the break-even point.*

6. Illustrate how economic losses will disappear in the long run.

Figure 31.6

From Short-Run Losses to Long-Run Equilbrium

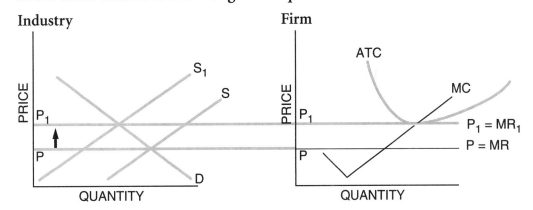

Explanation: *Firms within an industry cannot continue to operate at a loss in the long run. Therefore, the least-efficient firms will exit the industry first, thus shifting the industry supply curve to the left and raising price. Firms that survive will move to their break-even long-run equilibrium.*

The Monopoly Firm

Introduction and Description

In Lesson 3, the students learned why perfect competition leads to an optimum allocation of resources in the long run. They found that even though the perfect competitor's goal is to maximize profits, in the long run the perfect competitor makes no economic profits-only normal profits. The perfect competitor also is productively (technically) and allocatively efficient. All rejoice when the perfectly competitive firm seeks to maximize profits.

When a monopolist attempts to maximize profits, the result is a misallocation of resources. In long-run equilibrium, the monopoly may make an economic profit and is not allocatively or productively efficient. All (except the monopolist) can complain when a monopoly attempts to maximize profits.

Activity 32 is a key to understanding monopoly behavior. The cost concepts for all types of market structures are conceptually the same. But a monopolist is a price seeker (price searcher). The monopolist's demand curve is downward sloping, and marginal revenue is less than price. Therefore, marginal revenue and price are different for a monopoly.

Activity 33 illustrates long-run equilibrium for a monopolist. Students should see that a monopoly will charge a higher price, produce less, and be less productively and allocatively efficient than a perfect competitor.

Activity 34 reinforces how monopolies determine price and output and how this affects society by changing consumer and producer surplus.

Objectives

1. Define *marginal revenue.*
2. Calculate marginal revenue from a schedule of output and total revenue, and plot marginal revenue and price.

3. Explain why the marginal revenue curve lies below the demand curve when plotted on a graph.
4. Explain why a monopoly firm should never operate on the inelastic portion of its demand curve.
5. Given cost and demand information, find the monopolist's profit-maximizing output.
6. Calculate the monopoly firm's profit or loss at its profit-maximizing output.
7. Compare and contrast the monopolist's profit-maximizing price, output and profit with those of a perfect competitor.
8. Describe the effect of a monopoly on consumer and producer surplus.

Time Required

Three class periods or 135 minutes

Materials

1. Activities 32, 33 and 34
2. Visuals 3.10 and 3.11

Procedure

1. Use Visual 3.10 to explain that a monopolist is a price seeker (price searcher). The monopoly firm can charge any price it wants, but it cannot repeal the law of demand: If the monopolist raises its price, it will sell less. If it lowers its price, it will sell more.

2. Now use Visual 3.10 to explain why marginal revenue for the monopolist is less than price. This is because if the monopolist lowers the price to sell more Greebes, it must lower the price on all the Greebes it sells. Price cuts will apply not only to the extra output sold but also to all other Greebes that the monopolist could have sold at a higher price.

3. Assign Activity 32. In plotting the curves, the students have to add points or dots: four on the

demand curve and three on the marginal revenue curve. Students sometimes incorrectly connect the points on the demand curve with the points on the marginal revenue curve. Make sure they connect the points on the two curves correctly.

4. Discuss Activity 32. Here are some points to make in the discussion:

(A) Begin with a schedule of output and total revenue or, equivalently, a demand schedule since price (P) x quantity demanded (Q) = TR.

(B) Calculate the change in total revenue (ΔTR) over each quantity interval (ΔQ).

(C) Calculate the change in the number of units of output over each quantity interval (ΔQ).

(D) Marginal revenue equals the change in total revenue divided by the change in quantity:
MR = ΔTR / ΔQ
Changes in TR = MR if ΔQ = 1.

(E) Plot the MR just calculated at the midpoint of the quantity level. For example, over the quantity interval from 300 to 400 units, total revenue increases from $2,700 to $3,000. The change in TR is ($3,000 – $2,700) = $300. The change in quantity (ΔQ) is (400 – 300) = 100. Then marginal revenue is $300 Δ $100 = 3. The midpoint of the quantity interval from 300 to 400 is 350, and the marginal revenue figure of $3 is plotted at quantity level 350 units.

(F) As explained in the third paragraph of Activity 32, if a monopolist sees a downward sloping demand curve, and if the monopolist has to charge everyone the same price, it must lower the price to increase the quantity sold. The marginal revenue on an additional unit at the lower price can never equal the old (higher) price, so the marginal revenue curve will always lie below the demand curve.

(G) As indicated on the answer key, a monopolist will never operate on the inelastic por-

tion of the demand curve. Reducing output in the inelastic region will increase total revenue and reduce total cost at the same time. Since increasing revenue and reducing cost are bound to increase profit, a monopolist will never operate in the area where demand is inelastic (MR < 0). It will try to keep reducing output until the demand curve becomes elastic (MR > 0). Or, put another way, since MC is always greater than 0, the MC = MR profit-maximizing rule requires that MR > 0, and this means that demand is elastic since total revenue increases with an increase in output.

5. Now use Visual 3.11 to explain the monopolist's profit-maximizing price and output. The monopolist will produce 500 Greebes because it maximizes profits by producing where MR = MC. It is a good idea to ask the students why a monopoly maximizes profits where MR = MC. The price will be $122. To determine price, the students must go to the demand curve at an output of 500 Greebes. First determine output where MC = MR, and then determine price. The demand curve is the price curve. This yields a profit of $28 per Greebe (P – ATC), or $14,000 total profit (ATC x output).

6. Use Visual 3.11 to compare the output of the monopolist with that of the perfect competitor. A perfect competitor would operate where P = MC = ATC. This is at the bottom of the ATC curve or at an output of 700 Greebes. The price would be about $100. Compared with the perfect competitor, the monopolist operates at a higher price, a lower output and where P > MC, or an allocatively inefficient output.

7. Have the students complete Activity 33.

8. Discuss the answers, and pay attention to these points:

(A) The profit-maximizing monopolist finds the output where MC = MR. In the MC and

MR columns on the first page of the activity, MC and MR are equal only at an output of four units where MC = MR = $300.

(B) To calculate the monopolist's profit or loss, the profit-maximizing output must be determined first. Then, at four units, the table gives the value for price and average cost.

Profit per unit = (Price – ATC)
= ($750 – $600) = $150

Total profit = (P – ATC) x (Q)
= ($150) x (4) = $600

(C) Finally, compare the equilibrium of the monopolist with that of a perfect competi-

tor. The perfect competitor would produce five units at a price of $600. The perfect competitor would produce more at a lower price.

9. Assign Activity 34 to reinforce these concepts and to illustrate the effects of monopoly on consumer and producer surplus. The activity illustrates that when a monopoly replaces a perfectly competitive firm, some of the consumer surplus is transferred from consumers to the monopoly firm.

10. Discuss Activity 34.

Marginal Revenue for an Imperfect Competitor

Fill in the blanks on the table, and plot both the demand curve and the marginal revenue curve on Figure 32.2. Label the demand curve D and the marginal revenue curve MR. (**Note:** Plot the marginal revenue data midway between the quantity levels shown in the second column of the table.) Then answer the following two questions.

1. Notice that the price points show $1.50 changes. By how much does marginal revenue change for each change in price points? ___*$3.00*___

2. For a firm large enough to see the whole demand curve, marginal revenue is positive when the demand curve is price elastic. Marginal revenue becomes negative when the segment of the demand curve becomes price inelastic. Will a single-price monopoly ever operate on the inelastic portion of its demand curve? Why or why not? *No. As long as demand is inelastic, marginal revenue is negative, and a reduction in output will increase total revenue and reduce total cost at the same time. An increase in output would decrease total revenue and increase cost. Therefore, the monopolist would increase price and reduce output until it is on the elastic portion of its demand curve.*

❋ Figure 32.1
Average Revenue and Marginal Revenue for a Monopoly

Price (Average Revenue)	Quantity Demanded (Q)	Total Revenue (R)	Change in Total Revenue (ΔR)	Marginal Revenue (ΔR / ΔQ)
$13.50	0	$0		
12.00	100	1,200	$1,200	$12.00
10.50	200	2,100	900	9.00
9.00	300	2,700	*600*	*6.00*
7.50	400	*3,000*	*300*	*3.00*
6.00	500	3,000	0	0
4.50	600	2,700	−300	−3.00

Figure 32.2
**Plotting Average Revenue and
Marginal Revenue for a Monopoly**

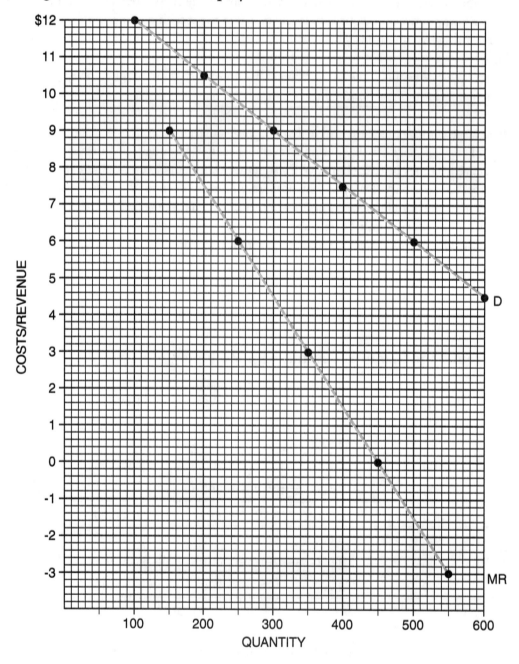

Pure Monopoly

Like other producers in a market economy, a pure monopolist tries to maximize profit by producing at an output where marginal cost (MC) equals marginal revenue (MR). For a firm in a competitive market, price and marginal revenue are the same; but for a monopolist, who "sees" the entire market demand curve and who must charge all buyers the same price, marginal revenue is below price. This activity considers the monopolist's choice of output level.

Part A

1. Figure 33.1 presents a summary of the relevant cost and revenue data facing a pure monopoly firm. Fill in the blanks on the table.

2. Plot the data for MC, MR, ATC (average total cost) and AR (average revenue) on Figure 33.2. (**Note:** For this problem plot MR and MC on the number.)

Figure 33.1
Pure Monopoly: Cost and Revenue Data

Quantity of Output	Total Cost	Marginal Cost	Average Total Cost	Total Revenue	Marginal Revenue	Average Revenue (Price)
0	$0	—	$0	$0	—	$0
1	900	$900	900	1,200	$1,200	1,200
2	1,600	700	800	2,100	900	1,050
3	2,100	*500*	700	2,700	*600*	900
4	2,400	*300*	*600*	3,000	300	*750*
5	3,000	600	*600*	3,000	*0*	*600*
6	4,200	1,200	*700*	2,700	−300	*450*

Part B

After you have completed the table and the graph, answer these questions by filling in the blanks and shading in the area indicated in Question 7. In this problem, plot the MC and MR data at each quantity rather than at the midpoint. This is just for simplicity and does not change the fundamental analysis.

3. A profit-maximizing monopolist would produce an output of __*4*__ units.

4. At this level of output, MC is __*$300*__ per unit and MR is __*$300*__ per unit.

5. At this level of output, ATC is __*$600*__ per unit, and AR (price) is __*$750*__ per unit.

6. This gives the monopolist an economic profit of ___$150___ per unit for a total economic profit of ___$600 ($150 x 4)___.

7. Shade in the area on the graph that represents the total economic profit figure indicated in your answer to Question 6.

✳ Figure 33.2
Profit-Maximizing Equilibrium for a Monopoly

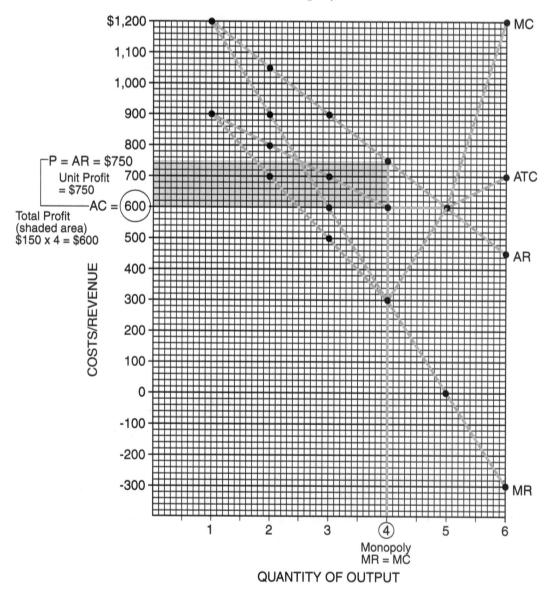

Monopoly Pricing

Part A
Equilibrium for the Perfectly Competitive Industry

Consider Figure 34.1. Assume that the market described by the figure is perfectly competitive, and MC represents the horizontal summation of marginal cost curves and, therefore, the market supply curve. Use Figure 34.1 to answer the following questions.

✳ Figure 34.1
Perfect Competition

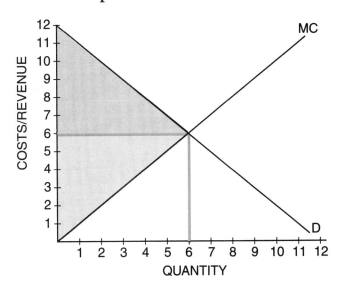

1. What quantity of output will be produced? ___6___

2. What price will the market establish? ___$6.00___

3. Calculate the amount of the consumer surplus. Darkly shade the area of consumer surplus.
   _1/2 (6) (6) = $18.00_

4. Calculate the amount of the producer surplus. Lightly shade the area of producer surplus.
   _1/2 (6) (6) = $18.00_

Part B
Equilibrium for the Monopolist

Now consider the same demand and cost curves, but assume the market is a monopoly. Therefore, MR represents the monopolist's marginal revenue curve and MC represents the monopolist's marginal cost curve. Using Figure 34.2, answer the following questions.

Figure 34.2
Monopoly

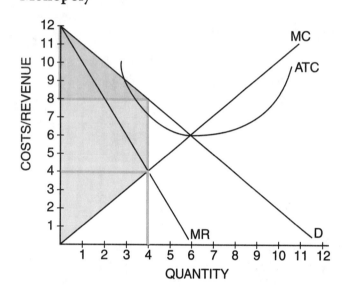

5. What quantity of output will be produced? ___4___ Why? *MR = MC at this quantity.*

6. What price will the monopolist establish? ___$8.00___ Why? *This is the maximum price the monopolist can charge and still sell four units of output.*

7. Calculate the amount of the consumer surplus. Darkly shade the area of consumer surplus.
   ¹/₂ (4) (4) = $8.00

8. Calculate the amount of the producer surplus. Lightly shade the area of producer surplus.
   4 (4) + ¹/₂ (4) (4)
   *   16   +   8   = $24*

9. How does the price and output of a monopolist differ from that of the perfectly competitive industry? *Price is higher and output is lower.*

10. What portion of the consumer surplus in the competitive situation was transferred to the firm in the monopoly situation? *$8 was transferred ($2 x $4 = $8). Total consumer surplus was $18, so* $8/_{18}$ *or* $4/_9$ *was transferred to producer.*

11. How does a monopoly affect consumer surplus? Is this good or bad?
    Consumer surplus is transferred from the consumer to the producer. This is bad for the consumer.

Regulating Monopoly: Antitrust Policy in the Real World

Introduction and Description

Because a monopoly produces an inefficient level of output, government often tries to regulate monopoly or break up a monopoly into several firms.

Without using graphs, Activity 35 illustrates why unregulated monopolies have undesirable outcomes. Students must go beyond graphs to really understand the behavior of monopolies. In discussing this activity, you might also insert some current case studies on monopoly. We have not included these to keep the workbook from becoming dated.

A monopoly or any firm with market power can practice *price discrimination*. Price discrimination occurs when a producer is able to charge consumers with different tastes and preferences different prices for the same good. Price discrimination works well only if the good-or more likely the service-cannot be resold.

Activity 36 analyzes the effects of price discrimination on consumer surplus.

Activity 37 shows how government regulates natural monopolies. Be sure the students can differentiate among the *unregulated* price, the *fair-return* price (P = ATC) and the *socially optimal* price (P = MC).

Activity 38 is a brain teaser. If the students can answer these problems, they really understand the interrelationship between revenue and costs for a monopoly firm. Activity 38 would be a good group exercise.

Finally, Activity 39 compares monopoly and perfect competition. It is a review exercise designed to bring closure to the topics of monopoly and perfect competition.

Objectives

1. Analyze the effects of pure monopoly on the price of the product, the quantity of the product produced and the allocation of society's resources.
2. Identify the socially optimal and fair-return price for a regulated monopoly.
3. Identify the characteristics of a natural monopoly and discuss why natural monopolies occur.
4. Describe price discrimination and analyze its effects on society.
5. Given data, recommend the proper price and output for a monopoly.
6. Compare and contrast the effects of perfect competition and monopoly on society.

Time Required

Three class periods or 135 minutes

Materials

Activities 35, 36, 37, 38 and 39

Procedure

1. Assign Activity 35, and have the students answer the questions that follow the article.

2. Discuss the answers to Activity 35. Many of these examples are not pure monopolies, but the monopoly model is useful in analyzing the effects of these cases. Be sure to bring out the reasons why monopolies harm society. Also be sure to pay particular attention to price discrimination and its effects.

3. Give a lecture on price discrimination. Emphasize the characteristics necessary for price discrimination and the effects of price discrimination on consumer surplus.

4. Have the students complete Activity 36, and discuss the answers.

5. Give a lecture on regulation of natural monopolies. Discuss these points:

   (A) Why natural monopolies occur

   (B) The advantages and disadvantages of regulating monopolies at the fair-return price

   (C) The advantages and disadvantages of regulating monopolies at the socially optimal price

6. Assign Activity 37, and discuss the answers.

7. Assign Activity 38 as homework, or have the students work in groups to answer the questions. In discussing the answers, show how each case is solved.

   Case No. 1

   (A) *MC = MR; therefore, the firm is in the best possible position.*

   (B) *To determine TC, multiply ATC by Q.*

   (C) *TC-FC = VC = $13,000*

   (D) *TR = P x Q = $12,500*

   (E) *Revenue does not cover VC; therefore, this firm should shut down.*

   Answer: *3*

   Case No. 2

   (A) *Find ATC by TC ÷ Q.*

   (B) *When ATC is at its minimum, it equals MC; therefore, MC = $4.*

   (C) *MR = MC; therefore, the firm is in the best possible position.*

   (D) *The firm is in the correct position.*

   Answer: *2*

Case No. 3

MR may not exceed P; therefore, this case is nonsense.

Answer: *1*

Case No. 4

(A) *MR = MC; therefore, the firm is in the best possible position.*

(B) *Check to see if the firm is covering VC; it is since P is above ATC.*

(C) *Therefore, the firm is in the correct position.*

Answer: *2*

Case No. 5

(A) *Find P by TR ÷ Q.*

(B) *Since you know MR is less than P, it follows that MC, which is equal to P, is greater than MR.*

(C) *Therefore, the firm should reduce production and increase price.*

Answer: *5*

Case No. 6

(A) *MR is greater than MC.*

(B) *Therefore, increase production and decrease P.*

Answer: *6*

Case No. 7

Fixed costs are fixed; they don't decline. Therefore, this case is nonsense.

Answer: *1*

8. Assign Activity 39, and go over the answers.

9. Conclude by summarizing the differences in price, output and efficiency between a perfectly competitive firm and a monopoly firm.

Let's Play Monopoly

1. Do you agree or disagree with the final contestants for the monopoly award? Explain. *Answers will vary but should include discussion on the runners-up as well as the contestants that were selected. Include the characteristics of a monopoly and how the selected contestants fit that description.*

2. How might e-mail change the market for first-class mail? *E-mail has created competition for first-class mail service by offering consumers a faster and inexpensive alternative. Fax machines are another alternative to mail.*

3. What prevents a cartel, particularly OPEC, from maintaining a long-run monopoly? What would help to make it more successful? *Because of the voluntary participation of members, cartels may have a very difficult time convincing all members of the benefits of playing by the rules. Particularly with OPEC, the economic incentives to members to undercut the cartel's pricing system are too great. To prevent this, there must be greater restrictions on members and better enforcement of the rules.*

4. What are the standard arguments against monopolies? What example is provided in the reading that emphasizes these arguments? *Monopolies are traditionally known for poor service and high prices. An example of this in the reading is cable TV.*

5. What is price discrimination and under what conditions is it successful? *Price discrimination is selling the same service for different prices. It is effective when offering a service that cannot be resold. For example, hotel rooms, airline fares and college scholarships are all examples of price discrimination. This is a good place to discuss price discrimination. It increases a monopoly's output and profits. Ironically, it also makes the monopoly more allocatively efficient.*

6. Why doesn't the NCAA have competition in providing a forum for young athletes to play sports? *Discuss reasons that other leagues have not formed and the barriers to their formation. Include costs and indicate which groups would benefit and which groups would be harmed.*

7. How does leaving college early to go pro or going pro directly from high school affect the NCAA monopoly? *It may make it more difficult not to pay the athletes. In fact, in 2002 there was a proposal to give college athletes $20,000 interest-free loans.*

8. Why are monopolies considered to be bad? Be sure to discuss price, output and efficiency in your answer. *A monopoly produces a lower output and charges a higher price than a perfect competitor. It also is allocatively and productively less efficient than a perfect competitor.*

Price Discrimination

When producers have market power and they sell a good that cannot be resold, the possibility for price discrimination arises. Price discrimination occurs when a producer is able to charge consumers with different tastes and preferences, different prices for the same good.

We know profit maximization for a firm that is able to set a single price occurs when the firm produces the quantity at which MR = MC. If a producer is able to price discriminate, however, then profits can be even higher.

Part A
Pricing with Market Power and Consumer Surplus

Pat's Patriotic Tattoos is the only tattoo parlor in town. Pat tattoos only images of the American flag. There are 20 consumers who are willing to buy a tattoo. Each consumer is interested in buying only one tattoo, but they vary in their willingness to pay. One consumer is willing to pay $20 for a tattoo; another is willing to pay $19; a third, $18, down to the consumer least willing to pay who has a reservation price of $1.

1. The demand schedule is given below in Figure 36.1. Complete the table.

Figure 36.1
Demand Schedule

Price	Quantity	Total Revenue	Marginal Revenue
$20	1	$20	—
19	2	38	$18
18	3	54	16
17	4	68	14
16	5	80	12
15	6	90	10
14	7	98	8
13	8	104	6
12	9	108	4
11	10	110	2
10	11	110	0
9	12	108	−2
8	13	104	−4
7	14	98	−6
6	15	90	−8
5	16	80	−10
4	17	68	−12
3	18	54	−14
2	19	38	−16
1	20	20	−18

2. Recalling Rules: Underline the correct answer.

   (A) A perfectly competitive firm would produce the output at which price is equal to
   (AC / <u>MC</u> / MR).

   (B) A monopolistic firm would produce the output at which MC is equal to (AC / P / <u>MR</u>).

Part B
First-Degree Price Discrimination

3. Prove to yourself that a market price of $17 will generate a total consumer surplus of $6.
   Hint: The consumer surplus generated by the consumer willing to pay $20 is $(20 - 17) \times 1 = 3$.

   $CS = (20 - 17) + (19 - 17) + (18 - 17) = 3 + 2 + 1 = \$6$

4. Assume that the average and marginal costs are constant and equal to 14. If Pat produces the perfectly competitive quantity and charges the perfectly competitive price,

   (A) what price will Pat charge for a tattoo? __$14__

   (B) what quantity will Pat supply? __7__

   (C) what is the amount of consumer surplus generated? __$21__

   $CS = (20 - 14) + (19 - 14) + (18 - 14) + (17 - 14) + (16 - 14) + (15 - 14)$
   $= 6 + 5 + 4 + 3 + 2 + 1 = \$21$

5. Assume that the average and marginal costs are constant and equal to 14. If Pat produces the monopoly quantity and charges the monopoly price,

   (A) what price will Pat charge for a tattoo? __$17__

   (B) what quantity will Pat supply? __4__

   (C) what is the amount of consumer surplus generated? __$6__

   $CS = (20 - 17) + (19 - 12) + (18 - 17) = 3 + 7 + 1 = \$11$

6. Again, assume that the average and marginal costs are constant and equal to 14. Now assume that Pat knows the tastes and preferences of all consumers and that the conditions that allow price discrimination apply.

   (A) What quantity will Pat supply? __7__

   (B) At what prices will she sell tattoos?

   __$20__ , __$19__ , __$18__ , $17, __$16__ , __$15__ , __$14__

   (C) What is the amount of consumer surplus generated? __0__

   $CS = (20 - 20) + (19 - 19) + (18 - 18) + (17 - 17) + (16 - 16) + (15 - 15) + (14 - 14) = 0$

Advanced Placement Economics Teacher Resource Manual © National Council on Economic Education, New York, N.Y.

7. Without calculating profit, explain how Pat's profits differ among cases 4, 5 and 6.
   Pat's profits will be highest in case 4 with the discriminating monopoly, lowest in case 2 with the perfect competitor and the nondiscriminating monopoly in between.

Part C
The Effects of Price Discrimination

Use the example of Pat's Patriotic Tattoos to make some conclusions about the effects of price discrimination.

8. What happens to consumer surplus if a firm successfully price discriminates? *Consumer surplus decreases.*

9. What happens to the firm's profits if it successfully price discriminates? *Its profits increase.*

10. What happens to the quantity supplied by a successful price-discriminating monopoly firm compared with a nonprice-discriminating monopoly firm? *The quantity supplied is greater.*

11. How does the quantity supplied by a successful price-discriminating monopoly firm compare with the quantity supplied by firms in a perfectly competitive industry? *It is the same.*

12. How does price discrimination affect economic efficiency? *It improves it because output is increased and price is closer to marginal cost.*

Part D
Real Examples of Price Discrimination

13. Pat's Patriotic Tattoos is a fictional case. What are some real examples of price discrimination?
    This question provides the opportunity to discuss real examples and the results of price discrimination. Here are some examples:

    ■ *Charging higher tuition for college juniors and seniors than for freshmen and sophomores*

    ■ *Charging different airline passengers different prices for the same ticket*

    ■ *Providing discounts on cars by negotiating with each consumer on an individual basis*

    ■ *Providing college scholarships for low-income students but not for wealthier ones*

    ■ *Selling hardcover and paperback books*

    ■ *Providing discounts for senior citizens*

14. Use your examples to determine which factors make price discrimination easier.

   ■ *An inelastic demand curve*

   ■ *The product or service cannot be resold easily.*

   ■ *Categories of consumers can be separated in the market.*

15. Is price discrimination a good thing or a bad thing? *Answers will vary. On the negative side, it reduces consumer surplus and increases a firm's profits. On the positive side, it increases output over pure monopoly pricing. More consumers will now buy the product. It results in a more efficient level of output.*

Regulating Monopoly

1. If this monopolist is not regulated, what will be the level of

    (A) output? *About 1,500 units*

    (B) price? *$4.00*

    (C) total revenue? *$6,000 ($4.00 x 1,500)*

    (D) total costs? *$4,500 ($3.00 x 1,500)*

    (E) profit or loss? *$1,500 profit ($6,000 – $4,500)*

2. If this monopolist is regulated by marginal cost pricing (i.e., the socially optimal price), what will be the level of

    (A) output? *About 3,000 units*

    (B) price? *$1.50*

    (C) total revenue? *$4,500 ($1.50 x 3,000)*

    (D) total costs? *About $7,500 (3,000 x $2.50)*

    (E) profit or loss? *$3,000 loss ($7,500 – $4,500)*

    (F) Will the monopoly need a subsidy? *Yes*

    (G) If so, how much? *$3,000*

3. If cost-of-service regulation (fair-return price or average cost pricing) is imposed on this monopolist, what will be the level of

    (A) output? *2,500 units*

    (B) price? *$2.50*

    (C) total revenue? *$6,250 ($2.50 x 2,500)*

    (D) total costs? *$6,250 ($2.50 x 2,500)*

    (E) profit or loss? *0*

4. What are the advantages and disadvantages of marginal cost pricing? *The firm operates at its most allocatively efficient output, but the government must subsidize the firm.*

5. What are the advantages and disadvantages of cost-of-service regulation? *Output is higher and price is lower compared with an unregulated firm. The firm, however, is not operating at its most efficient output. Nevertheless, no government subsidy is required.*

Monopoly Consultants, Inc.

You have been retained by seven corporations to advise them on their future output and price decisions. These firms are listed on Figure 38.1. Each firm is a pure monopoly and desires to maximize its profits or minimize its losses. Before making your recommendations, fill in as much of the incomplete data in the table as possible. Although you may not be able to fill in every box, there are sufficient data in each case to recommend action that is in the best interest of the firm.

After you have analyzed each case, decide which statement below is the best course of action for the firm involved. Place the number of the statement in the answer column.

1. Nonsense: The information is inconsistent and could not be correct.
2. This firm is in the correct position.
3. This firm should shut down in the short run because its revenue does not exceed variable cost.
4. This firm should shut down in the long run because its revenue does not exceed variable cost.
5. This firm should reduce production and increase price.
6. This firm should increase production and reduce price.

 Figure 38.1

Monopoly Consultants Inc. Monopoly Model

Case	Price	Marginal Revenue	Quantity Output	Total Revenue	Total Cost	Fixed Cost	Average Total Cost	Marginal Cost	Answer
1	$1.25	$1.00	10,000	*$12,500*	*$15,000*	$2,000	$1.50	$1.00	*3*
2	5.00	4.00	1,000	*5,000*	4,000		4.00 minimum level	*4.00*	*2*
3	1.50	2.00	10,000				2.00	2.00	*1*
4	above marginal revenue	5.00					5.00	5.00	*2*
5	*2.00*		4,000	8,000	7,200			2.00	*5*
6	7.00	4.00	2,000		*8,000*			3.00	*6*
7			5,000	9,000	10,000	declining	minimum level		*1*

A Quick Review of Perfect Competition and Monopoly

✳ Figure 39.1

Graphs of Monopoly and Perfect Competition

Monopoly

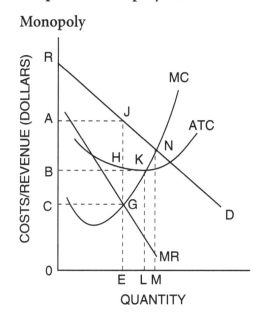

Perfect Competition

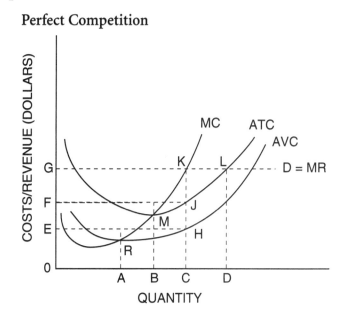

These questions are based on Figure 39.1. Underline the correct answer. Assume that the monopoly can set only one price. Both the monopoly and the perfect competitor seek to maximize profits.

1. A monopoly firm will maximize profits at what price?

   (A) 0A (B) 0B (C) 0C (D) 0R

2. Economic profits for the monopoly firm are represented by the area of which rectangle?

   (A) 0CGE (B) 0AJE *(C) AJHB* (D) BAJN

3. Total costs for the monopoly firm are represented by the area of which rectangle?

   (A) BKL0 (B) CGE0 (C) AJE0 *(D) BHE0*

4. The total revenue for the monopoly firm is represented by the area of which rectangle?

   (A) 0CGE *(B) 0AJE* (C) AJHB (D) BAJH

5. The perfect competitor will maximize profits at what output level?

   (A) 0A (B) 0B *(C) 0G* (D) 0D

6. The perfect competitor will shut down below which price-output relationship?

   (A) K   (B) M   (C) L   *(D) R*

7. At price 0G, the area of which rectangle represents total revenue for the profit-maximizing perfect competitor?

   (A) 0GKC   (B) 0FJC   (C) FGKJ   (D) EFJH

8. At output 0C, total variable cost is represented by the area of which rectangle?

   (A) 0GKC   (B) FGKJ   *(C) 0EHC*   (D) 0FJC

9. At price OG, profits for the perfect competitor are represented by the area of which rectangle?

   (A) 0GKC   (B) 0FJC   *(C) FGKJ*   (D) 0EHC

10. At what price-output relationship will a perfect competitor operate in the long run?

    (A) K   (B) L   *(C) M*   (D) R

11. For the monopolist, what is the area of consumer surplus?

    (A) ABHJ   (B) AJGC   *(C) ARJ*   (D) ARJE

Monopolistic Competition and Oligopoly

Introduction and Description

Perfect competition and monopoly give us some of the basic tools needed to understand how product price and output are determined. Although they simplify reality, perfect competition and monopoly identify conditions that affect consumers' and producers' behavior. Perfect competition and monopoly, however, are the exception in the U.S. economy. Most market structures are between these two extremes, and they are the focus of this lesson.

Today the U.S. economy is dominated by *oligopolies* and *monopolistically competitive* firms. An oligopolistic industry is dominated by a few large firms that act interdependently in output and pricing decisions. Monopolistic competition is a market in which a relatively large number of firms of small and moderate size offers similar but not identical products. Most retailing in the United States is conducted under conditions of monopolistic competition. In contrast, manufacturing typically occurs under conditions of oligopoly.

Activity 40 provides an overview of monopolistic competition and compares it to perfect competition and monopoly.

Game theory is used to explain the behavior of oligopolists. John Nash of *A Beautiful Mind* fame won the Nobel Prize in economics for his contributions on game theory. Game theory is the study of situations in which the outcome depends jointly on the actions of each of the participants. The optimum strategy or mix of strategies is delivered by the *minimax* principle: Each participant lists the worst possible results that an opponent could inflict. Then the participants try to realize the best outcome from this list. When both players have found their optimum strategies, the game is solved. Game theory also explains why collusion among oligopolists does not work in the long run.

Activity 41 provides an overview of game theory.

Objectives

1. Define and discuss the nature of *monopolistic competition.*
2. When given cost and price data, determine the output and price charged by a monopolistic competitor in the short run and in the long run.
3. Identify the wastes of monopolistic competition, and explain why product differentiation may offset these wastes.
4. Define and discuss the nature of *oligopoly.*
5. When given cost and price data, determine the output and price charged by an oligopolist in the short run and in the long run.
6. Discuss the role of nonprice competition in oligopoly.
7. Describe the types of nonprice competition used by oligopolists.
8. Discuss the mutual interdependence of oligopolists and analyze how this provides incentives to cheat on a collusive agreement.
9. Use game theory to illustrate how the prisoner's dilemma affects collusive and competitive strategies.

Time Required

Two class periods or 90 minutes

Materials

1. Activities 40 and 41
2. Visual 3.12

Procedure

1. Use Visual 3.12 to describe the characteristics of monopolistic competition.

   (A) Give specific examples of monopolistic competition.

   (B) Explain why the demand curve of a monopolistic competitor is downward sloping but not as steep as that of a monopolist.

(C) Explain that monopolistic competition is very similar to perfect competition except for a differentiated product.

(D) Explain why a monopolistic competitor can have profits and losses in the short run.

(E) Explain why a monopolistic competitor breaks even in the long run but does not operate at the most efficient point either allocatively or productively.

2. Have the students complete Activity 40, and discuss the answers.

3. Give a lecture on game theory. Because the activity that follows is fairly complex and detailed, make sure the students understand why economists study game theory.

(A) Game theory is used to explain the strategic behavior of oligopolistic firms. It is a way of explaining the effects of oligopolistic firms being highly interdependent.

(B) Game theory is similar to a card game in which a player's strategy depends on the cards he or she is dealt.

(C) A *dominant strategy* is one that is best for one player regardless of any strategy the other player follows.

(D) A *dominated strategy* is one whose outcome depends on the strategy the other player uses. It can be a good strategy if the player can predict the other players's move.

(E) A *Nash Equilibrium* is a combination of strategies that is the best response for a player given the other player's best response. It does not always provide the best result for society.

4. Have the students read the introduction to Activity 41, and discuss the basics of game theory.

(A) What is a payoff matrix? *It describes the payoffs in a game for possible combinations of strategies.*

(B) What is the dominant strategy? *A strategy that is best for one player regardless of any strategy the other player follows.*

(C) What is the Nash Equilibrium? *Any combination of strategies that is a best response for a player, given the other player's best response to this combination of strategies.*

5. Have the students complete Activity 41, and discuss the answers.

6. Apply game theory to collusion as a strategy to deal with the pricing dilemma. Discuss strategies such as these:

(A) Overt collusion

(B) Price leadership

(C) Cost-plus pricing

Monopolistic Competition

✳ Figure 40.1
Monopolistically Competitive Firm in the Short Run

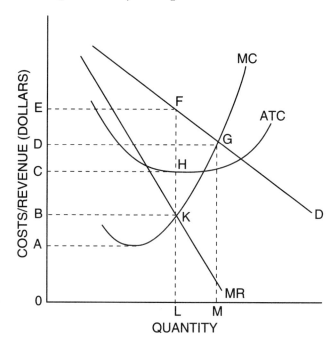

1. Use Figure 40.1 to answer these questions.

    (A) At what level of output will this firm operate? ___*0L*___

    (B) What is marginal revenue at this level of output? ___*0B*___

    (C) What price will this firm charge for its product? ___*0E*___

    (D) The area of which rectangle is equal to total revenue? ___*0EFL*___

    (E) What is the firm's average total cost? ___*0C*___

    (F) The area of which rectangle is equal to the firm's total cost? ___*0CHL*___

    (G) Is the firm making profits or incurring losses? ___*Making economic profits*___

    (H) The area of which rectangle is equal to profits or losses? ___*CEFH*___

2. Would the demand curve for a monopolistic competitor be more or less elastic than the demand curve for a monopolist? Justify your answer. *More elastic. Because there are many competitors, the monopolistic competitor will lose sales to these producers if it raises prices.*

3. What are the characteristics of a monopolistically competitive market? In what sense is there competition and in what sense is there monopoly in this type of market structure? *Monopolistic competition is characterized by many firms selling a differentiated but similar product. It is similar to monopoly because the firm has some control over price. It is similar to perfect competition because there are few barriers to entry, many competitors and long-run profits may exist but probably will be low.*

4. What are three examples of monopolistically competitive markets? *Almost all retailing is done under conditions of monopolistic competition.*

5. True, false or uncertain, and why? "Monopolistic competition is just another form of pure monopoly." *False. It has many characteristics of perfect competition.*

6. True, false or uncertain, and why? "Monopolistic competition is even better than perfect competition." *Uncertain. Monopolistic competition does allow price and quality competition. Consumers have a wider choice under monopolistic competition. However, price is higher and output lower than under perfect competition. Monopolistic competition also creates excess capacity.*

7. True, false or uncertain, and why? "In the long run, monopolistic competitors produce at their most efficient point." *False. Monopolistic competitors do not operate at the bottom of their average cost curve (productive efficiency) or where P = MC (allocative efficiency).*

Game Theory

Part B
The Prisoner's Dilemma Game

One classic type of game is the *prisoner's dilemma game.* Prisoner's dilemma games are games in which each player has a dominant strategy; and when both players play the dominant strategy, the payoffs are smaller than if each player played the dominated strategy. The dilemma is how to avoid this bad outcome.

The basics of the prisoner's dilemma game are as follows: Two prisoners have the option to confess or not confess to a crime they committed. The prosecutor has only enough information to convict both criminals of a minor offense and is, therefore, relying on a confession. The minor offense carries one year in jail. The prisoners are questioned in different cells, without the ability to communicate. They are told that if one prisoner confesses while the other remains silent, the prisoner confessing will go free and the prisoner remaining silent will serve 20 years in jail. If both prisoners confess, both prisoners will serve three years in jail.

If a player goes free, the payoff is 0. If a player serves one year in jail, the payoff is –1. If a player spends 20 years in jail, the payoff is –20. Use these numbers in your payoff matrix. Note that the negative numbers come from losing years of freedom.

1. Determine the three basic elements of the game.

    (A) The players: *Prisoner 1 and Prisoner 2*

    (B) The strategies for each player: *Confess or Not Confess*

    (C) The payoffs for each player: *If one confesses, he or she goes free, and the other gets 20 years in jail. If both confess, both get three years in jail. If neither confesses, both get one year in jail.*

2. Create a payoff matrix for the prisoner's dilemma game.

		Prisoner 2	
		Confess	*Not Confess*
Prisoner 1	*Confess*	*–3, –3*	*0, –20*
	Not Confess	*–20, 0*	*–1, –1*

3. Identify any dominant strategies. *Prisoner 1: Confess. Prisoner 2: Confess*

4. Identify any dominated strategies. *Prisoner 1: Not Confess. Prisoner 2: Not Confess*

5. Find the Nash Equilibrium. *Both Confess.*

Part C
Variation of the Prisoner's Dilemma Game

You are in a class with one other student. It is the end of the semester, and final exams are in a week. Your teacher has said the final exam will be graded so that anyone who scores the class average on the final exam will receive a "B" in the class. Anyone who scores above the average will receive an "A" in the class, and anyone who scores below the average will fail the class. You would certainly score higher on the exam than the other student. You and the other student have made an agreement not to take the final exam so that the class average is zero and you both receive "B" grades.

6. Determine the three basic elements of the game.

   (A) The players: *You and the Other Student*

   (B) The strategies for each player: *Take the Exam or Not Take the Exam*

   (C) The payoffs for each player: *If both players take the exam, you receive an A and the Other Student receives an F. If both players do not take the exam, both receive a B. If you take the exam and the Other Student does not take the exam, you receive an A and the Other Student receives an F. If the Other Student takes the exam and you do not take the exam, you receive an F and the Other Student receives an A.*

7. Create a payoff matrix for this game.

		Other Student	
		Take the Exam	*Not Take the Exam*
You	*Take the Exam*	*A, F*	*A, F*
	Not Take the Exam	*F, A*	*B, B*

8. What is your dominant strategy? (Underline the correct answer.)
   <u>Take the Exam</u> or Not Take the Exam

9. Using a four-point scale (A = 4, B = 3, C = 2 and D = 1), which choice results in the highest class GPA? *Both players do not take the exam because B + B = 3 + 3 = 6 class GPA is higher than A+ F = 4 + 0 = 4 class GPA.*

If you finished Parts B and C correctly, you will realize that when each player chooses his or her dominant strategy, the result is unattractive to the group.

The key to avoiding the prisoner's dilemma outcome of lower payoffs for both players is to find a way for players to credibly commit to playing a dominated strategy. Merely having both prisoners agree to Not Confess or both students to Not Take the Exam will not work. This results because it is always optimal for Prisoner 1 (or Prisoner 2) to still play the Confess strategy, and it is always optimal for the better student to play the Take the Exam strategy. One possible way to have credible commitment in the prisoner's dilemma game would be to have both prisoners reveal another past crime they committed, thus ensuring that if they confess to this crime, the other prisoner will have additional information to punish the prisoner who cheats on an agreement to not confess.

One way to do this is to form a *cartel*. A cartel is a coalition of firms that coordinate their decisions to reach a more optimal solution for all members of the group by finding ways to credibly commit players to play their dominated strategies. Cartels, however, are not always successful in maintaining their agreements because there may be an incentive for a member to cheat on the cartel.

Part D
Questions

10. Is the Coke and Pepsi advertising game a prisoner's dilemma game? Explain why or why not. *Yes, it is optimal for both players to play their dominated strategies and be at the Don't Advertise/Don't Advertise corner, earning 100 each.*

11. Interpret "standing at a concert" in terms of the prisoner's dilemma game. *If one person stands, he or she gets a better view of the concert. If the person in front of someone stands, then that person's best response is also to stand, or he or she will not be able to see the concert. However, if all people sat, then everyone would be able to see the concert and would not have to get tired standing.*

12. Explain at least one way the optimal outcome for players, which would be for all players to play the dominated strategy, can be reached in Question 11. What are the possible commitment problems? *The concert hall could require people at the concert to remain seated. However, this implies an external enforcer. If an external enforcer cannot be used, the group may collectively decide legal ways to punish those who stand. The punishment could range from throwing food at violators to physically assaulting them. The key is to make the commitment credible.*

13. A rivalry exists between the U.S. jet producer Boeing and the European jet producer Airbus. Each government has the opportunity to subsidize its jet producer to give it a competitive edge in the global market. Using game theory, explain what you would expect to observe in practice. *Both countries would subsidize their producers. However, this costs money and lowers the price of jets for the rest of the world without either firm ultimately receiving a competitive advantage (the same outcome for both firms if there were no subsidies at all). This is another example of the prisoner's dilemma game.*

Analyzing Market Structure

Introduction and Description

This lesson helps the students apply their knowledge of market structure to conventional and unconventional situations. Activity 42 can be assigned as homework or completed in groups. It is good practice for the complex application questions that are emphasized on the AP test.

Objectives

1. Use the concepts of the theory of the firm to analyze a variety of issues.
2. Analyze the behavior of perfect and imperfect competitors.

Time Required

One class period or 45 minutes

Materials

Activity 42

Procedure

1. Assign Activity 42 a few days before it is due, or have the students complete it in groups.
2. Go over the answers to Activity 42.

Market Structure and Business Decision Making

Answer the questions and briefly explain your answers. Use diagrams to illustrate your point.

1. True, false or uncertain, and explain why? "Monopolies always charge the highest possible price."
   False. The monopolist will try to charge a price where marginal revenue equals marginal cost. This is a higher price than a perfect competitor would charge if the monopoly and competitive firm have the same costs. However, monopolists can't repeal the law of demand. If the monopolist charges too high a price, profits will not be maximized. Students may define "highest possible price" where MR = MC; this answer might be correct.

2. True, false or uncertain, and explain why? "To find a monopoly, look for bigness. For example, monopoly is more likely to be found in the oil business than in the dry-cleaning business."
   False. Look for oneness, not bigness. Examples of small monopolies are toll-road restaurants and ballpark concessions.

3. True, false or uncertain, and explain why? "If all the firms in an industry raise their prices at the same time, one can be pretty sure that there is collusion or monopoly behavior in this industry."
   False. If they were perfect competitors, they would all raise their prices at the same time because they have no control over price. If they were oligopolists, their pricing would be interdependent.

4. After several losing seasons, a college is considering dropping football. The college has concluded it needs an athletic director for other sports. To what extent should the college's decision makers consider the following budget items? (Hint: Consider variable and fixed costs.)

   (A) Tuition scholarships *Tuition scholarships are a variable cost and should be considered.*

   (B) Payments on the stadium's mortgage *Mortgage payments are a fixed cost and should not be considered.*

   (C) Free tickets to the games for the students *A variable cost. If students didn't get free tickets, some would pay for them.*

   (D) Salary of the athletic director *A fixed cost although with less responsibilities, he or she might be paid less.*

   (E) Salary of the football coach and assistant coaches *A variable cost; it should be considered.*

5. True, false or uncertain, and explain why? "The marginal-cost curve for a perfectly competitive firm is the same thing as its supply curve." *Uncertain. The marginal cost curve is the same thing as the supply curve for the firm as long as it is above the average variable cost curve. Where price = marginal cost, the firm will produce or supply at that output because it maximizes profits there. With a price below the AVC curve, the firm will shut down. A market supply curve is the sum of all the firms' marginal cost curves. Both are upward sloping. This is also why changes in costs shift a market supply curve.*

6. True, false or uncertain, and explain why? "If marginal cost equals marginal revenue, a firm must be breaking even because costs and revenue are equal." *False. This statement confuses marginal cost and average total cost. A firm maximizes profits or minimizes losses where marginal revenue equals marginal cost. The firm could be making a profit, breaking even or losing money where MR = MC. However, it is doing better there than at any other output level unless price is less than AVC, in which case the output should be zero.*

7. The Crazy Toy Company produces yo-yos. Figure 42.1 gives the total revenue and total cost associated with the production of a certain number of yo-yos. Fixed costs are $1,200.

Figure 42.1
Crazy Toy Company Yo-Yo Schedule

Number of Yo-Yos Produced	Total Revenue	Marginal Revenue	Total Cost	Marginal Cost
0	$0	—	$1,200	—
1	150	$150	1,300	$100
2	275	125	1,350	50
3	375	100	1,425	75
4	460	85	1,505	80
5	540	80	1,595	90
6	600	60	1,700	105
7	640	40	1,820	120
8	670	30	1,960	140

Advanced Placement Economics Teacher Resource Manual © National Council on Economic Education, New York, N.Y.

(A) What are the fixed and variable costs associated with each level of output? *Fixed cost is $1,200. Fixed costs do not vary with output and exist even if the output level is zero. All other costs are variable. For example, at an output of two, fixed cost is $1,200 and variable costs are $150.*

(B) What is the optimal production level for the firm? *Four units of output*

(C) In the short run, should the firm shut down? Explain your answer. *The firm should operate where MR = MC. This is at an output of four and a loss of $1,045. (You can figure this out by comparing MC and MR at output of three, four and five. They do not have to be exactly equal at four.) However, this loss is less than the $1,200 the firm would lose if it shut down. The firm is covering variable costs, so it should remain open in the short run.*

8. Why do airlines charge a discounted fare to passengers who stay over on a Saturday night? (Hint: Consider price discrimination.) *Many airline costs are fixed. The additional passengers probably provide more revenue (MR) than the additional cost (MC), as long as a lower-priced passenger does not replace a higher-priced passenger. Because air travel is a service and cannot be resold, airlines can price discriminate.*

9. Assume your economics teacher got a scholarship to study in Europe this summer. Therefore, the teacher's family wants to rent its house for the summer. They figure if no one rents it, it will still cost them $700 a month in principal, interest, and property insurance. It will cost them an additional $200 a month to maintain it if someone occupies it.

   (A) How much rent must they charge to cover all costs?   *$900 (TR = TC)*

   (B) What is the minimum rent they should be willing to accept before they would leave the house unoccupied?   *$200.01*   Why? *They would lose less money than they would if they left the house empty. This assumes that the $200 in variable costs includes wear and tear on the house.*

10. True, false or uncertain, and explain why? "Without government regulations most firms in a capitalist market system would be monopolies." *False. It is very hard to maintain barriers to entry. High profits will attract other firms to the industry. Very few monopolies have been broken up by government. Yet, except for regulated monopolies, few, if any, monopolies exist in the United States except in local markets. In fact, some foreign governments pass rules that help monopolies stay that way. Government regulations sometimes make competition more difficult.*

11. Draw a graph illustrating a monopoly market. Include the demand curve, the marginal revenue curve and the marginal cost curve.

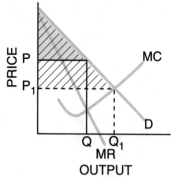

(A) Indicate the equilibrium quantity for the monopolist and label it Q.

(B) Indicate the equilibrium price and label it P.

(C) Shade the area of consumer surplus for the monopolist market.

(D) Indicate the equilibrium price and quantity, if your diagram indicates conditions of perfect competition, and label them respectively P_1 and Q_1.

(E) Using diagonal lines, indicate the area of consumer surplus if the monopoly were actually a perfectly competitive industry.

(F) Does the monopoly model exhibit allocative efficiency? Why or why not?
No. It does not produce where price = MC.

(G) Does a perfectly competitive industry exhibit allocative efficiency? Why or why not?
Yes. It does produce where price = MC.

12. Why is game theory important to an oligopolist? *It explains interdependent pricing and output decisions.*

Answers to Sample Multiple-Choice Questions

1. E	13. D	24. D	35. E
2. C	14. B	25. D	36. B
3. D	15. B	26. B	37. E
4. C	16. C	27. D	38. E
5. C	17. C	28. B	39. A
6. D	18. E	29. D	40. C
7. E	19. C	30. C	41. A
8. A	20. C	31. C	42. E
9. C	21. B	32. A	43. A
10. E	22. C	33. C	44. B
11. E	23. B	34. D	45. A
12. D			

Answers to Sample Short Free-Response Questions

*1. "A monopolist charges the highest price the market will bear, whereas a perfect competitor does not." Explain in detail why you agree or disagree with this statement. As part of your answer, be sure to describe how a monopolist determines the profit-maximizing price.

9 points: Talks about and relates the following three main points of the question:

(A) How a monopoly sets the price

(B) How a perfect competitor sets the price

(C) Defines the "highest price the market will bear" and relates the above discussion to the quotation.

8 points: Firm grasp of the concept of profit maximization. May have a minor error. May not relate answer to question asked.

7 points: Graph of perfect competition and monopoly models or verbiage. Can explain the idea of profit maximization.

6 points: No (C) as explained in 9 points. Monopoly model is OK but perfect competition is incomplete. Must discuss profit maximization. To receive a 6 and above, the concept of a monopoly must be correct.

5 points: Neither model is correct, or significant errors exist.

4 points: More errors than in 5

3 points: One logical, consistent argument

2 points: Contains one distinction between monopoly and perfect competition but is riddled with errors and confusions.

1 point: Anything that is correct and at all relevant

Note: Question 1 was a nine-point-scale AP question; the students were given 15 minutes to answer the question.

---

* Actual free-response question from a past AP test. Reprinted by permission of the College Entrance Examination Board, the copyright owner. For limited use by NCEE.

---

*2. A single airline provides service from City A to City B.

(A) Explain how the airline will determine the number of passengers it will carry and the price it will charge.

(B) Suppose fixed costs for this airline increase. How will this increase in fixed costs affect the airline's price and output decisions in the short run?

Grading Rubric: Basically the point distribution is 3 points for Part (A) and 2 for Part (B).

Part (A)

The airline is operating as a monopoly; the monopolist determines quantity by equating MR = MC and price from the downward-sloping demand curve.

1 point: Indicates this is a monopoly explicitly or draws a downward sloping demand curve for the picture.

2 points: Output is determined by MR = MC.

3 points: Price is determined from the demand curve at the output where MR = MC.

Part (B)

The increase in fixed costs increases ATC but leaves the MC curve in the same place. Thus, since marginal cost and demand have not changed, the profit-maximizing price and output do not change.

1 point: Price and output remain the same.

2 points: Increase in fixed cost does not change MC.

---

* Actual free-response question from a past AP test. Reprinted by permission of the College Entrance Examination Board, the copyright owner. For limited use by NCEE.

UNIT
3 Microeconomics
SHORT FREE-RESPONSE
SAMPLE QUESTIONS
Answer
Key

*3. Assume that Star Inc. is a monopoly. Explain each of the following for this firm.

(A) Why marginal revenue and demand are not equal

(B) How the profit-maximizing level of output and the price are determined in the short run

(C) Why economic profits continue to exist in the long run

> *Grading Rubric: Basically the point distribution is 2 points for Part (A), 2 for Part (B) and 1 for Part (C).*
>
> *Part (A): 2 points*
>
> *The marginal revenue curve lies below the demand curve because downward-sloping demand curve, price maker/price seeker or the firm is the market; and the firm must decrease price on all units in order to sell additional units.*
>
> *1 point: Some version of downward-sloping demand curve and a marginal revenue curve that lies below it (a graph is sufficient).*
>
> *1 point: Firm must decrease price on all units or on all previous units sold in order to sell additional units.*
>
> *Part (B): 2 points*
>
> *Profit-maximizing output is determined where MR = MC, and price is read off the demand curve for this output.*
>
> *1 point: Quantity is determined where MR = MC.*
>
> *1 point: Price comes from demand curve at MR = MC quantity.*
>
> *Part (C): 1 point*
>
> *1 point: Economic profits can continue to exist in the long run because of barriers to entry. An example of a barrier to entry is sufficient.*

4. What is the long-run equilibrium condition for a perfectly competitive firm? Is the long-run equilibrium condition of a perfect competitor allocatively and/or technically (productively) efficient? Why or why not?

   A perfectly competitive firm is in long-run equilibrium where price equals marginal cost and where price equals average total cost. In addition, the perfectly competitive firm operates at the lowest point on its average total cost curve. In the long run, the perfectly competitive firm is allocatively efficient (P = MC) and technically efficient (minimum ATC).

---

* Actual free-response question from a past AP test. Reprinted by permission of the College Entrance Examination Board, the copyright owner. For limited use by NCEE.

---

5. Why do oligopolists prefer to use nonprice competition rather than price competition?
Oligopolists are characterized by mutual interdependence. If the oligopolist raises its price, rivals will not follow and will therefore gain market share. If the oligopolist lowers its price, rivals will have to lower their prices in order to keep from losing market share. Therefore, the oligopolist often prefers nonprice competition as a safer way of competition.

6. What is the long-run equilibrium position for a monopolistically competitive firm? How does the long-run equilibrium position of a monopolistically competitive firm compare with the long-run equilibrium position of a perfectly competitive firm?
A monopolistic competitor in long-run equilibrium operates where price equals average total cost, so it earns zero economic profit in the long run. This long-run equilibrium occurs because one of the characteristics of monopolistic competition is that firms can easily enter or leave the industry (free entry). If monopolistic competitors are earning short-run economic profits, more firms will enter the industry. This increases industry supply, lowers price and eliminates economic profit. On the other hand, if monopolistically competitive firms are experiencing short-run economic losses, firms will leave the industry to seek economic profits elsewhere or existing firms will cut production. This decreases industry supply, raises price and restores normal profits in the long run to the firms remaining in the industry. The monopolistic competitor faces a downward-sloping demand curve because of product differentiation. The perfect competitor faces a horizontal demand curve because there is no product differentiation. Because marginal revenue is lower than price and because profits are maximized where marginal revenue equals marginal cost, the monopolistically competitive firm is not allocatively efficient. Because price and marginal revenue are equal, a perfectly competitive firm does operate where P = MC and is allocatively efficient. The monopolistically competitive firm also does not operate at the bottom of its average total cost curve so it also is not productively or allocatively efficient. The perfect competitor does operate at the bottom of its average total cost curve.

7. Why will a firm maximize profits where marginal revenue equals marginal cost? Under what conditions, if any, will a firm not operate where marginal revenue equals marginal cost? Explain.

When MR is greater than MC, each additional unit of output adds more to total revenue than total cost, causing losses to decrease or profits to increase. When MR is less than MC, each unit produced adds more to total cost than to total revenue, causing profits to decrease or losses to increase. Therefore, profit maximization occurs where MR = MC.

8. Consider two firms in a market. Each firm must decide whether to market a new product. The profit earned from marketing the new product depends on whether one or both firms market the product. If one firm markets the product, the firm will earn a profit of $2 million. If both firms market the product, they split the profits of $3 million.

(A) Identify the players, actions and payoffs in this game and construct a payoff matrix. Call the firms A and B. The first number in each square should represent the payoff for Firm A.

(B) Does Firm A have a dominant strategy in this game? If so, what is it?

(C) Does Firm B have a dominant strategy in this game? If so, what is it?

		Firm A	
		Produce	*Don't Produce*
Firm B	*Produce*	*1.5, 1.5*	*2, 0*
	Don't Produce	*0, 2*	*0, 0*

Firm A has a dominant strategy: produce.

Firm B has a dominant strategy: produce.

Note: Students may come up with different labels for the matrix. For example, they may use "market" rather than "produce." Make sure their answers for 8(B) and 8(C) are consistent with their labels.

9. A firm is operating in a perfectly competitive market where price is equal to average variable cost in the short run.

   (A) Draw and correctly label a graph for this firm, indicating each of the following:
      (i)   Marginal revenue
      (ii) Average variable cost
      (iii) Average cost
      (iv) Marginal cost
      (v)   Price

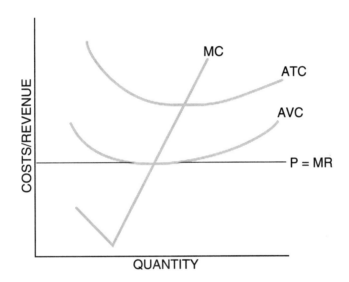

   (B) Describe the profit situation for the firm. *It is not making a profit.*

   (C) If industry price decreases, explain in the short run how this will affect the firm shown in your graph. *Price will decrease and equal marginal cost below average variable cost. The firm will shut down.*

UNIT
3 Microeconomics
SHORT FREE-RESPONSE
SAMPLE QUESTIONS
Answer
Key

*10. Assume that in a perfectly competitive market, a firm's costs and revenue are

Marginal cost = average variable cost at $20

Marginal cost = average total cost at $30

Marginal cost = average revenue at $25

(A) How will this firm determine the profit-maximizing level of output?

The firm will maximize profits by operating where MC = MR = P.

Grading Rubric: Part (A) = 1 point

MC = MR = P or MR = MC or P = MC

(B) What price will this firm charge? Explain how the firm determined this price. *The firm will charge $25; the price is determined by the market, not the firm.*

Grading Rubric: Part (B) = 2 points

1 point: Price equals $25.

1 point: Market/industry determines the price (simply saying that the firm is a price taker in a competitive industry is not acceptable) OR Price may be used to link marginal revenue to average revenue (simply asserting that MR = 25 is insufficient).

(C) Should this firm produce in the short run? Why or why not?

Yes, the firm should operate in the short run because it is covering all of its variable costs and some of its fixed costs; price is greater than average variable cost.

Grading Rubric: Part (C) = 1 point

Yes and reason P > AVC or TR > TVC is acceptable. (1 point) (Price or average revenue greater than total variable cost is unacceptable; total revenue greater than average variable cost is unacceptable. A comparison of a total concept with an average concept is incorrect.)

(D) Will this firm earn a profit or incur a loss? Why?

The firm will earn an economic loss because average revenue (price) is less than average total cost.

Grading Rubric: Part (D) = 1 point

Loss and reason P < AVC or TR < TC is acceptable. (Price or average revenue loss less than total cost is unacceptable; total revenue less than average total cost is unacceptable.) Revenue less than cost is acceptable.

Notes on scoring: Besides counting points, the answer may be looked at as a whole and ultimately judged by its overall quality. This is particularly true if the total point count includes a half. The final total should mean something in terms of the overall quality of the answer. A score of 5 points should reflect an excellent answer but not necessarily perfect, 4 an excellent answer with a flaw, 3 a good answer, 2 an adequate answer, 1 a seriously deficient answer but still an answer, 0 no relevant economic answer to the question.

---

* Actual free-response question from a past AP test. Reprinted by permission of the College Entrance Examination Board, the copyright owner. For limited use by NCEE.

UNIT
3 Microeconomics
LONG FREE-RESPONSE
SAMPLE QUESTIONS
Answer
Key

Answers to Sample Long Free-Response Questions

*1. In a particular product market, there is only one seller and there are significant barriers to entry.

(A) Explain how this firm determines its equilibrium output and price.

(B) Explain whether this firm is producing the economically efficient level of output. In your answer include a brief definition of economic efficiency.

Grading Rubric: Part (A) = 6 points, Part (B) = 3 points

Part (A) Components of a good answer:

(i) *Because the firm is a monopoly, it faces a downward-sloping demand curve.*

(ii) *Because its demand curve is negatively sloping, its marginal revenue curve will be more steeply sloping downward.*

(iii) *Bring in marginal cost to determine output at $MR = MC$.*

(iv) *Recognize that the profit-maximizing point is $MR = MC$.*

(v) *Read price from the demand curve at the output where $MR = MC$.*

In allocating points for Part (A), give 1 point for each of (i) through (iv) and 2 points for (v).

Part (B) Components of a good answer:

(i) *A definition of economic efficiency (either allocative efficiency requires $P = MC$ or productive efficiency is producing at minimum ATC)*

(ii) *Correctly relating the definition to the monopoly situation. A monopolist is not efficient by either definition.*

In allocating points for Part (B), give 1 point for the efficiency definition and 2 points for correctly relating the monopolist situation to the definition of efficiency.

Special situations:

(1) *There is a possibility that an answer will have efficiency, meaning that a producer operates at the least ATC for a given level of output, and hence the monopolist could be productively efficient. That's okay! Give 3 points.*

(2) *Answer states that the monopolist is not efficient because it produces too little output and charges too high a price, or the monopolist restricts output. Give 1 point for this line of "reasoning."*

(3) *If a rudimentary concept of inefficiency is recognized, give 1 point.*

---

* Actual free-response question from a past AP test. Reprinted by permission of the College Entrance Examination Board, the copyright owner. For limited use by NCEE.

*2. Assume that initially, a perfectly competitive industry is in long-run equilibrium.

(A) For the typical profit-maximizing firm in this industry, explain the following:
   (i) How the firm determines its level of output
   (ii) What the level of profit is and why it is at this level

(B) A change occurs that reduces the variable costs of production for all firms in this industry. Explain how and why this decrease in variable costs affects each of the following in the short run:
   (i) The typical firm's level of output
   (ii) The industry price and level of output

Grading Rubric: Part (A) = 4 points, Part (B) = 5 points

Part (A) Components of a good answer:

(i) Identification of the output at which price or marginal revenue equals marginal cost at the profit-maximizing output, and

(ii) Identification of long-run equilibrium as zero economic profits (or only normal profits — the exact wording is not important) and an explanation of why there are zero economic profits in long-run equilibrium.

The allocation of 4 points for Part (A) would be 2 for (i), 1 for identification of the zero-profit condition and 1 for the explanation of why zero profits exist in long-run equilibrium.

Part (B) Basic points the answer should make:

(i) The reduction in variable costs would reduce marginal cost, which would cause marginal revenue to equal marginal cost at a higher level of output (in other words, the student should use a marginal revenue and marginal cost argument to motivate the increase in the firm's output caused by the reduction in variable costs).

(ii) The increase in output of the individual firms will result in an increase in industry supply, and

(iii) The increase in industry supply will cause industry output to increase and thus industry output to fall.

The allocation of the 5 points for Part (B) would be 2 for (i), 1 for (ii) and 2 for (iii). If the student simply says that a decrease in costs will cause a producer to increase her output, that would be only 1 point for (i). A student who says that all of this will increase the output of the product and reduce the price of the product without using an increase in supply to motivate these events would receive only 1 point for (iii). If the student starts the answer with a nice clear graph for a monopolist and proceeds to answer the question as if it applied to a monopoly instead of to a perfectly competitive industry, 2 would be the maximum possible number of points that could be given for an answer, and these 2 points would be for an identification of the MR = MC position as a maximum profit position. The rest of the question would not effectively apply to a monopolist.

---

* Actual free-response question from a past AP test. Reprinted by permission of the College Entrance Examination Board, the copyright owner. For limited use by NCEE.

*3. A retail industry is perfectly competitive and in long-run equilibrium.

(A) The wholesale price increases. Explain what happens initially to the retail industry's output and price.

(B) In reaction to the changes above, the government imposes a retail price ceiling on the product at its original price level. What will be the effect of the price ceiling on the quantity demanded and supplied in the retail industry?

(C) Given the effect of the price ceiling on the typical firm's profits, will firms in the retail industry have an incentive to enter or exit this industry in the long run? Explain.

Grading Rubric: Each part is worth 3 points.

Part (A) The components of a good answer include

(i)   an increase in factor input prices increases the cost of production and shifts the industry supply curve to the left (upward)

(ii) equilibrium quantity decreases and

(iii) equilibrium price increases.

Allocate 1 point for each correct part. There does not have to be an explicit recognition that the wholesale price is a cost.

Part (B) Components of a good answer:

(i)   Recognizes that the quantity demanded is greater (movement along the demand curve)

(ii) Recognizes that there is movement along the supply curve (decrease in the quantity supplied)

(iii) Recognizes that what happens in (i) and (ii) creates a disequalibrium situation, which could be identified as a shortage or excess demand. The precise language is not crucial. What is important is that the answer recognizes that the price ceiling has changed an equilibrium situation into one of disequalibrium. Allocate 1 point for each correct part.

Special cases:

(1) If merely shortage is mentioned, give it 1 point.

(2) If the standard price ceiling diagram indicating a shortage or disequalibrium or demand/supply imbalance is given, give the answer 3 points.

---

* Actual free-response question from a past AP test. Reprinted by permission of the College Entrance Examination Board, the copyright owner. For limited use by NCEE.

Part (C) Components of a good answer:

(i)   There is recognition that, since originally the industry was in long-run equilibrium, the increase in costs coupled with the price ceiling results in losses (not merely a decrease in profits).

(ii) The losses will drive firms out of the industry (firms will exit).

Allocating the points:

(1) If the answer indicates that profits are lower and that firms will exit the industry, give 1 point.

(2) If the answer indicates that the firms are earning less than normal profits (or economic losses) as the result of the price ceiling and hence will exit the industry in the long run, give 3 points.

(3) If the answer indicates that firms will exit and states that more than profits have declined, such as "the firm is losing money" or "the firm can now do better than someone else," then 2 points is an appropriate score.

(4) If there is a general statement about exit or entry into an industry correctly related to the profit/loss situation, give 1 point.

*4. A perfectly competitive manufacturing industry is in long-run equilibrium. Energy is an important variable input in the production process, and therefore the price of energy is a variable cost. The price of energy decreases for all firms in the industry.

(A) Explain how and why the decrease in this input price will affect this manufacturing industry's output and price in the short run.

(B) What will be the short-run effect on price, output and profit of a typical firm in this manufacturing industry? Explain.

(C) Will firms enter or exit this manufacturing industry in the long run? Why?

Grading Rubric: Basically the point distribution is 3 points for Part (A), 4 for Part (B) and 2 for Part (C).

Part (A)

The industry's supply curve shifts to the right, resulting in an increase in equilibrium output and a decrease in equilibrium price. The supply curve shifts to the right because of the decrease in input cost (energy prices).

1 point: An explanation that the industry supply curve shifts to the right because of a decrease in costs

1 point: Price declines as a result.

1 point: Quantity increases as a result.

---

* Actual free-response question from a past AP test. Reprinted by permission of the College Entrance Examination Board, the copyright owner. For limited use by NCEE.

Advanced Placement Economics Teacher Resource Manual © National Council on Economic Education, New York, N.Y.

Part (B)

For the firm: The price decline from the industry carries over to the firm, the MC curve must shift to the right, average costs must decline, profit-maximizing output must increase. The profit situation depends on how the student draws the curves. (Yes, I know it depends on the elasticity of the industry demand curve, but they do not!)

1 point: *The firm, as a price taker, has a lowered price equivalent to the decrease in industry price.*

1 point: *Firm produces an increased quantity at MR = MC, as indicated by the new marginal cost curve.*

1 point: *Explains why the marginal cost curve has shifted downward (to the right).*

1 point: *Coherent (consistent) statement about the firm's profits, i.e.*
- *The firm may show an economic profit if price decreases less than average cost decreases OR*
- *Profits may be uncertain since both price and average cost decrease OR*
- *Profits decrease since the price decrease is greater than the average cost decrease, but this condition still requires that output increase.*

The maximum points for Part (B) are 2 if the MC curve doesn't move!!!

Part (C)

Profit situation must be consistent with Part (B) and explanation include entrance if economic profits, uncertainty if profit situation is uncertain and exit if losses.

1 point: *Impact on isndustry, whether firms enter, exit or is uncertain is consistent with previous discussion.*

1 point: *Correct and consistent explanation for assertion about profits*

*5. Peaches and nectarines are substitute goods, and both are produced under conditions of competitive long-run equilibrium.

(A) Joyce, a producer in the peach industry, discovers a technological breakthrough that reduced only the cost of producing peaches. Explain how the change in technology will affect each of the following for Joyce.
   (i)   Quantity of peaches produced
   (ii) The price of peaches
   (iii) Short-run profits

(B) Now assume that all other peach-producing firms adopt the new technology. Explain how the adoption of the new technology will affect each of the following in the peach-producing industry.
   (i)   The price of peaches
   (ii) Quantity of peaches produced

* Actual free-response question from a past AP test. Reprinted by permission of the College Entrance Examination Board, the copyright owner. For limited use by NCEE.

(C) This new technology is not applicable to the production of nectarines. Explain how the changes that occurred in the peach industry will affect each of the following in the nectarine industry.
(i) The price of nectarines
(ii) Quantity of nectarines

Grading Rubric: Part (A) = 3 points

The technological breakthrough, which reduces the costs of producing peaches, lowers the average total cost curve and marginal cost curve, resulting in a greater output at the same price. The reduction in average costs, the increase in Joyce's production and the price remaining constant combine to increase short-run profits.

1 point: An explanation that costs have decreased, shifting the marginal cost curve and resulting in a new profit-maximizing higher level of output

1 point: Price remains constant because of perfect competition. Thus, Joyce cannot affect the market price.

1 point: The student must show, convincingly, that short-run profits increase. One of the following explanations is acceptable.
  - *Price is constant and costs decrease.*
  - *Costs have decreased while total revenue has increased because of constant price and increased input.*
  - *If the student has indicated above that price has decreased, then the student must argue that average costs decrease more than price decreases (or equivalent) to get an increase in Joyce's profits.*

Grading Rubric: Part (B) = 2 points

The new technology spreads to the entire peach industry, resulting in a rightward shift of the industry supply curve. Price decreases and quantity increases.

1 point: For indicating graphically or verbally that the industry supply curve shifts to the right.

1 point: For equilibrium price and quantity effects. $1/2$ point for price decrease and $1/2$ point for quantity increase

Grading Rubric: Part (C) = 2 points

Given that peaches and nectarines are substitutes, a decrease in the price of peaches results in a decrease in the demand for nectarines. A leftward shift in the demand curve for nectarines results in a decrease in the equilibrium price and quantity.

1 point: For a decrease in demand resulting from the price decrease in peaches and the fact that peaches and nectarines are substitutes. The reason must be given.

$1/2$ point: Decrease in nectarine equilibrium price

$1/2$ point: Decrease in nectarine equilibrium quantity

*6. In the country of Lola, sugar had always been produced in a perfectly competitive industry until a dictator seized power and monopolized the production of sugar.

(A) Draw a graph that shows the output and price the monopolist would choose to maximize profits.

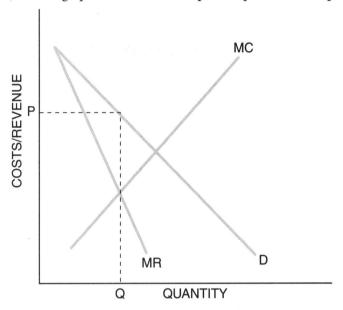

The people of Lola revolt, imprison the dictator and repeal the law restricting the number of sellers of sugar.

(B) Explain two conditions that might lead to an increase in the number of sugar sellers after the repeal of the law.

Conditions that might lead to an increase in the number of sellers:
(i)   Reduction in the barriers to entry
(ii) Profits that were earned by the monopolist
(iii) Returning property rights to original owners

Grading Rubric: 2 points

1 point: For each correct condition, up to a maximum of 2 points (Appealing but irrelevant responses such as technological progress, subsidies and population growth are not acceptable.)

(C) Describe how an individual seller would determine the profit-maximizing output level of sugar if the sugar industry were perfectly competitive.

An individual will determine the profit-maximizing output by equating marginal revenue to marginal cost (MC = MR). For a competitive firm, price equals marginal revenue (P = MR). Price is determined in the market or industry and is not determined by the individual seller. Merely asserting that the firm is a price taker is insufficient for credit.

---

* Actual free-response question from a past AP test. Reprinted by permission of the College Entrance Examination Board, the copyright owner. For limited use by NCEE.

Grading Rubric: 2 points

1 point: Recognizing that output is produced where MC = MR

1 point: Recognizing in some form that P = MR

(D) Given your answers in Parts (A) and (C), is the repeal of the law likely to make the sugar industry more efficient? In your explanation, be sure to include an explanation of economic efficiency.

Under perfect competition, the industry is operating more efficiently. Economic efficiency includes having P = MC (allocative efficiency) and P = min ATC (production efficiency).

Grading Rubric: 2 points

1 point: Some correct definition of economic efficiency (P = MC or P = min ATC)

1 point: Correct explanation that the firm will operate where P = MC and at min ATC

Different Types of Market Structures

Characteristics

Market Structure	Number of Firms	Differentiated or Homogeneous Product	Ease of Entry
Perfect Competition	*Very many*	*H*	*Very easy*
Monopolistic Competition	*Many*	*D*	*Relatively easy*
Oligopoly	*Few*	*H/D*	*Not easy*
Monopoly	*One*	*Only product of its kind (no close substitute)*	*Impossible*

Results

Market Structure	Price-Setting Power	Nonprice Competition	Allocative and Productive Efficiency	Long-Run Profits	Examples
Perfect Competition	*Nil (price taker)*	*None*	*Highly efficient*	*0*	*Doesn't exist; agriculture close*
Monopolistic Competition	*Somewhat*	*Considerable*	*Less efficient than PC*	*0*	*Fast food, retail stores, cosmetics*
Oligopoly	*Limited*	*Considerable for a differentiated oligopoly*	*Less efficient than PC*	*Positive*	*Cars, steel, soft drinks, cereals, computers*
Monopoly	*Absolute (price maker)*	*Somewhat*	*Inefficient*	*High*	*Small-town newspaper, rural gas station*

Marginal Product and Marginal Cost

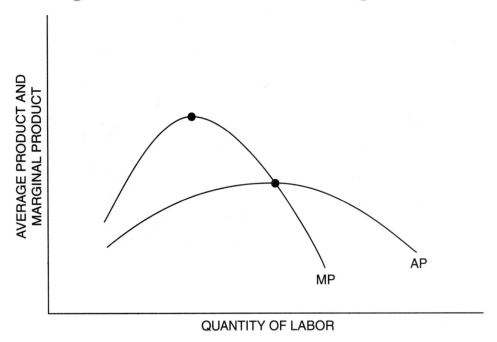

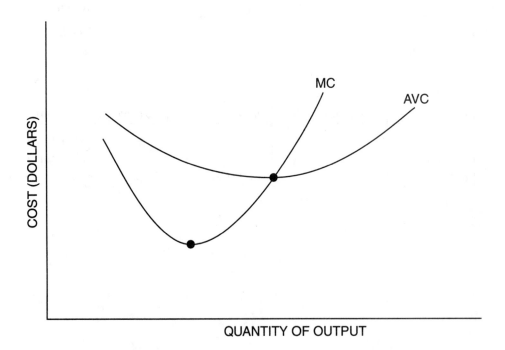

Total Fixed, Total Variable, and Total Costs

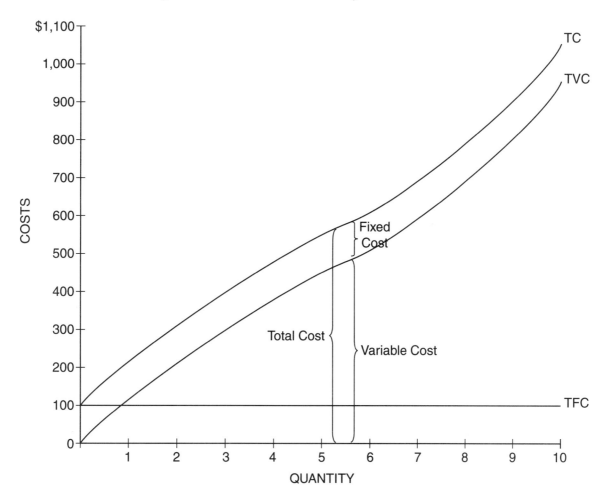

Average Fixed, Average Variable and Average Costs

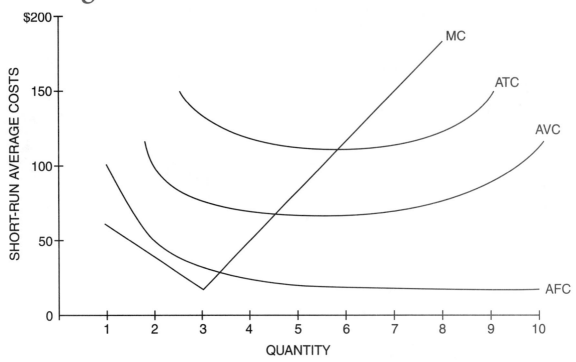

The Perfectly Competitive Firm and Industry in Short-Run Equilibrium

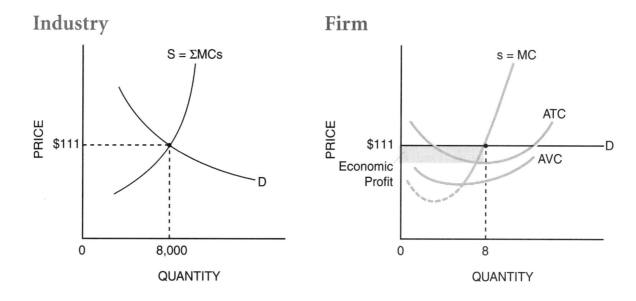

Profit, Loss and Shutdown

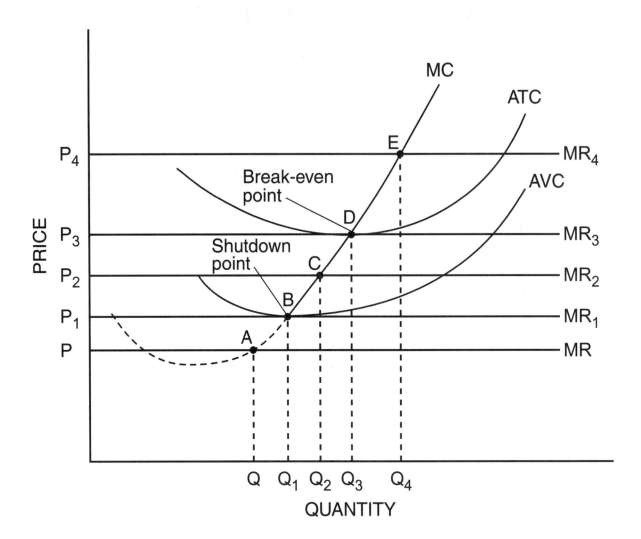

Advanced Placement Economics Teacher Resource Manual © National Council on Economic Education, New York, N.Y.

The Perfectly Competitive Firm in Long-Run Equilibrium

Firm

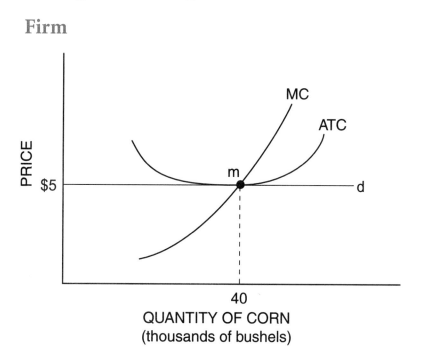

QUANTITY OF CORN
(thousands of bushels)

Industry

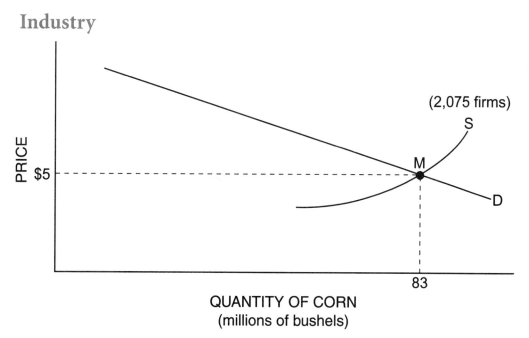

QUANTITY OF CORN
(millions of bushels)

How an Increase in Demand Changes Long-Run Equilibrium for the Firm and Industry

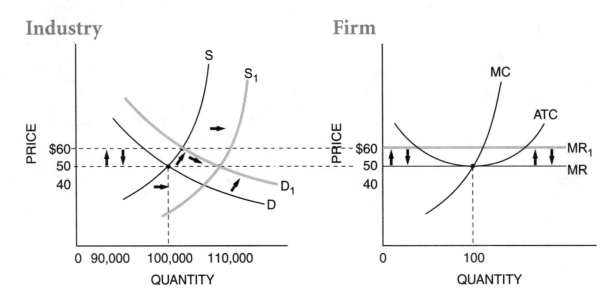

How a Decrease in Demand Changes Long-Run Equilibrium for the Firm and Industry

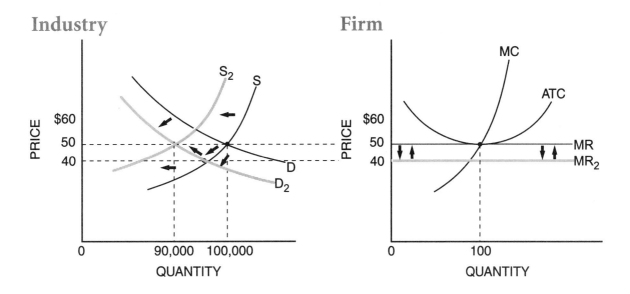

Price and Marginal Revenue for a Monopolist

Demand and Marginal Revenue Curves

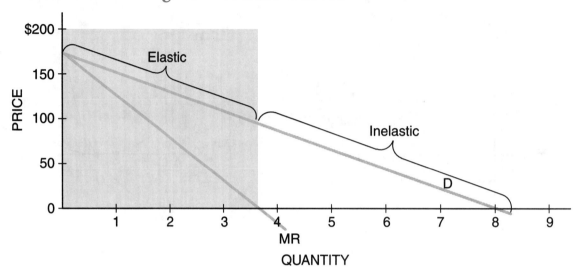

Total Revenue Curve

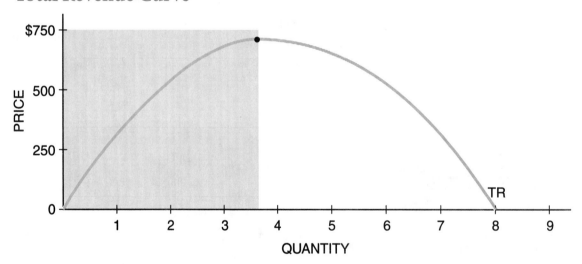

The Profit-Maximizing Position of a Monopoly

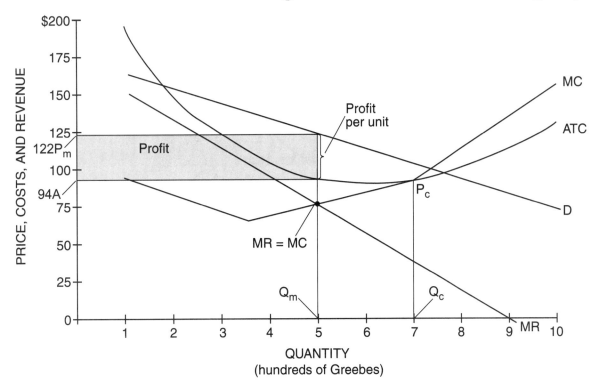

Short-Run and Long-Run Equilibrium for a Monopolistic Competitor

Short-Run Profits

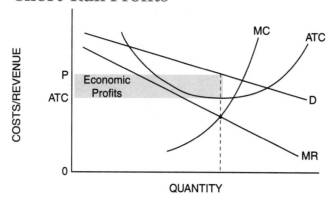

Short-Run Losses

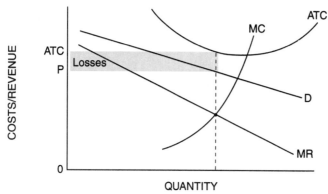

Long-Run Equilibrium

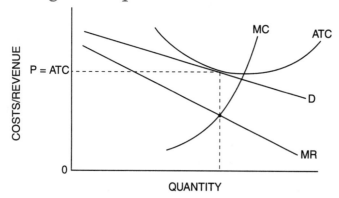

From Campbell R. McConnell and Stanley L. Brue: *Economics,* 12th ed. Copyright © by McGraw-Hill, New York, 1993. All rights reserved.

Microeconomics | Unit 4

Factor Markets

12 class periods or 540 minutes
(16 percent of course time)

Unit Overview

The basic analytical framework for examining factor markets uses concepts similar to those used in the supply and demand unit and the theory of the firm unit. Supply, demand, equilibrium, marginalism and profit-maximizing are all analyzed again in this unit. The only difference is that they are applied to inputs rather than outputs. Students do not have to learn a lot of new concepts in this unit. Rather, they must apply to the factor or resource markets the concepts they already learned in studying product markets.

The demand curve for a resource, however, is derived from the product that the resources can produce. This is important, and every year AP test questions involve examples relating the demand in the product market to the demand in the resource market.

A key concept in the study of factor markets is marginal productivity analysis, which is used to analyze how wages, rents, interest and profits are determined. Following the procedure used in most textbooks, this unit stresses wage determination and uses it as an example to show how the factors of production are priced. The key is that a firm will hire inputs until marginal revenue product equals marginal resource cost.

Another part of this unit covers how wages are determined in a perfectly competitive labor market and in a monopsonistic labor market. The unit analyzes the effects of minimum-wage laws and union activities using both competitive and monopsonistic models.

Although the major emphasis of the AP Exam will be on labor markets, there may also be questions on the other factors of production: land, capital and entrepreneurship.

Some of these activities get fairly detailed; be sure to have your students focus on the key ideas. Activity 51, "Problems Dealing with Factor Markets," will test their knowledge of these concepts.

The Lesson Planner

Lesson 1 returns to the circular flow to show the differences between factor markets and product markets. It also introduces key concepts in factor markets. It uses **Activity 43** and **Visual 4.1**.

Lesson 2 examines how marginal productivity theory determines how resource prices are established. It uses **Activities 44, 45, 46** and **47. Visuals 4.2** and **4.3** help explain this.

Lesson 3 analyzes how wages are determined in competitive labor markets and in monopsonistic labor markets. This lesson uses **Activities 48** and **49** and **Visuals 4.4** and **4.5**.

Lesson 4 discusses the concept of economic rent and uses **Activity 50** and **Visual 4.6**.

Lesson 5 uses thought questions to apply factor-market concepts to a variety of conventional and unconventional situations. It uses **Activity 51**.

Week 1

Day 1

(A) Use the circular flow diagram to distinguish factor markets from product markets.

(B) Have the students complete Activity 43 and discuss the answers.

(C) Use Visual 4.1 to present a lecture on major ideas in factor markets.

Day 2

(A) Use Visual 4.2 to explain how many workers are hired under certain conditions in a firm that is perfectly competitive in the resource and factor markets.

(B) Use Visual 4.3 to discuss how many workers a firm hires if it is perfectly competitive in the factor market but imperfectly competitive in the product market.

(C) Assign Activity 44 as homework.

Day 3

(A) Go over Activity 44.

(B) Have the students complete Activity 45, and discuss the answers.

(C) Assign Activity 46 as homework.

Day 4

(A) Discuss the answers to Activity 46.

(B) Have the students complete Activity 47.

Day 5

(A) Discuss the answers to Activity 47.

(B) Review the basic concepts discussed so far.

Week 2

Day 6

(A) Use Visual 4.4 to show how wages are determined in a competitive labor market for both the industry and firm.

(B) Use Visual 4.5 to show how wages are determined in a monopsonistic labor market.

(C) Have the students complete Activity 48 and discuss it.

Day 7

(A) Have the students complete Activity 49 and discuss it.

(B) Assign Activity 51 for Day 9.

Day 8

(A) Use Visual 4.6 to introduce economic rent.

(B) Have the students complete Activity 50 and discuss it.

Day 9

Go over Activity 51.

Day 10

Review for tests.

Week 3

Day 11

Give free-response test.

Day 12

Give multiple-choice test.

An Introduction to Factor Markets

Introduction and Description

Students can understand factor or resource markets better if they gain an overall perspective before getting into the details of marginal productivity theory. In this lesson, the students learn that a firm is both a seller in product markets and a buyer in factor markets. This lesson also brings out some key ideas to give structure to the lessons that follow.

Objectives

1. Describe the difference between *factor markets* and *product markets.*
2. Describe the difference between a *monopsony* and a *monopoly.*
3. Provide examples of what is bought and sold in a product market and in a factor market.
4. Obtain an overview of the factor market unit.

Time Required

One class period or 45 minutes

Materials

1. Activity 43
2. Visual 4.1

Procedure

1. Use the circular flow diagram in Activity 43 to introduce the difference between product markets and factor markets.

2. Have the students complete Activity 43, and discuss the answers.

3. Use Visual 4.1 to present an overview of factor markets.

"As the 'Circular Flow' Turns"

Part A

1. The circular flow diagram in Figure 43.1 provides a visual representation of economic activity between product and factor markets. Study the diagram and then fill in the table on the top of the next page by determining

   ■ whether the activity takes place in the product or factor *market.*

   ■ what the *role* of the participant is in terms of supply or demand.

   ■ whether the *price* is a product price, a wage, interest or rent.

Activity	Market	Role	Price
Cashier at work	*Factor*	*Supply*	*Wage*
A student buying a hamburger	*Product*	*Demand*	*Product price*
A business paying rent	*Factor*	*Demand*	*Rent*
A firm hiring workers	*Factor*	*Demand*	*Wage*
A firm selling T-shirts	*Product*	*Supply*	*Product price*

Part B

2. A study announces increased cancer risk from drinking coffee.

Primary market	*Product*	Other market	*Factor*
Affects supply or demand	*Demand*	Affects supply or demand	*Demand*
Influence on price (increase / decrease)	*Decrease*	Influence on price (increase / decrease)	*Decrease*

3. There is an increase in the number of people looking for work.

Primary market	*Factor*	Other market	*Product*
Affects supply or demand	*Supply*	Affects supply or demand	*Supply*
Influence on price (increase / decrease)	*Decrease*	Influence on price (increase / decrease)	*Decrease*

4. Price in the labor market is called a ___*wage*___ .

How Resource Prices Are Determined: Marginal Productivity Theory

Introduction and Description

Marginal productivity theory is the heart of the factor market unit. Students must master the details of marginal productivity and complex terminology such as *marginal physical product, marginal revenue product, marginal resource cost* and the *MRP = MRC* rule before they can grasp the main concepts. Furthermore, the students must understand that the demand for a resource is derived from the demand for the goods and services produced by that resource. Finally, the students must understand how a firm hires resources when more than one resource is involved. The material covered in this lesson is the most heavily emphasized among the factor-market questions on the AP test.

Objectives

1. Define *derived demand, marginal revenue product, marginal physical product* and *marginal resource cost.*
2. Given data, construct a marginal physical product schedule and a marginal revenue product schedule for a resource purchased in a perfectly competitive resource market when the product is sold in a perfectly competitive product market.
3. Given data, construct a marginal physical product schedule and a marginal revenue product schedule for a resource purchased in a perfectly competitive resource market when the product is sold in an imperfectly competitive product market.
4. State the principle employed by a profit-maximizing firm to determine how much of a resource it will employ.
5. Given data, determine how much of a resource the firm will employ and what price it will pay.
6. Given data, state and use the principle employed by a firm to develop the least-cost profit-maximizing combination of resources.
7. Predict the effect of various events on the demand for a resource.

Time Required

Four class periods or 180 minutes

Materials

1. Activities 44, 45, 46 and 47
2. Visuals 4.2 and 4.3

Procedure

1. Use Visual 4.2 to explain how many workers a firm will hire if it is perfectly competitive in both the resource market and the factor market. Organize your lecture around questions such as these:

   (A) What is marginal physical product?

   (B) Why does marginal physical product decline as input increases?

   (C) What is marginal revenue product?

   (D) How is marginal revenue product calculated?

   (E) Why does marginal revenue product decline as input increases?

2. Explain the profit-maximizing rule for employing resources: MRP = MRC.

3. Now use Visual 4.3 to discuss how a firm maximizes profits if it is a perfect competitor in the resource market but sells in an imperfectly competitive market. Ask questions such as these:

   (A) What is the evidence that this is an imperfectly competitive product market?

   (B) Why does the MRP of the imperfectly competitive firm fall more rapidly than the MRP of the perfect competitor?

   (C) What are the implications of this?

4. Still using Visual 4.3, ask how many workers would be hired if the wage were

   $13.95 *One worker* $11.95 *Two workers*

   $9.95 *Two workers* $7.95 *Three workers*

5. Ask: Given the same costs, what can we conclude about the number of workers hired in perfectly competitive markets compared with imperfectly competitive product markets? *More workers will be hired under perfectly competitive product markets.*

6. Assign Activity 44 as homework.

7. Discuss the answers to Activity 44.

8. Have the students complete Activity 45.

9. Go over Activity 45. In discussing the answers, be sure to review these points:

   (A) Why is the MRP or the demand for a resource downward sloping?

   (B) The factors that can shift the demand for a resource:
       (i) Change in the product price
       (ii) Change in productivity
       (iii) Changes in the price of substitute or complementary resources depending on the substitution effect and the output effect

   (C) The determinants of the elasticity of resource demand:
       (i) Rate of MRP decline
       (ii) Elasticity of product demand
       (iii) Ease of resource substitutability
       (iv) The proportion of total costs that the resource represents

10. Assign Activity 46 as homework.

11. Discuss the answers to Activity 46. In the discussion, be sure to make the main point that a monopoly firm will hire fewer workers than a perfectly competitive firm. Also make sure the students understand that these examples compare monopoly and perfectly competitive firms in the product markets even though the analysis is in the factor markets.

12. Have the students complete Activity 47, and discuss the answers. This is a summary of everything they studied so far and reinforces their learning.

Advanced Placement Economics Teacher Resource Manual © National Council on Economic Education, New York, N.Y.

How Many Workers Should Be Hired?

 Figure 44.2

How Many Workers to Hire per Day for $2 Yo-Yos

Number of Workers Hired (inputs)	Level of Output (number of yo-yos produced per day) (Q)	Marginal Physical Product (MPP)	Price at Which Yo-yos Can Be Sold	Total Revenue (P x Q)	Marginal Revenue Product (MPP x MR)
0	0	—	$2.00	$0	—
1	20	20	2.00	40 = 2 x 20	$40
2	50	30	2.00	100	60
3	70	20	2.00	140	40
4	85	15	2.00	170	30
5	95	10	2.00	190	20
6	100	5	2.00	200	10

1. Why does the number of extra yo-yos produced decrease as more workers are hired?
   Because of diminishing marginal returns

2. If the wage is $30 per day, how many workers should Acme hire? Why?
   Acme should hire four workers. Profit is maximized where MRP = wage. At four workers, MRP is $30 and the wage is $30. At five workers, MRP is $20 and the wage is $30. It does not pay to hire the fifth worker.

3. If the demand for yo-yos increases so that Acme can sell as many yo-yos as it wants for $3 each, what effect will this have on Acme's level of employment?
   It will now hire five workers. At $3, MRP for five workers is $30 rather than $20 (P x MPP) so the higher price makes it profitable to hire the fifth worker.

4. To make as much profit as possible, in this case a firm should hire an additional worker as long as that worker's ___*marginal revenue product*___ is greater than his or her ___*wage*___.

The Derived Demand for a Resource

The key to understanding resource prices in factor markets is to see the relationship between demand in the factor market and demand in the product market. You should review the definitions of marginal physical product (MPP), marginal revenue (MR) and marginal revenue product (MRP).

The demand for a resource (land, labor, capital or entrepreneurship) is called *derived demand* because it is derived (comes) from the demand for the goods and services that are produced by these resources.

1. Complete Figure 45.1. The yo-yo manufacturer operates in a perfectly competitive factor market and in a perfectly competitive product market. In a perfectly competitive factor market, market supply and demand determine the price of the factors of production. In a perfectly competitive product market, supply and demand determine the price of the product.

Figure 45.1
Data for a Yo-Yo Manufacturer

Units of Resource	Total Product	Marginal Physical Product (MPP)	Price at Which Yo-Yos Can Be Sold	Total Revenue (P x Q)	Marginal Revenue Product (MPP x MR)
0	0	—	$2.00	$0	—
1	8	8	2.00	16	16
2	14	6	2.00	28	12
3	19	5	2.00	38	10
4	23	4	2.00	46	8
5	26	3	2.00	52	6
6	28	2	2.00	56	4
7	29	1	2.00	58	2

The marginal revenue product (MRP) shows the additional revenue the firm will receive from the additional output produced by adding another unit of the factor / resource. This can be calculated as ΔTR / ΔResource or MPP x P. This is the firm's demand curve for the resource.

2. Use the answers in the last column of Figure 45.1 to graph marginal revenue product on Figure 45.2. Label the MRP curve MRP = D. Plot each number on the line, not at the midpoint.

Figure 45.2
Price and Quantity for a Resource

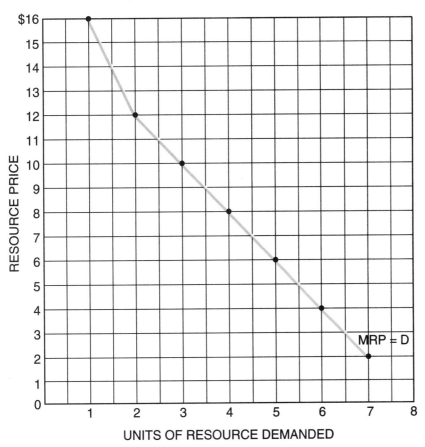

3. MRP depends on two variables. One is marginal physical product (MPP), sometimes referred to as *marginal product*. The second variable is the price of the good or service being produced. For each of the following situations, identify whether MPP of the factor or P of the product is affected and indicate whether the demand for a resource would increase or decrease.

Situation	Marginal Physical Product	Price	Demand for labor (inc. / dec.)
(A) A new yo-yo machine increases productivity of labor	X		*Increase*
(B) The price of yo-yos increases		X	*Increase*
(C) Better training increases the output of yo-yo labor	X		*Increase*
(D) The demand for yo-yos increases		X	*Increase*
(E) New technology increases the output of yo-yo labor	X		*Increase*
(F) Consumers become sick of yo-yos		X	*Decrease*

The Only (Yo-Yo) Game in Town

 Figure 46.2

How Many Workers to Hire per Day for Varying Prices of Yo-Yos

Number of Workers Hired (inputs)	Level of Output (number of yo-yos produced per day) (Q)	Marginal Physical Product (MPP)	Price at Which Yo-yos Can Be Sold	Total Revenue (P x Q)	Marginal Revenue Product (change in TR from previous level)
0	0	—	$0.00	$0	—
1	20	20	5.00	$100 = $5 x 20	$100
2	50	30	4.00	200	100
3	70	20	3.50	245	45
4	85	15	3.00	255	10
5	95	10	2.00	190	–65
6	100	5	1.00	100	–90

1. How is Acme's demand schedule for labor different now from when it sold all its product for $2 each? *Acme's demand schedule for labor, which is its MRP schedule, now declines both because of the law of diminishing returns and because Acme must lower its price to sell more. The demand for labor is less elastic because the demand for Acme's product is less elastic. The demand curve now is steeper.*

2. Acme's decision-making rule is the same: If an additional worker adds more to revenue than cost, this worker should be hired. If Acme can still hire workers at $30 per day, how many workers should Acme hire? Why? *Three workers. Beyond this level, workers do not generate enough additional revenue to cover the cost of hiring them.*

3. How does the number of workers hired by the monopolist differ from the number in Activity 45? *It hires fewer workers.*

Factor Market Pricing

Suppose that the Acme Belt Company (ABC) is a price taker in both the input and output markets — that is, it sells belts in a perfectly competitive market and purchases labor in a perfectly competitive market.

Part A

1. Fill in the blank spaces in Figure 47.1. Note that marginal data are placed between levels of employment.

 Figure 47.1

Labor Demand for the Perfectly Competitive Firm

Employment Number of Workers (L)	Total Output Per Day (Q)	Marginal Physical Product (MPP) ($\Delta Q / \Delta L$)	Marginal Revenue Product (MPP × P) $P_B = \$2.00$	$P_B = \$2.50$
0	0		—	—
1	10	10	$20.00	$ 25.00
2	30	20	40.00	50.00
3	70	40	80.00	100.00
4	105	35	70.00	87.50
5	135	30	60.00	75.00
6	160	25	50.00	62.50
7	180	20	40.00	50.00
8	195	15	30.00	37.50
9	205	10	20.00	25.00
10	205	0	0	0
11	195	−10	−20.00	−25.00

An individual firm's factor demand curve is restricted to a range of the MRP_L curve that is downward sloping, beginning at L = 3 for ABC.

2. If the marginal resource cost, or wage, faced by ABC is $20 and the price of belts is $2 per belt, then the quantity of labor demanded by ABC is __9__.

3. If the marginal resource cost, or wage, faced by ABC is $20 and the price of belts is $2.50 per belt, then the quantity of labor demanded by ABC is __9__.

Part B

Now suppose that ABC is one of 1,000 identical firms that purchase labor in this perfectly competitive labor market. To get the market demand curve for labor, we need to sum over each individual firm's MRP_L curve at each given wage. Given our assumption that the firms are identical, we can simply multiply the quantity of labor demanded by a single firm by the number of firms in the market. In Figure 47.2, data are for P = $2.00 and P = $2.50.

Figure 47.2

The Labor Market

	P = $2.00				P = $2.50		
Wage	Number of Workers Demanded By Firm ABC ($P_b = \$2$)	Number of Workers Demanded In the Market ($P_b = \$2$)	Number of Workers Supplied	Wage	Number of Workers Demanded By Firm ABC ($P_b = \$2.50$)	Number of Workers Demanded In the Market ($P_b = \$2.50$)	Number of Workers Supplied
$20	9	9,000	3,000	$25.00	9	9,000	3,500
30	8	8,000	4,000	37.50	8	8,000	4,750
40	7	7,000	5,000	50.00	7	7,000	6,000
50	6	6,000	6,000	55.00	6.5	6,500	6,500
60	5	5,000	7,000	62.50	6	6,000	7,250
70	4	4,000	8,000	75.00	5	5,000	8,500
80	3	3,000	9,000	87.50	4	4,000	9,750
				100.00	3	3,000	11,000

4. If the wage is $20 and the price of belts is $2 per belt, then the quantity of labor demanded in the market is 1,000 x __9__ = __9,000__ units of labor.

Figure 47.3 shows the market labor supply curve as well as the firm and market demand curves when P_B = \$2. The supply curve shows that, *ceteris paribus*, as the wage increases, more workers are willing to supply their labor to this market, and existing workers in this market are willing to supply more labor.

Figure 47.3
Market and Firm Demand for Labor

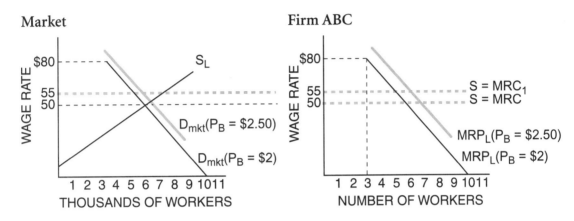

5. On the graphs in Figure 47.3 and the table in Figure 47.2, the equilibrium wage in the market is ___$50___. The equilibrium quantity of labor in this market is ___6,000___ workers.

6. Given that this is a competitive labor market, ABC faces a marginal resource cost, or wage, of ___$50___.

7. Because ABC can purchase as much or as little labor as it wants without affecting the market, it is said to face a perfectly elastic labor supply curve. Draw the labor supply faced by the firm in the *Firm ABC* graph above.

8. Using a different color pen or pencil, graph ABC's and the market's labor demand curves in Figure 47.3, given that the price of a belt has increased to \$2.50.

9. Designate the new market equilibrium based on Figure 47.2. The equilibrium wage in the market is now ___$55___. The equilibrium quantity of labor in this market is now___6,500___ workers.

10. What has happened to the labor supply curve faced by the firm? *It shifted up to a higher wage rate.*

Competition vs. Monopsony: The Effects of Resource Market Structure on Wages and Employment

Introduction and Description

Until now, the students have studied only the perfectly competitive resource market. What happens if the resource market is not perfectly competitive? This lesson compares *monopsony* with perfect competition. To illustrate the differences between these markets, the students study the effects of minimum wages and union activities in competitive and monopsonistic markets.

Objectives

1. Understand what determines the wage rate and level of employment in competitive labor markets.
2. Understand what determines the wage rate and level of employment in monopsonistic labor markets.
3. Compare the wage level and employment level in a competitive labor market with the wage level and employment level in a monopsonistic labor market.
4. Analyze the effects of a minimum-wage law in competitive and monopsonistic labor markets.
5. Analyze the effects of labor-union tactics in competitive and monopsonistic labor markets.

Time Required

Two class periods or 90 minutes

Materials

1. Activities 48 and 49
2. Visuals 4.4 and 4.5

Procedure

1. Use Visual 4.4 to show how wages are determined in a competitive labor market for both the industry and the firm. Ask questions such as these:

   (A) What determines the wage in a competitive labor market?

(B) Why is the supply curve for an individual firm in a competitive labor market horizontal or perfectly elastic?

(C) Why is the market supply curve for labor upward sloping?

(D) Why are the demand curve for labor and the MRP for labor the same thing?

(E) Why is the market demand curve for labor downward sloping?

2. Use Visual 4.5 to show how wages are determined in a monopsonistic labor market. Ask questions such as these:

   (A) Why is the MRC higher than the firm's supply of labor curve?

   (B) What would be the wage level and employment level if this firm were buying labor in a perfectly competitive market?

   (C) What quantity of labor would the firm purchase in a monopsonistic labor market? Why?

   (D) What is the wage level in a monopsonistic labor market? Why?

3. Have the students complete Activity 48 in class and discuss the answers.

4. Have the students complete Activity 49 in class and discuss the answers.

5. Using the answers to Activity 49, discuss the effects of unions on competitive and monopsonistic markets with questions such as these:

   (A) Which of the union goals has the most favorable impact on existing employees? *To increase wages and employment of union members. Hence any strategy that attempts to increase the demand for labor would be most favorable for existing members. Yet it may be argued that collective-bargaining strategies that negotiate a wage rate higher than the previous equilibrium may be beneficial to employees but sacrifice the opportunities of future union members or members with the least seniority.*

(B) Which of the union goals is most restrictive in the number of people who might want to enter the labor market? *To restrict the number of employees in the profession. Hence state certification requirements and occupational licensing restrict future entry into the professions.*

(C) Which union goal seems to have an effect similar to a minimum wage? *When unions attempt to negotiate wages in competitive labor markets above the equilibrium wage rate. Some members may receive a higher wage rate but only at the cost of employment of other members.*

(D) Which union goal has the largest positive effect on the wage rate and the number of laborers employed? *Increasing the demand for labor, either by increasing the product price or by increasing the productivity of workers. Given that labor unions are only a small share of the product market, it is not probable that they can easily influence the*

demand for — and hence the price of — the product. However, some unions have supported advertisements for their products. The increase in productivity of laborers is also difficult to accomplish, given that the increases in productivity are the result of changes in technology and the amounts of capital used in the production process. Education and training — investments in human capital — can also increase productivity. Labor unions have little influence on shifts in the demand curve because of these factors.

(E) "Unions can increase wage levels and employment." To what extent is this claim true? *All other things equal, the extent to which unions can increase wage levels and employment depends on the type of labor market. In bargaining for wages, labor unions would have more success in monopsonistic labor markets because they are able to increase wages and employment opportunities. They are least successful in competitive labor markets, where a union may bargain for a wage rate above equilibrium, causing some unemployment. Yet unions that attempt to increase the overall demand for labor by promoting increases in productivity of their members may positively influence wages and employment.*

How Wages Are Determined in Competitive Labor Markets

❋ **Figure 48.1**
Wages and Labor

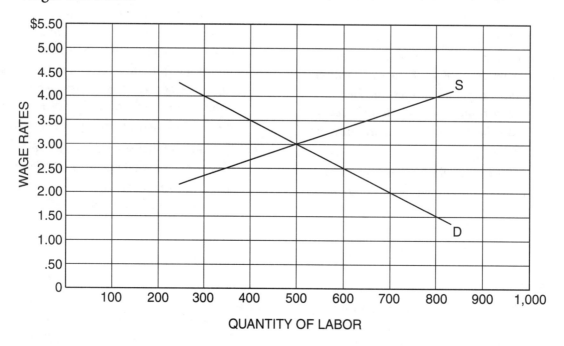

Use Figure 48.1, which shows the supply and demand curves for a perfectly competitive labor market in a perfectly competitive product market, to answer these questions:

1. What two factors affect the demand for labor? *The price of the product produced by that labor and the productivity of the labor*

2. How does marginal revenue product affect the demand for labor? *A firm will hire labor until the wage = MRP. The perfectly competitive firm cannot control the wage; so where wage = MRP, the amount of labor demanded is determined. The MRP is the demand curve for labor. A firm will hire workers as long as the workers contribute more to TR than to TC. To calculate how much a worker contributes to TR, multiply the MPP of the factor by the price of the good in the output market, which is MRP. MRP and demand are necessarily the same.*

3. Why is the demand curve for labor downward sloping? *Because under perfect competition the product price is constant, diminishing marginal returns is the reason the demand curve is downward sloping.*

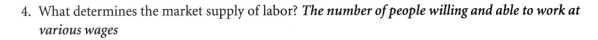

4. What determines the market supply of labor? *The number of people willing and able to work at various wages*

5. Why is the market supply curve for labor upward sloping? *More people are willing to work if they are paid more. The cost of not working, or leisure, increases.*

6. What is the equilibrium wage in this labor market? __*$3.00*__

7. How many workers will be hired in this labor market? __*500*__

8. If a minimum-wage law raises the minimum wage to $4.00 an hour, what quantity of labor will be supplied? __*800*__

9. At a minimum wage of $4.00 an hour, what quantity of labor will be demanded? __*300*__

10. How many workers would be laid off or would lose their jobs because of this minimum wage? __*200*__

11. How many workers entered the labor force seeking a job because of this minimum wage? __*300*__

12. If the demand for labor were more inelastic, would more or fewer workers lose their jobs because of this minimum wage? __*Fewer*__

13. Would skilled or unskilled workers be more likely to lose their jobs because of a minimum-wage law? __*Unskilled*__

14. Who benefits from the minimum wage? *Skilled workers and unskilled workers who keep their jobs*

15. Who is hurt by the minimum wage? *Unskilled workers who lose their jobs*

16. Do you favor a higher minimum wage? Why or why not? *Answers will vary. Although the minimum wage does lead to higher wages for unskilled workers who keep their jobs, it hurts unskilled workers who lose their jobs. The least skilled and youngest workers are hurt most. Victims of discrimination are also hurt by the minimum-wage laws because a large pool of unskilled workers allows employers to pick and choose among the available job hunters.*

The Effects of Unions on Wages and Employment in Competitive and Monopsonistic Labor Markets

Assume two labor markets: Market 1 is competitive, and Market 2 is monopsonistic. Assume each market is in an initial equilibrium illustrated by the graphs. Assume further that a union exists in each of the markets.

For each scenario below, you have been given the market supply and demand curves for a labor market before a union is formed. For each scenario and each market, identify how the actions of the union affect the supply and demand curves. Then indicate whether, as a result of these actions, the wage rate and level of employment will be higher, lower or indeterminate.

SCENARIO 1: The union is successful in requiring that new teachers pass a state competency test to be employed.

Figure 49.1
Competency Test Required

Competitive

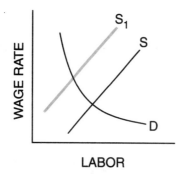

Wage Rate _Higher_
Employment _Lower_

Monopsonistic

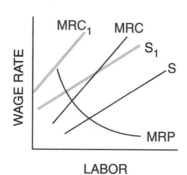

Wage Rate _Higher_
Employment _Lower_

SCENARIO 2: The labor union conducts a successful national advertising campaign urging people to buy union-made goods.

 Figure 49.2
National Advertising Campaign

Competitive

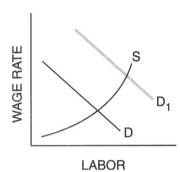

Wage Rate *Higher*
Employment *Higher*

Monopsonistic

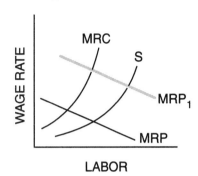

Wage Rate *Higher*
Employment *Higher*

SCENARIO 3: The labor union educates workers in new methods of production, which leads to increased productivity.

 Figure 49.3
Increased Productivity

Competitive

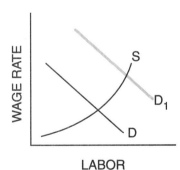

Wage Rate *Higher*
Employment *Higher*

Monopsonistic

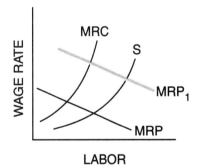

Wage Rate *Higher*
Employment *Higher*

SCENARIO 4: The labor union promotes national legislation to increase quotas and/or tariffs on foreign competitors.

 Figure 49.4
Quotas/Tariffs on Foreign Competition

Competitive   Monopsonistic

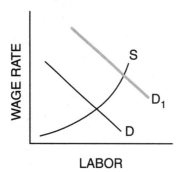   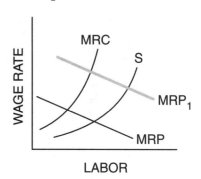

Wage Rate *Higher*   Wage Rate *Higher*
Employment *Higher*   Employment *Higher*

SCENARIO 5: The labor union bargains for and wins an increase in the wage rate above the equilibrium wage rate.

 Figure 49.5
Wage Increase Above Equilibrium Rate

Competitive   Monopsonistic

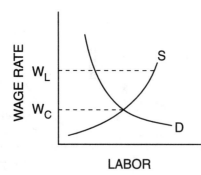   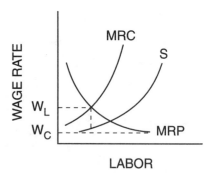

Wage Rate *Higher*   Wage Rate *Higher*
Employment *Lower*   Employment *Indeterminate*

SCENARIO 6: The labor union signs an agreement with employers that forces employers to hire only union members who have gone through the union's apprenticeship program.

 Figure 49.6
Only Union Members Hired

Competitive

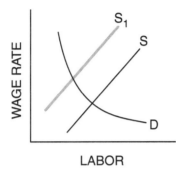

Wage Rate *Higher*
Employment *Lower*

Monopsonistic

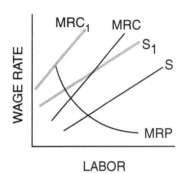

Wage Rate *Higher*
Employment *Lower*

Economic Rent and Return for Other Factors of Production

Introduction and Description

The factor-market questions on the AP test will place the heaviest emphasis on labor markets because labor accounts for almost 75 percent of payments to factors of production. However, there also may be questions on payments to other factors of production. Although rent is the smallest payment to any factor of production, the concept of economic rent provides insights into any input, such as land, whose supply is fixed. Interest rates, determined by the supply of and demand for borrowed funds, are important influences on the ability of firms to raise money for business investment. Economic profits create the incentive in a capitalist economy and influence both the use and allocation of resources.

Objectives

1. Define *economic rent*, and explain what determines the amount of economic rent paid.
2. Explain why the owners of land do not all receive the same amount of economic rent.
3. Apply the concept of economic rent (economic surplus) to the salaries of professional athletes.
4. Describe why the interest rate is the return on borrowed funds.
5. Define *economic profit* and distinguish between normal profit and economic profit.

Time Required

One class period or 45 minutes

Materials

1. Activity 50
2. Visual 4.6

Procedure

1. Use Visual 4.6 to explain what determines economic rent. Ask questions such as these:

    (A) Why is the supply curve for land vertical?

    (B) What determines the amount of rent if the supply of land is perfectly inelastic (vertical)?

    (C) What effect will an increase in the demand for land have on the amount of land available?

2. Explain the unique aspect of economic rent. Here is one approach to this explanation:

The determination of rent, like wages, occurs within a context of supply and demand factors and institutional circumstances.

Rent is usually accorded special treatment because of the inelasticity of the supply of land and other natural resources. This aspect of natural resources has attracted the attention of economists since the days of the Physiocrats and has led to controversial issues in economic theory and public policy (such as Henry George's single-tax movement, urban-renewal programs, and "obscene profits" of landlords and the oil industry).

The major theoretical point for the students to understand is that when the supply of a factor is perfectly inelastic, the price paid to that factor cannot provide an incentive to produce more. Thus, economists refer to such a factor as a *surplus* or as *economic rent*.

The amount of economic rent received by owners of land and other factors fixed in supply is determined by the productivity of each factor.

Henry George and others argued that, since a tax on land or any other factor with a fixed supply doesn't affect the amount of that factor available to society, all economic rent could be taxed away with no cost to society.

Critics of this theory point out that rent is a cost to individuals because the supply of land *for any one use* is not perfectly inelastic. Users of land, just as with other factors of production, must bid the land away from alternative uses. Thus, rent is merely a cost of production.

One approach to dealing with this topic is to do the following:

(A) Make the definitions clear for the meanings of *fixed supply* and *economic surplus.*

(B) Minimize the theoretical discussion, which can become extremely complex.

(C) Focus on discussions of public-policy questions that involve considerations of equity, efficiency and attitudes about wealth. For example, the following scenarios could be topics for this discussion or debate:

Agricultural land near a large city was selling for $3,000 an acre last year. Now a subdivision is being developed on this land, and it is selling for $50,000 an acre. Why did the price rise so dramatically? Do you think it is fair that the owners of this land reaped such a large and sudden return for no effort on their part? *Some students will think that when an investor buys anything, he or she is taking a risk of a loss and a chance of a gain. If a purchase increases in value, the investor is entitled to the benefit. Other students will think that dumb luck should not be rewarded so generously. This is an example of a return that is a mixture of rent and profits — and possible interest and wages.*

A professional basketball player earns $850,000 a year. The next-best alternative for this player might be as a high school coach for $40,000 a year. Should $810,000 of his current salary be considered wages or rent (an economic surplus)? If a large part of the wages and salaries of many highly paid athletes, entertainers and others is considered as economic-surplus payments (not necessary to attract people into a particular line of work), does this suggest that such incomes should be taxed heavily? *Again, answers will vary. The major point is probably not whether answers are yes or no but whether economic reasoning is used in reaching a conclusion.*

3. Assign Activity 50.

4. Discuss the answers to Activity 50.

5. Discuss the role of interest rates in a market economy. Make these points:

(A) The interest rate is the price paid for the use of money (loanable funds).

(B) Like other prices, the price of money (an interest rate) is determined by the supply of and demand for loanable funds.

(C) A real interest rate is the nominal rate of interest minus inflation.

(D) Real interest rates influence investment decisions.

6. Discuss the role of profits in a market economy.

The Story of Economic Rent: What Do Land, Athletics and Government Have in Common?

Economic rent is defined as a return over and above opportunity cost or the "normal" return necessary to keep a resource in its current use. Economic rent is any payment made to a resource above the amount necessary to induce any amount of the resource to be employed. Economic rent can also be defined as the amount over and above the opportunity cost necessary to keep the resource in its current use.

Part A

1. Assume that the quantity of a certain type of available land is 300,000 acres and the demand for this land is the data given in Figure 50.1.

Figure 50.1
Demand for Land at Varying Prices

Pure Land Rent Per Acre	Acres of Land Demanded
$350	100,000
300	200,000
250	300,000
200	400,000
150	500,000
100	600,000
50	700,000

(A) Plot on Figure 50.2 the supply and demand curves for this land.

(B) The pure rent per acre on this land will be __$250__.

(C) The total quantity of land rented will be __300,000__ acres.

(D) If landowners were taxed at a rate of $250 per acre for their land, the pure rent on this land after taxes would be __$0__, but the number of acres rented would be __300,000__.

Figure 50.2
Plotting Demand Curves for Land

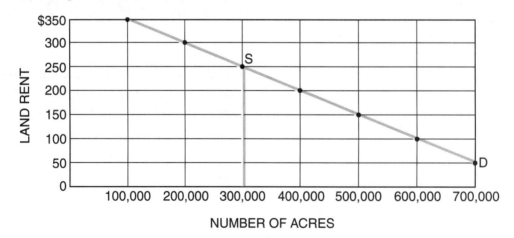

2. Figure 50.3 gives the yields, or output per acre, in bushels on three grades of land resulting from varied amounts of expenditure on workers, fertilizer, etc. (Use only these data; don't try to estimate what would happen if other amounts are expended.) To answer the questions below, apply your marginal-analysis skills to the data in the table.

Figure 50.3
Yield per Acre on Three Grades of Land

| | Expenditure per Acre | | | | | | |
Land Quality	$0	$100	$200	$300	$400	$500	$600
Grade A Land	0	175	325	450	525	575	615
Grade B Land	0	160	290	375	445	490	525
Grade C Land	0	120	210	290	330	360	385

(A) If the product sells for $1.00 a bushel, how many dollars per acre should be spent on

Grade A land? __*$300*__   Grade B land? __*$200*__   Grade C land? __*$100*__

(B) In a competitive market, what do you think the rental price would be for an acre of

Grade A land? __*$150*__   Grade B land? __*$90*__   Grade C land? __*$20*__

(Note: Economic rent is defined as a return over and above opportunity cost of the "normal" return necessary to keep a resource in its current use. Using this logic, you can approach Question 2(B) by asking: "What is the most someone would be willing to pay for the right to use an acre of each type of land?")

Part B

Land is not the only resource with a fixed supply. For example, the supply of a star athlete is fixed. Suppose Tiger Woods earns $50 million a year.

3. Assume that Tiger Woods' next-best option after playing golf is to work as a high school teacher and coach. He could earn $50,000 a year in this job. How much economic rent is involved in Tiger's salary as a golfer? __*$4,950,000*__

4. Now assume that someone else is as good at soccer as Tiger Woods is at golf. If this person wanted to play soccer in the United States, would this player receive more or less economic rent than Tiger does for playing golf? Support your answer. *The soccer player would receive less economic rent. Professional soccer is not as popular as golf in the United States.*

Analyzing Factor-Market Concepts

Introduction and Description

This lesson helps the students to apply their knowledge of factor markets to conventional and unconventional situations. Activity 51 can be assigned as homework or completed in groups. It is good practice for the complex application questions that are emphasized on the AP test.

Objective

1. Use factor-market concepts to analyze a variety of issues.

Time Required

One class period or 45 minutes

Materials

Activity 51

Procedure

1. You may assign Activity 51 as homework a few days before it is due. An alternative is to have the students work on the problems in groups.

2. Discuss the answers.

Problems Dealing with Factor Markets

Part A

Answer the questions and briefly explain your answers. Feel free to use diagrams to illustrate your points.

1. Why are some basketball players paid more than brain surgeons? Explain using the concept of marginal revenue product. *A professional basketball team will pay for a player until MRP = the wage. A star player can generate a lot of extra revenue for a team. People place a high value on watching basketball relative to the number of basketball players. They place a high value on brain surgery as well, but not in comparison with the availability of brain surgeons.*

2. True, false or uncertain, and explain why? "If it were not for unions pushing up wages, we'd all be working 60 hours a week for $100 a month just like people did a century ago." *False. Although unions may raise the wages of their members, the biggest factor in increasing real wages is higher productivity. Increases in real wages depend on increases in real output. Unions may have been responsible for social legislation, but increasing MRP is much more important.*

3. Use a graph to explain why firms that want to maximize their profits use a resource until the marginal revenue product of this resource equals the marginal resource cost. *If MRP is greater than MRC, the firm will improve its profits by hiring the resource. If MRP is less than MRC, the firm will be adding more to TC than to TR by hiring the extra resource. Thus profits will decrease. The firm will maximize profits where MRP = MRC. This logic is the same in the product market: A firm maximizes profits where MR = MC.*

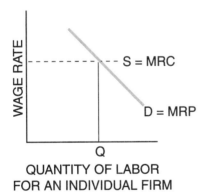

This graph is the simplest way to illustrate this. When MRP > MRC, it pays to hire an additional worker. When MRP < MRC, it does not pay to hire an additional worker. Therefore, the firm will hire Q workers.

Note: Students could also illustrate this in a monopsonist labor market, but MRC would be less than supply.

4. True, false or uncertain, and explain why? "American workers who are paid $10 an hour cannot possibly compete with workers who are paid $1 an hour in developing countries."
False, or we would be buying all our goods from developing countries. Americans are paid more because their productivity is higher. Increases in real wages depend on increases in real output.

5. Why might a university pay a Nobel Prize-winning faculty member more than its president? Does this make sense economically for the university? Support your answer.
The Nobel Prize winner increases the reputation of the university and attracts more students, increasing revenue. Therefore, because the MRP of the professor is greater than the MRP of the president, the wage rate of the professor would be greater.

6. What are the effects of a minimum wage that is above the equilibrium wage in a perfectly competitive market? What about in a market in which the employer is a monopsonist? Give an example of a relatively competitive labor market and a less competitive labor market.
In a competitive labor market, a minimum wage increases the number of workers who want to work (quantity supplied) and decreases the amount of workers employers want to employ (quantity demanded). The result is greater unemployment. For a monopsonist, MRC is above the supply curve for labor, and this results in a lower wage and lower employment than if the firm were a perfect competitor in the labor market. Raising the minimum wage will increase employment and wages until the wage becomes greater than the point where MRC = MRP. Most economists believe that labor markets are closer to perfect competition than to monopsony. There are numerous examples of competitive labor markets. An example of a monopsonistic labor market might be a specialized company in a small town or a supplier to a rural military base.

Advanced Placement Economics Teacher Resource Manual © National Council on Economic Education, New York, N.Y.

7. The National Collegiate Athletic Association (NCAA) regulates all college athletics in the United States. It sets the amount of scholarships, the number of scholarships granted and the regulations for recruiting athletes. The NCAA has hundreds of rules regulating intercollegiate athletics.

(A) What effect do these regulations have on who receives the economic rent from college athletics? *They set the level of the athletes' benefits and salaries so the universities receive the economic rent.*

(B) Which colleges have greater incentives to cheat? Why? *Colleges that do not have national academic prestige and cannot recruit against the colleges that do. Colleges with big arenas and stadiums that they need to fill. A star athlete can increase MRP a lot.*

(C) Who would gain if the NCAA could no longer set rules for college athletics? Why? *Probably the athletes who would receive higher salaries and not just standard scholarships. Players in major-revenue sports would be helped, and players in low-revenue sports would be hurt.*

(D) Who would lose if the NCAA could no longer control college athletics? Why? *The universities that would have to pay a wage determined by supply and demand*

(E) True, false or uncertain, and why? "The NCAA is a champion for amateur athletics, and its rules protect the rights of college athletes." *False or uncertain. The NCAA does champion the cause of amateur athletics, but this may benefit the universities more than the athletes. A case can be made that the NCAA is a champion for the majority of amateur athletes, who are not in major-revenue sports. In the absence of the NCAA, athletes who are less successful would not be able to participate. To the extent this is true, the NCAA helps. But successful athletes are harmed by the NCAA in the interest of universities.*

Part B

Figure 51.1 gives you information about a firm operating in a competitive product market. Consider all factors of production fixed, with the exception of labor. The other factors of production cost the firm $50 a day, which may be thought of as a fixed cost. Assume the firm is a profit maximizer.

 Figure 51.1

Firm Operating in a Competitive Product Market

Labor Input (workers per day)	Total Physical Product (units per day)	Marginal Physical Product (units per day)	Marginal Revenue Product ($ per worker)
0	0	—	—
1	22	22	66
2	40	18	54
3	56	16	48
4	70	14	42
5	82	12	36
6	92	10	30
7	100	8	24
8	106	6	18

Fill in the answer blanks or underline the correct words in parentheses.

8. Assume the firm sells its output at $3 per unit. Complete the last two columns in the table.

   (A) If the equilibrium market wage is $36 per day, the firm will hire __5__ workers per day and produce __82__ units of output.

   (B) Given your answer to the preceding question, the firm will have total revenue of __$246__ per day and total cost of __$230__ per day.

   (C) The above will result in a (**profit** / loss) of __$16__ per day.

9. Suppose you work for a firm that sells its output in a monopoly market. Answer the following questions.

   (A) If you hire an additional worker, output goes up by 50 units to 125 units per day. If you want to sell the additional 50 units, you must lower your price from $3 per unit to $2 per unit. What is the wage you would be willing to pay the additional worker? __$25__

   $$TR_1 = 75 \times 3 = 225$$
   $$TR_2 = 125 \times 2 = 250 \quad > 25 = MRP$$

(B) Assume that you hired the additional worker and output now stands at 125 units per day. If you hire another worker, output rises to 165 units per day. Given the demand curve for your product, you know that to sell the additional output, price will have to be dropped from $2 per unit to $1 per unit. What is the maximum wage you would be willing to pay *this* additional worker? ___*$0*___ Would you hire this additional worker? ___*No.*___ Why or why not? ***You would not pay the extra worker a wage because MRP is negative.***

10. Use a graph to explain why "monopsonists will always hire fewer workers and pay lower wages than firms operating in competitive labor markets." (Assume that the monopsonistic and competitive firms have the same costs.)

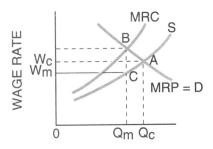

If the monopsonist increases the wage of the last worker, it must increase the wage of all previous workers. Therefore, MRC is above supply at each amount of labor. The monopsonist hires workers such that MRC = MRP (demand) but sets the wage for these workers according to the supply curve. The firm wants to pay the lowest wage it can and still have Q_m workers. This is at a lower number of workers and lower wage than a competitive firm would pay its workers. On the graph above, the perfect competitor hires Q_c and pays W_c. This is because the supply curve is the MRC, and MRC and MRP intersect at Q_c and W_c. The monopsonist hires where MRC = MRP, or an input of Q_m. However, it hires labor where the wage equals supply or W_m. Therefore, the monopsonist hires fewer workers at a lower wage.

UNIT
4 Microeconomics
MULTIPLE-CHOICE
SAMPLE QUESTIONS
Answer
Key

Answers to Sample Multiple-Choice Questions

1. A	8. E	14. D	20. E
2. A	9. E	15. E	21. B
3. E	10. C	16. B	22. C
4. D	11. B	17. D	23. B
5. D	12. B	18. A	24. C
6. A	13. D	19. C	25. B
7. E			

Advanced Placement Economics Teacher Resource Manual © National Council on Economic Education, New York, N.Y.

UNIT
4

Microeconomics

SHORT FREE-RESPONSE
SAMPLE QUESTIONS

Answer
Key

Answers to Sample Short Free-Response Questions

1. What determines the demand for a resource (factor of production)? Why is the demand for a resource downward sloping? What determines the elasticity of demand for a resource (factor of production)? *The demand for a resource is derived from the demand for a good or service that is produced with the resource. The demand for resources is affected by the price of the good or service and the marginal productivity of labor. Because the marginal productivity decreases as output increases, marginal revenue product decreases. MRP is the demand for the resource. In addition, if the firm is operating in an imperfect product market, the price of the product will decrease as output decreases. This also decreases MRP. The elasticity of demand for the factor depends on the rate of decline of MRP, the elasticity of the demand for the product, ease of resource substitutability and proportion of total costs that the factor represents.*

2. List three factors that would increase the demand for a resource, and explain why the factors would increase demand.

    Students may use several examples, which should relate to these categories:

    (A) The demand for, and therefore the price of, the product produced by the resource increases.

    (B) The productivity of the resource increases.

    (C) The price of a substitute resource decreases, as long as the output effect is greater than the substitution effect.

    (D) The price of a substitute resource increases, as long as the substitution effect is greater than the output effect.

    (E) The price of a complementary resource decreases.

3. Assume a monopsonistic labor market is in equilibrium. What are the effects on wages and employment if workers organize themselves into a labor union and demand an increase in wages? *The wage will increase. As long as the increase is less than the point where MRC = MRP, employment will increase as well.*

4. Compare the wage level and employment level of a firm in a perfectly competitive labor market with the wage level and employment level of a firm in a monopsonistic labor market. Both firms have similar costs and sell their goods in a perfectly competitive product market.
    The monopsonist will hire fewer workers and pay a lower wage. This is because the MRC is greater than the supply curve. MRC is above supply, so the firm is less likely to hire an extra worker, all things equal.

5. What is economic rent? Draw a supply curve and a demand curve for land. Now show the effects of an increase in the demand for land. What happens to the amount of economic rent if the demand for land increases?

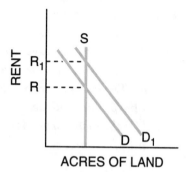

Economic rent is the price paid for the use of land and other natural resources that are completely fixed in supply. Therefore, the demand for the fixed land determines its rent. As demand increases from D to D_1, the amount of rent per acre increases from R to R_1.

*6. Use the table below to answer this question.

Production Table for Company X

Number of Workers	Total Product
0	0
1	20
2	50
3	70
4	80
5	86
6	88
7	87

(A) Given this information, what is the marginal product of the second worker? *30 (1 point)*

---

*Actual free-response question from a past AP test. Reprinted by permission of the College Entrance Examination Board, the copyright owner. For limited use by NCEE.

Advanced Placement Economics Teacher Resource Manual © National Council on Economic Education, New York, N.Y.

(B) Define the law of diminishing returns, and explain fully why diminishing returns occurs. *According to the law of diminishing returns, as one adds more of a variable input to fixed factors (inputs), the increase to total product (or marginal product) declines. (1 point)*

Diminishing returns occur because the existence of fixed capital means less capital per worker. (1 point)

(C) In the table above, diminishing returns sets in with the addition of which worker? *The third worker (1 point)*

(D) Why does the addition of the seventh worker result in a decline of total product? Explain fully why this decline occurs. *Overcrowding becomes so serious that ultimately the additional worker has no capital to use; he gets in the way of other workers and interferes with their production, so total production drops. (1 point)*

Grading Rubric: 5 points

Answers to Sample Long Free-Response Questions

*1. Initially a country's labor market is competitive and in long-run equilibrium. Now assume that new workers enter the labor market.

(A) Assuming no other changes, explain how the increase in the number of workers will affect each of the following in the short run:
   (i)   The wage rate of workers
   (ii) The costs of production for a typical firm
   (iii) The price of goods produced by the workers

(B) Assume that the demand for the goods produced by the workers in Part A decreases. Explain the effect of this decrease on each of the following:
   (i)   The price of goods produced by the workers
   (ii) The demand for labor
   (iii) The wage rate of workers

(C) Now assume that legislation requiring the establishment of a national minimum wage is proposed. Explain at what level this minimum wage would need to be set to be effective.

(D) Explain how the imposition of the minimum wage in Part C would affect each of the following:
   (i)   The number of workers employed in the labor market
   (ii) The costs of production for a typical firm

Grading Rubric: Basically the point distribution is 3 points for Part (A), 3 for Part (B), 1 for Part (C) and 2 for Part (D).

Part (A) = 3 points

The labor supply curve shifts to the right, resulting in a decrease in the equilibrium wage. The supply curve shifts to the right because of the influx of workers. The decrease in the wage rate reduces the costs of production for the firm using the labor, resulting in an increase in supply for the product, or a rightward shift of the product supply curve.

1 point: An explanation that the labor supply curve shifts to the right (1/2 point) because of an influx of labor → wage rate declines (1/2 point)

1 point: Firm's costs decline because wage rate declined.

1 point: Show supply curve of product increases (1/2 point) and the equilibrium product price declines (1/2 point)

Part (B) = 3 points

The demand for goods declines, resulting in a product-price decrease. The product-price decline causes the MRP$_L$ to decrease (shift to the left) because labor is a derived demand.

Wage rate declines.

1 point: Product price declines, with explanation or graph ($1/2$ point for price decrease, $1/2$ point for decrease in demand)

1 point: MRP$_L$ declines. Must link product-price decline to the decrease in demand for labor. (The use of the term derived demand or indicating product Q decreases → need for labor decrease is inadequate.) Grading here will be either zero or one — that is, a half point is not an option.

1 point: Wage rate declines ($1/2$ point) as a result of decrease in the demand for labor ($1/2$ point).

Part (C) = 1 point

The minimum wage must be set above the equilibrium wage rate.

Once again, either a zero or a one should be allocated — that is, a half point is not an option.

Part (D) = 2 points

If the minimum wage is above the equilibrium wage, then there will be a decrease in employment and the firm's costs of production will increase.

1 point: Decrease in employment ($1/2$ point) and $1/2$ point for explanation

1 point: Increase in costs of production

Once again, point allocation will be either a zero or a one.

In Part (D) we are looking for a consistent answer with what they said in Part (C). Consistency is rewarded.

Note: May make efficiency-wage argument: Higher wage results in higher productivity, less turnover, greater "loyalty" to firm, etc. So costs might not rise.

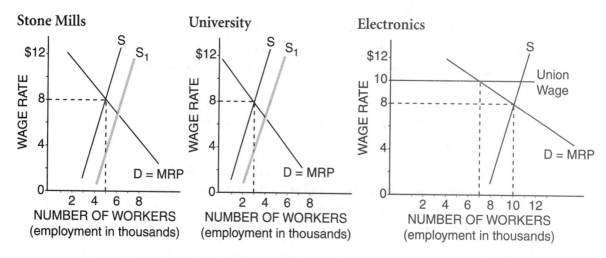

2. Suppose that University City has a perfectly competitive labor market in which there are only three kinds of employment for a certain type of labor. Also suppose that the demand for and supply of this type of labor in each market are as shown above. Total employment is 18,000 persons, as shown, and the average wage rate in each kind of employment is the same: $8 per hour. Now imagine that there is a strong union covering workers in the electronics industry and that it succeeds in negotiating with the employers in this industry an average wage of $10. Show on the graphs the effect this will have on the whole University City labor market, and discuss your analysis by indicating who gains and who loses from the increase in the wages of electronics workers.

Note the graphs above. With no change in the basic underlying demand conditions or productivity of workers, employment at the $10 wage in the electronics industry will be reduced by 3,000 workers who are working at a wage of $8. These workers will show up at the stone mills and the university looking for work at $8. This increased supply of labor will put downward pressure on wages and tend to increase employment in these locations. (No exact numbers needed here. In the graphs, supply was increased at $8 and other wages by increased numbers of workers looking for work at both the stone mills and the university.)

Winners

1. *Electronics workers who are still employed at $10 and people who receive the extra income these electronics workers spend*

2. *Stone mills and the university, which gain as employers hire more workers at a lower wage*

Losers

1. *People laid off at the electronics plant; employees at the stone mills and the university who feel the effect that this cutback has in their consumption spending*

2. *Purchasers of electronics products if the higher wage costs lead to higher product prices*

UNIT
4 Microeconomics
LONG FREE-RESPONSE
SAMPLE QUESTIONS
Answer
Key

*3. In the United States, textiles are sold in two separate and perfectly competitive markets. The textiles produced in the United States are sold in Market A, and imported textiles are sold in Market B.

(A) Explain how the supply curve for textiles produced in the United States will be affected by each of the following:
   (i)   A decrease in the number of firms in the United States producing textiles
   (ii) An increase in the price of textiles
   Assume that the textiles produced in Market A and Market B are close substitutes.

With fewer firms producing textiles, the supply of textiles is reduced; the supply curve shifts to the left (inward). With a high price for textiles, the quantity supplied increased along an unchanged supply curve.

Grading Rubric: Part (A) = 2 points
   (i)   inward shift in supply; a decrease in supply (1 point)
   (ii) movement along the supply curve; an increase in the quantity supplied or supply curve does not change (1 point)

(B) Using one graph for Market A and another for Market B, show and explain how a substantial increase in the tariff on textiles imported into the United States will affect each of the following:
   (i)   Equilibrium price and quantity of textiles sold in Market B (imported textiles)
   (ii) Equilibrium price and quantity of textiles sold in Market A (textiles produced in the United States)

The tariff raises the per-unit supply price of all units of imported textiles; the supply curve in Market B shifts to the left (inward), leading to a higher equilibrium price and a lower equilibrium quantity of imported textiles. Since imported and domestically produced textiles are close substitutes, the increase in the price of imported textiles leads to an increase in the demand for domestically produced textiles (Market A). The Market A demand curve shifts outward. Both the equilibrium price and quantity increase in Market A.

Grading Rubric: Part (B) = 4 points
   (i)   Import Market B: shift inward (decrease) in supply; need correct graph (1 point) leading to increased price and reduced quantity in Market B (either in a correct graph OR a verbal explanation) (1 point)
   (ii) Domestic Market A: shift out (increase) in demand; need correct graph, plus verbal linkage to the price increase in import Market B (Part (B)(i) above) (1 point) leading to increased price and increased quantity in Market A (either a correct graph OR a verbal explanation) (1 point)

---

*Actual free-response question from a past AP test. Reprinted by permission of the College Entrance Examination Board, the copyright owner. For limited use by NCEE.

4. Use the table below to answer this question.

Production Table for Company X

Number of Workers	Total Product	Marginal Product
0	0	0
1	10	10
2	25	15
3	45	20
4	60	15
5	70	10
6	75	5
7	77	2

(A) Calculate the marginal product of each worker. *(1 point)*

(B) Draw a graph plotting marginal product. *(1 point)*

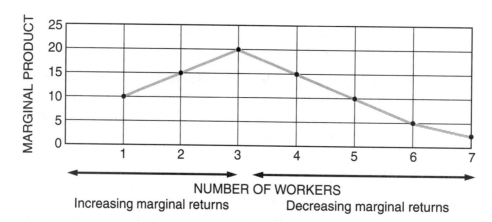

(C) On the marginal product graph you drew in Part (B), indicate the range of the following:
  (i)   Increasing marginal returns
        See graph in Part (B) (1 point)
  (ii) Decreasing marginal returns
        See graph in Part (B) (1 point)
  (iii) Negative marginal returns
        There are no negative returns (1 point)

Grading Rubric: Part (C) = 3 points

UNIT
4 Microeconomics

LONG FREE-RESPONSE
SAMPLE QUESTIONS

Answer
Key

(D) State the law of diminishing marginal returns, and explain fully why diminishing marginal returns occurs.

Grading Rubric: Part (D) = 2 points

As additional units of a variable resource, in this case workers, are added to a fixed resource such as capital, at first production increases at an increasing rate; however, at some point, the addition of another unit of the variable results in production increasing at a decreasing rate. (1 point)

Diminishing returns occurs because the addition of units of the variable resource to a fixed resource, such as capital, means that the amount of fixed resource available for each worker decreases. (1 point)

(E) Explain what happens to total product where each of the following occurs:
  (i)   Marginal product is rising.
        Total product increases at an increasing rate. (1 point)
  (ii) Marginal product is falling but positive.
        Total product increases at a decreasing rate. (1 point)
  (iii) Marginal product is negative.
        Total product decreases. (1 point)

(F) Should Company X hire the fourth worker? Explain fully why or why not.

Grading Rubric: Part (F) = 1 point

The marginal product of the fourth worker is 15 units of product. If the revenue generated by the sale of these 20 units is equal to or greater than the cost to produce these units, that worker should be hired. If not, the worker should not be hired. (1 point) (Also acceptable: There is not enough information to answer the question.)

Total points for Question 4 = 11

Big Ideas about Factor, or Resource, Markets

1. The economic concepts are similar to those for product markets.

2. The demand for a factor of production is derived from the demand for the good or service produced from this resource.

3. A firm tries to hire additional units of a resource up to the point where the resource's marginal revenue product (MRP) is equal to its marginal resource cost (MRC).

4. In hiring labor, a perfectly competitive firm will do best if it hires up to the point where MRP = the wage rate. Wages are the marginal resource cost of labor.

5. If you want a high wage:

   (A) Make something people will pay a lot for.

   (B) Work for a highly productive firm.

   (C) Be in relatively short supply.

   (D) Invest in your human capital.

6. Real wages depend on productivity.

7. Productivity depends on real or physical capital, human capital, labor quality and technology.

The Demand for a Resource: Perfect Competition in the Sale of the Product

(1) Units of Resource	(2) Total Product	(3) Marginal Physical Product (MPP) or Δ(2) / Δ(1)	(4) Product Price	(5) Total Revenue or (2) x (4)	(6) Marginal Revenue Product (MRP) or Δ(5) / Δ(1)
0	0		$2	$0	
1	7	7	2	14	$14
2	13	6	2	26	12
3	18	5	2	36	10
4	22	4	2	44	8
5	25	3	2	50	6
6	27	2	2	54	4
7	28	1	2	56	2

From Campbell R. McConnell and Stanley L. Brue: *Economics*, 12th ed. Copyright © by McGraw-Hill, Inc., New York, 1993.
All rights reserved.

The Demand for a Resource: Imperfect Competition in the Sale of the Product

(1) Units of Resource	(2) Total Product	(3) Marginal Physical Product (MPP) or Δ(2) / Δ(1)	(4) Product Price	(5) Total Revenue or (2) x (4)	(6) Marginal Revenue Product (MRP) or Δ(5) / Δ(1)
0	0		$2.80	$0	
1	7	7	2.60	18.20	$18.20
2	13	6	2.40	31.20	13.00
3	18	5	2.20	39.60	8.40
4	22	4	2.00	44.00	4.40
5	25	3	1.85	46.25	2.25
6	27	2	1.75	47.25	1.00
7	28	1	1.65	46.20	−1.05

Advanced Placement Economics Teacher Resource Manual © National Council on Economic Education, New York, N.Y.

The Supply of and Demand for Labor in a Competitive Labor Market

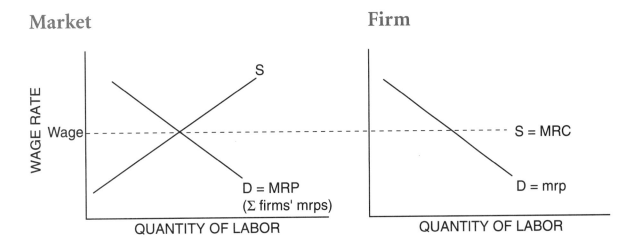

Market

Firm

The Wage Rate and Level of Employment In a Monopsonistic Labor Market

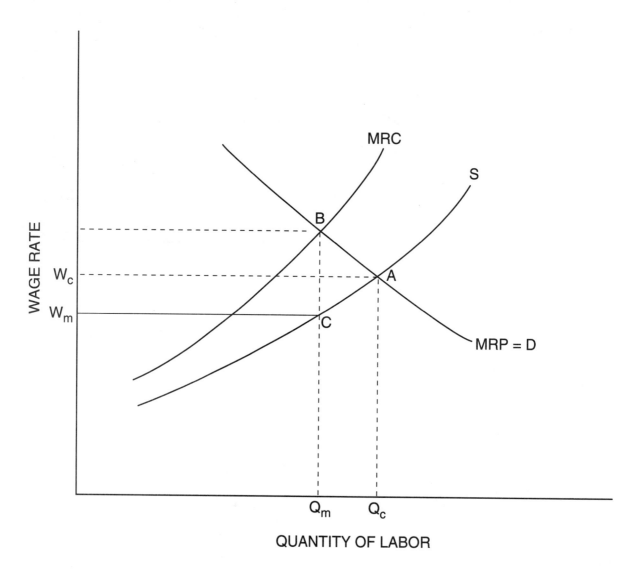

Advanced Placement Economics Teacher Resource Manual © National Council on Economic Education, New York, N.Y.

The Determination of Economic Rent

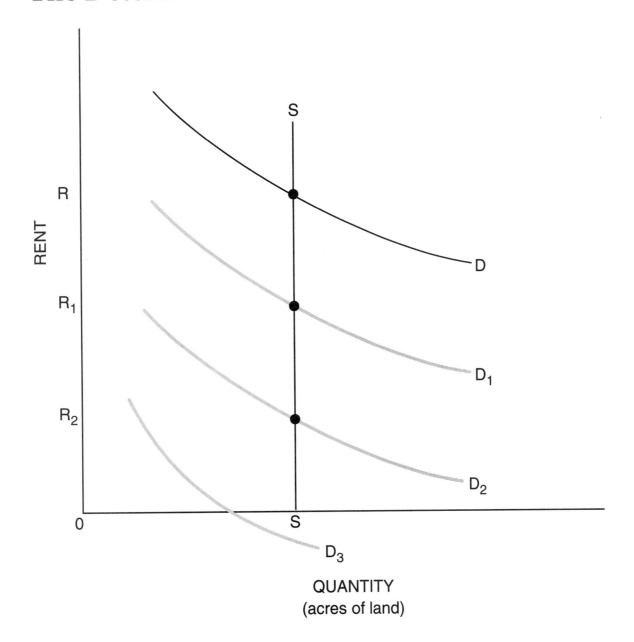

The Role of Government

11 class periods or 495 minutes
(15 percent of course time)

Unit Overview

In this unit the students develop criteria to determine which activities government should undertake and to evaluate how well government performs these activities.

The students first learn that governments must provide public goods. Pure public goods are rare and must meet the criteria of shared consumption and nonexclusion.

Governments also correct market failures. A market failure occurs when the private market produces too much or too little of a good because of negative and positive externalities. Market failures also occur when people in markets do not have sufficient information, and this is also used to justify government intervention.

Of course, governments also have less-than-perfect information. Although government intervention may correct market failures, government policies can also fail. Public-choice theorists believe politicians and government officials are as self-interested as businesspeople. However, instead of trying to maximize profits, "political entrepreneurs" seek to maximize power, salaries, prestige and votes. This behavior results in government waste and inefficiency. Public-choice theory provides balance to a discussion of the role of government.

Finally, some people believe that governments should make the distribution of income more equal. Governments do this through taxation policies, although these policies do not always have the desired effects.

The Lesson Planner

Lesson 1 explains the conditions under which a good or service should be provided by the private sector or by government. The activities describe the characteristics of public goods and private goods. The lesson uses **Activities 52** and **53** and **Visual 5.1**.

Lesson 2 is all about externalities. A market externality refers to a situation in which some of the costs or benefits from an activity fall on someone other than the one pursuing the activity. Governments intervene to make the allocation of these goods more efficient. The lesson also discusses information-cost problems. It uses **Activities 54, 55, 56** and **57** as well as **Visuals 5.2** and **5.3**.

Lesson 3 focuses on public-choice economics. Although governments have important economic functions, they sometimes perform these functions poorly. In addition to market failures, there are government failures. The lesson uses **Activity 58** and **Visual 5.4**.

Lesson 4 discusses the economics of taxation. Governments use taxes to alter the distribution of income in a society. This lesson discusses who actually pays income taxes and how this affects the distribution of income. **Activities 59** and **60** comprise this lesson. There are no activities on shifting tax incidence in this unit. You may want to use **Activity 21** in Unit 2 here.

| Week 1 | Week 2 |

Week 1

Day 1

(A) Give lecture on economic role of government, using Visual 5.1.

(B) Give a lecture on public goods.

(C) Have the students complete Activity 52 and discuss it.

Day 2

(A) Have the students complete Activity 53 and discuss it.

(B) Discuss externalities, using Visuals 5.2 and 5.3.

Day 3

Have the students complete Activity 54 and discuss it.

Day 4

(A) Describe the Coase Theorem.

(B) Have the students complete Activity 55 and discuss it.

(C) Review marginal analysis.

(D) Assign Activity 56 as homework.

Day 5

(A) Discuss answers to Activity 56.

(B) Discuss information costs with an emphasis on the importance of marginal analysis in making cost-benefit decisions.

(C) Have the students complete Activity 57 and discuss answers.

(D) Conduct a lecture and discussion about why markets fail and how government can correct these failures.

Week 2

Day 6

(A) Use Visual 5.4 to discuss why government fails.

(B) Have the students work in groups to solve the mysteries in Activity 58.

Day 7

(A) Have the students report on their solutions and discuss them.

(B) Discuss progressive, proportional and regressive taxes.

Day 8

(A) Have the students complete Activity 59 and discuss it.

(B) Discuss the equity versus efficiency issue.

(C) Discuss how government tax policies affect the distribution of income.

Day 9

(A) Have the students complete Activity 60 and discuss it.

(B) Review for test.

Day 10

Give multiple-choice test.

Week 3

Day 11

Give free-response test.

Public vs. Private Goods

Introduction and Description

In the United States, most economic decisions are made in the marketplace through the interaction of buyers and sellers. Some goods and services, however, can be provided only by government. The students should know the criteria that should be used to judge whether a good or service should be provided by the private sector or by government. They must know the characteristics of public goods and private goods.

Objectives

1. Define *public good.*
2. Describe the characteristics of a public good.
3. Develop a rationale for determining which goods should be produced by the private sector and which by the public sector.

Time Required

One and one-half class periods or 68 minutes

Materials

1. Activities 52 and 53
2. Visual 5.1

Procedure

1. Ask the students to brainstorm jobs that government does. Have them list as many functions of local, state and federal governments as they can.

2. Give a lecture on the economic role of government, using Visual 5.1.

3. Introduce the concept of a public good. Explain that a public good has both shared consumption and nonexclusion. You might ask the students to classify some goods using

    (A) exclusion

    (B) nonexclusion

    (C) nonshared consumption (rival good)

    (D) shared consumption (nonrival good)

    Some possibilities are

    (A) hamburger: exclusion and rival

    (B) TV show: exclusion but nonrival

    (C) park: exclusion but nonrival

    (D) education: exclusion but nonrival

    (E) national defense: nonexclusion and shared consumption (nonrival)

4. Discuss the problem of free riders when people cannot be excluded from using goods.

    (A) Ask what happens if a person does not contribute to public television.

    (B) Offer to sell a grade for the highest price. But once the first grade is sold, everyone in the class gets this same grade. Who will buy the grade? Will all the students join together to buy it? What if one student refuses to pay? Compare the results with selling a private good.

5. Have the students read Activity 52 and answer the questions.

6. Discuss the answers to Activity 52. There might be some discussion on shared consumption. For example, a private amusement park is shared consumption until it is full. Health care is shared consumption in some areas (public health) and not in others. This is a good opportunity to show these decisions are difficult.

7. Have the students complete Activity 53 and discuss the answers. These are opinions, but goods produced by government should meet the criteria of nonexclusion and shared consumption.

Private or Public? Public Goods and Services

1. What is the difference between the private and public sectors of our economy? *The public sector is government: federal, state and local. The private sector consists of decisions in the marketplace made between buyers and sellers.*

2. What are the characteristics of a pure private good? *It is traded through voluntary exchange. People who are not part of the transaction can be excluded from the transaction. Pure private goods, such as haircuts, cannot be characterized by shared consumption.*

3. What are the characteristics of a pure public good? *Nonexclusion, shared consumption*

4. Place each of the goods and services in the list below into one of the four boxes in Figure 52.2. Circle the box that contains pure private goods. Then draw two circles around the box that contains pure public goods.

 Figure 52.2
Determining Combinations of Exclusion and Shared Consumption

		Shared Consumption	
		No	Yes
Exclusion	Yes	*(B) Electric power* *(C) A haircut* *(H) Canine rabies shots* *(O) Potato chips* *(P) Auto airbags*	*(A) A college education* *(E) A private amusement park* *(G) Cable television* *(J) The St. Lawrence Seaway* *(K) Public toll roads and bridges* *(M) Health care* *(N) National forest campgrounds*
	No		*(D) National defense* *(F) Spraying for mosquitoes* *(I) Street lights* *(L) Police and fire protection*

5. What is a free rider? Select three goods from the list in Question 4 that could have free riders. *Someone who uses the good or service but doesn't pay for it. Free riders occur when there are nonexclusion and shared consumption. This occurs for all public goods. Examples from the list are spraying for mosquitoes, police and fire protection, national defense and street lights.*

When Markets Fail

Introduction and Description

Some government intervention in the economy is designed to remedy problems arising from third-party costs and benefits of private activities or transactions. Students who understand third-party effects, often called *externalities,* can analyze the need for and effect of such government interventions. Activity 54 provides an overview of the externality problem.

When a government tries to correct a negative externality, it can choose to intervene in a number of ways, or the problem may be corrected by private negotiations, which is the basis for the Coase Theorem (Activity 55). When government does intervene, its objective is to use marginal analysis so the marginal social benefit of the last unit produced equals the unit's marginal social cost. Activity 56 provides practice in doing this type of analysis. Finally, competitive markets can fail because of information cost, which is the basis of Activity 57.

Objectives

1. Explain how private market activities can cause externalities.
2. Define and give examples of *third-party costs* or *negative externalities.*
3. Define and give examples of *third-party benefits* or *positive externalities.*
4. Analyze ways positive and negative externalities can cause overproduction or underproduction of goods and services.
5. Analyze the effectiveness of government policies designed to remedy problems caused by positive or negative externalities.
6. Describe the Coase Theorem and use it to analyze how negotiations among private-property owners can resolve market-allocation problems.
7. Analyze how marginal analysis can determine the optimum amount of pollution cleanup.
8. Describe the information-cost problem, and analyze the effectiveness of government policies to correct it.

Time Required

Three and one-half class periods or 158 minutes

Materials

1. Activities 54, 55, 56 and 57
2. Visuals 5.2 and 5.3

Procedure

1. Begin with a discussion on the external effects of production and some common-sense examples of positive and negative externalities.

   (A) Smoking creates external costs. The smoker is satisfied, and the tobacco company gains; but third parties often have to cope with smell and litter, as well as the hazard to health from breathing secondary smoke.

   (B) People who drive under the influence of alcohol are much more likely to cause accidents than other drivers. These accidents cause third parties to suffer personal injury and/or property damage.

   (C) The productive work of maintaining one's house is an example of an external benefit provided by a consumer who also acts as a producer. If people landscape their yards, paint and otherwise maintain their houses, the whole neighborhood looks better. The houses are then usually worth more than houses in comparable neighborhoods where the owners do not maintain their houses to an equal extent.

   (D) Education provides third-party benefits. On the whole, people's productivity increases with their level of education. A higher level of education also tends to be correlated with better health and a lower crime rate. Third parties benefit from this greater productivity through fewer demands on health-care services and the lower burden on the police and judiciary.

   (E) If you teach in a public school, ask the students why taxpayers should pay for their education. One reason is the third-party benefits that education creates.

2. Now use graphical analysis to illustrate negative and positive externalities and how these externalities can be corrected.

   (A) Use Visual 5.2 to illustrate the effects of a negative externality.

   (B) Use Visual 5.3 to illustrate the effects of a positive externality.

3. Have the students complete Activity 54 and discuss the answers.

4. Discuss the Coase Theorem. Ronald Coase is a Nobel Laureate in economics. His theory has many practical applications. The key is that resources can be allocated efficiently if private ownership rights are assigned and when there are no transaction costs. Most importantly, Coase maintained that no matter who receives the legal rights to ownership, the assignment will have no effect on the way economic resources are used.

Your students may wonder why this is a big deal, particularly because all transactions do have costs. The excitement is that the Coase Theorem changes the way people look at economic problems. There is less need for government intervention. In any economic transaction, solutions that can benefit most parties can be achieved by negotiations. For example, environmental problems can be resolved if property rights are assigned rather than relying on government command and control.

5. Have the students complete Activity 55 and go over the answers.

6. Now that we have established that markets fail because of externalities, how should government treat the problem? The environment is an important issue. Is it always a good idea to clean up the environment as much as possible? This would ignore the opportunity cost of the cleanup. Therefore, the environment should be cleaned up

to the point where the marginal social benefit equals the marginal social cost of the cleanup.

7. Have the students complete Activity 56 and discuss the answers. Keep these points in mind as you discuss the answers:

Question 1(A). Correctly interpreted, it costs Firm 1 $160 to reduce pollution emissions by the first unit. The marginal benefit from this emission reduction is $350. Thus, it clearly pays to reduce emissions by this first unit.

Question 1(B). Similarly, it costs Firm 1 $360 to reduce pollution emissions by the fifth unit, while the marginal benefit from this damage reduction is $150. Thus, it clearly does not pay to reduce emissions by this fifth unit of pollution.

Question 2(A). With MSC of $160 less than MSB of $200, it pays for Firm 2 to reduce pollution emissions by the fourth unit.

Question 2(B). The MSC of $160 is greater than the MSB of $150, so it does not pay Firm 2 to eliminate the fifth unit of foul sludge emissions.

The explanations for Questions 3 and 4 are shown on the answer key. Since the basic logic of "keep reducing so long as MSB > MSC, and stop reducing when MSB < MSC" lends itself to graphical exposition — and since a graph helps illustrate the social optimum of MSB = MSC — two graphs of the numerical data in this problem are in the answer key for Activity 56.

8. Another reason a market can fail is because of information costs. If either the buyer or seller has better information, market efficiency may suffer. Although an answer may be government regulation, this should be tempered by the fact that governments also have less-than-perfect information.

9. Have the students complete Activity 57 and go over the answers.

10. Conduct a general discussion about why markets fail and how government can correct these failures.

Externalities

Figure 54.1
External Benefits

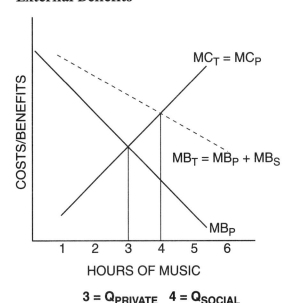

3 = Q~PRIVATE~   4 = Q~SOCIAL~

Figure 54.2
External Costs

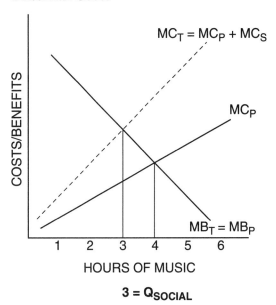

3 = Q~SOCIAL~

1. Imagine you live with a roommate in a college residence hall. Your roommate has brought an expensive stereo system to play in your room. Figure 54.1 shows your roommate's private marginal cost (MC_P) and marginal benefit (MB_P) curves for music played on the stereo system. Based on your roommate's private costs and benefits from playing music, answer the following questions.

   (A) If your roommate considers only the private costs and benefits from playing music, how many hours of music are played? ___*Three hours*___ Label the number of hours $Q_{PRIVATE}$ on the graph.

   (B) Assume that your roommate plays music only at times that do not disturb you and plays only music that you also enjoy. The dashed line shows that MB_T exceeds MB_P. Therefore, how do total benefits (social benefits plus private benefits) differ from private benefits? ***They are greater.*** If your roommate considers the social benefits from playing music as well as the private benefits, what happens to the quantity of music played? ***It increases to four hours.*** Label the number of hours Q_{SOCIAL} on the graph.

   (C) Now assume that your roommate plays music only at times that you are trying to study and plays only music that you hate. The dashed line on Figure 54.2 shows that MC_T exceeds MC_P. If your roommate considers the social costs from playing music as well as the private costs, what happens to the quantity of music played? ***It would be less (three hours).*** Label the number of hours Q_{SOCIAL} on the graph.

   (D) When your roommate does not consider your external benefits in the absence of external costs from playing music, the number of hours played is (*efficient* / *too high* / ***too low***). When your roommate does not consider your external costs in the absence of external benefits, the number of hours played is (*efficient* / ***too high*** / *too low*).

(E) How can government regulation (in this case, residence-hall rules) assure the efficient quantity of music? Consider the circumstances under which prohibiting stereos or imposing daily "quiet hours" are efficient ways to regulate stereo use in the hall. Does economics suggest a more-efficient approach to stereo regulation? *Prohibiting stereos or imposing quiet hours will not result in an efficient level since marginal benefits and marginal costs are not considered. A more efficient approach would be to issue "rights" to play stereos. You could issue property rights and negotiate how many hours stereos could be played. For example, the stereo owner could pay the third party if there is a negative externality, and the owner could charge if there is a positive externality.*

2. For each of these activities, explain whether there is a positive or negative externality:

   Private high school education
   Positive. The students become better citizens.

   Smog from an electric power plant
   Negative. The waste causes health problems.

   Your neighbor's yappy dog
   Negative. The dog's bark keeps the neighbors awake at night and makes them less productive.

   Prekindergarten measles vaccinations
   Positive. There is less disease spread.

3. The Women's National Basketball Association (WNBA) has awarded a new franchise for a basketball team to be established in Metropolis, but only if the new team has a new arena in which to play. Proponents of the franchise argue that the team will generate new business, provide jobs, increase tax revenue and promote tourism in Metropolis. Opponents argue that most of the money spent on basketball games will come from Metropolis-area residents who will simply reduce their spending on other activities. Thus there will be few new jobs, little increase in tax revenue and few new tourists coming to Metropolis. Others say the new stadium will cause property values to fall and create traffic, parking and noise problems.

   Voters have the following three proposals before them:

   Proposal 1: No city money should be used in the construction of the arena.

   Proposal 2: The city should place a tax on each ticket sold to pay for the arena.

   Proposal 3: The city should build the arena and lease the right to play there to the basketball team at a subsidized rate.

   Using your knowledge of externalities, answer the following questions.

   (A) What assumption does Proposal 1 make about the size of external costs compared with external benefits? Explain. *There are no externalities. It is a market transaction.*

(B) How does Proposal 2 change the composition of total costs and benefits to adjust for externalities (both positive and negative)? *There are negative externalities that must be paid for by taxing tickets.*

(C) What assumptions does Proposal 3 make about external costs and benefits to reach an efficient solution? *There are positive externalities, so the activity should be subsidized.*

Summary

4. When positive externalities are involved, private markets (**_underproduce_** / overproduce).

5. When negative externalities are involved, private markets (underproduce / **_overproduce_**).

6. Why do economists refer to the presence of an externality as a *market failure*? *The private market does not produce the correct allocation of resources.*

7. How would a tax remedy a negative externality? *It would raise the cost of production to reduce quantity.*

8. How would a subsidy mitigate underproduction in the presence of a positive externality? *It would lower the cost of production or increase revenue, so production increases.*

Private or Public? The Coase Theorem

 Figure 55.1
Profits per Month

	With Dumping	Without Dumping
Grunge Inc.	$2,300	$2,000
White Water Expeditions	$1,500	$2,000

1. What are the total returns to both companies with and without dumping? Which situation (dumping or no dumping) is socially optimal — in other words, provides the highest combined returns?

   With dumping: $3,800

   Without dumping: $4,000

   The highest combined returns are without dumping.

2. If there is no government intervention in the market, and the two companies do not communicate, will Grunge dump waste into the river? Why or why not? *Yes, because Grunge's returns are higher.*

3. What is the cost to Grunge not to dump waste into the river? How much would White Water have to pay to clean up the waste?   *$300*

4. What is the cost of the pollution to White Water each month? How much would White Water be willing to pay Grunge to stop dumping waste into the river?   *$500*

5. If Grunge and White Water could negotiate, at no cost, could they come to an agreement that would eliminate the externality problem and result in the efficient outcome? If not, why not? If so, what would the payment be? *They should come to an agreement. The payment would be between $301 and $499. Otherwise both parties would not gain.*

6. Does it matter who has the property right: Grunge to dump or White Water to have clean water? Explain. *No, it does not matter. If Grunge has the right, White Water will pay Grunge not to dump. If White Water has the right, then Grunge will clean up at a cost of $300.*

Economic Efficiency and the Optimum Amount of Pollution Cleanup

 Figure 56.1
Firm 1

Reduction of Foul Sludge Emissions	Total Social Benefit of Cleanup	Marginal Social Benefit of Cleanup	Total Social Cost of Cleanup	Marginal Social Cost of Cleanup
0	0		0	
1	350	350	160	160
2	650	300	370	210
3	900	250	630	260
4	1,100	200	940	310
5	1,250	150	1,300	360

1. Using the data from Figure 56.1, fill in the blanks or underline the correct words in parentheses.

   (A) The marginal social benefit (MSB) of reducing emissions by the first unit of foul sludge is ___**$350**___, and the marginal social cost (MSC) of reducing pollution emissions by the first unit is ___**$160**___. The marginal social benefit (MSB) is (**_greater than_** / equal to / less than) the marginal social cost (MSC), so it (**_would_** / would not) be economically efficient from society's perspective to require Firm 1 to reduce pollution emission by the first unit.

   (B) The MSB of eliminating the last (fifth) unit of foul sludge is ___**$150**___, and the MSC of reducing pollution emissions by the last (fifth) unit is ___**$360**___. The MSB is (greater than / equal to / **_less than_**) the MSC, so it (would / **_would not_**) be economically efficient from society's perspective to require Firm 1 to reduce pollution emission by the fifth unit.

 Figure 56.2
Firm 2

Reduction of Foul Sludge Emissions	Total Social Benefit of Cleanup	Marginal Social Benefit of Cleanup	Total Social Cost of Cleanup	Marginal Social Cost of Cleanup
0	0		0	
1	350	350	160	160
2	650	300	320	160
3	900	250	480	160
4	1,100	200	640	160
5	1,250	150	800	160

2. Using the data from Figure 56.2, fill in the blanks or underline the correct words in parentheses.

(A) The marginal social benefit (MSB) of eliminating the fourth unit of foul sludge is ___*$200*___, and the marginal social cost (MSC) of reducing pollution emissions by this fourth unit is ___*$160*___. The MSB is (**_greater than_** / equal to / less than) the MSC, so it (**_would_** / would not) be economically efficient from society's perspective to require Firm 2 to reduce pollution emissions by four units.

(B) The MSB of eliminating the fifth (last) unit of foul sludge is ___*$150*___, and the MSC of reducing pollution emissions by this fifth (last) unit is ___*$160*___. The MSB is (greater than / equal to / **_less than_**) the MSC, so it (would / **_would not_**) be economically efficient from society's perspective to require Firm 2 to reduce pollution emissions by five units.

3. If this community decides to adopt a pollution-control ordinance aimed at maximizing economic efficiency, how should it evaluate each of the following three proposals, all of which are based on the data presented above? Write a brief economic evaluation in the space provided after each of the proposals. Be sure to use the concepts of marginal social benefit and marginal social cost in your analysis.

Proposal A. "Foul sludge emissions should be reduced (by five units) to zero for each firm because we should eliminate all pollution from our lakes regardless of the cost." This proposal (would / **_would not_**) maximize economic efficiency, because *economic efficiency considers marginal social costs and marginal social benefits. MSB < MSC after Firm 1 reduces two units. MSB < MSC after Firm 2 reduces four units. For five units, MSC > MSB for both firms. Therefore, it would not be economically efficient to make either firm reduce five units because the MSB would be less than the MSC.*

Proposal B. "Firm 2 should be forced to reduce emissions (by five units) to zero because the total social benefit of cleanup ($1,250) exceeds the total social cost of cleaning up ($800). But Firm 1 should not be forced to clean up at all, because the total social benefit of cleanup ($1,250) is less than the total social cost of reducing emissions to zero ($1,300)." This proposal (would / **_would not_**) maximize economic efficiency, because *it is marginal (not total) benefits and marginal (not total) costs that count in finding the optimum point of economic efficiency. If Firm 2 reduces five units and Firm 1 reduces zero units, the total net gain is $450 ($1,250 − $800) from Firm 2. However, if Firm 2 reduces only four units and Firm 1 reduces two units, the total net gain is $740:*

Firm 1: $650 − $370 = $280
Firm 2: $1,100 − $640 = $460
                                          $740

Proposal C. "In the interest of equal treatment for all, each firm should be forced to clean up (reduce emissions) by three units." This proposal *(would / **would not**)* maximize economic efficiency because *making Firm 1 reduce a third unit would result in MSB < MSC. Stopping Firm 2 at three units would leave MSB > MSC. Efficiency would increase if Firm 1 cut back to reducing two units, and Firm 2 continued reducing to a fourth unit. With each reducing three units, the total net gain is $690:*

Firm 1: $900 – $630 = $270
Firm 2: $900 – $480 = $420
                          $690

With Firm 1 reducing two units and Firm 2 reducing four units, the total net gain is $740:
Firm 1: $650 – $370 = $280
Firm 2: $1,100 – $640 = $460
                          $740

4. Using the data presented above, what do you think is the optimum level of emissions reduction for each firm? Explain briefly why you chose these numbers.

Firm 1: ___2___ units

Firm 2: ___4___ units

The optimal level of emissions is the output where MSB = MSC. For Firm 1, MSB > MSC up to a reduction of two units; beyond this point MSB < MSC. For Firm 2, MSB > MSC up to a reduction of four units; beyond this point MSB < MSC. No other combination yields a net gain greater than $740.

The Economics of Information

1. Determine which of the following packages of identical laundry detergent is the best buy.

Size	Weight	Price	Price per Ounce
Jumbo	25.0 oz.	94 cents	*3.76 cents*
Large	1.4 lbs.	85 cents	*3.79 cents*
Grande	25.5 oz.	97 cents	*3.80 cents*

   (A) Were you able to determine the best buy? *Depends on the student. Actually, they are all about the same price per ounce, although the jumbo size is slightly less expensive; see the "Price per Ounce" column in the table above.*

   (B) Are you likely to take the time needed to determine the best buy for each product you purchase? *This depends on the person, the amount of time he or she has and his or her access to information. You might ask the class for their opinions.*

   (C) If you don't determine the best buy for each product, what happens to market efficiency? *Market efficiency is less.*

2. The government has established regulations for product labels to help provide consumers with the information necessary to make efficient decisions in the market. Give an example of information that could be put on a product label to address each of the information asymmetries below.

   (A) You want to purchase the best buy in the laundry-detergent example above. *Price per ounce*

   (B) You want to buy a candy bar, and you are allergic to peanuts. *List of ingredients*

   (C) You are on a special diet that requires you to eat 24 grams of fiber each day. *Nutrition facts*

   (D) You want to buy fresh cottage cheese. *Date of production; last date to be sold or used*

   (E) You want to purchase a car that keeps your gas costs low. *Miles per gallon*

3. Assume you are in the market for a new car.

   (A) Do you have perfect information about the performance and safety of the car? Why or why not? *No, much of the information is technical or complicated.*

   (B) How does a competitive market help provide this information? *There are brand names and the manufacturer's reputation. Some print and online publications such as Consumer Reports sell the information, although there is a free-rider problem.*

   (C) How can government help provide this information? *Government can require auto makers to provide consumers with miles per gallon and crash-test results. Government may also require standard safety equipment, but this goes beyond information.*

When Government Fails

Introduction and Description

Lessons 1 and 2 stress the economic functions of government, with particular emphasis on market failures. This lesson deals with government failure and provides balance in evaluating the role of government.

Throughout their education, the students have been told that democratic governments try to improve society. They learn that some political leaders may be stupid, incompetent or corrupt; but a responsible electorate can vote them out of office. Furthermore, poor leadership is often blamed on political apathy. Most civics and government classes stress the reasons why citizens should vote and actively participate in the political process.

Public-choice economists believe that all this good-government stuff is bunk and that when political activity is studied with the tools of economics, government will be seen to fail more often than markets will. Their analysis shows why there is not much difference between the political parties, why special interests prevail over the public good, why it is rational not to vote and why bureaucrats are inefficient. It is *not* a matter of getting the right people in government. Rather, government fails because politicians and bureaucrats are trying to maximize their ability to gain votes and power. Their behavior is as self-interested as anyone else's.

This lesson should increase the students' skepticism toward government. They may agree with Winston Churchill, who said that democracy is the worst form of government except for the alternatives.

Objectives

1. Describe the basic tenets of the public-choice model of government behavior.
2. Analyze the reasons why self-interest leads to the public good in a private market but does not lead to the public good in the government sector.

3. Analyze political behavior using the theory of public choice.

Time Required

One and one-half class periods or 68 minutes

Materials

1. Activity 58
2. Visual 5.4

Procedure

1. Begin the lesson with an idea suggested by Ralph Byrns and Gerald Stone in *Great Ideas for Teaching Economics*, 5th ed. (New York: Harper-Collins, 1992):

   A quick poll of the students in virtually any college classroom will reveal a widespread call for "lower taxes and less government." After ascertaining that this is true through a show of hands in your class, either list a large number (20 or so) of present or proposed government activities (e.g., national health care, national defense) on a chalkboard or pass out detailed lists of such activities (perhaps to have the students take home to record their responses). One activity at a time, have the students indicate by a show of hands whether they favor: (a) eliminating the specific activity by government; (b) substantially decreasing the funding for the activity; (c) keeping the activity at present levels; or (d) increasing the government's participation in this area. They will be surprised (and you may be as well) when virtually all classes vote for substantial net expansions of many, or even most, government programs. When asked to account for this seeming paradox, some students may argue that most people want greater efficiency — more and better quality government services at lower tax costs. You can question whether a greater efficiency in government is likely, regardless of who holds office, and then contrast the efficiency of marketplace resource allocations with those resulting from public sector decision making. We have found that this exercise invariably generates enthusiastic class participation.

2. Give a lecture on the basic ideas of the public-choice school of economics using Visual 5.4. Here are some points to make.

Question 1: Is it rational for government leaders to favor special interests over the general public interest?

This is an important point in the public-choice doctrine. The idea is that special interests have a big stake in government. Therefore, they take a big interest in government. When they give politicians contributions and support, the politicians know it. Each member of the public may lose just a little when a special interest gets its way, so the public doesn't pay attention. Furthermore, the public is ignorant. Therefore, the politician goes with the special interest. The more concentrated the benefit for the special interest and the more diffused the cost to the public, the more likely the special interest will get its way.

Question 2: Why are politicians mainly in the middle of the road?

The median-voter hypothesis predicts that politicians, regardless of party, will appeal to the median voter in the constituency they represent. It also predicts that politicians will take a more extreme position in the party primary election (when they are appealing to the median voter in the party) than in the general election.

Question 3: Are people rational or irrational when they spend little time evaluating candidates before they vote and when they don't vote?

This is known as rational ignorance. Why be informed about the candidates when your vote counts so little? Why even vote? If this is true, why do so many people vote? The public-choice answer is that voting is a consumption activity. Voting gives people a feeling that they did their civic duty. By voting, they can complain without guilt when they don't like a government policy.

Question 4: What is the effect of bureaucratic entrepreneurs on government?

A business is successful if it can maximize profits. A bureaucrat is successful if he or she can maximize power. Bureaucrats are rewarded when they expand the duties and clientele of their departments. A bureaucrat will have a smaller department if it becomes more efficient. Bureaucrats have an incentive to expand their departments, not to reduce them. With larger departments come more power, a bigger office, a higher salary and a larger pension.

3. Have the students read the beginning of Activity 58 (up to the mystery activity), and answer any questions they have.

4. Divide the class into groups, and have each group try to solve the mysteries.

5. Have the groups report their solutions and discuss them.

Public-Choice Economics

1. The Electoral College Mystery

Why does a democratic country tolerate an undemocratic institution?

Politicians ordinarily want to be reelected. Their wish to be reelected creates a strong incentive for them to keep the voters back home happy. For members of Congress who represent states with relatively small populations — for example, Alaska, Delaware, Hawaii, Maine, New Hampshire, Montana, Nevada, New Mexico — one way to keep the voters at home happy is to preserve the Electoral College, since the Electoral College guarantees that even the least-populous state will have some clout (no fewer than three electoral votes) in presidential elections.

But why don't members of Congress from large-population states do away with the Electoral College by proposing the necessary action and then outvoting the others? It would take a constitutional amendment to get rid of the Electoral College, and passing a constitutional amendment would require support from the members of Congress who represent small-population states. Besides, large-population states also benefit from the Electoral College, since presidential candidates make special efforts to win in large states such as California, New York, Pennsylvania and Texas, and thus capture the many electoral votes these states control.

Even presidents are apt to see something good in the Electoral College. For newly-elected presidents, the winner-take-all nature of the Electoral College state-by-state elections may convey a stronger impression of a voter mandate than the total popular vote would convey.

2. The Mystery of the Voter Who Doesn't Vote

Why don't more Americans vote?

People decide whether or not to vote, taking into account the costs and benefits associated with their choice. What does it cost to vote? Some time and effort spent registering, gathering information about the candidates or issues, waiting in line at the polling station and so forth. Not a high cost, you might say, especially not for citizens who value their participation in the electoral process. But many citizens see little benefit in such participation. The odds are that no single vote will determine the outcome of an election, they say, and the outcomes don't matter all that much to them anyway. Any cost at all, then, seems too much. Let others do the voting, these nonvoters say, in effect; we'll "free ride" on the good citizenship of the voters and benefit as much or as little as they do from the outcomes.

Just for fun, you might invite your class to discuss possible ways of reducing the cost of voting. For example: what might be the effect of holding major elections on national holidays? Would scheduling a change of this sort increase or decrease the cost to voters?

3. The Mystery of Too Much Milk

Why would members of Congress fail to pass a law that saves their taxpayer and consumer constituents money?

   The reason is that the program has a large benefit for dairy farmers and a small cost for each consumer. Therefore, districts with dairy farms support the legislation, and districts without them trade their votes for a vote that will provide a big benefit to a special interest in their districts. This is why price floors exist even if they cause surpluses.

4. The Urban Housing Mystery

Why do some New Yorkers face a housing crisis while others are secure in choice apartments, paying low monthly rent?

   Building apartments and renting them out to tenants involves making choices. The money put into apartments could be put somewhere else. Rent controls affect the decisions people make in these cases. A ceiling on rental rates creates a disincentive, discouraging some people from entering or staying in the rental-properties business. As a result, some existing apartments will fall into disrepair, and fewer new apartments will be built. At the same time, rents for nonrent-controlled apartments will be bid up, owing to the shortage created by the rent controls. So why doesn't the City of New York abandon rent controls? Tenants who live in rent-controlled apartments benefit greatly from paying below-market rates. They support rent controls, and they put pressure on government officials to keep the current system in place.

5. The Trade Barrier Mystery

Why would nations pass laws that lower their standards of living?

   Some individual firms and employees get relatively large benefits from tariffs and quotas. These benefits have costs, and consumers pay more for the goods. For example, consumers paid $42,000 for every textile job saved by trade barriers, $105,000 for every auto job saved and $750,000 for every steelworker's job saved. Because these costs are spread over millions of consumers and most of them don't even notice the higher prices, legislators vote in favor of the trade restrictions to please the few people who receive large benefits.

Efficiency, Equity, and the Effects of Government Policies

Introduction and Description

Previous lessons have examined the role or size of government. This unit looks at the distribution of income and the effects of government policies to change it. The controversy weighs efficiency against equity. Markets work. In a world of scarce resources, higher productivity is better than lower productivity. Markets create incentives that increase productivity and the size of the pie.

It also may be true that the poor are needier than the rich. Markets create inequalities, and governments use taxes and transfer payments to redistribute income. These very policies, however, may create serious disincentives that damage efficiency and shrink the size of the pie.

What should be the trade-off between efficiency and equity? Are there policies that can improve both? Can government create hard-headed and soft-hearted policies?

Objectives

1. Define and differentiate between the *ability-to-pay* and the *benefits-received* theories of taxation.
2. Define and differentiate among *progressive, proportional* and *regressive taxes.*
3. Describe the distribution of income in the United States.
4. Describe who pays income taxes and which income earners bear the greatest burden of income taxes.
5. Analyze the effects of government redistribution policies.

Time Required

Two and one-half class periods or 113 minutes

Materials

Activities 59 and 60

Procedure

1. Have the students read Activity 59 until they reach the questions.

2. Give a lecture-discussion on tax equity that covers these points:
   (A) The difference between the *ability-to-pay* and the *benefits-received* theories of taxation
   (B) The difference between a *nominal* and an *effective tax rate*
   (C) The definitions of *progressive, proportional* and *regressive taxes.* Be sure to make clear that the rate must be an effective rate applied against income. Students confuse an income-tax base with other tax bases, such as consumption or wealth. For example, they might incorrectly conclude that the sales tax is a proportional tax since the rate is the same for everyone. They will not distinguish between a consumption base and an income base.

3. Have the students answer the questions on Activity 59 and discuss them.

4. Now bring up the question of whether the federal income tax is progressive, proportional or regressive.

5. Have the students complete Activity 60 and discuss the answers.

6. Be sure to make the big point that the federal income tax is progressive. In 1997, the top 1 percent of taxpayers paid 33.2 percent of the taxes. Their tax rate was 27.7 percent. The bottom 50 percent of taxpayers paid 4.3 percent of taxes. Their tax rate was 4.5 percent.

7. Discuss the following philosophical issues:
   (A) Why is efficiency important?
   (B) Why is equity important?
   (C) Do policies that redistribute income hurt efficiency, or are there policies that can improve both equity and efficiency?

What Is a Fair Tax?

1. A tax that requires each person to pay 3 percent regardless of income is a __*proportional*__ tax.

2. A tax levied at 1 percent on the first $1,000 of income, 2 percent on the next $1,000 and so on is a __*progressive*__ tax.

3. A tax levied at 15 percent on the first $1,000 of income, 12 percent on the next $1,000 and so on is a __*regressive*__ tax.

4. If it is true that a person with an income of $20,000 a year typically buys 10 gallons of gasoline per week and a person with an income of $40,000 typically buys 15 gallons of gasoline per week, this suggests that an excise tax of 40 cents per gallon would be a __*regressive*__ tax. Explain.
   The richer person has double the income but buys only 50 percent more gasoline. Therefore, the poorer person pays a greater percentage of his or her income on the gasoline tax.

5. Rick Morales has an income of $50,000 but spends only $40,000 on taxable goods. Chet Burton has an income of $25,000 and spends it all on taxable goods. Assuming an 8 percent sales tax, Mr. Morales will pay __*$3,200*__ in sales taxes, which is __*6.4*__ percent of his total income. On the other hand, Mr. Burton will pay __*$2,000*__ in sales taxes, which is __*8*__ percent of his total income. Therefore, we can conclude that the sales tax is __*regressive*__.

6. Since the sales tax has the same nominal or legal rate based on sales, why is it regressive? What steps could be taken to make it less regressive? *The sales tax base is consumption, not income. Most states do not include services in their sales tax base. Since the rich purchase more services, taxing services would make the tax less regressive. It would also raise more revenue. Since the poor pay a greater percentage of their income on food, exempting food also makes the tax less regressive. Several states exempt food from sales taxes. The government could tax income, or exempt the first portion of expenditures, or eliminate the sales tax on necessities such as food.*

7. Suppose that the government runs a pension fund to which all workers must contribute. The employee contribution rate is 6.2 percent on the first $84,900 of income. All income in excess of $84,900 is not taxed for pension purposes.

   (A) What was the effective pension tax rate for a person earning $20,000 a year? __*6.2%*__

   (B) What was the effective pension tax rate for a person earning $84,900? __*6.2%*__

   (C) What was the effective pension tax rate for a person earning $169,800? __*3.1%*__

   (D) Therefore, the pension tax is a *(progressive / __proportional__ / regressive)* tax up to $84,900 of income. For incomes above __*$84,900*__, the tax is *(progressive / proportional / __regressive__)*.

   (E) In addition to the pension tax, people must pay 1.45 percent of their income for medical benefits. There is no income limit on the medical-care tax. Does this make the total tax for pension and medical care more or less regressive? Why? *Less regressive because high-income people must pay the medical-care tax on their entire income, but they must pay the pension tax on their income up to only $84,900.*

Who Pays the Income Tax?

Part A

Figures 60.1 and 60.2 contain information from the Tax Foundation regarding shares of income, taxes and tax rates for federal income-tax returns in 1987 and 1997. Use the tables to answer the questions.

 Figure 60.1
Table of Federal Individual Income-Tax Return Data 1987

Percent of All Taxpayers	Income Range	Group's Share of Total Income (AGI)	Group's Share of Total Taxes	Group's Average Tax Rate
Top 1%	Above $139,289	12.3%	24.8%	26.4%
Top 5%	Above $68,414	25.7%	43.3%	22.1%
Top 10%	Above $52,921	36.9%	55.6%	19.8%
Top 25%	Above $33,983	60.8%	76.9%	16.6%
Top 50%	Above $17,768	84.4%	93.9%	14.6%
Bottom 50%	Below $17,768	15.6%	6.1%	5.1%
All Taxpayers		100.0%	100.0%	13.1%

 Figure 60.2
Table of Federal Individual Income-Tax Return Data 1997

Percent of All Taxpayers	Income Range	Group's Share of Total Income (AGI)	Group's Share of Total Taxes	Group's Average Tax Rate
Top 1%	Above $250,736	17.4%	33.2%	27.6%
Top 5%	Above $108,048	31.8%	51.9%	23.6%
Top 10%	Above $79,212	42.8%	63.2%	21.4%
Top 25%	Above $48,173	65.0%	81.7%	18.2%
Top 50%	Above $24,393	86.2%	95.7%	16.1%
Bottom 50%	Below $24,393	13.8%	4.3%	4.5%
All Taxpayers		100.0%	100.0%	14.5%

1. Suppose you defined "the rich" as the top 10 percent of all income earners. In 1997, what was the minimum income that you had to earn to be "rich"?

   (A) $33,983   (B) $52,921   *(C) $79,212*   (D) $250,736

2. What percentage of total income taxes did the top 1 percent of income earners pay in 1997?

   (A) none   (B) 1 percent   (C) 27.6 percent   *(D) 33.2 percent*

3. In 1997, the bottom half of all income earners paid what percentage of total income taxes?

   (A) 4.3 percent   (B) 6.1 percent   (C) 16.1 percent   (D) 50 percent

4. In 1997, the average U.S. taxpayer paid 14.5 percent of his or her income in taxes. Based on the information in the table, how would you classify U.S. income taxes (as discussed in Activity 59)?

   (A) Regressive   (B) Proportional   *(C) Progressive*

5. Compare 1987 with 1997. What is the best description of what happened to income tax burdens over this 10-year period?

   (A) The rich paid a smaller share, and more taxes fell on lower-income earners.

   (B) The income tax became more progressive, and the rich paid a larger share.

   (C) There was little change in the relative tax burdens of the rich and lower-income earners between 1987 and 1997.

Part B

Many people are concerned that "the rich are getting richer and the poor are getting poorer." Using the data in Figures 60.1 and 60.2, answer the following questions:

6. Is there evidence that the rich got richer and the poor got poorer between 1987 and 1997? Defend your answer. *This is a subjective answer, but the data seem to support this. In 1987, the top 1 percent had 12.3 percent of the nation's income; in 1997, it grew to 17.4 percent, so the rich share of the pie is bigger. Also, the bottom half's share of income fell from 15.6 percent to 13.8 percent during the same period. Also, the threshold to be rich (top 1 percent) increased from $139,289 to $250,736, or by 80 percent. The bottom half threshold increased from $17,768 to $24,393, or by 37 percent.*

7. Many politicians argue that the wealthy are not paying their "fair share" of taxes. Based on the data, do you agree or disagree? Why? Be sure to specify the criterion you are using. *Again, subjective answer. However, the top 1 percent of income earners have 17.4 percent of all income but pay 33.2 percent of all taxes. Also, they have a tax rate that is more than six times that of the bottom half. However, one could also argue that they have a much higher ability to pay, and even 33.2 percent is not their "fair" share.*

8. Would you argue that the U.S. progressive income tax hinders or promotes income equality? Why? *The U.S. tax system appears to promote equality because it increases the tax burden as one's income grows: The higher the income, the higher the effective tax rate. However, this also makes it hard to move up the income ladder: As you work hard and start to earn, the government takes more of your income. Also, redistribution results from both taxing and spending; these data deal only with the tax side. If tax revenue is not redistributed to people with lower incomes, then the system will not promote equality. Overall, other things equal, the U.S. progressive income tax promotes equality.*

Answers to Sample Multiple-Choice Questions

1. B	8. C	14. C	20. C
2. D	9. B	15. C	21. A
3. C	10. C	16. C	22. C
4. B	11. E	17. B	23. D
5. E	12. A	18. E	24. C
6. B	13. B	19. D	25. C
7. A			

Answers to Sample Short Free-Response Questions

1. Is elementary and secondary education a public good? Evaluate education by the criteria of a public good. *Education meets the criterion of shared consumption, and it may create positive externalities. However, education is not a pure public good because it does not meet the criterion of nonexclusion. People can be excluded from an educational system by imposing tuition, which many private schools do.*

2. Use a supply and demand graph to illustrate a negative externality. Explain your graph.

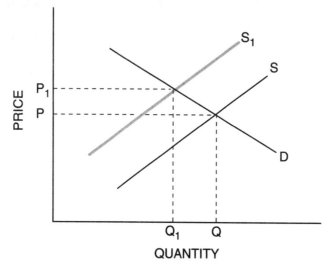

The correct output for society is Q_1. However, because of externalities, the actual output is Q and the price is P. Taxing the emissions would decrease supply from S to S_1. This would increase the price and reduce the output to the level where all externalities would be internalized. Without considering the negative externalities, the price is too low and the output too high for an efficient allocation of resources.

3. Use a supply and demand graph to illustrate a positive externality. Explain your graph.

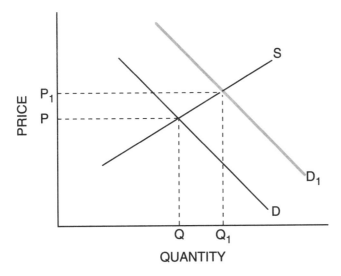

Because the positive externalities are not considered, the demand based on buyer benefits is only D. If societal benefits were considered, the demand would be greater, shifting to D_1. Without consider-ing external benefits, both the price and output are too low for an efficient allocation of resources.

4. The city council in Portland, Ore., must decide on a tax increase to finance a new airport. What advice would you give if you believed in the benefits-received theory of taxation? What advice would you give if you believed in the ability-to-pay theory? *According to the benefits-received theory, those who gain from the airport should pay for it. This could be done through landing fees for aircraft, taxes on passenger travel to and from the airport, fees for taxicabs picking up airport passengers and taxes on hotel rooms adjacent to the airport. Application of the benefits-received theory is difficult, however, as many people other than those listed above will benefit. Under the ability-to-pay theory, the airport should be financed out of progressive income-tax revenue, which collects the most money from those who are most able to pay. However, this will also reduce incen-tives and ability to produce.*

5. How could you change a 6 percent sales tax on all purchases to make it less regressive? *Food and other necessities could be exempted from the tax. Because the poor spend a larger percentage of their income on necessities, this would make the sales tax less regressive. Also, luxuries could be taxed at a higher rate. However, determining what a "luxury" is can be difficult.*

UNIT
5 Microeconomics
LONG FREE-RESPONSE
SAMPLE QUESTIONS
Answer
Key

Answers to Sample Long Free-Response Questions

1. One approach to the problem of pollution control in a market economy is the selling of pollution "credits" known also as *externality rights*. The pollution-control agency of Big Falls has determined that 500 tons of pollutants may be discharged into the Fox River each year because this is the determined recycling capacity of the river. Accordingly, 500 pollution credits entitling the owners to dump one ton of pollutants into the river in a year are available. The city intends to make 500 pollution credits available each year.

(A) What would be the shape of the supply curve for pollution credits in 2004? Why?

(B) What would be the shape of the supply curve for pollution credits in 2009? Why?

(C) Draw and label the demand curve for pollution credits in 2004. Why would it assume this shape?

(D) On the same graph, draw and label the demand curve for pollution credits in 2009. Explain what would happen to the demand over time.

(E) What would happen to the equilibrium price for pollution credits over time? Why?

(F) What are the costs and benefits of this approach to pollution control for producers, consumers and the public?

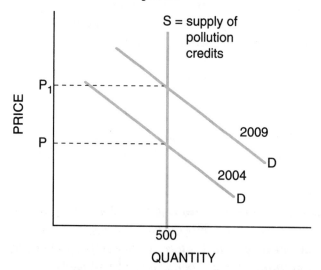

(A) *The supply curve for pollution credits would be a straight line and perfectly inelastic because the city decided to set an upper limit on these rights at 500.*

(B) *It would be the same: 500 per year.*

(C) *The demand curve in 2004 would assume the same downward slope as a demand curve for any other factor of production. Polluters therefore would have the choice of paying P for their credits or finding ways of polluting less.*

UNIT
5 Microeconomics
LONG FREE-RESPONSE
SAMPLE QUESTIONS

Answer
Key

(D) By 2009, we can assume that population growth and increased production by factories would increase the demand for pollution credits. Because credits remain fixed by the city's edict, the price would rise.

(E) The demand curve would move to the right, and the new equilibrium price would rise to P_1. The increased demand for a fixed supply would necessarily drive the price to a higher level.

(F) The costs to producers will almost always rise when government imposes an upper limit on pollution levels. Producers will have to cope with higher and higher prices for the right to dump waste, or they will have to explore new technologies to deal with it. Either way, their costs of production will go up in the short run (unless there is a technological breakthrough that costs very little to implement). A benefit to the public is a cleaner environment although goods will cost more.

2. Assume that the government places a 50 percent tax on Greebes. Neither the demand for Greebes nor the supply of Greebes is perfectly inelastic or perfectly elastic. With the use of graphs, explain what will determine the incidence of this tax on Greebes.

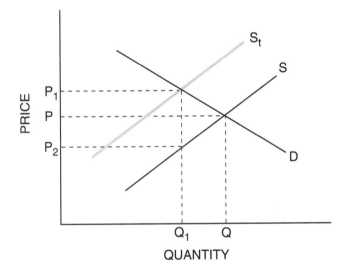

The incidence of the tax will be on both consumers and producers. The tax raises the costs of production, which decreases the supply. This decrease in supply causes the price to rise from P to P_1. This higher price is paid by consumers. However, the quantity of Greebes purchased falls from Q to Q_1. This decrease in the quantity of Greebes purchased means less after-tax revenue for the producers. The incidence of the tax is determined by the price elasticity of the demand curve. The incidence of the tax to consumers is represented by the distance $P_1 - P$ and to producers by the distance $P - P_2$.

---

3. What is the difference between the ability-to-pay theory of taxation and the benefits-received theory? Give an example of a tax that meets the criteria of the ability-to-pay theory and a tax that meets the criteria of the benefits-received theory.

The ability-to-pay theory says that the tax rate should depend on a person's ability to pay the tax. The effective tax rate for higher incomes should be greater than for lower incomes.

Large-income families should pay a higher tax rate than small-income families. The federal income tax meets the criteria of the ability-to-pay theory. There is an exemption for each family member, and the effective tax rate rises as income rises. Any progressive tax tends to meet the criteria of the ability-to-pay theory. Wealth should be considered in trying to adjust for ability to pay; differences in wealth are not always reflected fully in income.

The benefits-received theory of taxation holds that people who benefit from a government service should pay the tax. People who benefit more should pay higher taxes. The gasoline tax meets the criteria of the benefits-received theory. The gasoline tax funds highways. The more a person drives, the more gas he or she must buy and the more gas tax paid.

The Economic Functions of Government

1. Enforce laws and contracts.

2. Maintain competition.

3. Redistribute income. Provide an economic safety net.

4. Provide public goods:
   - Nonexclusion
   - Shared consumption

5. Correct market failures:
   - Provide market information.
   - Correct negative externalities.
   - Subsidize goods with positive externalities.

6. Stabilize the economy:
   - Fight unemployment.
   - Encourage price stability.
   - Promote economic growth.

Illustrating a Negative Externality

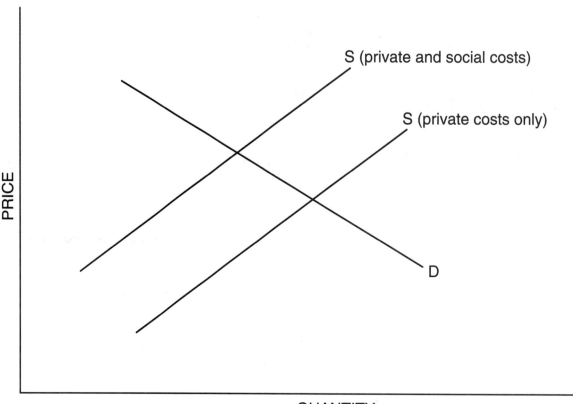

Illustrating a Positive Externality

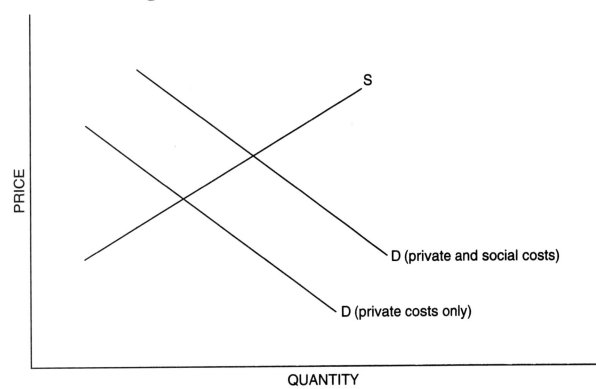

Key Ideas in Public-Choice Economics

1. Is it rational for government leaders to favor special interests over the general public interest?
   - Concentrated vs. special interests
   - Information costs

2. Why are politicians mainly in the middle of the road?
   - Median-voter model of political behavior

3. Are people rational or irrational when they spend little time evaluating candidates before they vote and when they don't vote?

4. What is the effect of bureaucratic entrepreneurs on government?

Advanced Placement

ECONOMICS

Macroeconomics
Teacher Resource Manual

Outline for an Advanced Placement Macroeconomics Course

75 class periods of 45 minutes each

Unit 1 Basic Economic Concepts
    (10 class periods or 450 minutes)
A. Scarcity: The Nature of Economic Systems
   1. Opportunity costs
   2. Production possibilities curves
B. Specialization, Trade and Comparative Advantage
   1. Determining comparative advantage with input information
   2. Determining comparative advantage with output information
C. Demand
   1. Relationship between price and quantity demanded
   2. Determinants of demand
   3. Changes in quantity demanded vs. changes in demand
D. Supply
   1. Relationship between supply and quantity supplied
   2. Determinants of supply
   3. Changes in quantity supplied vs. changes in supply
E. Introduction to Elasticity of Demand and Supply

Unit 2 Measuring Economic Performance
    (8 class periods or 360 minutes)
A. Circular Flow of Income
B. Macroeconomic Goals
C. Macroeconomic Measurement
   1. Gross domestic product
   2. Economic growth
   3. Price level
   4. Employment
D. Inflation and Price Indexes
   1. Difference between price level and inflation
   2. Different price indexes
   3. Nominal vs. real quantities
E. Unemployment
   1. Unemployment rate
   2. Labor force participation rate
   3. Types of unemployment
F. Business Cycles
   1. Phases of business cycle
   2. Definition of recession

Unit 3 Aggregate Demand and Aggregate Supply: Fluctuations in Outputs and Prices
(23 class periods or 1,035 minutes)

A. Aggregate Expenditure
   1. Keynesian Equilibrium
   2. Government expenditure, investment and tax multipliers
   3. Effects of investment spending decisions on national output
   4. Inventory changes in response to difference between aggregate expenditures and income
B. Aggregate Demand
   1. Difference between aggregate demand and microeconomic concept of demand
   2. Components of aggregate demand
   3. What effects each of the components of aggregate demand
   4. Determinants of the slope of the aggregate demand curve
   5. Determinants of shifts in the aggregate demand curve
C. Aggregate Supply
   1. Determinants of aggregate supply
   2. Alternative aggregate supply curve shapes
   3. Effects of the labor market on aggregate supply
   4. How wages are determined
D. Macroeconomic Equilibrium
   1. Aggregate demand and aggregate supply together
   2. Short-run equilibrium
   3. Effects of aggregate supply and aggregate demand shocks
   4. Long-run equilibrium and production possibilities curve
   5. Analysis of the economy moving from the short-run to the long-run equilibrium
E. Fiscal Policy
   1. Effects of changes in government spending
   2. Effects of changes in taxation
   3. Automatic stabilizers
   4. Short-run effects on output and the price level of fiscal policy

Unit 4 Money, Monetary Policy and Economic Stability
(14 class periods or 630 minutes)

A. Money and the Banking System
   1. Definitions of money
   2. Functions of money
   3. Relationship of money supply to nominal gross domestic product
   4. Creation of money and the deposit expansion multiplier
B. Monetary Policy and Aggregate Demand
   1. Tools of the central bank
   2. How the Federal Reserve's tools change the money supply
   3. How the interest rate is determined in the money market
   4. The transmission mechanisms of changes in the money supply to output and the price level

C. Real versus Nominal Interest Rates
   1. Definition of real and nominal interest rates
   2. Fisher equation showing the relationship between real and nominal interest rates
   3. Short-run effects of monetary policy on real and nominal interest rates
   4. Long-run effects of monetary policy on real and nominal interest rates

**Unit 5 Monetary and Fiscal Policy Combinations:
Stabilization Policy in the Real World**
   (13 class periods or 585 minutes)
A. Monetary and Fiscal Policy
   1. Monetary and fiscal policy working together
   2. The loanable funds market and relationship to the money market
   3. The interest rate effects of fiscal policy
B. Trade-off between Inflation and Unemployment
   1. Short-run Phillips curve
   2. Long-run Phillips curve
   3. Effect of expectations
C. Economic Growth
   1. Sources of economic growth
   2. What policies promote economic growth
   3. Showing economic growth using aggregate demand and aggregate supply analysis
   4. Showing economic growth using the production possibilities curve
D. Reasons for disagreements among economists about macroeconomic policies and effects of the
   policies

Unit 6 International Economics
   (7 class periods or 315 minutes)
A. International Trade
   1. Comparative advantage
   2. Gains from trade
   3. Consequences of government intervention into international trade
B. International Finance
   1. The current account, capital account and the balance of payments
   2. Exchange markets
   3. How domestic and foreign economies affect the exchange rate
C. Domestic Monetary and Fiscal Policy and International Economics
   1. Income effects
   2. Price effects
   3. Interest rate effects

Macroeconomics | Unit 1

Basic Economic Concepts

10 class periods or 450 minutes
(13 percent of course time)

Unit Overview

Unit 1 focuses on the fundamental concepts in economics. These concepts form 5 percent to 10 percent of the Advanced Placement Macroeconomics Examination. If the students are unable to explain and apply these concepts, they will have difficulty throughout the Macroeconomics Course because they will not understand the basis of the models discussed later. The topics covered in Unit 1 are the basic microeconomic concepts that underlie macroeconomics.

Scarcity is the concept that motivates the entire study of economics. If society could meet all the wants of people with existing resources, the discipline of economics would probably never have developed. However, people have unlimited wants and limited resources to meet these wants. Thus, people have to make choices. The students must understand scarcity, opportunity cost and the trade-off between choices. The production possibilities curve is used to demonstrate society's choices between two goods.

The production possibilities curve is also used to illustrate the advantages of specialization and trade. The concept of comparative advantage forms the basis for determining specialization and trade.

Because of scarcity and the need for society to make choices among the products to be produced, society must have a mechanism for deciding what will be produced, how it will be produced and who receives the goods and services. In a market system, the price mechanism is used to answer these questions. Unit 1 presents the key concepts of demand and supply. An understanding of demand, supply and equilibrium is essential to student understanding of economics and the market system. The final concept introduced is elasticity of demand.

If the students have taken an Advanced Placement Microeconomics Course, you may want to reduce the time you spend on Unit 1 and have the students do the activities as a refresher. The extra time should be spent on Units 3, 4 and 5.

The Lesson Planner

Lesson 1 emphasizes scarcity, opportunity cost, production possibilities curves and comparative advantage. It uses **Activities 1** and **2** and **Visuals 1.1** through **1.4**.

Lesson 2 introduces the concept of demand and the factors that shift the demand schedule. It uses **Activities 3** and **4** and **Visuals 1.5** and **1.6**.

Lesson 3 introduces the concept of supply and the factors that shift the supply schedule. It uses **Activities 5** and **6** and **Visuals 1.7** and **1.8**.

Lesson 4 brings the concepts of demand and supply together to determine equilibrium price and quantity. It uses **Activity 7** and **Visual 1.9**.

Lesson 5 demonstrates a variety of results given different elasticities of demand and supply curves. It uses **Activity 8** and **Visuals 1.10, 1.11** and **1.12**.

Week 1

Day 1

(A) Lecture on scarcity, opportunity costs and production possibilities curves using Visuals 1.1 and 1.2.

(B) Assign Activity 1 for homework.

Day 2

(A) Review Activity 1 answers.

(B) Lecture on trade and absolute and comparative advantage using Visuals 1.3 and 1.4.

(C) Assign Activity 2 for homework.

Day 3

(A) Review the students' answers to Activity 2.

(B) Lecture on demand using Visuals 1.5 and 1.6.

(C) Begin Activity 3 in class; have the students complete Activity 3 for homework.

Day 4

(A) Review Activity 3.

(B) Use Visual 1.6 to emphasize determinants of shifts in the demand curve.

(C) Have the students complete Activity 4 in class.

Day 5

(A) Review the students' answers to Activity 4.

(B) Lecture on supply using Visuals 1.7 and 1.8.

(C) Begin Activity 5 in class; have the students complete Activity 5 for homework.

Week 2

Day 6

(A) Review Activity 5.

(B) Use Visual 1.8 to emphasize the determinants of shifts in the supply curve.

(C) Have the students complete Activity 6 in class.

Day 7

(A) Review Activity 6.

(B) Lecture on market equilibrium using Visual 1.9.

(C) Have the students begin Activity 7 in class and complete for homework.

Day 8

(A) Review Activity 7.

(B) Lecture on elasticity using Visuals 1.10, 1.11 and 1.12.

(C) Have the students begin Activity 8 in class and complete for homework.

Day 9

(A) Review Activity 8.

(B) Review for unit test.

Day 10

Give unit test.

Scarcity, Opportunity Cost, Production Possibilities and Comparative Advantage

Introduction and Description

This lesson uses the concept of opportunity cost to develop a production possibilities curve. The production possibilities curve represents the choices that society faces. Opportunity cost is a fundamental concept in economics and includes not only out-of-pocket costs but also the cost to society of not using the resources to produce an alternative product or service. Alternative forms of the production possibilities curves illustrate different trade-offs. Activity 1 reinforces the concept of opportunity cost and investigates the alternative shapes of the production possibilities curve.

We use production possibilities curves to illustrate the economic situation that nations face and the advantages that exist if people or nations specialize in the production of specific goods and services and then trade for the goods and services they want. The concept of comparative advantage underlies trade and exchange within an economy and between different economies. Activity 2 provides practice at determining absolute and comparative advantage.

Objectives

1. Define *scarcity* and *opportunity cost*.
2. Apply scarcity and opportunity cost to a number of everyday situations.
3. Construct production possibilities curves using hypothetical data.
4. Apply the concept of opportunity cost to a production possibilities curve.
5. Analyze the different locations of points on, outside and inside a production possibilities curve.
6. Demonstrate and explain different shaped production possibilities curves.
7. Define *absolute advantage* and *comparative advantage*.
8. Determine comparative advantage when given data.
9. Explain how both parties gain from specialization and exchange.

Time Required

Two class periods or 90 minutes

Materials

1. Activities 1 and 2
2. Visuals 1.1, 1.2, 1.3 and 1.4

Procedure

1. Give a lecture on *scarcity* and *opportunity cost*.

   (A) People have unlimited wants.

   (B) Resources to fulfill these wants are limited. Resources are land, labor, capital and entrepreneurship.

   (C) Here are some examples of scarcity you might want to use:

   (i) A teenager wants to go to a soccer game on Saturday night but also wants to catch up on late school assignments. The teenager encounters the scarcity of time.

   (ii) A family wants to take a vacation to Mexico and build an addition on the house. They experience scarcity because family income will not permit both to occur.

2. Individuals and society must choose between the competing wants. They must make decisions. *Opportunity cost* emphasizes that people are making *choices*. People choose to do one activity and the cost is giving up another activity.

3. Use Visual 1.1 of a production possibilities curve (PPC) and emphasize the following points.

   (A) The PPC is drawn assuming that

(i) all resources (land, labor, capital, entrepreneurship) are fully employed.

(ii) the technology is constant.

(B) The shape of the PPC (bowed out or concave to the origin) determines the trade-off in the production of the two commodities. Note that the trade-off is not constant but increasing as we move along the curve.

(C) What other shapes could the PPC take, and what do the shapes imply about the trade-off? *The PPC can be either a straight line, representing constant opportunity costs, or convex to the origin, representing decreasing costs. Visual 1.2 provides alternative shapes.*

(D) If the factors of production were not fully utilized, where on the graph would an economy be? *The economy would be interior to the PPC, that is, between the origin and the PPC.*

4. Have the students complete Activity 1 as homework.

5. When reviewing Activity 1, emphasize these points:

(A) If the cost of obtaining one more unit of a good is increasing as you move down the PPC, then the cost of obtaining more of the other good must also be increasing as you move up the curve.

(B) The assumptions that determine the location of the PPC curve

(C) What determines if an economy is on the PPC curve, inside (in the region between the curve and the origin) or outside (beyond) the curve

6. Begin with a discussion of trade. Ask the students what life would be like if they could consume only the goods produced by the state they live in. How would production in the state change if each state had to be self-sufficient? Emphasize the point that it is individuals, not nations or states, that trade.

7. Use Visual 1.3 to distinguish between *absolute advantage* and *comparative advantage*. Discuss the examples on Visual 1.3.

(A) What if an economics professor can do word processing faster than any secretary the professor could hire? The professor has an absolute advantage in teaching economics and in word processing. Should she do her own typing? *No. The opportunity cost of the professor's time spent as a secretary is very high, perhaps $75 an hour. She should hire a secretary to do the typing because a secretary's wage is significantly less than $75 an hour.*

(B) The auto-mechanic and doctor situation is the same as the professor/secretary situation.

8. Use Visual 1.4 to illustrate absolute and comparative advantage using outputs. Calculate the opportunity cost of corn and of sunscreen for the students. This will help the students do Activity 2. Demonstrate that comparative advantage is based on the lower opportunity cost. Mexico has the absolute advantage and comparative advantage in the production of corn. Neither has an absolute advantage in the production of sunscreen. France has a comparative advantage in producing sunscreen.

9. Have the students complete Activity 2 for homework.

10. Review the answers to Activity 2.

Scarcity, Opportunity Cost and Production Possibilities Curves

Scarcity necessitates choice. Consuming or producing more of one commodity or service means consuming or producing less of something else. The opportunity cost of using scarce resources for one commodity or service instead of something else is often represented in graphical form as a *production possibilities curve.*

Part A

Use Figures 1.1 and 1.2 to answer Questions 1 and 2. Fill in the answer blanks, or underline the correct answer in parentheses.

※ Figure 1.1
Production Possibilities Curve 1

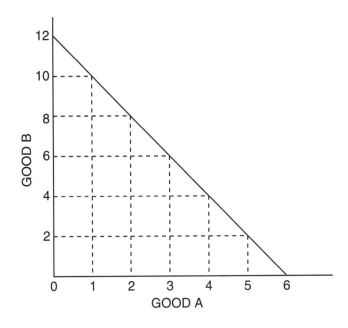

1. If the economy represented by Figure 1.1 is presently producing 12 units of Good B and zero units of Good A:

    (A) The opportunity cost of increasing production of Good A from zero units to one unit is the loss of ____*two*____ unit(s) of Good B.

    (B) The opportunity cost of increasing production of Good A from one unit to two units is the loss of ____*two*____ unit(s) of Good B.

    (C) The opportunity cost of increasing production of Good A from two units to three units is the loss of ____*two*____ unit(s) of Good B.

    (D) This is an example of (*__constant__* / increasing / decreasing / zero) opportunity cost per unit for Good A.

✳ Figure 1.2
Production Possibilities Curve 2

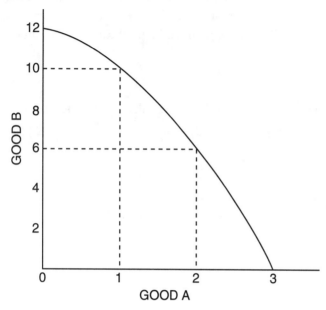

2. If the economy represented in Figure 1.2 is presently producing 12 units of Good B and zero units of Good A:

(A) The opportunity cost of increasing production of Good A from zero units to one unit is the loss of ___*two*___ unit(s) of Good B.

(B) The opportunity cost of increasing production of Good A from one unit to two units is the loss of ___*four*___ unit(s) of Good B.

(C) The opportunity cost of increasing production of Good A from two units to three units is the loss of ___*six*___ unit(s) of Good B.

(D) This is an example of (constant / ***increasing*** / decreasing / zero) opportunity cost per unit for Good A.

Part B

Use the axes in Figures 1.3 and 1.4 to draw the type of curve that illustrates the label above each axis.

✳ Figure 1.3

Production Possibilities Curve 3

Increasing opportunity cost per unit of Good B

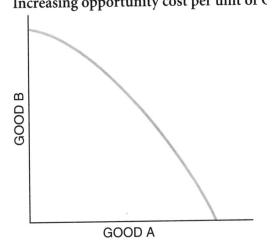

GOOD A

✳ Figure 1.4

Production Possibilities Curve 4

Constant opportunity cost per unit of Good B

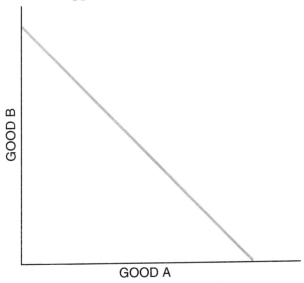

GOOD A

Part C

Use Figure 1.5 to answer the next five questions. Each question starts with Curve BB' as a country's production possibilities curve.

Figure 1.5

Production Possibilities Curve: Capital Goods and Consumer Goods

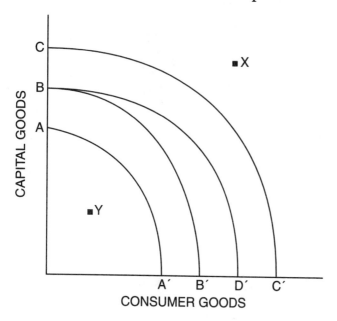

3. Suppose there is a major technological breakthrough in the consumer-goods industry, and the new technology is widely adopted. Which curve in the diagram would represent the new production possibilities curve? (Indicate the curve you choose with two letters.) ___*BD'*___

4. Suppose a new government comes into power and imposes a significant tax on the use of automated machinery and modern production techniques in all industries. Which curve in the diagram would represent the new production possibilities curve? (Indicate the curve you choose with two letters.) ___*AA'*___

5. Suppose massive new sources of oil and coal are found within the economy, and there are major technological innovations in both industries. Which curve in the diagram would represent the new production possibilities curve? (Indicate the curve you choose with two letters.) ___*CC'*___

6. If BB' represents a country's current production possibilities curve, what can you say about a point like X? (Write a brief statement.) *It is impossible for a country by itself to attain with existing resources and technology.*

7. If BB' represents a country's current production possibilities curve, what can you say about a point like Y? (Write a brief statement.) *The economy is not fully using existing resources and technology. An example of Point Y is the Great Depression of the 1930s.*

Opportunity Cost and Comparative Advantage

Part B: Questions

1. What is the difference between comparative advantage and absolute advantage? *Absolute advantage states that a particular individual or country can produce more of a specific commodity than another individual or country using the same amount of resources. Comparative advantage states that a particular country or individual can produce a specific commodity at a lower opportunity cost (in terms of forgone production in an alternative commodity) than another country or individual.*

2. You're given the following information about a newlywed couple and the time it takes each of them to do two different chores: vacuuming a room or washing a load of dishes.

	Mike	Debbie
Vacuum a room	60 minutes	45 minutes
Wash a load of dishes	30 minutes	45 minutes

(A) What is Mike's opportunity cost of vacuuming in terms of washing dishes?
Washing two loads of dishes

(B) What is Mike's opportunity cost of washing dishes in terms of vacuuming?
Vacuuming 1/2 of a room

(C) What is Debbie's opportunity cost of vacuuming in terms of washing dishes?
Washing one load of dishes

(D) What is Debbie's opportunity cost of washing dishes in terms of vacuuming?
Vacuuming one room

(E) Who has the *absolute* advantage in vacuuming? _____ *Debbie* _____

(F) Who has the *absolute* advantage in washing dishes? _____ *Mike* _____

(G) Who has the *comparative* advantage in vacuuming? _____ *Debbie* _____

(H) Who has the *comparative* advantage in washing dishes? _____ *Mike* _____

(I) Who should do which chore and why? Base your answer only on the information above and on comparative advantage considerations. *Mike should wash dishes and Debbie should vacuum. They will finish their chores sooner by specializing according to their comparative advantage. The person with the lower opportunity cost should perform the chore.*

3. Now, you're given the following information about Andy and Hannah and the time it takes each of them to clean an office and clean a jail cell:

	Andy	Hannah
Cleaning offices	60 minutes	20 minutes
Cleaning jail cells	30 minutes	15 minutes

(A) What is Andy's opportunity cost of cleaning offices in terms of cleaning jail cells?
Cleaning two jail cells

(B) What is Hannah's opportunity cost of cleaning offices in terms of cleaning jail cells?
Cleaning 4/3 of a jail cell

(C) What is Andy's opportunity cost of cleaning jail cells in terms of cleaning offices?
Cleaning 1/2 of an office

(D) What is Hannah's opportunity cost of cleaning jail cells in terms of cleaning offices?
Cleaning 3/4 of an office

(E) Who has the *absolute* advantage in cleaning offices?_____*Hannah*_____

(F) Who has the *absolute* advantage in cleaning jail cells?_____*Hannah*_____

(G) Who has the *comparative* advantage in cleaning offices?_____*Hannah*_____

(H) Who has the *comparative* advantage in cleaning jail cells?_____*Andy*_____

(I) Who should do which chore and why? Base your answer only on the information above and on comparative advantage considerations. *Hannah should clean offices and Andy should clean jail cells, and they will finish sooner. The person with the lower opportunity cost should perform the chore.*

4. Consider the following two countries. Assume they produce only these two goods. *Note that productivity is now measured in how many goods can be produced per hour*, the opposite of how we measured it in Questions 2 and 3.

	United States	Japan
Cars	12	10
Computers	4	6

(A) What is the United States' opportunity cost of making cars?
For every car, it must give up 1/3 of a computer.

(B) What is Japan's opportunity cost of making cars?
For every car, it must give up ³/₅ of a computer.

(C) What is the United States' opportunity cost of making computers?
For every computer, it must give up three cars.

(D) What is Japan's opportunity cost of making computers?
For every computer, it must give up ⁵/₃ of a car.

(E) Which country has the *absolute* advantage in cars? _____*United States*_____

(F) Which country has the *absolute* advantage in computers? _____*Japan*_____

(G) Which country has the *comparative* advantage in cars? _____*United States*_____

(H) Which country has the *comparative* advantage in computers? _____*Japan*_____

(I) Which country should produce which good and why? Base your answer only on the information above and on comparative advantage considerations. *The United States should produce cars, and Japan should produce computers because cars and computers would then be produced by the lower-cost country. The total output of cars and computers will be higher.*

5. Use the law of comparative advantage to explain why self-sufficiency leads to a lower standard of living. *If people and nations do not trade on the basis of comparative advantage, there will be fewer goods and services for people to enjoy. People will be poorer. Less trade or self-sufficiency means a lower standard of living.*

Demand

Introduction and Description

This lesson introduces the market system. Demand is half of a market and a demand schedule represents the quantities that people are willing and able to buy at alternative prices. The demand curve is a graphical representation of the demand schedule. Understanding a market is essential to success in AP Economics.

Activity 3 has the students graph a demand schedule and helps them understand the implications of a shift in the demand curve. The activity then focuses on the factors that shift the demand curve. Activity 4 reinforces the factors that cause a demand curve to shift, the direction of the shift and whether the shift represents an increase or decrease in demand.

Objectives

1. Define *demand schedule* and *demand curve.*
2. Construct a demand curve using hypothetical data.
3. Explain why consumers buy more of a good or service when the price decreases.
4. Explain the difference between a shift in the demand curve and a movement along the demand curve.
5. Describe and analyze the forces that shift the demand curve.
6. Explain why a demand curve would shift to the right or left given a scenario.

Time Required

Two class periods or 90 minutes

Materials

1. Activities 3 and 4
2. Visual 1.5 and Visual 1.6

Procedure

1. Begin with a discussion of demand. Have the students tell you how much they are willing to pay for various quantities of a commodity. One possibility is to use one student and tell this student that he or she has $10 to buy candy. Offer this student a candy bar and ask how much he or she would be willing to pay for it; then ask how much he or she would be willing to pay for two, etc. Write the quantities and prices down; create a demand schedule and graph it. *Note: The willingness to pay must be constrained by the $10 the student has as "income."*

2. Use Visual 1.5 and note that as the price decreases, the quantity demanded increases.

3. Use Visual 1.6. Show that an increase in demand is a shift to the right (and a decrease in demand is a shift to the left), and discuss the factors that will shift the demand curve. Changes in preferences, incomes, expectations, population or prices of complementary or substitute goods will shift the demand curve.

4. Have the students start Activity 3 in class and complete it for homework.

5. Review the answers to Activity 3.

6. Review the factors that shift the demand curve.

7. Have the students complete Activity 4 in class.

8. Review the answers to Activity 4.

Demand Curves, Movements Along Demand Curves and Shifts in Demand Curves

Part A

Figure 3.1 shows the market demand for a hypothetical product: Greebes. Study the data, and plot the demand for Greebes on the axes in Figure 3.2. Label the demand curve D, and answer the questions that follow. Write the correct answer in the answer blanks, or underline the correct words in parentheses.

Figure 3.1
Demand for Greebes

Price ($ per Greebe)	Quantity Demanded (millions of Greebes)
$.10	350
.15	300
.20	250
.25	200
.30	150
.35	100
.40	50

Figure 3.2
Demand for Greebes

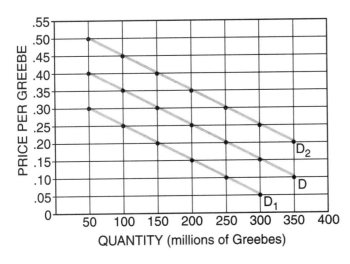

QUANTITY (millions of Greebes)

1. The data for demand curve D indicate that at a price of $0.30 per Greebe, buyers would be willing to buy ____150____ million Greebes. Other things constant, if the price of Greebes increased to $0.40 per Greebe, buyers would be willing to buy ____50____ million Greebes. Such a change would be a decrease in (demand / **quantity demanded**). Other things constant, if the price of Greebes decreased to $0.20, buyers would be willing to buy____250____ million Greebes. Such a change would be called an increase in (demand / **quantity demanded**).

2. Now, let's suppose there is a dramatic change in federal income-tax rates that affects the disposable income of Greebe buyers. This change in the *ceteris paribus* (all else being equal) conditions underlying the original demand for Greebes will result in a new set of data, shown in Figure 3.3. Study these new data, and add the new demand curve for Greebes to the axes in Figure 3.2. Label the new demand curve D₁ and answer the questions that follow.

Figure 3.3
New Demand for Greebes

Price ($ per Greebe)	Quantity Demanded (millions of Greebes)
$.05	300
.10	250
.15	200
.20	150
.25	100
.30	50

3. Comparing the new demand curve (D₁) with the original demand curve (D), we can say that the change in the demand for Greebes results in a shift of the demand curve to the *(**left** / right)*.

Such a shift indicates that at each of the possible prices shown, buyers are now willing to buy a *(**smaller** / larger)* quantity; and at each of the possible quantities shown, buyers are willing to offer a *(higher / **lower**)* maximum price. The cause of this demand curve shift was a(n) *(**increase** / decrease)* in tax rates that *(increased / **decreased**)* the disposable income of Greebe buyers.

4. Now, let's suppose that there is a dramatic change in people's tastes and preferences for Greebes. This change in the *ceteris paribus* conditions underlying the original demand for Greebes will result in a new set of data, shown in Figure 3.4. Study these new data, and add the new demand curve for Greebes to the axes in Figure 3.2. Label the new demand curve D₂ and answer the questions that follow.

Figure 3.4
New Demand for Greebes

Price ($ per Greebe)	Quantity Demanded (millions of Greebes)
$.20	350
.25	300
.30	250
.35	200
.40	150
.45	100
.50	50

Comparing the new demand curve (D₂) with the original demand curve (D), we can say that the change in the demand for Greebes results in a shift of the demand curve to the *(left / **right**)*.

Such a shift indicates that at each of the possible prices shown, buyers are now willing to buy a *(smaller / **larger**)* quantity; and at each of the possible quantities shown, buyers are willing to offer a *(lower / **higher**)* maximum price. The cause of this shift in the demand curve was a(n) *(**increase** / decrease)* in people's tastes and preferences for Greebes.

Part B

Now, to test your understanding, underline the answer you think is the one best alternative in each of the following multiple-choice questions.

5. Other things constant, which of the following would *not* cause a change in the demand (shift in the demand curve) for mopeds?

    (A) A decrease in consumer incomes

    (B) A decrease in the price of mopeds

    (C) An increase in the price of bicycles, a substitute for mopeds

    (D) An increase in people's tastes and preferences for mopeds

6. "Rising oil prices have caused a sharp decrease in the demand for oil." Speaking precisely, and using terms as they are defined by economists, choose the statement that best describes this quotation.

    (A) The quotation is correct: An increase in price always causes a decrease in *demand*.

    (B) The quotation is incorrect: An increase in price always causes an increase in *demand*, not a decrease in *demand*.

    (C) The quotation is incorrect: An increase in price causes a decrease in the quantity demanded, not a decrease in demand.

    (D) The quotation is incorrect: An increase in price causes an increase in the *quantity demanded*, not a decrease in *demand*.

7. "As the price of domestic automobiles has inched upward, customers have found foreign autos to be a better bargain. Consequently, domestic auto sales have been decreasing, and foreign auto sales have been increasing." Using only the information in this quotation and assuming everything else constant, which of the following best describes this statement?

    (A) A shift in the demand curves for both domestic and foreign automobiles

    (B) A movement along the demand curves for both foreign and domestic automobiles

    (C) A movement along the demand curve for domestic autos, and a shift in the demand curve for foreign autos

    (D) A shift in the demand curve for domestic autos, and a movement along the demand curve for foreign autos

8. You hear a fellow student say: "Economic markets are like a perpetual see-saw. If demand rises, the price rises; if price rises, then demand will fall. If demand falls, price will fall; if price falls, demand will rise and so on forever." Dispel your friend's obvious confusion in no more than one short paragraph below.

The student is confusing a change in "demand" (shift in the curve) with a change in "quantity demanded" (a movement along the curve). Part of the second sentence — "if price rises, then demand will fall" — is wrong: The quantity demanded will fall; and since this is not a change in demand, the rest of the statement does not follow.

Reasons for Changes in Demand

Part A

Read the eight newspaper headlines in Figure 4.2, and use the table to record the impact, if any, of each event on the demand for beef. Use the first column to the right of the headline to show whether the event causes a change in demand. Use the next column to record whether the change is an increase or a decrease in demand. In the third column, decide whether the demand curve shifts left or right. Finally, write the letter for the new demand curve. Use Figure 4.1 to help you. **Always start at curve B**, and move only one curve at a time. One headline implies that the demand for beef does not change.

Figure 4.1
Beef Consumption in May

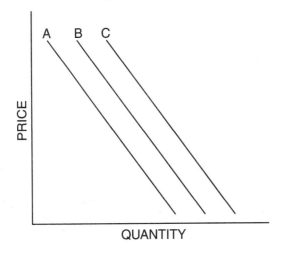

Figure 4.2

Headline	Demand Shift? (Y / N)	If Demand Shifts, Inc / Dec	Curve Shifts Left / Right	New Curve
1. Price of Beef to Rise in June	Y	Inc.	R	C
2. Millions of Immigrants Swell U.S. Population	Y	Inc.	R	C
3. Pork Prices Drop	Y	Dec.	L	A
4. Surgeon General Warns That Eating Beef Is Hazardous to Health	Y	Dec.	L	A
5. Beef Prices Fall; Consumers Buy More	N	—	—	—
6. Real Income for U.S. Drops for Third Month	Y	Dec.	L	A
7. Charcoal Shortage Threatens Memorial Day Cookouts	Y	Dec.	L	A
8. Nationwide Fad: The Disco-Burger	Y	Inc.	R	C

Part B

Categorize each change in demand in Part A according to the reason why demand changed. A given demand curve assumes that consumer expectations, consumer tastes and preferences, the number of consumers in the market, the income of consumers, and the prices of substitutes and complements are unchanged. In the table below, place an X next to the reason that the event described in the headline caused a change in demand. One headline will have no answer because it is a change in quantity demanded.

 Figure 4.3

↓ Reason Headline Number →	1	2	3	4	5	6	7	8
A change in consumer expectations	x							
A change in consumer tastes				x				x
A change in the number of consumers in the market		x						
A change in income						x		
A change in the price of a substitute good			x					
A change in the price of a complementary good							x	

Advanced Placement Economics Teacher Resource Manual © National Council on Economic Education, New York, N.Y.

Supply

Introduction and Description

Lesson 2 introduced demand. This lesson introduces supply, the other half of the market system. A supply schedule represents the quantities that firms are willing and able to supply at alternative prices. A supply curve is a graphical representation of the supply schedule. Understanding a market is essential to success in AP Economics.

Activity 5 has the students graph a supply schedule and helps them understand the implications of a shift in the supply curve. The activity then focuses on the factors that shift the supply curve. Activity 6 reinforces the factors that cause a supply curve to shift, the direction of the shift and whether the shift represents an increase or decrease in supply.

Objectives

1. Define *supply schedule* and *supply curve.*
2. Construct a supply curve using hypothetical data.
3. Explain why producers are willing to supply more of a good or service when the price increases.
4. Explain the difference between a shift in the supply curve and a movement along the supply curve.
5. Explain the difference between an increase in supply and an increase in the quantity supplied.
6. Describe and analyze the forces that shift the supply curve.
7. Explain why a supply curve would shift to the right or left given specific changes in the economy.

Time Required

Two class periods or 90 minutes

Materials

1. Activities 5 and 6
2. Visual 1.7 and Visual 1.8

Procedure

1. Begin with a discussion of supply. Ask the students what factors they think determine how much a firm will produce. Be sure to emphasize that supply is not inventory or stock, but the amount producers are willing and able to bring to market at alternative prices.

2. Use Visual 1.7 and note that as the price decreases, the quantity supplied decreases.

3. Use Visual 1.8. Show that an increase in supply is a shift to the right (and a decrease in supply is a shift to the left), and discuss the factors that will shift the supply curve.

4. Have the students start Activity 5 in class and complete it for homework.

5. Review the answers to Activity 5.

6. Review the factors that shift the supply curve.

7. Have the students complete Activity 6 in class.

8. Review the answers to Activity 6 with the students.

Supply Curves, Movements Along Supply Curves and Shifts in Supply Curves

In this activity and those that follow, we will assume that the long-run supply curve of Greebes is typically upward sloping.

Part A

Study the data in Figure 5.1 and plot the supply of Greebes on the axes in Figure 5.2. Label the supply curve S and answer the questions that follow. Write the correct answer on the answer blank, or underline the correct answer in parentheses.

 Figure 5.1
Supply of Greebes

Price ($ per Greebe)	Quantity Supplied (millions of Greebes)
$.15	100
.20	150
.25	200
.30	250
.35	300

 Figure 5.2
Supply of Greebes

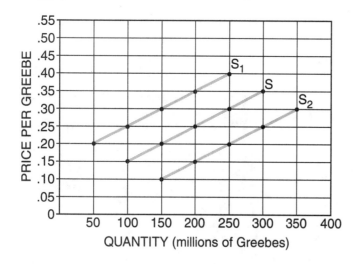

1. The data for supply curve S indicate that at a price of $0.25 per Greebe, suppliers would be willing to offer ____200____ million Greebes. Other things constant, if the price of Greebes increased to $0.30 per Greebe, suppliers would be willing to offer ____250____ million Greebes. Such a change would be an increase in (supply / **quantity supplied**).

Other things constant, if the price of Greebes decreased to $0.20 per Greebe, suppliers would be willing to offer ____*150*____ million Greebes. Such a change would be called a decrease in *(supply / **quantity supplied**)*.

2. Now, let's suppose that there is a dramatic change in the price of several of the raw materials used in making Greebes. This change in the *ceteris paribus* conditions underlying the original supply of Greebes will result in a new set of data, such as that shown in Figure 5.3. Study the data, and plot this supply of Greebes on the axes in Figure 5.2. Label the new supply curve S_1 and answer the questions that follow.

Figure 5.3
New Supply of Greebes

Price ($ per Greebe)	Quantity Supplied (millions of Greebes)
$.20	50
.25	100
.30	150
.35	200
.40	250

3. Comparing the new supply curve (S_1) with the original supply curve (S), we can say that a change in the supply of Greebes results in a shift of the supply curve to the (***left*** / right). Such a shift indicates that at each of the possible prices shown, suppliers are now willing to offer a (***smaller*** / larger) quantity; and at each of the possible quantities shown, suppliers are willing to accept a (***higher*** / lower) minimum price. The cause of this supply curve shift was a(n) (***increase*** / decrease) in prices of several of the raw materials used in making Greebes.

4. Now, let's suppose that there is a dramatic change in the price of Silopanna, a resource used in the production of Greebes. This change in the *ceteris paribus* conditions underlying the original supply of Greebes will result in a new set of data shown in in Figure 5.4. Study the data, and plot this supply of Greebes on the axes in Figure 5.2. Label the new supply curve S_2 and answer the questions that follow.

Figure 5.4
New Supply of Greebes

Price ($ per Greebe)	Quantity Supplied (millions of Greebes)
$.10	150
.15	200
.20	250
.25	300
.30	350

Comparing the new supply curve (S_2) with the original supply curve (S), we can say that the change in the supply of Greebes results in a shift of the supply curve to the *(left / **right**)*. Such a shift indicates that at each of the possible prices shown, suppliers are now willing to offer a *(smaller / **larger**)* quantity; and at each of the possible quantities shown, suppliers are willing to accept a *(**lower** / higher)* minimum price. The cause of this supply curve shift is a(n) *(increase / **decrease**)* in the price of Silopanna, a resource used in the production of Greebes.

Part B

Now, to check your understanding, underline the answer you think is the one best alternative in each of the following multiple-choice questions.

5. Other things constant, which of the following would *not* cause a change in the long-run supply of beef?

    (A) A decrease in the price of beef

    (B) A decrease in the price of cattle feed

    (C) An increase in the price of cattle feed

    (D) An increase in the cost of transporting cattle to market

6. "Falling oil prices have caused a sharp decrease in the supply of oil." Speaking precisely, and using terms as they are defined by economists, choose the statement that best describes this quotation.

    (A) The quotation is correct: A decrease in price always causes a decrease in *supply*.

    (B) The quotation is incorrect: A decrease in price always causes an increase in *supply*, not a decrease in *supply*.

    (C) The quotation is incorrect: A decrease in price causes an increase in the *quantity supplied*, not a decrease in *supply*.

    (D) The quotation is incorrect: A decrease in price causes a decrease in the quantity supplied, not a decrease in supply.

7. A multiyear drought in Florida has dried the land so that rampant wildfires have destroyed many orange groves. Florida oranges supply much of the nation's orange juice. Which statement below is correct?

    (A) The price of orange juice will rise because of a movement up the supply curve.

    (B) The price of orange juice will rise because the supply curve will shift to the left.

    (C) The price of orange juice will fall because of a movement down the supply curve.

    (D) The price of orange juice will fall because the supply curve will shift to the right.

8. A popular movie star wears a certain style of sunglasses. If her fans want to copy her look,

    (A) the price of the movie star's brand of sunglasses will rise because of a movement up the supply curve.

    (B) the price of the movie star's brand of sunglasses will rise because the supply curve will shift to the left.

    (C) the price of the movie star's brand of sunglasses will fall because of a movement down the supply curve.

    (D) the price of the movie star's brand of sunglasses will fall because the supply curve will shift to the right.

Reasons for Changes in Supply

Part A

Read the eight newspaper headlines in Figure 6.2, and record the impact, if any, of each event on the supply of cars. Use the first column to the right of the headline to show whether the event will cause a change in supply. Use the next column to record whether the change is an increase or a decrease in supply. In the third column, decide whether the supply curve shifts left or right. Finally, write the letter for the new supply curve. Use Figure 6.1 to help you. **Always start at curve B**, and move only one curve at a time. Two headlines imply that the supply of cars does not change.

Figure 6.1
Supply of Foreign and Domestic Cars

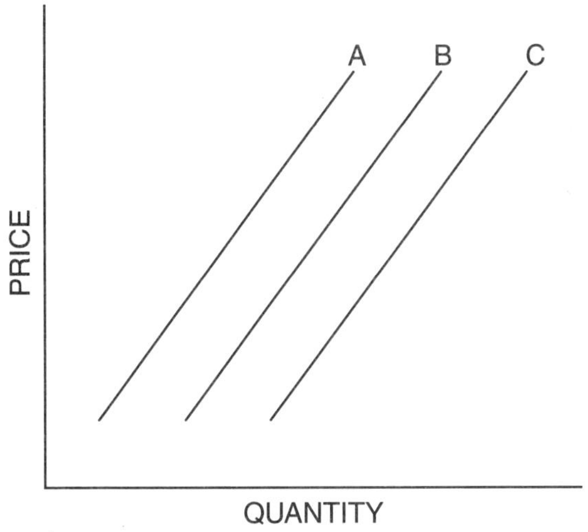

Figure 6.2

Headline	Supply Shift? (Y / N)	If Supply Shifts, Inc / Dec	Curve Shifts Left / Right	New Curve
1. Auto Workers' Union Agrees to Wage Cuts	*Y*	*Inc.*	*R*	*C*
2. New Robot Technology Increases Efficiency	*Y*	*Inc.*	*R*	*C*
3. Nationwide Auto Strike Began at Midnight	*Y*	*Dec.*	*L*	*A*
4. New Import Quotas Reduce Foreign Car Imports	*Y*	*Dec.*	*L*	*A*
5. Cost of Steel Rises	*Y*	*Dec.*	*L*	*A*
6. Auto Producer Goes Bankrupt; Closes Operation	*Y*	*Dec.*	*L*	*A*
7. Buyers Reject New Models	*N*	—	—	—
8. National Income Rises 2%	*N*	—	—	—

Part B

Categorize each change in supply in Part A according to the reason why supply changed. In Figure 6.3, place an X next to the reason that the event described in the headline caused a change in supply. In some cases, more than one headline could be matched to a reason. Two headlines do not indicate a shift in supply.

 Figure 6.3

↓ Reason Headline Number →	1	2	3	4	5	6	7	8
A change in costs of inputs to production process	x	x			x			
A change in technology		x						
A change in the number of producers in the market			x	x		x		
Government policies				x				

Equilibrium Price and Quantity

Introduction and Description

In this lesson we bring the two sides of the market — demand and supply — together to determine the equilibrium price and quantity. The students should understand that unless there are forces operating to change supply or demand, the price and quantity will remain at the equilibrium.

Activity 7 brings the supply and demand sides of the market together and helps the students understand equilibrium price and quantity. The factors that shift supply and demand are also used to emphasize the impact of supply or demand on the equilibrium price and quantity. The second part of Activity 7 has the students work through changes in supply and demand and the effects in related markets.

Objectives

1. Define *equilibrium price* and *equilibrium quantity*.
2. Determine the equilibrium price and quantity when given the demand for and supply of a good or commodity.
3. Explain why, at prices above or below the equilibrium price, market forces operate to move the price back toward equilibrium price.
4. Predict the equilibrium price and quantity if there are changes in demand or supply.
5. Given a change in supply or demand, explain which curve shifted and why.
6. Explain how markets act as rationing devices.

Time Required

One class period or 45 minutes

Materials

1. Activity 7
2. Visual 1.9

Procedure

1. Begin with a discussion of equilibrium. Review the importance of the market as a price determination mechanism.

2. Use Visual 1.9 to explain market equilibrium.

   (A) What happens if the price is $10? *The quantity supplied is 100, and the quantity demanded is 60. Therefore, there is excess supply.*

   (B) What happens if the price is $6? *The quantity demanded is 100, and the quantity supplied is 60. Therefore, there is excess demand.*

   (C) What happens if the price is $8? *The quantity that producers want to sell is exactly equal to the quantity that buyers want to buy. The market is in equilibrium.*

3. Have the students start Activity 7 in class and complete it for homework.

4. Review with the students the answers to Activity 7.

Equilibrium Price and Equilibrium Quantity

Part A

Figure 7.1 below shows the demand for Greebes and the supply of Greebes. Plot these data on the axes in Figure 7.2. Label the demand curve D and label the supply curve S. Then answer the questions that follow. Fill in the answer blanks, or underline the correct answers in parentheses.

Figure 7.1
Demand for and Supply of Greebes

Price ($ per Greebe)	Quantity Demanded (millions of Greebes)	Quantity Supplied (millions of Greebes)
$.15	300	100
.20	250	150
.25	200	200
.30	150	250
.35	100	300

Figure 7.2
Demand for and Supply of Greebes

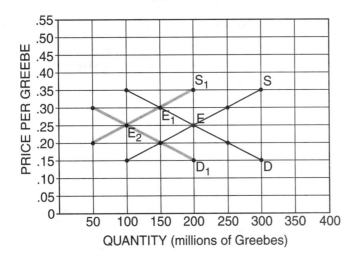

1. Under these conditions, competitive market forces would tend to establish an equilibrium price of _____ $ 0.25 _____ per Greebe and an equilibrium quantity of _____ 200 _____ million Greebes.

2. If the price currently prevailing in the market is $0.30 per Greebe, buyers would want to buy _____ 150 _____ million Greebes and sellers would want to sell _____ 250 _____ million Greebes. Under these conditions, there would be a (*shortage* / *surplus*) of _____ 100 _____ million Greebes. Competitive market forces would tend to cause the price to (*increase* / *decrease*) to a price of _____ $0.25 _____ per Greebe.

   At this new price, buyers would now want to buy _____ 200 _____ million Greebes, and sellers now want to sell _____ 200 _____ million Greebes. Because of this change in (*price* / *underlying conditions*), the (*demand* / *__quantity demanded__*) changed by ___*50*___ million Greebes, and the (*supply* / *__quantity supplied__*) changed by ___*50*___ million Greebes.

3. If the price currently prevailing in the market is $0.20 per Greebe, buyers would want to buy ___*250*___ million Greebes, and sellers would want to sell ___*150*___ million Greebes. Under these conditions, there would be a (*__shortage__* / surplus) of ___*100*___ million Greebes. Competitive market forces would tend to cause the price to (*__increase__* / decrease) to a price of ___*$0.25*___ per Greebe. At this new price, buyers would now want to buy ___*200*___ million Greebes, and sellers now want to sell ___*200*___ million Greebes. Because of this change in (*__price__* / underlying conditions), the (*demand* / *__quantity demanded__*) changed by 50 million Greebes, and the (*supply* / *__quantity supplied__*) changed by ___*50*___ million Greebes.

4. Now, suppose a mysterious blight causes the supply schedule for Greebes to change to the following:

Figure 7.3
New Supply of Greebes

Price ($ per Greebe)	Quantity Supplied (millions of Greebes)
$.20	50
.25	100
.30	150
.35	200

   Plot the new supply schedule on the axes in Figure 7.2 and label it S_1. Label the new equilibrium E_1. Under these conditions, competitive market forces would tend to establish an equilibrium price of ___*$0.30*___ per Greebe and an equilibrium quantity of ___*150*___ million Greebes.

   Compared with the equilibrium price in Question 1, we say that because of this change in (*price* / *__underlying conditions__*), the (*__supply__* / quantity supplied) changed; and both the equilibrium price and the equilibrium quantity changed. The equilibrium price (*__increased__* / decreased), and the equilibrium quantity (*increased* / *__decreased__*).

5. Now, with the supply schedule at S_1, suppose further that a sharp drop in people's incomes as the result of a prolonged recession causes the demand schedule to change to the following:

Figure 7.4
New Demand for Greebes

Price ($ per Greebe)	Quantity Demanded (millions of Greebes)
$.15	200
.20	150
.25	100
.30	50

Plot the new demand schedule on the axes in Figure 7.2 and label it D_1. Label the new equilibrium E_2. Under these conditions, with the supply schedule at S_1, competitive market forces would tend to establish an equilibrium price of ___*$0.25*___ per Greebe and an equilibrium quantity of ___*100*___ million Greebes. Compared with the equilibrium price in Question 4, because of this change in (*price* / ***underlying conditions***), the (***demand*** / *quantity demanded*) changed. The equilibrium price (*increased* / ***decreased***), and the equilibrium quantity (*increased* / ***decreased***).

6. The movement from the first equilibrium price and quantity to the new equilibrium price and quantity is the result of a (*price* / ***nonprice***) effect.

Part B

The following questions refer to a group of related markets in the United States during a given time period. Assume that the markets are perfectly competitive and that the supply and demand model is completely applicable. The figures show the supply and demand in each market *before* the assumed change occurs. Trace through the effects of the assumed change, *other things constant*. Work your way from left to right. Shift only one curve in each market. For each market, draw whatever new supply or demand curves are needed, labeling each new curve S_1 or D_1. Then circle the correct symbol under each diagram (↑ for increase, — for unchanged, and ↓ for decrease). Remember to shift only one curve in each market.

7. Assume that a new fertilizer dramatically increases the amount of wheat that can be harvested with no additional labor or machinery. Also assume that this fertilizer does not affect potato farming and that people are satisfied to eat either bread made from wheat flour or potatoes.

 Figure 7.5

Effects of a New Fertilizer

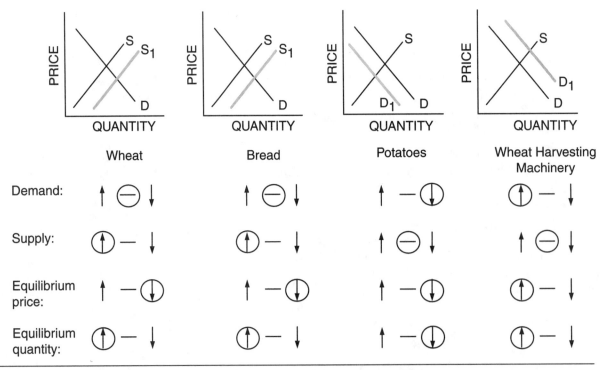

    Advanced Placement Economics Teacher Resource Manual © National Council on Economic Education, New York, N.Y.

8. Assume that a heavy frost destroys half the world's coffee crop and that people use more cream in coffee than they do in tea.

Figure 7.6
Effects of a Loss of Coffee Crop

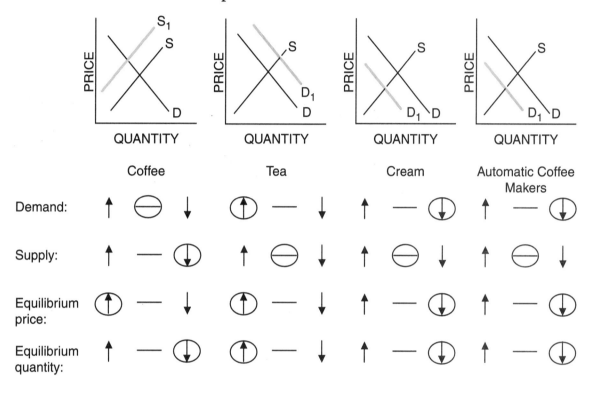

9. Assume beef and pork are perfect substitutes. The price of pork rises dramatically. Catsup is a complement to beef; mustard is a complement to pork.

Figure 7.7
Effects of a Change in the Price of Pork

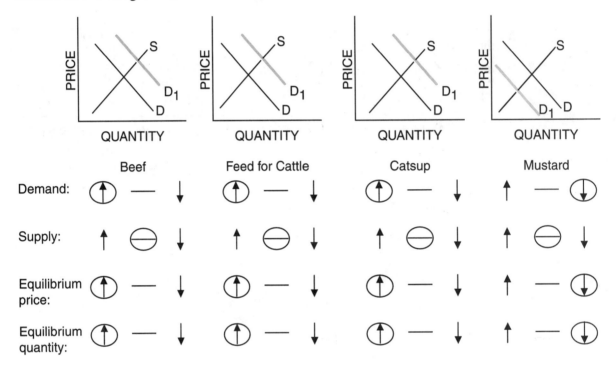

Elasticity

Introduction and Description

In many economic situations, producers and policy makers want to know more than simply the direction in which price or quantity will move. The law of demand tells producers that if price increases, the quantity demanded will decrease. This law doesn't tell the producers by *how much* the quantity demanded will decrease. The responsiveness of one variable to changes in another variable is important information. Elasticity is a measurement of how much one variable will change if another variable changes.

Activity 8 focuses on the definition of elasticity and the calculation of the coefficient of elasticity. The activity then has the students see the difference between elasticity of a curve and the slope of a curve.

Objectives

1. Define *price elasticity of demand* and *price elasticity of supply.*
2. Calculate price elasticity using the arc method.
3. Predict the effect on price and quantity given demand curves with different elasticities.
4. Explain the difference between slope of a line and the elasticity between two points on a line.

Time Required

One class period or 45 minutes

Materials

1. Activity 8
2. Visuals 1.10, 1.11 and 1.12

Procedure

1. Begin with a discussion of elasticity. Review the importance of the market as a price-determination mechanism.

2. Provide several examples and demonstrate the method to calculate the elasticity of each curve. Be sure to show elastic as well as inelastic demand curves. Visual 1.10 contains two examples. Be sure to emphasize that demand elasticity is always negative and supply elasticity is always positive. For this reason, we look at the absolute value of the coefficient of elasticity and always talk about positive values.

3. Emphasize by working through an example that elasticity and slope are different concepts. Use Visual 1.11 to show that the elasticity of a straight line is not constant. Use this example to show that slope of a straight line is constant. Emphasize that slope and elasticity are not the same concept. The slope is 1 at both ends of the demand curve.

4. Use Visual 1.12 to explain the effects of changes with demand curves with different elasticities.

   (A) Which demand curve is more inelastic? *D*

   (B) What happens to the equilibrium price and quantity with an elastic demand curve if supply increases? *With an elastic demand curve, the price effect is smaller and the quantity effect is larger than with an inelastic demand curve.*

   (C) What happens to the equilibrium price and quantity with an inelastic demand curve if supply increases? *With an inelastic demand curve, the price effect is greater and the quantity effect is smaller than with the elastic demand curve.*

5. Have the students start Activity 8 in class and complete it for homework.

6. Review with the students the answers to Activity 8.

Elasticity: An Introduction

Part A
Problems Involving Extra Credit

1. Now, suppose that your economics teacher currently allows you to earn extra credit by submitting answers to the end-of-the-chapter questions in your textbook. The number of questions you're willing to submit depends on the amount of extra credit for each question. How responsive you are to a change in the extra-credit points the teacher gives can be represented as an *elasticity*. Write the formula for the elasticity of extra-credit problems submitted:

$$\varepsilon_{ps} = \frac{percentage\ change\ in\ number\ of\ questions}{percentage\ change\ in\ extra\text{-}credit\ points}$$

2. Now, consider that your teacher's goal is to get you to submit twice as many questions: a 100-percent increase. Underline the correct answer in parentheses.

   (A) If the number of chapter-end questions you submit *is* very responsive to a change in extra-credit points, then a given increase in extra credit elicits a large increase in questions submitted. In this case, your teacher will need to increase the extra-credit points by (*more than* / **_less than_** / *exactly*) 100 percent.

   (B) If the number of chapter-end questions you submit *is not* very responsive to a change in extra-credit points, then a given increase in extra credit elicits a small increase in questions submitted. In this case, your teacher will need to increase the extra-credit points by (**_more than_** / *less than* / *exactly*) 100 percent.

Part D
Problems Involving Coffee

Suppose Moonbucks, a national coffee-house franchise, finally moves into the little town of Middle-ofnowhere. Moonbucks is the only supplier of coffee in town and faces the following demand schedule each week. Write the correct answer on the answer blanks, or underline the correct answer in parentheses.

 Figure 8.3

Cups of Coffee Demanded per Week

Price (per cup)	Quantity Demanded
$6	80
5	100
4	120
3	140
2	160
1	180
0	200

3. What is the arc price elasticity of demand when the price changes from $1 to $2? ___*.18*___

$$\varepsilon_d = \frac{\dfrac{\Delta Q}{(Q + Q_1)/2}}{\dfrac{\Delta P}{(P + P_1)/2}} = \frac{\dfrac{20}{170}}{\dfrac{1}{1.5}} = \frac{.12}{.67}$$

So, over this range of prices, demand is (*elastic / unit elastic / __inelastic__*).

4. What is the arc price elasticity of demand when the price changes from $5 to $6? ___*1.22*___

$$\varepsilon_d = \frac{\dfrac{\Delta Q}{(Q + Q_1)/2}}{\dfrac{\Delta P}{(P + P_1)/2}} = \frac{\dfrac{20}{90}}{\dfrac{1}{5.5}} = \frac{.22}{.18}$$

So, over this range of prices, demand is (*__elastic__ / unit elastic / inelastic*).

Note: Because the relationship between quantity demanded and price is inverse, price elasticity of demand would always be negative. Economists believe using negative numbers is confusing when referring to "large" or "small" elasticities of demand. Therefore, they use absolute or positive numbers, changing the sign on the negative numbers.

Part E

Now, consider Figure 8.4, which graphs the demand schedule given in Figure 8.3.
Recall the slope of a line is measured by the rise over the run: slope = rise / run = $\Delta P / \Delta Q$.

Figure 8.4
Elasticity of Demand for Coffee

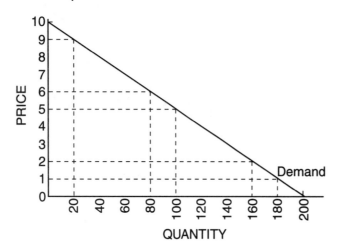

5. Using your calculations of ΔP and ΔQ from Question 3, calculate the slope of the demand curve.
   <u>   1/20 or .05   </u>

6. Using your calculations of ΔP and ΔQ from Question 4, calculate the slope of the demand curve.
   <u>   1/20 or .05   </u>   *This is the same slope as for Question 5. These calculations help the students to understand in Question 7 that a demand curve of constant slope has several varying elasticities.*

7. The law of demand tells us that an increase in price results in a decrease in the quantity demanded. Questions 5 and 6 remind us that the slope of a straight line is *constant everywhere along the line.* Along this demand curve, a change in price of $1 generates a change in quantity demanded of 20 cups of coffee a week.

   You've now shown mathematically that while the slope of the demand curve is related to elasticity, the two concepts are not the same thing. Briefly discuss the relationship between where you are along the demand curve and the elasticity of demand. How does this tie into the notion of *responsiveness? At a higher price, you are in the price elastic portion of the demand curve. As you move to a lower price along a demand curve, the demand curve becomes more price inelastic. Thus, at a high price, a small percentage change in price leads to a large percentage change in quantity. As the price decreases, the same percentage change in price generates a smaller percentage change in quantity, so the elasticity of demand decreases.*

Answers to Sample Multiple-Choice Questions

1. D	13. C	25. C
2. B	14. C	26. E
3. E	15. C	27. C
4. B	16. D	28. D
5. D	17. D	29. B
6. C	18. E	30. B
7. E	19. C	31. A
8. B	20. C	32. D
9. B	21. A	33. C
10. C	22. C	34. D
11. B	23. C	35. E
12. A	24. A	36. C

Answers to Sample Short Free-Response Questions

1. True, false or uncertain, and explain why? "The economic concept of scarcity is not relevant to the study of a modern economy such as that of the United States because the existence of unsold stocks of goods (books, cars, homes) is vivid evidence that we are surrounded by plenty, not scarcity."
   False. Economic scarcity refers to the fact that there are a limited number of productive resources available to satisfy the unlimited wants of society.

2. A newspaper headline says, "The Coldest Winter in 20 Years Brings Record Prices for Heating Oil."
   (A) Using a graph of home heating oil, show and explain how price changed.
   The record cold increases the demand for heating oil to run heaters, so the demand increases, raising the price and quantity sold.

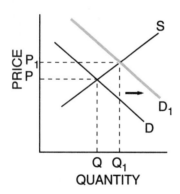

   (B) What other factors could cause the price of heating oil to increase?
   Any factor that increased demand could increase price and quantity.
   Any factor that decreased supply could increase price and decrease quantity.

      Advanced Placement Economics Teacher Resource Manual © National Council on Economic Education, New York, N.Y.

3. In a recent year, the price of wheat fell. For each of the following, draw a supply and demand graph showing a decrease in prices with the stated impact on quantity.

(A) The quantity of wheat decreasing

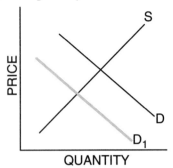

(B) The quantity of wheat increasing

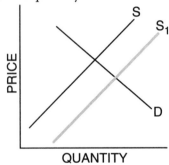

(C) The quantity of wheat staying the same

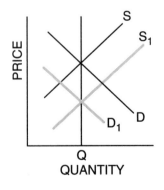 OR 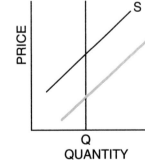 OR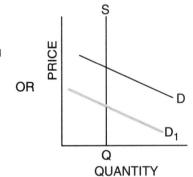

4. True, false or uncertain, and explain why? "If you won $1 million in the lottery, you wouldn't have the economic problem of scarcity." *False. People with $1 million cannot spend more than $1 million. Even if people had all the money they could use, time to use it would be scarce.*

5. Explain what would have to be true in each case for the production possibilities curves to be shaped as they are in Graphs I, II and III.

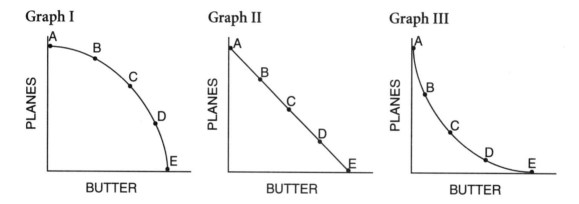

Graph I   Graph II   Graph III

In Graph I there are increasing costs. To move from B to C to D, the economy must give up increasing numbers of planes. The factors that produce butter and planes are not equally efficient in the production of both commodities.

In Graph II there are constant costs. To move from B to C to D, the economy must give up the same number of planes to gain the same amount of butter — for example, one plane for 25 pounds of butter.

In Graph III there are decreasing costs of production. To move from B to C to D, the economy has to give up decreasing numbers of planes to get the same amount of butter. In this situation, the economy would end up at one end or the other: at either Point A or Point E.

Answers to Sample Long Free-Response Questions

1. Every society has the fundamental problem of scarcity.

   (A) What is scarcity? *Scarcity exists because there are limited resources to fulfill unlimited wants.*

   (B) What three questions must every society answer because of scarcity? *What to produce and how much of each good or service to produce, how to produce, and for whom to produce*

   (C) What are the three ways societies have dealt with the scarcity problem? *Tradition, command and market*

   (D) Give one example of how each way is used in the United States. *Answers will vary.*

2. Hightechland produces two commodities: movies and computers. Hightechland's resources include workers, factories, electricity and so on. The following schedule indicates some of the points on Hightechland's production possibilities curve.

Commodity	A	B	C	D	E
Movies	100	75	50	25	0
Computers	0	30	55	70	80

   (A) Does movie production exhibit increasing, decreasing or constant per-unit opportunity costs? How do you know? *Movie production indicates increasing per-unit opportunity costs. As more movies are produced, increasingly more computers must be sacrificed.*

   (B) Graph Hightechland's production possibilities curve, and label it AA.

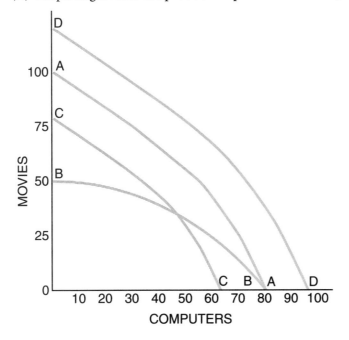

UNIT
1
Macroeconomics
LONG FREE-RESPONSE
SAMPLE QUESTIONS
Answer
Key

(C) Suppose Hightechland is operating at Point C but would like to alter production to Point D. What would be the per-unit opportunity cost of producing more computers? *With a move from Point C to Point D, the per-unit opportunity cost of producing one additional computer is 1 ²/₃ movies.*

(D) Suppose Hightechland is operating at Point C but would like to alter production to Point B. What would be the per-unit opportunity cost of producing more movies? *The per-unit opportunity cost of producing one more movie as we alter the production from Point C to Point B is one computer.*

(E) What will happen to Hightechland's production possibilities curve if many of its movie sets are destroyed by fire? (Assume that the sets are not used in the production of computers.) Using the same graph you drew for Question 2(B), draw Hightechland's new production possibilities curve and label it BB. *The point on the axis will shift inward for the movie production, but the point on the axis corresponding to computer production will not change.*

(F) What will happen to Hightechland's production possibilities curve if all the country's resources are reduced (perhaps by natural disaster or war)? Using the same graph as in Question 2(B), draw Hightechland's new production possibilities curve and label it CC. *Shift the production possibilities curve to the left or inward.*

(G) What will happen to Hightechland's production possibilities curve if technology improves both the production of movies and the production of computers? Using the same graph as in Question 2(B), draw Hightechland's new production possibilities curve and label it DD. *Shift the production possibilities curve to the right or outward.*

3. The market for many commodities is seasonal in nature. Their sales (equilibrium quantity) increase dramatically during certain times of the year. Christmas cards and fresh strawberries, at least in the North, are two examples. Christmas card sales increase during the last three months of the year, and the sales of fresh strawberries in the North increase during the summer months. But the (equilibrium) price movement of these two commodities is quite different during their peak sales season: Christmas cards increase in price during the last three months of the year, whereas strawberries decrease in price during the summer.

(A) Show on the graph below how there can be an increase in the equilibrium quantity and an increase in the equilibrium price of Christmas cards during the last three months of the year, and briefly explain what has happened.

Christmas Card Market

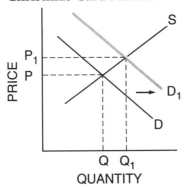

With other things constant, there is an increase in the demand for Christmas cards in the last three months of the year. This causes a rightward shift of demand and causes the price and quantity sold to increase.

(B) Change the graph below for fresh strawberries in the North to show how there can be an increase in the equilibrium quantity and a decrease in the equilibrium price of strawberries in the summer, and briefly explain what has happened.

Other things constant, there is an increase in the supply for fresh strawberries in the northern areas of the United States in the warmer months when the berries are harvested in the northern areas. This causes a rightward shift in the supply curve and causes the price to fall and the quantity sold to increase.

Strawberry Market in the North

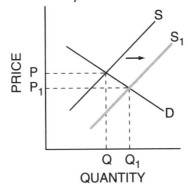

UNIT
1
Macroeconomics
LONG FREE-RESPONSE
SAMPLE QUESTIONS
Answer
Key

4. Explain how each of the following may affect the production possibilities curve of the United States or the point at which the economy is operating. Draw a production possibilities curve; put "Capital Goods" on the vertical axis and "Consumer Goods" on the horizontal axis. Now, add a PPC curve or point to the graph to illustrate each scenario.

(A) The Congress and the president decide to provide more funding for higher education with more students attending college and graduating. *More education increases human capital, a resource, and moves the curve outward.*

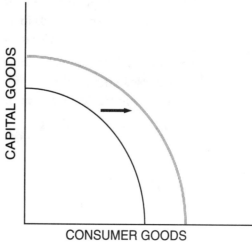

(B) New advances in medicine allow for a healthier lifestyle. *Better medicine improves human capital, a resource, and moves the curve outward.*

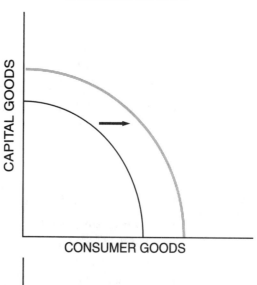

(C) The United States agrees to be a part of a world-trade agreement that will foster international trade. *International trade increases output because of the law of comparative advantage and moves the curve outward.*

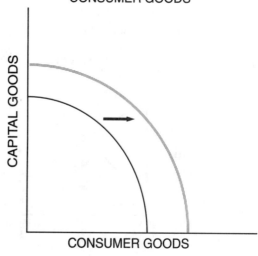

Advanced Placement Economics Teacher Resource Manual © National Council on Economic Education, New York, N.Y.

UNIT
1 Macroeconomics

LONG FREE-RESPONSE
SAMPLE QUESTIONS

Answer
Key

(D) The unemployment rate increases in the economy from 4.2 percent to 5.1 percent of the labor force. *The increase in the unemployment rate results in underemployed resources, which is illustrated by a point inside the curve. The resources (workers) are still available but are not being employed.*

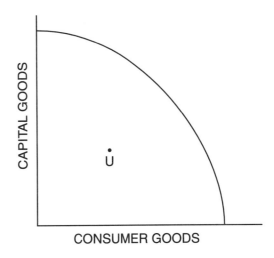

(E) Computer viruses are out of control, and efficiency and output in the economy fall. *The computer viruses take computers out of commission, which shifts the curve inward.*

Production Possibilities Curve

Increasing Opportunity Costs

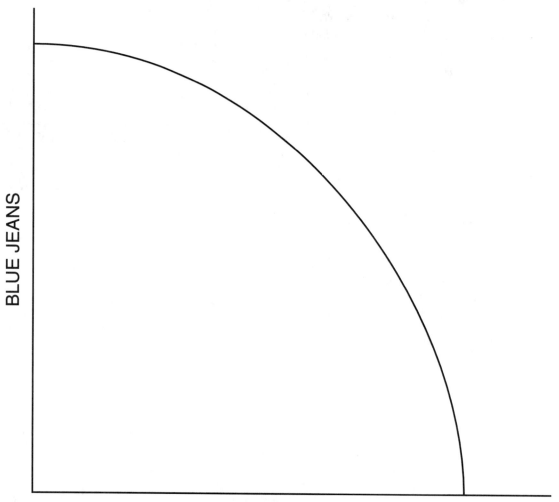

BLUE JEANS

FIRE ENGINES

Production Possibilities Curve

Constant Opportunity Cost

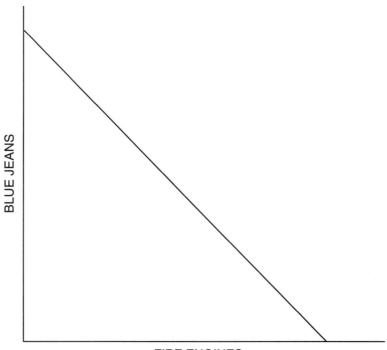

Decreasing Opportunity Cost

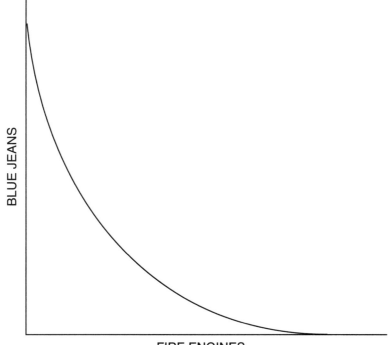

Absolute Advantage and Comparative Advantage

ABSOLUTE ADVANTAGE

- One individual or nation can produce more output with the same resources as another individual or nation.

COMPARATIVE ADVANTAGE

- One individual or nation can produce a good at a lower opportunity cost than another.

EXAMPLES OF COMPARATIVE ADVANTAGE

- Economics professor and secretary
- Auto mechanic and medical doctor

Determining Comparative Advantage (Output Method)

	Corn (bushels per year)	Sunscreen (gallons per year)
Mexico	300	150
France	200	150

1. Which nation has an absolute advantage in producing corn?

2. Which nation has an absolute advantage in producing sunscreen?

3. Which nation has a comparative advantage in producing corn?

4. Which nation has a comparative advantage in producing sunscreen?

5. Should Mexico specialize in corn or sunscreen?

6. Should France specialize in corn or sunscreen?

Movement Along a Demand Curve

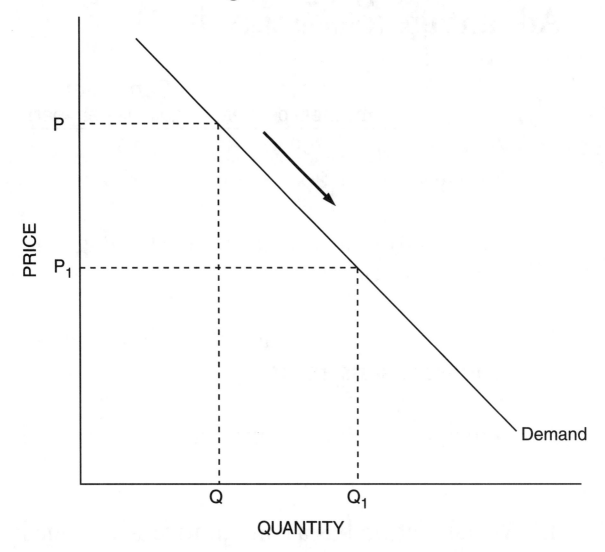

As the price declines from P to P_1, the quantity increases from Q to Q_1.

Shift in Demand

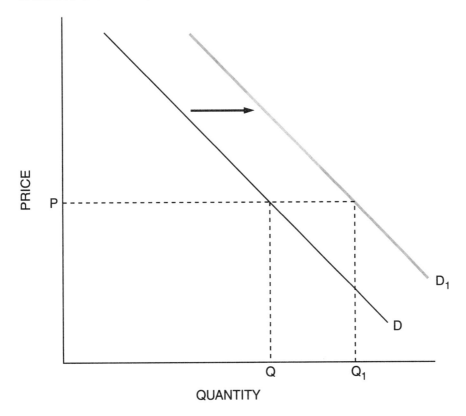

Increase in demand from D to D_1 shows that at the same price (P), the quantity increased from Q to Q_1.

Factors that shift demand:

1. Number of consumers

2. Price of complementary good

3. Price of substitute good

4. Consumer income

5. Expectations about income or prices

Movement Along a Supply Curve

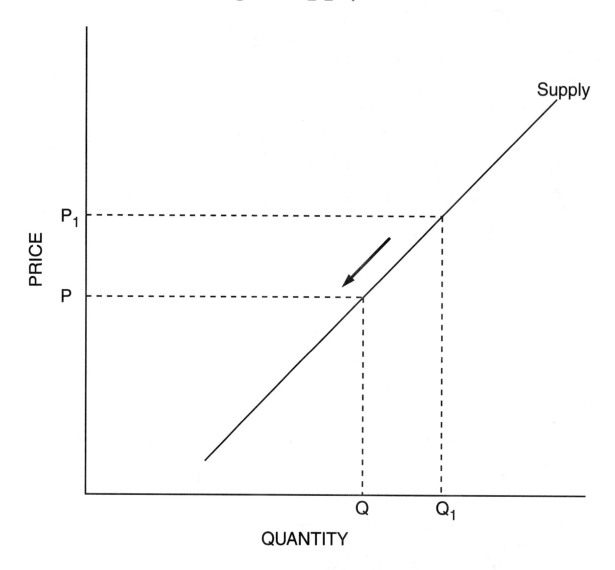

As the price declines from P_1 to P, the quantity decreases from Q_1 to Q.

Shift in Supply

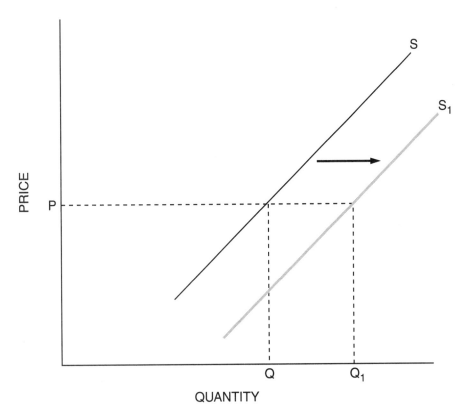

Increase in supply from S to S_1 shows that at the same price (P), the quantity increased from Q to Q_1.

Factors that shift supply:

1. Number of suppliers

2. Prices of resources used to produce good

3. Prices of related goods produced

4. Technology

5. Expectations about future prices

Equilibrium Quantity and Price

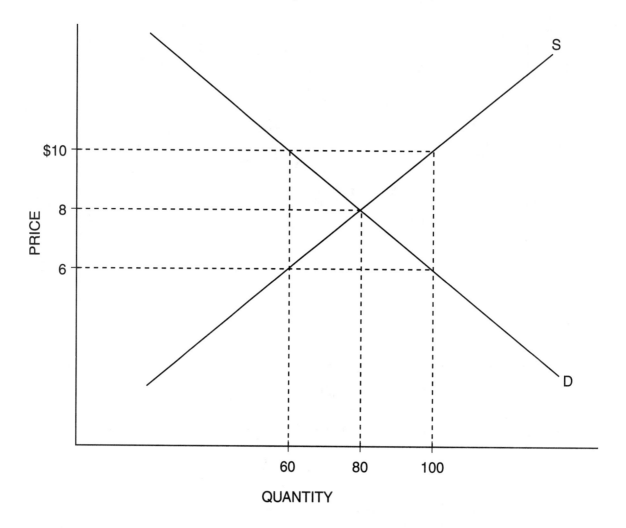

What happens if the price is $10?

What happens if the price is $6?

What happens if the price is $8?

Advanced Placement Economics Teacher Resource Manual © National Council on Economic Education, New York, N.Y.

Calculation of Price Elasticity of Demand

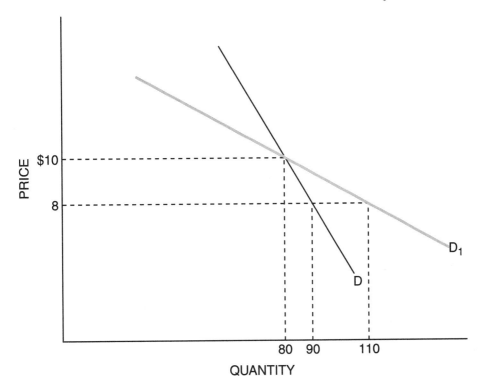

Arc price elasticity for demand curve D

The price decreases from $10 to $8.

$$\varepsilon_d = \cfrac{\cfrac{10}{85}}{\cfrac{2}{9}} = \frac{.12}{.22} = 0.55$$

Arc price elasticity for demand curve D_1

The price decreases from $10 to $8.

$$\varepsilon_d = \cfrac{\cfrac{30}{95}}{\cfrac{2}{9}} = \frac{.32}{.22} = 1.45$$

Price Elasticity along a Demand Curve

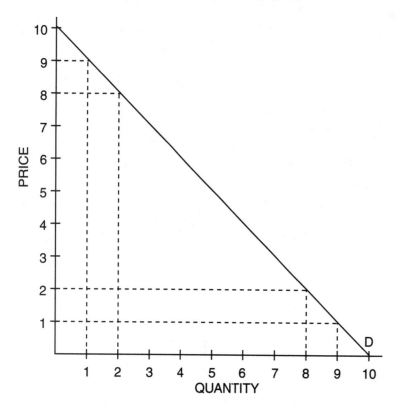

Arc elasticity from P = 9 to P = 8 is

$$\varepsilon_d = \cfrac{\cfrac{1}{1.5}}{\cfrac{1}{8.5}} = \frac{.67}{.12} = 5.58$$

Arc elasticity from P = 2 to P = 1 is

$$\varepsilon_d = \cfrac{\cfrac{1}{8.5}}{\cfrac{1}{1.5}} = \frac{.12}{.67} = 0.18$$

Effects of Different Demand Elasticities

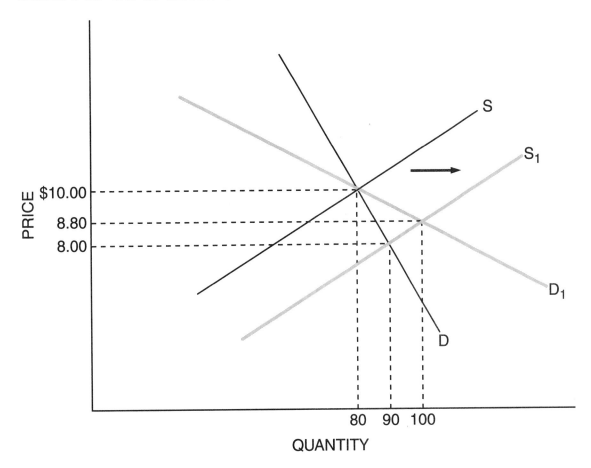

Which demand curve is more inelastic?

What happens to the equilibrium price and quantity with an elastic demand curve if supply increases?

What happens to the equilibrium price and quantity with an inelastic demand curve if supply increases?

Macroeconomics | Unit 2

Measuring Economic Performance

8 class periods or 360 minutes
(11 percent of course time)

Unit Overview

Unit 2 introduces the students to the goals of macroeconomic policies and the basic definitions of macroeconomic terms and explains how macroeconomics affects people's lives. The College Board attempts to have 8 percent to 12 percent of the Advanced Placement Examination based on this unit. A student's understanding of the definitions of macroeconomic terms is essential for the analysis that comes in Units 3 through 6. Without an understanding of the definitions and goals of macroeconomic policies, the students cannot analyze the effects of different policies.

There are some critical points to be made in this unit. The AP Examination will probably never ask the students to calculate gross domestic product, net national product and the other national income accounting concepts. Still, the students should know what is included in national income accounting concepts, what is not and why. They need to know the relationships to understand other key concepts such as aggregate expenditures and the impact of changes in taxes on gross domestic product. The students should also be able to explain

- why there is unemployment at full employment,
- the difference between a price level and inflation,
- how price indexes are computed and
- the difference between fluctuations in output and long-term economic growth.

The Lesson Planner

Lesson 1 defines macroeconomics and describes the main components of the economy and their interaction. It uses **Activities 9** and **10** and **Visuals 2.1, 2.2** and **2.3.**

Lesson 2 focuses on measuring key economic variables. It uses **Activities 11** and **12** and **Visual 2.4.**

Lesson 3 addresses a key macroeconomic goal in looking at the effects of inflation and how a price index is created. It uses **Activities 13, 14** and **15.**

Lesson 4 delves into how unemployment, employment and labor-force participation are defined. This lesson uses **Activity 16** and **Visuals 2.5** and **2.6.**

Lesson 5 looks at the business cycle and pulls together all the concepts about economic growth, inflation and unemployment. It uses **Activities 17** and **18** and **Visual 2.7.**

Week 1

Day 1

(A) Introduce macroeconomics using Visuals 2.1 and 2.2.

(B) Have the students complete Activity 9.

(C) Discuss answers to Activity 9.

(D) Use Visual 2.3 to discuss circular flow.

(E) Have the students complete Activity 10.

(F) Review Activity 10.

Day 2

(A) Use Visual 2.4 to discuss economic goals.

(B) Lecture on measuring key macroeconomic variables.

(C) Have the students complete Activity 11.

(D) Review Activity 11.

(E) Have the students complete Activity 12 for homework.

Day 3

(A) Review Activity 12.

(B) Lecture on price indexes and inflation.

(C) Have the students complete Activity 13 in class.

(D) Review Activity 13.

Day 4

(A) Play the Inflation Game (Activity 14).

(B) Have the students complete Activity 15 for homework.

Day 5

(A) Review Activity 15.

(B) Lecture on unemployment using Visuals 2.5 and 2.6.

(C) Have the students complete Activity 16 in class.

(D) Review Activity 16.

Week 2

Day 6

(A) Lecture on business cycles, using Visual 2.7.

(B) Have the students complete Activity 17 in class and discuss answers.

Day 7

(A) Have the students complete Activity 18 as initial step in review for unit test.

(B) Review Activity 18.

Day 8

Give unit test.

Macroeconomics and the Circular Flow

Introduction and Description

This lesson defines macroeconomics, presents the important macroeconomic questions and explains the different sectors of a macroeconomic model of the economy. The circular flow model shows the household sector, the business sector and the government sector with the basic interactions among the sectors.

Activity 9 asks the students to think about current economic issues, the ideas frequently expressed and the economic basis for each of these ideas. The activity draws on their understanding of a few basic economic concepts. Activity 10 has the students use the circular flow concepts to gain understanding about the movement of money and goods and services in the economy.

Objectives

1. Define *macroeconomics.*
2. Explain the important macroeconomic issues.
3. Describe the circular flow of goods, services and payments in the macroeconomy.
4. Describe the major sectors of the macroeconomy.

Time Required

One class period or 45 minutes

Materials

1. Activities 9 and 10
2. Visuals 2.1, 2.2 and 2.3

Procedure

1. Project Visual 2.1 and discuss the importance of each question. Here are some ideas for each question on the transparency.

   ■ **Why does output fluctuate?**

   Use Visual 2.2, a graph of real gross domestic product from 1952 to 2001, to show how output has fluctuated. As output rises and falls,

the amount of goods and services people have increases and decreases. Thus, the standard of living rises and falls, and people are better off or worse off. The changes in output cause changes in the number of people employed. Macroeconomics looks at the determinants of output fluctuation and how these factors can be controlled.

■ **What determines economic growth?**

Just as fluctuations in output affect the standard of living from year to year, the long-run growth in output is important for society's welfare. Growth in an economy depends on the number of workers, the education and training of workers, the technological advances, the amount of machinery and technology labor has to work with, and the basic material resources. Macroeconomics addresses how society can encourage the development of these factors, which determine economic growth.

■ **Why do we have unemployment, and why is unemployment a problem?**

The unemployed are people who are actively seeking jobs or are temporarily laid off. The question usually arises, "Why won't these people work for a lower wage and thus get a job?" Some unemployed people do not have the skills firms require and are unable to find a job even at a lower wage. Some unemployed people do have skills and want to be paid the market wage for these skills, and they are willing to continue to search for a job until they find one. Some of these people are unemployed because firms do not have the need for additional workers because demand for their product is down. Firms will typically not fire existing workers to hire new workers at a lower wage because doing so endangers worker loyalty and also increases the firm's training costs. Unemployment is not simply a problem for the unemployed. Unemployment means that society has fewer products because these workers are not working. Unemployment also imposes social and psychological costs on society.

■ **Why do we have inflation, and why is inflation a problem?**

Inflation is an increase in the average price level over time. One of the difficulties with inflation is its unpredictability. If people knew what inflation was going to be, they could build in adjustments for its effects. Macroeconomics studies the causes of inflation, the misallocation of resources that result from inflation and methods for controlling inflation.

■ **Which government policy affects output, growth, unemployment and inflation?**

Fiscal policy is a summary of the government's decisions about expenditures and taxation. Government decisions about taxes and about how much it will spend affect the level of output, growth, unemployment and inflation.

■ **How do changes in the amount of money in the economy affect output, growth, unemployment and inflation?**

The decisions of the central bank — the Federal Reserve in the United States — determine the amount of money in the economy. The amount of money in the system determines to

a great extent the level of economic activity. The amount of money in the economy (money supply) in conjunction with how much money society wants to use determine the interest rate. Monetary policy is a summary of the Federal Reserve's decisions about money and interest rates.

■ **How do domestic economic activities affect other countries and our trade?**

A nation's economy does not operate independent of other countries' economies. Trade policies, monetary policies, and fiscal policies all affect the impact of the domestic economy on the economies of other nations. In the next lesson the economic basis for trade is explained.

2. Now have the students work on Activity 9 either as a quiz or as a worksheet. Discuss the answers to Activity 9. This will help the students start to learn the definitions of the macroeconomic terms they have heard on television or read in the print media.

3. Project Visual 2.3. Discuss the flows of goods and services and the reverse flow of payments. Be sure the students understand that the three sectors of the economy are households (resource owners), businesses and government.

4. Have the students complete Activity 10 and discuss the answers.

Test of Macroeconomic Thinking

All the answers are false. The reasoning for each false statement follows.

1. *Scarcity is a relative concept. As our resources and output increase, so do our wants for goods and services.*

2. *Given the limited resources and unlimited wants of people, we would find new ways to use our resources if the world disarmed. Military expenditures are made for defense reasons, not for economic reasons.*

3. *Money is not a resource. If money were a resource, the country would be better off if we made more money. If the country prints more money, the result will be inflation. Money is a tool that serves as a medium of exchange, a store of value and a standard of value.*

4. *GDP is a measure of economic activity. The level of GDP does not measure economic welfare or the distribution of the goods and services among the people.*

5. *At full employment, unemployment is not zero. Frictional unemployment (people moving from one job to another) and structural unemployment (people having skills — repairing typewriters, for example — that are no longer in demand) are always present in the economy. At full employment, cyclical unemployment is zero. Cyclical unemployment results from changes in the business cycle.*

6. *Inflation was below 3 percent for several periods during the 1950s, 1990s and 2000s.*

7. *Debtors are helped by unanticipated inflation because the value of the money with which they repay their debt is less than the value of the money they borrowed. Conversely, savers and people on fixed incomes are hurt by unanticipated inflation because they can no longer purchase the same amount of goods and services.*

8. *Most of the money supply consists of demand deposits (checking accounts) and is created by banks through lending.*

9. *Gold has not been used to determine the international value of the U.S. dollar since 1971. The value of money is determined by what it can buy.*

10. *Economists think that government taxing and spending decisions (fiscal policy) affect the health of the economy. Further, some taxation is imposed to curb particular expenditures — for example, cigarette taxes.*

11. *The Federal Reserve System controls the money supply and affects the economy by changes in the money supply. It also provides services to financial institutions, such as check clearing and loans. The Federal Deposit Insurance Corporation insures deposits of most financial institutions.*

12. *Tariffs may save jobs in a specific industry. In general, tariffs raise the price of goods for consumers and interfere in the efficient allocation of resources, thus hurting the economy as a whole. Furthermore, because of the higher prices, employees in other industries may lose their jobs.*

Understanding the Circular Flow of the Macroeconomy

Part A

Each of the flows in the circular flow diagram in Figure 10.1 is numbered. Identify which number matches the transaction described in the statements below. Consider only the first transaction — not the return flow.

1. David buys a CD at the local store for $9.99. _____ 4 _____

2. Emily earns $6.50 per hour entering data at the music conservatory. _____ 1 _____

3. Maria pays her federal income tax. _____ 5 _____

4. Jagdish receives $15,000 in profits from his half-ownership of a coffee shop. _____ 1 _____

5. Keisha makes decorative pillows that she sells for $30.00. _____ 3 _____

6. Mammoth Toys Inc. hires 100 new employees. _____ 2 _____

7. The National Park Service opens two new campgrounds in Yellowstone National Park. _____ 6 _____

Part B

Write T if the statement is true and F if the statement is false.

8. Money flows are clockwise. _____ T _____

9. Goods and services flows are clockwise. _____ F _____

10. The resource market determines the price per acre of farmland. _____ T _____

11. The product market determines the price of a computer. _____ T _____

12. Firms sell resources in the resource markets. _____ F _____

13. Government buys resources and households sell resources. _____ T _____

14. Government buys products, and firms sell products. _____ T _____

15. The product market determines the salary of the C.E.O. of a firm. _____ F _____

16. The resource market determines the price of soda. _____ F _____

17. The resource market determines the price of soda-bottling equipment. _____ T _____

Macroeconomic Goals and GDP

Introduction and Description

The goals of U.S. macroeconomic policy makers are captured in two laws: the Employment Act of 1946 and the Full Employment and Balanced Growth Act of 1978 (Humphrey-Hawkins Act). The 1946 law committed the federal government to maximize employment and economic growth, and maintain a stable price level. The 1978 law went further and committed the government to reach an unemployment rate of 4 percent, to stabilize the price level with a target inflation rate of zero percent and to maintain steady economic growth. In this lesson the students should learn the components of gross domestic product and how we measure the economy to see if we are meeting macroeconomic policy goals. This lesson continues an emphasis on definitions and describes the limitations of the measures of macroeconomic activity.

In Activity 11, the students practice calculating the unemployment rate, the labor force participation rate, a price index and the short-run change in output. Activity 12 helps the students determine what is included in gross domestic product (GDP) and what is included in government spending, household spending and business spending. It also asks them to explain the basic reasoning for inclusion or exclusion of economic activity in GDP.

Objectives

1. Describe the economic goals of U.S. society.
2. Define *full employment*, *inflation* and *economic growth*.
3. Explain the methods of measuring macroeconomic goals.
4. Describe the construction of a price index.
5. Explain the difference between real GDP and nominal GDP.
6. Explain the importance of GDP as a measure of economic activity.

Time Required

One class period or 45 minutes

Materials

1. Activities 11 and 12
2. Visual 2.4

Procedure

1. Project Visual 2.4. Discuss each goal and why it is important. Discuss the variables used to evaluate the performance of the U.S. economy at different times. In general, the goals conflict, and society is faced with trade-offs among the goals. If the students understand the goals and validity of the measurement of economic variables, it will help them understand the implications of the trade-offs among goals.

2. Have the students read the Activity 11 overview and discuss macroeconomic policy goals. Stress that the unemployment rate is a broad measure of economic activity. However, if policy makers are going to create and implement programs to help the unemployed, they need to know more about the unemployed: skill level, ethnic and racial groups, and age groups. Have the students complete Part A and review the answers.

3. Have the students complete Activity 11 and review the answers. Here are the critical issues:

   (A) The CPI measures the price level; and from this, the inflation rate can be calculated.

   (B) The CPI is only one of several price level measures.

   (C) There is discussion about how well the CPI measures the inflation that most people experience. The CPI includes items that people don't buy every year: house, car, etc. Thus, the CPI may overstate the actual change in the cost of living.

(D) The growth rate in real GDP is a better measure of the change in the macro-economic conditions than the growth rate of nominal GDP because nominal GDP includes the effects of inflation. The growth rate in real GDP per capita captures a measure of changes in the standard of living.

4. The students should understand the difference between fluctuations in output (short-run economic growth) and long-run economic growth. Fluctuations in output are measured by the changes in real gross domestic product from quarter to quarter or year to year. In general, fluctuations in output are caused by greater or lesser utilization of the existing capital stock and technology. So we are actually measuring changes in real output because of more or less labor applied to the existing level of technology and plant and equipment. Long-run economic growth refers to changes in the productive capability of the economy through changes in the amount of plant and equipment and technology.

Economists use the term *economic growth* to refer to long-run economic growth and *fluctuations in real output* to refer to the short-run phenomenon. However, the media frequently refer to short-run changes in output as economic growth. The Advanced Placement Examination uses the term *economic growth* to refer to the long-run changes in the economy's ability to produce.

5. Have the students read in their text about GDP and national income accounting, then complete Activity 12 for homework.

6. Review Activity 12 to ensure the students understand that only *final goods and services* are included in GDP, that only market activities are included and that financial transactions are not included. The students must understand the identity GDP = C + I + G + NX and what types of expenditures are included in each component. This is the point of Part B of Activity 12.

7. Review the answers to Activity 12 with the students.

Measuring Broad Economic Goals

Part A
Measuring Employment

The *unemployment rate* (UR) is defined as

$$UR = \frac{\text{number of unemployed}}{\text{labor force}} \times 100$$

The *labor force participation rate* (LFPR) is defined as:

$$LFPR = \frac{\text{number in labor force}}{\text{adult population}} \times 100$$

How well has the U.S. economy met the goal of full employment? Use the formulas just given to fill in the last three columns of Figure 11.1. All of the population and labor-force data are in millions.

Figure 11.1
Civilian Employment 1960 to 2000

Year	Civilian Noninstitutional Population Aged 16 and Over	Civilian Labor Force			Unemployment Rate	Labor Force Participation Rate
		Employed	Unemployed	Total		
1960	117	66	4	70	5.7%	60%
1970	137	79	4	83	4.8%	61%
1980	168	99	8	107	7.5%	64%
1990	188	117	7	124	5.6%	66%
2000	209	135	6	141	4.3%	67%

1. In which year was the economy very close to full employment as indicated in the Humphrey-Hawkins Act? *2000. The unemployment rate was the lowest in that year.*

2. Why has the labor force participation rate increased since the 1960s? *More women and retirees have entered or re-entered the labor force.*

3. Do the data on the national unemployment rate in Figure 11.1 reflect the extent of unemployment among a particular group in our society, such as teenagers aged 16 to 19? Explain. *No, the data are too aggregated. The data do not provide information for different demographic groups.*

Part B
Measuring Price Changes

$$\text{Price change} = \frac{\text{change in CPI}}{\text{beginning CPI}} \times 100$$

Here's the calculation for the example above:

$$\text{Price change} = \frac{165 - 150}{150} \times 100 = 10\%$$

Fill in the blanks in Figure 11.2, and then use the data to answer the questions.

 Figure 11.2

Prices of Three Goods Compared with Base-Year Price

	Quantity Bought in Base Year	Unit Price in Base Year	Spending in Base Year	Unit Price in Year 1	Spending in Year 1	Unit Price in Year 2	Spending in Year 2
Whole pizza	30	$5.00	*$150*	$7.00	*$210*	$9.00	*$270*
Prerecorded audio cassette	40	6.00	*$240*	5.00	*$200*	4.00	*$160*
Six-pack of soda	60	1.50	*$90*	2.00	*$120*	2.50	*$150*
Total	—	—	*$480*	—	*$530*	—	*$580*

4. What is the total cost of buying all the items in Year 2? ___*$580*___

5. What is the CPI for Year 2? ___*120.8 [(580 / 480) x 100]*___

6. What is the percentage increase in prices from the base year to Year 2? ___*20.8%*___

7. In August 2000 the CPI was 172.8, and in August 2001 the CPI was 177.50. What was the percentage change in prices for this 12-month period? ___*2.7%*___

Advanced Placement Economics Teacher Resource Manual © National Council on Economic Education, New York, N.Y.

Part C
Measuring Short-Run Economic Growth

Figure 11.3
Nominal and Real GDP

	Nominal GDP	Price Index	Population
Year 3	$5,000	125	11
Year 4	$6,600	150	12

8. What is the real GDP in Year 3? ___*$4,000 [(100 x $5,000) / 125]*___

9. What is the real GDP in Year 4? ___*$4,400 [(100 x $6,600) / 150]*___

10. What is the real GDP per capita in Year 3? ___*$364 ($4,000 / 11)*___

11. What is the real GDP per capita in Year 4? ___*$367 ($4,400 / 12)*___

12. What is the rate of real output growth between Years 3 and 4?
    ___*10% [(4,400 – 4,000) / 4,000] x 100*___

13. What is the rate of real output growth per capita between Years 3 and 4?
    (Hint: Use per-capita data in the output growth rate formula.)
    ___*0.82% [(367 – 364) / 364] x 100*___

All About GDP

Part A
Is This Counted as Part of GDP?

Which of the following are *included* and which are *excluded* in calculating GDP? Explain your decisions.

1. A monthly check received by an economics student who has been granted a government scholarship *Excluded: transfer payment from government to an individual*

2. A farmer's purchase of a new tractor *Included: business fixed investment*

3. A plumber's purchase of a two-year-old used truck *Excluded: Truck was not produced in current year.*

4. Cashing a U.S. government bond *Excluded: Bond is a financial asset.*

5. The services of a mechanic in fixing the radiator on his own car *Excluded: This is a nonmarket activity.*

6. A Social Security check from the government to a retired store clerk *Excluded: transfer payment from government to an individual*

7. An increase in business inventories *Included: Inventory is an investment.*

8. The government's purchase of a new submarine for the Navy *Included: government purchase of a good*

9. A barber's income from cutting hair *Included: income from services provided*

10. Income received from the sale of Nike stock *Excluded: Stock is a financial asset.*

Part B
GDP: Is It Counted and Where?

For each of the following items, write one of the following in the space provided:

C if the item is counted as *consumption spending.*
I if the item is counted as *investment spending.*
G if the item is counted as *government spending.*
NX if the item is counted as *net exports.*
NC if the item is *not counted* in GDP.

_C_ 11. You spend $7.00 to attend a movie.

_I_ 12. A family pays a contractor $100,000 for a house he built for them this year.

_NC_ 13. A family pays $75,000 for a house built three years ago.

_C_ 14. An accountant pays a tailor $175 to sew a suit for her.

_G_ 15. The government increases its defense expenditures by $1,000,000,000.

_NC_ 16. The government makes a $300 Social Security payment to a retired person.

_NC_ 17. You buy General Motors Corp. stock for $1,000 in the stock market.

_I_ 18. At the end of a year, a flour-milling firm finds that its inventories of grain and flour are $10,000 above the amounts of its inventories at the beginning of the year.

_NC_ 19. A homemaker works hard caring for her spouse and two children.

_I_ 20. Ford Motor Co. buys new auto-making robots.

_C_ 21. You pay $300 a month to rent an apartment.

_I_ 22. Apple Computer Co. builds a new factory in the United States.

_NC_ 23. R.J. Reynolds Co. buys control of Nabisco.

_NX_ 24. You buy a new Toyota that was made in Japan.

_C_ 25. You pay tuition to attend college.

Part C
Why Are Items Counted or Not Counted in GDP?

26. We count only the final retail price of a new good or service in GDP. Why? *To avoid double counting*

27. A purely financial transaction will not be counted in GDP. Why? *A financial transaction does not involve production of a good or service. It is a transfer of assets.*

28. When a homeowner does home-improvement work, the value of the labor is not counted in GDP. Why? *The labor does not involve a market transaction, and it is difficult to compute the value.*

Price Indexes and Inflation

Introduction and Description

At various points in the economic history of the United States, inflation has been a major economic problem. The high inflation rates of the late 1960s and 1970s led to the severe recession of the early 1980s. This experience has had a major impact on our economic policy today. Monetary policy under Alan Greenspan's chairmanship of the Federal Reserve System has revolved around controlling inflation. In this lesson, the measurement of prices is reviewed and the impact of unanticipated inflation is explored.

Activity 13 provides practice in creating a price index, changing the base year of a price index and examining the results of changing the base year. Activity 14 is a classroom game to help the students understand the effects of inflation on individuals. The students use their knowledge of the effects of unanticipated inflation to evaluate different scenarios, and they explain their analysis in Activity 15.

Objectives

1. Demonstrate how to change the base year of a price index.
2. Define anticipated versus unanticipated inflation.
3. Explain the impact of unanticipated inflation.

Time Required

Two class periods or 90 minutes

Materials

1. Activities 13, 14 and 15
2. Inflation Game cards

Procedure

1. Review the construction of a price index. Point out the current base year used in the government's reporting of macroeconomic statistics. You can find this information in the *Economic*

Report of the President, the *Federal Reserve Bulletin* or in several places on the Internet.

2. Have the students complete Activity 13 in class. Review the answers with the students.

3. Discuss the difference between *anticipated inflation* and *unanticipated inflation. Anticipated inflation* represents the level of inflation people expect to occur and have built into their economic decisions. Unanticipated inflation is the level of inflation that is not expected or is unforeseen.

4. Wage contracts and long-term loan contracts are usually the source for judging the expected inflation rate. Unanticipated inflation causes economic costs because people have not adjusted earnings and expenditures for this level of inflation. High levels of anticipated inflation also have economic costs. One economic cost of anticipated high inflation is transactions costs referred to as *boot-leather costs* because people run around trying to avoid losses from the declining value of money. A second economic cost is the distortion of incentives generated by the tax system. For example, anticipated inflation increases the dollar return on investments. As these dollar returns are taxed, the effective tax rate rises. The third economic cost is the result of the uncertainty of how and when policy makers will respond to the high level of inflation.

5. Play the Inflation Game: Royalty for a Day (Activity 14). This is a role-play. The instructions are on the activity Answer Key. You will need to prepare ahead of time cards for each speaker and scorecards for the audience if the students do not have their own books.

6. Have the students complete Activity 15 for homework. Review the answers with the students.

Price Indexes

There is more than one method for constructing a price index. The easiest to understand is probably the *weighted-average* method explained in this activity. This method compares the total cost of a fixed market basket of goods in different years. The total cost is weighted by multiplying the price of each item in the basket by the number of units of the item in the basket and then adding up all the prices. The cost of the basic market basket in the current year is then expressed as a percentage of the cost of the basic market basket in the base year using this formula:

$$\text{index number} = \frac{\text{current-year cost}}{\text{base-year cost}} \times 100$$

Multiplying by 100 converts the number so it is comparable to the base-year number. The base year always has an index number of 100 since the current-year cost and the base-year cost of the market basket are the same in the base year.

Part A
Constructing a Price Index

Using this information, let us now construct a price index. Fill in the blanks in Figure 13.1.

 Figure 13.1
Constructing a Price Index

Basic Market Basket Item	No. of Units	Year 1 Price Per Unit	Year 1 Cost of Market Basket	Year 2 Price Per Unit	Year 2 Cost of Market Basket	Year 3 Price Per Unit	Year 3 Cost of Market Basket
Cheese	2 lbs.	$1.75	$3.50	$1.50	$3.00	$1.50	$3.00
Blue Jeans	2 pair	12.00	24.00	15.50	*31.00*	20.00	40.00
Gasoline	10 gals.	1.25	12.50	1.60	16.00	2.70	*27.00*
Total Expenditure	—	—	$40.00	—	$50.00	—	*$70.00*

1. We now have the information needed to construct a price index. The first step is to pick a base year and apply the formula. If Year 1 is selected as the base year, the index number for Year 1 is ($40 / $40) x 100 = 100. The index number for Year 2 is ($50 / $40) x 100 = 125 and the index number for year 3 is (__$70__ / $40) x 100 = __175__ .

2. These index numbers indicate that there was a 25 percent increase in prices between Year 1 and Year 2.

   (A) What is the percentage increase between Year 1 and Year 3? __75%__

   (B) What is the percentage increase between Year 2 and Year 3? __40% [(175 – 125) / 125]__

Part B
Changing the Base Year

We need not have chosen Year 1 to be our base year. To determine if our choice of base year influenced the results, let's use Year 2 as our base year and recompute both the index numbers and the percentage changes between years. The first percentage change in prices has been done for you.

 Figure 13.2

Changing the Base Year of a Price Index

Year	Index Numbers (Year 2 = Base)	Percentage Change in Prices (calculated by using changes in index numbers)	
Year 1	($40 / $50) x 100 = 80	Between Yr. 1 and Yr. 2	[(100 − 80) / 80] x 100 = 25%
Year 2	($50 / $50) x 100 = 100	Between Yr. 2 and Yr. 3	*[(140 − 100) / 100] x 100 = 40%*
Year 3	($70 / $50) x 100 = 140	Between Yr. 1 and Yr. 3	*[(140 − 80) / 80] x 100 = 75%*

3. Do the index numbers change when the base year is changed from Year 1 to Year 2?___*Yes*___

4. Does the percentage change in prices between years change when the base year is changed from Year 1 to Year 2?___*No*___ Why or why not?
Only the base is changed. The relative price changes are the same.

5. Would the price index numbers you have computed above change if a different set of expenditure patterns were selected for weighting? ___*Yes*___ Why?
The index numbers depend on the weights and the price changes.

6. Under what conditions would each price index number computed above be a cost-of-living index?
To be a cost-of-living index, the number would have to include all major expenditure items consumers purchase. The quantity of the items purchased could not have changed over time, and the quality of the items could not have changed.

7. Would each price index number computed above be accurate if the quality of the goods in the basic market basket changed? ___*No*___ Explain why.
Because the true weights would be different.

8. How do you know if the quality of a product changes for the better? For the worse?
The product quality will have improved if the product yields more utility or satisfaction. The product will yield less satisfaction if the quality has deteriorated.

Inflation Game: Royalty for a Day

Introduction

Prices usually rise over a period of time. The same items you bought a few years ago may cost more now. For example, a restaurant menu lists its finest steak entrée at $22; however, two years ago the same steak was only $20. *Inflation* is the term used to describe an increase in the overall level of prices. It's an important concept to understand because it's discussed so frequently in the media: Price indexes and inflation measurements are reported almost daily in the financial pages, politicians constantly announce programs to control inflation and economists endlessly debate inflation's effects on economic growth.

In general, people don't like inflation because higher prices mean they can purchase less for the same income. However, inflation does not affect everyone in the same way. While many people are hurt by inflation, especially when it is unexpected, others may actually benefit.

This activity is designed to teach the students the effects of inflation on different segments of the population: Who is hurt by unanticipated inflation and who benefits?

Time Required

One class period

Overview of the Game

This activity is modeled after an ancient (1950s) television game show called "Queen for a Day," in which (women) contestants took turns describing their lives of tragedy, hardship and sorrow. After all had shared their misery, the sympathetic audience voted for the most deserving by applauding. An "applause meter" measured the sound. The winner was crowned "Queen for a Day" and presented with a robe, crown and many prizes. In this modern version, male and female economics students compete for the honor of "Royalty for a Day" by convincing the audience how much they are suffering because of inflation.

Materials

1. 12 individual contestant sheets describing the role of the contestant. These are set up as cards at the end of this activity.
2. Audience scorecards
3. Crown and robe for winning contestant (or other symbols of royalty)

Procedure

1. Arrange the classroom so the front of the room is the stage and the audience sits facing the stage.

2. Begin the activity by reviewing the concept of inflation and explaining the game's purpose using the Introduction and Overview.

3. The teacher performs the role of host, announcer and applause meter.

4. Select 12 students to be contestants and hand out role cards. Ask each student to study the role he or she is asked to play. The students may improvise as long as they communicate the basic message. The "contestants" will be called individually to "perform" their role in front of the audience. They will each have approximately 60 seconds to perform.

5. The remainder of the class participates as the audience. Hand each student an audience scorecard. (Audience scorecards are in Part A of the student book.) They are to complete the scorecard as each contestant performs. Tell the students to assume the inflation rate is 5 percent. Note that this is key to understanding the gain or hurt perspective of some contestants.

6. Begin the game. Call the contestants to the stage to perform one at a time. Allow approximately 60 seconds for each. Make sure the students in the audience have sufficient time between contestants to mark their scorecards.

7. At the end of all the contestants' performances, present a brief reminder of the purpose of the game and recap each of the 12 contestants by asking questions such as "Who has been most hurt by inflation?" "Who will be crowned 'Royalty for a Day?' Will it be Priscilla the homeowner or Mr. Mayor or Peter the storeowner? Or possibly it will be Theresa the union member at the auto factory or Jerry the real-estate speculator?" Then ask the students in the audience to review their scorecards individually and select the candidate they feel is most hurt by inflation.

8. Then read each contestant's name. Ask the students in the audience to rate each contestant with applause. The audience must applaud each contestant, but the louder the clapping, the greater the rating. *Suggestion for increased frivolity: Act as a human applause meter by placing your hands together above your head. Start in a sideways bent position (9:00) and gradually point straight up as applause increases (12:00). For truly thunderous applause, continue bending to the 3:00 position.*

9. The contestant with the greatest rating (loudest clapping) is crowned, robed and proclaimed "Royalty for a Day."

10. Conduct Part B. Do not get hung up on the exact position of each person. Instead, emphasize the reasoning behind why the students position the people as they do.

11. Conduct a post-game discussion:
    (A) Using a blank audience scorecard on an overhead projector or on the board, have the students volunteer their answers about how inflation affected each contestant.
    (B) "Inflation reduces the value of money." Have the students use the contestants as a basis for discussion. (Lucy, Elmer)
    (C) "When people's incomes increase more slowly than the inflation rate, their purchasing power declines." Have the students use the contestants as a basis for discussion. (Mr. Sad Class)
    (D) Discuss how the costs of inflation are different for different groups of people. "Unexpected inflation hurts savers and people on fixed incomes; it helps people who have borrowed money at a fixed rate of interest."
    (E) Discuss how inflation imposes costs on people beyond its effects on wealth distribution because people devote resources to protect themselves from expected inflation. Have the students use the contestants as a basis for discussion. (cost-of-living allowances or COLAs, long-term contracts, fixed interest rates)
    (F) Give a brief explanation about measuring inflation. "The consumer price index (CPI) is the most commonly used measure of price-level changes. It can be used to compare the price level in one year with price levels in earlier or later years."
    (G) Give a brief explanation to the class about how "expectations of inflation may lead to higher interest rates."

Part A
Audience Scorecard

Contestant	Gain or Hurt by Inflation?	Reasoning
Priscilla *Homeowner / Worker*	*Gain*	*Wages increase above inflation rate.* *Could cause cost-push inflation*
Mayor *Government official*	*Gain*	*Higher tax receipts and able to repay debt / loan with lower purchasing-power dollars*
Peter *Store owner*	*Hurt*	*Costs are rising faster than revenue.*
Theresa *Auto worker /* *Union member*	*Gain*	*COLA keeps wages equal to inflation; pay raise results in wages above inflation rate. Cost-push inflation possible*
Jerry *Real-estate developer /* *Speculator*	*Gain*	*Money borrowed is repaid with dollars that have less purchasing power.*
Elmer *Retiree*	*Hurt*	*People on fixed income find the purchasing power of savings decreases.*
Mr. Sad Class *Teacher*	*Hurt*	*Wages are not keeping up with inflation.*
Lucy *High school senior*	*Hurt*	*Saved dollars have less purchasing power.*
Bernie *Bank president*	*Hurt*	*Bank loans are paid back with inflated dollars, which buy less.*
Helga *Retiree*	*Hurt*	*Saved dollars have less purchasing power.*
Jerome *Potential homeowner /* *Borrower*	*Uncertain, depends on future price-level changes*	*Will gain if real interest rate falls. Will be hurt if real interest rate rises.*
Lawrence *British businessowner*	*Gain*	*Signed contract that locked in lower price for an extended period of time.*

Part B
Spectrum Technique for Analyzing Contestants

Distribute the contestants along the spectrum, and explain why you think each should be located where you put him or her.

 Figure 14.1
Spectrum Technique for Analyzing Contestants

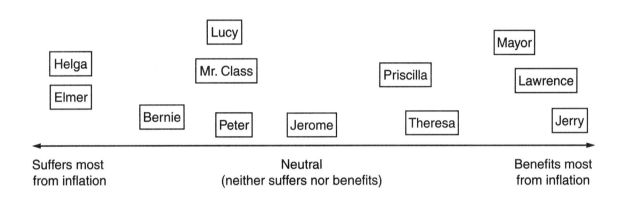

Priscilla
Homeowner / Worker

I'm Priscilla, a homeowner. I used to think that this inflation stuff was just a bunch of media hype. All the stuff I have to buy to keep my house going is costing me more each year. Now my income is buying fewer goods and services than it used to. Let me give you an example. My lawnmower broke, and I had to buy a new one last week. The new one is just like the old one, except it cost 50 percent more than the old one did 10 years ago. And here's another thing: The state says my house is worth more because house prices in general have risen. How does that affect me? Because my house is worth more, my property taxes have gone up. Now I must pay more in taxes to live in the same house. That's not fair — I feel like I'm living in the poor house. But I got lucky at work. I told my boss that I deserved a 6 percent raise because of all this inflation going on. You know that I couldn't afford to live here anymore unless I got the raise. He moaned and groaned — you should have heard him — but he gave it to me. So I just went out and celebrated!

Mayor
Government official

Hello there. I'm the mayor. I know some people don't like inflation. I'm not crazy about it — makes me look bad to the voters. You know, when prices go up, everyone seems to blame the government. And I don't want to look bad to the voters because I need to get re-elected. But ssshhh. I'll tell you a secret. Overall, higher prices for everything people buy result in higher sales-tax receipts. And this gives the city more money to spend on things the voters want, like recreation programs and road improvements. Not only this, remember that skateboard park the town built and financed with municipal bonds? Well, inflation means that we'll pay back those bonds with cheaper dollars. So, inflation actually helps us a bit. I just hope those voters don't blame me for the higher prices.

Peter

Store owner

My name's Peter. I run an "Everything for a Buck" store. I advertise all kinds of wonderful treasures for $1 or less. Catchy name, don't you think? I used to do really well, but I'm not earning as much profit as I used to. Lots of folks complainin' about inflation these days. And rightfully so; it's a MESS. The wholesale prices I pay for merchandise keep goin' up and up, but I gotta keep my prices at $1 because that's my niche and why folks shop at my store. And it's not just the merchandise that costs me more, it's my employees, too. They threatened me with quitting if I didn't give them a 5 percent raise. Understand employees gotta make a livin', but so do I. Can't run the store without employees. My costs are going up, but I can't raise my prices — people won't pay over a buck for my merchandise. What can I do?

Theresa

Auto worker / Union member

My name is Theresa. I'm an auto worker at the car factory. My company is high tech and has automated our production line. I have an important job because the buttons I push determine how your car interior is made. Yep, one button selects the type of seats, another button determines the color of the seat fabric and the last button plops the seat on the car frame. It's a boring job but important because it must be done carefully. If I make a mistake, it's very expensive for the company to correct it after the car has left the factory. I'm proud to be part of the auto-workers' union because it really cares about its members. The union just negotiated a new five-year labor contract with a hefty raise *plus* an annual cost-of-living adjustment — what they call a COLA, and no, it's not a type of soft drink. Let me tell you why I am so excited about our new contract: My wages are guaranteed to keep up with the inflation rate, no matter what it is, and I get an annual raise on top of it. I'm a great supporter of my union!

Jerry

Real-estate developer / Speculator

My name is Jerry. All this moaning and groaning about inflation. Just a bunch of worry for nothing. Let me tell you how I feel about inflation: I love it! That's right. You see, I'm a real-estate speculator. I buy houses and apartments and rent them out. I borrow as much money as I can to buy these places, so I don't have to tie up my own money. Then, thanks to inflation, the prices rise and I raise the rents. Then after a few years, I can sell the buildings at a handsome profit. The beauty is that the rents I charge cover my costs; and when I sell, I get to keep all the profits. The banks put up the money, but I get the profits. Pretty good deal, don't you think? And then I just start over and do it all again. I use some of my profits as down payment to borrow more money and buy more real estate. My business just keeps expanding and growing. Of course, if this inflation ever stops, I might be in a bit of a bind. But that will never happen — we always have inflation, right?

Elmer

Retiree

My name is Elmer. Don't know how long I'm going to be able to last with this here inflation. When I was working, I put what I thought was a lot of money into a savings plan. I was self-employed, so no company pension. Thought I was being smart because my savings grew every year. Now I'm retired, and the value of my savings in terms of what it will buy is shrinking and shrinking. I'm withdrawing the same amount every month for living expenses, but it buys less and less. A few more years of inflation like this and I won't have anything left. That's a fine "How do you do!" Man works hard all of his life, scrimps and saves, eats all that hamburger instead of steak and look what happens. Soon I won't be able to afford even tomato soup!

Mr. Sad Class

Teacher

I'm Mr. Sad Class, a poor starving high school teacher. My classes are boring, my students hate me and my dog just had puppies — and they just bit me, one by one, all 12 of them. On top of all that, the school district board of trustees just voted to give teachers a 2 percent raise. They thought they were generous. BIG DEAL! Inflation is 5 percent. Guess who loses? Do you really think I got a raise? I think I'll give my students a really rotten exam.

Lucy

High school senior

I'm Lucy, a high school senior. I love all the senior activities, but they are costing me plenty. I've got to buy a dress for the prom and also pay for graduation announcements and the senior all-night party. My older sister told me exactly how much it cost her, so I made a budget and have been saving my money since I was a freshman. Last weekend I went looking for a prom dress. Wow! Every dress I saw would cost me more money than what my sister paid. I don't have that much money. Well, I know from my economics class that there's an opportunity cost associated with everything and that I have choices. I thought about the opportunity cost of not going to the prom and decided it was enormous. So I just took a counter job at the Hot Dog Haven in the mall. My manager makes me wear a yellow mustard-colored shirt, red ketchup-colored shorts and a hot-dog-shaped hat. I would die if any of my friends see me. But it's worth it because I'm going to the prom. Also, when I took the job, I forgot that some of my wages would be deducted each month to pay taxes. It's going to take me a little longer to get enough money for the dress.

Bernie
Bank president

I'm Bernie, the president of ABC Bank. Why the name ABC? Because ABC is listed first in the telephone directory, and everyone will see my financial institution first. Pretty clever, huh! I had to think of ways to fight those big corporate banks. My bank has a good reputation. People like to come to ABC because we give low fixed interest rate loans. Our competitors give only variable interest rate loans. Hey, just thought of something. With all this talk of inflation here, the loans ABC makes will be repaid in dollars that are worth less than the dollars originally loaned. Oh dear — we're going to lose money!!!!

Helga
Retiree

I'm Helga. I'm 80 years old. When my dear, darlin', wonderful, lovin' late husband passed away — bless his soul — I thought he'd left me enough money to live for the rest of my life. But now prices are out of sight. At the grocery store they charged me 79 cents for celery, and it was a dinky bunch of celery at that! I can remember when a bunch of celery cost only 5 cents. Now, those were the good old days. But what is going to happen to me if the prices keep goin' up? I may not be able to buy even a dinky bunch of celery. And the electric company and the phone company keep charging me more, yet I'm using less power, and hardly ever talk on the phone. What's a person like me goin' to do?

Jerome
Potential homeowner / Borrower

I'm Jerome, and I just went to the bank to get a loan for a new house. The loan officer told me I couldn't get a mortgage at a fixed rate of interest. I would have to get an adjustable rate. Said something about the bank can lend money only when the interest rates can be adjusted as inflation rates change. This is a big risk for me. I can afford monthly payments of only a certain amount, and I need to know exactly how much I'm going to pay before I sign the papers. The adjustable interest rate stuff is horrible — if the bank "adjusts" my payments above my limit, I might have to default and lose my house. I'm not too sure about all this.

Lawrence
British businessowner

I'm Lawrence, a British businessowner. My U.K. corporation negotiated a sweet deal: a five-year contract to purchase some computers from a U.S. computer company. The chaps from the U.S. were quite genteel. They allowed us to buy computers for the next five years at the current U.S. prices as long as we promised to buy a certain quantity. This means we've got price protection — they've guaranteed us the same price for five years, even if the company raises prices next year. Now mind you, the inflation rate has remained stable in Britain these past five years. So guess what? My company gained on this contract. Can't say I mind inflation in the U.S. I'll drink a cup of tea to that.

Who Is Hurt and Who Is Helped by Unanticipated Inflation?

In Questions 1 through 15, decide which people or groups are hurt by unanticipated inflation and which benefit from unanticipated inflation. Circle the correct response, and explain why you answered as you did.

      H means the person or group is *hurt* by unanticipated inflation.

      G means the person or group *gains* from unanticipated inflation.

      U means it is *uncertain* if the person or group is affected by unanticipated inflation or if the effects are unclear.

1. Banks extend many fixed-rate loans.

    (H)   G   U

    Explain: *The money the bank receives for the loan repayment will be less in real terms (purchasing power) than the loan amount.*

2. A farmer buys machinery with a fixed-rate loan to be repaid over a 10-year period.

    H   (G)   U

    Explain: *Farmer makes payments that are less in real terms than the loan amount.*

3. Your family buys a new home with an adjustable-rate mortgage.

    H   G   (U)

    Explain: *It depends on what happens to the future interest rate relative to the inflation rate. If the real interest rate rises, the family will be hurt.*

4. Your savings from your summer job are in a savings account paying a fixed rate of interest.

    (H)   G   U

    Explain: *The return from savings will be worth less because of inflation and the fixed rate of return.*

5. A widow lives entirely on income from fixed-rate corporate bonds.

    (H)   G   U

    Explain: *The purchasing power of the income will be less as inflation continues to deflate the value of the dollar.*

6. A retired couple lives entirely on income from a pension the woman receives from her former employer.

   H   G   (U)

   Explain: *It depends on whether the pension has a cost-of-living adjustment. If it does not, then the purchasing power of the pension payment will be less as inflation continues.*

7. A retired man lives entirely on income from Social Security.

   H   G   (U)

   Explain: *It depends on whether the Social Security payments are fully indexed for inflation. If Social Security payments do not increase at the same rate as inflation, then the retired man is hurt by inflation because he cannot puchase the same amount of goods and services.*

8. A retired bank official lives entirely on income from stock dividends.

   H   G   (U)

   Explain: *It depends on the growth in stock dividends relative to the inflation rate. In general, stock dividends increase with inflation while bond interest rates are fixed; however, the increase does not have to match the inflation rate.*

9. The federal government has a $5,000,000,000 debt.

   H   (G)   U

   Explain: *The government will repay the debt with money that has less purchasing power.*

10. A firm signs a contract to provide maintenance services at a fixed rate for the next five years.

    (H)   G   U

    Explain: *Revenue from contract will be worth less.*

11. A state government receives revenue mainly from a progressive income tax.

    H   G   (U)

    Explain: *It depends on how much tax revenue increases relative to inflation.*

12. A local government receives revenue mainly from fixed-rate license fees it charges businesses.

    (H)   G   U

    Explain: *Revenue will have a smaller purchasing power.*

13. Your friend rents an apartment with a three-year lease.

    H   (G)   U

    Explain: *Rent payments will be lower in real terms.*

14. A bank has loaned millions of dollars for home mortgages at a fixed rate of interest.

    (H)   G   U

    Explain: *Loan repayments will have less value or purchasing power.*

15. Parents are putting savings for their child's college education in a bank savings account.

    H   G   (U)

    Explain: *It depends on the return on the savings relative to the inflation rate.*

16. What conclusions can you draw about who is helped and who is hurt by unanticipated inflation?
    Individuals who receive fixed incomes are hurt by inflation — for example, lenders and savers. People who make fixed payments gain — for example, borrowers.

17. If you were certain that the inflation rate would be 10 percent a year for the next 10 years, how might your behavior change? Does your answer depend on who you are? Student? Worker?
    If you are a borrower, you would borrow money to buy real assets particularly if you could borrow at interest rates that did not reflect the high (10 percent) inflation rate. If you are a lender, you would adjust interest rates by the anticipated inflation of 10 percent.

Unemployment

Introduction and Description

Unemployment is always a major economic issue. Economic history seems to show that there is a short-run trade-off between inflation and unemployment. Understanding the types of unemployment is essential to analyzing unemployment reduction policies.

Activity 16 has the students identify the unemployment situation and determine whether it represents frictional, cyclical or structural unemployment.

Objectives

1. Define *unemployment, employment, labor force* and *labor force participation rate.*
2. Explain the issues in measuring unemployment.
3. Define the types of unemployment.

Time Required

One class period or 45 minutes

Materials

1. Activity 16
2. Visuals 2.5 and 2.6

Procedure

1. Project Visual 2.5. Discuss the important points:

   (A) Unemployment includes people who are *actively* looking for work. People who have stopped looking are not counted as unemployed.

   (B) The labor force consists of the employed and the unemployed.

   (C) The labor force participation rate is the proportion of the population over age 16 who are looking for work or who are working.

2. One issue associated with the definition of unemployment is *discouraged workers*: people who were looking for work but gave up because they didn't succeed in finding a job. The unemployment rate underestimates, by the number of discouraged workers, the number of people who would like to work.

3. A second issue is *underemployed* workers: people who are working part time but would like to work full time, or who hold a job that requires a lower skill level than they possess. These people are considered employed, but they could be more productive in a different job.

4. A third issue is that different groups within the economy experience vastly different rates of unemployment. The groups may be age cohorts, or race or ethnic categories. Knowing the distribution of unemployment by a particular characteristic is important in constructing policies to help the unemployed.

5. Project Visual 2.6. The important point is that there are different types of unemployment. The primary type that macroeconomic policy makers address is *cyclical* unemployment.

   The other terms on the visual are *natural rate of unemployment* and *full employment*. The natural rate of unemployment is the level of unemployment when there is no cyclical unemployment; frictional and structural unemployment may exist at the natural rate of unemployment. The "full-employment" level of employment occurs when the economy is at the natural rate of unemployment.

6. Have the students complete Activity 16. Review the answers to Activity 16 with the students.

Types of Unemployment

There are three types of unemployment:

- *Frictional unemployment* includes people who are temporarily between jobs. They may have quit one job to find another, or they could be trying to find the best opportunity after graduating from high school or college.

- *Cyclical unemployment* includes people who are not working because firms do not need their labor due to a lack of demand or a downturn in the business cycle. For example, if people are not buying many goods and services, workers are laid off.

- *Structural unemployment* involves mismatches between job seekers and job openings. Unemployed people who lack skills or do not have sufficient education are structurally unemployed.

At full employment, we have frictional and structural unemployment, but cyclical unemployment would be zero. At full employment, the level of unemployment is called the *natural rate of unemployment.*

For each of the following situations, put the appropriate letter before the example.

F if it is an example of *frictional* unemployment.

C if it is an example of *cyclical* unemployment.

S if it is an example of *structural* unemployment.

_C_ 1. A computer programmer is laid off because of a recession.

_F_ 2. A literary editor leaves her job in New York to look for a new job in San Francisco.

_F_ 3. An unemployed college graduate is looking for his first job.

_S_ 4. Advances in technology make the assembly-line worker's job obsolete.

_C_ 5. Slumping sales lead to the cashier being laid off.

_F_ 6. An individual refuses to work for minimum wage.

_S_ 7. A high school graduate lacks the skills necessary for a particular job.

_C_ 8. Workers are laid off when the local manufacturing plant closes because the product made there isn't selling.

_S_ 9. A skilled glass blower becomes unemployed when a new machine does her job faster.

Business Cycles

Introduction and Description

The study and control of business cycles are the heart of macroeconomics. The discipline of macroeconomics started as business cycle theory. The business cycle is a problem because of the by-products of output fluctuations: unemployment and inflation. Fluctuations in output and employment created major economic problems during the Great Depression and after World War II. Fluctuations in the economy before World War II led to the Employment Act of 1946; and the business cycles in the post-war period led to discussions of the trade-offs between the goals of economic growth, price stability and unemployment, and to passage of the Humphrey-Hawkins Act.

Objectives

1. Define and describe the phases of the business cycle.
2. Define *recession*.
3. Recognize the trade-offs between goals.

Time Required

Two class periods or 90 minutes

Materials

1. Activities 17 and 18
2. Visual 2.7

Procedure

1. Start by asking the students, "What causes output to rise and fall?" and "What causes unemployment to rise and fall?"

2. Explain that the business cycle describes economic fluctuations: the rising and falling of output in relation to potential output. Potential output is the level of output that the economy can sustain given the capital stock, technology and full employment.

3. Use Visual 2.7 to discuss the phases of the business cycle. *Recession* is defined as two consecutive quarters (six months) of negative growth in real GDP. The point at which output starts to decline is called the *peak* of the cycle, or the beginning of the recession. The point at which output starts to increase is called the *trough*, or the end of the recession. As the economy moves forward, the period between the trough and the next peak is called the *recovery period* or *expansion*.

4. Business cycles are defined in terms of output; however, other variables follow the movement of output. Investment and consumption both rise and fall with movements in real GDP. Inflation typically declines during recessions and increases as the economy approaches the peak. The unemployment rate rises sharply in recessions.

Interesting phenomena occur with the unemployment rate over a business cycle. Initially, the unemployment rate rises. If the recession lasts a long time, the unemployment rate remains at a high level or might actually decline as discouraged workers leave the ranks of the unemployed. As the recovery begins, the unemployment rate may remain very steady at a high level. As the economy recovers and people find jobs, other people enter the labor market looking for work and thus the unemployment rate remains steady.

5. Emphasize these points about business cycles:
   - There is no consistent length of time for each phase.
   - Business cycles are unpredictable. After the fact, economists can identify some of the causes of business cycles but are notoriously poor at predicting the actual downturn.
   - Some variables are *countercyclical*: move in the opposite direction from real GDP. Some variables are *procyclical*: move in the same direction as real GDP.

6. Have the students complete Activity 17 and review the answers with the students.

7. Have the students complete Activity 18, and review the answers with the students.

The Business Cycle

✳ Figure 17.1
The Business Cycle

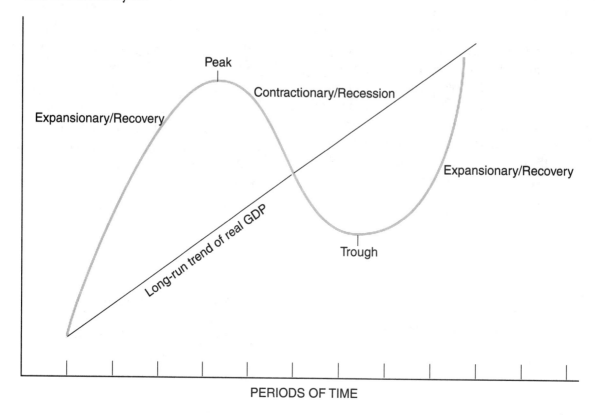

The curved line on Figure 17.1 shows a sample business cycle for an economy. The straight line represents the long-run trend of real GDP.

The business cycle can conveniently be divided into four phases:

1. **Expansionary or recovery phase.** Real output in the economy is increasing and the unemployment rate is declining. As the economic expansion continues, inflation may begin to accelerate.

2. **Peak.** Real output, GDP, is at its highest point of the business cycle.

3. **Contractionary or recession phase.** Real output in the economy is decreasing, and the unemployment rate is rising. As the contraction continues, inflationary pressures subside. If the recession continues long enough, prices may actually start to fall, a situation known as deflation.

4. **Trough.** The lowest point of real GDP reached during the business cycle is known as the trough. If the trough is particularly deep, it may be called a depression. A depression is an economic situation where the level of output falls to especially low levels and unemployment climbs to very high levels relative to the historical average. There is no precise decline in out-

put at which a serious recession becomes a depression. However, most business cycles do not end in a depression. The most recent depression the United States experienced was during the 1930s.

1. Figure 17.2 contains information for the U.S. economy from 1980 through 2001. For each quarter, first identify whether the economy was in an expansionary (E) or a contractionary (C) phase. Go back and pick out the quarters that correspond with a business cycle peak, and mark them with a P. Then find the quarters that correspond with a trough, and mark them with a T. Some of the answers have been provided for you.

Using your answers from Question 1, answer the following questions.

2. How many business cycles did the U.S. economy have between 1980 and 2001? __*2*__

3. In how many quarters was output expanding? __*76*__

4. In how many quarters was output contracting? __*10*__

5. Which expansion looks best to you? Explain. *The period from 1992 through 2001 had low unemployment and inflation rates.*

6. Which contraction looks worst to you? Explain. *1980. Both unemployment and inflation rates were very high.*

7. During quarters in which real GDP fell, what happened to the unemployment rate compared with the previous quarter? Why? *The unemployment rate was higher. As real GDP fell, the unemployment rate increased; because of rising inventories, workers were laid off.*

8. Look at the unemployment rate in quarters corresponding to a business cycle peak. Why do you think there was still some unemployment in these quarters? *There is unemployment even at full employment because of frictional and structural unemployment.*

9. Look at the unemployment rate in quarters corresponding to recoveries. Why do you think the unemployment rate remained high? *Unemployment remains high for two reasons: (1) frictional and structural employment and (2) with an expanding economy, more people move into the labor force looking for work.*

10. Based on the years 1980 to 2001, how does the rate of inflation correspond with the business cycle? *The inflation rate decreases during contractions but fluctuates during recoveries.*

✳ Figure 17.2

The U.S. Economy from 1980

Year	Real GDP in 1996 Dollars (billions)	% Change From Previous Quarter	Civilian Unemployment Rate	Inflation Rate (CPI)	Phase of Business Cycle
1980q1	4,958.9	0.33	6.30	3.91	E
1980q2	4,857.8	−2.04	7.32	3.67	C
1980q3	4,850.3	−0.15	7.68	1.83	C, T
1980q4	4,936.6	1.78	7.40	2.64	E
1981q1	5,032.5	1.94	7.43	2.65	E
1981q2	4,997.3	−0.70	7.40	2.32	C
1981q3	5,056.8	1.19	7.42	2.82	E, P
1981q4	4,997.1	−1.18	8.24	1.44	C
1982q1	4,914.3	−1.66	8.84	0.82	C
1982q2	4,935.5	0.43	9.43	1.52	E
1982q3	4,912.1	−0.47	9.94	1.88	C
1982q4	4,915.6	0.07	10.68	0.24	E, T
1983q1	4,972.4	1.16	10.39	−0.07	E
1983q2	5,089.8	2.36	10.10	1.26	E
1983q3	5,180.4	1.78	9.36	1.18	E
1983q4	5,286.8	2.05	8.54	0.90	E
1984q1	5,402.3	2.18	7.87	1.12	E
1984q2	5,493.8	1.69	7.48	1.08	E
1984q3	5,541.3	0.86	7.45	1.10	E
1984q4	5,583.1	0.75	7.28	0.73	E
1985q1	5,629.7	0.83	7.28	0.63	E
1985q2	5,673.8	0.78	7.29	1.23	E
1985q3	5,758.6	1.49	7.21	0.71	E
1985q4	5,806.0	0.82	7.05	0.89	E
1986q1	5,858.9	0.91	7.02	0.21	E
1986q2	5,883.3	0.42	7.18	−0.21	E
1986q3	5,937.9	0.93	6.99	0.73	E
1986q4	5,969.5	0.53	6.83	0.55	E
1987q1	6,013.3	0.73	6.62	1.12	E

Figure 17.2 (continued)

Year	Real GDP in 1996 Dollars (billions)	% Change From Previous Quarter	Civilian Unemployment Rate	Inflation Rate (CPI)	Phase of Business Cycle
1987q2	6,077.2	1.06	6.28	1.31	E
1987q3	6,128.1	0.84	6.01	1.15	E
1987q4	6,234.4	1.73	5.87	0.84	E
1988q1	6,275.9	0.67	5.73	0.61	E
1988q2	6,349.8	1.18	5.49	1.26	E
1988q3	6,382.3	0.51	5.49	1.33	E
1988q4	6,465.2	1.30	5.35	1.04	E
1989q1	6,543.8	1.22	5.22	1.11	E
1989q2	6,579.4	0.54	5.24	1.64	E
1989q3	6,610.6	0.47	5.28	0.81	E
1989q4	6,633.5	0.35	5.37	0.96	E
1990q1	6,716.3	1.25	5.30	1.72	E
1990q2	6,731.7	0.23	5.34	1.02	E, P
1990q3	6,719.4	−0.18	5.69	1.73	C
1990q4	6,664.2	−0.82	6.11	1.62	C
1991q1	6,631.4	−0.49	6.57	0.82	C, T
1991q2	6,668.5	0.56	6.82	0.59	E
1991q3	6,684.9	0.25	6.85	0.79	E
1991q4	6,720.9	0.54	7.10	0.76	E
1992q1	6,783.3	0.93	7.38	0.70	E
1992q2	6,846.8	0.94	7.60	0.82	E
1992q3	6,899.7	0.77	7.63	0.79	E
1992q4	6,990.6	1.32	7.41	0.71	E
1993q1	6,988.7	−0.03	7.15	0.85	C
1993q2	7,031.2	0.61	7.07	0.77	E
1993q3	7,062.0	0.44	6.80	0.39	E
1993q4	7,168.7	1.51	6.62	0.69	E
1994q1	7,229.4	0.85	6.56	0.64	E
1994q2	7,330.2	1.39	6.17	0.64	E
1994q3	7,370.2	0.55	6.00	0.88	E

✳ Figure 17.2 (continued)

Year	Real GDP in 1996 Dollars (billions)	% Change From Previous Quarter	Civilian Unemployment Rate	Inflation Rate (CPI)	Phase of Business Cycle
1994q4	7,461.1	1.23	5.62	0.47	E
1995q1	7,488.7	0.37	5.48	0.82	E
1995q2	7,503.3	0.19	5.68	0.88	E
1995q3	7,561.4	0.77	5.66	0.44	E
1995q4	7,621.9	0.80	5.57	0.48	E
1996q1	7,676.4	0.72	5.55	0.91	E
1996q2	7,802.9	1.65	5.47	0.99	E
1996q3	7,841.9	0.50	5.26	0.53	E
1996q4	7,931.3	1.14	5.31	0.72	E
1997q1	8,016.4	1.07	5.23	0.67	E
1997q2	8,131.9	1.44	4.98	0.40	E
1997q3	8,216.6	1.04	4.86	0.40	E
1997q4	8,272.9	0.69	4.68	0.39	E
1998q1	8,396.3	1.49	4.64	0.27	E
1998q2	8,442.9	0.56	4.42	0.54	E
1998q3	8,528.5	1.01	4.53	0.39	E
1998q4	8,667.9	1.63	4.43	0.35	E
1999q1	8,733.5	0.76	4.26	0.39	E
1999q2	8,771.2	0.43	4.26	0.97	E
1999q3	8,871.5	1.14	4.25	0.62	E
1999q4	9,049.9	2.01	4.10	0.62	E
2000q1	9,102.5	0.58	4.02	0.99	E
2000q2	9,229.4	1.39	4.00	1.06	E
2000q3	9,260.1	0.33	4.06	0.80	E
2000q4	9,303.9	0.47	3.97	0.54	E
2001q1	9,334.5	0.33	4.19	0.96	E
2001q2	9,341.7	0.08	4.47	1.04	E

Test Your Understanding of Macroeconomic Indicators

Answer the questions and briefly explain your answers.

1. The unemployment rate and employment both go up. Ellen says that it is not possible for both to rise at the same time. Is Ellen correct or incorrect? Why? *Ellen is incorrect. If more people enter the labor force and most of them do not find jobs, both employment and unemployment rates will rise.*

2. True, false or uncertain, and explain why? "Gross domestic product measures the amount of wealth in the economy." *False. GDP measures a stream of production or income in a particular year or time period. Wealth includes the current value of goods and services produced in past years.*

3. True, false or uncertain, and explain why? "A decrease in gross domestic product must reduce a person's standard of living." *False. GDP measures the production of the nation. Even during recessions, many people's real incomes rise.*

4. True, false or uncertain, and explain why? "If nominal GDP increases by 5 percent and the price level increases by 7 percent, real GDP has decreased." *True. Real GDP would fall by about 2 percent because the inflation rate is higher than the rate of growth in nominal GDP.*

5. True, false or uncertain, and explain why? "In preparing an index of prices, it is important that all commodities entering the index be given equal weight." *False. Commodities should enter the index with the weight that represents the proportion the item represents in people's actual pattern of consumption or use. Different groups have different consumption patterns. An index cannot capture everyone's cost of living.*

6. True, false or uncertain, and explain why? "*Frictional* and *structural* unemployment are two words for the same thing." *False. Structural unemployment occurs because people do not have the skills necessary for the jobs available. Frictional unemployment occurs when people are between jobs. They will find employment, but it will take time to match them with job vacancies.*

7. Why does unanticipated inflation help borrowers and hurt lenders? *Borrowers pay back a fixed number of dollars, but these dollars are worth less. This means that the purchasing power of the dollars that lenders receive is lower than the purchasing power of the dollars in the original loan. If the loan has a variable interest rate and inflation causes nominal interest rates to rise, the lender will not be hurt as badly because the lender can raise the interest rate on the loan.*

8. True, false or uncertain, and explain why? "Inflation always increases when unemployment decreases." *False. Although this is sometimes the case, look at the data in Activity 17 to illustrate that this is not always true. During 1983q2 to 1987q1, the unemployment rate was decreasing and inflation was highly variable.*

9. True, false or uncertain, and explain why? "If the economy is at full employment, the unemployment rate is zero." *False. At full employment, we have frictional and structural unemployment. Frictional unemployment occurs when people are between jobs; structural unemployment occurs when people do not have the skills for the jobs that are available.*

10. True, false, or uncertain, and explain why. "Seasonal unemployment is a continual worry because some people are out of work on a regular basis." *Uncertain. For the seasonally unemployed person it can be a worry. However, stimulating the economy may not change the situation. Seasonal workers are people who work only during particular seasons of the year such as Christmas time or harvest time.*

Answers to Sample Multiple-Choice Questions

1. *D*

2. *C*

3. *C*

4. *D*

5. *B*

6. *A*

7. *E*

8. *B*

9. *A*

10. *C*

11. *B*

12. *D*

13. *C*

14. *A*

15. *B*

16. *D*

17. *A*

18. *A*

19. *A*

20. *A*

Answers to Sample Short Free-Response Questions

1. Answer the following questions about GDP.

   (A) Explain whether this statement is true, false or uncertain: "To ignore the production of inter-mediate goods when measuring the total product of a country means ignoring the work, the efforts and the incomes of millions of citizens. This is a mistake and can be rectified only by including intermediate goods production in GDP figures." *False. The value of intermediate goods is captured in the value of the final good. Thus, the effort of intermediate goods producers is not ignored in the GDP numbers.*

   (B) Give two reasons for using real GDP per capita as a measure of the standard of living for a nation. *Real GDP per capita is a good measure because it gives us some idea of the income people would have if we divided production equally among all people. It is also a consistent measure over a long period of time, which allows us to observe changes in the average standard of living.*

   (C) Give two reasons why real GDP per capita is not a good measure of the standard of living for a nation. *Real GDP per capita does not measure all of the nonmarket production that goes on in households. It also does not recognize the fact that income is not equally distributed among the nation's citizens.*

2. Explain the statement "A man diminishes GDP by marrying his cook."
   It demonstrates how omitting nonmarket activities affects real GDP. The man pays his cook for her services, and her salary enters into GDP. However, once she becomes his wife and continues to cook for him, her services are no longer included in GDP because they are nonmarket activities.

    Advanced Placement Economics Teacher Resource Manual © National Council on Economic Education, New York, N.Y.

UNIT
2 Macroeconomics

SHORT FREE-RESPONSE
SAMPLE QUESTIONS

Answer
Key

3. You read the headline: "Real GDP Rises 3% This Year; Further Increases Likely Next Year, Econo-mists Say."

(A) What does this headline mean? Be specific.
The output of the nation, accounting for the change in the price level, has increased and is expected to continue to increase.

(B) Why do people care about the growth in real GDP?
It could mean more job opportunities or fewer job losses. Continued increases in real GDP could lead to inflation.

(C) What is the difference between real GDP and nominal GDP?
The real indicator accounts for price-level changes, which means it gives a clearer picture of actual changes in output. Nominal GDP is simply price times quantity. Nominal GDP increases could be caused by price increases, output increases or a combination of the two.

4. In a certain year, the annual unemployment rate was 6.1 percent. Define the term *unemployment rate*, and explain its meaning. What other information do you want to know before recommending a policy to reduce unemployment? Explain why you would want to know this information.
The unemployment rate is the percentage of the labor force that is looking for work. Before devising a policy, you would want to know what part of the unemployment is frictional, structural or cyclical. You would want to know this information because only cyclical unemployment is directly affected by changes in the policy. You might also want to know if the labor force participation rate has changed — that is, if more people are entering the labor force. Actual employment could be increasing while the unemployment rate is rising. Additionally, you might want to know whether particular groups are experiencing higher unemployment rates. If specific groups are, you might want to propose programs to help reduce unemployment in these groups: retraining programs for coal miners, for example.

5. You read the following headline: "Inflation Rate at 1.1% — Lowest Rate in 2 Decades."

   (A) What is meant by *inflation*? **Inflation is the rate of increase in the average price level.**

   (B) How did the statisticians arrive at 1.1 percent? What measure did they probably use?
   They probably used the consumer price index. Inflation = [P(t) – P(t – 1)] / P(t – 1)

   (C) What does this headline imply about inflation during the previous 20 years?
   The inflation rate has been higher than 1.1% during the last 20 years.

6. The following table shows a price index for a five-year period.

   (A) Using 2000 as the base year, calculate the price index for each year.

Year	Price Index (1999 = 100)	Price Index (2000 = 100)
1998	88	*73.3 (88 / 120)*
1999	100	*83.3 (5 / 6)*
2000	120	*100 (100)*
2001	132	*110 (132 / 120)*
2002	140	*116.7 (140 / 120)*

   (B) If 2001 nominal GDP were $400 billion and 2002 nominal GDP were $420 billion, what was the growth rate for the economy from 2001 to 2002? *The real GDP in 2001 is $363.6 billion and real GDP in 2002 is $360 billion. Thus, the growth rate is –1.01 percent. The economy actually experienced negative growth even though nominal GDP increased. Answers may differ because of rounding. The major point is that because of inflation, real GDP declined slightly even though nominal GDP increased.*

7. Assume the inflation rate is 2 percent. How is this rate measured, and what does this rate of inflation mean to the average citizen? *This is probably a CPI (consumer price index) measurement. The CPI is constructed by measuring the prices of goods and services that consumers typically buy. The index is based on a market basket of 400 goods and services. To average consumers, the 2 percent rate means that generally what they purchased before for $100 will now cost $102.*

Answers to Sample Long Free-Response Questions

1. Define *unanticipated inflation*. How does unanticipated inflation affect lenders, borrowers, home-owners and the federal government? *Inflation reduces the purchasing power of money received in the future. When inflation is unexpected or unanticipated, people have not made certain choices that would protect them against inflation of the specific rate. In general, people who borrow money will gain at the expense of lenders. The premium (the interest rate) charged for a loan may not be enough to cover the loss in purchasing power at the time of repayment. Thus, buyers are paying back with dollars that have a reduced purchasing power. Homeowners are usually borrowers, so they would gain if they had a fixed-rate mortgage. The federal government would gain until it reissues its bonds. The federal government would gain from its bond sales because it receives money that has greater purchasing power than the money it pays bondholders when the bonds mature.*

2. You read the following information about the economy:

   ■ Real GDP up 3 percent from a year ago

   ■ Unemployment rate of 4.6 percent

   ■ Consumer price index up 6 percent from a year ago

   ■ Index of leading indicators up for the last six months

   ■ Prime interest rate of 10 percent, up from 7 percent a year ago

   (A) Explain what each of these economic indicators measures and the significance of the current data for the economy. *Output of goods and services in this economy has increased by 3 percent in real terms, or accounting for price changes. The percentage of the labor force that is currently looking for work is 4.6. The general level of prices of items typically purchased by consumers has increased 6 percent. This means that what was purchased last year for $100 now costs $106. The index of leading indicators is constructed of the economic variables that generally lead the business cycle. In other words, it is a composite of variables that appear to predict what will happen to the economy. Here the leading economic indicators have increased, indicating that the economy is in a recovery or expansionary phase of the business cycle. The interest rate for the best customers has increased. This is particularly bad news for the business sector of the economy, which does much of its capital improvement with borrowed money. The increase in interest rates means that any investment expenditures are going to cost more; thus, firms will spend less on capital goods.*

   (B) These indicators should paint a picture of the entire economy. Describe this picture. *The data indicate that this economy is in the expansionary phase of a business cycle. The unemployment rate is relatively low; output is growing in real terms but inflation is rather high. The increase in the prime rate is historically high and may mean that the economy is about to turn down.*

Macroeconomic Questions

Why does output fluctuate?

What determines economic growth?

Why do we have unemployment, and why is unemployment a problem?

Why do we have inflation, and why is inflation a problem?

Which government policy affects output, growth, unemployment and inflation?

How do changes in the amount of money in the economy affect output, growth, unemployment and inflation?

How do domestic economic activities affect other countries and our trade?

Real GDP 1952-2001
(in billions of 1996 dollars)

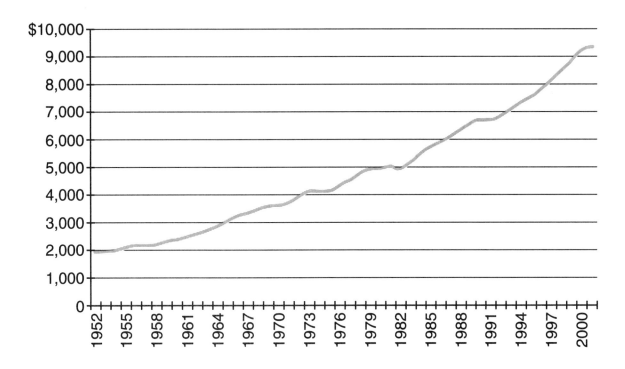

Circular Flow

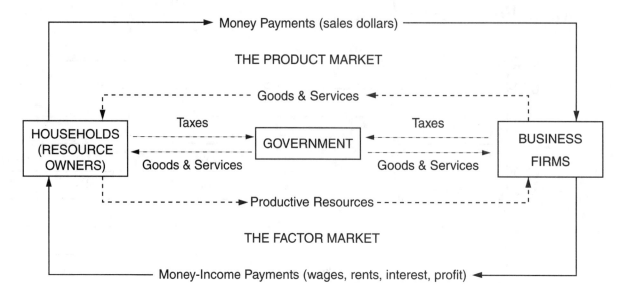

Macroeconomic Goals

Full Employment

Price Stability

Economic Growth

Definitions of Employed, Unemployed and Unemployment Rate

Employed $=$ everyone currently working, including part-time workers

Unemployed $=$ people looking for work or temporarily laid off from work

$$\text{Unemployment rate} = \frac{\text{unemployed}}{\text{labor force}}$$

Labor force $=$ employed + unemployed

$$\text{Labor force participation rate} = \frac{\text{labor force}}{\text{population aged 16 and older}}$$

Types of Unemployment

- ▓ Frictional Unemployment

- ▓ Structural Unemployment

- ▓ Cyclical Unemployment

Other Employment Concepts

- ▓ Natural Rate of Unemployment

- ▓ Full Employment

Phases of the Business Cycle

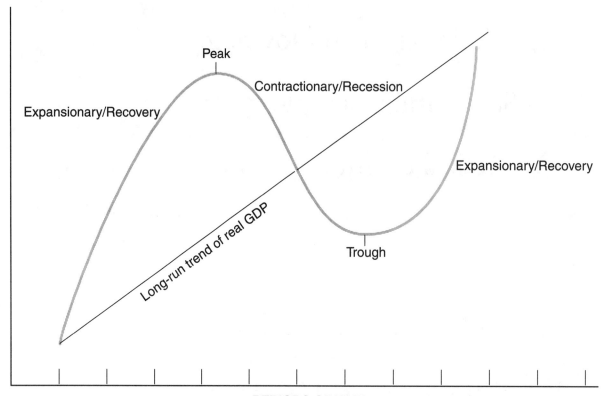

Peak

Contractionary/Recession

Expansionary/Recovery

Expansionary/Recovery

Long-run trend of real GDP

Trough

PERIODS OF TIME

Aggregate Demand and Aggregate Supply: Fluctuations in Outputs and Prices

23 class periods or 1,035 minutes
(31 percent of course time)

Unit Overview

This unit forms the core of the study of macroeconomics. The students must be able to use the models and the methods of analysis presented here.

The simple Keynesian model is presented as the transition from national income accounting to modeling the economy. This model also provides a clear mechanism for discussing the consumption function and the multiplier process. The Keynesian model holds the price level constant, which is not a realistic representation of the economy. The aggregate demand and aggregate supply model, where the price level and output are determined, is the central model for macroeconomic analysis. The students will have to use this model throughout the Advanced Placement Examination. They will have to interpret it; they will have to use the model to analyze problems. Most importantly, the students will have to present answers to questions by providing the graphical analysis of the aggregate demand and aggregate supply model. Initially, the short-run version of this model is presented. The analysis to transition the economy from the short run to the long run is presented later in the unit. The unit concludes with analysis of fiscal policy. Unit 3, in combination with Unit 4 on the monetary sector, provides the students with the essential macroeconomic model and policy analysis mechanisms.

The students may feel overwhelmed by the amount of material in this unit. It is essential that you spend sufficient time on Units 3 and 4 for the students to be able to analyze monetary and fiscal policy in the short run and the long run, and to understand the fundamental workings of the economy. The material presented here may be presented in a different order in the textbook you are using. Therefore, you may have to rearrange the order in which you use the activities. The material in this unit includes several of the content areas in the course outline presented by the College Board's Advanced Placement material.

The Lesson Planner

Lesson 1 develops a simple Keynesian model of the economy. It uses **Activities 19, 20** and **21** and **Visuals 3.1** through **3.4.**

Lesson 2 looks at investment: the expenditures of the business sector. It uses **Activity 22** and **Visuals 3.4** through **3.6.**

Lesson 3 develops aggregate demand. It uses **Activity 23** and **Visuals 3.7** and **3.8.**

Lesson 4 looks at the basic determinants of short-run aggregate supply. It uses **Activity 24** and **Visuals 3.9** and **3.10.**

Lesson 5 brings aggregate demand and aggregate supply together and relates this model to the simple Keynesian model. It uses **Activities 25** and **26** and **Visuals 3.11** and **3.12.**

Lesson 6 investigates many aspects of the aggregate demand and aggregate supply model including the responses of the economy to outside shocks and to other changes. It uses **Activities 27** and **28** and **Visual 3.13.**

Lesson 7 relates the long-run aggregate supply curve and the economy's production possibilities curve. It uses **Activity 29** and **Visual 3.14.**

Lesson 8 initiates the study of stabilization policy by discussing fiscal policy. It uses **Activities 30, 31, 32** and **33.**

Week 1	Week 2

Day 1

Lecture on simple Keynesian model using Visuals 3.1 and 3.2.

Day 2

(A) Have the students complete Activity 19.

(B) Review Activity 19.

Day 3

(A) Discuss consumption and savings using Visual 3.3.

(B) Have the students complete Activity 20 for homework.

Day 4

(A) Review Activity 20.

(B) Use Visual 3.4 to show effect of increase in investment on aggregate expenditure and to introduce the multiplier.

(C) Have the students complete Activity 21 for homework.

Day 5

(A) Review Activity 21.

(B) Discuss investment expenditures using Visuals 3.4, 3.5 and 3.6.

(C) Have the students complete Activity 22 for homework.

Day 6

(A) Review Activity 22.

(B) Discuss aggregate demand using Visual 3.7.

Day 7

(A) Continue discussion of aggregate demand using Visual 3.8.

(B) Have the students start Activity 23 in class and complete for homework.

Day 8

(A) Review Activity 23.

(B) Discuss aggregate supply and labor market using Visual 3.9.

Day 9

(A) Review aggregate supply using Visual 3.10.

(B) Have the students start Activity 24 in class and complete for homework.

Day 10

(A) Review Activity 24.

(B) Lecture on macro equilibrium, using Visual 3.11.

(C) Use Visual 3.12 to study an increase in AD.

(D) Have the students complete Activity 25 for homework.

Week 3

Day 11

(A) Review Activity 25.

(B) Show parallels between the Keynesian and the AD and AS models.

(C) Have the students complete Activity 26 for homework.

Day 12

(A) Review Activity 26.

(B) Review shifts in the AD curve.

(C) Discuss demand shocks.

(D) Have the students complete Part A of Activity 27.

(E) Review Part A of Activity 27.

Day 13

(A) Discuss shifts in the AS curve.

(B) Discuss supply shocks.

(C) Have the students complete Part B of Activity 27 .

(D) Review Part B of Activity 27.

(E) Assign Part C of Activity 27 as homework.

Day 14

(A) Review Part C of Activity 27.

(B) Discuss AD and AS model adjustments using Visual 3.13.

Day 15

(A) Continue discussion of the self-correcting or dynamic AD and AS model.

(B) Have the students complete Activity 28.

Week 4

Day 16

(A) Review Activity 28.

(B) Discuss LRAS and review production possibilities curve using Visual 3.14.

(C) Have the students complete Activity 29 for homework.

Day 17

(A) Review Activity 29.

(B) Discuss tools of fiscal policy.

(C) Have the students complete Activity 30.

Day 18

(A) Review Activity 30.

(B) Continue discussion of fiscal policy.

(C) Have the students complete Activity 31.

Day 19

(A) Review Activity 31.

(B) Discuss the Keynesian and the AD and AS models.

(C) Have the students complete Activity 32.

Day 20

(A) Review Activity 32.

(B) Have the students complete Activity 33.

Week 5

Day 21

(A) Review Activity 33.

(B) Review for unit test.

Day 22

Give multiple-choice portion of unit test.

Day 23

Give free-response portion of unit test.

Note: You may want to expand this unit to a full five weeks by providing additional tests and quizzes at appropriate places. For example, you could test the Keynesian model at the end of Week 1, and you could test the AD and AS model at the end of Week 3.

Keynesian Model

Introduction and Description

This lesson establishes fundamental macro concepts. The Keynesian model is the simplest macro model and is the starting point from the national income accounting identity: GDP = C + I + G + NX. The lesson describes the equilibrium between production and planned expenditures, and investigates the way economic agents react when planned expenditures do not equal production. The consumption function is presented and this leads to a discussion of average and marginal propensities to consume. The discussion then turns to the impact on the equilibrium if consumption or government spending changes.

Activity 19 gives the students practice using the Keynesian model, finding the equilibrium income and understanding the relationship among the concepts of income, consumption and saving. The students calculate APS, APC, MPS and MPC in Activity 20 and see the relationship among those concepts. The students practice calculating various multipliers and using the multiplier concept in Activity 21.

Objectives

1. Develop the Keynesian model.
2. Explain the four sectors of the Keynesian model.
3. Explain equilibrium in the Keynesian model.
4. Explain the economy's response if income is not at the equilibrium level.
5. Explain the difference between equilibrium output and full-employment output.
6. Explain the *consumption function*.
7. Describe the relationship between average and marginal propensities to consume and save.
8. Explain the *multiplier process*.

Time required

Four class periods or 180 minutes

Materials

1. Activities 19, 20 and 21
2. Visuals 3.1, 3.2, 3.3 and 3.4

Procedure

1. Tell the students the purpose of the lesson is to develop a simple model of the economy. Start with the national income identity: GDP = C + I + G + NX. By definition, this is always true. From here, planned aggregate expenditures are equal to the sum of planned consumption, planned investment, government spending and net exports. Planned consumption (C), government spending (G) and net exports (NX) always occur. Planned investment (I) does not necessarily occur. Sometimes inventories accumulate more than businesses planned, and sometimes businesses draw down inventories more than planned.

2. Use Visual 3.1 to explain the Keynesian model. **Note:** The price level is held constant in this model. Point out the following:

   (A) The 45° line shows all of the points where real GDP = planned aggregate expenditure.

   (B) Equilibrium is the intersection of the 45° line and the C + I + G + NX line.

   (C) Equilibrium does not have to be at full-employment real GDP.

3. Next discuss equilibrium and disequilibrium in the Keynesian model. Project Visual 3.2. The equilibrium output level is Y. Here aggregate expenditures equal output. At Y_1, the total output produced is 0B and the total expenditures are 0A. 0B is greater than 0A; therefore, more is produced than is demanded. Firms experience a build-up of inventories: More product is unsold and sitting in the warehouse. Firms will respond by producing less and usually laying off workers.

The output will decrease and move the economy toward the equilibrium level of output Y.

4. Now draw a vertical line at a level of output below Y. Ask the students to explain what is going on in the economy. More is demanded than is supplied; firms will be experiencing unplanned inventory reduction. Firms will respond by increasing production and employment. The economy will move toward Y.

5. Now look at one component of aggregate expenditures: consumption. Explain that consumption can be represented by the equation $C = a + bY$, where Y is income or output. The b is the marginal propensity to consume (MPC). It shows the amount by which consumption will increase if income increases by \$1. MPC = change in consumption / change in income.

6. Have the students complete Activity 19, and review the answers.

7. In the simplest model, households have only two things they can do with their income: consume or save. Thus, $Y = C + S$. Use Visual 3.3 to show savings and dissavings. In addition, since households have the choice only to consume or save, the marginal propensity to consume plus the marginal propensity to save must equal 1, or MPC + MPS = 1.

8. Have the students complete Activity 20, and review the answers.

9. Use Visual 3.4 to show what happens if businesses decide to spend more on investment goods. Point out that output goes up. By how much does output rise? Explain the multiplier process to the students. Demonstrate that the result depends on the MPC.

10. Expand on the idea of consumption and make it more realistic by introducing the concept of taxes. The consumption relationship now becomes $C = a + b\ YD$, where YD is disposable income. Disposable income = $Y - T$ where T represents taxes. Thus, households have three ways to spend income: consume, save and pay taxes.

11. Note that if the students are good at algebra, you can show them how to find the different multipliers by using the following simple equation system and substituting

$$C = a + b(Y - T)$$
$$I = I_0$$
$$G = G_0$$
$$NX = NX_0$$
$$Y = C + I + G + NX$$

Here's how to derive the various multipliers:

Substitute the values for C, I, G and NX into the equilibrium condition:

$$Y = a + b\ (Y - T) + I_0 + G_0 + NX_0$$

Collecting like terms, we have:

$$Y - bY = a - bT + I_0 + G_0 + NX_0$$

Solving for Y, we have:

$$Y = \frac{a}{(1-b)} - \frac{bT}{(1-b)} + \frac{I_0 + G_0 + NX_0}{(1-b)}$$

Holding T, G and NX constant, a change in I will change Y by

$$\Delta Y = (1/[1-b])\ \Delta I$$

We then arrive at the investment multiplier:

$$\frac{\Delta Y}{\Delta I} = \frac{1}{(1-b)}$$

Likewise we can derive the lump-sum tax multiplier and arrive at

$$\frac{\Delta Y}{\Delta T} = \frac{-b}{(1-b)}$$

12. Have the students complete Activity 21, and review the answers.

Advanced Placement Economics Teacher Resource Manual © National Council on Economic Education, New York, N.Y.

Keynesian Equilibrium

This activity is designed to give you practice with manipulations of the aggregate expenditure model. It shows you how the expenditure schedule is derived and how it helps to determine the equilibrium level of income. This activity assumes that the price level is constant with the consumer price index or price level having a value of 100. All numbers in Figure 19.1 are in billions of constant dollars.

✳ Figure 19.1
Income-Expenditure Schedule

Income (Output)	Consumption Spending	Investment Spending	Government Spending	Total Spending (Aggregate Expenditure)
$2,400	$2,500	$300	$100	*$2,900*
2,600	2,600	300	100	*3,000*
2,800	2,700	300	100	*3,100*
3,000	2,800	300	100	*3,200*
3,200	2,900	300	100	*3,300*
3,400	3,000	300	100	*3,400*
3,600	3,100	300	100	*3,500*
3,800	3,200	300	100	*3,600*

1. Use the data on consumption spending and income to draw the consumption function on the graph in Figure 19.2. Label the function C.

2. Using the consumption function you have just drawn and the data on investment and government spending, draw the aggregate expenditure schedule on the same graph. Label it AE (C + I + G). What is the difference between the aggregate expenditure schedule and the consumption function? *$400: the sum of government spending (G) and investment spending (I)*

3. Now draw a line representing all the points at which total spending and income could be equal. Label this the 45° line.

4. The 45° line represents all the points that *could be* the equilibrium level of total spending. Now circle the one point that *is* the equilibrium level of total spending. What is the equilibrium level of total spending on your graph? _____ *$3,400 billion* _____

✳ Figure 19.2

Aggregate Expenditure Model

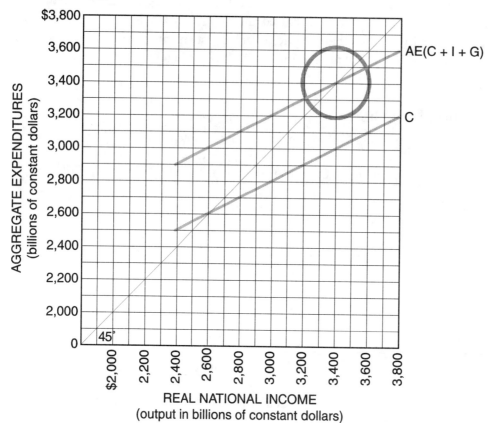

5. Based on the data in Figure 19.1, and assuming that the full-employment level of total spending is $3,600 billion, what conclusions can you draw about the equilibrium level of total spending? *The equilibrium level of total spending is below the full-employment level of total spending. There is unemployment of resources; the economy is in a recession.*

6. Based on the data in Figure 19.1, and assuming that the full-employment level of total spending is $3,200 billion, what conclusions can you draw about the equilibrium level of total spending? *The equilibrium level of total spending is above the full-employment level of total spending.*

7. If government spending increased by $100 billion, what would be the new equilibrium level of total spending? ___*$3,600 billion*___ For the increase of $100 billion in government spending, total spending increased by ___*$200 billion*___. Explain why this occurs. *The new equilibrium level of total spending is $3,600 billion. The increase in government spending becomes income to other people who in turn spend a portion of the increase in income, etc. The total effect of the $100 billion increase in government spending is an increase in total spending of $200 billion.*

Practice with APC, APS, MPC and MPS

Part A
Average Propensities

The *average propensity to consume* (APC) is the ratio of consumption expenditures (C) to disposable income (DI), or APC = C / DI.

The *average propensity to save* (APS) is the ratio of savings (S) to disposable income, or APS = S / DI.

1. Using the data in Figure 20.1, calculate the APC and APS at each level of disposable income given. The first calculation is completed as an example.

 Figure 20.1
Average Propensities to Consume and to Save

Disposable Income	Consumption	Saving	APC	APS
$0	$2,000	−$2,000	—	—
2,000	3,600	−1,600	1.8	−0.8
4,000	5,200	−1,200	*1.30*	*−0.3*
6,000	6,800	−800	*1.13*	*−0.13*
8,000	8,400	−400	*1.05*	*−0.05*
10,000	10,000	0	*1.00*	*0*
12,000	11,600	400	*0.97*	*0.03*

2. How can savings be negative? Explain. *People are borrowing or reducing their savings to be able to consume at the particular level of income.*

Part B
Marginal Propensities

The *marginal propensity to consume* (MPC) is the change in consumption divided by the change in disposable income. It is a fraction of any change in DI that is spent on consumer goods: MPC = ΔC / ΔDI.

The *marginal propensity to save* (MPS) is the fraction saved of any change in disposable income. The MPS is equal to the change in saving divided by the change in DI: MPS = ΔS / ΔDI.

3. Using the data in Figure 20.2, calculate the MPC and MPS at each level of disposable income. The first calculation is completed as an example. (This is not a typical consumption function. Its purpose is to provide practice in calculating MPC and MPS.)

Figure 20.2

Marginal Propensities to Consume and to Save

Disposable Income	Consumption	Saving	MPC	MPS
$12,000	$12,100	−$100	—	—
13,000	13,000	0	0.90	0.10
14,000	13,800	200	0.80	0.20
15,000	14,500	500	0.70	0.30
16,000	15,100	900	0.60	0.40
17,000	15,600	1,400	0.50	0.50

4. Why must the sum of the MPC and MPS always equal 1? *The only choice people have is to consume or to save. Thus an additional dollar in income must result in a change in consumption and/or a change in savings. The sum of the change must be one.*

Part C

Figure 20.3

Changes in APC and MPC as DI Increases

Disposable Income	Consumption	Savings	APC	APS	MPC	MPS
$10,000	$12,000	−$2,000	1.20	−0.20	—	—
20,000	21,000	−1,000	1.05	−0.05	0.90	0.10
30,000	30,000	0	1.00	0	0.90	0.10
40,000	39,000	1,000	0.975	0.025	0.90	0.10
50,000	48,000	2,000	0.96	0.04	0.90	0.10
60,000	57,000	3,000	0.95	0.05	0.90	0.10
70,000	66,000	4,000	0.94	0.06	0.90	0.10

5. Complete Figure 20.3, and answer the questions based on the completed table.

6. What is the APC at a DI level of $10,000? __*1.20*__ At $20,000? __*1.05*__

7. What happens to the APC as DI rises? _____*It decreases.*_____

8. What is the MPC as DI goes from $50,000 to $60,000? __*0.90*__ From $60,000 to $70,000? __*0.90*__

9. What happens to MPC as income rises? _____*It remains constant.*_____ What happens to MPS as income rises? _____*It remains constant.*_____

10. What is the conceptual difference between APC and MPC? *The APC measures the average consumption at any level of disposable income. The MPC measures what proportion of each additional dollar of income consumers will spend.*

The Magic of the Multiplier

The people in Econoland live on an isolated island. One year a stranger arrived and built a factory to make seashell charms. The factory is considered an investment on Econoland. If the marginal propensity to consume on the island were 75 percent, or 0.75, this would mean that Econoland residents would consume or spend 75 percent of any change in income and save 25 percent of any change in income. The additional spending would generate additional income and eventually a multiple increase in income. This is called the *multiplier effect*. When they heard about this multiplier effect, the islanders were thrilled about the new factory because they liked the idea of additional income.

The residents of Econoland wanted to know what would eventually happen to the levels of GDP, consumption and saving on the island as the new spending worked its way through the economy. Luckily there was a retired university economist who had settled on Econoland who offered a brief statement of the multiplier. "It's simple," he said: **"One person's spending becomes another person's income."** The economist began a numerical example. "This shows the process," he said. The rounds refer to the new spending moving from resident to resident. He stopped his example at four rounds and added the rest of the rounds to cover all Econoland's citizens.

Figure 21.1

Changes in Econoland's GDP, Consumption and Saving

Round	Income (GDP)	Consumption Spending	Saving
Round 1	$1,000	0.75 of $1,000 = $750	0.25 of $1,000 = $250
Round 2	One person's spending becoming another person's income: $750	0.75 of $750 = $562.50	0.25 of $750 = $187.50
Round 3	The next person's spending becoming another person's income: $562.50	0.75 of $562.50 = $421.88	0.25 of $562.50 = $140.62
Round 4	The next person's spending becoming another person's income: $421.88	0.75 of $421.88 = $316.41	0.25 of $421.88 = $105.47
Rounds continue	• • •	• • •	• • •
All rounds	**Final outcome for income (GDP)** **1 / (1 − 0.75) x $1,000 = 4 x $1,000 = $4,000**	**Final outcome for consumption spending** **0.75 of $4,000 = $3,000**	**Final outcome for saving** **0.25 of $4,000 = $1,000**

The retired economist then summarized the multiplier effect for the assembled crowd of Econolanders. "This shows us that the factory is an investment that has a multiplied effect on our GDP. In this case, the multiplier is 4." He added, "It appears to be magic, but it is simply that *one person's spending becomes another person's income.*" There were some nods of agreement but also many puzzled looks, so the old professor asked the citizens a series of questions. Answer these questions as if you were an Econolander.

1. Would the multiplier be larger or smaller if you saved more of your additional income? *Smaller*

2. What do you think would happen if all Econolanders saved all of the change in their incomes? *There would not be any change in output from consumption.*

3. What would happen if you spent *all* of the change in your income? *There would be an infinite change in output from consumption.*

The professor broke out into a smile as the answers all came out correct.

The economist reminded the islanders about the multiplied effect on GDP that a new road around the island would have. That new bridge built by the island government over the lagoon would also have a multiplied effect on GDP. This time there were many more nods of approval and understanding.

The economist also indicated that if the government of Econoland lowered taxes, the citizens would have more income to spend, which would cause a multiplier effect. He said there was another side to this: If the taxes were raised, there would be a multiplier effect, which would decrease income and GDP by a multiple amount.

The King of Econoland commissioned the old economist to write a simple explanation about multipliers so all the citizens of Econoland would understand. He told the old economist: "If you succeed in helping all citizens understand the multiplier in simple terms, you will be rewarded. If not, you will be banished from the island."

The economist started banging away on an old rusting typewriter since he did not want to be banished from this island paradise. The result follows:

The Professor's Treatise on Multipliers

MULTIPLIER FORMULAS AND TERMS

Marginal propensity to consume (MPC) = change in consumption divided by change in income

Marginal propensity to save (MPS) = change in saving divided by change in income

Investment Multiplier = 1 / (1 – MPC) or simply 1 / MPS

How to use the investment multiplier: change in GDP = change in investment times investment multiplier

When to use the investment multiplier: when there is a change in investment such as a new factory or new equipment

Government Spending Multiplier = 1 / (1 – MPC) or simply 1 / MPS

How to use the government spending multiplier: change in GDP = change in government spending times government spending multiplier

When to use the government spending multiplier: when there is a change in government spending such as a new road or bridge

Tax Multiplier = – MPC / (1 – MPC) = – MPC / MPS

How to use the tax multiplier: change in GDP = change in taxes times tax multiplier

When to use the tax multiplier: when there is a change in lump-sum taxes. Remember that the tax multiplier has a negative sign.

Figure 21.2
Multiplier Table
(Derived from using the formulas above)

MPC	Investment Multiplier	Government Spending Multiplier	Tax Multiplier
0.90	10.0	10.0	–9.0
0.80	5.0	5.0	–4.0
0.75	4.0	4.0	–3.0
0.60	2.5	2.5	–1.5
0.50	2.0	2.0	–1.0

"ALWAYS" RULES (A surefire way to remember multipliers)

■ The investment multiplier is *always* equal to the same value as the government spending multiplier.

■ The investment and government spending multipliers are *always* positive.

■ The tax multiplier is *always* negative.

The King took the treatise and had it printed for every islander. He then ordered the old professor to make up a series of questions to see if the subjects understood the multiplier.

Answer the questions on the professor's test.

The Econoland Test

1. What is the value of the tax multiplier if the MPC is 0.80? _____−4_____

2. What is the value of the government spending multiplier if the MPC is 0.67? ___3___

3. What is the tax multiplier if the MPS is 0.25? _____−3_____

4. How could the multiplier be used to explain wide swings in income (which could be called business cycles) in Econoland? *Small changes in expenditure are magnified by the multiplier effect.*

5. The numerical value for the investment and government spending multiplier increases as the
   (A) value of the marginal propensity to save decreases.
   (B) value of the average propensity to consume increases.
   (C) value of the marginal propensity to consume decreases.
   (D) value of the marginal propensity to save increases.
   (E) value of the average propensity to consume decreases.

6. If the government spending multiplier is 5 in Econoland, the value of the tax multiplier must be
   (A) 5
   (B) 4
   (C) 1
   (D) −4
   (E) −5

Econoland has the following values for income and consumption. Use this data to answer questions 7, 8 and 9.

Income	Consumption
100	150
200	225
300	300
400	375
500	450
600	525

7. The government spending multiplier in Econoland is

(A) 3

(B) 4

(C) 5

(D) 10

(E) 30

8. If there is an increase in taxes of $200 in Econoland, the decrease in GDP will be

(A) $100

(B) $200

(C) $400

(D) $600

(E) $800

9. If there is an increase in government spending of $100 and an increase in taxes of $100 in Econoland, then the change in GDP will be

(A) $50

(B) $100

(C) $200

(D) –$100

(E) –$200

10. Why do the people of Econoland need to understand multipliers? *Understanding multipliers allows people to understand the impact of fiscal policy and changes in autonomous components of consumption, investment and government spending on total income.*

Investment

Introduction and Description

In the last lesson, the focus was on a simple Keynesian model of the economy and consumption. In this lesson, the determinants of investment — spending by businesses to replace or increase the capital stock — are described. In contrast to consumption, investment spending in the United States changes greatly from year to year. Keynes referred to the cause of the great variability in investment as the "animal spirits of business."

Activity 22 presents an opportunity for students to use knowledge about business investment to determine whether a project should be undertaken and to calculate the effects of changes in interest rates for investment functions with different elasticities.

Objectives

1. Define investment.
2. Differentiate between investment in capital stock and financial investment.
3. Describe the determinants of investment.
4. Explain why changes in the interest rate change the level of investment.
5. Describe the effects of different interest elasticities of investment demand.

Time Required

One class period or 45 minutes

Materials

1. Activity 22
2. Visuals 3.4, 3.5 and 3.6

Procedure

1. Tell the students what this lesson is about. Define investment. To an economist, investment is spending on plant and equipment: the machinery and the buildings that a firm uses to produce output. Investment is *not* the purchase of stocks and bonds or any other financial instrument.

2. Discuss the determinants of investment: output and interest rate. Real GDP determines investment because it is a measure of the level of demand for the product. Businesses have a range of investment opportunities; for example, they can buy a new machine that produces more than an older machine, or they can build a whole new factory. A business will calculate the expected profitability of the investment alternatives. To be able to make an investment, the business must have the money. It can use its profits, or retained earnings, or it can borrow the money. Either way the interest rate will determine whether the business invests. The interest rate represents the opportunity cost of using the money to buy investment goods. To decide whether to invest, businesses will compare the interest rate to the expected profit rate of the new plant and equipment. If the expected profit is greater than the interest rate, firms will invest. Thus, as the interest rate goes down, more investment opportunities will be available and firms will invest more. Project Visual 3.5, which shows that investment is an inverse function of the interest rate: As the interest rate goes down, the level of investment goes up.

3. Use Visual 3.4 to explain that if the interest rate goes down, the aggregate expenditure curve in the Keynesian model will shift up. The multiplier process will work, and real GDP will increase.

4. The students may ask how much investment will increase as the interest rate decreases. The answer depends on the elasticity of the investment function. Project Visual 3.6. There are two investment functions: I_A and I_B. I_A is more interest elastic than I_B. Thus, the same decrease in the interest rate from r to r_1 will result in two different levels of investment, I_1 and I_2.

5. Have the students complete Activity 22. Review the answers with the students.

Investment Demand

Investment spending consists of spending on new buildings, machinery, plant and equipment. Investment spending is a part of total spending or aggregate expenditures. Any increase in investment spending would necessarily increase total spending or aggregate expenditures.

Decisions on investment spending are based on a comparison of marginal cost and marginal benefit: If you expect a particular project to yield a greater benefit than cost, you will undertake it. One of the costs associated with investment spending is the interest expense on borrowed money to engage in the project.

Part A

1. Figure 22.1 lists the expected cost of various projects and the associated expected benefit. Fill in the decision column with Yes if you would undertake the project and No if you would not. The first example has been completed for you.

Figure 22.1
Comparison of Costs and Benefits of Different Projects

Cost	Benefit	Decision
$65	$20	No
$55	$30	*No*
$45	$40	*No*
$35	$50	*Yes*
$25	$60	*Yes*

2. If interest rates fell and the cost associated with the project fell by $15 at each level, indicate in Figure 22.2 which projects you would undertake. The first example has been completed for you.

Figure 22.2
Comparison of Project Costs and Benefits with Decrease in Costs

Cost	Benefit	Decision
$50	$20	No
$40	$30	*No*
$30	$40	*Yes*
$20	$50	*Yes*
$10	$60	*Yes*

Part B

Figure 22.3 lists the dollar value of investment projects that would be profitable at each interest rate.

Figure 22.3

Country A and Country B Investment Data

Interest Rate	Country A Investment	Country B Investment
10%	$10	$70
8	50	75
6	90	80
4	130	85
2	170	90

Figure 22.4

Investment Demand Curves

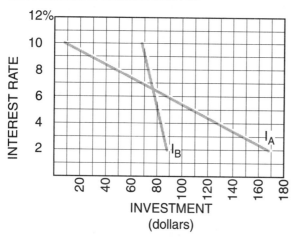

3. Plot the investment demand curve for Country A on Figure 22.4 and label it I$_A$.

4. Plot the investment demand curve for Country B on Figure 22.4, and label it I$_B$.

5. Which country would experience the larger increase in the amount of investment spending if interest rates in each country dropped from 8 percent to 6 percent? *Country A*

6. How would you characterize the responsiveness of investment spending to the interest rates in Country A compared with Country B? *In Country A, investment demand is more interest elastic.*

7. Assuming an MPC of 75 percent, what would be the effect on real GDP in Country A and Country B if real interest rates decline from 8 percent to 6 percent? *In Country A, real GDP would increase by $160 ($40 x 4); in Country B, real GDP would increase by $20 ($5 x 4).*

8. What conclusions can be reached about the elasticity of the investment demand curve and the effect a given change in interest rates would have on equilibrium real GDP? *The more inelastic the investment demand, the smaller the impact on investment of a given change in interest rates and, thus, a smaller impact on real GDP.*

9. Looking at the graph you drew, the investment demand curve is downward sloping in both Country A and Country B. Why does the investment demand curve have a downward slope? *As the interest rate declines, more investment opportunities become profitable because the cost of borrowing has declined.*

Part C

Use Figure 22.5 to help answer questions 10, 11 and 12.

✳ Figure 22.5
Shift in Investment Demand Curve

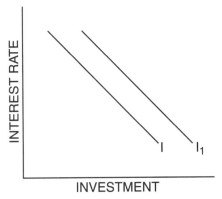

10. If interest rates rise, will the investment demand curve shift to a new location? If so, in what direction? *No. A change in interest rates is a movement along the investment curve.*

11. The shift in the investment demand curve shown in Figure 22.5 (I to I_1) represents a new location for the entire curve. How would you interpret the difference between movement along an existing investment demand curve and a shift in the location of the curve? *A movement along the curve is caused by a change in interest rates. A shift in the curve results from factors other than interest rate. For example, business confidence may increase and cause the investment curve to shift to the right.*

12. List two factors that could cause a shift in the investment demand curve as shown in Figure 22.5.
Change in business conditions
Change in expected profitability of an investment project

Aggregate Demand

Introduction and Description

Aggregate demand represents the sum of consumption (C), investment (I), government expenditures (G) and net exports (NX). The quantity of real GDP demand is the total of all final goods and services that households, businesses, governments and foreigners plan to buy. This lesson explains the factors that determine aggregate demand. Just as in microeconomics, the students should understand the difference between a shift in a curve and movement along a curve. This lesson helps the students differentiate the two situations when applied to the aggregate demand curve.

Activity 23 provides practice with the aggregate demand curve and distinguishing between movements along and shifts in the aggregate demand curve.

Objectives

1. Define aggregate demand.
2. Explain why the aggregate demand curve is downward sloping.
3. Describe the factors that affect aggregate demand.
4. Explain what factors will shift the aggregate demand curve.

Time Required

Two class periods or 90 minutes

Materials

1. Activity 23
2. Visuals 3.7 and 3.8

Procedure

1. Tell the students that this lesson begins to develop a more complex economic model. Define aggregate demand. It is the sum of planned consumption, investment, government and export minus import expenditures on final goods and services.

2. Project Visual 3.7. Explain that the aggregate demand function is an inverse function between the price level and output: As the price level rises, the level of output demanded decreases. Explain the three factors that affect aggregate demand: the interest-rate effect, the wealth effect and the net-export effect. Assume that nominal money supply is constant.

   (A) The *interest-rate effect* is defined as a decrease in households' and businesses' plans to buy capital and consumer durables because a price level increase will increase the interest rate. A price level increase decreases the purchasing power of money. With a smaller amount of real money available, financial institutions raise the interest rate.

   (B) The *wealth effect* is defined as a decrease in the real value of cash balances as the price level increases. Faced with this decrease in real wealth, people decrease consumption and increase savings to restore their real wealth to the desired level. An alternative term is the *real balance effect*.

   (C) The *net export effect* is defined as a decrease in domestic output demanded with an increase in the domestic price level because domestic products are more expensive to foreign buyers and foreign goods are less expensive to domestic consumers.

   These three effects combine to produce a downward sloping aggregate demand curve. Emphasize that these are different reasons than those that create a downward sloping demand curve for a single commodity.

3. Use Visual 3.8 to work through increases and decreases in aggregate demand. Discuss the following changes and their effects on aggregate demand.

   (A) Changes in expectations of future income, inflation or profits

   (B) Changes in government spending or taxes

   (C) Changes in the money supply

   (D) Changes in the foreign exchange rate or foreign income

4. Have the students do Activity 23. Review the answers with the students.

An Introduction to Aggregate Demand

Part A
Why Is the Aggregate Demand Curve Downward Sloping?

 Figure 23.1
Aggregate Demand Curve

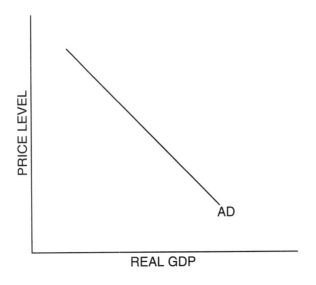

1. According to the AD curve, what is the relationship between the price level and real GDP?
   There is an inverse relationship: the lower the price level, the higher the real GDP or real national output.

2. Explain how each of the following effects helps explain why the AD curve is downward sloping.

   (A) Interest rate effect *A lower price level decreases the demand for money, which decreases the equilibrium interest rate and increases investment and interest-sensitive components of consumption and, therefore, the real output.*

   (B) Wealth effect or real-balance effect *As the price level falls, cash balances will buy more so people will spend more, thus increasing the real output.*

   (C) Net export effect *A lower U.S. price level means prices for goods produced in the United States are lower relative to the prices in foreign countries. Thus, people will buy more U.S.-produced goods and fewer foreign produced goods. This increases net exports, a component of real GDP.*

3. In what ways do the reasons that explain the downward slope of the AD curve differ from the reasons that explain the downward slope of the demand curve for a single product? *The demand curve for a single product is downward sloping because of diminishing marginal utility and income and substitution effects for the individual at a specified level of income. For macro aggregate demand, the reasons are the interest rate effect, the wealth effect and the net export effect.*

Part B
What Shifts the Aggregate Demand Curve?

Figure 23.2
Shifts in Aggregate Demand

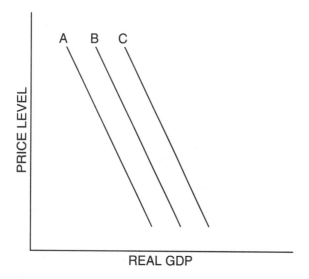

4. Using Figure 23.2, determine whether each situation below will cause an increase, decrease or no change in AD. Always start at curve B. If the situation would cause an increase in AD, draw an up arrow in column 1. If it causes a decrease, draw a down arrow. If there is no change, write NC. For each situation that causes a change in aggregate demand, write the letter of the new demand curve in column 2. Move only one curve.

Advanced Placement Economics Teacher Resource Manual © National Council on Economic Education, New York, N.Y.

Situation	1. Change in AD	2. New AD Curve
(A) Congress cuts taxes.	↑	C
(B) Autonomous investment spending decreased.	↓	A
(C) Government spending to increase next fiscal year; president promises no increase in taxes.	↑	C
(D) Survey shows consumer confidence jumps.	↑	C
(E) Stock market collapses; investors lose billions.	↓	A
(F) Productivity rises for fourth straight year.	NC	
(G) President cuts defense spending by 20 percent; no increase in domestic spending.	↓	A

Note: (F) does not shift the aggregate demand curve. We will see that productivity changes affect the aggregate supply curve.

Aggregate Supply

Introduction and Description

Aggregate supply is the quantity of output that firms are willing and able to produce for the economy. In the long run, the level of output depends on the capital stock, the labor force and the level of technology. In the short run, the level of output depends on the amount of labor employed with a given level of capital and technology. The students should understand the aggregate supply curve and its determinants because the adjustment process in the economy to changes in aggregate demand or aggregate supply depends on understanding the determinants of aggregate supply. The aggregate supply curve is derived in the Appendix to this lesson.

Activity 24 provides practice with the aggregate supply curve and understanding movements along and shifts in the aggregate supply curve.

Objectives

1. Define aggregate supply.
2. Explain why the aggregate supply curve is upward sloping.
3. Describe the factors that affect aggregate supply.
4. Explain what factors will shift the aggregate supply curve.

Time Required

Two class periods or 90 minutes

Materials

1. Activity 24
2. Visuals 3.9 and 3.10

Procedure

1. Tell the students that this lesson develops the other side of the macroeconomy: aggregate supply. Define aggregate supply: Aggregate supply is the total supply of all goods and services in the economy. The aggregate supply curve shows the relationship between total quantity of output supplied by all firms and the overall price level.

Point out that the aggregate supply curve is not the sum of individual firm supply curves. In microeconomics, a firm's supply curve is derived by changing price and holding all other variables constant, including costs. However, if there is an increase in the overall price level, it is unrealistic to assume that costs are constant for individual firms. The aggregate supply curve is the relationship between production and the price level; it is sometimes called a *price-output adjustment curve.*

2. Explain that aggregate supply, or real gross domestic product (GDP), depends on the quantity of labor, the quantity of capital and the level of technology. In the short run, the capital and level of technology are fixed, and only the quantity of labor changes. A short-run aggregate supply (SRAS) curve assumes the money wage, resource prices and potential GDP are constant. With the money wage, resource prices and potential GDP constant, as the overall price level rises, firms will produce more output. The short-run aggregate supply curve can be shaped as a horizontal line, a vertical line or a positively sloped line. We usually draw the aggregate supply curve as positively sloped, as seen in Visual 3.9.

3. Still using Visual 3.9, explain that the long-run aggregate supply (LRAS) curve is vertical at full employment, or potential GDP. If there is an increase in the overall price level that is matched by equal percentage increases in the money-wage rate and other resource prices, the economy will remain at potential GDP. Following adjustments, the SRAS and AD curves intersect along the LRAS curve.

4. Explain that the SRAS will change (a shift in the curve) if the potential GDP changes, or if money wages or other resource prices change. Changes in potential GDP can occur if there is a change in the full-employment quantity of labor, a change in the quantity of capital or a technological advance. Visual 3.10 summarizes the effects for an increase in the long-run aggregate supply. We can also use Visual 3.10 to show a decrease in money-wage rates. A decrease in money-wage rates shifts the SRAS but not the LRAS because a change in the money-wage rate is matched by an equal change in the price level in the long run.

A graphical derivation and discussion of the aggregate supply curve is provided in the Appendix to this lesson. This discussion is for the benefit of the teacher and may be provided to the students at the teacher's discretion.

5. For the second day, propose various scenarios and have the students tell you in which direction the SRAS curve moves and why it moves in that direction. Here are some examples of shifts in SRAS:

   - An increase in labor productivity will shift SRAS to the right.
   - An increase in the average wage rate will shift SRAS to the left.
   - An increase in technology will shift SRAS to the right.

6. Have the students complete Activity 24. Review the answers with the students.

Appendix to Lesson 4

In this appendix we show the derivation of the short-run aggregate supply curve, the long-run aggregate supply curve and the use of these models to show economic growth.

The Short-Run Aggregate Supply Curve

The aggregate supply curve represents the relationship between the price level and the level of production. We can look at the microfoundations of the aggregate supply curve by looking at Appendix Figure 4.1. In Appendix Figure 4.1, the top left graph is the short-run production function; the bottom left graph is the labor market. The top right graph is a 45° line; this graph is used only to transfer real GDP from the vertical axis to the horizontal axis. The bottom right graph is the short-run aggregate supply curve.

 Appendix Figure 4.1
Deriving the SRAS Curve

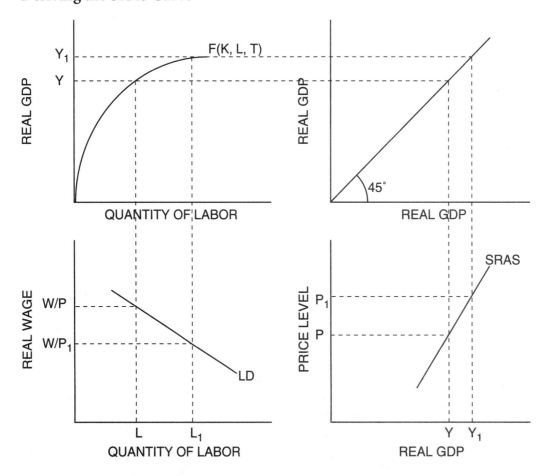

This appendix was written by Rae Jean Goodman, U.S. Naval Academy, Annapolis, Md., and Charles Orvis, Rhodes College, Memphis, Tenn.

Looking at Appendix Figure 4.1, we have the short-run production function, which is a function of the amount of labor input (L), capital (K) and technology (T). Capital and technology are fixed in the short run. From the production function, assuming a perfectly competitive labor market, we can derive the marginal product of labor, which is the slope of the production function (which equals the change in output / change in labor = $\Delta Y / \Delta L$) and is the demand curve for labor. If the real wage is W / P, firms will hire L amount of labor and produce Y real GDP. We then have one point on the SRAS: Y and P.

If the price level increases to P_1, the real wage falls to W/P_1; firms will hire L_1 quantity of labor and produce Y_1: real GDP. This gives us a second point on the SRAS curve: Y_1 and P_1. Thus, the short-run aggregate supply curve SRAS is determined by the nominal wage, W, and the given technology and capital stock.

Changes in the nominal wage (or other resource prices), in the capital stock or in technology will shift the short-run aggregate supply curve. If we look at Appendix Figure 4.2, we can see the effects of a change in the nominal wage. We show the derivation of the first SRAS curve. Now if nominal wages rise to W_1 such that $W_1 / P_1 = W / P$, we trace out a point on a new SRAS curve; the point involves a nominal wage (W_1), a price level (P_1,) and real output of Y. This shows that with an increase in the nominal wage, the short-run aggregate supply curve shifts leftward to $SRAS_1$.

Appendix Figure 4.2
New SRAS with Increase in Nominal Wage

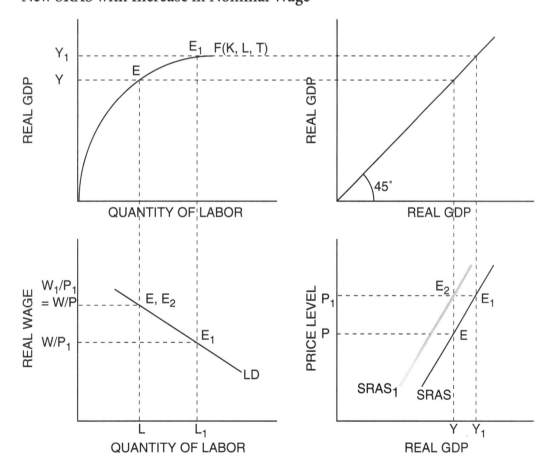

We can examine other changes such as a change in technology or a change in the capital stock in the same manner. The difference is that changes in capital or technology will cause a shift in the production function and thus will cause the SRAS and the LRAS curves to shift. This is discussed later in this appendix.

The Long-Run Aggregate Supply Curve

There can be short-run changes in the aggregate demand curve, which will increase or decrease output along a fixed short-run aggregate supply curve (SRAS) without affecting the wage rate. The reasons that wages are not affected in the short run include explicit or implicit labor contracts, workers do not recognize that the change in the price level affects their real wage, the efficiency-wage model or imperfect competition.

Using Appendix Figure 4.3, we add a labor supply curve and an aggregate demand curve (AD). The labor supply curve intersects the labor demand curve at the real wage, W / P; and the AD curve intersects the SRAS curve at the corresponding level of output, Y*. Equilibrium is labeled E.

Appendix Figure 4.3
Long-Run Aggregate Supply Curve

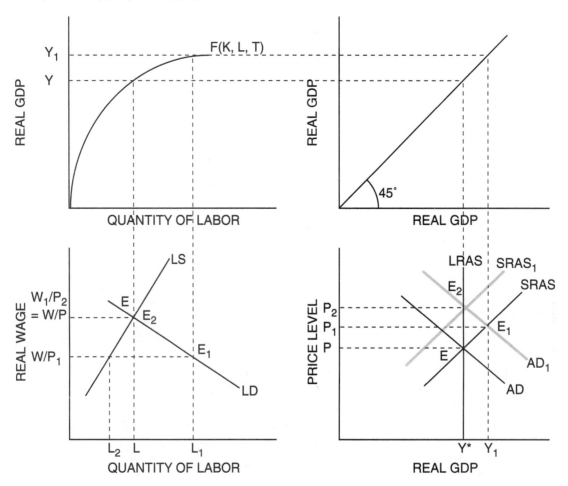

Now assume there is an increase in AD to AD_1. AD may increase because of an increase in the money supply by the Federal Reserve or an increase in any one of the components of aggregate demand: consumption, investment, government spending or net exports. The increase in AD will cause both real GDP and the price level to increase to Y_1 and P_1, respectively. The increase in P will reduce the real wage to W / P_1 and move the labor market to a shortage position on the labor demand curve but off the labor supply curve. L_1 is the quantity of labor demanded; L_2 is the quantity supplied; the shortfall is $(L_1 - L_2)$. The resulting shortage of labor will cause the nominal wage rate to rise until equilibrium is restored in the labor market. This increase in the nominal wage will cause the SRAS curve to shift to the left until output is back to its starting level at Y^*. Equilibrium is E_2.

Note the result: Any movement away from equilibrium in the labor market will be temporary, and the economy will return to that level of output consistent with labor market equilibrium with a different (higher, in this case) price level (P_2) and nominal wage rate (W_1) such that the original equilibrium real wage rate is restored. The vertical line at this full employment level of output, Y^*, is our long-run aggregate supply (LRAS) curve.

For a decline in AD that creates a short-run equilibrium level of output that is below full-employment GDP, the result is the same. The difference is that there is a surplus of labor in the short run, which causes the nominal wage to fall and thus shift the SRAS curve to the right until equilibrium is restored at full-employment GDP. The labor market will also be in equilibrium.

Economic Growth

Now we will extend the SRAS, LRAS, AD model to illustrate the process of economic growth.

We know that we can use the production possibilities curve model to demonstrate growth, defined as an increase in the capacity of the economy to produce GDP. In this model, we can show that an increase in resources, an increase in the stock of capital or an in increase in technology will cause the PPC to shift outward.

We can show this same result in our AD and AS model. Appendix Figure 4.4 presents the following analysis.

An increase in the stock of capital or an increase in technology will cause the production function for the economy to shift (rotate) upward to F_1, showing a greater level of output for every level of labor employed. This upward rotation of the production function will raise the slope of the production function. This slope is the marginal productivity of labor, which is the labor demand curve in a perfectly competitive labor market. Thus the labor demand curve will shift upward to LD_1. The labor demand curve increases because every unit of labor will have more capital (or technology) to work with so its productivity will be higher.

This upward shift in the labor demand curve will create a higher equilibrium real wage (W_1 / P_1) and a higher equilibrium level of employment (L_1) in the labor market. Since the position of the LRAS curve is based upon the equilibrium level of employment, you can trace through the model from this new equilibrium employment up to the new higher production function to determine the position of the new LRAS curve to the right of the original LRAS curve. This is the increase in the productive capacity of the economy. The new LRAS is labeled $LRAS_1$.

✳ Appendix Figure 4.4
New LRAS with Increase in Capital Stock

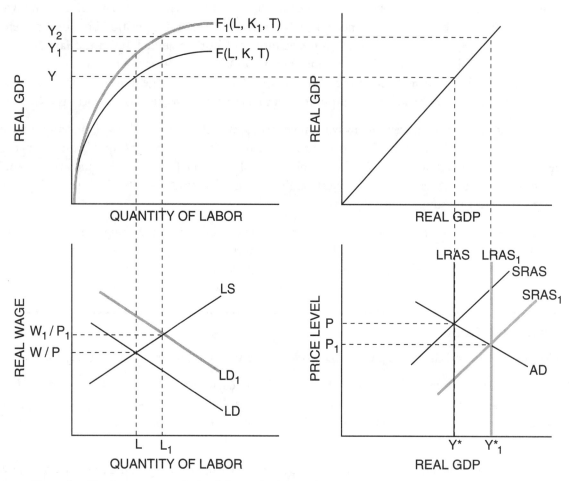

Since the SRAS curve was derived from the labor demand curve, there will also be a new SRAS curve with the nominal wage rate constant, which lies to the right of the original SRAS curve. The new short-run equilibrium between the new SRAS curve and the fixed AD curve will create a lower equilibrium price level. Eventually, the economy will be in LR equilibrium where AD = SRAS = LRAS and the labor market is back in equilibrium. The new SRAS is labeled $SRAS_1$ and intersects with the AD and $LRAS_1$ curve.

We show the derivation of the new SRAS after an increase in labor demand in Appendix Figure 4.5.

To determine one point on the new SRAS curve, you hold the real wage constant to determine a level of employment on the new labor demand curve. The new amount of labor demanded is L_2. From there you can trace through the model using the new production function to determine the level of output, Y_2, at the original price level for that nominal wage rate. This gives you one point on the new SRAS curve, labeled A, and allows you to approximate the balance of the new SRAS curve for a fixed nominal wage rate.

✳ Appendix Figure 4.5
SRAS for Increase in Labor Demand

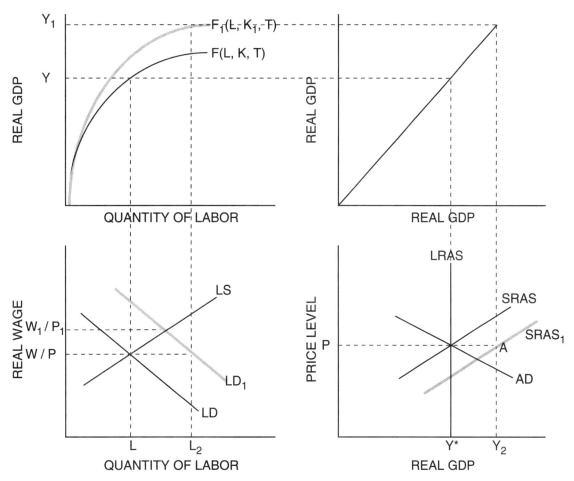

The intersection of the SRAS$_1$ and AD curves is at a new lower price level. This lower price level will increase the real wage toward the new higher equilibrium real wage rate in the labor market. If the short run AD-SRAS equilibrium output level is below full employment, there will be a surplus of labor, which will in time cause the nominal wage rate to decline. This decline in the nominal wage rate will cause the SRAS curve to shift to the right until the economy is back in long-run equilibrium where aggregate demand, short-run aggregate supply and long-run aggregate supply intersect, and the labor market is back in equilibrium.

An increase in the supply of labor will also cause the LRAS curve to shift to the right since it will create a new, higher equilibrium level of employment. The difference here is that the production function and the labor demand curve are fixed. Thus the SRAS curve will not shift with the shift of the LRAS. Since only the labor supply curve increased, there will now be a surplus of labor and a new lower equilibrium real wage. The nominal wage will then fall, causing the SRAS curve to shift to the right until equilibrium is restored in the labor market and in the output market. The new output equilibrium will, given a fixed AD curve, be at a lower price level. Since the real wage must also be lower, the nominal wage must fall more than the decline in the price level at the new LR equilibrium.

An Introduction to Short-Run Aggregate Supply

Part A
Why Can the Aggregate Supply Curve Have Three Different Shapes?

 Figure 24.1
Possible Shapes of Aggregate Supply Curve

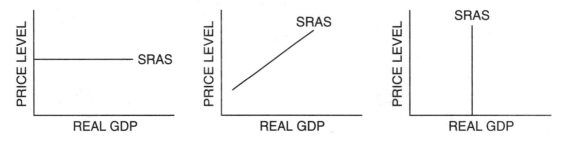

1. Under what conditions would an economy have a horizontal SRAS curve? *When there are a lot of unemployed resources or a constant price level as in a recession or depression*

2. Under what conditions would an economy have a vertical SRAS curve? *AS is vertical when real GDP is at a level with unemployment at the full-employment level and where any increase in demand will result only in an increase in prices. The economy is unable to produce any more goods and services for a sustainable period of time.*

3. Under what conditions would an economy have a positively sloped SRAS curve? *In this range, resources are getting closer to full-employment levels, which creates upward pressure on prices. The upward pressure on prices is caused by rising costs of doing business. Sticky wages and/or sticky prices cause the AS curve to be positively sloped. Wages and prices may be slow to adjust, or sticky, if firms or workers lack information.*

4. Assume AD increased. What would be the effect on real GDP and the price level if the economy had a horizontal SRAS curve? A positively sloped SRAS curve? A vertical SRAS curve? *With a horizontal SRAS curve, an increase in AD results in an increase in real GDP and no change in the price level. With a positively sloped SRAS curve, an increase in AD results in increases in real GDP and the price level. With a vertical SRAS curve, an increase in AD results in no change in real GDP and an increase in the price level.*

5. What range of the SRAS curve do you think the economy is in today? Explain. *Answer depends on current economic conditions.*

Part B
What Shifts the Short-Run Aggregate Supply Curve?

Figure 24.2
Shifts in Short-Run Aggregate Supply

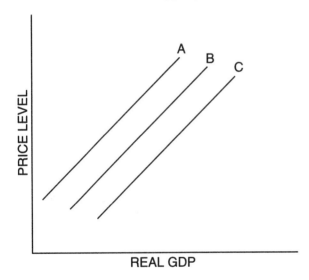

6. Using Figure 24.2, determine whether each situation below will cause an increase, decrease or no change in short-run aggregate supply (SRAS). Always start at curve B. If the situation would cause an increase in SRAS, draw an up arrow in column 1. If it causes a decrease, draw a down arrow. If there is no change, write NC. For each situation that causes a change in SRAS, write the letter of the new curve in column 2. Move only one curve.

Situation	1. Change in SRAS	2. New SRAS Curve
(A) Unions grow more aggressive; wage rates increase.	↓	A
(B) OPEC successfully increases oil prices.	↓	A
(C) Labor productivity increases dramatically.	↑	C
(D) Giant natural gas discovery decreases energy prices.	↑	C
(E) Computer technology brings new efficiency to industry.	↑	C
(F) Government spending increases.	NC	
(G) Cuts in tax rates increase incentives to save.	NC	
(H) Low birth rate will decrease the labor force in future.	NC	
(I) Research shows that improved schools have increased the skills of American workers and managers.	↑	C

Note: (F) and (G) do not affect the aggregate supply curve. They do shift the aggregate demand curve. (H) will not affect aggregate supply for 16 years or more.

Short-Run Equilibrium

Introduction and Description

In this lesson, the focus is on the short-run equilibrium between aggregate supply and demand, on the changes in output and price level if aggregate supply or aggregate demand changes, and on the students' ability to explain correctly why the curve shifted in a specific direction. The relationship between the simple Keynesian model and the aggregate supply-aggregate demand model is explored.

Activity 25 provides the students with practice at manipulating the aggregate demand and aggregate supply model and interpreting the effects on the price level and real GDP. Students who perform well on this activity have an excellent foundation for the rest of the course. Activity 26 relates the Keynesian simple model and the AD and AS model.

Objectives

1. Explain the macroeconomic equilibrium.
2. Explain what happens to the equilibrium price level and quantity with a change in aggregate demand.
3. Explain what happens to the equilibrium price level and quantity with a change in aggregate supply.
4. Explain what happens to the equilibrium price level and quantity with a change in aggregate demand and aggregate supply.
5. Explain the relationship between the simple Keynesian model and the AD and AS model.
6. Distinguish among equilibrium below, above and at full employment.

Time Required

Two class periods or 90 minutes

Materials

1. Activities 25 and 26
2. Visuals 3.11 and 3.12

Procedure

1. Project Visual 3.11 and focus on the top graph. Short-run macroeconomic equilibrium occurs when real GDP demanded equals real GDP supplied. This is Point A in the graph, or the level of output Y.

   If the price level (P_1) is above the equilibrium, then the aggregate supply (Y_2) is greater than the aggregate demand (Y_1). Firms experience an accumulation of inventory; they cut production and employment; output decreases toward the equilibrium level. Have the students tell a comparable story if the price level is below equilibrium.

2. Explain that the long-run macroeconomic equilibrium occurs at point B in the lower graph of Visual 3.11.

3. Use Visual 3.12 to examine what happens if there is an increase in aggregate demand. The new equilibrium is at a higher price level and a higher level of output. In response to the increase in demand, firms increase production and price. Go through decreases in aggregate demand, decreases in aggregate supply and increases in aggregate supply and have the students explain what happens in the economy.

4. Have the students complete Activity 25. Review the answers with the students.

5. Review the simple Keynesian model. Remember that in the simple Keynesian model, the price level is held constant. Show the relationship among changes in components of aggregate expenditures, aggregate demand and the effects on equilibrium real GDP.

6. Have the students complete Activity 26. Review the answers with the students.

Short-Run Equilibrium Price Level and Output

Part A
Equilibrium

  Figure 25.1
Equilibrium Price and Output Levels

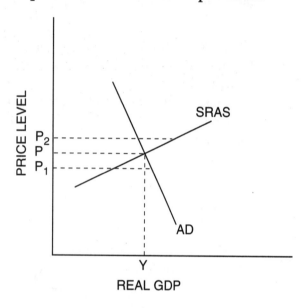

1. What are the equilibrium price level and output?   *P and Y*

2. What would eventually happen to the price level and output if the initial price level were P_2 rather than P? Why would this happen? *There is excess supply of goods and services. Inventories are building up. To reduce the inventory levels, firms will cut prices and output. The price level will fall, and real output will decrease. This would happen because higher inventories will cause sellers to reduce prices; lower prices will provide fewer incentives to increase production. However, consumers will purchase more output at lower prices.*

3. What would eventually happen to the price level and output if the initial price level were P_1 rather than P? Why would this happen? *There is excess demand. Inventories are below intended levels. Firms will seek to increase inventory levels, prices will rise and output will increase. This would happen because competition among buyers will increase the price level; increased prices will encourage producers to increase their output and consumers will buy less.*

Part B
Changes in the Equilibrium Price Level and Output

For each situation described below, illustrate the change on the AD and AS graph and describe the effect on the equilibrium price level and real GDP by circling the correct symbol: ↑ for increase, ↓ for decrease, or — for unchanged.

4. Congress passes a tax cut for the middle class, and the president signs it.

Middle Class Tax Cut

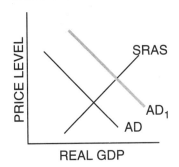

Price level: ↓ —

Real GDP: ↓ —

5. During a recession, the government increases spending on schools, highways and other public works.

Increased Government Spending

Price level: ↑ ↓ —

Real GDP: ↑ ↓ —

6. New oil discoveries cause large decreases in energy prices.

New Oil Discoveries

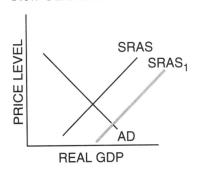

Price level ↑   —

Real GDP   ↓ —

7. Illustrate the effects of an increase in aggregate demand.

Effects of an Increase in AD

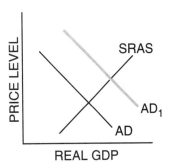

Price level   ↓ —

Real GDP   ↓ —

8. Illustrate the effects of increases in production costs.

Effects of Increases in Production Costs

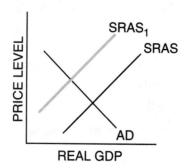

Price level   (↑)   ↓   —

Real GDP   ↑   (↓)   —

9. New technology and better education increase productivity.

Effects of New Technology and Better Education

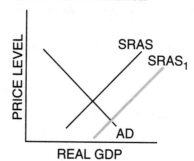

Price level   ↑   (↓)   —

Real GDP   (↑)   ↓   —

10. A new president makes consumers and businesses more confident about the future economy. **Note:** Show the change in AD only.

Increased Confidence for Future Economy

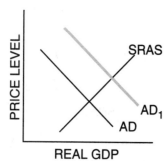

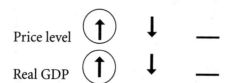

Price level   (↑)   ↓   —

Real GDP   (↑)   ↓   —

11. With the unemployment rate at five percent, the federal government reduces personal taxes and increases spending. **Note:** Show the change in AD only.

Reduced Taxes and Increased Government Spending

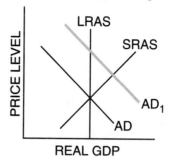

Price level   (↑)   ↓   —

Real GDP   (↑)   ↓   —

Part C
Summarizing Aggregate Demand and Aggregate Supply Shifts

For each of the events below, make additions to the graph to illustrate the change. Then indicate the response in terms of shifts in or movements along the aggregate demand or aggregate supply curve and the short-run effect on real GDP and the price level. Indicate *shifts* in the curve by S and movements *along* the curve by A. Indicate the changes in price level, unemployment and real GDP with an up arrow for an increase and a down arrow for a decrease.

	1. Increase in labor productivity due to technological change	2. Increase in the price of inputs used by many firms	3. Boom in investment assuming some unemployed resources are available	4. A major reduction in investment spending
	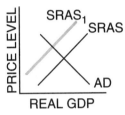	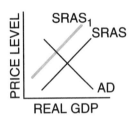		
AD Curve	A	A	S	S
AS Curve	S	S	A	A
Real GDP	↑	↓	↑	↓
Price Level	↓	↑	↑	↓
Unemployment	↓	↑	↓	↑

Reconciling the Keynesian Aggregate Expenditure Model With the Aggregate Demand and Aggregate Supply Model

Now it is time to reconcile the Keynesian aggregate expenditure model with the aggregate demand and supply model. We find both differences and similarities when comparing the two models:

■ The Keynesian model is a fixed, or constant, price model while the AD and AS model is a variable-price model. The vertical axis of the Keynesian model is *aggregate expenditure* while the vertical axis of the AD and AS model is *price level*.

■ Aggregate expenditure (C + I + G + Net Exports) on the Keynesian model is aggregate demand on the AD and AS model. A shift upward in aggregate expenditure is the same as a shift outward in aggregate demand. A shift downward of aggregate expenditure is the same as a shift inward of aggregate demand.

■ The ADs and AS model can account for shifts in aggregate supply. The Keynesian model cannot do so.

■ In the Keynesian model, a shift in aggregate expenditures results in the full multiplier effect, and the multiplier can easily be calculated from the graphs. In the AD and AS model, the multiplier is not at full strength on the positively sloped and vertical AS curves.

■ In the AD and AS model, the increase in the price level diminishes the impact of the multiplier.

For each of the following situations, illustrate the indicated change on both the AD and AS model and the Keynesian model.

1. The economy is at less than *full* employment. An increase in consumer confidence moves the economy to *full* employment.

Figure 26.1

An Increase in Consumer Confidence

Less Than Full Employment
Using the AD and AS Model

Less Than Full Employment
Using the Keynesian Model

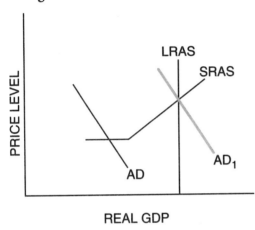
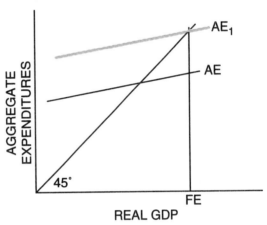

2. The economy is at full employment but businesses begin to believe that a recession is ahead.

Figure 26.2

Businesses Believe a Recession Is Coming

Full Employment
Using the AD and AS Model

Full Employment
Using the Keynesian Model

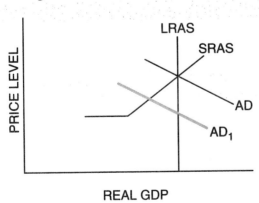
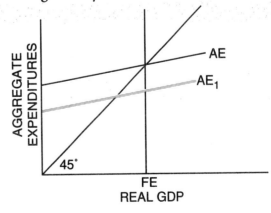

Aggregate Supply and Aggregate Demand Analysis Continued

Introduction and Description

Manipulation of the aggregate demand and aggregate supply model continues in this lesson. In particular, the students will practice shifting each curve and explaining why the curve shifted. The lesson then explores how the economy moves from the short run to the long run. In order for the students to explain the move from the short run to the long run, it is essential that they understand the framework of aggregate demand and aggregate supply.

Activity 27 provides the students with practice interpreting scenarios and determining the effects on aggregate demand, aggregate supply, the price level and the level of output. The students work through the transition of the economy from the short run to the long run and explain the process in the economy in Activity 28.

Objectives

1. Explain the shifts in aggregate demand.
2. Explain the shifts in aggregate supply.
3. Explain the price and output effects of shifts in aggregate demand and aggregate supply.
4. Explain the effects on price and output as the economy moves from the short run to the long run.
5. Explain the effects on nominal wage, real wage and employment of the movement from the short run to the long run.

Time Required

Four class periods or 180 minutes

Materials

1. Activities 27 and 28
2. Visual 3.13

Procedure

1. Review the factors that shift the aggregate demand curve. These factors include changes in autonomous consumption, changes in autonomous investment, changes in government spending, changes in taxes and changes in the money supply. Have the students complete Part A of Activity 27. Review the answers with the students.

2. Review the factors that shift the short-run aggregate supply curve. These factors include changes in resource prices, changes in technology, changes in capital stock and changes in expectations. Have the students complete Part B of Activity 27 in class and discuss the answers.

3. Now have the students put short-run aggregate supply and demand together to illustrate the effects of shifts of AD and AS on the price level and real GDP. Have the students complete Part C of Activity 27. Review the answers.

4. Throughout this unit, the discussion has focused on short-run changes in the economy. We now turn to the long run. What happens after the initial effects in the aggregate demand and aggregate supply model? Project Visual 3.13.

   (A) The economy is initially at full employment output: Y^*.

   (B) There is an increase in aggregate demand: $AD \rightarrow AD_1$.

   (C) Output increases to Y_1, and the price level increases to P_1.

   The increase in the price level means that real wages have fallen. Labor will push for higher nominal wages to compensate for the higher price level. The increase in nominal wages will shift the aggregate supply curve to the left. Eventually, the economy will return to the potential output level, Y^*, but at a higher price level, P_2. This is the process of adjustment over the long run.

5. Go back to some of the supply shocks discussed in Activity 27 and have the students work through the changes that would occur in the long run. Note that over time the economy will end up at the full-employment level of output along the LRAS curve.

6. Have the students complete Activity 28 for homework.

7. Review Activity 28.

Manipulating the AD and AS Model: Exogenous Demand and Supply Shocks

Part A
Exogenous Demand Shocks

An *exogenous demand shock* is a change in an exogenous variable — a variable determined outside the model — that affects aggregate demand. Read the description of each exogenous demand shock, and then draw a new AD curve that will represent the change the demand shock caused. Label the new curve AD_1. Then briefly explain the reason for the change in the graph.

1. **Exogenous Demand Shock:** Economic booms in both Japan and Europe result in massive increases in orders for exported goods from the United States.

EXPLANATION: *Increased orders for exports will cause more people to be hired and their increased income will result in increased consumer spending. AD will increase.*

2. **Exogenous Demand Shock:** As part of its countercyclical policy, the government both reduces taxes and increases transfer payments.

EXPLANATION: *With increased discretionary incomes, taxpayers will increase comsumption. AD will increase.*

3. **Exogenous Demand Shock:** While the United States was in the midst of the Great Depression, a
   foreign power attacked. Congress declared war and more than 1,000,000 soldiers were drafted in
   the first year, while defense spending was increased several times over.

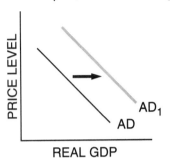

EXPLANATION: *Now consumers who had been unemployed or reluctant to spend their savings will respond by
purchasing many goods they had postponed buying. The
government is also increasing spending and its demand
for goods and services. AD will increase.*

4. **Exogenous Demand Shock:** To balance the budget, the federal government cuts Social Security
   payments by 10 percent and federal aid to education by 20 percent.

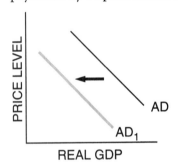

EXPLANATION: *Recipients of Social Security will have
less income to spend. Local school districts will cut back
by laying off teachers or will raise taxes. Either action
will reduce discretionary income, and, thus consumption
decreases. In turn, AD will decrease.*

Part B
Exogenous Supply Shocks

The cause of an *exogenous supply shock* is the change in an exogenous variable — a variable determined
outside the model — that affects aggregate supply. Read the description of each exogenous shock to
short-run aggregate supply, and then draw a new SRAS curve that will represent the change caused by
the shock. Label the new curve SRAS$_1$. Then briefly explain the reason for the change in the graph.

5. **Exogenous Supply Shock:** New environmental standards raise the average cost of autos and trucks 5 percent.

EXPLANATION: *The new standards result in increases in the costs of producing automobiles and trucks. This decreases AS.*

6. **Exogenous Supply Shock:** Fine weather results in the highest corn and wheat yields in 40 years.

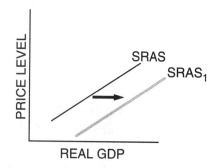

EXPLANATION: *The fine weather will increase the supply of corn and wheat, and if demand remains constant, the price will decrease. This in turn will decrease the price of inputs for many food-related industries. The SRAS curve will shift to the right.*

7. **Exogenous Supply Shock:** Because of decreased international tension, the government sells off thousands of army surplus Jeeps and trucks at prices that are far less than the market price for their commercial counterparts.

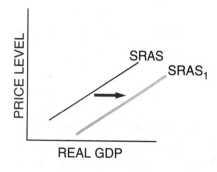

EXPLANATION: *The reduction in transportation costs will mean lower operating costs for industries using the Jeeps and trucks. The SRAS curve will shift to the right.*

8. **Exogenous Supply Shock:** An enemy power sets up a blockade of the sea lanes leading to a country, and most ships refuse to deliver cargo through the blockade.

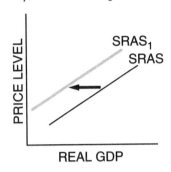

EXPLANATION: *A significant decrease in foreign goods, including inputs to American industries, will increase the cost of production. The SRAS curve will shift to the left.*

Part C
Manipulating the Aggregate Supply and Demand Model

Read each of the scenarios below, and explain the impact the exogenous shocks will have on short-run aggregate supply and aggregate demand. Then draw a correctly labeled aggregate demand and aggregate supply graph to illustrate each short-run impact.

9. During a long, slow recovery from a recession, consumers postponed major purchases. Suddenly they begin to buy cars, refrigerators, televisions and furnaces to replace their failing models.

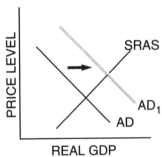

EXPLANATION: *AD will increase as a result of increased autonomous consumer spending.*

10. With no other dramatic changes, the government raises taxes and reduces transfer payments in the hope of balancing the federal budget.

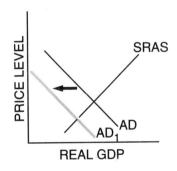

EXPLANATION: *Higher taxes and a reduction in transfer payments reduce disposable income, which reduces consumption spending.*

11. News of possible future layoffs frightens the public into reducing spending and increasing saving
for the feared "rainy day."

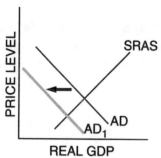

EXPLANATION: *A decrease in consumer confidence
decreases consumption spending.*

12. Because of rising tensions in many developing countries, firms begin to build new factories in
Econoland and to purchase sophisticated machinery from Econoland businesses that will enable
them to produce in Econoland at prices that are competitive.

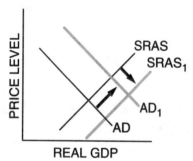

EXPLANATION: *The increase in investment spending
will increase AD. The increase in machinery increases
SRAS.*

13. Brazil solves its foreign debt and inflation problems. It then orders $10 billion worth of capital
machinery from Econoland. Draw the AD and short-run AS graph for Econoland.

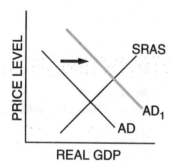

EXPLANATION: *Econoland's exports increase. AD
increases.*

Advanced Placement Economics Teacher Resource Manual © National Council on Economic Education, New York, N.Y.

The Macroeconomic Model: Short Run to Long Run

Part A

1. In the following graph, suppose the aggregate demand shifts from AD to AD_1. How will the economy react over time? Assume that no monetary or fiscal policy is undertaken.

Figure 28.1

**Increase in Aggregate Demand
Starting at Full Employment**

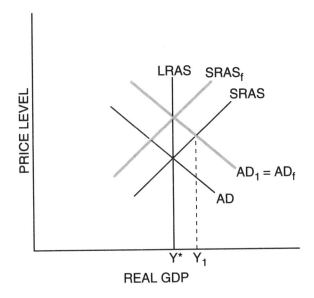

(A) What will happen to output in the short run? Explain. *Output initially increases to Y_1 in response to the increase in aggregate demand.*

(B) What will happen to output as the economy moves to the long-run equilibrium? Explain. *Over time, labor realizes that the real wage has decreased and demands a higher nominal wage. The increase in the nominal wage causes the short-run aggregate supply curve to decrease, and output returns to Y^*.*

(C) What will happen to the price level? Explain. *The price level increases initially because firms are paying overtime and are using less-productive resources to produce beyond full-employment output. The price level will continue to rise to cover increased labor costs.*

(D) What will happen to wages? Explain. *With the increase in AD, the price level rises and the real wage decreases. Once labor realizes that the real wage has decreased, it demands higher nominal wages, forcing the real wage to return to the original level. In response to the increase in nominal wages, firms increase price and the SRAS shifts leftward.*

(E) In the graph, draw the shifts in AD and SRAS that you think will occur. Indicate the final aggregate demand and short-run aggregate supply curves by labeling them as AD_f and $SRAS_f$. *There are many shifts in the short-run aggregate supply curve between the original and $SRAS_f$ depending on how long it takes the economy to adjust. The economy will return to full employment.*

2. In the following graph, suppose the aggregate supply shifts from SRAS to $SRAS_1$. How will the economy react over time? Assume that no monetary or fiscal policy is undertaken.

✳ Figure 28.2
Change in Short-Run Aggregate Supply

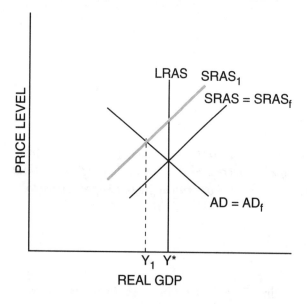

(A) What will happen to output in the short run? Explain. *Output will decrease to Y_1 because of the decrease in short-run aggregate supply.*

Advanced Placement Economics Teacher Resource Manual © National Council on Economic Education, New York, N.Y.

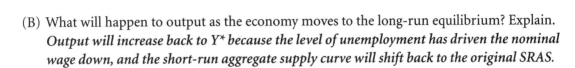

(B) What will happen to output as the economy moves to the long-run equilibrium? Explain. *Output will increase back to Y* because the level of unemployment has driven the nominal wage down, and the short-run aggregate supply curve will shift back to the original SRAS.*

(C) What will happen to the price level? Explain. *The price level initially increases because of the forces that caused the aggregate supply curve to shift to the left. Then the price level will fall as nominal wages decrease.*

(D) What will happen to wages? Explain. *Initially, nominal wages do not change and real wages decrease. But as the level of unemployment eventually increases, nominal wages will decrease.*

(E) In the graph, draw the shifts in AD and SRAS that you think will occur. Indicate the final aggregate demand and short-run aggregate supply curves by labeling them as AD_f and $SRAS_f$. *There are many shifts in the short-run aggregate supply curve between the original and $SRAS_f$ depending on how long it takes the economy to adjust. The economy will return to full employment.*

Part B

Read the description of each exogenous shock to aggregate supply and aggregate demand. Draw a new SRAS or AD curve that represents the change caused by the shock in the short run. Explain the reasons for the change in the graph, and then explain what happens in the long run if no stabilization policy is implemented. Identify the final AD curve as AD_f and the final SRAS curve as $SRAS_f$. If there is a change in LRAS, show the change and label the new curve $LRAS_f$.

3. The government increases defense spending by 10 percent a year over a five-year period.

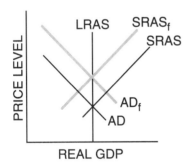

EXPLANATION: *Higher government spending increases the AD in the short run. Over the medium run, nominal wages increase to maintain real wages, and the SRAS decreases. The final result is on the LRAS at $SRAS_f$ and AD_f.*

4. OPEC cuts oil production by 30 percent, and the world price of oil rises by 40 percent.

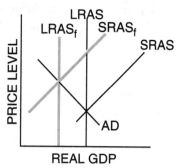

EXPLANATION: *Higher production costs decrease SRAS to $SRAS_f$. If the increase is permanent, the LRAS will also decrease to $LRAS_f$, if the capital stock can't be modified to use an alternative fuel.*

5. The government increases spending on education, health care, housing and basic services for low-income people. No increase in taxes accompanies the program.

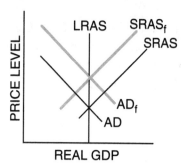

EXPLANATION: *Higher government spending increases the AD in the short run. Over the longer run, nominal wages increase to maintain real wages, and the SRAS decreases. The final result is on the LRAS at $SRAS_f$ and AD_f.*

6. Can the government maintain output above the natural level of output with aggregate demand policy? If the government attempts to, what will be the result?

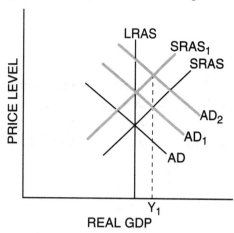

If the government wants to move the economy to Y_1, a level of output above the natural level of output, then it must increase aggregate demand to AD_1. There will be a tendency for the SRAS to shift to the left as labor demands higher nominal wages. The SRAS will shift to $SRAS_1$. The expansionary policy has resulted in increases in the price level. If the government wants to maintain a level of Y_1, then it must continue to implement additional expansionary policy as shown in AD_2. There will continue to be a tendency for the SRAS to shift left; the government must continue to implement expansionary policy to keep the economy at Y_1. This is shown in the graph.

The Long-Run Economy

Introduction and Description

The last lesson explored the movement of the economy from the short run to the long run. Here, we explore the long-run aggregate supply curve and its relationship with the economy's production possibilities curve, introduced in Unit 1.

Activity 29 draws together the relationship between the long-run aggregate supply curve and the production possibilities curve studied earlier.

Objectives

1. Review the process of moving from the short run to the long run.
2. Review the factors that shift the long-run aggregate supply curve.
3. Relate the long-run aggregate supply curve to the production possibilities curve.

Time Required

One class period or 45 minutes

Materials

1. Activity 29
2. Visual 3.14

Procedure

1. Review the process discussed in the last lesson of moving from the short run to the long run.

2. Explain that normally the economy will adjust and return to the original LRAS curve. However, if there is an adverse supply shock that results in a permanent decrease in resources, the LRAS curve could shift to the left. There is evidence that the OPEC oil price increases had exactly this impact in the 1970s.

3. Discuss the factors that will shift the LRAS curve to the right. These factors are increases in productivity of labor, increases in technology and increases in the capital stock. Discuss factors that might influence the productivity of labor (education), increases in technology (research and development expenditures) and increases in the capital stock of the economy (low, stable interest rates).

4. Project Visual 3.14. Demonstrate that increases in the factors that shift the LRAS curve will also shift the production possibilities curve for the economy. Factors that shift the LRAS curve to the right shift the production possibilities curve outward or to the right. Factors that shift the LRAS curve to the left shift the production possibilities curve inward or to the left.

5. Have the students complete Activity 29. Review the answers with the students.

Long-Run Aggregate Supply (LRAS) and the Production Possibilities Curve (PPC)

The long-run aggregate supply (LRAS) curve differs from the short-run aggregate supply (SRAS) curve. The LRAS curve is a vertical line at an output level that represents the quantity of goods and services a nation can produce over a sustained period using all of its productive resources as efficiently as possible with all of the current technology available to it. Long-run aggregate supply is at full employment. LRAS doesn't change as the price level changes. Developing more and better resources or improving technology will shift the LRAS curve outward, but it will still be vertical.

The LRAS curve represents a point on an economy's production possibilities curve. Remember that the production possibilities curve (PPC) represents the maximum output of two goods that can be produced given scarce resources. The economy could grow if the PPC shifts outward because of more resources or technological advances. For the same reason, the LRAS curve shifts outward if more resources are developed or if there are technological advances.

SRAS can actually be greater than LRAS. Resources can be used more intensively in the short run. For example, workers can work more hours and machines can operate for more hours. However, this output level cannot be sustained in the long run. Eventually, the equilibrium level of output will fall unless LRAS is increased. As an analogy on a personal level, you may pull an all-nighter to prepare for several exams on the same day. You cannot, however, work 24 hours a day all the time.

Now answer the questions that follow to be sure you understand these concepts. Use the graphs in Figure 29.1 in your answers.

✳ Figure 29.1
Aggregate Supply and Production Possibilities Curves

LRAS and SRAS Curves

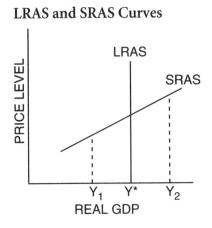

PPC Graph

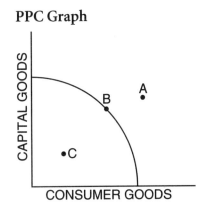

1. What information does a PPC provide for us about a nation's economy?
   The maximum possible combinations of two types of goods an economy can produce when the economy is fully employing all its resources in a given time period and with a given technology

2. What assumptions do you make about the use of available resources when drawing a PPC?
   When we are on a PPC, resources are fully employed and are being used in the most efficient way given the current state of technology.

3. What would cause a nation's PPC to shift? *Changes in the amount of resources or changes in technology*

4. What do you know about a nation's economy that is operating on the LRAS curve?
   The economy is fully employing its resources in the most efficient way given the current state of technology. It can't produce more of one good without producing less of another.

5. Under what conditions would an economy be on the LRAS curve?
   It would be fully employing all of its resources and be on its PPC.

6. If the price level rises, will LRAS shift? __*No*__ Will the LRAS curve shift if AD changes? __*No*__

7. If an economy finds that it faces a short-run equilibrium where real GDP is Y_1, how would you describe the condition of the economy? Given this equilibrium level of output, at what point would the economy lie on the PPC? Explain your answer. *Resources are unemployed. The economy is inside the PPC at a point like C. The economy can produce more consumer goods and more capital goods if all resources are fully employed.*

8. If an economy finds that it faces a short-run equilibrium where real GDP is Y^*, how would you describe the condition of the economy? Given this equilibrium level of output, at what point would the economy lie on the PPC? Explain your answer. *The economy would be operating on the PPC at Point B. All resources are fully employed.*

9. If an economy finds that it faces a short-run equilibrium where real GDP is Y_2, how would you describe the condition of the economy? Given this equilibrium level of output, at what point would the economy lie on the PPC? Explain your answer. *The condition of the economy is overheated and at Point A outside the PPC. The economy is working beyond the full-employment level of production and will not be able to sustain this level unless the LRAS increases, or shifts to the right.*

10. If the economy were producing at Y_2, what would happen in the long run? Why?
Eventually output will decrease. People and production facilities can work overtime without maintenance problems in the short run only. Eventually, the price level and nominal wages will increase.

11. What could cause a nation's LRAS to shift? *The development of more productive resources or an improvement in technology will cause LRAS to shift to the right. The capital stock increases.*

12. How would a rightward shift in LRAS be shown on the PPC? *The PPC would shift outward also.*

Fiscal Policy

Introduction and Description

Fiscal policy is one of the two demand management policies available to policy makers. Government expenditures and the level and type of taxes are discretionary fiscal policy tools. This lesson explores the effects of these tools on the economy, the existence of embedded tools and alternative ways to analyze fiscal policy.

Activity 30 provides the students with practice at manipulating the tools of fiscal policy and analyzing scenarios to determine appropriate fiscal policy. The students continue with fiscal policy analysis in Activity 31 and distinguish between discretionary fiscal policy tools and automatic stabilizers. The students analyze fiscal policy in the Keynesian and aggregate demand and aggregate supply models in Activity 32. Activity 33 serves as an excellent unit review by having the students analyze economic observations and scenarios.

Objectives

1. Explain the impact of government spending changes on the economy.
2. Explain the effect of changes in taxes on the economy.
3. Describe the embedded fiscal policy tools and explain how the tools adjust the economy.
4. Explore the alternative methods of analyzing fiscal policy effects.

Time required

Four class periods or 180 minutes

Materials

Activities 30, 31, 32 and 33

Procedure

1. Tell the students that the two primary fiscal policy tools are government spending and taxes. Government spending affects the economy directly by increasing the demand for goods and services. As soon as the government increases its spending, it initiates a multiplier process (practiced in Activity 21) that results in a greater increase in total spending than the initial increase in government spending. The increase in government spending increases aggregate demand, shifting the AD curve to the right. In the short run, the usual effects are an increase in real GDP and the price level.

2. Have the students work through the effects of a decrease in government spending.

3. Explain that changes in taxes do not directly change real GDP. Changes in taxes affect the disposable income of households or businesses. These changes are felt through consumption spending and investment spending. An increase in taxes decreases disposable income. A decrease in disposable income decreases consumption, but by less than the increase in taxes. Some of the additional tax bill is paid from savings. The multiplier process applies to the increase in taxes, and real GDP decreases by more than the tax increase.

4. Have the students complete Activity 30. Review the answers to the questions.

5. Besides the direct fiscal policy tools of government spending and taxes, there are many tools embedded in the economy that respond to the different phases of the business cycle. These tools are called automatic stabilizers. They are automatic because they adjust without an action by Congress or the president. They serve as stabilizers because they limit the increase in real GDP during expansions and reduce the decrease in real GDP during a recession.

6. Give examples of automatic stabilizers and explain how they work:

(A) Income tax system. As an individual's nominal income increases, he or she moves into higher tax brackets and pays more taxes, thus limiting the increase in disposable income and consumption.

(B) Unemployment compensation. As the economy slows and unemployment increases, the income of the unemployed does not fall to zero, which would have a significant negative effect on the economy. Unemployment compensation provides a base level of income, and the negative impact on real GDP is lessened.

(C) Stock and bond returns. Many corporations establish the dividends they pay on shares of stock and maintain this payout for several years. Thus dividends do not follow the swings of the business cycle. Bond payments are established at the time the bond is issued and remain throughout the life of the bond.

7. Have the students complete Activity 31. Review the answers with the students.

8. Review both the aggregate demand and aggregate supply model and the simple Keynesian model for analyzing the effect of discretionary fiscal policy.

9. Have the students complete Activity 32. Review the answers with the students.

10. Have the students complete Activity 33 as review for the unit test. Review the answers with the students.

Advanced Placement Economics Teacher Resource Manual © National Council on Economic Education, New York, N.Y.

The Tools of Fiscal Policy

Part A

Decide whether each of the following fiscal policies of the federal government is expansionary or contractionary. Write *expansionary* or *contractionary*, and explain the reasons for your choice.

1. The government cuts business and personal income taxes and increases its own spending. *Expansionary. The decrease in personal income taxes increases disposable income and thus increases consumption spending. The business tax cut increases investment spending, and the increase in government spending increases government demand.*

2. The government increases the personal income tax, Social Security tax and corporate income tax. Government spending stays the same. *Contractionary. Business income and personal disposable income decrease because of the tax increases, thus reducing consumption and investment spending. Government demand is unchanged.*

3. Government spending goes up while taxes remain the same. *Expansionary. Higher government spending without a corresponding rise in tax receipts increases aggregate demand in the economy.*

4. The government reduces the wages of its employees while raising taxes on consumers and businesses. Other government spending remains the same. *Contractionary. Reduction in government spending results in a decrease in AD. Increases in taxes on consumers reduce disposable income and consumption, and increased business taxes will reduce investment. The decrease in both consumption and investment will reduce aggregate demand.*

Part B

Test your understanding of fiscal policy by completing the table in Figure 30.1. Your choices for each situation must be consistent — that is, you should choose either an expansionary or contractionary fiscal policy. (Fiscal policy cannot provide a solution to one of the situations.) Fill in the spaces as follows:

Column A: Objective for Aggregate Demand
   Draw an up arrow if you wish to increase aggregate demand.
   Draw a down arrow if you wish to decrease aggregate demand.

Column B: Action on Taxes
   Draw an up arrow if you wish to increase taxes.
   Draw a down arrow if you wish to decrease taxes.

Column C: Action on Government Spending
   Draw an up arrow if you wish to increase government spending.
   Draw a down arrow if you wish to decrease government spending.

Column D: Effect on Federal Budget
   Write *toward deficit* if your action will increase the deficit (or reduce the surplus).
   Write *toward surplus* if your action will reduce the deficit (or increase the surplus).

Column E: Effect on the National Debt
   Draw an up arrow if you think the national debt will increase.
   Draw a down arrow if you think the national debt will decrease.

 Figure 30.1
Effects of Fiscal Policy

	(A) Objective for Aggregate Demand	(B) Action on Taxes	(C) Action on Government Spending	(D) Effect on Federal Budget	(E) Effect on the National Debt
1. National unemployment rate rises to 12 percent.	↑	↓	↑	*Toward deficit*	↑
2. Inflation is strong at a rate of 14 percent per year.	↓	↑	↓	*Toward surplus*	↓
3. Surveys show consumers are losing confidence in the economy, retail sales are weak and business inventories are increasing rapidly.	↑	↓	↑	*Toward deficit*	↑
4. Business sales and investment are expanding rapidly, and economists think strong inflation lies ahead.	↓	↑	↓	*Toward surplus*	↓
5. Inflation persists while unemployment stays high.	*Fiscal policy is unable to provide a solution to the situation of high inflation and unemployment: stagflation.*				

504   Advanced Placement Economics Teacher Resource Manual © National Council on Economic Education, New York, N.Y.

Discretionary and Automatic Fiscal Policy

Listed below are several economic scenarios. For each scenario, indicate whether it represents an automatic (A) or discretionary (D) stabilizer and whether it is an example of expansionary (E) or contractionary (C) fiscal policy. A sample has been completed for you.

Economic Scenarios	Automatic (A) or Discretionary (D)	Expansionary (E) or Contractionary (C)
Sample: Recession raises amount of unemployment compensation.	A	E
1. The government cuts personal income-tax rates.	*D*	*E*
2. The government eliminates favorable tax treatment on long-term capital gains.	*D*	*C*
3. Incomes rise; as a result, people pay a larger fraction of their income in taxes.	*A*	*C*
4. As a result of a recession, more families qualify for food stamps and welfare benefits.	*A*	*E*
5. The government eliminates the deductibility of interest expense for tax purposes.	*D*	*C*
6. The government launches a major new space program to explore Mars.	*D*	*E*
7. The government raises Social Security taxes.	*D*	*C*
8. Corporate profits increase; as a result, government collects more corporate income taxes.	*A*	*C*
9. The government raises corporate income tax rates.	*D*	*C*
10. The government gives all its employees a large pay raise.	*D*	*E*

Two Ways to Analyze Fiscal Policy

In Figure 32.1, assume an estimated full-employment national income of $400 billion for the economy and a horizontal SRAS.

 Figure 32.1
Aggregate Expenditure Function for a Hypothetical Economy

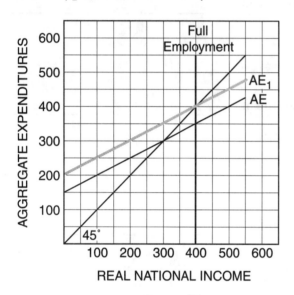

1. What will be the actual national income level in equilibrium? __*$300 billion*__

2. Given a marginal propensity to consume of 0.50, how much of an increase in aggregate expenditure would be needed to move the economy to full employment? (Hint: Calculate the MPC from the diagram using the rise divided by the run. Then calculate the multiplier that will operate on any change in AE.) __*$50 billion*__

3. How much will GDP increase if aggregate expenditure increases by $50 billion? Why?
   $100 billion because the multiplier is 2

4. What fiscal policy measures are available to deal with this situation? *Decrease in taxes or increases in government spending will help an economy reach the full-employment level of income.*

5. Draw in a new AE curve showing the elimination of the gap between the current equilibrium income and the full-employment level of income through the use of fiscal policy. Explain completely the policy you employed. *The new curve is AE₁ and results from either an increase in government spending or a decrease in taxes.*

Figure 32.2
Diagram of a Persistent Gap

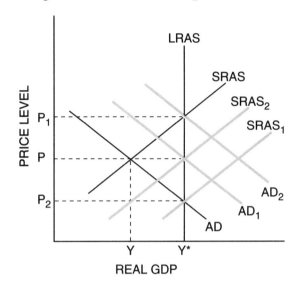

6. Assume a persistent gap between current equilibrium income, Y, and full-employment income, Y*, as shown in Figure 32.2.

   (A) If the government decided not to implement any fiscal policy, the unemployment of resources would eventually lead to a decrease in factor prices. Show diagrammatically that this could eliminate the gap. Label the new curve $SRAS_1$. The new price level would be _____P_2_____ .

   (B) A second possibility would be to depend on a smaller shift of aggregate supply and have a modest shift in aggregate demand by a discretionary fiscal stimulus so that the price level was maintained at P. Show these two changes in the graph. Label the curves $SRAS_2$ and AD_1.

   (C) A third possibility is that government would seek changes in taxes and/or expenditures that would rapidly bring the economy to full employment. Show this diagrammatically. Label the curve AD_2.

7. Assume that a hypothetical economy is currently at an equilibrium national income level of $1 trillion, but the full-employment national income is $1.2 trillion. Assume the government's budget is currently in balance at $200 billion and the marginal propensity to consume is 0.75. Fill in the answer blanks or underline the correct words in parentheses.

   (A) The gap between the equilibrium income and full employment is ___*$200 billion*___ .

   (B) The value of the multiplier is ___*4*___ .

   (C) Aggregate expenditures would have to be (***increased*** / decreased) by ___*$50*___ billion to eliminate the gap.

   (D) The government could attempt to eliminate the gap by holding taxes constant and (***increasing*** / decreasing) expenditures by___*$50*___billion.

   (E) Alternatively, the government could attempt to eliminate the gap by holding expenditures constant and (increasing / ***decreasing***) its tax receipts by ___*$66.7*___ billion.

Analyzing the Macroeconomy

Answer the following questions. In some cases, you may also want to include a graph to show your analysis.

1. True, false or uncertain, and explain why? "Regardless of our current economic situation, an increase in aggregate demand will always create new jobs." *False. At a level higher than full-employment output, workers will push for higher wages, which will shift the SRAS curve leftward; output and employment will decrease, and the price level will rise. Thus, as aggregate demand increases, an increase in output cannot be sustained and only prices increase.*

2. True, false or uncertain, and explain why? "In the long run, when nominal wages increase, everyone has more money to spend; therefore, the economy as a whole benefits." *False. If prices rise and the real wage is maintained, then there will be no change in the standard of living.*

3. True, false or uncertain, and explain why? "When unemployment rises, the price level falls. When unemployment falls, the price level rises. It is impossible to have a rising price level with rising unemployment." *False. The first sentence assumes a decrease in AD, which does lead to a decrease in prices and increase in unemployment. The second sentence refers to an increase in AD, which leads to an increase in prices and output, and a decrease in unemployment. However, if SRAS decreases, then the price level rises, output decreases and unemployment increases. The third sentence refers to a movement along the AD curve.*

4. True, false or uncertain, and explain why? "Our economy is able to adjust to a long-run equilibrium after a decrease in aggregate demand because prices and wages are sticky." *False. Sticky wages and prices make it more difficult for the economy to respond to a decrease in aggregate demand.*

5. True, false or uncertain, and explain why? "If we are in a recession, as long as we continue to increase aggregate demand, we can achieve full employment without driving up the inflation rate." *False. As aggregate demand increases and the economy starts to approach full employment, there will be a tendency for the price level to rise. The underlying cause is that less productive resources are being used.*

    Advanced Placement Economics Teacher Resource Manual © National Council on Economic Education, New York, N.Y.

6. True, false or uncertain, and explain why? "When the economy experiences an increase in aggregate demand, it will discover that its production possibilities curve has shifted outward."
   False. The nation's production possibilities curve shifts outward when it finds more resources or develops new technologies. These are the same elements that will cause the LRAS to shift outward.

7. Use short-run AD and AS analysis to illustrate the results of the following events. Then explain why these changes have taken place. Each answer should be accompanied by a clearly labeled diagram.

   (A) There is a 25 percent decrease in the price of crude oil.

   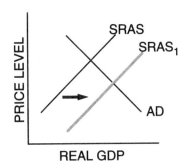

   Lower energy cost increases AS.

   (B) Price levels in Germany, Japan and Great Britain rise considerably, while price levels in the United States remain unchanged.

   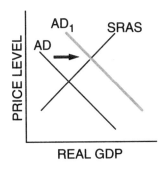

   More goods will be exported because they are less expensive when compared to foreign goods.

   (C) The federal government launches a major new highway-construction program.

   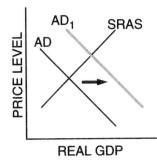

   Increased government spending increases AD.

(D) An insidious computer virus causes all IBM computers in the United States to crash.

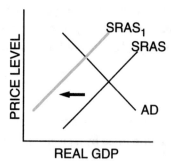

Capital is destroyed decreasing AS.

(E) There is an increase in worker productivity.

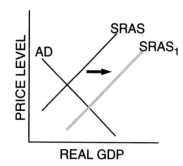

Higher productivity increases output using the same resources.

8. Illustrate the following fiscal policy using both the AD and AS model and the Keynesian aggregate expenditure model. In other words, draw two graphs for the fiscal policy change and give a brief explanation of each graph. In your explanation, be sure to emphasize the line of reasoning that generated your results; it is not enough to list the results of your analysis.

Fiscal Policy: At less than full employment, the federal government decreases taxes while holding government spending constant.

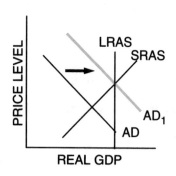

Lower taxes increase disposable income which increases consumption spending. Higher consumption spending increases AD or AE.

UNIT
3 Macroeconomics
MULTIPLE-CHOICE
SAMPLE QUESTIONS
Answer
Key

Answers to Sample Multiple-Choice Questions

1.	*E*	11.	*D*	21.	*B*
2.	*C*	12.	*C*	22.	*D*
3.	*C*	13.	*D*	23.	*D*
4.	*C*	14.	*B*	24.	*C*
5.	*D*	15.	*B*	25.	*B*
6.	*A*	16.	*B*	26.	*E*
7.	*B*	17.	*A*	27.	*D*
8.	*A*	18.	*E*	28.	*A*
9.	*D*	19.	*C*	29.	*E*
10.	*B*	20.	*C*	30.	*D*

UNIT
3
Macroeconomics

SHORT FREE-RESPONSE
SAMPLE QUESTIONS

Answer
Key

Answers to Sample Short Free-Response Questions

1. In the 1960s many newspaper reporters were accustomed to reporting a decrease in the unemployment rate when the overall price level increased. However, in the 1970s, when increases in the overall price level were accompanied by increases, not decreases, in the unemployment rate, some reporters went so far as to declare macroeconomics "bankrupt" and unable to explain this "mystery."

Using short-run aggregate demand and aggregate supply analysis, explain the "mystery" of why the increases in the overall price level during the 1960s might have been accompanied by decreases in the unemployment rate and the increases in the overall price level during the 1970s might have been accompanied by increases in the unemployment rate.

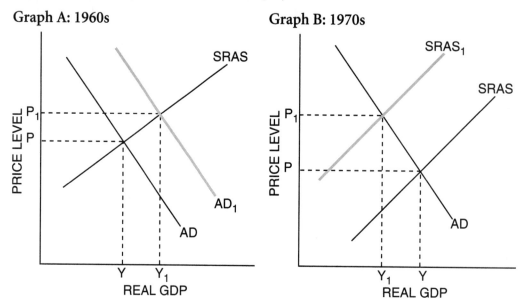

Graph A represents the 1960s. Increases in aggregate demand led to increases in the price level (inflation) (P to P_1), while at the same time the unemployment rate decreased as real GDP increased from Y to Y_1. Graph B represents the 1970s. Decreases in the short-run aggregate supply led to increases in the price level (inflation) (P to P_1) and decreases in real GDP (increases in the unemployment rate) as the level of output decreased from Y to Y_1. This situation is called stagflation.

Advanced Placement Economics Teacher Resource Manual © National Council on Economic Education, New York, N.Y.

UNIT
3 Macroeconomics

SHORT FREE-RESPONSE
SAMPLE QUESTIONS

Answer
Key

2. The U.S. stock market declined dramatically from 2000 to 2003.

   (A) What did this decline mean? *As the stock market declines, the value of the financial assets held by households decreases and, hence, the wealth that could be held if all financial assets were liquidated would decline.*

   (B) What were the possible effects of this decline on the U.S. economy's output, prices and employment? *A decrease in wealth will lead to a decrease in consumption expenditures, and a decrease in the stock market will lead to a decrease in investment by private firms, and thus a decrease in output (real GDP). U.S. output will decrease, employment will decrease and prices will decrease.*

3. Some economists claim that investment spending is more important than consumption spending in causing changes in the business cycle. However, investment spending is only one-fourth of consumption spending. Explain why investment spending can be so important if it is so much less than consumption spending. *Decisions regarding investment spending are a marginal cost-marginal benefit analysis. The benefit is the expected rate of return from the planned investment in capital and the cost is the rate of interest to borrow or lose from using saved funds. Investment spending is the unstable component of aggregate demand. Investment does not closely follow GDP, yet investment in capital goods provides the seeds of productivity gains, the implementation of technological advances and future increases in output. New investment increases the long-run aggregate supply curve and allows for more capacity.*

4. In 1981, factories used 79 percent of their capacity. In 1982, factories used 71 percent of their capacity. In which year do you think the economy was on a steeper portion of its short-run aggregate supply curve? Explain. *The economy would be on the steeper part of the aggregate supply curve in 1981 at a 79 percent capacity utilization rate. The economy would be approaching the potential level of output. In 1982, with a 71 percent capacity utilization rate, the economy would be further away from potential GDP. In addition, the price level was probably rising faster in 1981 than in 1982 because as the economy nears full employment (potential GDP), pressure on prices increases.*

5. Recently, an economist was asked if the Great Depression could occur again. The reply was, "It is possible, but we have many more automatic stabilizers today than we had in 1929." Describe three automatic stabilizers and explain how they might prevent a depression. *Automatic stabilizers cause changes in aggregate demand without changes in policy or laws. Four possible answers are:*

(A) *Social Security maintains the incomes of retired people during a recession. Total income does not fall as much as it might otherwise.*

(B) *The progressive personal income tax system decreases the marginal tax rate as income decreases. Thus, the amount of tax decreases more than proportionally as income declines.*

(C) *Unemployment compensation and other transfer payment programs maintain incomes as the economy slows and unemployment rises.*

(D) *Corporate dividend policy serves as an automatic stabilizer. In general, firms establish a level of dividends and continue to pay this level for several years unless there is a major drop in the demand for their products.*

6. A town's largest industry invests $50 million to expand its plant capacity. Without using a formula, explain how this expenditure will affect the town's economy through the multiplier effect. *Suppose that the plant expansion takes the form of adding a new building. Local construction firms will supply the labor for the construction and hence their incomes increase as do the number of laborers hired to build the new plant. In turn these people spend part of their new income in town to buy food and other consumer products. The incomes of stores increase and store owners in turn spend a proportion of their income and the process continues multiplying the initial $50 million expenditure.*

7. Throughout most of the decade of the 1990s, gains were made in productivity. What effect do these yearly gains have on the short-run aggregate supply curve? Is there any change in long-run aggregate supply? *Gains in productivity shift the short-run aggregate supply curve to the right. In turn, the long-run aggregate supply curve also shifts to the right.*

Answers to Sample Long Free-Response Questions

1. Assume you are a member of Congress. A member of your staff has just given you the following economic statistics:

	Year Ago Quarter	Last Quarter	Estimate for Quarter Now Ending
Real gross domestic product (in billions of 1997 dollars)	$2,789	$2,689	$2,598
Consumer price index	197	201	204
Unemployment rate	5%	8%	10.2%
Gross private investment (in billions of 1997 dollars)	$312	$300	$287

(A) What economic problem is this nation facing? *There is a recession. Real GDP is declining and unemployment is rising. Inflation is moderate, rising 3 percent in the last year.*

(B) Identify the fiscal policy actions you would recommend. *Policy recommendations are to decrease personal income taxes, decrease corporate income taxes and/or increase government spending.*

(C) What are the goals of your fiscal policy actions? *The goal would be to enact expansionary fiscal policy actions to raise employment and increase the level of real GDP, but to do so without causing more inflation.*

(D) Explain how each policy action you identified in Question 1(B) will fit the goals you stated in Question 1(C). *Decreasing personal income taxes will provide more disposable income available for consumption and saving. Higher consumption will increase aggregate demand and raise the level of real GDP and employment and possibly the price level. Because unemployment is high, the effect on the price level may be small. Some of the savings might find its way to financial markets and become investment.*

Decreasing corporate income taxes will give businesses more money for investment, raising aggregate demand, real GDP and employment. If businesses undertake purchases of new capital, this could increase the aggregate supply and the price level might fall.

Increasing government spending is an option. Government spending is a direct injection and none is lost to savings. Additional disposable income as it passes through the income stream will also add to real GDP and employment.

(E) Use a correctly labeled aggregate demand and aggregate supply graph to show the effects of your fiscal policy on the economy. Show the changes that will occur in the price level and the level of real GDP. *The rightward movement of aggregate demand results in increases in the price level and real GDP.*

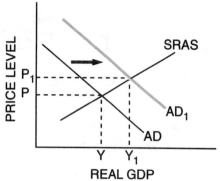

2. Assume you are a member of Congress. A staff member has just given you the following economic statistics:

	Year Ago Quarter	Last Quarter	Estimate for Quarter Now Ending
Real gross domestic product (in billions of 1997 dollars)	$2,356	$2,589	$2,752
Consumer price index	210	240	250
Unemployment rate	10%	6.5%	5.1%
Gross private investment (in billions of 1997 dollars)	$312	$340	$352

(A) What economic problem is this nation facing? *The main problem is inflation. Inflation rose almost 20 percent in the last year.*

(B) Identify the fiscal policy actions you would recommend. *Policy recommendations are to increase personal income taxes, increase corporate income taxes and/or decrease government spending.*

(C) What are the goals of your fiscal policy actions? *The goal would be to enact contractionary fiscal policy to lower inflation to a level that is acceptable. The fine line between lowering inflation and not causing lower employment and lower levels of real GDP is the difference between success and recession.*

(D) Explain how each policy action you identified in Question 2(B) will fit the goals you stated in Question 2(C). *Increasing personal income taxes will decrease disposable income available for consumption and saving. Lower levels of consumption will decrease aggregate demand to lower the level of real GDP and employment. If the economy is in the vertical range or upward-sloping range of AS, price levels will fall.*

Increasing corporate income taxes will give businesses less money for investment, reducing aggregate demand, real GDP and employment. Price levels will fall.

Decreasing government spending is an option. Raising taxes and cutting the budget may create a budget surplus. The loss of disposable income, as it passes through the income stream, will also lower real GDP and employment, but price levels will fall.

(E) Use a correctly labeled aggregate demand and aggregate supply graph to show the effects of your fiscal policy on the economy. Show the changes that will occur in the price level and the level of real GDP. *The leftward movement of aggregate demand results in a decline in the price level and real GDP.*

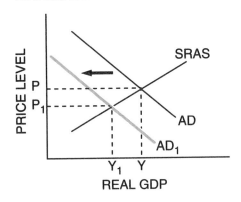

3. Assume that the economy has been operating at the full-employment levels of output and employment but has recently experienced a decrease in consumption spending because of a sharp decline in stock market indexes that has reduced the wealth of the nation by about 18 percent. Consumption expenditures have decreased at all levels of income.

(A) Use correctly labeled aggregate demand and aggregate supply graphs to illustrate the short-run effect of the decrease in consumption expenditures on each of the following:

(i) Output

(ii) Employment

(iii) The price level

The decline in consumption expenditures at each and every level of income will create an output gap at the full-employment level of output. As a result of this autonomous change in aggregate demand, the following will occur:

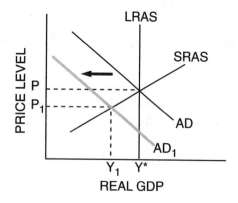

(i)   *Output will decline.*

(ii) *Employment will decline, and the unemployment rate will rise.*

(iii) *The price level will decline.*

(B) Identify two fiscal policy actions that could be used to counter the effects of the initial decrease in consumption spending. Explain, using correctly labeled aggregate demand and aggregate supply graphs, the short-run effects of each of your policies on each of the following:

(i)   Output

(ii) Employment

(iii) The price level

Fiscal-policy measures can include a cut in both personal and business taxes and/or increase in government spending. Another idea would be to raise taxes and increase government spending by equal amounts. This would result in an increase in real GDP.

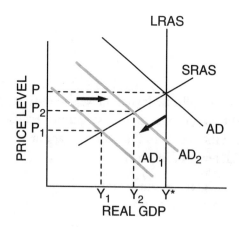

(i)   *Output will increase.*

(ii) *Employment will increase and the unemployment rate will fall.*

(iii) *The price level will increase.*

The decline in consumption moved the aggregate demand curve from AD to AD$_1$; the fiscal policy shifted the aggregate demand curve back to AD$_2$.

4. Assume that political problems restrict the supply of oil in international markets. Consequently, increased production costs result in the following economic conditions in the United States:

- The unemployment rate is 8 percent and rising.

- The CPI is rising 9 percent annually and accelerating.

- The annual rate of growth of real GDP is –1.5 percent.

(A) Identify and describe the major macroeconomic problems in the economy. Using correctly labeled aggregate demand and aggregate supply graphs, show the condition of the economy. *High rates of unemployment and negative growth rates combined with a high rate of inflation show that the economy is suffering from stagflation. The graph shows price levels increasing and unemployment rising.*

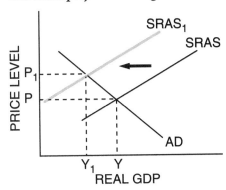

(B) With a federal budget deficit of nearly $350 billion, fiscal authorities are considering the following policy actions to address the existing economic problems:

Policy 1: Increase government expenditures.

Policy 2: Increase personal income taxes.

Policy 3: Decrease business taxes and regulations.

Describe the effect of each of the policies on the economy, and demonstrate each on an individual aggregate demand and aggregate supply graph. Be sure to include each of the following in your description:

(i) Output

(ii) Employment

(iii) The price level

Policy 1: *Increased government spending would move the AD curve to the right.*

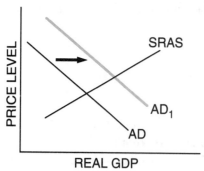

(i)   Output would increase.

(ii) Employment would increase.

(iii) The price level would increase.

Policy 2: *Increased personal taxes would move the AD curve to the left.*

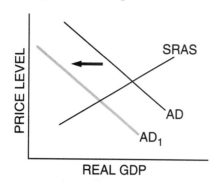

(i)   Output would decline.

(ii) Employment would decrease.

(iii) The price level would decrease.

Policy 3: *Decreased business taxes and decreased regulation would move the SRAS curve to the right.*

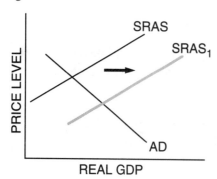

(i)   Output would increase if business expectations are positive.

(ii) Employment would rise if business expectations are positive.

(iii) The price level will fall as SRAS increases.

Simple Keynesian Model

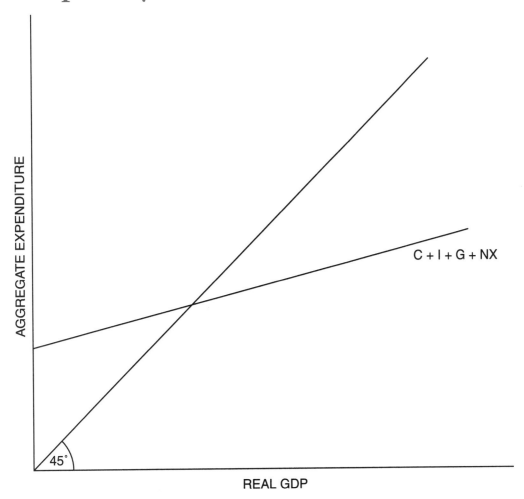

Planned aggregate expenditure = C + I + G + NX

45° line: all points where production (real GDP) = aggregate expenditure

Equilibrium occurs where planned aggregate expenditure equals production.

Equilibrium and Disequilibrium in the Keynesian Model

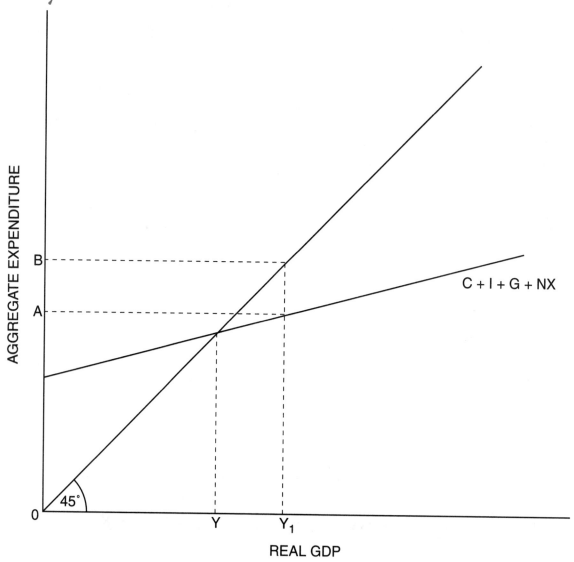

Advanced Placement Economics Teacher Resource Manual © National Council on Economic Education, New York, N.Y.

Saving and Dissaving

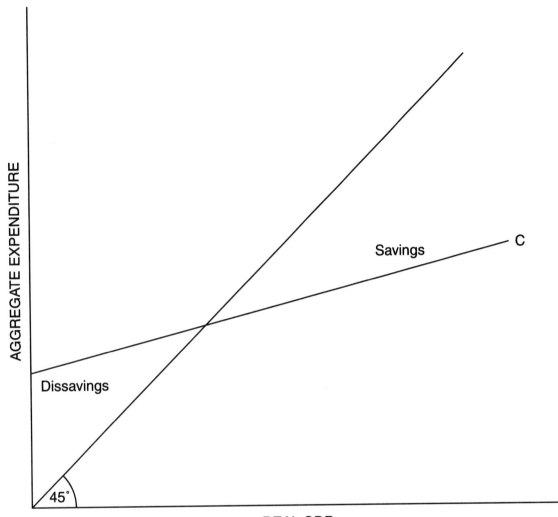

Increase in Investment

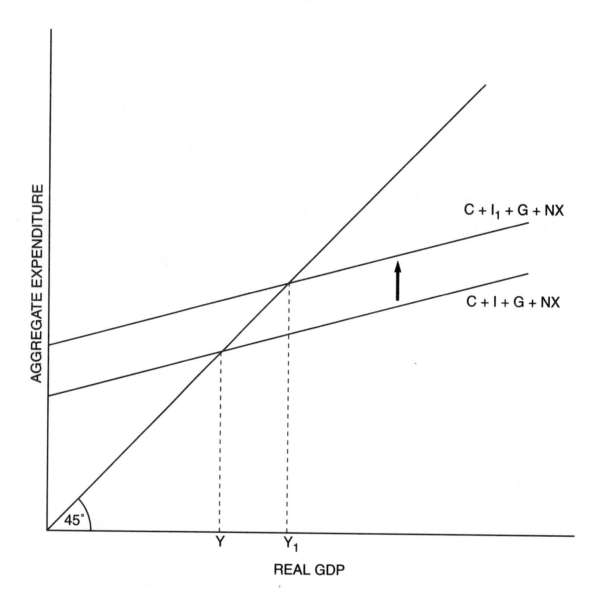

Investment increases from I to I_1.

Output increases from Y to Y_1.

Investment Demand

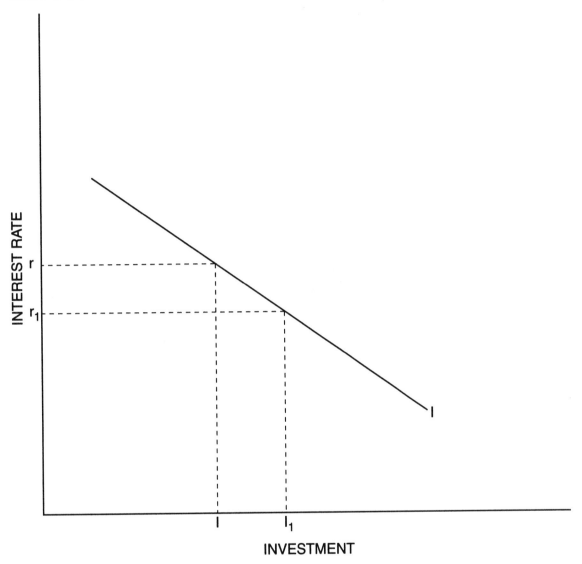

Interest rate decreases from r to r_1.

Investment increases from I to I_1.

Different Elasticities of Investment Demand

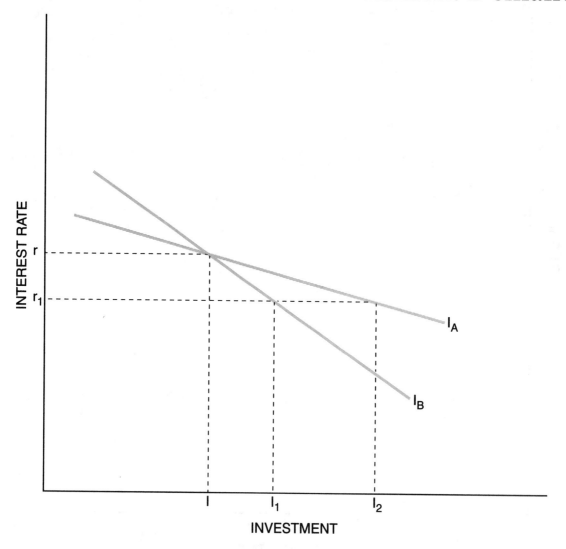

Decrease of interest rates from r to r_1.

With I_A, investment increases from I to I_2.

With I_B, investment increases from I to I_1.

I_A is more elastic than I_B.

Aggregate Demand

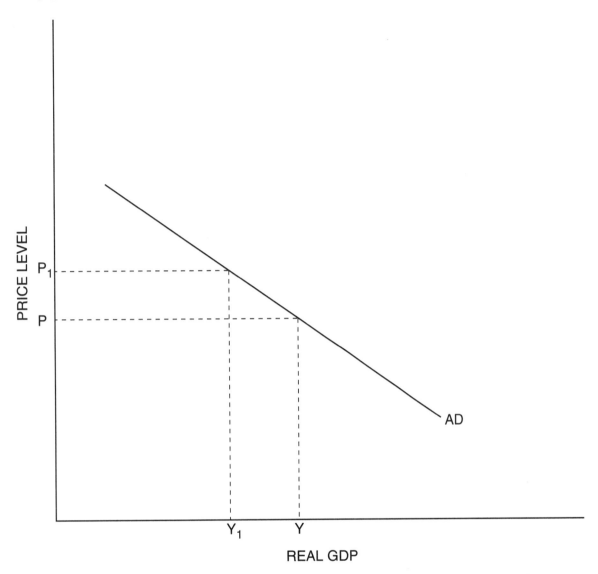

An increase in price from P to P_1 results in a decrease in real GDP from Y to Y_1.

Shifts in Aggregate Demand

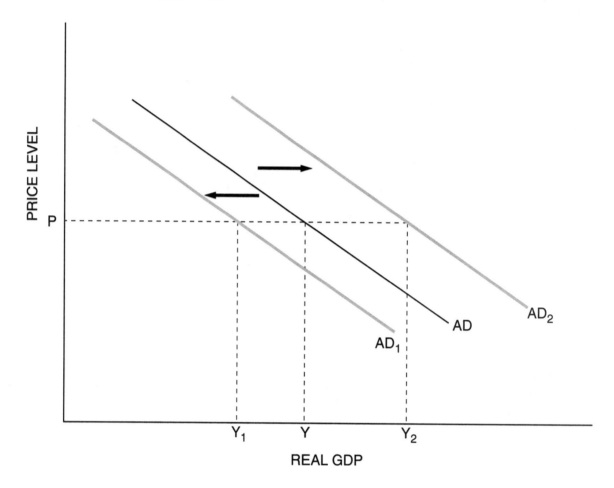

A decrease in expected future income, in government expenditures, in the money supply or an increase in taxes will cause the AD to shift from AD to AD_1.

An increase in expected future income, in government expenditures or in the money supply, or a decrease in taxes will cause the AD to shift from AD to AD_2.

Aggregate Supply

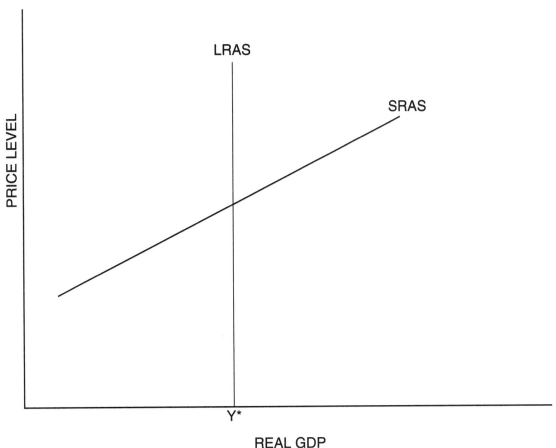

Y^* represents potential real GDP. It is full-employment output.

SRAS is the short-run aggregate supply curve.

Aggregate Supply

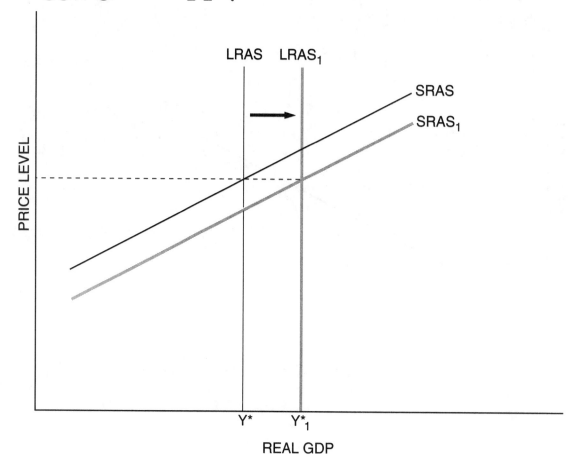

1. Potential GDP increases from Y* to Y*$_1$.
   The LRAS shifts to LRAS$_1$ and the short-run aggregate supply curve shifts to SRAS$_1$.

2. Decrease in resource prices will shift the SRAS to SRAS$_1$. A decrease in the money wage rate does not change the LRAS.

Aggregate Supply and Aggregate Demand

Graph A: Short-Run Equilibrium

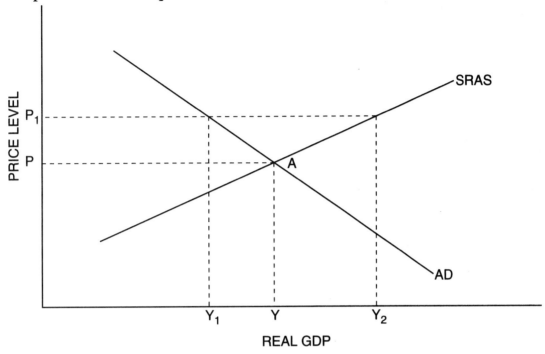

Graph B: Long-Run Equilibrium

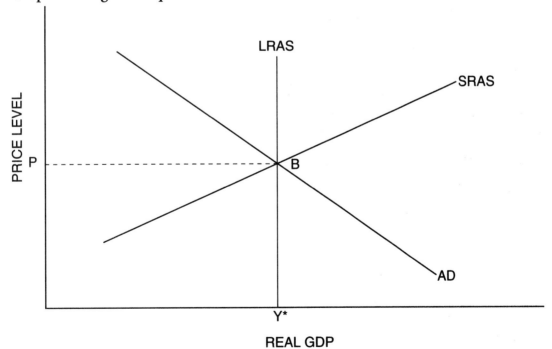

Change in Aggregate Demand

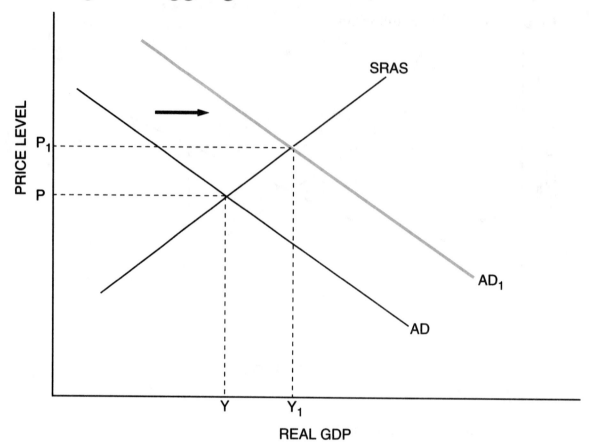

Advanced Placement Economics Teacher Resource Manual © National Council on Economic Education, New York, N.Y.

From the Short Run to the Long Run

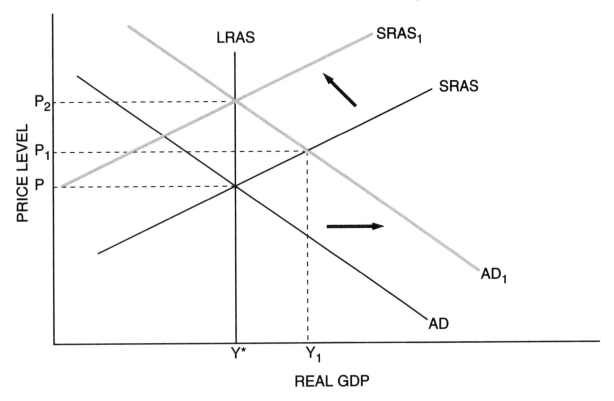

Initially the economy is at Y^*, potential GDP and P.

Aggregate demand increases from AD to AD_1 and the economy moves to Y_1 and P_1.

The final equilibrium is Y^* and P_2.

Long-Run Aggregate Supply and Production Possibilities Curves

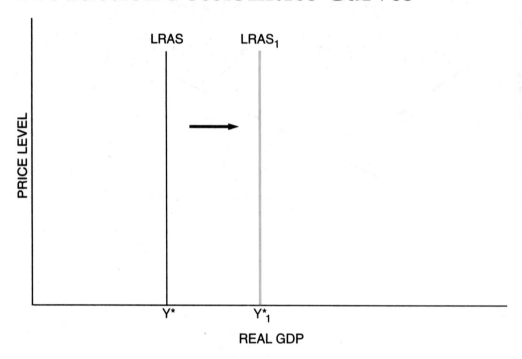

Money, Monetary Policy and Economic Stability

14 class periods or 630 minutes
(19 percent of course time)

Unit Overview

This unit explores the role of money in the economy. Basic concepts that are covered include the definition of money, the functions of money in the economy and how the money supply is influenced by the central bank and the banking system. The unit discusses how the banking system influences the money supply through loans to businesses and consumers and how the fractional reserve system works. It also examines the role of the Federal Reserve System, the central bank of the United States. Many misconceptions surround money and, by the end of this section of the course, the students should have a better grasp of the role of money and the relationships among monetary policy, the banking system and the economy.

The Lesson Planner

Lesson 1 looks at the properties of money, the functions of money and the definitions of money. It uses **Activities 34** and **35**.

Lesson 2 looks at the relationship between the money supply and gross domestic product. It uses **Activity 36**.

Lesson 3 examines financial institutions' ability to create money through loans to businesses and consumers. It uses **Activity 37**.

Lesson 4 explains the Federal Reserve System and its tools to control the money supply. It uses **Activity 38**.

Lesson 5 examines the money market and monetary policy. It uses **Activities 39** and **40** and **Visuals 4.1, 4.2, 4.3** and **4.4**.

Lesson 6 discusses real and nominal interest rates and examines the effects of monetary policy in the short run and long run. It uses **Activities 41** and **42** and **Visual 3.13**.

Week 1

■ Day 1

(A) Lecture on properties and functions of money.

(B) Have the students complete Activity 34.

(C) Review Activity 34.

■ Day 2

(A) Lecture on definitions of money.

(B) Have the students complete Activity 35.

(C) Review Activity 35.

■ Day 3

(A) Lecture on the equation of exchange.

(B) Have the students complete Activity 36.

■ Day 4

(A) Review Activity 36.

(B) Lecture on financial institutions and the money creation process.

■ Day 5

(A) Review money creation process

(B) Have the students complete Activity 37.

(C) Review Activity 37.

Week 2

■ Day 6

(A) Discuss Federal Reserve System and its tools to control money supply.

(B) Have the students complete Activity 38.

■ Day 7

(A) Review Activity 38.

(B) Use Visuals 4.1, 4.2 and 4.3 to develop the money market.

(C) Have the students complete Activity 39.

■ Day 8

(A) Review Activity 39.

(B) Lecture on monetary policy and its effects on the economy using Visual 4.4.

(C) Have the students complete Activity 40.

■ Day 9

(A) Review Activity 40.

(B) Lecture on real versus nominal interest rates and Fisher Effect.

■ Day 10

(A) Have the students complete Activity 41.

(B) Review Activity 41.

Week 3

Day 11

(A) Review factors that shift aggregate demand and aggregate supply in the short run and long run, using Visual 3.13.

(B) Have the students complete Activity 42.

Day 12

(A) Review Activity 42.

(B) Review for unit test.

Day 13

Give multiple-choice portion of unit test.

Day 14

Give free-response portion of unit test.

Money

Introduction and Description

The properties of money, the functions of money and the definitions of money are important concepts for the students to understand in the initial study of money. Money has existed for a long time, and a wide range of commodities have served as money in different countries and at different times. Before money, economies used a barter system. The principal problem with a barter system is the *double coincidence of wants* required for success. Double coincidence of wants means that you must find someone who wants what you want to trade and has what you want! This search could be extremely time-consuming and limiting to the development of an economy.

Activity 34 asks the students to demonstrate an understanding of the functions and properties of money and evaluate different commodities' performances as money. Activity 35 helps the students grasp the different definitions of money used in the United States and the importance of the differences.

Objectives

1. Describe the properties of money.
2. Describe the functions of money.
3. Explain the definitions of money used in the United States.
4. Explain the concept of near-monies.

Time Required

Two class periods or 90 minutes

Materials

Activities 34 and 35

Procedure

1. Provide a brief lecture on the properties of any commodity used as money. The properties discussed should include portability, unifor-

mity, durability, stability in value and acceptability.

2. Supply the students with examples of commodities that have served as money: cigarettes and chocolate bars in a prisoner of war camp, cattle and seashells. Ask them to indicate which properties the commodities have and which properties they do not have.

3. Provide a brief lecture on the functions of money: medium of exchange, store of value and unit of account.

   (A) The medium-of-exchange function eliminates the need for the double coincidence of wants.

   (B) The store-of-value function permits money to be held for use at a later time.

   (C) The unit-of-account, or standard-of-value, function means there is an agreed-to measure for stating the prices of goods and services. This simplifies price comparisons.

   Refer to the commodities listed in Procedure 2, and discuss how well they fulfill the functions of money.

4. Have the students start Activity 34 in class and complete for homework. Review the answers to the questions with the students.

5. Give a brief lecture on the definitions of money used in the United States today. Focus on M1, which consists of currency, traveler's checks and checkable deposits. Emphasize the function of medium of exchange in terms of each of the elements in M1. Now focus on M2, which includes M1 plus savings deposits, small time deposits, money market mutual funds and other deposits. Note that many items in M2 are constrained in the ability to serve as a medium of exchange. Time deposits may require a significant penalty if withdrawals are made before the maturity

date; frequently money market funds have a minimum withdrawal such as $500.

6. Present current data on M1 and M2. Emphasize here the proportion of M1 that checkable deposits represent. These data are available from the Federal Reserve.

7. Have the students complete Activity 35. Review the answers to the questions with the students.

Money

1. Use the table below to evaluate how well each item would perform the functions of money in today's economy. If an item seems to fulfill the function, put a **+** sign in the box; if it does not fulfill a function in your opinion, place a **−** sign in the box. Put a **?** sign in the box if you are unsure whether the item fulfills the functions of money. The item with the most **+** signs would be the best form of money for you. In the space below the table, list the top six forms of money, according to your evaluation.

Item	Medium of Exchange	Store of Value	Standard of Value
Salt	−	−	−
Large stone wheels	−	+	−
Cattle	−	−	−
Gold	+	+	+
Copper coins	+	+	+
Beaver pelts	−	−	−
Personal checks	+	+	+
Savings account passbook	−	+	+
Prepaid phone card	?	+	+
Debit card	+	+	+
Credit card	+	−	+
Cigarettes	−	−	−
Playing cards	−	−	−
Bushels of wheat	−	−	−
$1 bill	+	+	+
$100 bill	+	+	+

Your top six forms of money: *Gold, copper coins, personal checks, debit card, $1 bill and $100 bill.* *Answers may vary.*

2. After you finish the evaluation in Question 1, rate the various items in the table below. Evaluate how well they meet the characteristics of money. Again, if an item seems to fit a characteristic, use a **+** sign; if the item does not seem to fit a characteristic, use a **−** sign. If there is a difference of opinion or if you are uncertain, use a **?** sign. The item with the most **+** signs would best fit the characteristics of money. In the space below the table, list your six top items.

Item	Portability	Uniformity	Acceptability	Durability	Stability in Value
Salt	+	+	−	+	−
Large stone wheels	−	−	−	+	+
Cattle	−	−	−	?	−
Gold	+	+	?	+	−
Copper coins	+	+	?	+	−
Beaver pelts	+	−	−	+	?
Personal checks	+	+	?	+	+
Savings account passbook	+	+	−	−	+
Prepaid phone card	+	?	?	−	+
Debit card	+	+	+	+	+
Credit card	+	+	+	+	+
Cigarettes	+	−	−	−	−
Playing cards	+	−	−	−	−
Bushels of wheat	−	−	−	−	−
$1 bill	+	+	+	+	+
$100 bill	+	+	+	+	+

Your top six items: *Gold, copper coins, personal checks, debit card, $1 bill and $100 bill. Answers may vary.*

3. Why might factors such as ease of storage, difficulty in counterfeiting and security of electronic transfer of funds also be characteristics that you might use in evaluating money?
For an item to be a good medium of exchange, you would want to minimize the costs of holding or storing it. Counterfeiting and security affect the item's underlying value and might affect acceptability.

What's All This About the Ms?

1. What are the three basic functions of money? *Medium of exchange, a standard of value (unit of account), and a store of value*

2. Why is it important for the Fed to know the size and rate of growth of the money supply? *The size of the money supply and the rate at which it is growing can have a significant impact on the economic well being of the country.*

   (A) What are the effects if the money supply grows too slowly? *If the money supply is growing too slowly, the likelihood of recession increases because the demand for money will increase, driving interest rates up. As interest rates rise, investment declines, slowing the growth rate of real output.*

   (B) What are the effects if the money supply grows too rapidly? *If the money supply is growing too quickly, it could lead to inflation.*

3. Name a type of money that serves primarily as a medium of exchange. *Currency, coin, debit cards or checkable deposits*

4. Name a type of money that serves primarily as a store of value. *Savings account or money market mutual fund account*

5. With the use of credit cards becoming more prominent and the availability of credit broader than ever, why are credit cards not included in the Ms? *Credit cards are short-term loans. Credit-card bills are not directly subtracted from checking accounts. Instead the credit-card holder pays the bill from a checking or NOW account. Not only should loans NOT be counted as money, but if they were and the payment were also counted, one economic transaction would be double-counted in the money supply.*

6. Why is it difficult for the Fed to get an accurate measure of the money supply?
Because of the volume of transactions in the United States, which can range into the trillions on a daily basis, getting an accurate measure of each transaction can be an arduous task. The inputs are constantly changing as banks make new loans and people repay loans ahead of schedule.

7. Why must the Fed continue to develop new ways to track the money supply?
Because of technological innovation in the financial services industry and profit maximizing behavior on the part of commercial banks, the Fed must find new measures for tracking the money supply to assist with monetary policy.

8. Use the data in Figure 35.1 to calculate M1, M2 and M3. Assume that all items not mentioned are zero. Show all components for your answers.

Figure 35.1
Calculating the Ms

Checkable deposits (demand deposits, NOW, ATM and credit union share draft accounts)	$850
Currency	$200
Large time deposits	$800
Noncheckable savings deposits	$302
Small time deposits	$1,745
Institutional money market mutual funds	$1,210

M1 = * 850 + 200 = 1,050 *

M2 = * 1,050 + 1,745 + 302 = 3,097 *

M3 = * 3,097 + 800 + 1,210 = 5,107 *

Equation of Exchange

Introduction and Description

This lesson describes and explains the relationship between the money supply and gross domestic product. The equation of exchange is an identity and provides an understanding of the relationship between money and economic activity. The students demonstrate an understanding of the equation of exchange and the change in velocity over time in Activity 36.

Objectives

1. Define the equation of exchange.
2. Define the variables in the equation of exchange.
3. Explain how changes in the money supply are translated into changes in nominal GDP, prices and output.

Time Required

One class period or 45 minutes

Materials

Activity 36

Procedure

1. Present the equation of exchange: $MV = PQ$. This equation shows the relationship among the money supply, income velocity, the price level and real output. Define each of the terms in the equation. Stress that the equation of exchange is an accounting definition or an identity: It is always true.

2. There is evidence that income velocity (V) is highly predictable with its value remaining in a very narrow range over a multiyear period. Thus, changes in the money supply (M) result in changes in nominal GDP (P x Q). Depending on the state of the economy, the changes in the money supply can result in changes in prices only, in output only or in some combination of price and output.

3. Discuss the factors that affect income velocity and determine whether changes in the money supply are translated into changes in prices and/or output in the short run. Shift the aggregate demand curve over the three shapes of the aggregate supply curve. If the aggregate supply curve is horizontal, an increase in the money supply will cause the aggregate demand curve to shift to the right, and only output will increase. If the aggregate supply curve is vertical, an increase in the money supply will cause the aggregate demand curve to shift to the right, and only the price level will increase. If the aggregate supply curve is positively sloped, an increase in the money supply will cause the aggregate demand curve to shift to the right, and the economy will experience increases in both the price level *and* output.

4. Have the students complete Activity 36. Review the answers with the students. Please note that the students may get slightly different numbers for the PQ in Figures 36.1 and 36.2 if they multiply P x Q or M x V.

The Monetary Equation of Exchange

Part A

1. Define (in your own words and in one or two sentences each) the four variables in the equation of exchange.

   M = M1, stock of money

   V = income (GDP) velocity of circulation or average number of times $1 is spent on final goods and services in a particular time period

   P = average price level of final goods and services in GDP, also known as the GDP deflator

   Q = real output, the quantity of goods and services in GDP

2. The product of velocity (V) and the money supply (M) equals PQ. How can PQ be defined? *It can be defined as nominal GDP; Q is the current output at current prices (P).*

3. Suppose velocity remains constant, while the money supply increases. Explain how this would affect nominal GDP. *Nominal GDP (PQ) would increase. If the economy is not at full employment, both P and Q could increase. If the economy is operating at full employment, only P would increase. This action could lead to extreme inflation if the economy is at full employment.*

4. During the past 30 years, the use of credit cards has increased, and banks and financial institutions increasingly use computers for transactions. Explain how these changes might affect velocity. *V would increase. A given stock of M could "work harder" and finance more transactions more quickly.*

5. As the result of legislative and regulatory reform throughout the 1980s and 1990s, banks and other financial institutions began paying interest on a significant proportion of the checkable deposits in the M1 definition of the money supply. Explain how these changes might be expected to affect the velocity of M1. *V would decrease. People would be more willing to hold (not spend) M if it paid interest.*

Part B

The following tables give data on money supply, prices, real GDP and velocity for the U.S. economy for 14 recent years. Because of rounding, some totals may not come out exactly.

6. Complete the tables by filling in the blanks.

 Figure 36.1
M1 Chart

Year	M1 (billions of $)	V	P Implicit Price Deflator for GDP	Q Real GDP (billions of $)	PQ Nominal GDP (billions of $)
1987	$750	6.36	0.780	$6,114	$4,768.90
1988	786	6.48	0.800	6,370	5,096.00
1989	792	*6.93*	*0.830*	6,592	5,489.00
1990	824	7.00	0.860	6,707	5,768.00
1991	896	6.71	0.90	6,677	6,009.30
1992	1,024	6.18	0.920	6,880	6,329.60
1993	1,129	5.88	0.940	7,063	6,639.20
1994	1,150	6.13	0.960	*7,348*	7,054.30
1995	*1,125*	6.57	0.980	7,544	7,393.10
1996	1,080	*7.23*	1.000	7,813	7,813.00
1997	1,073	*7.76*	1.020	8,160	8,323.20
1998	1,097	7.99	1.030	8,510	*8,765.30*
1999	1,125	*8.28*	1.050	8,876	9,319.80
2000	1,088	*8.98*	1.0691	9,320	9,768.90

 Figure 36.2
M2 Chart

Year	M2 (billions of $; Dec. figures)	V	P Implicit Price Deflator for GDP	Q Real GDP (billions of $)	PQ Nominal GDP (billions of $)
1987	$2,830	1.68	0.78	$6,114	$4,769
1988	2,994	1.70	0.80	6,370	5,096
1989	3,158	*1.74*	*0.83*	6,592	5,489
1990	3,277	1.76	0.86	6,707	5,768
1991	3,377	1.78	0.90	6,677	6,009
1992	3,431	1.84	0.92	6,880	6,330
1993	3,484	1.91	0.94	7,063	6,639
1994	3,500	2.02	0.96	7,348	7,054
1995	3,642	2.03	0.98	7,544	*7,393*
1996	3,815	2.05	1.00	7,813	7,813
1997	4,032	2.06	1.02	*8,155*	8,318
1998	*4,395*	2.00	1.03	8,510	8,790
1999	4,653	*2.00*	1.05	8,876	9,299
2000	4,945	2.01	*1.07*	9,319	9,963

7. What might one infer from the changes of the 1980s and 1990s about the classical assumption that institutional factors determine velocity? *V does not remain constant when institutional factors change. In fact, it is increasing.*

8. Use the grid below and the M1 and M2 data to graph the income velocity from 1987 to 2000.

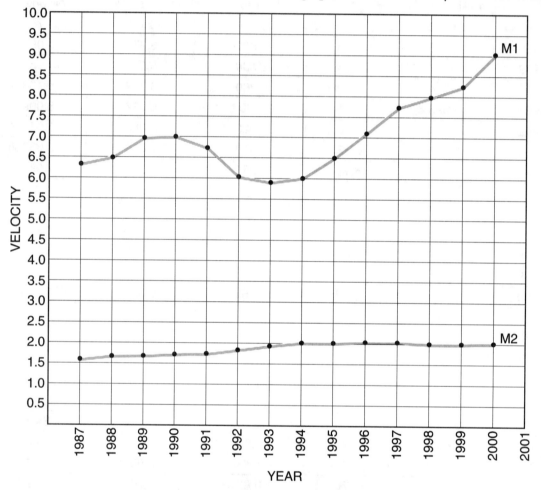

(A) What trends do you see? *Velocity is increasing slowly.*

(B) What is the difference in the value of M1 velocity and M2 velocity? Explain why they are different. *M1 velocity is much larger than M2 velocity. M1 is used for transactions, whereas a significant proportion of M2 is used for saving so it does not change on a daily or weekly basis.*

9. For a given money supply growth, a(n) (*increase* / decrease) in velocity will (*increase* / decrease) inflationary pressure. (Underline the correct word(s) in parentheses.)

Financial Intermediaries

Introduction and Description

Financial intermediaries act as the go-between borrowers and lenders. They take deposits from households and businesses and make loans to other households and businesses. Financial intermediaries include commercial banks, savings and loan associations, savings banks, credit unions and money market mutual fund companies.

This lesson focuses on demonstrating how banks create money. The term *banks* is used to mean any depository institution whose deposits are a part of M1. The concept of money creation is a difficult one for most students. Many students think that money is created only by the U.S. Mint or the Federal Reserve System. Student understanding of the money creation process is essential to understanding the economic effects of monetary policy. Thus, this lesson is very important. Activity 37 provides the students with practice in calculating the deposit expansion multiplier and an opportunity to understand it and its effect on the money supply.

Objectives

1. Explain the economic function of financial intermediaries.
2. Explain the fractional reserve system.
3. Explain the process by which banks create or destroy money and the factors that affect the increase or decrease in the money supply.
4. Define the *required reserve ratio, required reserves, excess reserves* and *deposit expansion multiplier.*

Time Required

Two class periods or 90 minutes

Materials

Activity 37

Procedure

1. Give a brief lecture on financial intermediaries. Define the role of financial intermediaries as bringing people who want to borrow funds together with people who want to lend funds. Give examples of financial intermediaries. Present the functions of financial intermediaries: liquidity creation, minimization of the cost of borrowing, minimization of the cost of monitoring borrowers and risk reduction through pooling.

2. Describe the fractional reserve system of banking in the United States. Banks are any institution holding deposits. People deposit money in a bank. Banks must hold a specific percentage of the deposit as reserves; this percentage is called the *required reserve ratio*. The deposit that is not part of required reserves is called *excess reserves*. The bank may loan excess reserves or buy government securities. A bank makes a loan by creating a checkable deposit for the borrower; this results in an increase in the money supply. The money supply, or M1, equals currency, checkable deposits and traveler's checks.

3. Present the entire money creation process. Most texts have a graphic. Stress that the total increase in the money supply may be less than predicted by the money expansion multiplier if

   - borrowers do not spend all of the money they borrow,

   - banks do not lend out all their excess reserves and

   - people hold part of their money as cash.

4. On the next day, review the money creation process and discuss how different required reserve ratios have different effects on the size of the money supply. Show that with a required reserve ratio of 1, all money deposited would be required reserves. The United States has a fractional reserve system because the required reserve ratio is not 1.

5. Have the students complete Activity 37. Review the answers with the students.

The Multiple Expansion of Checkable Deposits

Part A

Assume that

- the required reserve ratio is 10 percent of checkable deposits and banks lend out the other 90 percent of their deposits (banks wish to hold no excess reserves) and

- all money lent out by one bank is redeposited in another bank.

1. Under these assumptions, if a new checkable deposit of $1,000 is made in Bank 1,

    (A) how much will Bank 1 keep as required reserves? ___$ 100___

    (B) how much will Bank 1 lend out? ___$ 900___

    (C) how much will be redeposited in Bank 2? ___$ 900___

    (D) how much will Bank 2 keep as required reserves? ___$ 90___

    (E) how much will Bank 2 lend out? ___$ 810___

    (F) how much will be redeposited in Bank 3? ___$ 810___

2. Use your answers to Question 1 to help you complete the table in Figure 37.1. Fill in the blanks in the table, rounding numbers to the second decimal (for example, $59.049 = $59.05). After you have completed the table, answer the questions that follow by filling in the blanks or underlining the correct answer in parentheses so each statement is true.

 Figure 37.1

Checkable Deposits, Reserves and Loans in Seven Banks

Bank No.	New Checkable Deposits	10% Fractional Reserves	Loans
1	$1,000.00	$100.00	$900.00
2	900.00	90.00	810.00
3	810.00	81.00	729.00
4	729.00	72.90	656.10
5	656.10	65.61	590.49
6	590.49	59.05	531.44
7	531.44	53.14	478.30
All other banks combined	4,782.98	478.29	4,304.67
Total for all banks	$10,000.00	$1,000.00	$9,000.00

3. In this example:

   (A) The original deposit of $1,000 increased total bank reserves by __$1,000__ . Eventually, this led to a total of $10,000 expansion of bank deposits, __$1,000__ of which was because of the original deposit, while __$9,000__ was because of bank lending activities.

   (B) Therefore, if the fractional reserve had been 15 percent instead of 10 percent, the amount of deposit expansion would have been *(more / **less**)* than in this example.

   (C) Therefore, if the fractional reserve had been 5 percent instead of 10 percent, the amount of deposit expansion would have been *(**more** / less)* than in this example.

   (D) If banks had not loaned out all of their excess reserves, the amount of deposit expansion would have been *(more / **less**)* than in this example.

   (E) If all loans had not been redeposited in the banking system, the amount of deposit expansion would have been *(more / **less**)* than in this example.

4. Another way to represent the multiple expansion of deposits is through *T-accounts*. In short, a T-account is an accounting relationship that looks at changes in balance sheet items. Since balance sheets must balance, so, too, must T-accounts. T-account entries on the asset side must be balanced by an offsetting asset or an offsetting liability. A sample T-account is provided below. For the bank, *assets* include accounts at the Federal Reserve District Bank, Treasury securities and loans; *liabilities* are deposits and *net worth* is assets minus liabilities. Show how the $1,000 checkable deposit described in Question 1 would be listed in a T-account.

Assets		Liabilities	
Loans	*$900*	*Deposits*	*$1,000*
Reserves	*$100*		

Part B

5. Assume that $1,000 is deposited in the bank, and that each bank loans out all of its excess reserves. For each of the following required reserve ratios, calculate the amount that the bank must hold in required reserves, the amount that will be excess reserves, the deposit expansion multiplier and the maximum amount that the money supply could increase.

	Required Reserve Ratio					
	1%	5%	10%	12.5%	15%	25%
Required reserves	$10	$50	$100	$125	$150	$250
Excess reserves	$990	$950	$900	$875	$850	$750
Deposit expansion multiplier	100	20	10	8	6.67	4
Maximum increase in the money supply	$99,000	$19,000	$9,000	$7,000	$5,669.50	$3,000

6. If the required reserve ratio were 0 percent, then money supply expansion would be infinite. Why don't we want an infinite growth of the money supply? (Hint: remember the equation of exchange: MV = PQ.) *Based on the equation of exchange and assuming a constant velocity of money, an infinite increase in the money supply would translate into an infinite increase in nominal GDP. We know that real output cannot increase that rapidly; therefore the increase must be caused by increases in prices. Thus, we would have hyperinflation.*

7. If the Federal Reserve wants to increase the money supply, should it raise or lower the reserve requirement? Why? *The Federal Reserve should lower the required reserve ratio. Banks would have more excess reserves to lend out and, thus, the money supply could increase.*

8. If the Federal Reserve increases the reserve requirement and velocity remains stable, what will happen to nominal GDP? Why? *If the Federal Reserve increases reserve requirements, the money supply will decrease. Nominal GDP will decrease based on the equation of exchange (MV = PQ = nominal GDP): If M decreases, V stays constant and then PQ (nominal GDP) must decrease.*

9. What economic goal might the Federal Reserve try to meet by reducing the money supply? *Price stability*

10. Why might the money supply not expand by the amount predicted by the deposit expansion multiplier? *Several reasons: All money may not be deposited into the banking system; the banks may not be able to lend out all excess reserves because people do not want to borrow; banks may want to keep excess reserves as a precaution.*

The Federal Reserve System and Its Tools

Introduction and Description

The focus of this lesson is the Federal Reserve System: how its actions relate to the money creation process introduced in the last lesson and how its tools affect the money supply. The Federal Reserve System is the central bank for the United States. It has regulatory authority for many financial institutions that hold checkable deposits. It has the responsibility to control the money supply to promote the economic goals of full employment, price stability and stable economic growth. The Fed has three tools it can use to control the money supply: open market operations, the discount rate and the required reserve ratio. The primary tool the Fed uses is open market operations, or the buying and selling of Treasury securities. Activity 38 provides the students with practice using T-accounts and the mechanics of implementing monetary policy.

Objectives

1. Describe the structure of the Federal Reserve System.
2. Identify each of the tools of the Fed and explain how changes in each tool affect the money supply.
3. Explain basic balance sheets.

Time Required

One class period or 45 minutes

Materials

Activity 38

Procedure

1. Describe the structure of the Federal Reserve System including the Board of Governors and the Federal Open Market Committee. Be sure to discuss the role of the chairman of the Federal Reserve.

2. Discuss each of the tools of the Fed.

3. Ask the students to explain, based on their knowledge of the money creation process, how each tool can be used to change the money supply.

4. Explain basic balance sheets of the Fed, the banking system and the bank customers. Explain how changes are evidenced in the different balance sheets. Be sure to explain that the left side of a balance sheet shows the assets, and the right side shows the liabilities. Further, the two sides of the balance sheet, including net worth, must sum to each other — that is, net worth equals assets minus liabilities.

5. Have the students complete Activity 38. Review the answers with the students.

The Federal Reserve: The Mechanics of Monetary Policy

For Questions 1 through 4, start with the baseline case in Figure 38.1. The Fed wishes to *decrease* the money supply from $353 to $303 by open market operations. The reserve requirement is 10 percent.

1. Will the Fed want to buy or sell existing Treasury securities?___*Sell*___

2. What is the money multiplier?___*10*___

3. What is the value of Treasury securities that need to be bought or sold? ___*$5*___

4. Fill in Figure 38.3 to show the accounts after open market operations are finished and all changes have worked their way through the economy:

Figure 38.3
After Open Market Operations Are Finished

Assets			Liabilities
The Fed			
Treasury securities (–$5)	$78	$21	Reserve accounts of banks (–$5)
		$57	Federal Reserve notes
Banks			
Reserve accounts (–$5)	$21	250	Checkable deposits (–$50)
Federal Reserve notes	$4		
Loans (–45)	$360	$135	Net worth (to stockholders)
Bank Customers			
Checkable deposits (- $50)	$250	$360	Loans (–$45)
Federal Reserve notes	$53		
Treasury securities (+ $5)	$57		

Money supply = $303 ($250 + $53)

For Questions 5 through 7, suppose banks keep zero excess reserves and the reserve requirement is 15 percent.

5. What is the deposit expansion multiplier? ___*1 / 0.15 = 6.67*___

6. A customer deposits $100,000 in his checking account.

    (A) How much of this can the bank lend to new customers? __$85,000__

    (B) How much must the bank add to its reserves? __$15,000__

    (C) In what two forms can a bank hold the new required reserves? *As vault cash or reserve accounts (deposits at the District Federal Reserve Bank)*

7. Suppose that the $100,000 had previously been held in Federal Reserve notes under the customer's mattress and that banks continue to hold no excess reserves. By how much will the customer's deposit cause the money supply to grow? __$566,950__

8. A very low discount rate may (***encourage banks to borrow*** / *discourage banks from borrowing*) from the Federal Reserve. Underline the correct answer and explain why. *If banks are able to borrow from the Federal Reserve at a low interest rate and make loans at a higher rate, the banks will earn a profit and, hence, have an incentive to use the discount window.*

9. The federal funds rate is the interest rate at which financial institutions can borrow from other financial institutions. Suppose the federal funds rate is 5 percent and the discount rate is 4.5 percent. Why is it that a bank might choose to borrow in the federal funds market, rather than getting the lower interest rate available through the discount window? *Borrowing from another financial institution will have fewer transaction costs, plus the bank will not have the added scrutiny of its business practices that borrowing from the Federal Reserve will generate.*

10. In a foreign country, the reserve requirement is 100 percent. What will be the deposit expansion multiplier? __One__

11. If the Fed decided to implement a policy action designed to increase the money supply, in which direction would bank reserves and the federal funds rate change and why? *If the Fed wants to increase the money supply, it will institute a policy to increase reserves (giving banks an increased ability to make loans). Banks have more money to loan to other banks, businesses and consumers, so the federal funds rate is likely to decrease.*

12. Circle the correct symbol (↑ for increase, ↓ for decrease) in Figure 38.4.

Figure 38.4
Fed Actions and Their Effects

Federal Reserve Action	Bank Reserves	Money Supply	Fed Funds Rate
A. Sold Treasury securities on the open market	↑ (↓)	↑ (↓)	(↑) ↓
B. Bought Treasury securities on the open market	(↑) ↓	(↑) ↓	↑ (↓)
C. Raised the discount rate	↑ (↓)	↑ (↓)	(↑) ↓
D. Lowered the discount rate	(↑) ↓	(↑) ↓	↑ (↓)
E. Raised the reserve requirement	↑ (↓)	↑ (↓)	(↑) ↓
F. Lowered the reserve requirement	(↑) ↓	(↑) ↓	↑ (↓)

13. Indicate in the table in Figure 38.5 how the Federal Reserve could use each of the three monetary policy tools to pursue an expansionary policy and a contractionary policy.

Figure 38.5
Tools of Monetary Policy

Monetary Policy	Expansionary Policy	Contractionary Policy
A. Open market operations	*Buy Treasury securities*	*Sell Treasury securities*
B. Discount rate	*Lower the discount rate*	*Raise the discount rate*
C. Reserve requirements	*Lower the required reserve ratio*	*Raise the required reserve ratio*

14. Why do banks hold excess reserves, which pay no interest? *Banks are required by law to hold required reserves; they hold some excess reserves as a precaution in case of sudden withdrawals or changes in economic conditions.*

15. Why does the Fed rarely use the reserve requirement as an instrument of monetary policy?
Changes in the required reserve ratio cause radical or strong changes in the monetary system. It is difficult for financial institutions to adjust to changes in the required reserve ratio. In general, the Fed uses the tools of monetary policy to adjust the economy in smaller increments.

16. What does it mean to say that the Fed changes the discount rate mostly as a *signal* to markets?
The discount rate has no impact if banks do not borrow from the Federal Reserve; banks do not have to borrow because if they need funds, they can always go to the federal funds market. It signals to the banks and others how the Fed would like the money supply to change.

17. Why does the Fed currently target the federal funds rate rather than the money supply?
The Fed uses changes in reserves to affect the federal funds rate. It targets the federal funds rate because the Fed believes that this rate is closely tied to economic activity.

The Money Market and Monetary Policy

Introduction and Description

In this lesson, the demand for and supply of money are brought together in the money market. The effects of the Federal Reserve System's monetary policy are integrated into the money market and then linked to aggregate demand. The lesson then discusses the resulting impact on equilibrium output and price level. In Activity 39, the students practice manipulating the money market and understanding the impact of the Fed's actions in this market. Activity 40 provides practice in relating monetary policy to changes in the monetary variables such as the federal funds rate, the money supply and velocity.

Objectives

1. Define *transactions demand for money, precautionary (liquidity) demand for money* and *the speculative demand for money* and explain how each affects the total demand for money.
2. Discuss the motives for holding assets as money.
3. Identify the factors that cause the demand for money to shift and explain why the shift occurs.
4. Explain how interest rates are determined in the money market.
5. Describe Federal Reserve policy and the interest rate.
6. Explain how interest rates affect monetary policy.

Time required

Two class periods or 90 minutes

Materials

1. Activities 39 and 40
2. Visuals 4.1, 4.2, 4.3 and 4.4

Procedure

1. Project Visual 4.1 and discuss the sources of the demand for money. The students should recognize that individuals are faced with a simple decision: how much of their wealth do they want to hold as money and how much do they want to hold as interest-bearing assets? If you hold money, you are forgoing the interest you could earn on the money in an interest-bearing asset. There is an opportunity cost of holding money: the forgone interest. Visual 4.1 shows that as the interest rate decreases from r to r_1, the amount of money held by people increases from MD to MD_1.

2. Project Visual 4.2. Explain that the demand for money also depends on the price level and on the level of real GDP or real income. If prices double, a person will need twice as much money to buy groceries or other goods and services. People are most concerned with the real value of income: what the income can buy or its purchasing power. As income rises, the demand for money increases.

3. To complete the money market, we now add the supply of money, which is determined by the Federal Reserve through its tools. Visual 4.3 shows the money market. Explore what happens to the interest rate as prices rise (MD increases and the interest rate rises), income increases (MD increases and the interest rate rises) or the money supply increases (interest rate decreases).

4. Have the students complete Activity 39. Review the answers with the students.

5. Given the demand for money, by controlling the money supply, the Federal Reserve controls the interest rate in the short run. The interest rate affects the level of investment and a portion of the level of consumption. Using Visual 4.4, show how an increase in the money supply (MS to MS_1) causes the interest rate to decrease (r_1 to r) and investment (I to I_1) and consumption to increase. In turn, aggregate demand increases (AD to AD_1).

6. Have the students explain step-by-step what happens in the economy once the Federal Reserve decides to increase (decrease) the money supply. (Be sure the students understand why an increase in bond prices leads to a decrease in the interest rate.)

Fed purchases Treasury securities → Bond prices increase to entice households and businesses to sell Treasury securities → Money supply increases and interest rate decreases → Investment increases (and interest-sensitive components of consumption increase) → Aggregate demand increases → Output increases and the price level increases.

7. Explain the factors that affect the income velocity.

8. Have the students complete Activity 40. Review the answers with the students.

The Money Market

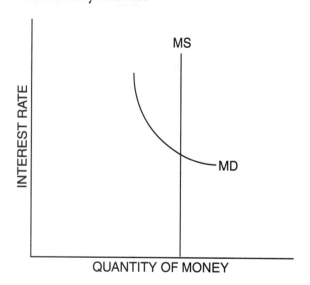

Figure 39.1
The Money Market

1. Suppose the Federal Reserve increases the money supply by buying Treasury securities.

   (A) What happens to the interest rate? *The interest rate decreases.*

   (B) What happens to the quantity of money demanded? *The quantity of money demanded increases.*

   (C) Explain what happens to loans and interest rates as the Fed increases the money supply. *As the Federal Reserve buys Treasury securities from the public, demand deposits in financial institutions increase. Thus financial institutions have more money to make loans. To encourage people to take out the loans, the financial institutions lower the interest rate.*

2. Suppose the demand for money increases.

   (A) What happens to the interest rate? *The interest rate increases.*

   (B) What happens to the quantity of money supplied? *The quantity of money supplied remains the same, as shown by the vertical money supply curve.*

   (C) If the Fed wants to maintain a constant interest rate when the demand for money increases, explain what policy the Fed needs to follow and why. *It must increase the money supply to meet the increase in the demand for money.*

   (D) Why might the Fed want to maintain a constant interest rate? *To stabilize the amount of investment in the economy*

Figure 39.2
Alternative Money Demand Curves

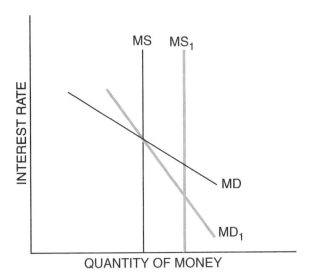

3. Suppose there are two money demand curves — MD and MD_1 — and the Fed increases the money supply from MS to MS_1 as shown in Figure 39.2.

   (A) Compare what happens to the interest rate with each MD curve. *The interest rate declines further with the more inelastic money demand curve (MD_1) than with the more elastic money demand curve (MD).*

   (B) Explain the effect of the change in the money supply on consumption, investment, real output and prices. Would there be a difference in the effects under the two different money demand curves? If so, explain. *With either demand curve, the increase in supply will cause interest rates to decline and investment and consumption — and thus real output — to increase. AD increases, so prices are likely to increase. For the interest-sensitive component of consumption and investment, there will be a greater increase (or decrease) with a greater decrease (or increase) in the interest rate. For example, a larger decrease in interest rates will usually lead to a greater increase in investment. The increase in investment will increase aggregate demand. Thus, the increase in the money supply will lead to an increase in AD, which will lead to an increase in real output and in the price level.*

   (C) How would you describe, in economic terms, the difference between the two money demand curves? *MD_1 is more interest inelastic than MD.*

   (D) If the Federal Reserve is trying to get the economy out of a recession, which money demand curve would it want to represent the economy? Explain. *The Fed would prefer the more-inelastic money demand curve because a given increase in the money supply will lead to a greater decrease in interest rates, which should stimulate the economy.*

The Federal Reserve: Monetary Policy and Macroeconomics

1. What is monetary policy? *Monetary policy is action by the Federal Reserve to increase or decrease the money supply to influence the economy.*

2. From 1998 to 2002, what was the dominant focus of monetary policy and why?
    From 1998 to 2001, the focus of monetary policy was to slow the growth of the economy to prevent an increase in inflation. In 2001 and 2002, the focus was to stimulate the economy without stimulating inflation.

3. Explain why the money supply and short-term interest rates are inversely related.
    When the Fed buys Treasury securities from the public, bank reserves increase. To decrease excess reserves and make loans, banks lower the interest rate to entice consumers and businesses to borrow.

4. What are some reasons for lags and imperfections in data used by central banks?
    Financial institutions report at specified periods, and the reporting time is not necessarily when the central bank can use the data. For short periods of time, the central bank collects data from only a sample of banks, and this leads to a certain amount of error in the data.

5. Why do many economists believe that central banks have more control over the price level than over real output? *Many economists believe that real output is determined by the level of capital stock and the productivity of workers. Thus, changes in the money supply affect prices more than real output.*

6. What might cause velocity to change? *Some factors that might cause velocity to change are changes in how money is transferred (institutional changes), changes in interest rates and changes in the price level.*

7. If velocity were extremely volatile, why would this complicate the job of making monetary policy? *One of the roles of monetary policy is stabilization of the price level. Thus, based on the equation of exchange (MV = PQ), changes in the money supply will yield a given change in PQ if velocity (V) is constant. If velocity is volatile, changes in the money supply may be either too small or too large, leading to inflation.*

8. What role does the money multiplier play in enabling the Fed to conduct monetary policy? *The money multiplier times the change in excess reserves yields the change in the money supply. Thus, if the Fed wants to change the money supply by a given amount, the money multiplier indicates by how much the excess reserves need to be changed.*

9. What is the fed funds rate? *The interest rate that financial institutions charge other financial institutions for short-term borrowing*

10. What happens to the fed funds rate if the Fed follows a contractionary (tight money) policy? *The federal funds rate increases.*

11. What happens to the fed funds rate if the Fed follows an expansionary (easy money) policy? *The federal funds rate decreases.*

12. Why do observers pay close attention to the federal funds rate? *It is an early indicator of monetary policy and provides a forecast of the direction for other interest rates and for Fed policy.*

Interest Rates and Monetary Policy in the Short Run and the Long Run

Introduction and Description

This lesson explores the relationship between the nominal interest rate and the real interest rate, the implications for monetary policy, and the short-run and long-run effects of monetary policy on real output and the price level. The students need to understand the relationship between real and nominal interest rates because the real interest rate determines the level of investment, whereas the nominal interest rate determines the demand for money. Further, the Fisher Effect demonstrates how changes in the money supply affect the nominal interest rate in the long run. The discussion of the short-run and long-run effects on interest rates leads to the discussion of the effects of monetary policy in the short run and long run. Student understanding of the dynamics of the macroeconomic model over time is essential to explaining the effects of monetary policy on the economy.

Activity 41 helps the students gain an understanding of the difference between nominal interest rates and real interest rates, and the effect of monetary policy on both in the short and long run. Activity 42 is designed to bring the dynamic macroeconomic model together with monetary policy actions and to help the students integrate the effects of monetary policy in the short and long run with their understanding of how the economy works. This will help them to analyze current monetary policy and understand monetary policy discussions.

Objectives

1. Define the real interest rate and the nominal interest rate.
2. Explain the relationship among the real interest rate, the nominal interest rate and the inflation rate. This is also known as the *Fisher Equation*.
3. Explain the *Fisher Effect*, or how changes in the

money supply are transmitted to the nominal interest rate in the long run.
4. Explain the effects of monetary policy in the short run and the subsequent changes in the model as the economy moves to the long run. Define *neutrality of money*.

Time Required

Three class periods or 135 minutes

Materials

1. Activities 41 and 42
2. Visual 3.13

Procedure

1. Define the *nominal interest rate* and the *real interest rate*. The nominal interest rate is the rate that appears on the financial pages of newspapers and on the signs and ads of financial institutions. Emphasize that the real interest rate is the increase in purchasing power the lender wants to receive to forego consumption now for consumption in the future.

2. Stress that there are two relationships between the real and nominal interest rates. There is the *ex ante* real interest rate, which is the expected interest rate and equals the nominal interest rate minus the expected inflation rate. There is the *ex poste* real interest rate, which is the real interest rate actually received and equals the nominal interest rate minus the actual rate of inflation. The *ex poste* real interest rate will equal the *ex ante* interest rate if people accurately anticipate the inflation rate. The relationship between the real and nominal interest rate is called the Fisher Equation.

3. Explain the Fisher Effect. Locking at the equation of exchange, we see that changes in the money supply — holding velocity and real out-

put constant — lead to changes in the price level. These changes in the price level change the nominal interest rate once they are anticipated.

4. Have the students complete Activity 41, and review the answers with the students. Emphasize the need to be able to work through and explain exactly the transmission mechanism of money supply changes to changes in the economy. This is an area where students frequently miss points in answering questions on the Advanced Placement Examination.

5. Review the effects of increases and decreases in the money supply in the short-run aggregate supply and aggregate demand model.

6. Project Visual 3.13. Have the students work through and explain money supply changes in the aggregate demand and aggregate supply model over the long run. The students should be able to do more than simply shift the curves; they should be able to explain why the curves shift. Emphasize that changes in the money supply over time result in changes in the price level and no change in the output level. Monetary policy is *neutral*. The Appendix to Lesson 4 in Unit 3 graphically presents the shifts in SRAS and the movement from the short run to the long run.

7. Have the students complete Activity 42. Review the answers to Activity 42 with the students.

Real Interest Rates and Nominal Interest Rates

Figure 41.1
Real and Nominal Interest Rates

Year	Nominal Interest Rate	Inflation Rate	Real Interest Rate
1991	5.41%	3.12%	*2.29%*
1992	3.46	2.30	*1.16*
1993	3.02	2.42	*0.60*
1994	4.27	2.05	*2.22*
1995	5.51	2.12	*3.39*
1996	5.02	1.87	*3.15*
1997	5.07	1.85	*3.22*
1998	4.78	1.14	*3.64*
1999	4.64	1.56	*3.08*
2000	5.82	2.29	*3.53*
2001	3.39	1.96	*1.43*

1. Figure 41.1 provides the nominal interest rates and inflation rates for the years 1991 through 2001.

   (A) Compute the actual real interest rates for 1991 through 2001.

   (B) Graph the nominal interest rates and the actual real interest rates on Figure 41.2.

Figure 41.2
Real and Nominal Interest Rates

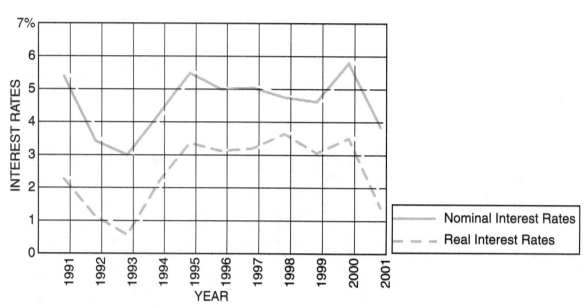

(C) Has the actual real interest rate stayed constant?___*No*___

(D) If it has not, explain why you think the real rate has not been constant. *The actual real interest rate has not been constant because the inflation rate has changed often. The money supply growth rate has also changed during the period shown in the graph.*

(E) For what years has the actual real interest rate remained nearly constant? *During the 1995 to 2000 period, the actual real interest rate fluctuated within a small range. The result is probably because of the reasonably steady inflation rate and the announced desire by the Fed to control inflation.*

2. Frequently, economists argue that the monetary authorities should try to maintain a steady real interest rate. Explain why you think a steady real rate of interest is important to the economy. *A steady interest rate is important to induce firms to invest and expand the capital stock.*

Figure 41.3
Expansionary Monetary Policy

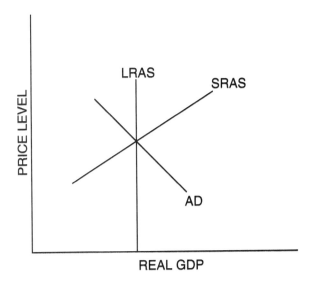

3. Suppose that initially the economy is at the intersection of AD and SRAS as shown in Figure 41.3. Now, the Fed decides to implement expansionary monetary policy to increase the level of employment.

(A) In the short run, what happens to real output? Explain why. *Real output should increase. With the decrease in interest rates because of the expansionary monetary policy, the interest rate sensitive components of aggregate demand (consumption and investment) will increase, thereby increasing output.*

(B) In the short run, what happens to the price level? Explain why. *The price level increases because the increase in demand can only be met if firms have the incentive to produce more. An increasing price level provides this incentive.*

(C) In the short run, what happens to employment and nominal wages? Explain why. *Employment increases and nominal wages remain the same. Employment increases because firms now have to produce more goods and services and they need people to do this. Nominal wages stay the same because people do not realize that the average price level has increased.*

(D) In the short run, what happens to nominal interest rates and real interest rates? *In the short run, the nominal and real interest rates decrease.*

(E) In the long run, what happens to real output? Explain why. *In the long run, the real output will be at the full-employment level. So real output will fall relative to the level of output in the short run. As employment increases, nominal wages increase, which raises the costs of production and the SRAS curve shifts to the left. The price level increases, and real output will fall back toward its original level.*

(F) In the long run, what happens to the price level? Explain why. *The price level rises in the long run because the SRAS curve shifted to the left in response to an increase in nominal wages.*

(G) In the long run, what happens to employment and nominal wages? Explain why. *Employment is at full employment and nominal wages have risen so that the real income of people has remained the same. To induce labor to work at the new higher level, firms must increase the nominal wage.*

(H) In the long run, what happens to the nominal interest rate and the real interest rate? *In the long run, the real interest rate goes to the long-run level and the nominal interest rate is the real interest rate plus the inflation rate. In the United States, the long-run real interest rate is about 2 percent to 3 percent.*

Monetary Policy

We now bring together all of the pieces of the process by which monetary policy is transmitted to the economy, and we examine both the short-run effects and the long-run effects of monetary policy.

 Figure 42.1
Effects of Monetary Policy

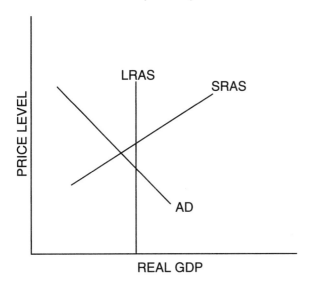

1. Suppose that initially the economy is at the intersection of AD and SRAS in Figure 42.1.

   (A) What monetary policy should the Fed implement to move the economy to full-employment output? _____*Expansionary monetary policy*_____

   (B) If the Fed is going to use open market operations, it should (*buy* / sell) Treasury securities.

   (C) What is the effect on Treasury security (bond) prices? *Bond prices should rise.*

   (D) In the short run, what is the effect on nominal interest rates? Explain. *Nominal interest rates should fall because financial institutions have more funds to lend out because people have sold their Treasury securities to the Fed.*

   (E) In the short run, what happens to real output? Explain how the Fed's action results in a change in real output. *Real output should increase. With the decrease in interest rates, the interest-rate sensitive components of aggregate demand (consumption and investment) will increase, thereby increasing output.*

UNIT
4 Macroeconomics   LESSON 6 ■ ACTIVITY 42   Answer Key

(F) In the short run, what happens to the price level? Explain how the Fed's action results in a change to the price level. *The average price level increases because the increase in demand can be met only if firms have the incentive to produce more. An increasing price level provides this incentive.*

✳ Figure 42.2
Moving to Full Employment

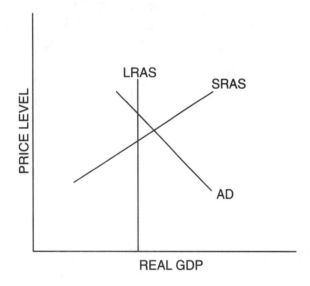

2. Suppose that initially the economy is at the intersection of AD and SRAS in Figure 42.2.

   (A) What monetary policy should the Fed implement to move the economy to full-employment output? _____*Contractionary monetary policy*_____

   (B) If the Fed is going to use open market operations, it should (*buy* / *sell)* Treasury securities.

   (C) What is the effect on Treasury security (bond) prices? *Bond prices will decline.*

   (D) In the short run, what is the effect on nominal interest rates? Explain. *In the short run, nominal interest rates will increase. When the public buys bonds, they pay for them by reducing their demand deposits, decreasing the supply of money, which means the interest rate will increase.*

   (E) In the short run, what happens to real output? Explain how the Fed's action results in a change in real output. *In the short run, real output will decline. As a result of the Fed's actions, interest rates have increased; therefore the interest-sensitive components of aggregate demand (consumption and investment) will decrease and thus, decrease aggregate demand. With a reduced aggregate demand, firms will experience an increase in inventories, which in turn leads to a decrease in production. Output decreases.*

572   Advanced Placement Economics Teacher Resource Manual © National Council on Economic Education, New York, N.Y.

(F) In the short run, what happens to the price level? Explain how the Fed's action results in a change to the price level. *The price level will fall as firms attempt to clear out inventory by reducing prices, having a sale.*

✴ Figure 42.3
Expansionary Monetary Policy

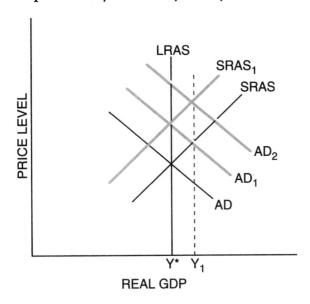

3. Suppose that in the situation shown in Figure 42.3, the aggregate supply and demand curves are represented by LRAS, SRAS and AD. The monetary authorities decide to maintain the level of employment represented by the output level Y_1 by using expansionary monetary policy.

(A) Explain the effect of the expansionary monetary policy on the price level and output in the short run. *In the short run, the monetary authorities (the Fed) will expand the money supply, which in turn increases the aggregate demand curve to AD_1. The price level and output increase.*

(B) Explain the effect on the price level and output in the long run. *The SRAS will shift leftward, leading to a decrease in output and an increase in price level. Given the Fed's desire to remain at Y_1, the Fed will continue to expand the money supply, shifting AD to AD_2. With the decrease in SRAS, the economy might be at a point like the intersection of AD_2 and $SRAS_1$. Thus, the price level will continue to rise and the economy will experience inflation.*

(C) Explain what you think will happen to the nominal rate of interest and the real rate of interest in the short run as the Fed continues to increase the money supply. Explain why.
In the short run, both the nominal interest rate and the real interest rate will decline. Consumers and financial intermediaries will not have correctly anticipated the inflation, and both interest rates will decline. As consumers and producers recognize that the price level is increasing, they will take steps to maintain their real income. Nominal wages will rise, and the nominal and real interest rates will start to rise.

(D) Explain what you think will happen to the nominal rate of interest and the real rate of interest in the long run. Explain why. *In the long run, the real interest rate will return to its long-run equilibrium, and the nominal interest rate will be the real interest rate plus inflation. Since inflation is increasing, the nominal interest rate will increase as well. Producers and consumers will adjust expectations to match reality.*

4. Many economists think that moving from short-run equilibrium to long-run equilibrium may take several years. List three reasons why the economy might not immediately move to long-run equilibrium.

Wages will adjust slowly to changes in prices (inflation) because of wage contracts.

Prices adjust slowly because business is slow to change prices to maintain customer loyalty.

Both labor and firms have inaccurate expectations about inflation.

5. In a short paragraph, summarize the long-run impact of an expansionary monetary policy on the economy. *In the long run, increases in the money supply translate into increases in the price level and no long-term increase in output. This is known as the neutrality of money. In the short run, nominal and real interest rates decline. In the long run, nominal interest rates follow the Fisher Equation and equal the real rate plus the inflation rate. Real interest rates return to their long-run level: the rate people require to forgo consumption now for consumption in the future.*

Answers to Sample Multiple-Choice Questions

1. *D*	8. *B*	15. *D*
2. *B*	9. *D*	16. *D*
3. *D*	10. *D*	17. *A*
4. *E*	11. *A*	18. *D*
5. *D*	12. *C*	19. *B*
6. *B*	13. *E*	20. *E*
7. *C*	14. *A*	

Answers to Sample Short Free-Response Questions

*1. The reserve requirement for the banking system is 20 percent. Currently Third National Bank has no excess reserves. Then Behroz deposits $100 in her checking account at Third National.

(A) Explain, without using a mathematical formula, why Behroz's deposit can lead to an increase in the money supply that is greater than $100. *The bank may make loans (or buy securities) based on excess reserves (80 percent of Behroz's deposit). The bank does make loans based on excess reserves, and the deposit created by the loan is redeposited in the banking system (fractional reserves). Answer must go one more step in loan and redeposit scenario: for example, show more than $100 of money created!*

Grading Rubric: Part (A) = 3 points

Loan equals deposit minus required reserves. (1 point)

Bank makes loan or buys securities. (1 point)

Loan is redeposited in banking system. (1 point)

(B) Discuss two limitations of this process.

The possible limitations to the process are

- *the bank willingly holds excess reserves.*
- *customers do not want to borrow.*
- *cash leakages.*

Grading Rubric: Part (B) = 2 points

One point for each correct limitation, up to two points.

Notes on scoring: Besides counting points, the answer may be looked at as a whole and ultimately judged by its overall quality. The final total should mean something in terms of the overall quality of the answer. A score of five points should reflect an excellent answer, but not necessarily perfect; four an excellent answer with a flaw; three a good answer; two an adequate answer; one a seriously deficient answer but still an answer; zero all else.

---

* Actual free-response question from a past AP test. Reprinted by permission of the College Entrance Examination Board, the copyright owner. For limited use by NCEE.

Advanced Placement Economics Teacher Resource Manual © National Council on Economic Education, New York, N.Y.

2. The Federal Reserve has three primary tools to expand or contract the money supply.

(A) List the three tools.

Open market operations (buying and selling Treasury securities)

Required reserve ratio

Discount rate

(B) Which tool does the Fed use most often? *Open market operations*

(C) Explain why the Federal Reserve uses the tool you indicated in Question 2(B).

With open market operations, the Fed has more immediate and more controlled influence on the money supply. If the money supply increases at a rate faster than output is increasing, it will be inflationary.

3. Milton Friedman has said, "Inflation is primarily a monetary phenomenon."

(A) Describe the conditions under which an increase in the money supply would be inflationary.

If the money supply increases at a rate faster than output is increasing, it will be inflationary.

(B) Use an aggregate supply and aggregate demand graph to show the conditions under which increases in the money supply are entirely inflationary.

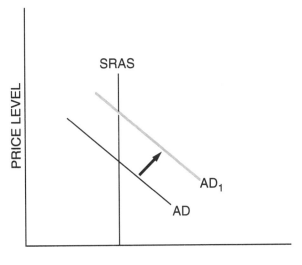

4. Explain the statement that the Federal Reserve can "target" the size of the money supply or the interest rate, but not both. *As we saw in our study of the money market, it is the interaction between the supply of money and the demand for money that determines the interest rate. The Fed controls the money supply. If the Fed targets the money supply, then as the demand for money changes, so will the interest rate. If the Fed targets the interest rate, it must change the money supply to adjust for changes in the demand for money to maintain the desired interest rate. Thus, the Fed cannot control both the money supply and the interest rate simultaneously.*

5. Suppose the required reserve ratio is 0.20.

   (A) What would be the value of the deposit expansion multiplier? ___5___

   (B) Discuss why it is unlikely that a new deposit of $1,000 to a checking account would result in the money supply fully increasing as indicated by the deposit expansion multiplier.
   Banks may choose to hold excess reserves, or borrowers may want fewer loans than banks have available. Or people may not redeposit the money in the banking system. Any one of these occurrences would limit the money expansion.

6. Banks can borrow reserves either at the federal funds rate or at the discount rate.

   (A) Define the federal funds rate. *The federal funds rate is the interest rate at which financial institutions can borrow short-term reserves from one another.*

   (B) Define the discount rate. *The discount rate is the interest rate at which financial institutions can borrow short-term funds from the Federal Reserve.*

   (C) Under what conditions would banks borrow at the discount rate? *In general, banks prefer to borrow in the federal funds market. Borrowing from the Federal Reserve, in general, means that the Federal Reserve will review the operations of the bank. Most banks would prefer not to come under this scrutiny. However, if the bank is able to loan the funds to earn a profit and the discount rate is much lower than the federal funds rate, or if the bank cannot borrow in the federal funds market, then the bank will borrow from the Federal Reserve.*

Answers to Sample Long Free-Response Questions

1. Suppose the economy is experiencing rising unemployment, slowing increases in real GDP and modest inflation. The Federal Reserve decides to follow an expansionary policy.

   (A) Describe what this policy might include. *The Federal Reserve could be buying bonds on the open market, reducing the discount rate or reducing the reserve requirement. Each of these actions is designed to stimulate an economy that is showing signs of entering a recession.*

   (B) If the policy is effective, explain the short-run effect it would have on each of the following:
      (i)   Interest rates
      (ii) Private investment
      (iii) GDP
      (iv) Employment

   These actions would
   (i)   reduce interest rates. More money is available for loans, and the price of this money would fall.
   (ii) With lower interest rates, investment and some consumption would increase.
   (iii) With an increase in investment and consumption, aggregate demand will increase and GDP will increase.
   (iv) As a result of the increase in aggregate demand and in GDP, employment will also increase to produce the larger output.

2. The Federal Reserve Board of Governors determines that it is currently appropriate to follow a contractionary policy.

(A) Use a correctly labeled aggregate demand and aggregate supply graph to illustrate the situation that would make this policy appropriate. *Graph must be properly labeled, showing output on the horizontal axis, price level on the vertical, an upward-sloping SRAS and some indication of potential. The intersection of SRAS and AD is beyond full employment or LRAS, illustrating an inflationary economy.*

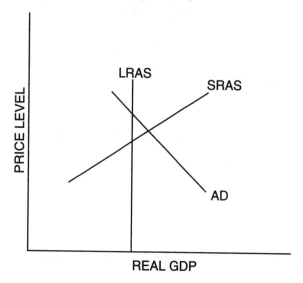

(B) Would the monetary policy be to increase or decrease the money supply? Explain. *The policy would be to reduce the money supply. By reducing the money supply, interest rates would rise and investment spending and other interest rate sensitive components of aggregate demand would decrease, reducing the upward pressure on prices. Or from the Monetarist view, the reduction in the money supply itself would reduce the price level (the SRAS being vertical, reduction in AD lowers price level).*

(C) Describe the policy the Federal Reserve is likely to take, and explain how its action achieves the goal of following a contractionary policy. Explain how the policy would affect each of the following:
(i)   Interest rates
(ii) Investment
(iii) Output
(iv) Price level
(v)   Employment

The Federal Reserve would most likely sell bonds on the open market, taking money directly and immediately out of circulation. Other actions the Federal Reserve could take are increasing the discount rate or raising the reserve requirement.

(i)   Any of these actions will cause interest rates to rise because the supply of money is decreasing.

(ii) As interest rates rise, investment looks less profitable and thus declines.

(iii) A decrease in investment leads to a decrease in AD. If the economy is on the upward-sloping portion of SRAS, output will decrease with the leftward shift of AD.

(iv) The goal of the policy is to lower the price level. On the upward-sloping SRAS, the price level will fall with less spending.

(v)   If on the upward-sloping SRAS, employment will decline with the decline in output.

UNIT
4 Macroeconomics
LONG FREE-RESPONSE
SAMPLE QUESTIONS
Answer
Key

3. Suppose the economy is at E in the graph below and the Federal Reserve decides to implement expansionary monetary policy to reduce the unemployment rate.

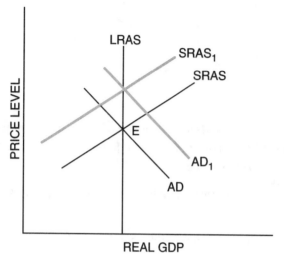

(A) Explain the short-run effect of the expansionary policy on each of the following:
  (i)   Nominal interest rates
  (ii) Real interest rates
  (iii) Output
  (iv) Price level
  (v)   Employment

The aggregate demand curve will shift to the right. See AD₁ in the graph. Nominal interest rates and real interest rates will decrease in the short run. The decrease in interest rates will lead to an increase in investment, which in turn increases aggregate demand. Output, the price level and employment will all increase.

(B) Explain the long-run effect of the expansionary policy on each of the following:
  (i)   Output
  (ii) Price
  (iii) Employment
  (iv) Nominal interest rates
  (v)   Real interest rates

In the long run, in response to the higher price level, workers will demand higher nominal wages. The higher nominal wages will increase the cost of production at every level of output, thus shifting the short-run aggregate supply curve to the left — shown in the graph above as SRAS₁. The higher costs of production resulting in higher prices will reduce the output demanded and, hence, reduce the level of employment. Over time, based on the Fisher Effect, the nominal interest rate will increase and equal the real rate of interest plus the inflation rate. The real interest rate will initially decrease and then return to its long-run equilibrium level.

Money Demand

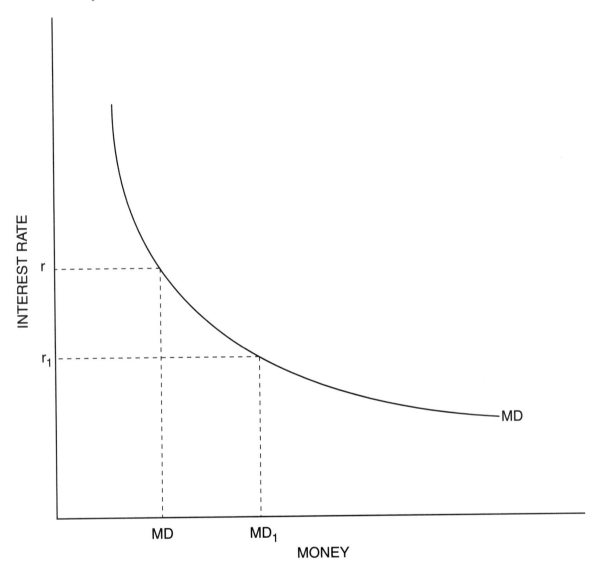

Factors Affecting Money Demand

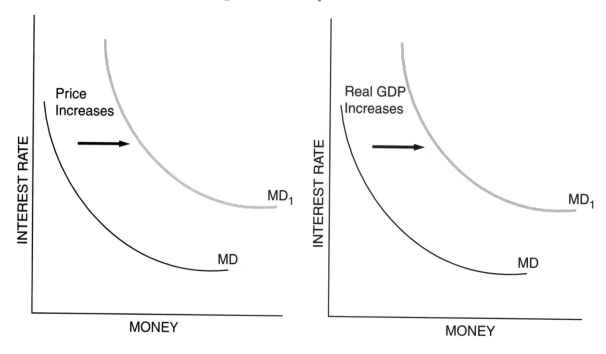

The Money Market

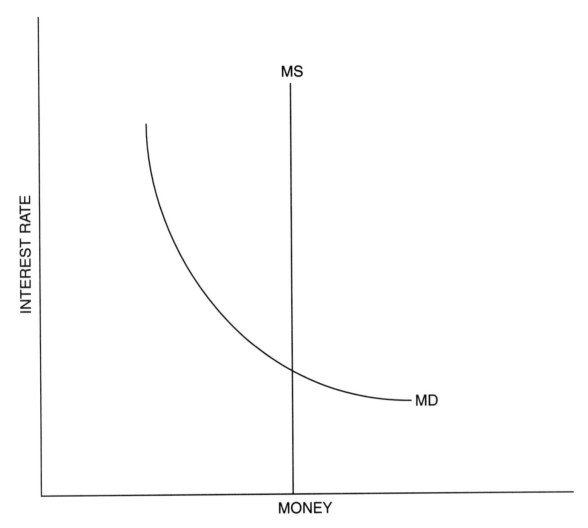

The Money Market, Investment and Aggregate Demand

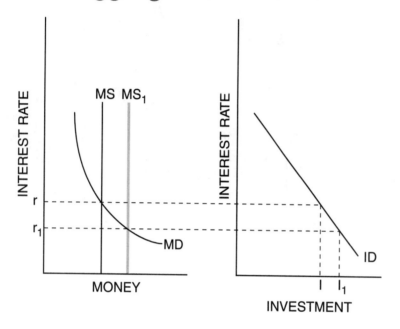
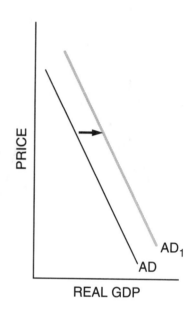

Monetary and Fiscal Policy Combinations: Stabilization Policy in the Real World

13 class periods or 585 minutes
(17 percent of course time)

Unit Overview

This unit brings the policy elements of Units 3 and 4 together, expands on related policy issues, introduces economic growth and provides the basis for policy discussions among economists.

Lesson 1 reviews monetary and fiscal policy tools and raises the issue of lags in policy decision making and implementation in the economy. The lesson continues with a discussion of crowding-out. Crowding-out is the primary argument some economists use to dismiss the effects of fiscal policy. The lesson then explores the interactions between monetary policy and fiscal policy. It explains different combinations of policies and their effects on the economy and explores the possibility of reinforcing or counteracting policies. The lesson then provides an examination of the short-run and long-run Phillips curve and the relationship to the aggregate demand and aggregate supply model. This policy section concludes with a discussion of the short-run and long-run effects of policy.

The second topic in this unit is economic growth, a long-run concept. What are the sources of economic growth? How do monetary and fiscal policies encourage economic growth? These are important policy issues that the students should be able to analyze. Economic growth determines our future standard of living, and the students need to understand that our future economic situation depends on current economic decisions.

Finally, this unit addresses the disagreements among economists about policy and explores the sources for the disagreements.

The Lesson Planner

Lesson 1 explains the lags associated with policy making, as well as the crowding-out effect. It uses **Activities 43** and **44** and **Visuals 5.1** and **5.2**.

Lesson 2 looks at the interaction of monetary and fiscal policies. It uses **Activity 45** and **Visual 5.3**.

Lesson 3 discusses the short-run and long-run Phillips curve and relates the Phillips curve to the aggregate demand and aggregate supply model. It uses **Activity 46** and **Visual 5.4**.

Lesson 4 examines the sources of economic growth and how monetary and fiscal policies contribute to long-term economic growth. It uses **Activity 47**.

Lesson 5 explains the reasons why there are differences among economists and the policies they advocate. It uses **Activity 48** and **Visuals 5.2, 5.3** and **3.13**.

Week 1

Day 1

(A) Review effects of monetary and fiscal policy on output, the price level and interest rates.

(B) Discuss lags associated with stabilization policy.

(C) Use Activity 43 to review monetary and fiscal policy.

Day 2

(A) Lecture on crowding-out, using Visual 5.1. Use aggregate demand and aggregate supply analysis to show the effects of crowding-out on output and the price level.

(B) Have the students do Part A of Activity 44 in class.

(C) Review Part A of Activity 44.

Day 3

(A) Use Visual 5.2 to discuss the loanable funds market.

(B) Have the students complete Activity 44 in class.

(C) Review Parts B and C of Activity 44.

Day 4

(A) Use Visual 5.3 to relate loanable funds, money markets and the economy.

(B) Lecture on monetary and fiscal policy interactions short run vs. long run.

(C) Have the students complete Activity 45 for homework.

Day 5

(A) Review Activity 45.

(B) Be sure that the students understand the relationships among the loanable funds market, the money markets, and the aggregate demand and aggregate supply model.

Week 2

Day 6

(A) Give a lecture on the short-run and long-run Phillips curve.

(B) Use Visual 5.4 to relate the Phillips curve and the economy, using aggregate demand and aggregate supply analysis.

Day 7

(A) Have the students complete Activity 46.

(B) Review Activity 46.

Day 8

(A) Lecture on economic growth, including sources of economic growth and measurement.

(B) Have the students complete Part A of Activity 47.

Day 9

(A) Review Part A of Activity 47.

(B) Review how policies affect the sources of economic growth and the effects on the production possibilities curve.

(C) Have the students complete Activity 47.

Day 10

(A) Review Parts B and C of Activity 47.

(B) Lecture on issues and sources of disagreement among economists, using Visuals 5.2 and 5.3.

(C) Have the students complete Activity 48.

Week 3

▩ Day 11

(A) Review Activity 48.

(B) Review for unit test.

▩ Day 12

Give multiple-choice portion of unit test.

▩ Day 13

Give free-response portion of unit test.

Policy Lags and Crowding-Out Effect

Introduction and Description

This lesson discusses the lags associated with monetary and fiscal policy making and analyzes the direct and indirect effects of government budget deficits. The direct effect of these deficits is an increase in interest rates. When the government borrows money to finance its deficit, this results in an increase in the demand for money, or, alternatively, the demand for loanable funds. This in turn results in an increase in the interest rate. A higher interest rate causes decreases in investment and other interest-sensitive components of aggregate demand. *Crowding-out* is the decrease in private demand for funds that occurs when the government's demand for funds causes the interest rate to rise: The demand by government for loanable funds decreases or *crowds-out* the private demand for loanable funds.

An indirect effect of government budget deficits is the possibility that these deficits will lead to an increase in private savings and a decrease in consumption that offset the predicted expansionary effects of expansionary fiscal policy. This is called the *Barro-Ricardo effect*.

Activity 43 should be used as a review of monetary and fiscal policy instruments and their effects on output and inflation. In Activity 44 the students work through the effects of crowding-out using both the money market and the loanable funds market.

Objectives

1. Explain inside and outside lags for monetary and fiscal policy.
2. Define the crowding-out effect.
3. Define the Barro-Ricardo effect.
4. Explain the effects of crowding-out within the short-run aggregate demand and aggregate supply model.
5. Explain how the Barro-Ricardo effect can

reduce the crowding-out effect while simultaneously reducing the effects of the fiscal policy.
6. Demonstrate the use of monetary policy to lessen or reinforce the crowding-out effect.

Time Required

Three class periods or 135 minutes

Materials

1. Activities 43 and 44
2. Visuals 5.1 and 5.2

Procedure

1. Discuss the lags associated with policy making. The *inside lag* consists of the time it takes for data to be collected, policy makers to recognize that policy action is necessary, the decision about which policy should be taken and the implementation of the policy. The *outside lag* is the time it takes the economy to respond to the new policy. These lags differ in length for monetary policy and fiscal policy.

2. Have the students complete Activity 43 and discuss the answers. Ask the students how the government could increase its spending (expansionary fiscal policy). This should lead to a discussion of increasing taxes or borrowing. This is an excellent opportunity to review the government spending multiplier and the tax-multiplier effects, which were introduced in Activity 21. Use the aggregate demand and aggregate supply graph to review the effects of monetary and fiscal policy on output and the price level.

3. Describe the sources of government borrowing: Treasury bills, notes or bonds. Describe the impact of government borrowing to finance an increase in spending. Use Visual 5.1 to show the interest-rate effect in the money market. Explain the impact on investment or other

interest-sensitive components of aggregate demand. Use an aggregate demand and aggregate supply graph to discuss the impact on the price level and real gross domestic product.

4. Reinforce the idea that, to this point, monetary policy has not changed; only fiscal policy became more expansionary. Ask whether the monetary authorities could do anything to prevent the reduction in investment.

5. Have the students complete Part A of Activity 44. Review Part A of Activity 44 with the students.

6. Project Visual 5.2. Describe the loanable funds market. Be sure to separate private and public demand for and supply of funds to this market. Note that the original demand curve is for the private sector only. At the beginning there is no borrowing or debt by the federal government. Show how an increase in government demand for funds crowds-out private investment. I_2 is the quantity of loanable funds demanded by the private sector at the new equilibrium because at i_1 (the equilibrium interest rate), I_2 is the quantity of investment funds the private sector demands, as shown by the private-sector demand curve.

7. Define the *Barro-Ricardo effect*. Use the loanable funds market graph to show the impact of the Barro-Ricardo effect. The supply curve for funds will shift rightward. The rightward shift in the supply curve reduces the increase in the interest rate and reduces the decrease in the private sector demand for funds. Thus, the crowding-out effect is reduced if there is a Barro-Ricardo effect. There is little evidence that the Barro-Ricardo effect is very large. However, crowding-out can be significant, depending on the elasticity of investment and interest-sensitive components of aggregate demand.

8. Have the students complete Activity 44. Review the answers to Parts B and C of Activity 44 with the students.

Monetary and Fiscal Policy

Part A
Tools of Monetary and Fiscal Policy

Both monetary and fiscal policy can be used to influence the inflation rate and real output. Indicate what effect each specific policy has on inflation and real output in the short run (nine to 18 months).

 Figure 43.1

Monetary Policy	Inflation	Real Output
1. (A) Buy government securities	*Increase*	*Increase*
(B) Sell government securities	*Decrease*	*Decrease*
2. (A) Decrease the discount rate	*Increase*	*Increase*
(B) Increase the discount rate	*Decrease*	*Decrease*
3. (A) Decrease reserve requirement	*Increase*	*Increase*
(B) Increase reserve requirement	*Decrease*	*Decrease*

Fiscal Policy	Inflation	Real Output
4. (A) Increase government spending	*Increase*	*Increase*
(B) Decrease government spending	*Decrease*	*Decrease*
5. (A) Increase taxes	*Decrease*	*Decrease*
(B) Decrease taxes	*Increase*	*Increase*

Part B
Lags in Policy Making

As the economic situation changes, policy makers must decide when to take action and which policy action to take. Then they must implement the policy. The economy then responds to the policy. The amount of time it takes policy makers to recognize and take action is called the *inside lag*. The amount of time it takes the economy to respond to the policy changes is called the *outside* or *impact lag*. The inside lag is estimated to be short for monetary policy but long for fiscal policy. The inside lag is long for fiscal policy because the legislative branch must come to agreement about the appropriate action. The outside lag, however, is long and variable for monetary policy but very short for fiscal policy.

6. Explain why the inside lag can be short for monetary policy but the outside lag is long and variable.
   The Federal Reserve can change the money supply on a daily basis through open market operations. Thus, once the Open Market Committee decides on a particular policy, the policy can be implemented immediately. However, monetary policy works through changes in interest rates and the response of interest-sensitive components of aggregate demand to the interest rate changes. The response of investment and consumption takes time.

7. Explain why the outside lag is short for fiscal policy. *The outside lag is short for fiscal policy for several reasons. (1) Fiscal policy has been debated in Congress and discussed extensively in the media. Thus, as soon as it is enacted, people can respond. (2) If the fiscal policy is a tax change, the effects will be felt within a year's time. (3) If the fiscal policy is an expenditure change, the effect will be felt almost immediately as the affected agency changes its spending pattern.*

8. Explain why lags are important to the discussion of stabilization policy. *The existence of policy lags implies that policy actions could be out of sequence with the economy. For example, expansionary policy might have its impact after the economy has started to recover from a recession. As a result, the expansionary policy may create inflation because it overstimulates the economy. This problem has led some economists to recommend policy rules. Examples of policy rules are that money supply should grow at 5 percent a year and nominal GDP should grow at 6 percent a year. There's a second reason why understanding lags is important for stabilization policy: Policy makers should not think that policy can fine-tune the economy at any point in time.*

Crowding-Out: A Graphical Representation

Part A
Using Aggregate Demand and Aggregate Supply Analysis

Figure 44.1
Crowding-Out Using Aggregate Demand and Aggregate Supply Analysis

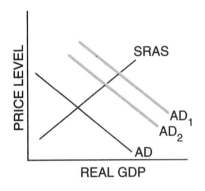 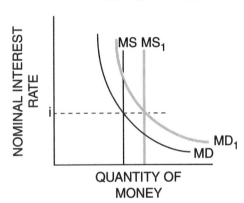

1. Assume fiscal policy is expansionary and monetary policy keeps the stock of money constant at MS. Shift one curve in each graph to illustrate the effect of the fiscal policy.

   (A) Which curve did you shift in the short-run aggregate demand and aggregate supply graph? What happens as a result of this new curve? *Shift the aggregate demand curve to AD$_1$, as a result of the expansionary fiscal policy. The price level and real GDP both increase.*

   (B) In the money market graph, which curve did you shift to demonstrate the effect of the fiscal policy? What happens as a result of this shift? *Shifted the money demand curve to the right; money demand increased because real GDP increased. Interest rates rise.*

(C) Given the change in interest rates, what happens in the short-run aggregate supply and aggregate demand graph? *Aggregate demand shifts back to AD_2 because the increase in interest rates reduces some private domestic investment and interest-sensitive consumer spending. This is crowding-out.*

(D) How could a monetary policy action prevent the changes in interest rates and output you identified in (B) and (C)? Shift a curve in the money market graph, and explain how this shift would reduce crowding-out. *Shift the money supply curve to MS_1. If the money supply is increased to MS_1, interest rates would move back to i. If interest rates are at i, there would be no crowding-out (or reduction) of investment spending, and the aggregate demand would be AD_1.*

Part B
Using the Loanable Funds Market

The loanable funds market provides another approach to looking at the effects of increases in the budget deficit. The *demand* for funds in the loanable funds market comes from the private sector (business investment and consumer borrowing), the government sector (budget deficits) and the foreign sector. The *supply* of funds in the loanable funds market comes from private savings (businesses and households), the government sector (budget surpluses), the Federal Reserve (money supply) and the foreign sector.

 Figure 44.2
Loanable Funds Market

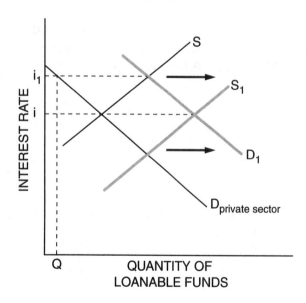

2. Shift one of the curves on Figure 44.2 to indicate what occurs in the loanable funds market if government spending increases without any increases in tax revenue or the money supply. *The demand increases, shifting the demand curve to D_1. D_1 represents the private plus public demand for loanable funds.*

(A) What happens to the interest rate as a result of this expansionary fiscal policy? Explain. *There is an increase in the demand for loanable funds to pay for the increased government spending. The interest rate rises to i_1.*

(B) Indicate on the graph the new quantity of private demand for loanable funds. *At the higher interest rate (i_1), the level of private demand for loanable funds is Q.*

(C) An accommodating monetary policy could prevent the effects you described in (A) and (B). Shift a curve in the diagram to show how the accommodating monetary policy would counteract the effects of crowding-out. Explain what would happen to interest rates and the level of private demand for loanable funds as a result of this new curve. *If the monetary authorities expanded the money supply to keep interest rates constant at the original level, a larger quantity of loanable funds would be available, and there would be no crowding-out. The new supply curve is S_1, interest rates return to i and the private sector receives the original level of loanable funds.*

Part C
Applications

3. Indicate whether you agree (A), disagree (D) or are uncertain (U) about the truth of the following statement and explain your reasoning. "Exhaustion of excess bank reserves inevitably puts a ceiling on every business boom because without money the boom cannot continue."
Uncertain. The answer depends on the assumptions that are made. The boom could continue to grow if the velocity of circulation increases. Increased demand for a fixed money stock would tend to increase interest rates, and increased velocity is associated with higher interest rates. However, the higher interest rates could cause investment to decrease and slow economic growth.

Answer the questions that follow each of the scenarios below.

4. The Federal Reserve Open Market Committee wishes to accommodate or reinforce a contractionary fiscal policy.

    (A) Would the Fed buy bonds, sell bonds or neither? *Sell bonds.*

    (B) What effect would this policy have on bond prices and interest rates? *Bond prices would decrease, and the interest rate would increase.*

    (C) What effect would this policy have on bank reserves and the money supply? *Bank reserves would decrease, and the money supply would decrease.*

    (D) What effect would this policy have on the quantity of loanable funds demanded by the private sector? *The bond sale would decrease the supply of loanable funds; the increase in the interest rate would decrease the quantity demanded of loanable funds (movement along the demand curve).*

    (E) What effect would the change in interest rates you indentified in (B) have on aggregate demand? *Aggregate demand would decrease because the higher interest rates would curtail the interest-sensitive components of consumption and investment.*

5. The Federal Reserve Open Market Committee wishes to accommodate or reinforce an expansionary fiscal policy.

    (A) Would the Fed buy bonds, sell bonds or neither? *Buy bonds.*

    (B) What effect would this policy have on bond prices and interest rates? *The price of bonds would increase, and the interest rate would decrease.*

    (C) What effect would this policy have on bank reserves and the money supply? *Bank reserves would increase and the money supply would increase.*

    (D) What effect would this policy have on the quantity of loanable funds demanded by the private sector? *The quantity demanded of loanable funds would increase.*

    (E) What effect would the change in interest rates you identified in (B) have on aggregate demand? *Aggregate demand would increase because of the lower interest rates and the resulting increase in interest-sensitive components of consumption and investment.*

Monetary and Fiscal Policy Interact

Introduction and Description

This lesson continues an examination of the interaction between monetary and fiscal policy in the short run. It examines the impact of monetary and fiscal policy on output, the price level, unemployment, interest rates and investment. Success on the Advanced Placement Examination depends on a student's ability to explain why economic variables are affected.

Activity 45 provides the students with an opportunity to work through the short-run effects of monetary and fiscal policy on important macroeconomic variables. The students continue to use the loanable funds market and the money market in this activity.

Objectives

1. Practice analytical skills with the AD and SRAS model and the money market.
2. Analyze the effects of combined monetary and fiscal policies on the loanable funds market.

Time required

Two class periods or 90 minutes

Materials

1. Activity 45
2. Visual 5.3

Procedure

1. Project Visual 5.3. Pose the following scenario: Suppose that, in response to the economic situation, the federal government decides to increase its spending without increasing taxes and the Fed keeps the money supply constant. There is no Barro-Ricardo effect. Explain what would happen in the three markets shown on the transparency.

   The aggregate demand curve should shift to the right. The students should then increase the demand for loanable funds by shifting the curve to the right. The demand for money should also shift to the right. The interest rates in the money market and loanable funds market should be equal.

2. Now ask what happened to each of the following variables and why:

   (A) Output (real GDP): *increased. Aggregate demand increased because of the increase in government spending.*

   (B) Employment: *increased. Aggregate demand increased because of the increase in government spending.*

   (C) Price level: *increased. Aggregate demand increased because of the increase in government spending.*

   (D) Interest rates: *increased. With the money supply held constant, the demand for money increased or the demand for loanable funds increased.*

   (E) Investment: *decreased because of the increase in interest rates*

3. Raise the issue of crowding-out. Have the students indicate how they know that crowding-out occurred. Have the students indicate on the loanable funds market graph the quantity of the federal government borrowing. Assume that there was no government borrowing prior to this.

4. Pose the following questions:

   (A) What could the Fed have done to prevent crowding-out? *The Fed could use expansionary monetary policy; thus the government's demand for funds would not result in an increase in interest rates.*

   (B) Are there certain conditions when the Fed should or should not prevent crowding-out? *If the economy were experiencing a recession, the Fed would want to prevent crowding-out, but if the economy were at or near full employment and government spending increased, the Fed might not want to prevent crowding-out.*

5. Have the students complete Activity 45 for homework.

6. Review Activity 45 with the students.

Graphing Monetary and Fiscal Policy Interactions

Illustrate the short-run effects for each monetary and fiscal policy combination using aggregate demand and supply curves, the money market and the loanable funds market. Once again, assume that there are no changes in the foreign sector. Circle the appropriate symbols (↑ for increase, ↓ for decrease, and **?** for uncertain), and explain the effect of the policies on real GDP, the price level, unemployment, interest rates and investment.

1. The unemployment rate is 10 percent, and the CPI is increasing at a 2 percent rate. The federal government cuts personal income taxes and increases its spending. The Fed buys bonds on the open market.

✳ Figure 45.1
Expansionary Monetary and Fiscal Policy

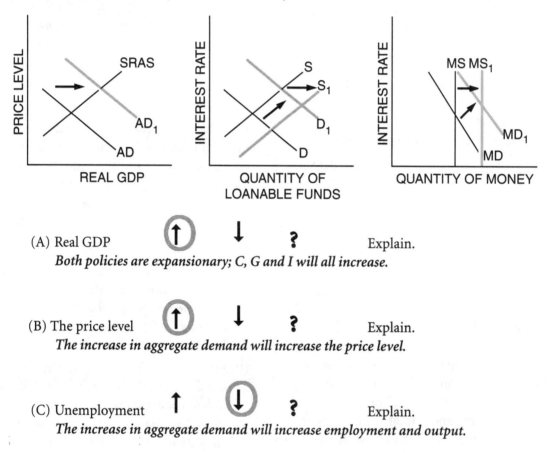

(A) Real GDP   (↑)   ↓   **?**   Explain.
Both policies are expansionary; C, G and I will all increase.

(B) The price level   (↑)   ↓   **?**   Explain.
The increase in aggregate demand will increase the price level.

(C) Unemployment   ↑   (↓)   **?**   Explain.
The increase in aggregate demand will increase employment and output.

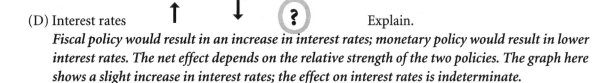

(D) Interest rates   ↑   ↓   (?)   Explain.
Fiscal policy would result in an increase in interest rates; monetary policy would result in lower interest rates. The net effect depends on the relative strength of the two policies. The graph here shows a slight increase in interest rates; the effect on interest rates is indeterminate.

(E) Investment   ↑   ↓   (?)   Explain.
Because we can't tell what happens to interest rates, we can't say what happens to investment because of changes in the interest rate.

2. The unemployment rate is 6 percent, and the CPI is increasing at a 9 percent rate. The federal government raises personal income taxes and cuts spending. The Federal Reserve sells bonds on the open market.

✳ Figure 45.2
Contractionary Monetary and Fiscal Policy

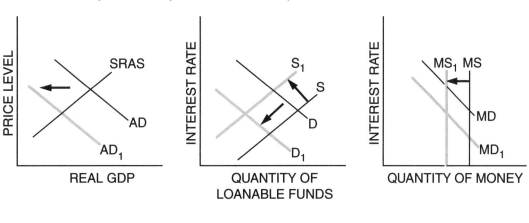

(A) Real GDP   ↑   (↓)   ?   Explain.
Decreased aggregate demand should lower GDP somewhat. AD decreases because of contractionary monetary and fiscal policy.

(B) The price level   ↑   (↓)   ?   Explain.
The decrease in aggregate demand should result in a lower price level.

(C) Unemployment ⬆ ⬇ ? Explain.
Lower output decreases employment on the SRAS curve.

(D) Interest rates ↑ ↓ ? Explain.
The Fed decreases the money supply, which should result in an increase in interest rates. The increase in taxes and decrease in government spending result in a decrease in interest rates since the demand for loanable funds by the government should decrease. The demand for money decreases because of the decrease in real GDP. Interest rates will be higher if the decrease in demand is less than the decrease in supply in the money market. The interest rate effect is indeterminate.

(E) Investment ↑ ↓ ? Explain.
If interest rates are higher, there would be a decrease in the level of investment. If interest rates are lower, there would be an increase.

3. The unemployment rate is 6 percent, and the CPI is increasing at a 5 percent rate. The federal government cuts personal-income taxes and maintains current spending. The Fed sells bonds on the open market.

Figure 45.3
Contractionary Monetary Policy and Expansionary Fiscal Policy

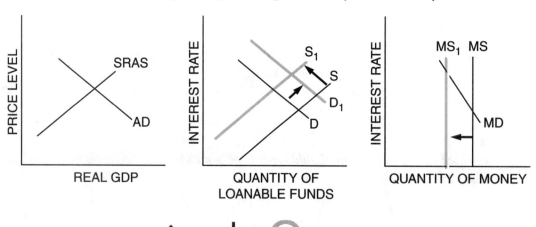

(A) Real GDP ↑ ↓ ? Explain.
The combined effect on aggregate demand is impossible to predict. The fiscal policy is expansionary, and the monetary policy is contractionary.

(B) The price level   ↑   ↓   (?)   Explain.

The impact on the price level is impossible to predict given the contradicting monetary and fiscal policies.

(C) Unemployment   ↑   ↓   (?)   Explain.

The impact on output and, hence, employment is impossible to predict given the contradicting monetary and fiscal policies.

(D) Interest rates   (↑)   ↓   ?   Explain.

Interest rates will rise because of the increased demand for and reduced supply of loanable funds.

(E) Investment   ↑   (↓)   ?   Explain.

The increase in interest rates will tend to decrease investment.

Phillips Curve and Stabilization Policy

Introduction and Description

The *Phillips curve* is an empirical relationship found by A.W. Phillips that shows the relationship between the unemployment rate and the rate at which wages change. He discovered that changes in wages were inversely related to the unemployment rate. Subsequent research established the same relationship between inflation and unemployment. During the 1960s, many economists and policy makers thought there was a consistent trade-off between price changes and unemployment. However, the trade-off is a short-run phenomenon, and inflationary expectations can shift the short-run Phillips curve. The long-run Phillips curve is a vertical line at the long-run aggregate supply curve.

In Activity 46, the students practice using the Phillips curve and the aggregate demand and aggregate supply model to investigate the effects of different economic scenarios in the short run and long run.

Objectives

1. Define the Phillips curve.
2. Demonstrate the short-run trade-off between unemployment and inflation.
3. Show how monetary and fiscal policy can help the economy move along the short-run Phillips curve.
4. Show how the short-run Phillips curve becomes a vertical long-run Phillips curve.

Time Required

Two class periods or 90 minutes

Materials

1. Activity 46
2. Visual 5.4

Procedure

1. Project Visual 5.4 and focus on the upper graph. The short-run Phillips curve (SRPC) shows the relationship between inflation and unemploy-

ment, holding the expected inflation rate and the natural rate of unemployment constant. Remember that the natural rate of unemployment is the rate of unemployment at full-employment output. Point A on the Phillips curve is the expected inflation rate-natural unemployment rate point. If there is an unanticipated increase in aggregate demand, then unemployment decreases and inflation increases: a movement up the Phillips curve toward Point A_2.

2. Focus now on the lower graph of Visual 5.4. The Phillips curve relationship can be explained using the aggregate demand and aggregate supply model. Suppose that aggregate demand and aggregate supply intersect at full employment. Suppose that aggregate demand is expected to increase. The AD curve shifts to AD_1. The money wage rate will rise because of the anticipated increase in prices: People want to maintain their real wage. The increase in the nominal wage rate shifts the SRAS to $SRAS_1$, and we are at Point A in both the Phillips curve graph and the AD and SRAS graph.

3. Now let's suppose that aggregate demand increases again. People thought AD would move to AD_1 but instead it increases to AD_2. The economy moves to Point A_2 in both graphs. Unemployment is below the natural rate, and inflation is above the expected rate of inflation. If policy makers attempt to keep the unemployment rate at the level associated with A_2, people will come to expect the inflation rate associated with A_2. As a result, the SRPC will shift upward and/or outward until the inflation rate associated with A_2 is at the natural rate of unemployment.

4. Ask the students what will happen if people expect the AD curve to increase and adjust their wages accordingly. But in reality AD does not

increase. *The economy moves to a point like A_3 in both figures.*

5. Summarize by saying that the short-run Phillips curve (SRPC) was drawn given an expected rate of inflation and a specific natural rate of unemployment. The SRPC will shift up if the expected inflation rate increases, as occurred in the 1970s. The SRPC will shift leftward if the natural rate of unemployment decreases.

6. Have the students complete Activity 46. Review the answers with the students.

Short-Run Phillips Curve

1. Suppose government policy makers want to increase GDP because the economy is not operating at its potential. They can increase aggregate demand by increasing government spending, lowering taxes or a combination of both. Using an AD and SRAS model, draw a new AD curve that will represent the change caused by government policy designed to increase real GDP.

Figure 46.2
Expansionary Fiscal Policy

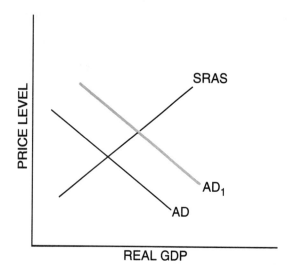

(A) What happens to the price level in the short run? _____*increases*_____

(B) What happens to real GDP in the short run? _____*increases*_____

(C) What happens to the rate of unemployment in the short run? _____*decreases*_____

(D) The Federal Reserve can use monetary policy to try to stimulate the economy. It can encourage bank lending by ____*purchasing*____ bonds on the open market, ____*decreasing*____ the discount rate, and/or ____*decreasing*____ the reserve requirements.

A Phillips curve would tell the same story. Inflation is low at high levels of unemployment, but inflation begins to increase as the unemployment rate decreases. The Phillips curve is useful for analyzing short-run movements of unemployment and inflation. See Figure 46.3.

2. Aggregate supply shocks resulting from the oil embargo imposed by Middle Eastern countries (OPEC) and worldwide crop failures helped to bring about higher inflation and higher unemployment rates. The economy, with rising prices and decreased output, was in a state of *stagflation*. Using an AD and SRAS model, draw a new SRAS curve that will represent the change caused by the OPEC oil embargo.

Figure 46.5
Effects of Oil Embargo

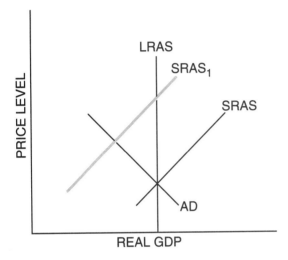

(A) In the short run, based on the new SRAS,

    (i)   what happens to the price level?____*increases*____

    (ii)   what happens to real GDP?____*decreases*____

    (iii) what happens to the rate of unemployment?____*increases*____

(B) As the economy moves to the long run,

    (i)   what happens to the wage rate? *The wage rate will decline in response to the increased unemployment rate.*

    (ii)   what happens to the price level? *The price level will return to the original level. As the wage rate declines, the SRAS shifts back toward the original SRAS.*

    (iii) what happens to real GDP? *The output level will eventually return to its original level.*

    (iv) what happens to the rate of unemployment? *The rate of unemployment will decline initially, then return to the original level of unemployment.*

3. Use the AD and SRAS model in Figure 46.6 to show the appropriate policy response to the oil-price increases in the following instances. Be sure to show on the graph the effects of the oil-price increase.

(A) If unemployment were the main concern of policy makers

(B) If inflation were the main concern of policy makers

(C) If inflation and unemployment were of equal concern

Figure 46.6
Policy Response to Oil Embargo

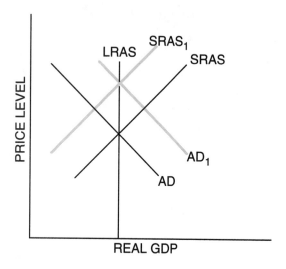

The increase in oil prices shifts the SRAS from SRAS to SRAS$_1$.

(A) If unemployment is the concern of policy makers, they will increase AD from AD to AD$_1$ using expansionary monetary and fiscal policy.

(B) If inflation is the concern, policy makers will probably maintain current policies and allow the self-correcting forces in the economy to move the economy back to the original price level and output.

(C) If inflation and unemployment are equally important, the authorities will carry out some expansionary policies but not to shift the aggregate demand as far as AD$_1$.

4. As inflation in the 1970s continued to increase, economists argued that, for a reduction in money growth to be fully effective in lowering inflation, the Federal Reserve would need to convince people it was serious about reducing money growth — in other words, the Fed would stick with a lower money growth policy until inflation decreased. Why would it be important for the Fed to establish this credibility? *If the public doesn't believe the Fed intends to maintain a low growth rate in the money supply, the public will simply demand higher wages, assuming the Fed will not be willing to live with a higher unemployment rate. The public expects continued inflation. The Fed would want to establish its credibility to reduce inflationary expectations and thus reduce wage demands.*

5. In 1980, the unemployment rate was no lower than it had been in 1960, but inflation was much higher. Between 1980 and 1982, the economy experienced a recession and unemployment rose. Explain the general effect of a recession on unemployment and inflation. Then explain why the recession of 1980-82 was accompanied by high inflation. *In general, if there are no policy changes, a recession will reduce inflation by decreasing the inflationary pressure of wage increases. During this period, the Fed did not accommodate the oil-price shocks and the economy sustained a high unemployment rate in conjunction with high inflation. This period lasted until the public believed that the Federal Reserve would not increase money growth to reduce unemployment. The public changed its inflationary expectations.*

6. Eventually the OPEC cartel was weakened, and energy prices decreased. Several U.S. industries, including communications and transportation, were deregulated. This caused greater competition. Explain and illustrate the effects of a weakened oil cartel and deregulation using both the aggregate demand and aggregate supply model and the Phillips curve. *A weakened oil cartel decreased energy prices and therefore production costs. Deregulation allows for greater competition, resulting in lower production costs and product prices. The short-run aggregate supply curve shifts to the right, and the short-run Phillips curve shifts to the left.*

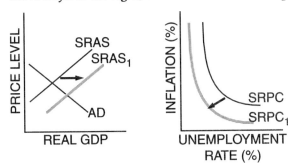

Economic Growth

Introduction and Description

In this lesson, the students learn the main sources of long-term economic or real GDP growth and the policies that governments might use to increase economic growth. The students should be aware that there is a difference between the short-term fluctuations in real GDP that result from the business cycle and the long-run growth in real GDP discussed here.

Activity 47 emphasizes the alternative measures of output growth and incorporates long-run economic growth into the aggregate demand and aggregate supply models. The activity also brings in the production possibilities curve discussed at the beginning of the course.

Objectives

1. Describe long-term growth trends in the United States.
2. Explain growth accounting.
3. Explain that growth accounting shows that to achieve increased economic growth, economies must increase the growth rate of capital stock or increase technological development.
4. Explain how policy can help achieve increases in the growth rate of the capital stock and increases in technological development.
5. Relate economic growth to the long-run aggregate supply curve and the production possibilities curve.

Time required

Two class periods or 90 minutes

Materials

Activity 47

Procedure

1. Summarize the long-term growth trend of the United States. The average growth rate in per-

capita real GDP has been above 2 percent a year for the last four decades. However, the annual rate of growth has varied considerably during this same period. The increase in the average standard of living represented by the increase in per capita real GDP is important. The distribution of the increase in real GDP is also important.

2. Explain that for growth to occur, economic agents — producers and consumers — must have the appropriate incentives. *Growth accounting* focuses on three sources of long-run economic growth: supply of labor, supply of capital and the level of technology. Increases in any one of these elements will increase real GDP. The growth in the supply of labor is primarily the population growth rate. Increases in capital or in technology increase labor productivity and thus increase real GDP. Have the students complete Part A of Activity 47. Review the answers with the students.

3. Explain how these *levers of growth* can be stimulated.

   (A) Increasing savings will increase the supply of loanable funds, decrease interest rates and spur investment or increases in the capital stock. In the United States, tax incentives are the principal method to increase savings. IRAs and Roth IRAs are examples. During the 1970s and 1980s, stockholders in gas and electric utility companies received a tax break if they reinvested their dividends in the companies.

   (B) Increasing government support for basic research will stimulate research and development. National Science Foundation grants are one mechanism used in the United States.

   (C) Getting the most from comparative advantage by encouraging international trade will also stimulate growth throughout the world.

(D) Growth can also be stimulated by improving the quality and capabilities of the labor force so workers can be more productive with a given level of capital and technology. Improving the quality of education is the primary tool used here. The United States has focused on improving the quality of public education and, using education IRAs, provides incentives for people to obtain more education.

4. Now relate the changes in the labor force and technology to the assumptions underlying a production possibilities curve (see Unit 1).

Increases in the labor force and advances in technology can be shown as an outward shift in the PPC or as an outward shift in the LRAS. Both shifts demonstrate that total output has increased.

5. Have the students complete Question 5 on Activity 47. Be sure they draw the curves on Figure 47.5. Go over the answers and discuss the relationship between shifts of the LRAS curve and shifts of the PPC curve.

6. Have the students complete Activity 47. Review the answers with the students.

Economic Growth and the Determinants of Productive Capacity

Part A
Measuring Economic Growth in Hamilton County and Jefferson County

 Figure 47.1

Year	Hamilton Real GDP	Hamilton Population	Jefferson Real GDP	Jefferson Population
1	$2.1 billion	70,000	$500,000	15
2	2.5 billion	80,000	525,000	16
3	2.8 billion	90,000	600,000	17
4	2.7 billion	86,000	650,000	18

1. Using Figure 47.1 as a reference, fill out the tables in Figures 47.2, 47.3 and 47.4.

 Figure 47.2

Time period	Hamilton % Change in Real GDP	Jefferson % Change in Real GDP
From Year 1 to Year 2	19%	5%
From Year 2 to Year 3	12%	14.3%
From Year 3 to Year 4	−3.6%	8.3%

 Figure 47.3

Year	Hamilton Per Capita Real GDP	Jefferson Per Capita Real GDP
1	$30,000	$33,333.33
2	31,250	32,812.50
3	31,111	35,294.12
4	31,395	36,111.11

 Figure 47.4

Time period	Hamilton % Change in Per Capita Real GDP	Jefferson % Change in Per Capita Real GDP
From Year 1 to Year 2	4.17%	−1.6%
From Year 2 to Year 3	−0.44%	7.56%
From Year 3 to Year 4	0.91%	2.31%

Advanced Placement Economics Teacher Resource Manual © National Council on Economic Education, New York, N.Y.

2. When did Hamilton County experience the largest growth in real GDP? *From Year 1 to Year 2*

   In per capita real GDP? *From Year 1 to Year 2*

   Are these growth rates different? Explain. *Both increased the most from Year 1 to Year 2. However, per capita real GDP increased by less than real GDP because of population growth.*

3. When did Jefferson County experience the largest growth in real GDP? *From Year 2 to Year 3*

   In per capita GDP? *From Year 2 to Year 3*

   Are these growth rates different? Explain. *The per capita growth rate is smaller than the GDP growth rate because the population has increased.*

4. The residents of Hamilton County believe they live in a wealthier community than small rural Jefferson County. Based on these numbers, do they? Explain. *No. Real GDP per capita is larger in Jefferson County than in Hamilton County.*

Part B
Analyzing the Reasons for Economic Growth

Economic growth can be illustrated by a rightward shift of the long-run aggregate supply curve or a shift outward of the production possibilities curve of consumption goods vs. capital goods.

5. Draw a graph that includes AD, SRAS and LRAS and then draw a graph of a PPC.

✳ Figure 47.5
Relationship Between LRAS and PPC:
Increased Investment in Education

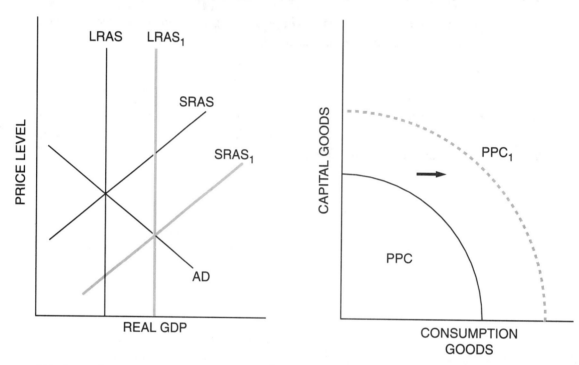

(A) On each graph you drew, show the effect of an increased investment in education that makes the work force more productive. Explain your reasoning. *Both long-run and short-run aggregate supply increase. The PPC shifts outward. The increase in education makes the labor force more productive with the same natural resources. This means that workers can produce more, thus increasing real GDP.*

(B) Of the five factors that affect economic growth, which factor is increased by this investment in education? *Human resources or human capital*

6. Explain how fewer government regulations will affect economic growth. Cite an example to support your explanation. Show the effect of fewer government regulations on the graphs in Figure 47.6.

❋ Figure 47.6
**Relationship Between LRAS and PCC:
Fewer Government Regulations**

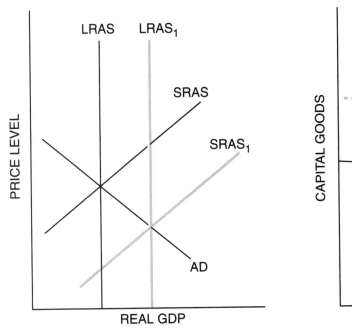
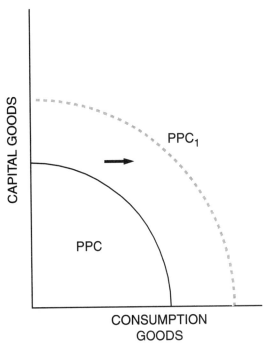

A reduction in government regulation will reduce the cost of production for firms. This will result in an increase in production at every price level, causing increases in short-run and long-run aggregate supply. The PPC curve will shift outward. Examples are a decrease in regulation of environmental pollution or a reduction in the required testing for new drugs.

7. Briefly explain how the following policies will affect economic growth and why.

(A) Higher taxes on businesses
   Economic growth would decrease because firms have fewer resources to invest in producing more products or in providing educational opportunities for employees.

(B) Improvements in technology

Economic growth should increase. Firms should be able to produce more with fewer resources.

(C) Less savings by people who want to enjoy the good life

Consumption expenditures increase, reducing the level of capital goods; thus, future production is reduced.

(D) Higher productivity of labor because of improved management styles

Economic growth would increase because labor can produce more with the same inputs.

(E) Lower interest rates

Lower interest rates sustained over time will encourage investment, which will increase the capital stock, and encourage people to invest in education.

Macroeconomic Theories

Introduction and Description

Listening to and reading analysis of the various policy proposals can confuse students who are learning economics for the first time. Here the current issues and sources of disagreement among economists should be presented. The students should recognize that most economists hold views that cannot be categorized into a particular school of thought but are a combination of different schools.

Activity 48 pulls many policy concepts together and serves to review and summarize stabilization policy.

Objectives

1. Explain the different types of lags in making policy and that there are different estimates about the length of these lags.
2. Describe the idea of crowding-out and that the extent of crowding-out can change depending on the responses of interest rates, consumption spending and business investment.
3. Explain the reasons why prices and wages do not adjust instantaneously.
4. Provide examples of conflicts among attaining economic goals.

Time Required

One class period or 45 minutes

Materials

1. Activity 48
2. Visuals 5.2, 5.3 and 3.13

Procedure

1. Give a lecture on the different lags in making policy: *inside lag, outside lag, recognition lag, decision* or *response lag,* and *transmission* or *impact lag.*

    (A) Recognition lag: the time it takes for policy makers to see that there is a problem with the economy. In general, the recognition lag is three to six months.

    (B) Decision or response lag: the time it takes policy makers to decide and implement the policy response to the current economic problem. This lag differs between monetary and fiscal policy. The monetary policy decision lag is usually very short (one quarter), while the fiscal policy decision lag can be several quarters to more than a year. These combined lags make up the inside lag referred to in Lesson 1 of this unit.

    (C) The transmission or impact lag (the outside lag): the time it takes the change in policy to have an effect on the economy. The transmission lag for monetary policy is long and variable because the change in the money supply affects interest rates, which in turn affect interest-rate sensitive components of aggregate demand. The transmission lag for fiscal policy in general is very short because fiscal policy is discussed in the media throughout the implementation process. People are ready to adjust as soon as the policy is enacted or may even act on the probability of enactment.

2. Use Visuals 5.2 and 5.3 to review the crowding-out effect: the impact of government borrowing to finance increases in government expenditure.

3. Discuss the reasons why prices and wages do not adjust quickly:

    (A) Menu costs: it costs firms money to change their prices — for example, to issue new catalogs or change price tags.

    (B) Labor contracts: multiyear contracts prohibit rapid changes in wages and may mandate cost-of-living-adjustments (increases to match inflation).

(C) Firms operating in imperfectly competitive markets worry about changing prices and getting into price wars with their competitors. Thus, firms may be slow to adjust prices to changes in costs or demand.

4. Review the dynamic macroeconomic model. Use Visual 3.13 to show that if the economy is already at full employment but policy makers think the unemployment rate is too high and carry out expansionary monetary policy, inflation will result. This demonstrates the conflict between the full-employment goal and the price stability goal. Another conflict to discuss might occur between the long-run economic growth goal (low real interest rates) and the price stability goal.

5. Have the students complete Activity 48 in groups during class and discuss the different views.

Why Economists Disagree

Part C
Analyzing Disagreements Among Economists

Professor T.X. Cut

Major point: *Tax cut will stimulate economy.*

Time period: *Present and near future (short run)*

Assumptions: *The administration's budget proposals are not inflationary because tax cuts balanced big spending cuts. Unemployment needs to decrease during a recession.*

Theoretical support: *Tax cuts stimulate business investment, as well as spending by all of the private sector and may encourage greater work effort.*

Values: *Economic freedom and distrust of big government*

Professor U.R. Nutts

Major point: *Higher interest rates will cause recovery to fail.*

Time period: *Next year (medium term)*

Assumptions: *Increases in government spending drive up interest rates, which in turn decreases private investment and interest rate sensitive components of consumption.*

Theoretical support: *Government borrowing is so large that it causes interest rates to rise and crowds-out consumer and business borrowing.*

Values: *Tax cuts must be fair, and fairness means taxing the wealthier more than the poorer. Government must maintain economic security for Americans with low incomes.*

Professor E.Z. Money

Major point: *Relatively free expansion of money will bring down interest rates and sustain recovery.*

Time period: *Near future (short run)*

Assumptions: *Relatively free expansion of money supply by Fed will sustain the recovery. Fed will support expansionary fiscal policy.*

Theoretical support: *Lower interest rates increase consumer spending and business investment. The primary effect of lower interest rates is on investment. Growth is more important than inflation.*

Values: *A growing economy is desirable.*

Professor Fred Critic

Major point: *There will be another recession. Fed will continue past policies — policies that have brought about periods of inflation and recession.*

Time period: *One to two years from now (long run)*

Assumptions: *Discretionary monetary policy is destabilizing because of the lags in policy and the inability to predict accurately the precise impact of changes in money supply on the economy.*

Theoretical support: *Not enough money growth causes recession; too much money growth causes inflation.*

Values: *Steady economic growth without inflation or recession is desirable.*

Advanced Placement Economics Teacher Resource Manual © National Council on Economic Education, New York, N.Y.

Answers to Sample Multiple-Choice Questions

1.	D	8.	B	15.	D
2.	B	9.	C	16.	B
3.	C	10.	D	17.	D
4.	E	11.	B	18.	D
5.	E	12.	B	19.	C
6.	D	13.	C	20.	E
7.	B	14.	A		

Answers to Sample Short Free-Response Questions

1. Using monetary and fiscal policies, outline an expansionary policy that would encourage long-run growth and explain why the policies will encourage this growth. *To encourage long-run growth, an expansionary policy should stimulate investment as much as possible. An expansionary monetary policy (lower discount rate, lower reserve requirement, buy bonds on the open market) will lower the interest rate and thus encourage investment. To stimulate investment, an expansionary fiscal policy should be directed toward business tax deductions. For these business tax deductions to have their full effect on investment, monetary policy would be needed to keep interest rates low. A combination of cutting business taxes and expanding the money supply will be good for economic growth.*

2. Some economists want to decrease government spending to reduce government budget deficits. Other economists want to reduce the size of the deficit by raising taxes. Compare these two points of view using aggregate supply and demand analysis. Illustrate the effects of each program using a correctly labeled aggregate demand (AD) and short-run aggregate supply (SRAS) graph.

Graph A

Graph B

- *Reducing government spending has a more powerful effect on aggregate demand than increasing taxes.*

- *Raising taxes reduces the level of disposable income, which means less consumption and less savings, depending on the marginal propensities to consume and save. Only the consumption reduction will be subject to the multiplier. Raising taxes will reduce aggregate demand.*

- *The effect of lower aggregate demand depends on the economy's position on the aggregate supply curve. The policy could reduce output, price level or both. Graph A indicates a reduction in both the price level and output.*

- *Increasing taxes might also decrease aggregate supply by decreasing people's incentive to work, save and invest, as shown in Graph B. The result is an increase in the price level and a decrease in output, also shown in the graph. Thus the tax increase may affect both aggregate demand and short-run aggregate supply. If so, the output level will fall, but the effect on the price level is indeterminate.*

3. Why is there a conflict between the Fed's attempts to control both the money supply and the interest rate? What is the implication of the Fed's attempt to control the money supply? *The interest rate is determined by the interaction between the supply of and demand for money in the money market. The supply of money is primarily controlled by the Fed; the demand for money is a function of the liquidity preferences of the private sector (households and businesses) and the public sector (governments). Thus, the Fed can either expand (or contract) the money supply to control the interest rate, or it can control the growth in the money supply and let the interest rate be established by the interaction of the money supply and money demand. When the Fed controls the money supply, the interest rate is allowed to fluctuate depending on the demand for money. If the interest rate fluctuates too much, this can lead either to fluctuations in investment or to a reduced level of business investment because of the uncertainty associated with interest rates. Fluctuations in investment can cause business cycles.*

4. Discuss the trade-off between unemployment and inflation in the short run. Why does this trade-off pose a dilemma for policy makers? What trade-off exists between inflation and unemployment in the long run? *The Phillips curve indicates that there is an inverse relationship between unemployment and inflation. The higher unemployment rate is associated with a lower inflation rate. The higher inflation rate is associated with a lower unemployment rate. This trade-off occurs because of the effects of aggregate demand on output, price level and employment. Increasing aggregate demand causes an increase in output and employment, but puts upward pressure on prices. Decreasing aggregate demand reduces inflation but can also decrease output and employment. The dilemma for policy makers is identifying which is more critical: inflation or unemployment. Even after the problem is identified, it is difficult to devise a strategy that corrects it: Too great a policy response could shift the trade-off back in the opposite direction.*

Most economists believe that the Phillips curve is vertical in the long run. Therefore, there is no trade-off between inflation and unemployment in the long run: As aggregate demand changes, only the price level changes.

5. As the national debt grows, one of the negative effects is crowding-out. Explain the meaning of this term. Identify two sectors of the economy that are involved in this crowding-out. Explain the activities of these two sectors, and show how they interact to create the crowding-out effect. Use a money market or loanable funds market graph to show crowding-out. Use an aggregate demand and aggregate supply graph to show the effects on the economy.

Graph A   Graph B

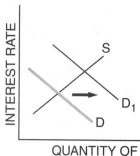
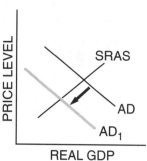

- *Greater borrowing by the federal government increases the demand for loanable funds, which will, other things constant, raise interest rates. These higher rates make it more expensive for consumers and businesses to borrow money, thus crowding them out of the market for loanable funds. Consumption (big-ticket items such as cars and homes) and investment such as new capital goods purchases will be reduced and aggregate demand will decrease.*

- *A reduction in investment also lowers the productive capacity of the economy in the future. Some of the positive effects of the expansionary fiscal policy are wiped out. Graph B shows the decrease in aggregate demand.*

- *Higher government demand for funds increases the demand for loanable funds and crowds-out private investment because of higher interest rates. This is shown in Graph A.*

Note, this crowding-out can also be shown in the money market by an increase in the demand for money, which raises interest rates (see Activity 44).

6. Explain the effects on long-term economic growth of using fiscal policy to fight recession and monetary policy to fight inflation.

- *Using expansionary fiscal policy to fight recession includes lowering taxes and increasing government spending. This strategy will cause crowding-out when government borrowing to cover the budget deficit raises the demand for loanable funds and, hence, interest rates rise. When interest rates rise, investment falls and reduces long-run economic growth.*

- *By using contractionary monetary policy, the Federal Reserve causes a decrease in the money supply. If the demand for money is constant, this new decrease in the money supply will force interest rates upward, and investment will be lower. When investment falls, long-run economic growth is reduced.*

*7. Using the aggregate supply and aggregate demand model, explain how the use of monetary policy to promote long-run economic growth will affect each of the following:

(A) Short-term interest rates

Expansionary monetary policy will decrease short-term interest rates by increasing the money supply. (1 point)

(B) The composition (mix) of aggregate expenditures

The decrease in interest rates results in an increase in investment and other interest-sensitive expenditures. The composition of GDP changes with the increase in investment. (2 points)

1 point: The decrease in interest rates increases investment and other interest-sensitive expenditures.

1 point: The increase in investment increases the investment component of aggregate expenditures relative to other components. There is a shift of the aggregate demand curve to the right because of the increase in investment.

(C) Potential gross domestic product

The increase in investment increases the capital stock, resulting in a rightward shift of the aggregate supply curve and an increase in potential GDP (rightward shift of LRAS). (2 points)

1 point: Shift in SRAS curve to the right

1 point: Increase in potential GDP; shift LRAS to right

---

*Actual free-response question from a past AP test. Reprinted by permission of the College Entrance Examination Board, the copyright owner. For limited use by NCEE.

Answers to Sample Long Free-Response Questions

*1. Suppose that the following statements describe the current state of an economy:

■ The unemployment rate is 5 percent.

■ Inflation is at an annual rate of 10 percent.

■ The prime interest rate is 11.5 percent.

■ The annual growth rate of real gross domestic product is 5 percent.

(A) Identify the major problem(s) the economy faces.

Inflation (1 point)

(B) Describe two fiscal policy actions that could be used to alleviate the problem(s). Using the aggregate supply and aggregate demand model, explain how the actions you identified will affect each of the following. Illustrate with a graph.

(i) Output and employment

(ii) The price level

(iii) Nominal interest rates

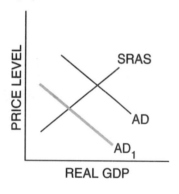
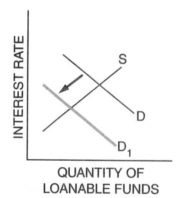
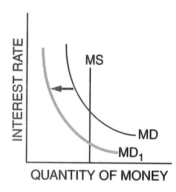

Decreasing government spending and increasing taxes are two fiscal policies that could allevi-ate the problem. A decrease in G will directly decrease AD. An increase in taxes will decrease C (or I if corporate taxes are discussed) and directly decrease AD. Output, employment and prices will decline. Interest rates will decline because (1) a decrease in government spending reduces the demand for funds in the bond market, and/or (2) decrease of income decreases the demand for money. Alternatively, if the student demonstrates an understanding of the rela-tionship between the inflation rate and the nominal interest rate and states that the reduction in inflation will reduce nominal interest rates, the answer may get credit. It will not receive credit, however, if the student states that high nominal rates are part of the problem in Part A.

---

*Actual free-response question from a past AP test. Reprinted by permission of the College Entrance Examination Board, the copy-right owner. For limited use by NCEE.

Advanced Placement Economics Teacher Resource Manual © National Council on Economic Education, New York, N.Y.

The student should show the effect of the fiscal policies in the aggregate demand and aggregate supply graph. The student can then go on to show the effect on interest rates using either the loanable funds market or the money market.

Grading Rubric: 4 points

1 point: Two correct fiscal policies ($1/2$ point for each policy)

1 point: AD decreases with an explanation of either the decrease in G or the increase in taxes is sufficient.

$1/2$ point: Output and employment decrease.

$1/2$ point: Price level decreases.

1 point: Nominal interest rates decline, with explanation.

(C) Instead of using fiscal policy to solve the country's problem(s), use only monetary policy. Describe two monetary policy actions that could be used to alleviate the problem(s). Using the aggregate supply and aggregate demand model, explain how the actions you identified would affect each of the following. Illustrate with a graph.

(i)   Nominal interest rates

(ii) Output and employment

(iii) The price level

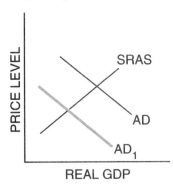
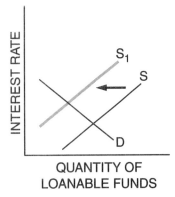
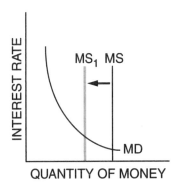

The student shows the effect of the monetary policies in the aggregate demand and aggregate supply graph. The student can then go on to show the effect on interest rates using either the loanable funds market or the money market.

The response must include two of the following monetary policies: selling government securities (OMO), increasing the reserve requirement, increasing discount rate, moral suasion, etc. Policies must be contractionary. The decrease in the money supply will result in an increase in the interest rate, which in turn decreases investment and/or interest-sensitive components of spending. The decrease in investment decreases AD, which drives employment, output and prices down.

The student should show the effect of the monetary policies on interest rates using either the loanable funds market or the money market. The student should show the effect of the monetary policies on the aggregate demand and aggregate supply graph.

Grading Rubric: 4 points

1 point: Two correct monetary policies (1/2 point per policy)

1 point: Increase in interest rate → Investment and other interest-sensitive expenditures decline, with correct explanation

1 point: Decrease in AD because of investment decline

1 point: Decrease in employment, output and price level

*2. Suppose that the following conditions describe the current state of the U.S. economy:

- The unemployment rate is 5 percent.

- Inflation is 2 percent.

- Real gross domestic product is growing at the rate of 3 percent.

(A) First, assume that the federal government increases its spending and increases taxes to maintain a balanced budget. Using aggregate supply and aggregate demand analysis, explain the short-run effects of these policies on each of the following:

   (i)   Output and employment

   (ii) The price level

   (iii) Interest rates

We would like the students to recognize that there is a balanced-budget multiplier effect so that this policy change will have a net positive impact on the AD curve. However, since we expect the students to address the increase in government spending and increase in taxes separately, we have set the grading standards to allow for partial credit for each change, with full credit given only if they show and/or explain that there is a net positive effect on AD. For full credit, the student must explain the interest rate effect.

Grading Rubric: 4 points

1 point: If the student shows or explains that the increase in G causes an increase in AD, which causes an increase in GDP and an increase in the price level

1 point: If the student shows or explains that increases in taxes cause a decrease in AD that causes a decrease in GDP and decrease in P. Alternatively, if the student asserts that the increase in G and increase in taxes have offsetting effects without discussing the effects on AD explicitly, give 1 point.

1 point: For explicit discussion of the balanced-budget multiplier or alternative explanation that shows the student understands that the positive effect of increases in G on AD exceeds the negative effect of increases in taxes on AD

1 point: Interest rate effect — they must explicitly state that there will be an increase in interest rates from the increase in the demand for money because of the increased output.

*Actual free-response question from a past AP test. Reprinted by permission of the College Entrance Examination Board, the copyright owner. For limited use by NCEE.

UNIT
5 Macroeconomics
LONG FREE-RESPONSE
SAMPLE QUESTIONS
Answer
Key

(B) Now assume instead that the Federal Reserve buys bonds on the open market. Analyze the impact of this action on each of the following:

(i)   Interest rates

(ii) Output and employment

(iii) The price level

The Federal Reserve buys bonds in OMO, thereby increasing the money supply. Interest rates decline because (1) the price of bonds increases or (2) more loanable funds are available. The decrease in interest rates stimulates investment and perhaps consumption spending, resulting in an increase in AD, which increases output and employment. The price level rises to induce additional output. So the increase in AD causes the price level to increase.

Grading Rubric: 4 points

1 point: Increase in the quantity of money decreases the interest rate.

1 point: Lower interest rate increases investment and interest-sensitive components of consumption.

1 point: Increase in investment shifts the AD so that GDP and employment increase.

1 point: Price level increases because of increase in AD.

(C) Using a graph, analyze the combined effect of the two policy actions described above on each of the following:

(i)   Output and employment

(ii) The price level

(iii) Interest rates

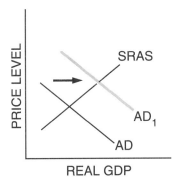 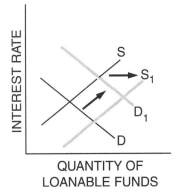 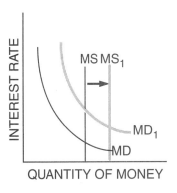

The combined effects of the two policies are (1) an increase in output, employment and the price level and (2) net effect on interest rates is indeterminate. In the graph on the left, the expansionary monetary and fiscal policies result in an increase in aggregate demand that increases output, employment and the price level. In the graph of the loanable funds market, the increase in demand for funds results from the increase in aggregate demand, and the increase in supply of funds results from the expansionary monetary policy. The same effects are shown in the graph on the right of the money market. A student could use either the loanable funds market or the money market to show the interest rate effects. (1 point)

3. Suppose that we have two countries: In Country A, the supply of loanable funds is relatively interest elastic; and in Country B, the supply of loanable funds is relatively interest inelastic. Assume that both countries are at the same initial equilibrium interest rate and quantity of loanable funds. Suppose that each government implements an expansionary fiscal policy and finances the same size deficit by issuing government securities.

(A) Draw the loanable funds market. Label Country A's supply of loanable funds S_A. Label Country A's new demand curve for loanable funds D_A. Label Country B's supply of loanable funds S_B. Label Country B's new demand for loanable funds D_B. Show the impact of the deficit financing.

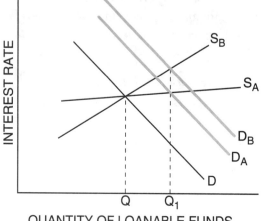

The effect of the deficit financing is to increase the demand for loanable funds from D to D_A for Country A and to D_B for Country B. Note that both countries have to borrow to finance the same size deficit. The amount of borrowing in both countries is $Q_1 - Q$. The interest rate increases in both countries, but it increases more in Country B.

(B) If investment in Country A is relatively interest inelastic and investment in Country B is relative interest elastic, explain the impact for each country on each of the following variables:
 (i) Investment
 (ii) Output
 (iii) Price level

Country A, with a relatively smaller increase in the interest rate, will experience a smaller decrease in investment than will Country B. Therefore, the decrease in aggregate demand caused by a decrease in investment will be smaller in Country A than in Country B. Output and the price level in Country A will decrease more than in Country B.

(C) Explain in which country crowding-out is greater. *Country A will have experienced smaller crowding-out than will Country B because the decrease in investment and resulting decline in aggregate demand will be less in Country A than in Country B.*

Government Demand for Funds Increases the Demand for Money

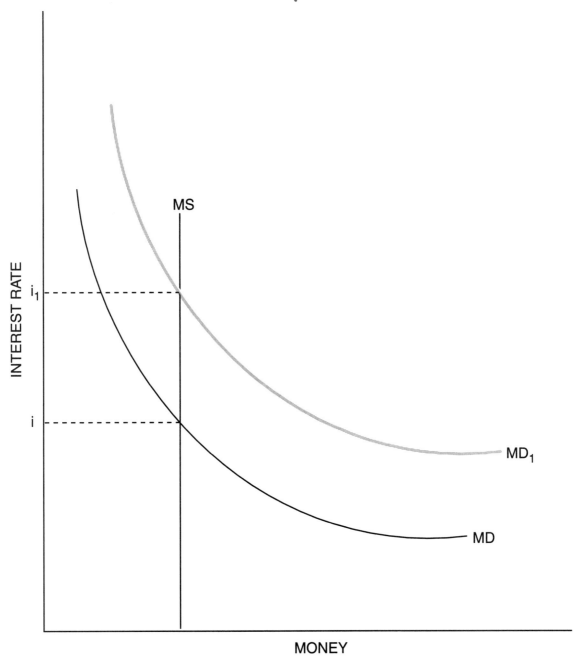

Loanable Funds Market

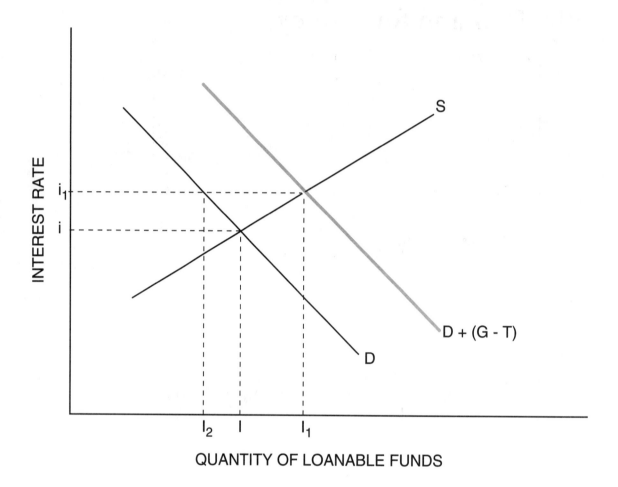

I and i are the initial equilibrium values.

D = private sector demand for funds (Investment)

D + (G–T) = private + government demand for funds

I_1 and i_1 are the new equilibrium values.

I_2 = new level of private investment

$I_1 - I_2$ = government demand for funds (G–T)

The Effects of Policy Changes in Multiple Markets

Aggregate Demand and Supply

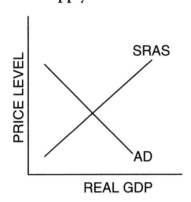

Loanable Funds Market

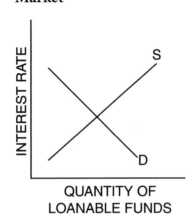

Money Market

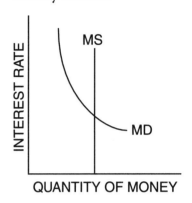

Short-Run Phillips Curve

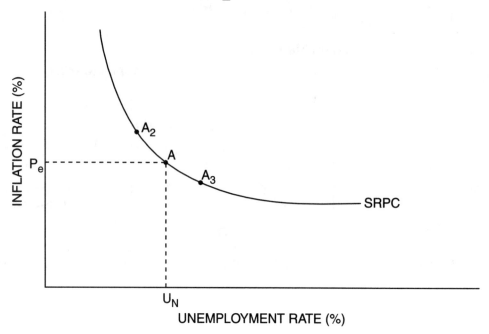

AD and SRAS and Short-Run Phillips Curve

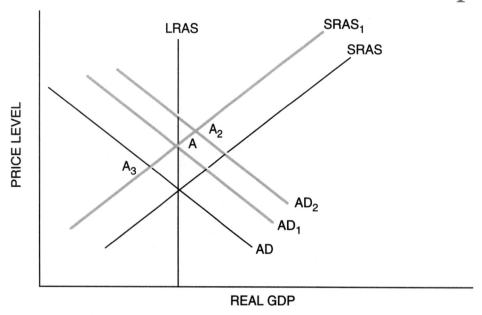

Holding constant

1. Expected inflation rate
2. Natural rate of unemployment

Macroeconomics | Unit 6

International Economics

7 class periods or 315 minutes
(9 percent of course time)

Unit Overview

Unit 6 introduces the international sector into the closed economy discussed in Units 1 through 5. The unit reviews the concepts of comparative advantage and production possibilities. Comparative advantage and the gains from trade motivate international trade. The unit presents the method to analyze the effects of government intervention in international trade and to examine the basic components of international finance. International finance includes the balance of payments accounts and analysis of the foreign exchange markets. In an increasingly integrated world, the students must have a good foundation in the concepts involved in international trade and finance and be able to analyze the effects of different policies in the international environment.

This unit investigates two types of policies: trade policies and domestic stabilization policies. It outlines the methods of analyzing the impacts of the policies. The activities give the students practice in analyzing the impacts of each type of policy. To be able to understand the influence of domestic monetary and fiscal policies on other countries, the students must have an understanding of the international financial system in terms of the balance of payments and foreign exchange markets.

The Lesson Planner

Lesson 1 reviews comparative advantage and production possibilities curves from Unit 1 and expands the idea of specialization and trade to have the students understand the actual gains that are possible from trade. It uses **Activities 49** and **50** and **Visuals 6.1** and **6.2**.

Lesson 2 examines the effects of government intervention on international trade. It uses **Activity 51** and **Visual 6.3**.

Lesson 3 introduces the basics of international finance in discussing the balance of payments and foreign exchange markets. It uses **Activities 52** and **53** and **Visual 6.4**.

Lesson 4 explains the interaction of domestic stabilization policy and international trade and finance. It uses **Activities 54** and **55**.

Week 1

■ Day 1

(A) Review comparative advantage and production possibilities using Visuals 6.1 and 6.2.

(B) Discuss the gains from trade.

(C) Have the students complete Activity 49 in class.

(D) Review Activity 49.

(E) Have the students complete Activity 50 for homework.

■ Day 2

(A) Review Activity 50.

(B) Give a lecture on barriers to trade using Visual 6.3.

(C) Have the students work on Activity 51 in class and complete for homework.

■ Day 3

(A) Review the answers to Activity 51.

(B) Give a lecture on international finance.

(C) Have the students complete Activity 52.

■ Day 4

(A) Review the students' answers to Activity 52.

(B) Review foreign exchange markets using Visual 6.4.

(C) Begin Activity 53; have the students complete Activity 53 for homework.

■ Day 5

(A) Review Activity 53.

(B) Review monetary and fiscal policy and their effects on interest rates.

(C) Have the students complete Activity 54.

Week 2

■ Day 6

(A) Review Activity 54.

(B) Use Activity 55 as a review for the unit test.

■ Day 7

Give multiple-choice and free-response portions of unit test.

International Trade

Introduction and Description

This lesson includes a review of comparative advantage and production possibilities curves. It then expands the concepts of specialization and trade to show the gains from international trade.

Activity 49 gives the students practice in determining comparative advantage using either the input or output method of presenting the information. In Activity 50, the students determine who has comparative advantage, explain the reasons behind their decision and then show the gains from trade when given the terms of trade.

Objectives

1. Define *comparative advantage, terms of trade* and *gains from trade.*
2. Explain comparative advantage using opportunity costs.
3. Demonstrate that specialization and trade allow consumption possibilities to exceed production possibilities.
4. Determine the terms of trade.

Time Required

One class period or 45 minutes

Materials

1. Activities 49 and 50
2. Visuals 6.1 and 6.2

Procedure

1. Project Visual 6.1 and work through the comparative advantage problem.

2. Project Visual 6.2, which shows the production possibilities curves for Israel and the United States as indicated on Visual 6.1. Answer the questions on Visual 6.1.

   (A) *For the United States, the opportunity cost of producing one bushel of oranges is two*

   bushels of avocadoes. For Israel, the opportunity cost of producing one bushel of oranges is four bushels of avocadoes. Thus, it is cheaper in terms of avocadoes for the United States to produce oranges. The United States has the comparative advantage in producing oranges.

   (B) *For the United States, the opportunity cost of producing one bushel of avocadoes is one-half a bushel of oranges. For Israel, the opportunity cost of producing one bushel of avocadoes is one-fourth of a bushel of oranges. Thus, it is cheaper in terms of oranges for Israel to produce avocadoes. Israel has the comparative advantage in producing avocadoes.*

3. Explain that the terms of trade are expressed in terms of the commodities to be exchanged. For each country there is a range of acceptable terms of trade. The United States is willing to trade one bushel of oranges for two or more bushels of avocadoes; Israel is willing to trade one bushel of oranges for less than four bushels of avocadoes. Thus, both the United States and Israel would be willing to trade one bushel of oranges for three bushels of avocadoes. Both countries gain from the trade.

4. Explain that before specialization and trade, the United States was producing 50 bushels of oranges and 50 bushels of avocadoes: Point A on Visual 6.2. If, after specialization and trade, the United States wants to continue to have 50 bushels of oranges — and the terms of trade are one bushel of oranges for three bushels of avocadoes — then the United States could trade 25 bushels of oranges for 75 bushels of avocadoes. Note that this combination — 50 bushels of oranges and 75 bushels of avocadoes — puts the United States outside of its production possibilities curve as indicated as point A' on the PPC in Visual 6.2.

Similarly, Israel would have 25 bushels of oranges and 325 bushels of avocadoes: Point B' after specialization and trade on the PPC in Visual 6.2. **Note:**

(A) Had Israel produced 25 bushels of oranges before specialization and trade, it would have had only 300 bushels of avocadoes (Point B on PPC in Visual 6.2).

(B) The combination of 25 bushels of oranges and 325 bushels of avocadoes (B') puts Israel outside of its production possibilities curve. Thus, the United States has gained 25 bushels of avocadoes, and Israel has gained 25 bushels of avocadoes.

5. Emphasize:

(A) The terms of trade can be anywhere between one bushel of oranges for two to four bushels of avocadoes. The actual terms of trade are based on market prices that reflect the opportunity costs.

(B) There is a wide range of solutions depending on the agreed-to terms of trade and the willingness to trade specific amounts of the commodities.

6. Have the students complete Activity 49 in class. Review the answers with the students.

7. The students should complete Activity 50 for homework. Review the answers with the students.

Determining Comparative Advantage

Part A
Productivity Measures and Example Problems

Output Method

| | Tons Produced per Hour | |
	Fish (A)	Cheese (B)
Ted	60	25
Nancy	45	40

For Ted, the opportunity cost of producing fish in terms of cheese is 60 fish = 25 cheese; therefore 1 fish = 5/12 cheese. On the other hand, 1 cheese = 12/5 fish. Similarly we can calculate the opportunity costs for Nancy. We summarize the opportunity cost information in the table below.

	Opportunity Cost (B / A) Fish	Opportunity Cost (A / B) Cheese
Ted	5/12 (0.42) cheese	12/5 (2.4) fish
Nancy	8/9 (0.89) cheese	9/8 (1.125) fish

Ted should produce fish because his opportunity cost in terms of cheese is less than Nancy's opportunity cost. Nancy should produce cheese because her opportunity cost in terms of fish is less than Ted's opportunity cost to produce cheese. Ted producing fish and Nancy producing cheese yields the *most* fish and cheese per hour of any combination of production.

Input Method

Acres Required to Produce One Bushel

	Apples (A)	Pears (B)
Tony	5	2
Chris	6	3

For the input method, the opportunity cost of producing one apple in terms of pears requires that we initially convert the input (acres) into output. For Tony, 5 acres = 1 apple; therefore, 1 acre = ⅕ apple. Also 2 acres = 1 pear; therefore, 1 acre = ½ pear. Now you can use the same method as for the output method: ⅕ apple = ½ pear; therefore 1 apple = 5/2 pear. Likewise 1 pear = ⅖ apple. We summarize the opportunity costs in the following table.

	Opportunity Cost (B / A) Apples	Opportunity Cost (A / B) Pears
Tony	5/2 (2.5) pears	2/5 (0.40) apples
Chris	6/3 (2) pears	3/6 (0.50) apples

Tony has the comparative advantage in producing pears. To produce one bushel of pears, Tony must give up 0.40 bushels of apples, whereas Chris has to give up half (0.50) of a bushel of apples. Thus, the opportunity cost of a bushel of pears is lower for Tony than for Chris, and so Tony should produce pears. Conversely, Chris should produce apples because he has the lower opportunity cost in terms of forgone bushels of pears.

Part B

Practice Problems

First decide whether the problem is an output or input problem; underline *output* or *input*. Then in the space below the table, calculate the opportunity cost of each product and indicate the product with the lower opportunity cost for each person, firm or country. The first one is completed for you.

1. Anna and Barry can grow the following amounts of potatoes and cabbage with the same amount of labor. Type of problem: (*output* / input)

	Potatoes	Cabbage
Anna	100	200
Barry	120	150

For Anna, the opportunity cost of one potato is two cabbages; for Barry, the opportunity cost of one potato is 1.25 cabbages. Barry has to give up fewer cabbages than does Anna to grow one potato. Thus, the opportunity cost of potatoes is lower for Barry than for Anna, so Barry should grow potatoes. Conversely, to grow one cabbage, Anna must give up one-half potato and Barry must give up 0.80 potato. Thus, the opportunity cost of growing cabbages is lower for Anna than it is for Barry, so Anna should grow cabbages.

2. Number caught per day. Type of problem: (**_output_** / input)

	Deer	Antelope
Henry	4	6
John	24	12

For Henry, the opportunity cost of one deer is 1.5 antelopes. For John the opportunity cost of one deer is 0.5 antelope. Conversely, for Henry the opportunity cost of one antelope is 2/3 of a deer. For John the opportunity cost of one antelope is two deer. John should hunt deer, and Henry should hunt antelope.

3. Days to produce one unit of each. Type of problem: (output / **_input_**)

	Cars	Planes
XYZ Corp.	8	10
QKFX Corp.	15	12

It takes XYZ Corp. eight days to produce a car and 10 days to produce a plane. Therefore, XYZ Corp.'s opportunity cost for one car is 0.8 plane. QKFX Corp.'s opportunity cost for a car is 1.25 planes. XYZ Corp.'s opportunity cost for producing one plane is 1.25 cars. QKFX Corp.'s opportunity cost of producing one plane is 0.8 car. XYZ Corp. should produce cars, and QKFX Corp. should produce planes.

4. Acres to produce 100 bushels. Type of problem: (output / **_input_**)

	Corn	Rice
India	9	3
China	8	2

On one acre of land, India can produce $100/9$ (11.11) bushels of corn or $100/3$ (33.33) bushels of rice. The opportunity cost of one bushel of corn is three bushels of rice; or, alternatively, the opportunity cost of one bushel of rice is 1/3 of a bushel of corn. On one acre of land, China can produce $100/8$ (12.5) bushels of corn or $100/2$ (50) bushels of rice. The opportunity cost of one bushel of corn is four bushels of rice, and the opportunity cost of one bushel of rice is 1/4 bushel of corn. Therefore, India has a comparative advantage in the production of corn and should produce corn, whereas China should produce rice.

5. To produce the following from one ton of olives. Type of problem: (***output*** / input)

	Cans of Olives	Bottles of Olive Oil
Zaire	60	10
Colombia	24	8

For Zaire, the opportunity cost of a can of olives is ¹/₆ of a bottle of olive oil. For Colombia, the opportunity cost of a can of olives is ¹/₃ of a bottle of olive oil. Conversely, for Zaire the opportunity cost of a bottle of olive oil is six cans of olives. For Colombia, the opportunity cost of a bottle of olive oil is three cans of olives. Zaire should produce cans of olives, and Colombia should produce bottles of olive oil.

6. Why should a person, firm or country produce the product that has the lower opportunity cost and trade for the other product? *Specializing in the product that has the lower opportunity cost produces more products than any other combination of production.*

Economic Efficiency and Gains from Trade

Underline the correct words in parentheses and complete the questions.

1. The following table gives the number of hours it takes in the United States and Scotland, using the same amount of resources, to produce a ton of oats or one bagpipe.

	Oats	Bagpipe
United States	3 hours	2 hours
Scotland	4 hours	5 hours

(A) (*The United States* / *Scotland*) has an absolute advantage in the production of oats.

(B) (*The United States* / *Scotland*) has an absolute advantage in the production of bagpipes.

(C) (*The United States* / *Scotland*) has a comparative advantage in the production of oats because *Scotland has a lower opportunity cost to produce oats in terms of bagpipes than the United States.*

(D) (*The United States* / *Scotland*) has a comparative advantage in the production of bagpipes because *the United States has a lower opportunity cost to produce bagpipes in terms of oats than does Scotland.*

(E) Based only on the data above and comparative advantage considerations, the United States should specialize in (*oats* / *bagpipes*).

(F) Based only on the data above and comparative advantage considerations, Scotland should specialize in (*oats* / *bagpipes*).

(G) Why will both Scotland and the United States be better off if they specialize and trade? *Total output will be greater using the same resources and trading.*

(H) Suppose that Scotland and the United States agree to specialize according to comparative advantage and to the following terms of trade: one ton of oats for one bagpipe. In a production period there are 60 hours, and before specialization Scotland produced 7.5 tons of oats and six bagpipes. After specialization and trade with the United States, Scotland wants to maintain the six bagpipes. How many tons of oats will it have? What are its gains from trade? *Scotland will have six bagpipes and nine tons of oats. Its gains from trade are 1.5 tons of oats.*

2. The following table gives the number of hours it takes in the United States and Canada, using the same amount of resources, to produce a ton of wheat or one bolt of cloth.

	Wheat	Cloth
United States	1 hour	2 hours
Canada	3 hours	4 hours

(A) (**_The United States_** / Canada) has an absolute advantage in the production of wheat.

(B) (**_The United States_** / Canada) has an absolute advantage in the production of cloth.

(C) (**_The United States_** / Canada) has a comparative advantage in the production of wheat because **_the opportunity cost of producing wheat is less than for Canada._**

(D) (The United States / **_Canada_**) has a comparative advantage in the production of cloth because **_the opportunity cost of producing cloth is less than for the United States._**

(E) Based only on the data above and comparative advantage considerations, the United States should specialize in (**_wheat_** / cloth).

(F) Based only on the data above and comparative advantage considerations, Canada should specialize in (wheat / **_cloth_**).

(G) Why will both Canada and the United States be better off if they specialize and trade? **_Using the same resources, total output will be greater._**

(H) Suppose that Canada and the United States agree to specialize according to comparative advantage and to the following terms of trade: three tons of wheat for two bolts of cloth. In a production period, there are 60 hours; and before specialization, Canada produced nine tons of wheat and 8.25 bolts of cloth. After specialization and trade with the United States, Canada wants to maintain the nine tons of wheat for each production period. How many bolts of cloth will it have? What are its gains from trade? **_Canada initially produces 15 bolts of cloth; it will trade six bolts of cloth for nine tons of wheat. Canada will have nine bolts of cloth. It will gain .75 bolts of cloth from specialization and trade._**

Advanced Placement Economics Teacher Resource Manual © National Council on Economic Education, New York, N.Y.

3. The following table gives the number of hours it takes in the United States and Japan, using the same amount of resources, to produce one computer or one auto.

	Computer	Auto
United States	2 hours	5 hours
Japan	1 hour	4 hours

(A) *(The United States /* ___Japan___*)* has an absolute advantage in the production of computers.

(B) *(The United States /* ___Japan___*)* has an absolute advantage in the production of autos.

(C) *(The United States /* ___Japan___*)* has a comparative advantage in the production of computers because ***the opportunity cost is less than for the United States.***

(D) *(___The United States___ / Japan)* has a comparative advantage in the production of autos because ***the opportunity cost is less than for Japan.***

(E) Based only on the data above and comparative advantage considerations, the United States should specialize in *(computers /* ___autos___*)*.

(F) Based only on the data above and comparative advantage considerations, Japan should specialize in *(___computers___ / autos)*.

(G) Why will both Japan and the United States be better off if they specialize and trade?
More automobiles and computers will be produced from the same resources.

(H) Suppose that Japan and the United States agree to specialize according to comparative advantage and to the following terms of trade: three computers for one auto. In a production period there are 60 hours; and before specialization, Japan produced 40 computers and five autos. After specialization and trade with the United States, Japan wants to maintain the five autos for each production period. How many computers will it have? What are its gains from trade? ***Japan will produce 60 computers in 60 hours; it will trade 15 computers to receive five automobiles. Japan will have 45 computers. Its gains from trade are five computers.***

Government Intervention in International Trade

Introduction and Description

The last lesson demonstrated the benefits of trade among nations, showing that total output increased. Nevertheless, most nations attempt to create barriers to trade using tariffs, quotas or regulations. Trade barriers limit the gains from trade and tend to reduce competition and economic efficiency.

Activity 51 presents a simple, single-graph model to analyze barriers to trade. The students work through the graphical analysis to determine the effects on the domestic economy.

Objectives

1. Define *tariffs, quotas* and *regulations to limit trade.*
2. Describe policies that are intended to protect the domestic economy from the effects of international trade.
3. Explain the effects of tariffs, quotas and subsidies on domestic production and the prices domestic consumers pay.
4. Explain the arguments for and against protectionist policies.

Time required

One class period or 45 minutes

Materials

1. Activity 51
2. Visual 6.3

Procedure

1. Review the definitions of tariffs, quotas and regulations to limit trade. Discuss some examples. For example, the United States imposes a tariff of more than 10 percent on imports of textiles and shoes. A good example of a quota is the voluntary export restraint (VER) Japan agreed to in the 1980s limiting the number of cars it exported to the United States. An example of a regulation to limit trade is the Federal Drug Administration's test requirements on pharmaceuticals imported into the United States.

2. Project Visual 6.3. Work through the imposition of a tariff to be sure the students understand the graph. Add the line "Total Supply with Tariff" to the graph between the "Domestic Supply" line and the "Total Supply" line. Discuss the total impact of the tariff on the quantity supplied by foreign companies and the quantity supplied by domestic firms. Emphasize that, for domestic consumers, the price is higher and the quantity available is smaller than under free trade.

3. Discuss the arguments in support of limitations on trade: the national defense argument, the infant industry argument, the "dumping" argument, preservation of domestic jobs, maintenance of a diverse and stable economy, and prevention of exploitation. Most of these arguments do not stand up to scrutiny. Limitations on trade fundamentally allow domestic producers to be inefficient and increase the costs to domestic consumers.

4. Review the history of tariffs in the United States. Make the following points:

   ■ With the Smoot-Hawley Act of 1933, tariffs reached a high average rate of 20 percent.

   ■ Over time, the United States has attempted to reduce tariffs using trade agreements such as the North American Free Trade Agreement. In the Uruguay Round (1986 to 1994) of World Trade Organization negotiations, the United States negotiated its lowest rate ever.

5. Have the students start Activity 51 and complete it for homework.

6. Review Activity 51.

Barriers to Trade

Part A
Quotas

1. Use Figure 51.3 to demonstrate what will happen to the domestic price, domestic production and the amount of imports if a quota is removed. The Domestic Supply and Total Supply curves on the graph are without any barriers to trade imposed. Be sure to show on the graph the supply curve with the quota. It is not on the graph now.

 Figure 51.3
Eliminating a Quota

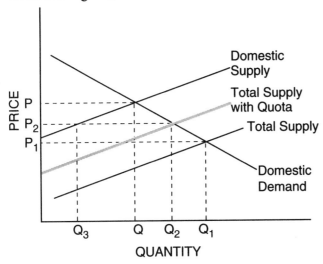

If there were a complete import ban, the equilibrium domestic price would be P and the equilibrium quantity would be Q with the commodity completely produced by the domestic industry. If there were a partial quota, the supply curve labeled Total Supply with Quota would be the relevant curve. The domestic price and quantity would be P_2 and Q_2. The amount of the quota would be $(Q_2 - Q_3)$. Domestic production will be Q_3. Removing the quota and moving to the free trade equilibrium, the domestic consumers will pay P_1 and purchase Q_1. Removal of a quota has led to a decrease in price and an increase in the quantity consumed. In the case illustrated, there will be zero domestic production under free trade.

2. Write a paragraph summarizing the advantages and disadvantages of a quota to the domestic economy. Be sure to discuss the impact on domestic consumers, domestic producers and foreign producers. *The advantages of a quota are that the domestic industry will be able to produce more and receive a higher price for the commodity relative to the free trade equilibrium, and employment in that industry is greater with a quota than without a quota. The disadvantages are that consumers pay a higher price and cannot consume as much of the commodity as at the free trade equilibrium. Foreign producers receive a higher price but produce less with a quota than under free trade.*

3. If a quota is imposed, explain the methods people would use to circumvent the effects of the quota. *An underground market may develop for the commodity. Foreign firms may open factories or assembly plants in the domestic nation and produce the commodity there so that production won't be subject to the quota.*

Part B
Tariffs

A tariff is a tax on an import. The imposition of a tax increases the cost of each unit, which is represented by a decrease in supply. This would result in an increase in equilibrium price and a decrease in equilibrium quantity.

4. Modify Figure 51.4 to show the effect of an import tariff of $T per unit. Be sure to show on the graph the amount of the tariff. Add one curve to the graph, and label it Total Supply with Tariff. After the imposition of the tariff, label the new equilibrium price P_T and the equilibrium quantity Q_T.

Figure 51.4
Effect of Import Tariff

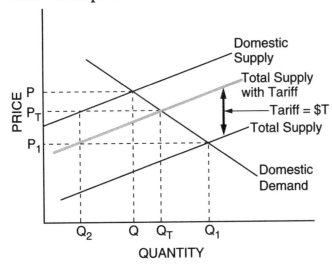

The imposition of a tariff causes the total supply to decrease because the tariff has caused the price to increase at every level of output. Q_2 is the amount of domestic production after the tariff. The tariff is the vertical distance between the Total Supply and the Total Supply with Tariff curves indicated by an arrow on the graph.

5. What is the effect of the tariff on the equilibrium price and quantity for domestic consumers compared with the free trade levels? *The equilibrium quantity decreases to Q_T, and the equilibrium price increases to P_T. Note that domestic firms are producing, whereas under the free-trade equilibrium price of P, the domestic industry is not producing. How far the curve shifts (how large the tariff is) determines whether domestic firms are producing any output.*

6. What are the similarities between the effects of a quota and those of a tariff?
   Both a quota and a tariff raise the price and limit the quantity to domestic consumers relative to the free trade equilibrium. Foreign firms produce less under either a quota or a tariff.

7. What is the primary difference between the effects of a quota and those of a tariff?
In both cases, the price increases. With a quota, all of the revenue generated by the price increase goes to the producers. With a tariff, the government receives the tax revenue.

8. Suppose a country can impose either a quota that raises the domestic price to P_2 as in Figure 51.2 or a tariff that raises the domestic price to P_2. Explain whether domestic consumers would prefer a tariff or a quota and why. *Domestic consumers would prefer a tariff because the domestic government receives the revenue as opposed to the producers (domestic and foreign). Consumers might expect that the overall level of taxes would then decrease. The tariff tax revenue would substitute for other tax revenue.*

Part C
Export Subsidies

Nations may choose to assist domestic industries by providing subsidies to an industry. The subsidies would lower the costs and permit the industry to sell at a lower price. This assistance is called an *export subsidy* because the industry can now compete on the world market and export some of its product to other nations.

9. Modify Figure 51.5 to show the effects of an export subsidy on domestic producers. Indicate as P_S and Q_S the equilibrium price and quantity for domestic consumers after an export subsidy. Add two curves to the graph: a Domestic Supply with Subsidy curve and a Total Supply with Subsidy curve.

Figure 51.5
Effects of a Subsidy

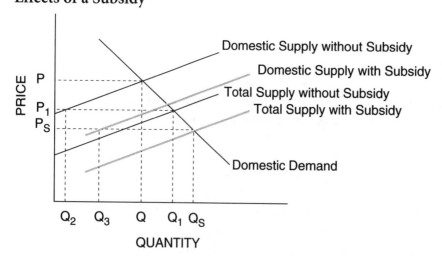

The equilibrium without subsidy would result in a price of P_1 and a quantity of Q_1, and the domestic economy would be producing Q_2. With the subsidy to the domestic industry, the equilibrium would result in a price of P_S and a quantity of Q_S, and the domestic economy would be producing Q_3. The quantity supplied by foreign producers is $(Q_S - Q_3)$.

According to Figure 51.5 with your modification, what would be the equilibrium price and quantity for

(A) a completely closed economy (no imports and no subsidy)? *P and Q*

(B) an open economy (completely free trade) with no export subsidy? *P₁ and Q₁*

(C) an open economy with a domestic export subsidy? *P_S and Q_S*

Note: The answers above are based on our labeling. Students may use different labels and still answer the questions correctly.

10. What is the effect of an export subsidy on the equilibrium price and quantity for domestic consumers relative to the free trade equilibrium without a subsidy? *The price is lower and the quantity is greater.*

11. If an industry receives a subsidy, what will happen at the equilibrium to domestic production and the amount of imports? *Refer to Figure 51.5. The free trade equilibrium without subsidy would result in a price of P₁ and a quantity of Q₁, and the domestic economy would be producing Q₂. With the subsidy to the domestic industry, the equilibrium would result in a price of P_S and a quantity of Q_S, and the domestic economy would be producing Q₃. With the subsidy, domestic production increases. The exact impact on imports depends on the extent of the subsidy and the demand curve for the commodity.*

Part D
Applications

12. One of the goals of the European Union is the elimination of trade barriers among the member nations. If this goal is achieved, which groups of people will benefit and which will not benefit?
Consumers who buy the commodity will benefit by having lower prices and a greater quantity of the commodity. Domestic producers of imported commodities will lose since the price will decrease as trade barriers are reduced and domestic producers will produce less at the lower price. A second result of the reduced production is that employment in this industry will decrease. However, the economy will be more efficient, and the standard of living will increase.

13. Identify the arguments frequently used to impose some type of trade barrier. Discuss the pros and cons of three arguments.

Protection of specific industries from foreign competition: An industry may argue that it cannot compete with foreign producers and that this competition will have an impact on wages and employment. The costs to domestic consumers are the higher prices and restricted quantity. Most governments that favor unrestricted trade will offer short-term protection to allow the industry to adjust.

National defense and other noneconomic considerations: Some industries produce defense items and thus should not be driven out of business by foreign competition. This is a noneconomic reason for protecting an industry. The problem with this argument is that the number of industries to which protection is extended may be quite large. The United States restricts endangered-species imports for noneconomic reasons.

Infant industry: Start-up industries argue that, to develop, they need protection from foreign competition. Support for this argument is valid only if the expected future benefits exceed the up-front costs of protectionism. Another argument against infant industry protection is that the industry may "never grow up."

Wage or employment protection: With low prices on imports, domestic workers will lose their jobs and unemployment will rise. The economy as a whole benefits from low prices and increased quantity of goods. The government response could be to retrain the affected workers and to provide adequate monetary and fiscal policies to maintain domestic growth and employment.

International Finance

Introduction and Description

International trade and the methods of limiting trade are extremely important to understanding much of the current discussions about the World Trade Organization (WTO) and the North American Free Trade Agreement (NAFTA). This lesson explains and uses for analysis the concepts of balance of payments and foreign exchange markets.

In Activity 52, the students apply their understanding of the balance of payments concepts. Activity 53 provides the students with practice using exchange rates and understanding the effects that changes in economic variables can have on exchange rates.

Objectives

1. Define *current account, capital account, balance of trade, balance of payments, debit* and *credit.*
2. Explain how international trade is financed.
3. Describe a country's balance of payments accounts.
4. Explain how international transactions affect the balance of trade and the balance of payments.
5. Explain how the international value of the dollar is determined.
6. Analyze how economic events affect the international value of the dollar.

Time Required

Two class periods or 90 minutes

Materials

1. Activities 52 and 53
2. Visual 6.4

Procedure

1. Use current newspaper headlines to show the students the need to understand the balance of trade and the balance of payments.

2. Give a brief lecture on the current account, the balance of trade, the capital account and the balance of payments. Explain the major components of each account, as well as which transactions are considered to be a debit and which are considered to be a credit.

3. Have the students read the introductory material of Activity 52. Answer any questions the students may pose, then have them complete Activity 52. Review the answers with the students.

4. Give a brief lecture on the foreign exchange market. Relate the demand for currency that can be used in trade to the supply and demand curves. Discuss the factors that shift these curves. Use Visual 6.4 and emphasize these points:

   - If the exchange rate increases, the quantity demanded falls and the quantity supplied increases.

   - A change in any factor other than the exchange rate will cause the demand curve or the supply curve to shift. For example, if France's income increases, then France's demand for U.S. dollars will increase because the French will want to buy more American goods.

   - If interest rates in the United States change relative to interest rates in other countries or if the expected future exchange rate changes, then the demand curve will shift.

5. Discuss fixed and flexible exchange rate systems.

6. Have the students begin Activity 53 in class.

7. Have the students complete Activity 53 for homework. Review the answers with the students.

Imbalance of Payments

Part A

To make sure you understand the components of the current account, the capital account and the difference between a credit (transaction that earns foreign exchange) and a debit (transaction that uses foreign currency), identify each of the following transactions on the U.S. balance of payments. Complete Figure 52.1 by putting check marks in the appropriate boxes for credit or debit and for capital or current account. The first one has been done for you.

 Figure 52.1
Transactions on the U.S. Balance of Payments

	Credit +	Debit −	Current Account	Capital Account
1. Harley Davidson USA purchases $25 million in production machinery from a Japanese company.		✓		✓
2. André Prenoor, U.S. entrepreneur, invests $50 million to develop a theme park in Malaysia.		✓		✓
3. A Chinese company sells $1 million worth of berets to the U.S. Army.		✓	✓	
4. BMW pays $1 million to a U.S. shipper for transporting cars from Germany to the United States.	✓		✓	
5. Each month, Ima Grent, who recently arrived in the United States, sends half her paycheck to her sister in Poland.		✓	✓	
6. Bank of America pays $5 million in interest to French depositors.		✓	✓	
7. Senor Ramos from Spain buys a shopping center in Florida.	✓			✓
8. A Brazilian investor buys five $10,000 U.S. Treasury bonds.	✓			✓
9. German tourists spend $3 million in the United States; U.S. tourists spend $5 million in Germany.		✓	✓	
10. Brit-Disz, a London record store, spends $10,000 on CDs by the Generic Gurls, a U.S. kiddy-pop group.	✓		✓	
11. Sam Boney, U.S. ice-rink magnate, buys stock in a Chilean ice-rink chain.		✓		✓

Advanced Placement Economics Teacher Resource Manual © National Council on Economic Education, New York, N.Y.

Part B

12. Analyze the data in Figure 52.2. Compute the missing figures, and answer the questions that follow.

Figure 52.2

2002 Balance of Payments, Z-Land

Current Account

Z-Land exports of goods	$ +300	
Z-Land imports of goods	−400	
Z-Land exports of services	+150	
Z-Land imports of services	−120	
Balance of trade		*−70*
Net investment income	+10	
Net transfers	−14	
Balance on current account		*−74*

Capital Account

Z-Land capital going abroad	−110	
Foreign capital coming into Z-Land	+160	
Balance on capital account		*+50*

Balance on Current Account Plus Balance on Capital Account	*−24*

Official Reserves Account

Official reserves transactions balance	*+24*
Total	$ 0

13. Does Z-Land have a current account deficit or surplus? How do you know? *Z-Land is running a current account deficit. Imports of goods and services exceed exports of goods and services.*

14. Without central bank intervention, does Z-Land carry a balance of payments surplus or deficit? How do you know? *Z-Land is running a balance of payments deficit because the capital account surplus (+$50) does not fully offset the current account deficit (−$84).*

15. If Z-Land runs a balance of payments deficit, how can this difference be made up? If it carries a balance of payment surplus, what will happen? *Z-Land must either borrow to bring its balance of payments deficit to $0, or it must use its official reserves to make up the difference. If Z-Land runs a balance of payments surplus, it can add the excess earned currency to its official reserves.*

Exchange Rates

People, firms and nations exchange products for money and use the money to buy other products or to pay for the use of resources. Within an economy, prices are stated in the domestic currency, such as U.S. dollars or European euros. Buyers use their currency to purchase goods. International markets are different. Producers in other countries who export goods want to be paid in their own currencies so they can carry out transactions. As a result, a *foreign exchange market* develops where national currencies can be exchanged. Such markets serve the need of all international buyers and sellers. The equilibrium prices in these markets are called *exchange rates.* An exchange rate is the rate at which the currency of one nation is exchanged for the currency of another.

Figure 53.1 shows the exchange rates for selected countries for May and August of the same year.

Figure 53.1
Exchange Rates

	Cost of Foreign Currency in U.S. Dollars (U.S. dollars / foreign currency)		Cost of U.S. Dollar in Foreign Currency (foreign currency / U.S. dollars)	
	May	Aug.	May	Aug.
British pound	1.4	1.8	0.71	0.56
Canadian dollar	0.64	0.63	1.5625	1.5873
European euro	0.87	0.91	1.149	1.099
Swedish krona	0.094	0.093	10.638	10.753
Japanese yen	0.0083	0.0090	120.482	111.111
Mexican peso	0.1101	0.1502	9.083	6.658

Part A

Using the data in Figure 53.1, calculate the cost of the following products in U.S. dollars. To solve, divide the cost of the product in the foreign currency by the cost of the U.S. dollar in the foreign currency.

	May	Aug.
1. A dinner for two that costs 500 Mexican pesos	*$55.05*	*$75.10*
2. A hotel room that costs 30,000 Japanese yen	*249.00*	*270.00*
3. A BMW that costs 85,000 euros in Germany	*73,977.37*	*77,343.04*
4. A pound of Swedish meatballs that costs 30 krona	*2.82*	*2.79*
5. A pair of pants that costs 72 pounds in London	*101.41*	*128.57*
6. A leather jacket that costs 1,800 Canadian dollars	*1,152.00*	*1,134.00*

A student may also multiply the cost of the product times the cost of foreign currency in U.S. dollars. This will yield slightly different numbers because of rounding.

7. Using the exchange table in Figure 53.1, calculate how much foreign tourists would have to pay in their own currency for an American meal that costs $60.00. To solve, divide the cost in U.S. dollars by the cost of the foreign currency in U.S. dollars.

	May	Aug.
British pound	42.86	33.33
Canadian dollar	93.75	95.24
European euro	68.97	65.93
Swedish krona	638.30	645.16
Japanese yen	7,228.92	6,666.67
Mexican peso	544.96	399.47

8. Did the value of the dollar appreciate (increase) or depreciate (decrease) against the following currencies between May and August?

	Appreciate	Depreciate
British pound		X
Canadian dollar	X	
European euro		X
Swedish krona	X	
Japanese yen		X
Mexican peso		X

Part B

Consider the following situations. In each case, an underlying event causes a change in the supply and demand for currencies. Indicate the impact of each scenario on each currency. The first example is done for you as a model.

9. The prices of U.S. goods rise relative to the prices of German goods.

 Figure 53.2

Prices of U.S. Goods Increase

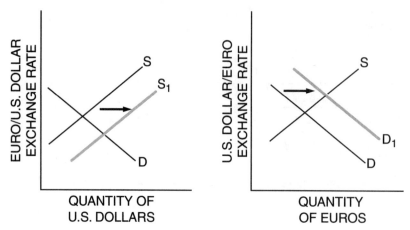

Rationale: *Americans will demand less expensive German goods, thereby increasing the demand for euros and supplying more dollars to the foreign exchange market. The U.S. dollar depreciates. The euro appreciates.*

10. Interest rates in the United States rise faster than interest rates in Canada.

 Figure 53.3

Interest Rates in the United States Increase

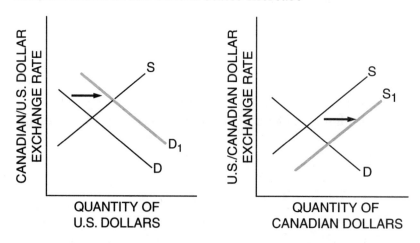

Rationale: *Canadian investors will demand U.S. dollars to purchase U.S. investments, causing the U.S. dollar to appreciate. The supply of Canadian dollars will increase because Canadians are trading Canadian dollars for U.S. dollars. The Canadian dollar will depreciate.*

11. French tourists flock to Mexico's beaches.

Figure 53.4
French Tourists Visit Mexico

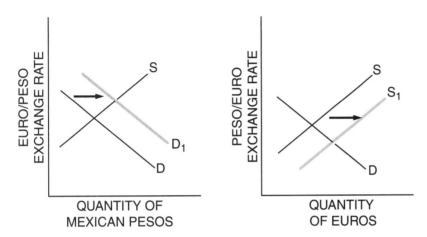

Rationale: *The demand for pesos increases to pay for the beach vacations. The supply of euros increases because the French are exchanging euros for Mexican pesos. The Mexican peso is appreciating, and the euro is depreciating.*

12. Japanese video games become popular with U.S. children.

Figure 53.5
U.S. Children Want Videos Produced in Japan

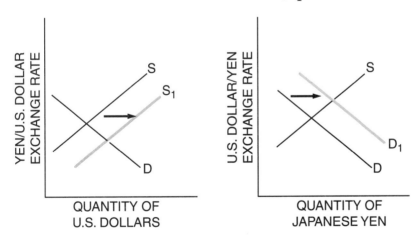

Rationale: *Demand for Japanese yen increases as U.S. children buy more Japanese video games; the supply of dollars to the exchange market increases. The U.S. dollar depreciates. The Japanese yen appreciates.*

Monetary and Fiscal Policy in a Global Economy

Introduction and Description

This lesson combines the knowledge of monetary and fiscal policy and the economy developed in Units 3 through 5 with the knowledge of international finance. It explains and analyzes the impact of domestic policy on the foreign exchange rate. It is essential that the students understand the interaction between the domestic economy and the international economy to understand the current policy discussions and to do well on the Advanced Placement Examination in Macroeconomics.

In Activity 54, the students work through the effects on the economy of stabilization policies, domestic or foreign, through the effects on exchange rates. Activity 55 is a review of the important international economic principles.

Objectives

1. Explain the effects of monetary and fiscal policy on foreign exchange markets.
2. Explain the effects of changes in the international value of the dollar on foreign trade.
3. Explain the effects of changes in net exports on domestic aggregate demand.

Time Required

Two class periods or 90 minutes

Materials

Activities 54 and 55

Procedure

1. Review the short-run effects of monetary and fiscal policy on the domestic interest rate.

   (A) Expansionary monetary policy decreases interest rates in the short run.

   (B) Expansionary fiscal policy increases interest rates if deficit financing is required.

2. Review the effects of a change in the difference between domestic and foreign interest rates.

3. Link these changes to changes in the international value of the dollar.

4. Discuss the relationship between the international value of the dollar and exports and imports.

5. Relate the change in net exports to changes in domestic aggregate demand.

6. Have the students work on Activity 54. Review the answers with the students.

7. Use Activity 55 as a review for the unit test.

How Monetary and Fiscal Policies Affect Exchange Rates

Changes in a nation's monetary and fiscal policies affect its exchange rates and its balance of trade through the interest rate, income and the price level. Changes in the value of a country's currency may affect the balance of trade and aggregate demand. The value of real output and price levels may also be affected. Domestic policies influence currency values, and currency values influence domestic policies. The complexity of the connection leads to careful evaluation of any change in domestic policy goals. Policy makers cannot ignore the international effects of changes in monetary and fiscal policies.

A series of situations is presented below. In each case:

■ Evaluate the expected effects on exchange rates in the United States and the other country. Use the currency graphs provided to reflect changes in the currency values.

■ Analyze the impact of the currency changes on the U.S. economy as it applies to net exports, balance of trade, aggregate demand and price levels. *Work out the situations in the short run only.*

1. The U.S. government initiates a personal income tax reduction plan, leaving every tax-paying American with more disposable income.

   (A) What will happen as a result to trade between the United States and Taiwan?
       Americans will buy more Taiwanese and domestic goods.

⁂ Figure 54.1
U.S. Government Reduces Taxes

Graph A

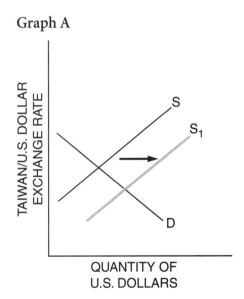

Graph B

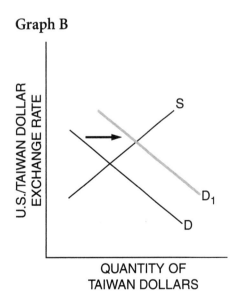

(B) In Graph A, what happens to the U.S. dollar?_____*It depreciates.*_____

(C) In Graph B, what happens to the Taiwanese dollar? _____*It appreciates.*_____

(D) As a result of the fiscal policy,

   (i)   U.S. aggregate demand shifts (*left* / *__right__*).

   (ii) Price levels in the United States (*__rise__* / *fall*).

   (iii) U.S. imports (*__increase__* / *decrease*). Explain why. *The increase in disposable income increases the demand for all goods, including foreign goods. Furthermore, the increase in U.S. prices makes foreign goods relatively less expensive.*

   (iv) U.S. exports (*increase* / *__decrease__*). Explain why. *The relative price to foreigners of U.S. goods has increased, so foreigners buy less.*

2. Japan's fiscal policies lead to an increase in Japan's real GDP.

   (A) What will happen as a result to trade between the United States and Japan? *Japan buys more U.S. goods because Japanese incomes rise.*

Figure 54.2
Japan's Real GDP Increases

Graph A

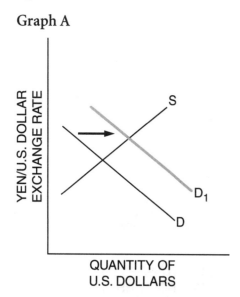

Graph B

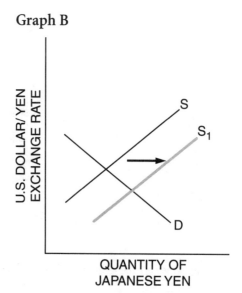

(B) In Graph A, what happens to the U.S. dollar? _____*It appreciates.*_____

(C) In Graph B, what happens to the Japanese yen? _____*It depreciates.*_____

(D) As a result of the changing value of the U.S. dollar,

    (i)   U.S. exports *(increase / **decrease**)*. Explain why. ***It takes more yen to buy each dollar; therefore U.S. goods cost more in yen than previously, and exports to Japan decrease.***

    (ii)   U.S. imports *(**increase** / decrease)*. Explain why. ***Each dollar buys more yen; therefore Japanese goods are cheaper in U.S. dollars, and imports from Japan increase.***

    (iii) U.S. aggregate demand shifts *(**left** / right)*.

    (iv) Price levels in the United States *(rise / **fall**)*.

3. The U.S. federal budget deficit increases, which causes increases in the interest rate. (Assume trade with Great Britain.)

    (A) What will happen as a result to trade between the United States and Great Britain? ***British investors will want to buy U.S. bonds.***

Figure 54.3
Interest Rates in the United States Increase

Graph A

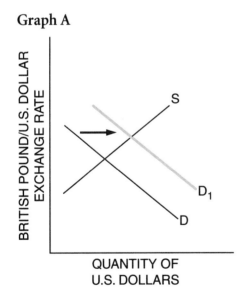

Graph B

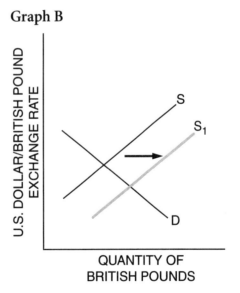

    (B) In Graph A, what happens to the U.S. dollar?____***It appreciates.***____

    (C) In Graph B, what happens to the British pound? ____***It depreciates.***____

(D) As a result of the changing value of the U.S. dollar:

   (i)   U.S. exports *(increase / **decrease**)*. Explain why. *It takes more pounds to buy each dollar; therefore U.S. goods cost more in pounds than previously, and exports to Great Britain decrease.*

   (ii) U.S. imports *(**increase** / decrease)*. Explain why. *Each dollar buys more pounds; therefore British goods are cheaper in U.S. dollars, and imports from Great Britain increase.*

   (iii) U.S. aggregate demand shifts *(**left** / right)*.

   (iv) Price levels in the United States *(rise / **fall**)*.

4. Europe's interest rates are increasing, while the U.S. interest rate remains relatively constant.

   (A) What will happen as a result to trade between the United States and Europe? *Europeans will sell U.S. bonds to buy European bonds.*

✳ Figure 54.4

Interest Rates in Europe Increase

Graph A

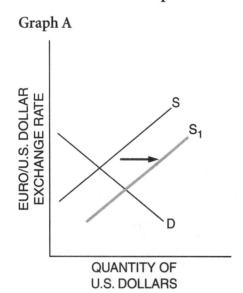

Graph B

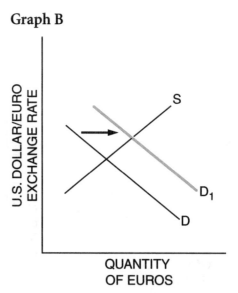

(B) In Graph A, what happens to the U.S. dollar? ____*It depreciates.*____

(C) In Graph B, what happens to the European euro?____*It appreciates.*____

(D) As a result of the changing value of the U.S. dollar,

    (i)   U.S. exports (*increase* / decrease). Explain why. *It takes more dollars to buy each euro; therefore U.S. goods cost less in euros than previously, and exports to Europe increase.*

    (ii)   U.S. imports (*increase* / **decrease**). Explain why. *Each dollar buys fewer euros; therefore European goods are more expensive in dollars, and imports from Europe decrease.*

    (iii)   U.S. aggregate demand shifts (*left* / **right**).

    (iv)   Price levels in the United States (**rise** / *fall*).

5. There is a rapid increase in the Canadian price level while the U.S. price level remains relatively constant.

    (A) What will happen as a result to trade between the United States and Canada? *Canadians will want to buy U.S. goods.*

✳ Figure 54.5
The Price Level in Canada Increases

Graph A

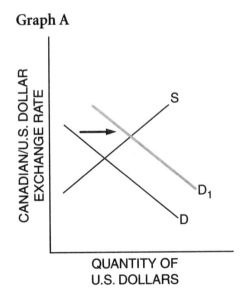

Graph B

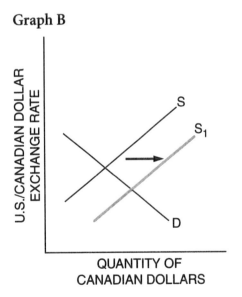

(B) In Graph A, what happens to the U.S. dollar? _____*It appreciates.*_____

(C) In Graph B, what happens to the Canadian dollar? _____*It depreciates.*_____

(D) As a result of the changing value of the U.S. dollar:

(i) U.S. exports *(increase / decrease)*. Explain why. *It takes more Canadian dollars to buy each U.S. dollar; therefore U.S. goods cost more in Canadian dollars than previously. Therefore exports to Canada decrease.*

(ii) U.S. imports *(increase / decrease)*. Explain why. *Each U.S. dollar buys more Canadian dollars; therefore Canadian goods are cheaper in U.S. dollars. Therefore imports from Canada increase.*

(iii) U.S. aggregate demand shifts *(left / right)*.

(iv) Price levels in the U.S. *(rise / fall)*.

The International Way of Thinking

1. True, false or uncertain, and explain why? "Nations do not trade; people trade."
   True. People make the decision to trade because two or more parties involved in the exchange expect to gain. For example, an American consumer buys a car made by Toyota in Japan. The consumer buys from Toyota. The United States does not buy from Japan.

2. Use one example from your own life when you specialized in doing something in which you had a comparative advantage and traded for something in which someone else had a comparative advantage. *There can be many different answers to this. The students should show that the exchange is based on relative opportunity costs.*

3. Assume the U.S. government has placed a high tariff on imported bicycles.

   (A) Use a supply and demand graph to show the effect of the tariff on the U.S. market for bicycles.

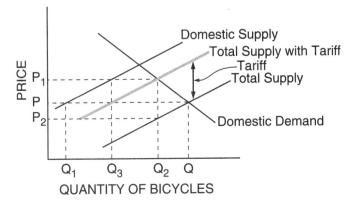

   In the graph above, before the tariff, the price was P and the equilibrium quantity was Q. The domestic producers were producing Q_1 and the foreign producers were producing $(Q - Q_1)$. The imposition of a tariff decreases the supply curve because of the increased cost of production to cover the tariff. The price of bicycles has increased and the quantity supplied, Q_2, to the U.S. market has decreased. However, the price received by the foreign suppliers has decreased because of the tariff. Domestic producers produce Q_3 after the tariff is imposed.

(B) Explain the effects of the tariff on the price and quantity of bicycles available to U.S. consumers. *Looking at the graph, the imposition of the tariff has increased the price. The price of bicycles has increased, and the quantity has decreased.*

(C) What are the effects of the tariff on

    (i)   foreign bicycle manufacturers? *Decrease in output and a decrease in after-tariff price. Although the price paid by the consumer has increased, the foreign producer must pay the tariff, and thus the real price of the bicycle received by foreign producers has decreased. In the graph, P_2 shows this after-tariff price.*

    (ii) domestic bicycle manufacturers? *Increased price and quantity produced; domestic producers are helped. Domestic producers initially produced Q_1; after the tariff they are producing Q_3.*

    (iii) U.S. consumers? *Consumers are hurt because they must pay a higher price and have fewer bicycles to buy.*

4. The table below shows how much wine and cheese Germany and France can produce in a day.

	Wine	Cheese
Germany	25 liters	30 kilos
France	50 liters	40 kilos

(A) Which country has an absolute advantage in wine production? Why? *France, because it produces more in one day.*

(B) Which country has an absolute advantage in cheese production? Why? *France, because it produces more in one day.*

(C) Which country has a comparative advantage in wine production? Why? *France. The opportunity cost of a bottle of wine in France is 4/5 of a kilo of cheese. In Germany it is 1.2 kilos of cheese.*

(D) Which country has a comparative advantage in cheese production? Why? *Germany. The opportunity cost of a kilo of cheese is 5/6 of a bottle of wine. In France, it is 1.25 bottles of wine.*

(E) Based on the data above and considering comparative advantage only, what should France import? What should France export? *France should import cheese and export wine.*

(F) Based on the data above and considering comparative advantage only, what should Germany import? What should Germany export? *Germany should import wine and export cheese.*

5. For each of the following situations, explain the effect of the event on the value of the U.S. dollar in relation to the Mexican peso. Draw a supply and demand graph to illustrate each situation.

(A) Americans increase their demand for Mexican tomatoes.

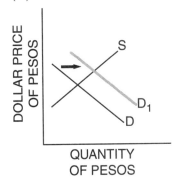

The value of the peso will increase because Americans will demand pesos to buy Mexican tomatoes. The peso will appreciate. The dollar will depreciate.

(B) Inflation in Mexico rises at a higher rate than in the United States.

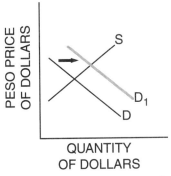

Mexicans will want to buy more American goods, so demand for the dollar will increase. The dollar will appreciate. The Mexican peso will depreciate.

(C) Americans increase their investments in Mexico because they feel the Mexican economy will be strong. *U.S. investors will have to buy pesos to invest in Mexico. This will increase the demand for the peso. The peso will appreciate; therefore, the dollar will depreciate relative to the peso. See the graph in the answer to Question 5(A).*

(D) Interest rates rise in the United States and have become relatively higher than Mexican interest rates. *Mexicans will invest in the United States to take advantage of higher interest rates, so demand for the dollar will increase. The dollar will appreciate. See the graph in the answer to Question 5(B).*

(E) Mexico becomes a much more popular tourist destination for Americans. *American tourists will have to buy pesos. The demand for the peso will increase; the peso will appreciate, and the dollar will depreciate. See the graph in the answer to Question 5(A).*

6. Explain three effects of a new law that would forbid U.S. citizens and businesses from trading with any other country.

Effects include:

- *Imports and exports would decrease because of retaliation by foreign countries.*
- *Prices would be higher because we would not benefit from the comparative advantage (lower opportunity cost) of producing goods in other countries.*
- *The standard of living would be lower.*
- *There would be far fewer goods and services and much less variety of goods and services.*

7. Assume that the United States increases its federal budget deficit, which causes interest rates to rise.

(A) What would be the effect of this on the international value of the dollar? Why? *Higher interest rates would attract foreign investment. The demand for the dollar would increase, and the value of the dollar would rise (appreciate).*

(B) What would be the effect of this on the U.S. balance of trade? Why? *A stronger dollar would make U.S. goods more expensive in foreign countries and foreign goods less expensive in the United States. This would decrease U.S. exports and increase U.S. imports. The trade balance (exports – imports) would adjust.*

(C) Would the budget deficit and higher interest rates tend to increase or decrease aggregate demand? Why? *The increase in the federal budget deficit would cause aggregate demand to increase. However, the increase in interest rates will cause investment and some parts of consumption to decrease. The decrease in exports would cause aggregate demand to decrease. The net effect is unknown given the information in the question.*

8. How could a nation have a negative balance of trade and still not have a deficit in its balance of payments? *The balance of payments includes the current and capital accounts. The current account is the balance of trade and considers the export and imports of goods and services only. Thus, the impact of capital inflows and outflows can outweigh the effects of imports and exports of goods and services.*

Answers to Sample Multiple-Choice Questions

1. *B*	8. *A*	14. *C*
2. *A*	9. *B*	15. *D*
3. *B*	10. *A*	16. *D*
4. *D*	11. *A*	17. *B*
5. *D*	12. *D*	18. *E*
6. *B*	13. *C*	19. *B*
7. *B*		

Advanced Placement Economics Teacher Resource Manual © National Council on Economic Education, New York, N.Y.

UNIT
6 Macroeconomics

SHORT FREE-RESPONSE
SAMPLE QUESTIONS

Answer
Key

Answers to Sample Short Free-Response Questions

1. In a recent year, the United States had a huge balance of trade deficit. Comment on the following policies designed to correct this deficit.

   (A) Limit foreign investment by U.S. firms in other countries. *A limit on foreign investment by U.S. firms would decrease the demand for foreign currencies, so the dollar would appreciate. An appreciated dollar would make U.S. exports more expensive and worsen the trade deficit.*

   (B) Sell dollars so the value of the dollar goes down. *Selling dollars would make exports less expensive in foreign countries and imports more expensive in the United States. This would improve the balance of trade deficit.*

   (C) Put high tariffs on autos, steel and consumer electronics. *High tariffs would initially cause Americans to buy less foreign currency, increase the value of the dollar and make U.S. exports more expensive in other countries. In addition, other countries might retaliate against the United States by increasing their tariffs on U.S. goods. The effect on the trade deficit is not clear because both imports and exports would fall.*

2. True, false, or uncertain, and explain why? "Tariffs actually increase domestic employment by reducing foreign competition and creating more jobs for American workers. Furthermore, more jobs means higher incomes with which Americans can buy more goods from abroad. Hence, instead of reducing foreign trade, tariffs tend to increase it." *False. High tariffs would make U.S. businesses less efficient, and the United States would obtain fewer goods and services from its scarce resources. Other countries might retaliate if the United States imposes tariffs.*

3. Assume that Liechtenstein and Andorra, with equal (and very few) resources, can produce the following:

	Grapes	Wool
Liechtenstein	100,000 kilos	100,000 kilos
Andorra	50,000 kilos	100,000 kilos

(A) Which nation has an absolute advantage in grapes? Why? *Liechtenstein; it produces more grapes.*

(B) Which nation has a comparative advantage in grapes? Why? *Liechtenstein; opportunity costs are lower. For each kilo of grapes, Liechtenstein must give up fewer kilos of wool compared to Andorra.*

(C) Should Liechtenstein specialize in grapes or wool? Why? *Grapes; Liechtenstein has a comparative advantage in the production of grapes. The opportunity cost of producing grapes in terms of wool is lower in Liechtenstein than in Andora.*

(D) Should Andorra specialize in grapes or wool? Why? *Wool; Andorra has a comparative advantage in the production of wool. The opportunity cost of producing wool in terms of grapes is lower in Andorra than in Liechtenstein.*

4. True, false or uncertain, and explain why? "If a nation has an expansionary fiscal policy and a contractionary monetary policy, the international value of its currency will appreciate." *Probably true. The policy will cause high interest rates, which will increase foreign investment in the United States. This will increase the demand for dollars and cause the dollar to appreciate. If the effect of the expansionary fiscal policy is greater, causing increased imports and decreased exports, then the value of the currency will fall.*

*5. Assume that labor in the United States becomes more productive because of major technological changes.

  (A) Using the aggregate supply and aggregate demand model, explain how the increased productivity will affect each of the following for the United States.

   (i) Output

   (ii) Price level

   (iii) Exports

---

*Actual free-response question from a past AP test. Reprinted by permission of the College Entrance Examination Board, the copyright owner. For limited use by NCEE.

   Advanced Placement Economics Teacher Resource Manual © National Council on Economic Education, New York, N.Y.

(B) Explain how the change in exports you identified in (iii) will affect the international value of the dollar.

Grading Rubric: Basically, the point distribution is 3 points for Part (A) and 2 for Part (B).

Part (A): 3 points

The major technological change increases productivity, which causes the aggregate supply curve to shift to the right, resulting in an increase in output and a decrease in price level. As a result, U.S. goods have become less expensive relative to foreign goods, thereby increasing the demand for U.S. goods → exports increase.

1 point: Aggregate supply shift with explanation. No credit should be given for an assertion without a graph.

½ point: Increase in output

½ point : Decrease in price level

1 point: Increase in exports with explanation that spells out relative prices

Part (B): 2 points

The increase in exports increases the demand for dollars, which raises the international value of the dollar.

1 point: Increase in international value of the dollar (value of the U.S. dollar appreciates)

1 point : Explanation

*6. Assume that in the United States, nominal wage rates rise faster than labor productivity. Analyze the short-run effects of this situation on each of the following.

(A) The general price level

(B) The level of exports

(C) The international value of the dollar

Grading Rubric: 5 points

Part (A): 1 point

Prices increase because of cost-push effects. Short-run aggregate supply shifts leftward.

1 point: must make a coherent statement about why prices rise: Costs rise.

Part (B): 2 points

U.S. goods are relatively more expensive than foreign goods; therefore exports decline.

1 point: Exports decline.

1 point: Explanation

---

* Actual free-response question from a past AP test. Reprinted by permission of the College Entrance Examination Board, the copyright owner. For limited use by NCEE.

UNIT
6 Macroeconomics

SHORT FREE-RESPONSE
SAMPLE QUESTIONS

Answer
Key

Part (C): 2 points

Given the decline in exports, the demand for U.S. dollars decreases, resulting in a decline in the international value of the dollar. A parallel argument is that there is an increase in imports because foreign goods are now relatively cheaper for U.S. buyers; and the supply of U.S. dollars increases, driving the international value of the dollar down.

1 point: Decline in the international value of the dollar

1 point: Explanation

Alternative Part (C): Inflation increases nominal interest rates (changing relative real interest rates) → *capital inflows to the United States, which increases the international value of the dollar.*

7. If the rate of inflation is higher in the United States than in other countries, analyze what will happen to

   (A) exports *Exports will decrease because U.S. goods will be more expensive relative to foreign goods.*

   (B) imports *Imports will increase because foreign goods will be less expensive relative to U.S. goods.*

   (C) the international value of the dollar *The dollar will depreciate because Americans will be demanding more foreign currency while foreigners will be demanding fewer U.S. dollars.*

8. Consider a simple model of the world economy in which there are two countries: the United States and Korea. Both produce cars and computers. The labor requirements for producing each good are given in the following table.

	Labor Hours Required	
	Cars	Computers
United States	80	20
Korea	60	10

   (A) Which nation has an absolute advantage in producing cars? Explain why. *Korea; given the same number of hours, Korea can produce more cars than the United States.*

Advanced Placement Economics Teacher Resource Manual © National Council on Economic Education, New York, N.Y.

(B) Which nation has a comparative advantage in producing cars? Explain why. *United States; it has to give up fewer computers than does Korea to produce each car.*

(C) Show that the nation with the comparative advantage in producing cars can gain from specialization and trade with the other. *Before specialization and trade, the United States faces a trade-off of one car for four computers. Korea will be willing to trade one car for five computers. Thus, the United States would gain from specializing in producing cars and trading with Korea for computers.*

Answers to Sample Long Free-Response Questions

1. The exchange rate between the Canadian dollar and other currencies has been free to fluctuate since the mid-1960s. For each of the following (in some cases hypothetical) events, indicate whether the value of the Canadian dollar in terms of the U.S. dollar will tend to appreciate, depreciate or remain unchanged. Explain your answer. Use a supply and demand graph to illustrate each situation.

(A) Montreal hosts the Olympics.

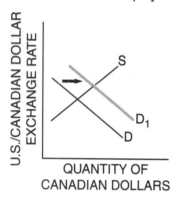

Appreciate. Visitors exchange their currency for Canadian dollars.

(B) The rate of inflation in Canada increases relative to the U.S. inflation rate.

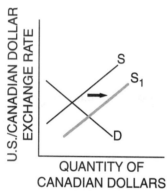

Depreciate. U.S. goods become relatively cheaper, stimulating imports by Canadians and reducing Canadian exports to the United States.

(C) Investors in Quebec purchase substantial real estate in nearby New England and New York.

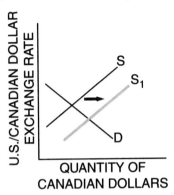

Depreciate. Outflow of investment funds requires U.S. dollars.

(D) A consortium of U.S. oil companies constructs a pipeline in Canada to transport natural gas to the United States.

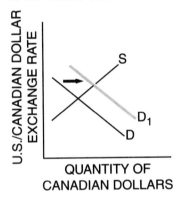

Appreciate. Investment funds shift from the United States to Canada.

(E) Interest rates rise in the United States relative to interest rates in Canada.

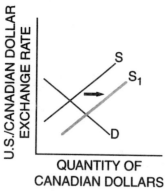

Depreciate. The United States should attract Canadian investment funds.

(F) New York and New England utilities contract to buy electricity from Canada's James River hydroelectric facility. *Probably unchanged until time of delivery, then appreciate because of increased exports. Consumer expectations could cause the demand for Canadian dollars to increase now. The graph should be consistent with the analysis.*

*2. The United States experiences an increase in exports because of changes in the tastes and preferences of foreigners for United States goods. As a result, the following occur:

■ The real gross domestic product rises by 3 percent.

■ The inflation rate rises from 5 percent annually to 10 percent annually.

■ The level of unemployment drops from 7 percent to 5 percent.

(A) Use aggregate demand and supply analysis to explain what has happened in the economy.

(B) Suppose the Federal Reserve decides to sell bonds in the open market. Analyze the short-run effects of this action on each of the following.

  (i) Interest rates

  (ii) Output and employment

  (iii) Prices

UNIT
6 Macroeconomics

LONG FREE-RESPONSE
SAMPLE QUESTIONS

Answer
Key

(C) Explain the effects of the change in interest rates caused by the Federal Reserve's action in (B) on each of the following.

(i)   The international value of the dollar

(ii) Imports

(iii) Exports

(D) Now the federal government increases taxes while keeping its expenditures unchanged. Analyze the short-run effects of this action on each of the following.

(i)   Output and employment

(ii) Prices

(iii) Interest rates

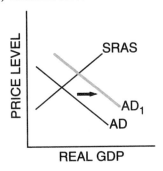

Grading Rubric: 9 points

Part (A): 2 points

An aggregate demand and aggregate supply graph shows that the changes in tastes and preferences of foreigners shifts the AD curve to the right (upward), causing a rise in output and employment and an increase in the price level, would be sufficient for two points. A verbal explanation of what the graph represents without the graph would also be worth two points. If the answer, either verbally or graphically, has the change in foreign tastes and preferences shifting the AS curve as well, the answer is worth only one point. If the answer is only about shifting the AS curve, the answer gets no points.

If Keynesian analysis is used with no price discussion but an increase in AD, give it one point. If Keynesian analysis is used and then the student goes on to the Phillips curve or some other correct price analysis to get the price effects, the answer should receive two points.

Part (B): 3 points

These are the basic points the answer should make:

(i)   The Fed's sale of bonds causes a decrease in the money supply, which increases the interest rates.

(ii) The increase in interest rates decreases the level of investment, thereby decreasing AD, which causes output and employment to decline.

(iii) The decrease in AD causes the price level to decline.

In allocating the three points for Part (B), (i) receives one point. Parts (ii) and (iii) receive two points; discretion is permitted because (ii) requires more reasoning than does (iii). If (i) states that the sale of bonds increases the money supply, but (ii) and (iii) are consistent with this incorrect answer for (i), then two points are given.

Part (C): 2 points

These are the basic points the answer should make:

(i)   *The increase in interest rates drives the international value of the dollar up as foreigners attempt to invest at the higher interest rates.*

(ii) *The increase in the international value of the dollar implies that the U.S. dollar can purchase more foreign currency, thus the relative price of foreign goods has declined. This causes an increase in the demand for foreign products, and thus imports increase.*

(iii) *The increase in the international value of the dollar implies that the foreign currency can purchase fewer U.S. dollars, thus the relative price of U.S. goods has increased, causing a decrease in the demand for U.S. goods by foreigners, thus exports decline.*

In allocating the two points: (1) one point for Part (i); (2) the effect on imports and exports must be consistent with the direction of the international value of the dollar to receive one point. But, the student loses one-half point for not explaining why the interest rate changes the international value of the dollar.

If Part (C) is consistent with the interest-rate direction in Part (B) but shows interest rates decreasing in Part (B), then the student may receive full credit for Part (C).

Part (D): 2 points

These points should be included in the answer:

(i)   *An increase in personal (corporate) taxes reduces disposable income (corporate income) thus reducing consumption (investment) and decreases AD. Thus, output and employment decrease.*

(ii) *The decrease in AD results in a price decrease. If the answer is on the Keynesian portion of the AS curve, explicitly stated, then prices will remain constant.*

(iii) *An increase in taxes, holding government expenditures constant, is contractionary fiscal policy, resulting in a decrease in interest rates. The decrease in interest rates is because of either a reduction in the government's demand for loanable funds or a fall in the transactions demand for money given the decrease in income.*

In allocating the two points, (i) is worth one point; (ii) and (iii) are each worth half a point.

Advanced Placement Economics Teacher Resource Manual © National Council on Economic Education, New York, N.Y.

*3. A series of natural disasters occurs that causes the following changes in the U.S. economy:

■ The real gross domestic product drops by 4 percent.

■ The inflation rate rises from 5 percent to 10 percent.

■ Unemployment increases from 6 percent to 10 percent.

(A) Use aggregate demand and supply analysis to explain what has happened in the economy.

(B) Suppose that the federal government, holding taxes constant, increases its spending and the Federal Reserve increases its purchases of bonds. Explain in detail the short-run effects of these actions on each of the following:

   (i)   Output and employment

   (ii) Prices

   (iii) Interest rate

(C) Explain how exports and imports will be affected by the changes in output and prices resulting from the policies described in (B).

Grading Rubric: 9 points

Part (A): 2 points

An AD and SRAS graph used to show the natural disaster shifting the AS curve to the left, causing a fall in output and an increase in the price level would be sufficient for two points. A verbal explanation of what the graph represents without the graph would also be worth two points. If the answer also shows the natural disasters shifting the AD curve as well as the AS curve, the answer is worth only one point. (A possibility: Output is cut, people lose their jobs and thus demand decreases.)

If the answer shifts only the AD curve, the answer receives no points.

Part (B): 5 points

The basic points should include:

(i)   The increase in government spending causes an increase in demand.

(ii) The Fed's purchase of government bonds increases the money supply, which causes the interest rate to fall, which causes investment spending to rise (or some version of more lending and less spending).

(iii) The actions of (i) and (ii), both causing an increase in demand, will cause output, employment and prices to rise (using an aggregate demand and aggregate supply diagram would be nice); the interest rate will fall because of the Fed's purchases of government securities.

In allocating the five points for Part (B), give one point for (i) and two points each for (ii) and (iii).

---

* Actual free-response question from a past AP test. Reprinted by permission of the College Entrance Examination Board, the copyright owner. For limited use by NCEE.

Part (C): 2 points

The question asks specifically how the change in prices and the change in output that occurred as a result of the actions taken in (B) will affect exports and imports. The increase in prices would make our goods less competitive and thus increase imports and decrease exports. The increased output would mean increased incomes, which would mean increased purchases of imported goods. It is also possible for the student to note that the lower interest rates will cause the price of the dollar to fall, which will make our goods more competitive. The really sophisticated student might also note that the higher prices, by decreasing exports and increasing imports, will create an excess supply of the dollar, thus causing a fall in the price of the dollar that would restore our competitiveness.

In the end, if the student addresses the effect of both prices and output on net exports, the answer is worth two points. If the student addresses one of these effects and also talks about one of the other possibilities mentioned above, give two points. Give one point for a correct discussion of one of the other possibilities alone.

4. Suppose the European Union (EU) has decided to impose trade restrictions on agriculture and some specific manufacturing industries. In fact, the EU has decided to subsidize some agricultural products from small farmers and to increase tariffs and quotas on the following key industries: steel, telecommunications, electronics, machine tools, computers and aerospace. The EU hopes these actions will make Europe less dependent on foreign producers for these essential goods.

(A) Which groups will gain and which will lose from these proposed restrictions?
Specific domestic manufacturing industries and agriculture would gain, and foreign manufacturing industries and agriculture would lose. Most importantly, European consumers will pay higher prices.

(B) What goals do governments intend to accomplish by imposing trade restrictions?
Governments want to keep domestic employment high and be less dependent on foreign producers.

(C) What are some of the costs that result from trade restrictions? *The standard of living will fall. Consumers will pay higher prices. The economy will be less efficient and jobs in export industries will be lost. New jobs will not be created because more resources must be used to make existing goods.*

(D) What would be the likely impact of restrictive trade policies on the total amount of trade between the EU and the rest of the world? *There would be less trade. If other nations cannot sell their goods to the EU, they will not have currency to buy EU goods. Other nations also might retaliate against the EU and raise their tariffs or impose quotas on EU goods.*

(E) Show graphically how quotas, tariffs and subsidies affect trade.

Effects of a Quota

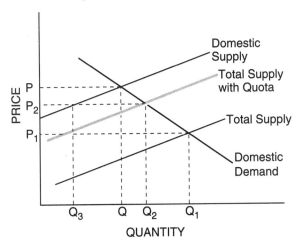

The imposition of a quota will result in an increase in price and a decrease in equilibrium quantity relative to the free trade equilibrium. P_2 price after quota and Q_2 quantity after quota. Free trade equilibrium would be P_1 and Q_1.

Effects of a Tariff

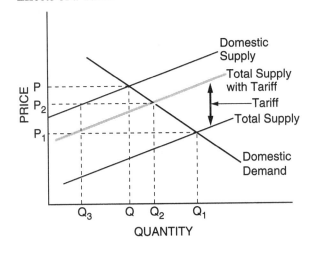

The imposition of a tariff will result in an increase in price and a decrease in equilibrium quantity relative to the free trade equilibrium. P_2 price after tariff and Q_2 quantity after tariff. Free trade equilibrium would be P_1 and Q_1.

Effects of a Subsidy

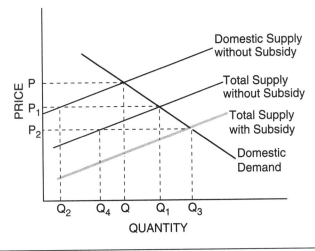

A subsidy will decrease the price and increase the equilibrium quantity relative to the free trade equilibrium. After a subsidy, the equilibrium price is P_2 and the equilibrium quantity is Q_3. The free trade price and quantity are P_1 and Q_1, respectively.

5. Consider a simple model of the world economy in which there are two nations. The United States produces computers and Mexico produces oil.

(A) Suppose now that the Mexican demand for computers increases while the United States' demand for oil remains unchanged. Use a graph to show what would happen to the value of the Mexican peso.

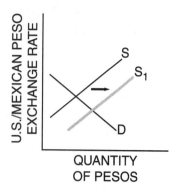

If the demand in Mexico for U.S. computers increases, so does the Mexican demand for the dollar (supply of pesos). The supply curve shifts rightward. The value of the peso will depreciate.

(B) Explain how the exchange rate changes in a flexible exchange rate system. *The supply of pesos in the exchange market increases as demand for the U.S. dollar increases. At the initial equilibrium exchange rate, the amount of pesos supplied is greater than the amount demanded. Thus the price of the peso will decline.*

(C) Explain how this change in the value of the peso affects Mexico's imports and exports. *The purchasing power of the peso has decreased, and so Mexican imports will drop. It is cheaper now to buy pesos than previously, so the rest of the world will demand more Mexican goods, and Mexican exports will increase.*

Production Possibilities
In One Day of Work

	Oranges	Avocadoes
United States	75 bushels	150 bushels
Israel	100 bushels	400 bushels

Which country has the comparative advantage in the production of oranges?

Which country has the comparative advantage in the production of avocadoes?

What is the range in terms of trade for the United States?

What is the range in terms of trade for Israel?

United States and Israel

United States

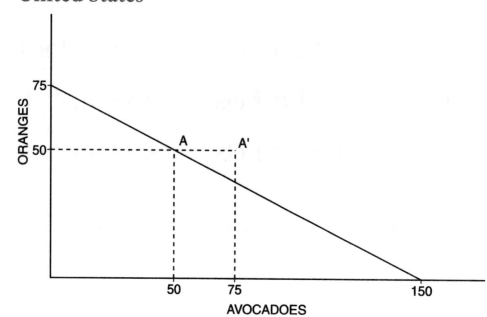

Israel

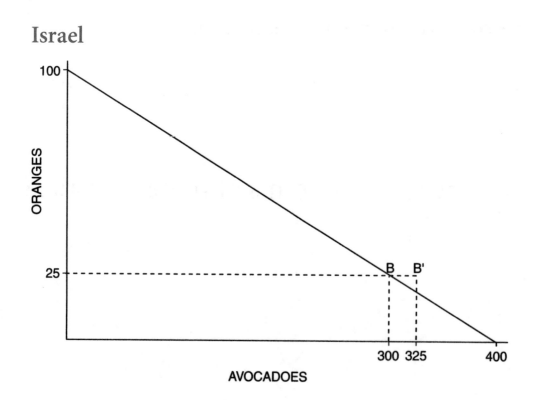

Domestic and Foreign Supply

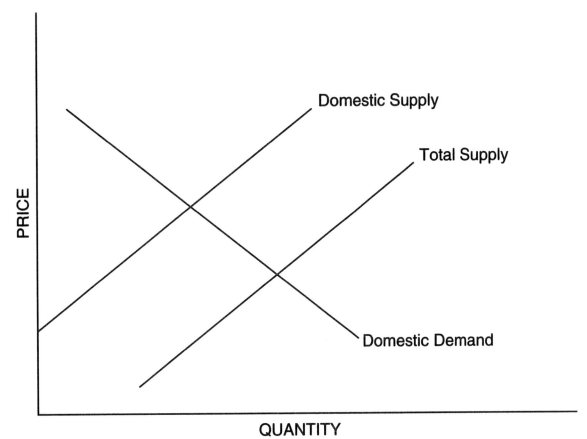

Supply of and Demand for Dollars

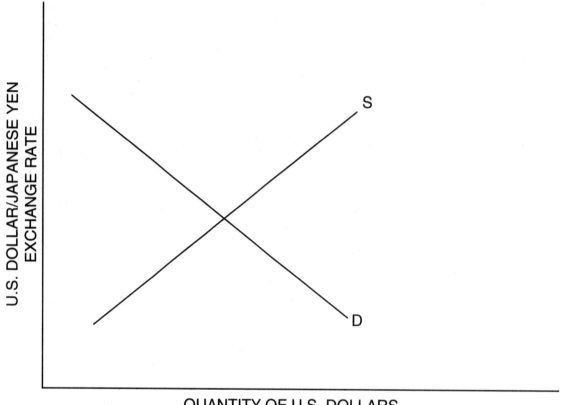

The supply of U.S. dollars is determined by U.S. demand for foreign goods, services and investments.

Demand for U.S. dollars is determined by foreign demand for U.S. goods, services and investments.